Management
of a Sales Force

Management of a Sales Force

Eleventh Edition

Rosann L. Spiro
Indiana University

William J. Stanton
University of Colorado

Gregory A. Rich
Bowling Green State University

**McGraw-Hill
Irwin**

Boston   Burr Ridge, IL   Dubuque, IA   Madison, WI   New York   San Francisco   St. Louis
Bangkok   Bogotá   Caracas   Kuala Lumpur   Lisbon   London   Madrid   Mexico City
Milan   Montreal   New Delhi   Santiago   Seoul   Singapore   Sydney   Taipei   Toronto

McGraw-Hill Higher Education

A Division of The **McGraw-Hill** *Companies*

MANAGEMENT OF A SALES FORCE

Published by McGraw-Hill/Irwin, a business unit of The McGraw-Hill Companies, Inc., 1221 Avenue of the Americas, New York, NY, 10020. Copyright © 2003, 1999, 1995, 1991, 1987, 1983, 1978, 1974, 1969, 1964, 1959 by The McGraw-Hill Companies, Inc. All rights reserved. No part of this publication may be reproduced or distributed in any form or by any means, or stored in a database or retrieval system, without the prior written consent of The McGraw-Hill Companies, Inc., including, but not limited to, in any network or other electronic storage or transmission, or broadcast for distance learning.

Some ancillaries, including electronic and print components, may not be available to customers outside the United States.

This book is printed on acid-free paper.

domestic   1 2 3 4 5 6 7 8 9 0 DOW/DOW 0 9 8 7 6 5 4 3 2
international   1 2 3 4 5 6 7 8 9 0 DOW/DOW 0 9 8 7 6 5 4 3 2

ISBN 0–07–239887-6

Publisher: *John Biernat*
Executive editor: *Gary Bauer*
Developmental editor II: *Barrett Koger*
Marketing Manager: *Kim Kanakes*
Producer, media technology: *Todd Labak*
Project manager: *Scott Scheidt*
Production supervisor: *Rose Hepburn*
Design team leader: *Mary Christianson*
Photo research coordinator: *Judy Kausal*
Photo researcher: *Robin Sand*
Supplement producer: *Betty Hadala*
Senior digital content specialist: *Brian Nacik*
Cover and interior freelance designer: *Jamie O'Neal*
Cover images: *©DigitalVisionOnline*
Typeface: *10/12 Century Schoolbook*
Compositor: *Carlisle Communications, Ltd.*
Printer: *R. R. Donnelley*

Library of Congress Cataloging-in-Publication Data

Spiro, Rosann L.
    Management of a sales force / Rosann Spiro, Gregory A. Rich. — 11th ed.
        p. cm. — (McGraw-Hill/Irwin series in marketing)
    Includes index.
        ISBN 0–07–239887-6 (alk. paper) — ISBN 0-07-119898-9 (international ed. : alk. paper)
        1. Sales management. I. Rich, Gregory A. II. Title. III. Series.
    HF5438.4 .S78 2003
    658.8'1—dc21
                                                    2002027887

INTERNATIONAL EDITION ISBN 0-07-119898-9
Copyright © 2003. Exclusive rights by The McGraw-Hill Companies, Inc. for manufacture and export. This book cannot be re-exported from the country to which it is sold by McGraw-Hill. The International Edition is not available in North America.

www.mhhe.com

To: Rockney, Imma, and Linda

This Book—Geared for the 21st Century

The new edition of *Management of a Sales Force* is coming out in the early years of a new century. The market environment in the new century is dramatically different from that in any preceding time. The age and ethnic mixes of the population of the United States are changing considerably; the population is getting older and less white. Many Americans are part of a minority group. People's values are changing as we show more concern for our social and physical environments and our overall quality of life. Along with these changes, we now expect that leaders in government, business, and other institutions adhere to higher standards of ethical and social responsibility than in the past. In this century, most businesses will be internationally oriented, buying from and/or selling to the global markets. Today the U.S. market has reached the saturation point for many consumer and industrial products; but new markets such as Eastern Europe and China have opened up. European, Asian, and U.S. trade agreements have made it easier for companies to sell products and services in Europe, Asia, Central and South America, and Canada. Growth for many American companies in the 21st century will come from the Asian, European, and South and Central American markets. At the same time, competition in the United States from foreign competitors has greatly intensified.

New developments in communication and information technology are changing our everyday lives and our business practices. Most salespeople now use some type of computer technology to assist them in serving their customers, and most sales managers use computer technology to assist them in managing their salespeople. Customers too are using new technologies, such as the Internet, to assist them in gathering product information and in making purchase decisions. Today's customers demand higher quality and greater levels of service.

As a result of these economic and competitive pressures and the social and cultural changes, companies are being forced to become more market oriented— more responsive to the customer. The role of the sales force is expanding greatly. The salesperson of the 21st century is a professional who is as much a marketing consultant as a salesperson. These new salespeople are engaged in consultative relationships with their customers. They are expected to solve customer problems, not just sell products. Their focus is on building long-term relationships with their customers. In many cases, companies respond to their customers' needs by using *selling teams*, rather than a single salesperson.

As the nature of personal selling changes, so does the role of the sales manager. Today's sales managers are viewed as *team leaders* rather than *bosses*. They empower and collaborate with their salespeople rather than controlling and dominating them. Managers in this century are being asked to manage multiple sales channels, such as telemarketing and electronic marketing as well as field salespeople. They are also assuming a greater responsibility for directing and coordinating the marketing efforts of their firms.

Your career success will depend greatly on your ability to adapt to the environmental challenges and changes that will occur throughout the coming decade. The contents of this book can be valuable to you because you will use the knowledge contained in your sales course fairly immediately. Within a very few years many of you may well be some type of sales force manager, perhaps at a district level. Even as salespeople, you may be called on to use material covered in this book. The year following your graduation, you may come back to your alma mater as a member of your firm's employee recruiting team. Or you may be called on for suggestions regarding a proposed compensation, expense, or quota plan. We wrote this book to help make the transition from college to a professional selling career easier for you.

What's New in This Edition

The most important change for this edition is that a new co-author, Greg Rich, has been signed on. Greg is a professor of marketing at Bowling Green State University, where he teaches sales and sales force management. He has particular interests in sales force leadership and technology. His entrance on this edition gives the book a fresh perspective in these and other areas.

The 11th edition has been substantially revised to reflect the changing social and technological changes that will affect sales force managers during the 2000s. Of the many new features in this edition, probably the most noticeable is the emphasis placed on *how the Internet is affecting personal selling and sales management practices*. Many of the chapters have a highlighted box or a specific section that discusses how the Internet has changed the way managerial activities are performed. The specific topics include:

- Customer relationship management.
- Sales force automation.
- The virtual office.
- Web-based recruiting.
- Web-based training.
- Global positioning systems.

In this edition, the chapter on personal selling has expanded discussions of relationship selling, team selling, and consultative selling. This chapter also provides additional information on sales follow-up, which is the stage of the selling process that is most closely associated with relationship selling.

The leadership chapter has been revised substantially. The new focus compares and contrasts management with leadership and emphasizes transformational leadership—a style that inspires sales organizations to perform above and beyond expectations.

The cases have always been a strength of this book. Out of 49 cases, the 11th edition contains 12 new cases. All of the other cases have been updated. These cases all involve sales management problems faced by real companies. Six of these are longer, integrative cases, which have been placed in an appendix at the end of the book. The accompanying case-by-chapter grid indicates the chapters for which cases are most appropriate. Several of the cases have data that are available on a supplementary Excel spreadsheet.

Many new figures, boxed materials, and other graphics have been added to make the book more readable and understandable. Internet exercises have been added to the end of the chapters. These supplement the experiential exercises that also appear at the end of the chapters. Many new company examples illustrate the principles discussed in the text, and a company index has been added that lists these companies for increased awareness and easy references. The authors have also developed PowerPoint slides that illustrate many of the principles discussed in the text. These are available as transparency masters as well.

Finally, some of the topics in the book have been reorganized to reduce the total number of chapters from 20 to 17. The topics of hiring, assimilation, and socialization have been integrated into the chapter on selection, now called "Selecting and Hiring Applicants." The discussion of sales force morale is now included in the leadership chapter. The topic of sales force quotas has been included in the chapter on compensation, and the sales budget development discussion has been added to the sales forecasting chapter.

Structure of This Book

Those who are familiar with the earlier editions will find that we have retained the features that have made this text an outstanding teaching and learning resource. The writing style continues to make the book clear and interesting to read. The section-heading structure makes for easier reading and outlining. We still have the excellent end-of-chapter discussion questions. Most of these questions are thought provoking and involve the application of text material, rather than being answerable right out of the book. The issue-oriented cases provide an opportunity for problem solving and decision making, rather than being simply a vehicle for long-winded discussion of a company's action.

We have also retained the basic scope and organization that have made this book the market leader in the sales management field for over 20 years. With respect to its scope, *this book still is concerned specifically with the management of an outside sales force and its activities.* Because outside salespeople—those who go to the customers—are distinguished here from over-the-counter salespeople to whom the customers come, the book deals largely with the management of sales forces of manufacturers and wholesaling intermediaries. Thus, the scope of this book does *not* include any significant treatment of the broader fields of marketing management.

The 11th edition continues the *real-world approach* that has successfully characterized previous editions. Students who learn from this book can talk to sales executives in the business world, and sales executives appreciate the material in this book. In fact, this book has been used in many executive development programs for sales managers.

The text is divided into five main parts:

1. **Introduction to sales force management.** The three chapters in this section set the scene for the rest of the book. Chapter 1 covers the nature, scope, and importance of personal selling and sales force management. This opening chapter also sets forth our basic managerial philosophy, which permeates the entire book. We believe that staffing—the selection of personnel at any level in organization—is the *most* important function of administrators. In Chapter 2 we discuss strategic planning and the role of sales force

planning as it relates to marketing planning and total-company planning. Chapter 3 presents the steps in the personal selling process.

2. **Organizing, staffing, and training a sales force.** Part 2 (Chapters 4 to 7) covers the first steps in operating a sales force. The major types of sales organizational structures and additional strategic organizational alternatives are treated in Chapter 4. The tasks of recruiting, selecting, hiring, and assimilating salespeople are discussed in some detail over the next two chapters. The development of a sales training program is the topic of Chapter 7.

3. **Directing sales force operations.** In this part (Chapters 8 to 11) we continue our discussion of operating a sales force. We start with the conceptual and practical aspects of sales force motivation. Another chapter is devoted to compensating a sales force, followed by a chapter on sales force expenses and transportation. We conclude Part 3 with a discussion of sales force leadership.

4. **Sales planning.** This part (Chapters 12 and 13) begins with an explanation of why we place sales planning after sales operations in the book. Part 4 covers sales planning activities, starting with sales forecasting and developing budgets. Then we discuss the design and coverage of sales territories.

5. **Evaluating sales performance.** The final stage in the management process of planning–implementation–evaluation is covered in Part 5 (Chapters 14 to 17). This part includes a sales volume analysis of an organization's total sales performance, a marketing cost and profitability analysis, and an evaluation of the performance of individual salespeople. The final chapter is a macro-evaluation of sales force management in which we discuss ethical and legal responsibilities facing sales managers.

Following the text are two appendixes:

Appendix A: Integrative cases. This appendix includes six lengthy integrative cases that may be used in conjunction with several different chapters. Included at the beginning of the appendix is a grid that suggests which chapters the integrative cases supplement.

Appendix B: Careers in sales management. This appendix discusses the opportunities and challenges of a career in sales management. It describes typical career paths and the everyday life of a sales executive. It also describes what it takes to be a successful sales manager.

Teaching Supplements

An extensive *Instructor's Teaching Supplement* has been prepared to accompany the 11th edition of *Management of a Sales Force*. The teaching supplement includes:

- Case notes.
- Answers to end-of-chapter questions.
- Suggestions for role-playing exercises.
- Spreadsheet analyses for several of the cases.
- PowerPoint slides, which are also available as transparency masters.

- An extensive, revised test bank of objective true–false and multiple-choice questions.
- Computest—a computerized version of the test bank available on request to all adopters. Computest allows the instructor to tailor and edit the exam questions to meet specific class needs.

Videotapes available with *Management of a Sales Force* depict selling and sales management situations. The *Sales Force–Sales Management Simulation* developed by Wesley Patton is also available as a teaching supplement.

Acknowledgments

Many people contributed directly to the improvements in this edition. Several of the cases were prepared by other professors and students, and in each instance their authorship is identified with the case. The concept of the Majestic Plastics Company problems and the first set of these incidents used in earlier editions were originally developed by Phillip McVey when he was at the University of Nebraska–Lincoln. George R. Cook of the Xerox Corporation contributed several ideas, as well as supplying the Xerox company forms that nicely illustrate several concepts in the sales force selection chapters. Dick Canada, a former Sales Training Manager for Xerox and currently Chairperson of Dartmouth Group, Ltd., contributed ideas for the training chapter.

Through the years, many sales executives, present and past colleagues, and other professors have contributed greatly to this book. Many of these debts are acknowledged in footnotes and other references throughout the text. Perhaps, however, our greatest debt is to our students who have used this text. Their suggestions, constructive criticisms—and yes, sometimes even their complaints—have led to many changes and improvements in the book. To all these people we are deeply grateful.

We would also like to extend our sincere thanks to all those people who offered valuable critiques and thoughtful recommendations in the reviewing process of the revision. Their efforts have helped to create a strong and effective 11th edition of *Management of a Sales Force*. We would especially like to thank the following people:

Ned J. Cooney, University of Colorado, Boulder

Joe Ellers, Palmetto Associates

Maryon F. King, Southern Illinois University

Cliff Olson, Southern Adventist University

Robert G. Roe, University of Wyoming

Finally, we would like to recognize, with grateful appreciation, the creative efforts of the people at McGraw-Hill. We especially want to thank Barrett Koger, our sponsoring editor, who did such a good job on this book that she got promoted. We also appreciate the efforts of Scott Scheidt, our project manager, for trying to keep us on schedule and for somehow pulling it all together to produce a great book.

Rosann L. Spiro
William J. Stanton
Gregory A. Rich

About the Authors

Rosann L. Spiro is a Professor of Marketing at the Kelley School of Business, Indiana University in Bloomington, Indiana, where she teaches Sales Management, Personal Selling, Business-to-Business Marketing, International Marketing, and Managerial Research in Marketing. After receiving her undergraduate degree in Economics and an M.B.A. in Marketing from Indiana, she joined the Shell Oil Company as a Senior Analyst/Statistician in the Economics and Planning Department. She then moved on to the more exciting area of sales: as the first woman to become a Shell Oil sales representative, she sold a wide variety of products to major industrial accounts.

In 1973, when the national oil crisis caused a shortage of products to sell, Rosann returned to school, earning a Ph.D. in Marketing from the University of Georgia. She then taught at the University of Tennessee and subsequently moved to Indiana University. She also spent a year at the University of Arhus in Denmark as a Visiting Professor of Marketing and a semester as a Visiting Professor at I.E.S.E. in Barcelona. She has lectured at universities and institutes in western, central, and eastern Europe as well as South Africa. Rosann is a well-known author whose work in marketing has appeared in numerous national and international publications. She won the Outstanding Article of the Year Award in the *Journal of Personal Selling & Sales Management* in 1996, 1986, and 1981. She also received the American Marketing Association Sales SIG's Excellence in Research Award in 2002. She is on the editorial review boards of the *Journal of Marketing*, the *Journal of Personal Selling & Sales Management*, and *Marketing Management*.

Currently Rosann is the Chairperson-Elect of the Sales SIG of the American Marketing Association. She has also served as President of the World Marketing Association and as Chairperson of the Board of the American Marketing Association as well as Vice President of the Education Division and as a member of the Advisory Board for the Business Marketing Division of AMA. Currently she serves on an advisory board to the U.S. Census Bureau. She is a frequent consultant to businesses and participates in national and international management development programs.

Outside of work Rosann enjoys her family, jogging, tennis, skiing, sailing, and reading.

William J. Stanton is Professor Emeritus of Marketing at the University of Colorado in Boulder. He earned his M.B.A. and Ph.D. at Northwestern University. For 35 years, Bill worked extensively with both undergraduate and graduate students at Colorado, developing teaching/learning materials and curricular programs.

As an extension of his teaching interests, he has worked in business and has taught in management development programs for sales and marketing executives. For many years he taught in management development programs sponsored by Sales and Marketing Executives–International, including the Field Sales

Management Institute (for middle-level sales executives) and the Graduate School of Sales and Marketing Management (for top-level sales and marketing executives).

Bill also designed, coordinated, and taught in the first management development programs sponsored by Advanced Management Research for sales executives. He has served as a consultant for business organizations and has engaged in research projects for the federal government.

Bill has lectured at universities in Europe, Asia, Mexico, and New Zealand and has written various journal articles and monographs. One of his other books, a widely used principles of marketing text, has been translated into Spanish, Portuguese, Italian, and Indonesian; and separate editions have been adapted (with co-authors) especially for students in Canada, Australia, and Italy.

In a survey of marketing educators, Bill Stanton was voted one of the top seven leaders in marketing thought. Recently, he was awarded the AMA Sales SIG Lifetime Achievement Award. He is listed in *Who's Who in America* and *Who's Who in the World.* In his "spare" time, Bill thoroughly enjoys jogging, downhill skiing, gardening, and traveling.

Gregory A. Rich is an Associate Professor of Marketing in the College of Business Administration at Bowling Green State University in Ohio. He earned his M.B.A. and Ph.D. at Indiana University.

Greg has a passion for teaching undergraduate students—especially in the area of selling and sales management. He is the faculty advisor to the BGSU Sales and Marketing Club; and has served as coach and chaperone to his students at the National Collegiate Sales Competition at Baylor University every year since its inception in 1999. He has a special interest in the impact of the Internet and computer-related technology on the sales force. He has published articles in this area, and was one of the first academics to develop and teach a course on Internet marketing.

In his primary research focus, Greg applies the principles of leadership theory to the field of sales management. His publication record includes articles in a number of prestigious outlets, and he is a regular presenter at national marketing conferences. He is on the editorial review board of the *Journal of Personal Selling & Sales Management.*

Greg also serves as a frequent consultant to sales organizations. He offers workshops that provide sales managers with specific feedback on how they can be more effective leaders of their sales force. Before entering academe, Greg was employed in the video production industry as a copywriter/producer of television commercials and other projects, including sales training videos. He worked closely with clients from a wide variety of industries. Current leisure activities include running marathons, playing guitar, coaching Little League baseball, and watching ice hockey.

Contents in Brief

Contents

PART 3

DIRECTING SALES FORCE
OPERATONS 220

List of Cases

Management of a Sales Force

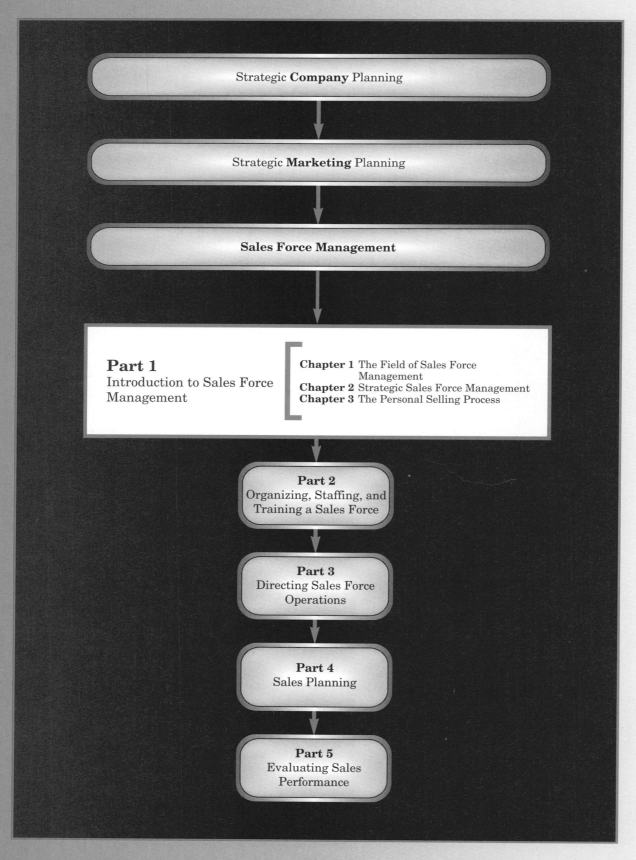

Strategic **Company** Planning

Strategic **Marketing** Planning

Sales Force Management

Part 1
Introduction to Sales Force Management

Chapter 1 The Field of Sales Force Management
Chapter 2 Strategic Sales Force Management
Chapter 3 The Personal Selling Process

Part 2
Organizing, Staffing, and Training a Sales Force

Part 3
Directing Sales Force Operations

Part 4
Sales Planning

Part 5
Evaluating Sales Performance

Introduction to Sales Force Management

For firms with an outside sales force, the activities involved in personal selling typically include more people and cost more money than any other phase of the firm's marketing program. Moreover, the success experienced by the salespeople usually is a major factor in determining the success enjoyed by the firm. Consequently, sales force management—the topic of this book—is a very important part of a company's total management effort.

Part 1 of this book, consisting of three chapters, introduces the field of sales force management. Chapter 1 starts with a statement of the scope and focus of this book. We then discuss the nature of personal selling—the wide variety of sales jobs and how they differ from other jobs. Next, we talk about sales managers—their role as administrators and how their job is distinctive. The chapter ends with a set of challenges sales managers are facing in the 21st century.

Before sales managers can make strategic decisions about their sales forces, they first should understand how the marketing system works in their companies. Chapter 2 deals with these relationships, starting with a marketing system and its environment. Objectives, strategies, and tactics then are discussed in relation to strategic planning and tactical operations. To conclude, we consider relationships in strategic planning at companywide, marketing, and sales force levels, and discuss the latest strategic trends in sales management. Chapter 3 details the eight steps of the sales process and highlights the differences between the simple one-time sale and more complex sales.

FIGURE 1

The management process

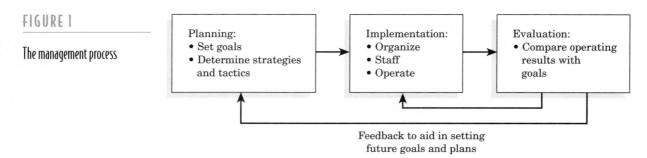

Feedback to aid in setting
future goals and plans

Plan of This Book

The management process in any organization consists basically of three stages, as shown in Figure 1: planning a program, implementing it, and evaluating its results. The **planning** stage includes setting goals and deciding how to reach them. **Implementation** includes organizing and staffing the organization and directing the actual operations of the organization. The **evaluation** stage is a good example of the interrelated, continuing nature of the management process. That is, evaluation is both a look back and a look ahead. Looking back, management compares the operating results with the plans and goals. Looking ahead, this evaluation is used as an aid in future strategic planning.

This book follows the management process as it relates to the strategic management of an outside sales force. The particular model we use to structure this book is shown in Figure 2. The general introductory chapters of Part 1 place sales force management within the context of marketing strategy and overall company strategy. The strategic planning stage of the management process is first addressed in Chapter 2, but continues throughout the book. Equally important introductory material is presented in Chapter 3, which describes each step of the personal selling process. To be effective at leading salespeople, a sales manager must understand what they do!

Parts 2 and 3 cover sales organization, staffing, and operations—the implementation stage of the management process. These topics typically generate the greatest student interest and embody the challenge and dynamism that is modern sales force management. Further, most middle-level and lower-level sales executives spend the bulk of their time engaged in these activities, which are by far the largest single marketing cost in most firms.

Part 4 then revisits planning—specifically focusing on some of the concepts and tools that sales managers must use to plan for the future. These include demand forecasting, budgeting, and territorial design techniques, which depend to an extent on the priciples of statistics and accounting.

FIGURE 2   The plan of this book

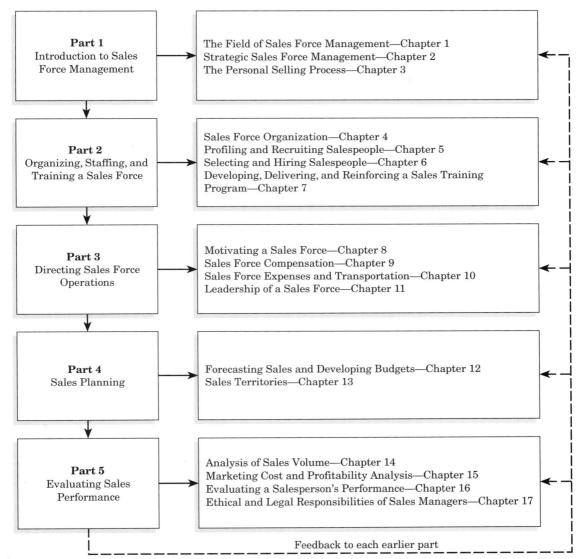

| Part 1
Introduction to Sales Force Management | The Field of Sales Force Management—Chapter 1
Strategic Sales Force Management—Chapter 2
The Personal Selling Process—Chapter 3 |

| Part 2
Organizing, Staffing, and Training a Sales Force | Sales Force Organization—Chapter 4
Profiling and Recruiting Salespeople—Chapter 5
Selecting and Hiring Salespeople—Chapter 6
Developing, Delivering, and Reinforcing a Sales Training Program—Chapter 7 |

| Part 3
Directing Sales Force Operations | Motivating a Sales Force—Chapter 8
Sales Force Compensation—Chapter 9
Sales Force Expenses and Transportation—Chapter 10
Leadership of a Sales Force—Chapter 11 |

| Part 4
Sales Planning | Forecasting Sales and Developing Budgets—Chapter 12
Sales Territories—Chapter 13 |

| Part 5
Evaluating Sales Performance | Analysis of Sales Volume—Chapter 14
Marketing Cost and Profitability Analysis—Chapter 15
Evaluating a Salesperson's Performance—Chapter 16
Ethical and Legal Responsibilities of Sales Managers—Chapter 17 |

Feedback to each earlier part

Appendix A: Integrated cases
Appendix B: Careers in Sales Management

Part 5 focuses on evaluating sales performance—the final stage of the management process. Of course, what sales managers learn in this stage is applied to the next round of planning as the mangement process is a never-ending cycle!

1 The Field of Sales Force Management

The best executive is the one who has enough sense to pick good people to do what he wants done and self-restraint enough to keep from meddling with them while they do it.

—Theodore Roosevelt—

The **Internet** is changing the way we do business in the 21st century. The impact of the Internet on sales and purchasing has been dramatic. Many companies have placed their product catalogs and product information online. Customers now have instantaneous access to product and pricing information from multiple suppliers, whereas in the past they needed to meet with at least one salesperson from each potential supplier to gain the same information. The Internet has made it easy for customers to compare potential suppliers. Business customers order commodity items or make repeat purchases online. Customers are able to track their orders, receive invoices, and make payments online.

So is the Internet going to replace salespeople? No, but it is redefining the sales job. In many cases, the salesperson will be forced to give up control of smaller accounts because the company can serve those accounts just as effectively and more efficiently online. This will give salespeople more time to develop relationships with the bigger, more complex, and more profitable accounts. Additionally, as seen in Figure 1–1, many companies are using the Internet to assist the salesperson with a wide variety of selling tasks, such as product explanation and proposal development. Dell Computer Corporation sales reps use their company's own internal website to access continually updated information on Dell products and prices. Using the Internet for routine tasks allows salespeople more time for building

FIGURE 1-1

Help on the Net
Source: "G-Business or Bust,"
*Sales and Marketing
Management*, June 2000,
pp. 64–65.

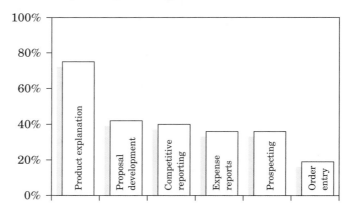

Percentage of Companies Using the Internet for Sales Activities

relationships and providing strategic value-added services to their customers. For most firms, the salesperson is and will remain the most important means of interacting with the customer. As noted by David Moore, the executive vice president of Kirkegaard & Perry Laboratories, a manufacturer of reagents and detection tools for biotech researchers, "There's always going to be a place for face-to-face selling, particularly when it comes to educating the customer."[1]

In a recent survey by Mercer Management Consulting of 60 sales organizations, 56 percent of the salespeople reported that the Internet had helped them increase their number of sales closed (i.e., completed sales) by 84 percent. Forty-one percent of the reps indicated that they had experienced an increase in average revenue per account by 21 percent due to Internet sales efforts.[2] Thus, the Internet is not replacing salespeople but rather is making them more productive.

The Internet is also driving shifts in the way customers, particularly business customers, buy products. Customers have greater access to information and have become more sophisticated and more demanding than in the past. They no longer focus just on buying products; instead, they are more interested in finding solutions to their business problems. To do so, they are forming strategic partnerships with a smaller set of suppliers that can work together to provide greater value to the end customer.

Along with using fewer sources of supply, business customers are increasingly purchasing some products from foreign producers. As businesses have narrowed their sources of supply and foreign companies have entered domestic markets, the competition among suppliers has intensified greatly. Adding to these competitive pressures is the rapid transfer of technology, which enables competitors to copy each other's products much more quickly than in the past. As a result, competing products are not as distinct as they used to be.

With less product differentiation and greater customer and competitive pressures, the selling task will become increasingly difficult and complex. Large accounts will require more sophisticated selling. The sales force must be able to identify and develop relationships with the high-profit-potential accounts. *Successful companies will distinguish themselves by the relationships they develop with their customers.* This means that managing the sales force will become more important to the ongoing success of most companies. *Sales management is ultimately responsible for what happens when the salesperson or selling team meets the customer.*

The success of sales executives will depend largely on their ability to enable, support, and assist salespeople in developing profitable relationships with their customers. We introduce the dynamic field of sales force management by explaining the scope and focus of this book.

Scope and Focus of This Book

This is a book about sales management—also called sales force management. *We define sales management as the management of the personal selling component of an organization's marketing program.* The central focus of the book is the design of sales management strategies and tactics that will help an organization achieve its marketing goals.

Specifically, this book deals almost entirely with the management of what is known as an **outside sales force,** that is, a sales force that calls on prospective customers. Outside selling stands in contrast with situations in which customers come to the salespeople—called across-the-counter selling. An outside sales force makes in-person sales calls, usually at the customer's home or place of business. Managing an outside sales force presents a unique set of problems, since most of the salespeople are geographically outside the organization's offices.

Most outside sales forces belong to producers and wholesaling intermediaries who sell to business, such as other producers, wholesalers, retailers, and institutions (e.g. schools and hospitals) rather than to household consumers (see Figure 1–2). However, as can be seen in the bottom section of Figure 1–2, an outside sales

FIGURE 1–2   Typical types of outside sales positions

Position	Product Examples	Customers	Selling Responsibility: To Increase Sales By
Industrial sales representative for a producer or a wholesaler	Industrial products Cummins Alcoa U. S. Steel Milacron Fanuc Microsoft	Producers Wholesalers	Providing technical information and assistance
Business products representative for a producer or a wholesaler	Business products and services Xerox Eli Lilly Lincoln National Insurance Consolidated Freightways Leo Burnett	Producers Wholesalers Retailers Institutions	Providing product information and assistance
Consumer products representative for a producer, wholesaler, retailer, or nonprofit organization	Consumer products and services Procter & Gamble Ford Motor Company General Electric Metropolitan Life Insurance Avon Products Sears American Cancer Society	Wholesalers Retailers Consumers	Providing product information, merchandising and promotional assistance, and management consulting

force also includes (1) producers, such as Metropolitan Life and Avon Products, who sell directly to household consumers; (2) retail salespeople, such as Sears heating and cooling representatives, who call on prospective customers; and (3) outside sales forces for nonprofit organizations, such as the American Cancer Society, who also call on the final consumer.

Many firms also contact customers by methods that are not face-to-face, such as **telemarketing,** where the telephone is used to contact customers, and **e-commerce,** where the Internet is used to contact customers. These systems are used as either the primary method or a supplemental method of interacting with customers.

The Nature of Personal Selling

We just said that sales management is the management of the personal selling effort in an organization. So let's begin by looking at some aspects of personal selling to see what it is that sales managers manage.

Personal Selling and the Marketing Mix

The term **marketing mix** describes the combination of the four ingredients that constitute the core of a company's marketing system. When these four—product, price, distribution, and promotion—are effectively blended, they form a marketing program that provides want-satisfying goods and services to the company's market.

Promotional activities form a separate submix that we call the **promotional mix,** or the **communications mix,** in the company's marketing program. The major elements in the promotional mix are the company's advertising, sales promotion, and personal selling efforts. Publicity and public relations are also part of the promotional activities, but typically they are less widely used than the first three elements. In the American economy, personal selling is the most important of the big three elements in terms of people employed, dollars spent, and sales generated.

Relationship Marketing and the Role of Personal Selling

In the face of intense competition, companies today are trying to improve their performance in every dimension of their operations. As a result, companies expect more from their suppliers. Salespeople who represent these suppliers are expected to make a contribution to their customers' success. To do this, salespeople must understand their customers' needs and be able to discover customers' problems and/or help solve those problems.

At the same time, companies are finding it harder to develop or sustain product-based competitive advantages. Most product-based advantages are soon copied by competitors. For example, Chrysler was the first to offer a van, but soon after other automobile manufacturers had vans in their lines as well. Thus, companies must focus on strengthening the value-added components of their offerings. **Value-added components** are those that augment the product itself, such as information and service.

To understand customer needs and to provide customers with value-added solutions to their problems, salespeople must develop close long-term relationships with their customers. These relationships are built on *cooperation*, *trust*, *commitment*, and *information*. The process by which a firm builds long-term relationships with customers for the purpose of creating mutual competitive advantages is called **relationship marketing,** or **relationship selling.** Salespeople who are engaged in relationship selling concentrate their efforts on developing trust in a few carefully selected accounts over an extended period, rather than calling on a large number of accounts. Relationship selling is distinct from the traditional **transaction selling,** whereby salespeople focus on the immediate one-time sale of the product. These differences are as follows:

Transaction Selling	Relationship Selling
Get new accounts	Retain existing accounts
Get the order	Become the preferred supplier
Cut the price to get the sale	Price for profit
Manage all accounts to maximize short-term sales	Manage each account for long-term profit
Sell to anyone	Concentrate on high-profit-potential accounts

Chapter 2 discusses relationship marketing in greater detail.

The Nature of Sales Jobs

In Figure 1–2 we identified different types of salespeople based on the different types of products they sell. However, most sales jobs, even within product categories, are quite different from one another and generally are different from non-sales jobs. Further, most sales jobs today are quite different from those of the past. Before we discuss each of these differences, we interject a note on pertinent terminology. The term *sales rep* will be used frequently throughout this book as a short form of *sales representative*. *Sales rep* is commonly used in business and parallels such titles as *factory rep* or *manufacturer's rep*. We shall treat the term *sales rep* as synonymous with *salesperson*, *saleswoman*, or *salesman*.

Wide Variety of Sales Responsibilities

No two selling jobs are alike. The types of jobs and the requirements needed to fill them cover a wide spectrum. The job of a Pepsi-Cola salesperson who calls in routine fashion on a group of retail stores is in another world from that of the IBM client manager who heads up a team of product specialists dedicated to serving the information needs of a specific industry. Similarly, an Avon Products representative who sells door-to-door has a job only remotely related to that of a Cessna Aircraft Company rep who sells airplanes to large firms.

One useful way to classify the different types of sales jobs is to look at them with regard to the amount of problem solving and selling required, from most complex to simple. One such classification is as follows:

- **Sales development.** Development salespeople initiate and generate sales for their companies. Reps in this group are sometimes called **order-getters.** In many cases order-getters call on customers with whom they have not done any previous business. This is the most difficult selling situation because the salesperson must be able to demonstrate how his or her company's products, services, or ideas will contribute to the customer's well-being or profit. In other cases the order-getter's objective is to gain greater sales at a current account by selling more of the same products or by selling products that the customer has not bought before. This is also a difficult challenge; the salesperson must take sales away from a competitor by providing a better solution to a customer problem. These positions require *creative, consultive, problem-solving selling.* Two strategic account managers at 3M recently worked with IBM to solve one of that company's biggest business problems. The 3M account reps helped redesign one of IBM's manufacturing processes with 3M materials that were less sensitive to static than the ones that had been in use. This cooperative problem-solving led to a much stronger relationship between the two companies and to a tenfold increase in 3M's sales to IBM.[3]

- **Sales support.** Support salespeople support the actual selling done by the reps in the other categories. Support personnel perform sales promotional activities and work with customers in training and educational capacities. Sometimes these reps may be part of the sales team brought in to assess customer needs and provide information before the sale or after the sale to help solve customer problems, but they are not responsible for *selling* the product.

  Some support people who are product specialists—**sales engineers**—work with customers to assist with technical problems. These reps may either help adapt a customer's system to the seller's products or help the seller design new products to fill the customer's particular needs. Shell Oil Company's sales engineers help out when the company's sales representatives need specialized expertise to solve a customer problem. Support personnel who introduce new lines of products to customers or assist in conducting special promotional activities are sometimes referred to as **missionary salespeople.** Essentially, all support reps assist in getting or keeping the customer by providing assistance and information about the products and their applications to customer needs.

- **Sales maintenance.** Maintenance salespeople facilitate sales to consumer or to business accounts that have already been established by taking orders and/or by delivering the product. Salespeople in these positions are sometimes referred to as **driver salespeople** or **order-takers.** Examples include Coca-Cola reps or Hostess brand food reps, who deliver product and stock shelves at retail food and drugstore chains. This work is fairly routine. Both selling and problem solving are left to national account salespeople higher in the organization, while the primary responsibility of the local reps is to ensure that their products are getting as much shelf space and promotional attention as possible.

Wide Variety of Companies, Products, and Customers

Salespeople have different responsibilities because they work for different types of companies, selling different types of products to different types of customers. For example, salespeople for Quaker Oats, Ford Motor Company, Eli Lilly, and Coca-Cola sell consumer products to wholesalers, institutions, or retailers. Mary Kay sells to the final consumer as well as to some retailers. Companies such as

FIGURE 1–3   Selected activities of salespeople

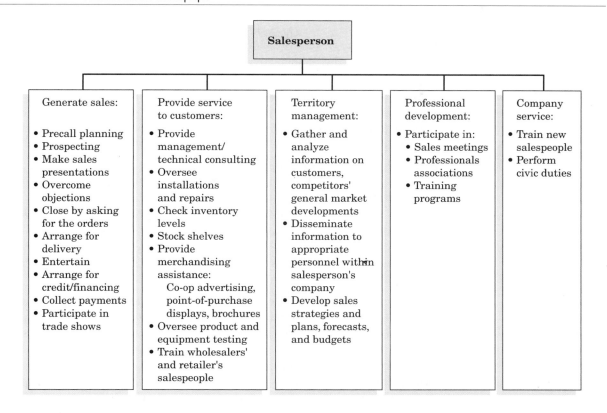

South-Western Educational Publishing sell only to the final consumer. The reps for any of these companies may be maintenance salespeople, developmental salespeople, and/or support salespeople.

Salespeople from Du Pont, Alcoa, Inland Steel, Textron, Georgia-Pacific, IBM, Xerox, Merck, and Airborne Express generally sell industrial and business products to manufacturers, wholesalers, and institutions such as universities, hospitals, or government agencies. These reps are usually developmental salespeople and sales support personnel. It should be noted that many companies, such as Eli Lilly and Ford, employ more than one type of salesperson because they sell to more than one type of customer.

How Sales Jobs Differ from Other Jobs

Why is it useful to study management of a sales force separately from the management of other classes of business personnel? Why are there no courses in the management of accountants or finance personnel? The answer is that a sales job is different from other jobs and is vital to a company's financial well-being. Figure 1–3 provides an overview of the activities for which a salesperson may be responsible. Not all reps perform all of these activities. Which activities they perform depends on the types of products they sell and the types of customers to whom they sell. Let's take a closer look at some of the key differentiating features of a sales job:

- *The sales force is largely responsible for implementing a firm's marketing strategies in the field.* Moreover, the sales reps generate the revenues that are managed by the financial people and used by the production people.

- *Salespeople are among the few employees authorized to spend company funds.* They are responsible for spending company money for entertainment, rooms, food, transportation, and so on. Their effectiveness in discharging this responsibility significantly influences marketing costs and profits.

- *Salespeople represent their company to customers and to society in general.* Opinions of the firm and its products are formed on the basis of impressions made by these people in their work and outside activities. The public ordinarily does not judge a company by its factory or office workers.

- *Salespeople represent the customer to their companies.* As noted earlier in the chapter, salespeople are primarily responsible for transmitting information on customer needs and problems back to the various departments in their own firms.

- *Sales reps operate with little or no direct supervision and require a high degree of motivation.* For success in selling, a sales rep must work hard physically and mentally, be creative and persistent, and show considerable initiative.

- *Salespeople are frequently required to develop innovative solutions to difficult problems.* Sales reps do not get the sale every time. They must be able to handle the negative feelings that come with "losing the sale."

- *Salespeople need more tact and social intelligence than other employees on the same level in the organization.* Many sales jobs require the rep to socialize with customers, who frequently are upper-level people in their companies. Considerable social intelligence may also be needed in dealing with difficult buyers.

- *Sales jobs frequently require considerable travel and time away from home and family.* This places additional physical and mental burdens on salespeople who already face much pressure and many demands.

- *Salespeople have large role sets.* The salesperson's role requires that individuals in this position interact with large numbers of people. At each customer firm, the salesperson usually works with many people, such as buyers, engineers, and production and finance personnel. In their own firms, they must also work with people from a variety of departments such as marketing research, product design, product management, finance, and production—as well as with other sales personnel.

- *Salespeople face role ambiguity, role conflict, and role stress.* As noted above, salespeople must often provide innovative solutions to problems and in doing so must satisfy many different people. As a result, salespeople often experience **role conflict,** whereby they feel caught in the middle between the conflicting demands of the people they must satisfy. Also, reps are not supervised very closely, so they frequently find themselves in situations where they are uncertain about what to do; thus, they experience **role ambiguity.** Because of role conflict and ambiguity, along with the expectation that salespeople will contribute increasing revenues to their companies, many sales positions have greater **role stress** than other jobs.

New Dimensions of Personal Selling: The Professional Salesperson

Personal selling today is quite different from what it was years ago. The cigar-smoking, backslapping, joke-telling salesman (and virtually all outside sales reps were men in those days) is generally gone from the scene. Moreover, his talents and methods would likely not be effective in today's business environment.

Instead, a new type of sales representative has emerged—a professional salesperson who is also a marketing consultant. This new breed works to relay consumer wants back to the firm so that appropriate products may be developed. Its representatives engage in a *total* consultative, non-manipulative selling job; they are expected to solve customers' problems, not just take orders. For example, Medtronics, a leader in the design and manufacture of high-tech surgical devices, sells to surgeons. These doctors often want the sales rep to be in the operating room during surgery to advise them in the best use of the product.[4] The vice president of sales and marketing for Lucent Technologies states that Lucent's overall goal is "to have all of our customers say that we are vital to their business success."[5] These are examples of relationship selling (described earlier in the chapter), in which salespeople succeed by enhancing their customers' performance.

The new-style reps also serve as *territorial profit managers.* They have the autonomy they need to make decisions that affect their own territory's profitability. Many decisions that in the past would have been made by the sales manager are today made by the salesperson. Salespeople are *empowered* to act in the best interests of their firms. A recent survey of salespeople's competencies found those salespeople who excel at aligning the strategic objectives of both customers and suppliers, and who understand the *business issues* underlying their customers' needs, are the most successful.[6] To a large extent, technology has empowered salespeople to increase the quality of contact and service they provide to their customers by allowing them to tap into huge data banks.

Whose sales forces best reflect this new professionalism? *Sales & Marketing Management* conducts an annual survey among sales executives to determine America's best sales forces. Results for 2000 are shown in Figure 1–4.

FIGURE 1-4   Best sales force programs, 2000

Company	Areas of Sales Excellence
Cisco Systems	Best trained salespeople
Philip Morris	Best international sales force
GM Isuzu Trucks	Best incentive plan
EMC Corporation	Best customer service

Source: *Sales & Marketing Management*, September 2001, pp. 28–30.

FIGURE 1-5

Sales management
responsibilities

The Nature of Sales Management

During the early stages in the evolution of marketing management, sales management was narrow in scope. The major activities were recruiting and selecting a sales force, and then training, supervising, and motivating these people. Today, personal selling and sales management have much broader dimensions. Many sales executives are responsible for strategic planning, forecasting, budgeting, territory design, and sales and cost analyses, as well as the more traditional activities. Sales managers must see that all of these tasks are integrated. Figure 1–5 illustrates how each of the sales management activities is linked with the others. If one of these activities is performed poorly, it will have a ripple effect on the others. For example, if the wrong people are hired, efforts to train and motivate them will almost always result in failure.

Furthermore, it is the sales manager's responsibility to see that all of the activities—such as production, advertising, and distribution—that support the sale of products and services are coordinated with the efforts of the sales department.

Role and Skills of a Sales Manager

As the role of the salesperson has changed, so has that of the sales manager. With high-quality empowered sales forces, sales managers are more likely to provide support and resources than to direct and control salespeople. They focus on internal coordination of the sales efforts so that their salespeople can spend more time with their customers. Increasingly, they will be asked to manage multiple sales channels—field sales as well as telemarketing and electronic marketing.

The demanding, controlling, volume-oriented sales manager is a dying breed. Today, the most successful sales managers are seen as *team leaders* rather than *bosses.* They still direct and advise people, but they do so through collaboration and empowerment rather than control and domination. To be successful in the 21st century, sales managers, like salespeople, will need to adapt their strategies, styles, and attitudes. Some of the critical changes are:

- Developing a detailed understanding of customers' business.
- Treating salespeople as equals and working with them to achieve profitability and customer satisfaction.
- Applying flexible motivational tools to a hybrid sales force of tellers, direct marketers, and field salespeople.
- Keeping up-to-date on the latest technologies affecting buyer–seller relationships.
- Working closely with other internal departments as a member of the corporate team seeking to achieve customer satisfaction.
- Continually seeking ways to exceed customer expectations and bring added value to the buyer–seller relationship.
- Creating a flexible learning and adapting environment.[7]

In terms of abilities, "people skills" are more important than analytical and evaluative skills. The ability to develop team-oriented relationships is particularly important. Today's sales manager must be sensitive to individual needs and skills, caring more about communicating and coaching than monitoring and controlling.

Administration—A Distinct Skill

A sales manager is first and foremost a manager—an administrator—and management is a distinct skill. Only during the past few decades has management, or administration (we use these terms synonymously), been recognized as a separate body of knowledge. One of the ironies of sales force management is that sales managers were usually promoted into the executive ranks because of their talent as salespeople. But from then on their success or failure depended on their administrative skills—skills that may or may not have been developed during their time as sales reps.

Sales Ability Is Not Enough

Although many people with outstanding technical abilities make good administrators, there is considerable evidence that sales talent does not necessarily correlate with managerial skill. The same concept holds true in many fields. In the sports world, for example, many successful managers and coaches were only average players, and some excellent players do not turn out to be excellent managers. In the sales field, it is widely recognized that the best salesperson may not even be a passable sales manager.[8] The very factors that create an outstanding salesperson often cause failure as an administrator. For example, many successful salespeople have strong, aggressive personalities. This can be a liability when working closely with others in an organization. Also, the detailed reporting that most sales personalities detest are essential duties of a sales manager. However, we should not jump to the conclusion that top sales producers never make good sales managers. A firm's top salespeople certainly should be considered when a management opportunity develops. In identifying a potential sales manager, particularly from among the ranks of salespeople, some important qualities to look for are:

- A willingness to share information.
- Structure and discipline in work habits.
- An ability to work well in teams or groups.
- Skill at selling internally.
- An ego that is not overinflated.[9]

While sales skills alone do not make a good administrator, some proficiency in the field is needed. It is difficult to imagine a successful sales manager who has little or no knowledge of selling. Also, the sales force must be confident that the sales manager can lead the group; successful sales experience can inspire such confidence.

Management Can Be Learned

One top executive who was a leader in the Young Presidents Organization confessed to a group of business students that she was a terrible manager in her first job. She set out to overcome this deficiency by volunteering for charitable work. In this way, she learned how to organize people and get them to cooperate.

Another young president reported that he learned a great deal about administration by studying executives and how they behaved in managing their enterprises. Observing the tactical behavior of both successful and unsuccessful managers helped him form ideas about managing people. The continuing growth of management development programs indicates that there is a body of management knowledge that can be taught and learned.

Levels of Sales Management Positions

In the administrative structure of many firms with outside sales forces, several executive levels are involved in sales force management, as shown in Figure 1–6. The title of *sales manager* may be applied to positions on any of these levels beyond that of salesperson. *Field sales manager* is a loosely used term typically applied to any sales executive who manages an outside (in-the-field) sales force or to an executive located in branch offices (in the field) away from company headquarters.

Lower-Level Sales Executives

The entry-level sales management position, especially in traditional firms with a large sales force, is typically that of a *sales supervisor*. This person provides day-to-day supervision, advice, and training for a small number of salespeople in a limited geographical area—usually part of a sales district. However, in some firms, this position has been eliminated because managers are relying on electronic communication and company databases to provide guidance and information. In firms that have adopted a team selling approach, the first managerial

FIGURE 1-6

The executive ladder in personal selling

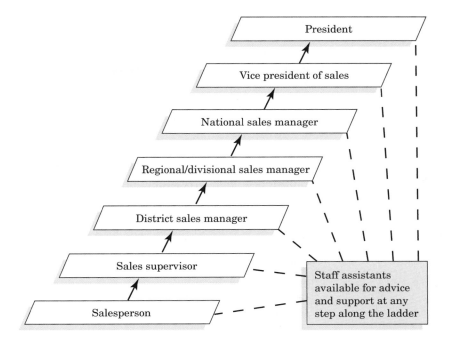

position is typically a *client team leader*, who coordinates the efforts of a multi-functional team. Usually these leaders are people with client sales or service experience.

The next step up the executive ladder is the position of *district sales manager*. This person manages the activities of sales supervisors or team leaders and also participates in some sales planning and evaluation activities in the district. In firms that do not have sales supervisors, district sales manager is the entry-level management position. In those firms that are primarily using team selling, the district manager position may be eliminated.

Middle-Level Sales Executives

Middle-level positions usually carry the title of *regional* or *divisional sales manager*. This executive normally is responsible for managing several sales districts. Sometimes this job title is *branch manager*, especially when the branch office carries product inventory and performs physical distribution activities. This position may also be eliminated in a firm that is using team selling.

Top-Level Sales Executives

The highest executive in sales management is most often called the *vice president of sales*. This executive reports to the vice president of marketing or directly to the president. The vice president of sales is responsible for designing an organization's long-run sales strategies and other companywide strategic sales planning activities. This executive acts as the sales department's liaison to the top executive in finance, production, and other major functional areas of the firm.

Just below the vice president of sales may be the *national sales manager*. The national sales manager heads the companywide sales force operations and is the executive to whom the regional sales managers report. The general sales manager thus acts as liaison between the *strategic* planning of top sales and marketing management and the *tactical* planning involved in operating regional sales forces.

Flatter Organizations

It is important to note that many organizations are becoming flatter; that is, they have eliminated some of the levels of management. Typically these are the organizations using cross-functional teams to serve their clients. As noted above, team leaders replace lower-level management positions, and often the middle levels are eliminated as well. Thus, the team leader may report directly to the vice president of sales or marketing (see Figure 1–7).

Staff Sales Management Positions

In addition to the sales management positions discussed above, most medium-sized and large companies employ staff executives to head activities that provide assistance to the sales executives and the sales force. Sales training, sales planning, and sales and marketing cost analyses are examples of these staff activities. A key point is that these executives have only an advisory relationship with the line sales executive and the sales force. Staff executives do not have line authority in the sales executive hierarchy. However, within a staff activity area—sales training, for example—the staff executives do have line authority over the people in that area.

FIGURE 1–7

The executive ladder in team selling

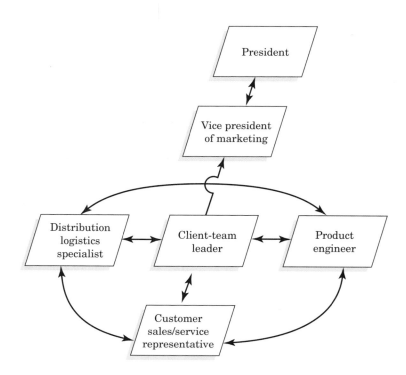

Most companies have international as well as domestic sales positions.

How Sales Managers' Jobs Differ from Other Management Jobs

Probably the most significant differentiating feature of an outside personal selling job is that the salespeople work away from the company's main facilities. Thus, sales managers cannot directly supervise each rep's work in person on a daily basis. The geographical deployment of an outside sales force makes sales managers' jobs different in several respects from other management jobs.

In sales training, for example, a sales manager can provide on-the-job training usually to only one person at a time, so other training tools and methods must be used. Communication with outside salespeople is often more difficult because it is not face-to-face communication. Similarly, motivating a sales force is a problem when a sales manager cannot regularly spend one-on-one time with the salespeople.

Another problem is evaluating a sales rep's performance when the sales manager cannot personally see the rep's work. It is also difficult to monitor the ethical behavior of workers who are geographically separated from the company. Finally, sales managers frequently face morale problems among outside salespeople. Being physically separated from co-workers, the sales reps don't have the same group morale support network as do inside employees.

Importance of Personal Selling and Sales Management

From any viewpoint in our total economy, in an individual organization, or even to you as a student, personal selling—and consequently its management—is tremendously important. As Red Motley, a noted sales trainer and writer, once said, "Nothing happens until somebody sells something."

In Our Economy

For the past 70 or so years, except during World War II and the immediate postwar period, a strong *buyers' market* has existed in the United States. That is, the available supply of products and services has far surpassed the demand. There has been relatively little difficulty in producing most goods. The real problem has been in selling them. Particularly during recessions, businesspeople soon realize that it is a slowdown in selling that forces cutbacks in production.

For further evidence of the importance of selling in our economy, take a look at the numbers. About 12 percent of the civilian working-age population is employed in sales occupations. That comes out to more than 26 *million* people. There are about 3 million outside sales jobs. Compare that to total employment in advertising, which is about 500,000.

In an Individual Organization

When a firm stresses marketing management, executive attention is devoted to sales and market planning. Such emphasis may be well placed, but ordinarily the sales force in the field must carry out the sales plan. No plan is of much value unless it is implemented properly. If salespeople cannot sell successfully because they are improperly selected, trained, or compensated, then the efforts devoted to sales planning are of little value. About the only exceptions are firms that do not rely on their own sales force but instead primarily use advertising or agent intermediaries, such as brokers or manufacturers' agents, to move the products. Since the sales force is critical to the success of a concern's marketing venture, sound management of these representatives is important.

The cost of managing and operating a sales force is usually the largest single operating expense for most firms. Public attention and criticism often focus on the amounts a firm spends for television or magazine advertising. Yet a firm's total advertising expenditures may be only 3 or 4 percent of net sales. The total expenses related to salespeople may be 15 or 20 percent of net sales.

To You, the Student

Okay, so selling and sales management are important in our economy and in an individual organization. But why should you study sales management? What's in it for you?

The primary benefit of studying sales management is related to your career aspirations. There are more positions available in sales than in any other professional occupation. As a result, there are also a lot of sales management jobs in today's world. A firm with a medium-sized or large sales force has many sales executive positions (sales supervisors, sales team leaders, district sales managers, regional sales managers) but only a few executives in finance, production, personnel, advertising, or marketing research. And the pay is usually much higher in sales management jobs than in other areas of management.

Within two or three years after graduation, you may be serving as a sales supervisor or a district sales manager. Even as a salesperson, you may engage in managerial activities, such as visiting your alma mater to do employee recruiting. You may be asked to do some sales forecasting for your territory or to offer suggestions regarding a proposed compensation or quota plan. All of these activities will require knowledge of sales management.

Sales Force Management Challenges in the 21st Century

Earlier in this chapter we noted that personal selling has assumed broader and more professional dimensions. We also observed that the people who manage the personal selling effort have significantly broadened their management activities. Now sales managers are planning for the early decades of the 21st century. To be successful in the competitive environment in the years ahead, sales executives must develop greater expertise in the following seven areas. Each of these areas is discussed in varying depth later in the book.

1. **Customer relationship management (CRM).** Seventy percent of the sales executives surveyed in a recent study stated that the biggest challenge facing them in the coming years will be to expand their relationships with existing customers.[10] Many companies have already initiated CRM programs specifically designed to expand relationships with existing customers. These companies recognize that getting new customers costs more than increasing sales with existing customers. This is a fundamental change in the way businesses serve both consumer and business-to-business markets.

2. **Sales force diversity.** The workforce is changing in many ways. The most important is the changing demographics of those individuals entering the profession and of those already in the profession. More women and minorities are embarking on careers in personal selling and are advancing into sales management positions. In the early 1980s only 10 percent of outside salespeople were women. Now that figure is at 24 percent.[11] Minority groups present another opportunity and a different set of challenges for sales management because minorities have been more difficult to recruit in large numbers for outside sales jobs. Not only have we long been a nation of ethnic diversity, but people of various minority groups are expected to become the majority in our country in the near future. To remain competitive, sales managers need to capitalize on the strengths of women and minorities in selling and to be aware of what these individuals want in a sales job.

   The bottom line for sales managers of women and minority groups is this: These groups are here to stay in selling, and they must be managed effectively. As a matter of self-interest, sales managers cannot afford to waste the brainpower (and selling power) of over half our population. Moreover, executives simply will not be able to adequately fill the available sales jobs in the foreseeable future unless they recruit qualified women and minorities.

   Additionally today's salespeople are much more educated than in the past. Over 65 percent of salespeople have college degrees, and the number holding postgraduate degrees has increased as well to 6.5 percent.[12] The more educated salesperson will desire challenges and rewards that differ from those his or her less educated counterpart desired in the past. Finally, as our population grows older, sales managers will be faced with managing a greater proportion of seniors in their sales forces. In many cases, these senior salespeople will place less emphasis on financial rewards than will their younger counterparts, but they will still need to be motivated to maintain and improve their performance.

3. **Electronic communication systems and computer-based technology.** In the United States, over 60 percent of salespeople are "connected."[13] The Internet, company intranets and extranets, desktop video conferencing, and other electronic technology all enable salespeople and sales managers to improve their productivity. To compete effectively, salespeople and managers alike will have to adopt the latest technologies. However, as noted earlier, technology can make some sales tasks more efficient, but it will not replace face-to-face contact in complex selling.

4. **Selling teams.** During the 21st century, more companies will respond to the changes in customer buying patterns by using selling teams. Coordinating the efforts of these teams and motivating them is a task very different from supervising and motivating the individual sales rep. Collaboration and consensus building will be essential skills for the manager in the new millennium.

5. **Complex channels of distribution.** Many sales managers will be asked to manage increasingly complex channels of distribution. They will oversee a hybrid sales force, which includes field sales reps, tellesellers, and electronic sellers. Their work—organizing and coordinating the efforts of these diverse salespeople—will become more strategic. The successful sales managers of the 21st century will be adaptive enough to handle both complexity and rapid change.

Many women and minorities are embarking on careers in sales.

6. **An international perspective.** Today the U.S. market has reached the saturation point for many consumer and industrial products. At the same time, many global markets are emerging and growing rapidly. Growth for many companies in the 21st century will come from their development of these international markets. Some companies, such as Coca-Cola, Colgate-Palmolive, and Avon, are already earning the greatest proportion of their revenues outside the United States. Differences in cultures and ways of doing business in foreign countries pose real challenges for American sales management.

   Additionally, in the United States, American sellers face increasing competition from many foreign firms. This competition is bound to increase (1) as economies expand in Asian and eastern European countries such as Korea, Taiwan, Thailand, China, Hungary, and Poland; (2) as a result of the European Union becoming a unified trading market; and (3) as a result of the North American Free Trade Agreement, signed in 1993, which eliminated many of the trade barriers between the United States, Canada, and Mexico. Sales executives must manage their sales forces to meet foreign competition in this country and to improve their company's personal selling efforts in other countries.

7. **Ethical behavior and social responsibility.** Each person in business operates within his or her own moral framework, the business ethical framework of the company and the industry, and a framework imposed by society. Of the topics covered in this final section of the chapter, this seventh topic of ethics is probably the most necessary—but also the most difficult to manage. Ethical standards differ among various companies and industries, and also among societies. Nevertheless, any institution in our socioeconomic system must operate within socially acceptable limits of ethical behavior; society will penalize any unethical institution and the people in it.

   For centuries, the institution of business, and especially its personal-selling component, has been accused periodically of unethical behavior. Yet it is commonly accepted that outside selling today is on an ethical plane far above that of a few decades ago and in a different world from that of a century or two in the past. Today, sales managers have no choice but to strive to maintain their ethical standards in personal selling and sales management, for the alternative can put them out of business or even into prison.

Summary

This is a book about managing a sales force—that is, managing the personal-selling component of an organization's marketing program. Specifically, this book deals with the management of an outside sales force where the salespeople go to the customer. Outside selling contrasts with across-the-counter selling, where the customers come to the salespeople. By any measure—people employed, dollars spent, or sales generated—personal selling is by far the most important element in a company's promotional mix.

In the face of intense competition, many companies today practice relationship marketing or relationship selling, which is very different from the traditional transaction-oriented selling that focused on the one-time sale of the product. In contrast, relationship selling focuses on developing trust in a few selected accounts over an extended period.

There are a wide variety of sales jobs in which salespeople work for a wide variety of companies, selling many different products, and serving a wide variety of customers. The sales job is also different in a number of ways from other jobs. Further, a new type of sales representative is emerging, one who acts as a marketing consultant for the customer and for his or her own firm.

The role of the sales manager is also expanding. Today, the most successful sales managers are seen as team leaders rather than bosses. They provide support and resources, and must often manage multiple channels of distribution.

Sales managers are administrators, and administration (management) is a distinct skill. Sales talent alone does not make a good manager, but management can be learned. There are several levels of sales management positions, and sales managers' jobs also differ from other management positions.

The importance of personal selling and sales management may be viewed from the perspective of our total economy; individual organizations; or you, the student. To manage a sales force effectively in the 21st century, sales executives must develop greater expertise in the following areas: (1) customer relationship management (CRM), (2) sales force diversity, (3) electronic communication systems and computer-based technology, (4) selling teams, (5) complex channels of distribution, (6) an international perspective, and (7) ethical behavior and social responsibility.

Key Terms

Communications mix
Driver salespeople
E-commerce
Internet
Marketing mix
Missionary salespeople
Order-getters
Order-takers

Outside sales force
Promotional mix
Relationship marketing
Relationship selling
Role ambiguity
Role conflict
Role stress
Sales development

Sales engineers
Sales maintenance
Sales support
Telemarketing
Transaction selling
Value-added components

Questions and Problems

1. Explain how the Internet makes salespeople more effective.

2. What is an outside sales force? Is this type of sales force used only by producers and wholesalers? Is it used only in business-to-business selling?

3. How can a salesperson add value to his or her customers' business?

4. How does relationship-oriented selling differ from transaction-oriented selling?

5. Based on the classification of sales development, sales support, and sales maintenance jobs listed in this chapter, answer these questions:
   a) In which types of jobs is the sales rep most free of close supervision?
   b) Which types of jobs are likely to be the highest paid?
   c) For which groups is a high degree of motivation most necessary?

6. We said that today's professional sales representative is a marketing consultant and a manager of a market—his or her territory. Explain how a sales rep can be a marketing consultant and a manager.

7. What can sales managers do to increase the professionalism of their salespeople?

8. How does a sales job differ from other jobs?

9. Assume that it is the year 2005 and you are a middle-level sales manager. Tell us something about your job.

10. Why do many successful salespeople fail to become successful sales managers?

11. Assume that you are a sales manager. What characteristics would you look for, or what criteria would you use, when promoting a salesperson to the position of district sales manager?

12. It has been said, "Nothing happens until somebody sells something." How would you explain this to a student who is majoring in accounting, finance, or engineering?

13. Should someone who is not majoring in marketing take a course in personal selling? In sales management?

14. Review your activities of the past week and identify those in which you did some personal selling.

15. Assume that your company, which sells paper products, has 60 percent of the business at your largest account. What factors would make it relatively easy for you to get a larger share of that customer's business, and what factors would make it harder?

Experiential Exercises

A. Interview sales managers from three different companies concerning their responsibilities and what they do. Compare and contrast their positions. Then explain which one you would prefer and why.

B. Interview a salesperson from each of three different companies about the nature of their selling responsibilities and their relationships with their customers. Then describe each of these sales positions and explain whether the selling is more similar to transactional selling or to relationship selling and why.

Internet Exercises

The following two websites focus on sales management:

Sales and Marketing Management Executives International (www.smei.org)

Sales & Marketing Management magazine (www.salesandmarketing.com)

A. Visit these sites and describe the information and services they offer, and how these services might be of use to sales managers.

B. Report on several current issues of importance to sales managers that are covered on *Sales & Marketing Management*'s website.

References

1. Quoted in Erika Rasmusson, "Watch This Channel," *Sales & Marketing Management*, June 2000, p. 88.

2. "E-Business or Bust," *Sales & Marketing Management*, June 2000, pp. 64–65.

3. Erika Rasmusson, "3M's Big Strategy for Big Accounts", *Sales & Marketing Management*, September 2000, p. 92.

4. James Champy, "Heading in New Directions," *Sales & Marketing Management*, January 1997, pp. 32–33.

5. Andy Cohen, "The Traits of Great Sales Forces," *Sales & Marketing Management*, October 2000, pp. 70–71.

6. Bernard L. Rosenbaum, "Seven Emerging Sales Competencies." *Business Horizons*, January/February 2001, pp. 33–36.

7. Chad Kaydo, "The New Skills of Top Managers," *Sales & Marketing Management*, May 2000, p. 16.

8. Erin Stout, "Movin' On Up," *Sales & Marketing Management*, March 2001, p. 63.

9. Ibid.

10. Eduardo Javier Canto, "Survey Says Where the Sales Are," *Sales & Marketing Management*, June 2001, p. 18.

11. Christian P. Heide, *Dartnell's 30th Sales Force Compensation Survey* (Chicago: Dartnell Corporation, 1999), p. 171.

12. Ibid., p. 173.

13. Ibid., p. 209.

G. W. PERGAULT, INC.

Salespeople Feeling Threatened by the Company Website

Ken Sutton, sales manager for G. W. Pergault, directly oversees 15 salespeople who serve clients in and around Milwaukee, Wisconsin. He is currently in a tough spot. The new president of the company, Celia Fiorni, has a vision for e-commerce that Sutton's salespeople strongly oppose. Sutton feels caught in the middle—between his boss and his subordinates.

Fiorni had become president of G. W. Pergault just six months ago. Her previous job was CEO/president of a very successful—but relatively small—technology firm that sold computer hardware to consumers. Fiorni is an enthusiastic, charismatic leader who has brought a fresh outside perspective to G. W. Pergault.

Given her background in the computer industry, Celia Fiorni is, not surprisingly, a fervent believer in new technology. Her first task was to spend over $20 million updating G. W. Pergault's website. With this accomplished, her next goal is to move a much larger percentage of the reps' sales to the company website. Further, she feels that company's salespeople should take the lead role in encouraging and training their customers to order products through the website.

G. W. Pergault is an established $4.2 billion supplier of maintenance, repair, and operations (MRO) products. The company sells pipe fittings, lightbulbs, ladders, and literally hundreds of thousands of other MRO products to business customers throughout North America. Established in 1952, G. W. Pergault traditionally has sold these products through its extensive mail-order catalog, which has grown to over 4,000 pages. In 1997, the catalog was put online. Although they have increased each year since, online sales are still dwarfed by catalog sales.

The business customers that buy the company's products vary greatly in size. Most are relatively small accounts that purchase supplies directly through either the paper catalog or the website without ever seeing or talking to a G. W. Pergault salesperson. Even though these smaller businesses represent about 80 percent of the customers, the aggregate sales generated from them is still only about 20 percent of G. W. Pergault's total sales.

Alternatively, the remaining 20 percent of the customers tend to be much larger accounts. The sales generated from these bigger customers represent about 80 percent of G. W. Pergault's total sales. These are the customers that are regularly called upon and serviced by G. W. Pergault's sales force. These sales reps personally process the vast majority of orders from their customers.

Celia Fiorni, however, believes that it is highly inefficient for these customers to order all their products through salespeople. First, it is needlessly time-consuming and keeps salespeople from their more important creative-selling activities. Second, it is costly. She feels that G. W. Pergault could save hundreds of thousands of dollars by insisting that existing customers reorder their supplies through the website. The savings, she says, will stem primarily from eliminating steps in the ordering process.

Currently, the ordering process starts as the G. W. Pergault sales rep personally meets with a purchasing agent from the customer firm. The sales rep writes up the order by hand as the purchasing agent makes his requests. After the meeting, the rep submits the order to G. W. Pergault—usually by fax. A member of G. W. Pergault's data-entry clerical staff receives the form, and enters the information into the system for delivery. The order is packaged and shipped, usually within three business days from when it was made.

The new company website, of course, provides an interface that allows customers to complete their own order, which then is directly entered into the system as soon as the customer clicks on the Submit button. This allows for quick order processing, saving at least one day in delivery time. In addition, it significantly reduces the chance of order-entry error by either the salesperson or the data-entry clerk. As Fiorni says, "It's a no-brainer. By ordering through the website, customers will not only get their supplies sooner, they can be much more assured that they will get exactly what they asked for."

Ken Sutton could see the logic in his new president's thinking. A recent customer satisfaction survey revealed that mistakes are made in about 1 out of every 20 orders that come in through salespeople. He feels that this error rate is much too high. Further, he believes that his sales reps are not even close to reaching the full potential for his market in and around Milwaukee. "The reps spend too much time taking orders, and not enough time explaining to customers how our *other products* can meet their needs," he says.

At the same time, his reps have expressed strong opposition to the plan. In fact, his top rep for the past two years had just called him yesterday. In a somewhat angry tone, the rep told him what he thought of the new president: "Fiorni doesn't understand that selling is about building personal relationships, and you can't have a relationship with a website. Customers buy from G. W. Pergault not just because they like our products but also because they like me. I'm sorry, but I refuse to tell my best customers, 'I'm too busy to take your order. Go surf the Internet.' "

Other reps have told Sutton that customers who had tried the new website did not like it. Some of the complaints were that it was too glitzy with too many distracting graphics. "We don't care about the bells and whistles; we just want to buy supplies in a convenient and quick way," said one purchasing agent. "It's so much easier to just meet with our rep and tell her what we want. Frankly, the website is too complicated and confusing."

Sutton thinks that customers might be less confused if their sales reps would do a better job of showing them how to use the website. After all, G. W. Pergault offers more than 500,000 different products, which can be overwhelming to sort through. Sutton believes that some of his reps may have trouble finding specific products on the website. He also acknowledges that G. W. Pergault has not made much of an effort to train its own sales force on the ins and outs of ordering online through the company website.

There are two other key issues that help explain why the sales force is so strongly opposed to the president's new vision. Ken Sutton believes these are the most critical reasons for the objections. First, over half of the typical salesperson's compensation is earned through commission. When customers buy through the website, reps don't earn any commission. Why would a sales rep convince a customer to do something that reduces the rep's pay?

Second, many of the reps feel that the website is a threat to their future with the company—even though Fiorni is on record saying that she does not want to eliminate the sales force. In a recent company address, she said, "G. W. Pergault needs more—not fewer—people selling. We simply need a shift of focus toward selling new products to our best customers. We also need sales to focus on opening new accounts." Nevertheless, some reps feel that this initiative is the first step to a pink slip.

Next week, Fiorni is scheduled to come to Milwaukee and talk to Sutton and his reps. She understands that her plan has not been well received by sales. G. W. Pergault reps from all around the country feel the same way that Sutton's reps do. In fact, Fiorni will be visiting various sales groups from around the country to try to get a better idea of why there is such resistance.

Sutton believes his new boss is a reasonable person, and he is looking forward to her visit. Through telephone conversations, he gets the sense that she will listen to his advice on the matter—but he is not sure exactly where he stands. All he knows is that Fiorni's e-commerce goal will not be achieved without salesperson buy-in, and that the salespeople are not buying the plan in its current form.

Questions:

1. What advice should sales manager Ken Sutton give to his company president, Celia Fiorni, in order to improve her e-commerce plan and make it successful?

2. What should Ken Sutton do to make his salespeople more accepting of the new initiative?

CASE 1-2   THOMPSON PLASTICS

Making the Transition from Salesperson to Sales Manager

Thompson Plastics is an $8 million family-owned corporation that takes pride in its quality products and customer relationships. The company manufactures plastics products, resins and adhesives, and custom moldings. The plastics, which are the largest part of Thompson's business, include polyvinyl chloride (PVC) sheets, acrylic sheets, acetate, polypropylene, and nylon. Thompson also manufactures 15 different resins and adhesives as well as custom-made vacuum molding products for other manufacturers.

Thompson sells its products to various manufacturers and retailers in the Buffalo, New York, metropolitan market. Sales to other manufacturers account for approximately 77 percent of its sales, and sales to retailers account for the remainder. Thompson has several competitors in the Buffalo market but has maintained slow, consistent growth over the past several years. Thompson's strategy is to maintain its market share by concentrating on its existing customers with quality products and personal service.

The company has a simple line-type organization that is relatively small. The president, John Thompson, heads up the organization. Reporting to him are the vice presidents of manufacturing, finance, operations, and marketing. The vice president of marketing is Lorna Kelley. Reporting to her is the sales manager, Ted Cook, who oversees the sales operations and the seven salespeople employed by Thompson.

Cook was recently promoted into the manager's job. Thompson has a policy of promoting from within, and Cook was selected from among the salespeople based on the strong recommendation of Lorna Kelley. She felt that even though he was not the top salesperson, he was the best choice to move into management. He clearly had the best administrative skills of the group, he often took a leadership role in helping the younger reps, and he was respected by all the other reps. In her mind, Ted had seemed to be the logical choice; but now she was wondering if she had made a mistake.

The sales manager for Thompson has a large amount of the responsibility for planning the sales effort and total responsibility for organizing and managing the sales force. In the area of planning, he (or she) assists in the preparation of the sales forecast. He compiles territory estimates by customer and by product, based on history, forecasts of economic conditions, and competitive developments. Based on the final forecasts, he also prepares the expense budgets and the sales quotas for the individual reps. He then breaks these budgets down into monthly and quarterly dollar figures, which he uses in evaluating the reps and determining their incentive pay.

The sales manager has total responsibility for recruiting and selecting new salespeople when there is an open territory. He places the advertisements in the local newspapers, screens the applicants based on their résumés, interviews those who appear to have the qualifications to fill the job, selects the candidate, and makes the job offer. The sales manager then spends two to three weeks training the new salesperson. This involves everything from acquainting the new rep with company objectives, production capabilities, and operating policies to teaching product knowledge and selling skills. During the training period, the new rep accompanies the manager on a number of typical sales calls.

Supervision, motivation, and evaluation are essential components of this position. The manager makes sure that the reps are allocating their time properly and that they are keeping current with regard to their product and industry knowledge. He is responsible for weekly sales meetings and continuing training programs. He must also spend time in the field with each rep in order to evaluate performance. In conjunction with the evaluation, he designs and administers the recognition and compensation programs. Of course, the sales manager also acts as a troubleshooter when any of the reps needs assistance with an account.

In the past, the sales managers at Thompson had always retained some of their key accounts. However, Lorna Kelley felt that because the size of the sales force had doubled in the last few years and because the responsibilities of the sales manager had expanded, it was time that the sales manager devote 100 percent of his time to managing the sales effort. Therefore, when she offered the manager's position to Ted Cook, she asked him to give up all of his selling responsibilities. His compensation package would consist of salary, a commission on all the reps' sales, and a bonus for making the sales and expense targets. This package would more than compensate for the loss of income from his sales commissions.

Cook was really excited about the opportunity to become Thompson's sales manager. But he was somewhat surprised that he had been chosen because he did not have seniority among the reps.

However, when Kelley told him about giving up all of his accounts, he countered that he didn't want to do that and that it was not in Thompson's best interests. Kelley recalled his comment: "If customer relationships are as important as we say they are, then I should retain several of my key accounts in which I have developed strong relationships over the past several years. I am certain we would lose our position as a favored supplier if we assigned these accounts to a new rep. It isn't that I'm any better than the next rep; it's just that it takes time to gain their trust and nurture these relationships."

Of course Cook had also wanted to know why there had been this change in policy. When Kelley explained her reasoning, Cook suggested that keeping several of his accounts would actually help him be a better manager because he would be more knowledgeable about what was going on in the marketplace. When Kelley relented, Cook took the job and kept his largest accounts. The smaller customers were split among the territories contiguous to his.

At first, this arrangement worked pretty well. However, in the last several months Cook began having problems with both the managing and the selling aspects of his job. His paperwork was way behind, his sales figures had slipped a little, and one of the reps had complained to Kelley about the lack of support from Cook.

Kelley did not have a good solution. If she forced Cook to give up his accounts, she thought there was a good chance he might quit Thompson. If he quit, she really did not have anybody else she felt she could put in his position. She would have both a manager and a rep to replace. If she asked him to give up the manager's job and go back into full-time selling, he might quit in that situation as well.

Question:

1. Should Lorna Kelley ask Ted Cook to give up his accounts? How do you think Kelley should handle this problem?

CASE 1-3   THE CORNELL COMPANY

Selection of a Sales Manager

Paula Ruiz, vice president of marketing for the Cornell Company of Chicago, Illinois, knew she had to make a decision on whom to select to manage the company's 56-person sales force. Seven months previously, the former sales manager resigned to accept the sales managership for Cornell's major competitor. Since that time Ruiz had assumed direct control of the sales force, but she clearly saw that in doing so she was not only neglecting her other responsibilities but also doing a poor job of managing the sales force. Ruiz's search for a new sales manager had narrowed down to two people,

Gordon Price and Janice Wilson, both of whom seemed eminently qualified for the job.

The Cornell Company was one of the nation's leading manufacturers of special-purpose metal fasteners and metal fastening systems used by metal fabricating manufacturers. The sales reps worked closely with both the engineers and purchasing agents of customers' organizations in developing product designs and specifications for solving their problems. While there was some calling on new accounts, the bulk of the sales reps' time was spent working with long-standing accounts.

The sales manager was charged with the full responsibility for maintaining an effective field sales force, which included hiring, firing, training, supervising, compensating, controlling, and evaluating the salespeople. The manager was accountable for all the department's paperwork, which included budget preparation, expense account auditing, and sales force planning. At times the manager had to work closely with sales reps in handling special accounts or particularly important or difficult contracts. There were no field supervisors to help the reps; however, close communications were maintained with them by the home office through the extensive use of modern electronic technology.

Each rep had a portable computer, mobile telephone, and fax machine, which allowed immediate contact with the home office and its databases. Technical information was immediately available to all sales reps by accessing the company's mainframe computer, which contained an extensive technical database. Every company employee could be accessed by electronic mail. The sales manager had an assistant in the home office who handled all communications between the reps and the manager. A large portion of the manager's time was spent in meetings with other members of management to coordinate sales force activities with all other functions of the business. The manager had to work particularly closely with Paula Ruiz.

Ruiz had taken the files on the two prospective managers home for the weekend to contemplate her decision. She had decided to announce her selection Monday morning.

As she reviewed Gordon Price's file, she fully realized that if Price were not made sales manager some repercussions might be felt. Price was not only the firm's best sales rep but also well regarded throughout the organization. He had sold for the company for 15 years and prior to that had worked in production for 4 years after graduation from high school. Now 37 years old, he had outsold all other reps for the last 10 years and always exceeded quotas by more than 20 percent, even in difficult times. Since the sales force was paid on a commission basis, Price had become moderately wealthy. His average earnings over the past decade exceeded $100,000; last year he earned $135,000. Price was married to an understanding woman of considerable charm. Their three children were in high school and, to Ruiz's knowledge, were outstanding youngsters. The Prices were extremely adept at entertaining and socializing with people. Hardly a month passed that they did not have some sort of social event at their home.

Although Gordon Price had not attended college, Paula Ruiz knew that he was intelligent and had acquired considerable business know-how. He had accumulated an impressive library of business books and had participated in many meaningful self-improvement programs.

When he learned of the previous sales manager's resignation, Price had come directly to Ruiz and requested the position. He outlined his achievements for the company and then gave a brief account of the goals that he would work toward as manager. Ruiz recalled acknowledging at the time that Price was certainly a prime candidate for the job and that he could be assured that he would be given every consideration. However, she told him that the decision was not entirely hers to make. The president had suggested that a thorough search be made in order to ensure that the best person available was placed in the position, since he felt keenly that the company had prospered largely because of its excellent sales force and he wanted to do nothing to jeopardize that success formula.

Privately, Ruiz had some reservations about making Price sales manager, but she was hesitant to bring her thoughts into the open for fear of engendering animosities that would later haunt her. First, she was fearful that if she promoted Price, she would be losing a good sales rep and getting a poor sales manager. She had seen it happen in other companies, and sales management literature was full of warnings that top salespeople may not make good sales managers. The two jobs required different skills. Second, Ruiz was worried that Price would be unhappy with the sales manager's salary of $90,000, despite his insistence that he would be happy with it. Third, she was afraid that Price's preference for customer contact would result in his not staying in the office enough to do the required paperwork. Finally, she was disturbed by Price's relationships with the other reps. He was extremely well liked by the men, who felt that he "would give you the shirt off his back" if you needed it. However, a few of the 14 women on the sales force had communicated to her that they felt that Price was a bit too macho for their liking.

However, none of the women had indicated that Price had been anything but very proper and pleasant in his behavior toward them.

Price had forced Ruiz to make a selection soon, appearing in her office Friday morning to issue a rather strong ultimatum: He had been offered a sales managership with a significant competitor and had to give an answer in two weeks. He made it clear that he did not want to leave but that he would do so to become a sales manager if that opportunity was not to be his with the Cornell Company. Ruiz inwardly rebelled at this holdup ploy but realized that it was a fair tactic. The last sales manager had given no warning of his impending departure. She thought that at least it was nice to be forewarned for a change.

Ruiz proceeded to review her other leading candidate, Janice Wilson, with whom she had been acquainted for more than four years. They were members of several clubs together and, while not close friends, had known each other from their college days. Wilson was the sales manager for an electronic instrumentation company and had developed an enviable reputation in the industry for building an outstanding sales force. She was 32 years old, married, with two young children. While she had a most agreeable disposition, all evidence indicated that she ran a tight ship. She demanded outstanding performance and seemed to get it.

Ruiz casually mentioned her job opening to Wilson one day at one of their club meetings on the off chance that she might know some outstanding person whom she could recommend for the job. Wilson had hesitated for a moment, then replied, "Let's talk."

She then confided that her firm was about to be acquired by a larger firm and she was not at all enthralled about what she knew of its management. "They are not my kind of people," she went on to say. "From what I know of you and your operation, I think I would like very much to be considered for the job."

After two hours spent contemplating the pros and cons of selecting each person, Paula Ruiz was still undecided.

Question:

1. Whom would you make sales manager?

2 Strategic Sales Force Management

You got to be very careful if you don't know where you're going, because you might not get there.

—Yogi Berra—

Developing a sound strategic plan for the future is critical to the success of any firm. It is a process that should occur in and be coordinated across the different functional areas of the company. That is, the actions of salespeople should be consistent with the strategic marketing plan, which should fit into the strategic plan for the total company. Too often, people think of sales as an activity that is separate from marketing strategy. In fact, marketing and sales often operate as if they are engaged in some sort of win–lose contest in which neither side cooperates with the other. The reality is that the marketing objectives can be achieved only when sales becomes an integral part of the marketing strategy—the part that carries out strategy. By working together as a team, marketing and sales personnel become key contributors to the success of the overall strategic plan for the business.[1]

A chief operating officer (COO) of a biotech enterprise whose 75-person sales force was fueling the company's rapid growth into the Fortune 500 noted, "I need many of my present salespeople to develop insights into the company's strategic plans so they can be my managers of the future. We're going to need dozens of them." This executive neatly highlighted the purpose of this chapter—to place sales force management within the context of the total marketing program. To make wise strategic decisions about the sales force, the sales manager must understand how the field-selling effort fits into the strategic marketing plan and how that fits into strategic planning for the total company.

FIGURE 2-1 A company's complete marketing system: a framework of internal resources operating within a set of external forces

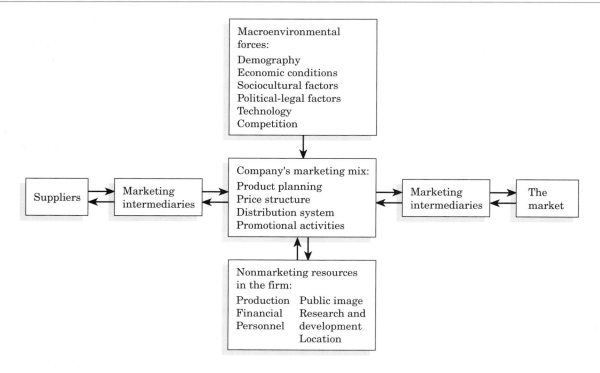

The Marketing System

A marketing system operates within a framework of forces—its environment. Two sets of these forces are external to the company, and another two sets are internal. Their relationship is seen in Figure 2–1.

External Environment

Six macroenvironmental forces impinge considerably on any company's marketing system, yet they generally are *not* controllable by management. These six forces are defined below, along with examples of how a company's marketing activities might be impacted by changes in these forces.

1. **Demography** is the measurement of basic characteristics of the human population, such as age, sex, race, income, and stage in family life cycle. Customer demographics can have a major impact on a firm's marketing system, which of course includes the sales force. For example, since the aging baby boomer generation will begin to retire in 10 to 15 years, sales opportunities are growing for those organizations that build and operate retirement communities. This is why Methodist Manor Retirement Community in Iowa solicited feedback from baby boomers while planning a new facility.[2]

2. **Economic conditions** simply refer to the overall health of the economy. In good economic times, for example, low mortgage rates and other positive indicators coincide with housing starts—leading to excellent selling opportu-

nities for real estate agents. Alternatively, slow economic times typically result in individuals and companies cutting back on expenses—yet this can provide opportunities for sales organizations in certain industries. In the downturn of 2001, Inceptor (a Massachusetts-based software and service provider) focused its sales strategy on how the company's product line can produce greater efficiency and revenue for customers.[3]

3. **Sociocultural factors** are the fundamental values and beliefs of society. Americans, for example, have placed a high priority on fitness and health in recent years. This trend facilitates those who sell memberships to fitness centers. Life Time Fitness Inc. has found success with a relatively new health club concept: a chain of family-oriented centers that offer lush decor, child care, restaurants, meeting rooms, and other amenities.[4]

4. **Political–legal factors**—laws, ordinances, regulations—can impact sales organizations in many ways. For example, selling educational children's books through its door-to-door sales force, South-Western Educational Publishing must abide by Green River Ordinances (i.e., laws unique to each city requiring an application process and permit to sell in that community). These laws are discussed in more detail in Chapter 17.

5. **Technology** includes inventions, innovations, and advances in scientific knowledge. Such advances have had a tremendous effect on day-to-day jobs of salespeople. For example, because of Internet technology, Encyclopædia Britannica eliminated its entire sales force! The encyclopedia is now sold through advertising and distributed via a website.[5] In fact, many observers originally thought that the Internet would replace face-to-face selling entirely. Instead, people who work in direct sales have learned to use technology to better serve their customers and enhance their productivity.[6]

6. **Competition** involves the marketing activities of rival firms. In most cases, this force has the greatest impact on the sales organization. In a recent survey of over 500 CEOs, "changes in type and/or level of competition" was identified as the top marketplace challenge (number two was "impact of the Internet").[7]

In addition to the six macroenvironmental forces, a company faces a set of three external forces that are a *direct* part of the firm's marketing system. These are the company's market, its suppliers, and its marketing intermediaries (primarily middlemen). While generally classed as uncontrollable, these three elements are susceptible to a greater degree of company influence than are the other six. Note the two-way flows between the company and these three external elements in Figure 2–1. The company receives products and promotional messages from its suppliers. In return, the company sends out payments and marketing information. The same types of exchanges occur between the company and its market. Any of these exchanges can go through one or more intermediaries.

Internal Variables

To reach its marketing goals, management has at its disposal two sets of internal, controllable forces: (1) the company's resources in nonmarketing areas and (2) the components of its marketing mix. Figure 2–1 shows these internal forces in relation to the forces in the external environment. The result is the company's total marketing system set within its environment.

Recall from Chapter 1 that the term *marketing mix* describes the combination of four ingredients that constitute the core of a company's marketing system. When effectively blended, these four—product, price, distribution, and promotion—form a marketing program designed to provide want-satisfying goods and services to the company's market. Also recall that promotional activities form a separate submix in the company's marketing program that we call the *promotional mix* or the *communications mix*. The major elements in the promotional mix are the company's advertising, sales promotion, and personal-selling efforts.

The Marketing Concept and Marketing Management

As businesspeople have come to recognize marketing's vital importance to a firm's success, a way of business thinking—a philosophy—has evolved. Called the **marketing concept,** this philosophy holds that *achieving organizational goals depends on the firm's ability to identify the needs and wants of a target market, and then to satisfy those needs and wants better than the competition does.* In order to do this, all activities throughout the entire company must be coordinated with each other and focused on the customer. An effective and efficient implementation of the marketing concept results in profitable sales volume and long-run success for the firm. Thus, as seen in Figure 2–2, the marketing concept is based on three fundamental beliefs:

1. Company planning and operations should be *customer* or *market oriented.*
2. Marketing activities in a firm should be *organizationally coordinated.*
3. The goal of the organization should be to generate *profitable sales volume over the long run.*

Firms have not always embraced the marketing concept—and many firms today still do not embrace it. Successful firms, however, use this philosophy as a guide to both the planning process and the implementation of strategies and tactics necessary for achieving goals.

Marketing Management and Its Evolution

For a business enterprise to realize the full benefits of the marketing concept, its marketing activities must be coordinated. The chief marketing executive is responsible for planning, implementing, and coordinating all marketing activities and integrating them into the overall operations of the firm. This process is called **marketing management.**

FIGURE 2–2

The marketing concept's three foundation stones

Marketing concept

| Customer/market orientation | Coordination of marketing activities | Profitable sales volume |

Marketing management in American business has evolved through four stages: production orientation, sales orientation, marketing orientation, and relationship orientation. The stages have direct implications for how salespeople deal with customers.

Each stage is described below, but first we present Figure 2–3, a cartoon demonstrating three distinct selling styles, which correspond to different marketing orientations. Interestingly, this cartoon is over 75 years old and thus was drawn in the production-orientation stage. It reveals that even before the Great Depression, progressive salespeople and managers understood the importance of identifying and satisfying customer needs. Such a revelation may seem to contradict the timeline presented in this and many other sales and marketing

FIGURE 2–3

Selling styles, 1927

Source: *52 Letters to Salesmen*, Chicago: Stevens-Davis Co., © 1926–1927.

textbooks when explaining when the marketing concept emerged. Although the timeline we present for the production, sales, marketing and relationship stages is *generally* correct, it is interesting and important to understand two things. First, salespeople have a long history of helping and solving problems for customers. Second, some people (including some salespeople) never learn—which is why The Drummer and Mr. "Stickem" are still around today!

Production-Orientation Stage

During the first stage, a company is typically production oriented. The executives in production and engineering shape the company's objectives and planning. The focus is on taking advantage of economies of scale and mass-producing a limited variety of products for as little cost as possible. The function of the sales department is simply to sell the production output at the price set by production and financial executives. With this stage, marketing is not recognized. In fact, the top "marketing" executive is the sales manager, who leads a sales department that is essentially within manufacturing. Most agree that this organizational pattern was predominant in the United States until about the start of the Great Depression.

Sales-Orientation Stage

The Depression made it quite clear that the main problem in our economy was no longer the ability to make or grow enough products. Rather, the problem was selling this output. Unfortunately, during this same period selling acquired much of its bad reputation. This was the age of the "hard sell," which dominated marketing into the 1950s. Even today, many organizations believe they must operate with a hard-sell philosophy. As long as this is so, there will be continued (and justified) criticism of selling and marketing.

Marketing-Orientation Stage

The marketing concept first emerged in marketing management's third stage, which began to take hold by 1960. With this orientation, companies use a coordinated marketing management strategy directed toward the twin goals of customer satisfaction and profitable sales volume. Attention focuses on marketing rather than on selling. The top executive is a marketing manager or the vice president of marketing. In this stage, several activities traditionally the province of other executives become the responsibility of the marketing manager. For instance, inventory control, warehousing, and aspects of product planning are often turned over to the marketing manager.

Ideally, a marketing-oriented firm goes beyond its own boundaries and coordinates its marketing activities with a select group of customers and suppliers. After all, customer needs and wants can be more easily understood and responded to if the selling firm has developed a close working relationship with its customers.

Relationship-Orientation Stage

The relationship-orientation stage is characterized by relationship building and is a natural extension of the marketing-orientation stage. Relationship-oriented firms continue to embrace the marketing concept. At the same time, the buyer and seller make a commitment to do business with each other *over a long time.* Thus, a given sale is not viewed as a discrete transaction. Salespeople become consultants to their customers. Their goal is to improve the customer's overall profitability rather than just to sell products. Over time, salespeople earn the customer's trust, which adds significant value to the relationship from the customer's perspective.[8] As noted in Chapter 1, this process of close cooperation and collaboration between the selling and buying firms is called *relationship marketing*. This orientation emerged in a widespread manner in the 1990s.

Relationship Marketing

Relationship marketing is a process of collaboration between the buying and selling firms that results in economic benefits for *both* firms. Instead of being adversarial, the relationship between firms is built on cooperation, trust, commitment, and information. Typically, the firms align their operating functions, such as order processing, accounting and budgeting, information systems, merchandising processes, and the like.

The sales manager and salespeople play a key role in these activities; and, thus, relationship marketing is often called relationship selling. In particular, sales must facilitate the following four key issues: promoting open communication, empowering employees, involving customers in the planning process, and working in teams.[9] Each of these is discussed below.

Open Communication

Because relationship marketing is often complex, the selling and buying firms must exchange extensive amounts of information. Open communication is the lifeblood of relationship marketing. It fosters trust and provides the information and knowledge necessary to carry out the cooperative and collaborative activities. Nobody in the selling firm knows more about the customer than the salesperson, who is therefore a key coordinator of the information flow. That is, a salesperson's responsibilities include collecting information from the customer and then dispensing that information to the appropriate person or department in their own organization. Of course, the salesperson also represents the firm and thus keeps the customer informed of events within that firm.

Empowering Employees

In relationship marketing, salespeople do more than simply sell their product to customers—they help solve customer problems. They can only do this if they have the skills, responsibility, and authority to make decisions and take action. Thus, companies must encourage and reward their salespeople for taking initiative and using creativity to solve customer problems. Further, managers must foster an environment in which salespeople do not fear losing their jobs if they make a mistake.

Customers and the Planning Process

Close, effective collaboration exists between firms when they agree on what tactics should be performed to carry out strategies that will lead to the accomplishment of goals. In other words, the selling firm should allow the customer to be involved in the seller's planning process. This ensures the customer's support in the implementation of the plan. In most cases, it is not feasible to involve all customers, but selling firms should at least solicit input from the larger firms among its customer base. Again, the salesperson is the key facilitator of this process; he or she is responsible for keeping the customer apprised of the latest planning decisions and for collecting feedback about those decisions.

Working in Teams

A firm engaged in relationship marketing must encourage teamwork—both among its own employees and among those of its partner firm. As indicated above, the relationship is often complex, with various operating processes of the two firms being closely aligned. Consequently, to effectively provide meaningful service and value to the buyer, the seller must involve a team of people with diverse, complementary skills. In addition to one or more salespeople, the selling team is composed of design engineers, financial experts, customer service representatives, quality control engineers—anyone and everyone who can contribute to solving customer problems and thus keeping the relationship on good terms. Salespeople play a key role in coordinating the many different actions of the diverse team, which interacts with an equally diverse group of individuals from the customer firm. This group or team of people from the customer firm is known as the **buying center.** The buying center is made up of functional specialists from purchasing, manufacturing, engineering, and/or product development who view the purchase from a strategic perspective. This practice of **team selling** is arguably the most widespread and significant strategic trend to influence sales in recent years.

Interestingly, these relationship marketing concepts, such as employee empowerment and working in teams, emerged in the 1990s as part of the **total quality management (TQM)** movement. TQM is the process by which a company strives to improve customer satisfaction through the continuous improvement of all its operations. The entire supply chain focuses on improving product quality

---

Teaching Teamwork

In today's selling environment, teamwork is more important than ever. Many sales organizations host creative exercises to build camaraderie and teach team members how to work and solve problems together. The following are five popular team-building exercises:

1. **Cooking class:** Members of the sales team are taken out of the office and into the kitchen for the opportunity to have fun and laugh together while tasting and learning how to make gourmet treats.

2. **Drum circle:** Team members sit around in a circle and bang on exotic drums from Africa and other parts of the world. Allows people to find their inner rhythm.

3. **Military exercise:** Team members partake in a wide range of physical exercises that a soldier might go through in boot camp, such as climbing

walls, navigating assault-style obstacle courses, and even driving military vehicles.

4. **Outdoor adventure:** For this, the team might go to a campground for a weekend and bicycle, boat, or snowmobile together. Often facilitated by an expert in organizational development.

5. **Ropes exercise:** In one of the more popular exercises, blindfolded team members each hold on to the same long rope, the two ends of which are tied together. The team works together to form a square, which sounds easier that it is!

In your opinion, which one of these (if any) would be most effective at teaching a salesperson how to be an effective member of a selling team? Discuss.

Source: Mark McMaster, "Roping In the Followers," *Sales & Marketing Management*, January 2002, pp. 36–41.

through eliminating manufacturing defects, which ultimately reduces costs. This requires extensive cooperation and collaboration with both customers and suppliers. Thus, firms that embrace the TQM philosophy are necessarily engaged in relationship marketing. Again, salespeople play a critical role in these relationships as they oversee the transfer of relevant, accurate, and timely information between firms.

If a company is successful in implementing a relationship marketing program, it can expect to have higher quality products, higher customer satisfaction, more loyal customers, and greater profitability.[10] As more and more companies focus on customer relations and satisfaction as a measure of the effectiveness of their marketing programs, sales managers and salespeople will be expected to assume greater responsibility for directing and coordinating the marketing efforts of the firm.

Integrating Marketing and Sales Functions

One common problem in marketing management is the lack of integration between a firm's marketing department and its sales function.[11] The marketing department typically develops a firm's overall marketing strategy, which includes decisions about how to promote, distribute, and price the product line. The salespeople ultimately determine success or failure of the strategy, because they have the responsibility of implementing it in the field. Thus, integration between the activities of the marketing and sales functions is critical to the success of the firm.

The marketing strategy can be effective only when it is clearly understood and embraced by the sales force. This is more likely to happen when salespeople are involved in the strategy development process. After all, salespeople are an invaluable source of information in this regard, given their unique position of working closely with customers. Further, the marketing department must assist the salespeople in carrying out the marketing strategy by providing them with the right marketing tools, such as advertising, support services, and sales promotions. But if salespeople don't like a particular tool, they probably won't use it— or at least they won't use it as effectively as they could.

One company that understands the importance of integrating marketing and sales is Ecolab Inc., which has a long history of manufacturing and selling detergents and other cleaning products to hotels and restaurants. Ecolab trains its salespeople to listen to customers, and then it listens to its salespeople in the development of marketing strategy. For example, one salesperson relayed to the company that many customers were having significant problems with insect control. Ecolab responded by creating its pest-elimination service, which is now one of the world's largest killers of cockroaches![12] Like many other companies embracing the marketing concept, Ecolab expects salespeople to do more than simply sell things—they solve customer problems.

Integrating Production and Sales

Coordinating the activities of the sales force and the production function is also critical to the overall success of the firm. Materials requirements and production schedules are developed according to sales forecasts. Therefore, firms avoid operational problems by integrating the plans of the production and sales functions.

When the amount sold exceeds production output, customers become dissatisfied because the products they ordered do not arrive on time. Of course, the opposite situation is also a serious problem, because high levels of unsold inventory become extremely costly to the firm.

In spite of the intuitive connection between production and sales, many companies do a poor job of coordinating the activities of these two business functions. The problem stems from the fact that salespeople for a given company are often dispersed across many different territories throughout the world. This makes it difficult for the company to keep up-to-date on the needs of each sales territory. A-dec, Inc., a dental equipment manufacturer, is one of many companies using Web-based technology to improve the coordination of its planning processes. Previously, A-dec would develop a sales forecast during its annual meeting—which was the one time all year when the sales managers from the company's 75 territories would come together. Typically, the forecast was extremely inaccurate, causing excess inventory for some products and long production lead times for others. The solution to these problems was a secure website. The site's advanced Web-based software application enabled sales managers from around the world to constantly update their sales forecasts—they can now communicate about the product mix they need, and when they need it. This technology-facilitated integration has led to many benefits for A-dec and its customers. Lead times are shorter, excess inventory has been eliminated, and customers get the right product at the right time.[13]

Strategic Planning

When shaping sales force management strategy, sales executives are guided and limited by both the firm's total company planning and its **strategic planning.** For example, in the early 1990s, IBM made some significant changes in its overall strategic approach to the personal computer market. For several years IBM concentrated on selling networks to big businesses and more or less ignored the individual, the educational, and the small-business market segments that Apple Computer solicited. However, Apple's success in its markets forced IBM to reconsider its own company strategies. IBM altered its marketing strategies accordingly, and IBM sales management planning also soon reflected the new company strategies.

Three concepts—objectives, strategies, and tactics—are the heart of planning at any level in the organizational hierarchy. All sales managers should have a thorough understanding of these concepts—what they are and how to use them.

Objectives

Objectives are the goals around which a strategic plan is formulated. Without goals, it is impossible to create a meaningful plan. Objectives must be more than platitudes. Such clichés as "We should be of service to our customers and treat our employees fairly" are only hazy guideposts for making business decisions. To be useful, objectives must be specific and measurable.

Once the firm's objectives are agreed on, all decisions should align with them. Decisions incompatible with the objectives only hinder the company's realization of its goals. This alignment seems simple and obvious, but it is not easy to achieve. For instance, goals of a 15 percent return on investment and a 10 percent annual growth rate can clash. Heublein, Inc., encountered this difficulty when it acquired Hamm's beer. One of Heublein's objectives was a 15 percent rate of return on its investment. It also had ambitious growth objectives. Hamm's large sales volume fit the company's growth objective. However, profits in the beer business are far less than 15 percent—Hamm's realized about a 5 percent return on investment. To satisfy its growth objective, Heublein would have had to sacrifice its profit objective. A few years after acquiring the brand, Heublein sold Hamm's at a loss.

Strategies

The terms *objectives*, *strategies*, and *tactics* gain more meaning when viewed in relation to each other, as in Figure 2–4. Companies set objectives first and then develop **strategies,** or plans of action, to achieve the objectives. For instance, the sales manager may have the goal of achieving a certain dollar volume of sales in a coming period. She proceeds to formulate strategies to accomplish this goal. These strategies may include entering new markets or covering the existing markets more intensely.

Strategies should be followed with some degree of perseverance. Some strategies require time to be effective. Impatient managers eager for results may not allow certain programs time to bear fruit. These managers often take new products off the market before the products have had a fair chance to develop a following. One sales manager fired a rep who had been sent to open up a new territory because dealers were not buying the product as fast as the manager had expected. The fault was not that the sales rep was inefficient, but rather that the manager had unrealistic expectations.

Tactics

After all the talking, the firm implements its chosen strategies. Some work must be done. **Tactics** are the activities that people must perform in order to carry out the strategy.

There are no perfect tactics, and in most situations there is no one best tactic that should always be used. Rather, managers must evaluate the situation and choose those tactics they feel are consistent with the strategy and have the highest probability of success at a given time.

Generally, when a company changes its strategies, it must also change its tactics. However, many administrators use the same tactics repeatedly, regardless of the circumstances, because those tactics worked for them in the past. But

FIGURE 2-4

Relationship of objectives, strategies, and tactics

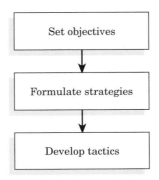

A diverse set of people with complementary skills, this sales team works together to solve problems for the customer.

success can be lulling. There comes a time when the tactic will not work, and that is usually the most critical time.

A classic example of using an inappropriate tactic occurs when a company changes its sales strategy from transactional selling to consultative selling yet does not make any changes in its compensation plan. The following discussion of strategic planning further illustrates the relationship among objectives, strategies, and tactics at different levels within the corporation.

Strategic Planning at the Company, Marketing, and Sales Force Levels

Several of the administrative concepts that we just discussed are involved in the strategic planning process for the total company, its marketing program, and its sales force operations. The strategic planning on all levels in a firm should be well integrated and highly coordinated.

Marketing must create a strategic plan that is consistent with the strategic plan of the total company. In turn, planning by the sales department is determined by the strategic marketing plan. In this sense, planning starts at the top and works its way down, guiding the entire organization.[14] At the same time, planning is a bottom-up process—those creating the strategic plan for the total company must listen carefully to the input of employees at all levels of the organization. Of course, this includes salespeople, who work closely with customers and thus have valuable insight into what direction the firm should take.

Strategic Planning for the Total Company

Strategic planning for the total company involves determining the organization's mission, the broad objectives (goals) that will enable the company to fulfill its mission, and the strategies and tactics needed to achieve the objectives. Thus, strategic planning starts with identifying the organization's fundamental **mission.** Management should ask two questions: "What business are we in?" and "What business should we be in?" The answers may or may not be the same. A television manufacturer may say it is in the "indoor entertainment" business. But after further analysis of its market opportunities, it may decide that it should be in the "entertainment and education" business.

Once it determines the company's mission, management can set objectives consistent with that mission. For example, the company may aim either to earn a 20 percent return on investment next year or to increase its market share from the present 8 percent to 20 percent in three years.

The next step is to select the strategy to be used to reach the objectives. As examples, consider the following relationships:

Objectives	Possible Strategies
1. Earn 20 percent return on investment next year.	*a.* Reduce production and marketing costs. *b.* Increase rate of capital turnover.
2. Increase market share from present 8 percent to 20 percent in three years.	*a.* Intensify marketing efforts in domestic markets. *b.* Expand into foreign markets. *c.* Buy out a competitor.

The tactics selected to implement the strategy depend, of course, on the strategy chosen. Thus, if the chosen strategy is to reduce marketing costs, management can use such tactics as cutting advertising expenses by 10 percent or closing two branch offices. To implement the strategy of intensifying the domestic marketing

An International Perspective

The international marketplace is booming, and thus strategic planning for most U.S. companies involves a global dimension. While the objectives or ultimate goals might be the same in all countries served, the best salespeople develop tactics unique to each specific culture.

For example, American salespeople generally find that the sales cycle is longer in almost every country outside the United States. That is, it takes more time for the salesperson to close a deal after making initial customer contact. This means that in order to be productive, American salespeople selling abroad must work simultaneously with more accounts than they would back home.

The reasons for the longer sales cycle tend to vary across cultures. The following observations are based on comments from salespeople with overseas experience:

In Germany, longer sales cycles stem from Germans' tendency to be thorough. Germans expect multiple references and do extensive background research on all competitive products before committing to the sale.

In Spain and Italy, customers expect weeks and weeks of schmoozing and entertaining before committing to the sale. In fact, U.S. salespeople are often asked to attend social gatherings with the customer's spouse, children, and maybe even siblings, parents, aunts, and uncles!

In England, the British do not commit before extensive negotiation about the price and thorough double-checking of facts and figures.

In Turkey, the sales cycle takes longer due to an unstable economy. American businesspeople have learned to ask for payment up front, and to insist on dealing with U.S. currency rather than the seriously devalued Turkish lira.

Note that these are general tendencies observed by a few salespeople. Clearly, not all customers in a given country or culture are identical!

Source: Lisa Bertagnoli, "Selling Overseas Complex Endeavor," *Marketing News* 35, no. 16 (July 30, 2001), p. 4.

effort, management might add 20 more sales reps or change the compensation plan to provide greater motivation for the sales force.

Strategic Marketing Planning

Once the total company planning process is completed, essentially the same procedure can be repeated for the marketing program. The objectives, strategies, and tactics at the marketing level are closely related to those at the corporate level. A corporate strategy often translates into a marketing strategy. To illustrate:

Company Objective	Company Strategy	Marketing Strategy
1. Earn 20 percent return on investment.	Cut marketing costs by 15 percent this year.	Reduce direct selling efforts by using wholesalers to reach small accounts.
2. Increase market share from present 8 percent to 20 percent.	Intensify marketing efforts in domestic markets.	Enter new markets.

Sales Force Strategy

Once the strategic planning process for the entire marketing program has been completed, the role of the sales force has largely been established. That is, the objectives, strategies, and tactics adopted by sales managers generally are limited and guided by the strategic marketing plan. To illustrate:

Company Objective	Company Strategy (Marketing Goal)	Marketing Strategy (Sales Force Goal)
Increase market share from 8 percent to 20 percent in two years.	Intensify market efforts in domestic markets to increase sales volume by $3 million next year.	a. Enter new geographic markets and sell to new types of customers, or b. Cover existing geographic markets more aggressively.

Now, whether the company elects to pursue marketing strategy (sales force goal) *a* or *b* will make a big difference in the choice of sales force strategies and tactics. Tactical decisions in the areas of organizational design, selection, training, compensation, supervision, and evaluation must all be aligned with the sales strategy. These principles may be illustrated as follows:

Marketing Strategy	Sales Force Strategy	Sales Force Tactics
a. Enter new markets.	Build long-term customer relations.	1. Stress missionary selling in sales training and supervision. 2. Stress salary element in compensation plan.
b. Sell aggressively in existing markets.	Increase sales force motivation.	1. Conduct more sales contests. 2. Stress commission feature in pay plan. 3. Increase field supervision.

In many companies, this strategic sales force planning is continued down the organizational hierarchy. That is, sales force goals and strategies are established for regional sales divisions, and even for individual sales reps and key accounts.

Strategic Trends

Several strategic trends emerging in the past decade continue to have a major impact on the sales strategies of today. These include Internet selling, multiple sales strategies, and multiple relationship strategies. We elaborate on each trend below.

Internet Selling

In the past few years, sales organizations have spent considerable time and money trying to figure out how to integrate the Internet into their sales processes. Many salespeople initially felt threatened by the Internet, fearing that their jobs would be replaced by an e-commerce website. After all, the Internet is a tremendous communications medium. Not only can a website provide relevant and timely product information, but it can also allow a company to process transactions 24 hours a day, seven days a week!

Most sales executives agree that the projected impact of the Internet on sales organizations was exaggerated—at least in the short term. Instead of threatening the salesperson's job, the Internet has become a tool that helps salespeople develop close relationships with their clients. Sales organizations are now cutting back the funding of technology and refocusing efforts on face-to-face sales.[15] In this era of relationship marketing, a website is no substitute for a competent, consultative salesperson intent on adding value and solving customer problems.

Sales organizations often make the mistake of not including salespeople in the process of designing their websites.[16] When left out of the loop, salespeople start expecting the worst. They begin to wonder if the website is intended to replace them, and they may even discourage their customers from using it. Firms must also consider how they will compensate salespeople when customers purchase products via the website. When buying household products from the Tupperware website, customers are asked who referred them to the site. The referring Tupperware sales rep gets full commission on the sale. This strategy helps the company maintain an energized and motivated sales force.

Customer Relationship Management

Combining relationship marketing practices with the latest advances in technology has resulted in the emergence of companywide software applications known as customer relationship management (CRM) systems. CRM applications aggregate all information about a customer into a single database. This gives both salespeople and customers access to timely and relevant information (typically via the Internet). CRM has become very popular because it allows for effective management of every aspect of the buyer–seller relationship.

However, CRM can be effective only if salespeople embrace it and are willing to use it. Consequently, sales managers must be passionate in communicating the benefits of CRM and in ensuring that all employees are properly trained in how to use the system.

Sources: William F. Brendler, "8 Critical Factors That Make or Break CRM," *Target Marketing*, April 2001, pp. 57–61; and Kathleen Cholewka, "CRM: The Failures Are Your Fault," *Sales & Marketing Management* 154, no. 1 (January 2002), pp. 23–24.

Multiple Sales Channels

To maintain existing customer bases, cut costs, and expand market coverage, many firms are restructuring their sales operations to use **multiple sales channels.** A company may employ a direct sales force as well as distributors. The same firm may also use direct mail, telemarketing, and electronic mail. These methods may be used to reach different segments of customers or to perform various selling tasks necessary to efficiently serve one segment.

Originally, IBM's selling tasks were handled by the company's direct sales force only. But as IBM faced increasing competition, it expanded its sales efforts to include independent dealers, catalogs, direct mail, and telemarketing. Apple Computer, in contrast, started with a dealer network and later added a direct sales force. Cosmetics seller Mary Kay Inc. has added telemarketing to its more traditional personal selling methods. Each of these companies created a *hybrid* sales system to reach different segments of buyers.

The objective in designing hybrid systems is to determine what mix of selling methods can best accomplish the selling tasks. Often it is possible to use less-expensive selling methods for tasks that do not require face-to-face contact. The trade-off that must be considered is between the need for personalized customer service and the cost of providing that service. Chapter 3 explores these options further.

The addition of new sales channels requires changes in the structure and policies of the sales organization. These changes may be accompanied by a certain amount of resistance from the existing salespeople. Sales managers must manage this conflict as well as the coordination within and across channels. Specific guidelines must be established that clearly delineate who is responsible for which customers and tasks in the hybrid system. Utilizing multiple channels undoubtedly makes the sales manager's job more complex. But in spite of the potential problems, the use of multiple channels is likely to increase throughout the next decade.

Multiple Relationship Strategies

Along with using multiple channels of distribution, many companies are segmenting their customers according to what kind of relationship the company has (or wants to develop) with them. In one segment the sale may be just an individual transaction, and in another the salesperson serves as a consultant and develops a close, long-term partnership with the customer.

On one end of the continuum, transaction selling (discussed in Chapter 1) is targeted at customers who are not interested in, or who are unable to afford, the value-added services offered by the selling firm. With this approach, the salesperson does not follow up with the customer after the sale and is not concerned about cultivating a long-term relationship.

Alternatively, **consultative selling** is used for those customers interested in the value-added services. Consultative selling involves salespeople who have in-depth knowledge of their customers' company and business. In fact, a team of individuals from the selling firm might be involved since it is often difficult for a single salesperson to provide all the necessary knowledge. Consultative salespeople or sales teams create value for their customers by identifying problems and finding mutually beneficial solutions.

A selling firm engages in a **multiple relationship strategy** when it reaches some customers through transaction selling and other customers through consultative selling. For example, Aeroquip (a division of Eaton Corporation) manufactures and sells fluid power components, such as high-pressure hydraulic hoses, to a wide variety of industrial distributors. Some distributors, which tend to be low-volume buyers, order Aeroquip products primarily through the telephone as needed—in fact, Aeroquip salespeople never visit them. Other distributors are called on frequently by Aeroequip reps, who provide these generally larger distributors with a wide variety of services (such as market research) to help them resell the product to the ultimate user. In another example of multiple relationship strategies, Microsoft has dramatically different selling relationships with its many business customers. Interestingly, the differences are not always due to the size of the customer—Microsoft has transactional relationships with some of its largest national accounts. Certain firms simply have corporate cultures that resist forming close partnerships and sharing proprietary information with vendors.[17]

Marketing Management's Social Responsibility

Global warming, toxic waste, pollution, and other concerns have led to another important development in the evolution of marketing management: Marketing executives in this era must act in a socially responsible manner if they wish to succeed, or even survive. External pressures—consumer discontent, concern for environmental problems, and political–legal forces—influence marketing programs in countless firms.

In response to great pressure from environmentalists, Arco developed and now markets an unleaded regular gasoline with low emissions. The auto industry made many technical and design changes in its products in response to governmental and public pressure for safer vehicles. Grocery chains responded quickly to complaints about harmful chemicals sprayed on produce. Ralph's, a California supermarket chain, promotes its produce as being free of such chemicals. This book is printed on partially recycled paper. It would be difficult to find any firm that has not somehow had to alter its marketing behavior in response to external pressures.

Viewed more broadly, there is a growing concern for the management of human resources. We sense a change in emphasis from materialism to humanitarianism in our society. One mark of an affluent society is a shift in consumption from products to services and a shift in cultural emphasis from things to people. As we progress in the 21st century, marketing management must be concerned not only with establishing a better material standard of *living* but also with creating and delivering a better quality of *life*.

Summary

Modern sales managers understand that they are but one link in the total marketing strategy for the firm. Moreover, they understand the place of the firm's marketing strategy within the company's total strategic plan.

In addition, both managers and reps should understand the external environmental forces that affect their operations. Specifically, they must monitor and respond to any changes in the demographics, economic conditions, sociocultural factors, political–legal factors, technology, and competition associated with their market. They must also understand their markets, their suppliers, and the marketing intermediaries (wholesalers and retailers).

To respond to their environment, managers can manipulate the variables of the marketing mix, which include product, price structure, distribution system, and promotional activities. Personal selling is a major element of promotion.

With the advent of the marketing concept and its acceptance by most businesses, the job of the sales manager has been changed and sales operations have become but one portion of the firm's total marketing program. Marketing has evolved through several stages. It is now in the relationship-orientation stage, in which buyers and sellers make long-term commitments to do business with each other. For effective relationship marketing, all functions of the selling firm must work together as a team to help solve customer problems.

Setting specific, clear-cut objectives is an essential step in the management of a company. Once the company's objectives are set, management can develop appropriate strategies. Tactics are the organizational behaviors that execute the strategy.

Strategic planning across all levels in a firm should be coordinated. Strategic decisions at the top of the organization dictate what goes in the strategic marketing plan, which in turn guides the activities of the sales force. At the same time, top-level executives cannot plan effectively without listening to lower-level employees such as salespeople.

Several strategic trends have emerged in the past decade and are shaping the strategy of sales organizations. The Internet has had a significant impact on sales strategy—though sales organizations have not completely grasped how best to use it. In response to intensified competition and changes in customer purchasing patterns, many firms are now using multiple sales channels to reach a broad customer base and multiple relationship strategies to sell to different customers. Finally, today's managers must act in a socially responsible manner if they wish to succeed.

Key Terms

Buying center
Competition
Consultative selling
Demography
Economic conditions
External environment
Goals
Internet selling
Marketing concept
Marketing management

Marketing mix
Marketing system
Mission
Multiple relationship strategy
Multiple sales channels
Objectives
Political–legal factors
Promotional mix
Relationship marketing
Relationship selling

Sociocultural factors
Strategic planning
Strategies
Tactics
Team selling
Technology
Total quality management (TQM)
Transactional selling

Questions and Problems

1. How can top management keep the sales manager abreast of changes in the environment that affect the company? How can the sales manager pass on such information to the sales force?

2. We said company planning should be customer oriented. Exactly what does that mean?

In what way or by what stretch of the imagination might the planning of the firm's employee benefit package be affected by customer considerations?

3. Why should a company be concerned about the profitability of its customers?

4. What are some ways in which sales managers can empower their salespeople?

5. How do marketing people depend on salespeople? How do salespeople depend on marketing people?

6. Why should a sales manager prepare an annual operating plan?

7. If you, as a sales manager, were required to prepare an annual operating plan, what would you include in the plan?

8. As a sales rep, you are required to develop an annual sales plan for your territory. What would you include in your plan? *Hint:* Think in terms of objectives, strategies, and tactics.

9. What role does the quality of the information you possess have in your tactical behavior?

10. In what way is the existence of a sales force the reflection of a strategy?

11. One management writer observed that it is folly to expect behavior A when rewarding behavior B. How might his insight be applied to the problem of aligning sales force behavior with corporate goals?

12. What are some of the ways sales managers can limit the amount of conflict between various distributors if their company is using a multiple-channel strategy?

13. How should a company decide whether to use transaction selling or consultative selling with each of its customers?

14. How does a manager reward the team members in a team-selling situation?

15. In what industries are salespeople's jobs most likely to change due to the increasing predominance of the Internet in our society? Elaborate on how the sales job will change.

Experiential Exercises

A. Interview a marketing or product manager. Ask him or her to identify the primary sales objective for one of the company's products. Ask a sales manager and a sales representative at that company the same question for the same product. Compare and contrast the three viewpoints.

B. Interview a salesperson on how the Internet has impacted her or his job responsibilities. Ask the salesperson if he or she has ever felt threatened by the Internet. Further, ask about the extent to which the company's website or e-mail system is critical to carrying out the strategic marketing plan of the organization. Combine the salesperson's answers into a written report.

Internet Exercises

A. Choose two companies and visit their websites. After examining each company's mission statement and other basic information, compare and contrast the marketing and sales strategies of the two companies. Which company is more customer-focused? Do the companies' sales organizations appear to use transaction selling or consultative selling?

B. Using a search engine (such as AltaVista or Yahoo!), enter "team-building exercises" or another similar search phrase. From the list of hits that is returned, find a few specific exercises that you feel would be most likely to help a sales team bond and work together, and describe these briefly. Then try to find price information. If you were a sales manager, would you pay to have your salespeople go through any such programs? Why or why not?

References

1. Stanley F. Slater and Eric M. Olson, "Strategy Type and Performance: The Influence of Sales Force Management," *Strategic Management Journal* 21, no. 8 (August 2000), pp. 813–29.

2. "Design Center," *Nursing Homes* 50, no. 1 (January 2001), p. 33.

3. Mark McMaster, "Don't Believe the Hype," *Sales & Marketing Management*, May 2001, p. 11.

4. Dick Youngblood, "Entrepreneur Gets Healthy Return on His Investment," *Star Tribune* (Minneapolis, MN), November 5, 2000, p. 1D.

5. Helan Jezzard, "Britannica Now Charging for Encyclopaedia Content," *Information World Review* 172 (September 2001), p. 8.

6. Gregory A. Rich, "The Internet: Boom or Bust to Sales Organizations?" *Journal of Marketing Management* 18 (April 2002).

7. Esther Rudis, Melissa A. Berman, and Chuck Mitchell, *The CEO Challenge: Top Marketplace and Management Issues 2001: A CEO Survey by Accenture and The Conference* Board (New York: Conference Board, 2001).

8. Sandy D. Jap, "The Strategic Role of the Sales-force in Developing Customer Satisfaction across the Relationship Lifecycle," *Journal of Personal Selling & Sales Management* 21, no. 2 (Spring 2001), pp. 95–108.

9. Atul Parvatiyar and Jagdish N. Sheth, "The Domain and Conceptual Foundations of Relationship Marketing," in *Handbook of Relationship Marketing*, ed. Jagdish N. Sheth and Atul Parvatiyar (Thousand Oaks, CA: Sage, 2000), pp. 3–38.

10. Joel R. Evans and Richard L. Laskins, "The Relationship Marketing Process: A Conceptualization and Application," *Industrial Marketing Management* 23 (1994), pp. 439–52.

11. Belinda Dewsnap and David Jobber, "The Sales-Marketing Interface in Consumer Packaged-Goods Companies: A Conceptual Framework," *Journal of Personal Selling & Sales Management*, Spring 2000, pp. 109–19.

12. Weld Royal, "Manufacturers Introduce Services to Boost Revenues and Give Salespeople Expanded Roles," *Industry Week*, March 5, 2001, p. 41.

13. "America's Largest Dental Equipment Manufacturer Creates 'Wow' Application with Comshare Business Intelligence Software," *Business Wire*, April 11, 2001.

14. William Strahle, Rosann L. Spiro, and Frank Acito, "Marketing and Sales: Strategic Alignment and Functional Implementation," *Journal of Personal Selling & Sales Management*, Winter 1996. pp. 1–20.

15. Andy Cohen, "Changing Channels," *Sales & Marketing Management*, April 2001, p. 11.

16. Melinda Ligos, "Clicks and Misses," *Sales & Marketing Management*, June 2000, pp. 68–76.

17. Neil Rackham and John R. DeVincentis, *Rethinking the Sales Force: Redefining Selling to Create and Capture Customer Value* (New York: McGraw-Hill, 1999), pp. 157–58.

CASE 2-1   CARDINAL CONNECTORS, INC.

E-Commerce and a Multiple Sales Channel Strategy

Sarah Miko, a sales manager for Cardinal Connectors Inc., is suddenly frightened about losing her job. She just stepped out of a meeting with her company's president, Bill Evans. In the meeting, Evans outlined a revolutionary e-commerce strategy that would dramatically alter Cardinal's distribution channel in the name of enhanced efficiency and overall productivity. That is, Evans has begun to believe that Cardinal's customers might be well served through a company website that actually replaces not only its current sales force but also its network of intermediary wholesalers.

With 100 employees and $10 million in annual sales, Cardinal Connectors Inc. is a relatively small manufacturer of custom-designed circuit-board connectors. Cardinal's loyal base of customers consists of firms in the telecom, networking, and auto industries. Currently, these customers are serviced through a multiple sales channel strategy. The bigger customers, which represent about 60 percent of total revenue, are dealt with directly through Cardinal's 15-person full-time sales force. The remaining 40 percent of revenue is generated from smaller customers, which buy the product indirectly through one of five intermediary electronics wholesaler firms.

Sarah Miko has been a loyal and successful sales executive for Cardinal Connectors for more than 20 years. She began as a sales representative with Cardinal right out of college and eventually came to be one of Cardinal's most consistent sales performers. Seven years ago, Miko was promoted to sales manager and has received consistently high evaluations from Evans, the company president.

Miko prides herself on her ability to train and coach young sales reps into being professional, consultative salespeople. Above all, Miko preaches about the importance of relationship selling and says that Cardinal's sales reps are not doing their job unless they are adding value to the interfirm relationship between buyer and seller. For a Cardinal sales rep, most of the creative selling effort involves showing existing customers how they can solve their problems through the purchase of more Cardinal products. Thus, the emphasis is on increasing customer share—as opposed to market share.

Cardinal's sales force, however, does not service all customers. As stated above, a significant portion of revenue is generated from smaller customers who buy Cardinal products through intermediaries. But again, Miko believes that these intermediaries provide end-user customers with a host of valuable services that Cardinal could never offer itself through any website. These services include access to inventory, parts delivery, engineering support, and chip programming.

Evans is not so sure that either the direct sales force or the intermediaries are truly adding value. Evans believes that Cardinal circuit-board connectors are unmatched in quality and performance, and thus current customers will remain loyal to Cardinal as the sales function is moved to the Internet. Evans says this will be especially true since the e-commerce strategy will result in cost savings that can be passed onto the customer. The savings will stem from two sources. First, Cardinal can eliminate the high costs of paying for salesperson compensation and benefits; and, second, it will no longer have to offer margins to intermediaries. In addition, Evans thinks that customers will prefer dealing with a well-designed, interactive website, which (unlike salespeople and intermediaries) can be reached from anywhere at any time. And because a website is a great way to organize information, customers can find out all they want about Cardinal products simply by surfing and clicking.

Further, Cardinal Connectors' competitors have started to move toward selling product through their own company websites. However, Evans is convinced that it is just a matter of time before that happens, and he wants to be the first in the industry to capitalize on the many new e-commerce tools and capabilities that are now available.

Although respectful of Evans's bold, future-oriented thinking, Sarah Miko still believes in the merits of many aspects of the current system. She feels that Evans's e-commerce initiatives are too extreme and should be downscaled and better integrated with the existing multiple sales channel strategy. At the same time, she knows it will take a convincing argument to persuade the very strong-minded Evans to consider anything else.

Evans has called another meeting in a few days to discuss the specifics of his strategy. Of course, Miko is greatly troubled by the thought of eliminating Cardinal's direct sales force. She is proud of the effort and accomplishments of her salespeople—many of whom she has personally trained. But, in addition, Miko truly believes that Evans's e-commerce strategy is not in the best interests of Cardinal Connectors Inc. Consequently, she wants to come to that meeting prepared to make a case for the benefits of their current strategy.

Questions:

1. What are the pros and cons of Bill Evans's e-commerce strategy?

2. What is the best argument that Sarah Miko can make to keep her sales force intact?

3. In your opinion, should Cardinal Connectors Inc. eliminate its sales force? Explain.

CASE 2-2   MATSUSHITA ELECTRIC CORPORATION OF AMERICA

Sales Force Strategy

John Cunningham was the national sales manager of the Lighting Products Department, Special Products Division, of Matsushita Electric Corporation, a huge industrial complex in Japan with total sales worldwide of ¥ 6,660 billion ($60 billion). He was immediately concerned with the operational sales strategy for a new line of compact, energy-efficient, fluorescent lightbulbs (lamps) for both the consumer and industrial markets. The company had many years of experience selling lamps in Asia, where it was a major factor in the market. For strategic reasons, Matsushita marketed its wide line of consumer and industrial products in the United States under the trade name Panasonic.

John Cunningham, after graduating as a marketing major from the University of South Florida in 1988, began his career selling lightbulbs for Westinghouse and subsequently North American Phillips when it purchased the lamp division from Westinghouse. His outstanding sales record attracted the attention of Mitsubishi, which was trying to build distribution for a new line of energy-efficient lightbulbs it had developed. However, that venture was terminated when the new bulbs were found to infringe on patents held by Phillips. Mitsubishi transferred Cunningham to selling its gigantic Diamond Vision television screens now seen in most of the sports stadiums in the country. His outstanding performance attracted the attention of the managers of Matsushita's lightbulb operations, who were looking for someone to manage sales and distribution in the United States.

After much conversation, several interviews, and a thorough investigation, Cunningham was hired. While his previous experience working for a Japanese company and his knowledge of the Japanese business culture were important factors in his selection, his outstanding sales record and establishment of a distribution network with Mitsubishi's compact fluorescent lamp operation was instrumental in the hiring decision.

Matsushita's basic marketing strategy was to introduce compact, energy-efficient fluorescent lamps. A 15-watt fluorescent lamp would provide the same lumens (light) as a 75-watt incandescent lamp, thus yielding significant savings in power consumption. Such savings were important in the Far East markets, where electricity costs were much higher than in the United States. Further, the life of the lamp was about 10 times that of an incandescent lamp. Research in the United States indicated that most people considered longevity the product's prime benefit. Social, political, and economic forces strongly supported such energy-saving innovations.

Despite Cunningham's outstanding performance, Panasonic's share of the U.S. consumer lamp market was small. Panasonic was a new player in a very competitive market dominated by such powerful names as General Electric and Phillips. Even such a name as Westinghouse had been driven out of the business. At a meeting at the company's headquarters in Osaka, Japan, in late 2000, he was asked a direct question by one of the firm's top executives: "What would it take for us to significantly increase our share of the market for our fluorescent bulbs?"

Cunningham knew that he was expected to make the company a major player in the market; Matsushita management did not like being a minor factor in any of its markets. Cunningham had studied the situation intensely and was waiting with his answer: "We need to develop an electronic chip to replace the ballast. Present ballasts hum, flicker when started, are bulky, and are not rheostatic. They are either off or on. If a small electronic chip could be designed to replace the traditional ballast, we'd have a technological feature that would significantly increase our market share."

Cunningham's superiors took note of his request and within a short time the company R&D people gave him exactly what he had requested—a small electronic chip to replace the ballast in fluorescent bulbs. It could be available for distribution in about 10 months. A planning meeting was held in Osaka at which Cunningham was asked to provide sales forecasts and budgets for marketing the new line of lamps. Cunningham was responsible only for the marketing of lamps under the Panasonic brand name. Matsushita also sold huge quantities of goods directly to other manufacturers and to large distributive organizations that sold them under their own brand names. For example, while Matsushita sold compact disc machines under its brand name Panasonic, it also made essentially the same product, with minor cosmetic alterations, for many other companies to market under their brand names. Matsushita company policy was to encourage original equipment manufacturer (OEM) sales since it was felt that by so doing the company would be able to sell a much larger portion of the total market.

One basic corporate goal was to keep the factories in Japan busy, at full employment. Matsushita was not caught up with the penchant of many American corporations for controlling significant shares of a market through their own brands. It would sell to any firm that could provide significant volume for the factories.

Cunningham was informed at the meeting that the new technology would be offered to all other manufacturers. General Electric would have the same technology to sell as Panasonic. Cunningham was somewhat dismayed but knew that he could do nothing about the policy. However, he negotiated two concessions. First, he was able to have his sales quotas reduced in view of the increased

competition. Second, he was able to get a one-year lead time over the competition. Panasonic would have the innovation exclusively for one year before Matsushita would sell it to anyone else. Cunningham had some sales force planning to do.

The new bulbs would be sold through the channels that traditionally sold lightbulbs: hardware stores, discount stores, supermarkets, drugstores, light fixture outlets, electrical wholesalers, industrial distributors, and so on. Many of these retail markets were dominated by huge and powerful mass merchandising firms such as Wal-Mart, Home Depot, and the drug and grocery chains. All of these firms were national accounts. The task before Cunningham was to get adequate distribution of the new bulb in such distributive systems quickly while Panasonic had exclusive control of the product. It would require building a large sales system quickly.

Cunningham was inclined to build the sales system using manufacturers' rep organizations that had existing relationships with the target distributive organizations. Using such rep organizations was within Panasonic policy. Its small-appliance division sold Panasonic's wide line of appliances through independent sales reps who called on essentially the same trades targeted by the lamp division.

However, one of Cunningham's peers in the Panasonic organization initiated a casual conversation at a company social event during which he suggested that perhaps now would be a good time for the company to consider hiring its own salespeople to sell directly to the particularly large national accounts such as Wal-Mart, Sears, Home Depot, and others of such size. Such a sales force could also sell to the distributors that sold to smaller retail groups and could cover OEM buyers. He argued, "It's time for us to get some experience in managing a sales organization and we could well afford it on the 5 percent of sales we would have to pay the reps. And we'd have more control over them than we would the reps!" John Cunningham nodded but said nothing.

Questions:

1. Should Panasonic initiate some efforts to build its own sales force to sell to selected target markets and distributor networks?

2. If not, what course of action would you recommend to John Cunningham?

The Personal Selling Process

3

The sales process itself plays an increasing role in creating customer value.

—Neil Rackham—

It is difficult to manage a sales force intelligently without a good grasp of the selling process. While heated debates over the sales manager's need for significant and successful sales experience have raged off and on in marketing for decades, good judgment favors the manager who is competent and knowledgeable about the field being administered. Thus, some exposure to selling seems warranted for students of sales management. Additionally, sales training programs basically teach selling. It would be difficult to plan and conduct a sales training program without knowing how to sell.

In Chapter 1, we noted the wide array of activities that salespeople perform. In this chapter we focus on just those activities related to generating sales and satisfying customers. These selling activities are known as the steps of the **personal selling process.** The typical salesperson spends about 70 percent of his or her time engaged in one of these steps. The remaining time is split between two general categories of nonselling activities: (1) doing paperwork and other administrative tasks, and (2) traveling and waiting to see customers.[1] Consequently, a sales organization cannot be successful without a thorough understanding of the selling process.

Sales reps should know, however, that there is nothing magic about the personal selling process. That is, no one method can be used to close every sale. The process is simply a recommended set of techniques that experience has indicated seem to work better than others in certain situations.

The actual selling process can be likened to a chain, each link of which must be closed successfully or the seller will fail to get the order. However, each step overlaps others, and their sequence may be altered to meet the situation at hand.

The eight steps of the sales process are:

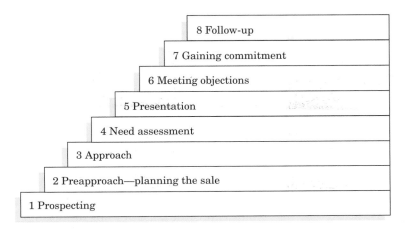

8 Follow-up

7 Gaining commitment

6 Meeting objections

5 Presentation

4 Need assessment

3 Approach

2 Preapproach—planning the sale

1 Prospecting

Prospecting

Succeeding in today's competitive environment means that a company must constantly find new customers. A salesperson's basic strategy should be to spend as much time as possible with excellent prospects—people who recognize their need and are ready to buy. As Phil Clark, an IBM regional sales manager in Dallas, succinctly told his sales force, "The idea is that through our advertising and promotional efforts we stand on a ladder shouting loudly all over Dallas, 'Everyone who is ready to buy a computer please raise their hands.' Then we go sell one to each person who responds."

Prospecting is the method or system by which salespeople learn the names of people who need the product and can afford it. There are two steps in successful prospecting. The first step is **identifying leads**—generating potential customers. The second step is **qualifying leads** according to who is most likely to buy.

Identifying Leads

Names and addresses of good prospects can be obtained in a number of ways:

- *Referrals from customers.* Salespeople indicate that their number one source of referrals is their existing customers, who provide nearly two-thirds of their leads.[2] Referrals from customers are arguably the best, most credible source of leads. "If you provide valuable, worthwhile products and services to your clients, they will want to share you with others," says Maribeth Kuzmeski, founder and president of Red Zone Marketing. "It's just human nature! But sometimes they need a little nudge. So whatever your business is, you should have a system in place for promoting this positive 'word of mouth.' "[3]

FIGURE 3-1   Sample record of a lead from GoLeads.com

Advantage Coupons	Business: **Direct Mail Advertising**
11932 Arbor Street Springfield, ME 18144 (203) 555-3550	Employee Size: **1–9 Employees** Key Contact: Carl Kenton

Source: www.goleads.com, accessed September 7, 2001 (contact information modified to disguise business's identity).

- *Referrals from internal company sources such as the sales manager, the marketing department, or the telemarketing department.* Customer inquiries may be generated from company advertising, direct mail, company websites, trade shows, and teleprospecting efforts. Salespeople report that these sources provide approximately 23 percent of their leads.[4]

- *Referrals from external referral agencies.* Some companies turn to outside agencies for the generation and qualification of leads. This trend is on the upswing due to an increasing number of dot-com businesses, which typically provide a list of leads for reasonable fees. Figure 3–1 shows a sample record of a lead from GoLeads.com, which provides its customers access to over 12 million U.S. businesses.

- *Published directories.* Trade associations, the government, local chambers of commerce, and the yellow pages all are good sources of prospects. Many of the directories are available on the Internet.

- *Networking by the salesperson.* Salespeople often use their friends and acquaintances to make new contacts. Many salespeople join professional and civic organizations in part to meet new people who may be potential customers or who may be able to provide leads.

Impact of Technology on Prospecting

The Internet and related technology are having a big impact on the way sales organizations generate and maintain their list of prospects and business contacts. Three examples follow:

1. In 2000, Ford Motor Company collected an estimated half-million online leads from website visitors who volunteered personal information. The names were passed on to Ford dealers— generating sales of more than 50,000 vehicles.

2. Insurance agents and many other types of salespeople are using the power of the Internet to gather the names, addresses, telephone/fax numbers, and e-mail addresses of potential customers. Free leads can be generated through search engines (e.g., Yahoo!, Google) or online databases focused on providing lists of businesses and/or individuals along with street-level maps (e.g., BigBook.com, QwestDex.com). Customized lists can also be purchased through a wide variety of online direct marketing companies (e.g., Acculeads.com, GoLeads.com, and Technology Sales Leads).

3. Self-updating electronic business cards were developed to save salespeople and their support staff time in keeping contact lists up-to-date. The new technology is especially helpful for organizations such as executive recruiting firms and university alumni associations, which depend on current databases for their lifeblood.

Sources: Jean Halliday, "Ford Finds E-Leads Productive," *Advertising Age* 72, no. 4 (January 22, 2001), p. 28; Marty Shanton, "Free Leads and Purchased Leads," *Broker World* 21, no. 6 (June 2001), pp. 84–86; and Gabrielle Birkner, "Tech Tools: Keeping Up with Contacts," *Sales & Marketing Management* 153, no. 8 (August 2001), p. 24.

- *Cold canvassing.* Salespeople make unannounced calls on businesses that may need the products the rep sells. The popularity of this approach is declining because it is very time-consuming and not very cost-effective due to the high rejection rate. This approach does not allow the salesperson to *qualify* the account before calling. However, for certain widely used products, such as office supplies, this approach can work well.

Qualifying Leads

Whatever the source of the lead, it is important that the lead be qualified. Philosophically, professional salespeople do not want to bother people who have no need for their products. Moreover, it is very expensive for salespeople to make calls that have little chance of success because the customer does not need, does not want, or cannot afford the products. In order to qualify a prospect, the salesperson or the person providing the referral should determine whether the prospect is a good one. To determine this, the prospect must satisfy three conditions:

1. The customer has a need for the products being sold.
2. The customer can afford to buy the products.
3. The customer is receptive to being called on by the salesperson.

Traditionally, sales reps were expected to find their own prospects. That was part of the selling process, part of the job—a most important part of it. Today, however, many companies realize that the marketing department is in the best position to develop effective prospecting systems for the sales force. Surveys have shown that 45 percent of the people who make an inquiry to a company about a product or service buy it from that company or a competitor within 12 months. Another 25 percent are planning on buying it (see Figure 3–2). So in fact these leads are hot prospects. Moreover, the success of company promotional programs in generating good leads (prospects) has centralized the prospecting systems. Today many companies use telemarketing to help salespeople identify and qualify customers.

Sales reps generally appreciate being relieved of the burden of developing a prospecting system, and the company benefits when its reps can spend more time actually making sales presentations to qualified prospects. Yet reports suggest that only 10 to 15 percent of all business and industrial leads receive

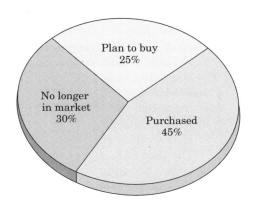

FIGURE 3-2

Lead conversion ratio: inquiry to decision 12 months after inquiring

Source: Bob Donath, James K. Obermayer, Carolyn K. Dixon, and Richard A. Crocker, "When Your Prospect Calls," *Marketing Management* 3, no. 2 (1994), pp. 26–37.

FIGURE 3–3

The value of inquiry follow-up
Source: Bob Donath, James K.
Obermayer, Carolyn K. Dixon,
and Richard A. Crocker, "When
Your Prospect Calls,"
Marketing Management 3, no.
2 (1994), pp. 26–37.

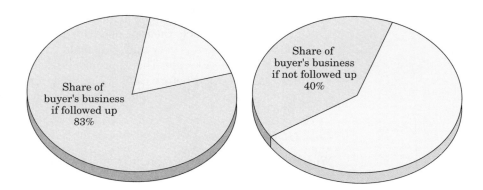

personal follow-ups.[5] To convert a qualified lead to a sale, salespeople must follow up the lead. In general, salespeople get more than 80 percent of the business if they follow up a customer inquiry (see Figure 3–3).

Preapproach: Planning the Sale

The preapproach step includes all the information-gathering activities salespeople perform to learn relevant facts about the prospects, their needs, and their overall situation. Then, based on this information, salespeople plan their sales presentations, selecting the most appropriate objective for each call.

Customer Research

The sales rep should learn everything possible about the prospective customer's business—its size; its present purchasing practices; the location of its plants; the names of its executives; and, most important, the *names of people who make the buying decision as well those who influence the purchase.* It is also helpful to learn something about the buyers' backgrounds, such as their education, social affiliations, or personalities. If the prospective buyer has been having problems, the seller should, if possible, become familiar with those problems.

When researching a current customer or one that has been called on previously by a salesperson from your company, start by reading the company files. They should provide a wealth of background information on the company and possibly on the buyers as well—sales records, correspondence, past sales call reports, and other relevant information. Many companies store information about their customers in a database to which their salespeople have easy access using laptop or notebook computers.

For new customers, you can easily obtain a great deal of information by using the Internet or online information services such as LexisNexis, Dialog, and Dow Jones News/Retrieval. Other sources include trade magazines, industrial directories, magazine and newspaper articles, chambers of commerce, and government publications, as well as the annual reports of companies. Sometimes the company's current suppliers, customers, and certain employees can provide information.

The goal of customer research is for salespeople to know as much as they can about the company, the decision makers, and their needs before making that first call. As Kenneth Ranucci, a senior account executive at Contempo Design, says, "In-depth research into prospects makes salespeople stand out."[6]

Planning the Sales Presentation

The most important part of planning the sales presentation is defining the objective or goal for the particular call. The goal is not necessarily to close or complete the sale on each call. In fact, salespeople report that, on average, it takes four calls to close a sale.[7] However, on each call the salesperson does want to obtain from the buyer some *type of commitment for action that moves the sale forward*. For example, the salesperson may try to obtain a list of the customer's vendor selection criteria or get the buyer to set up a meeting with some of the other people who will be involved in the decision. The objective may be any agreement on an action that moves the sale forward.

Salespeople may also plan how they are going to approach the buyer and what kind of questions they want to ask. It is important that salespeople recognize differences across selling situations and adapt their presentations accordingly. Based on their precall customer research, they will make a tentative judgment as to which of their products best meet their customers' needs and then formulate a tentative plan for presenting the features and benefits of those products. Of course, the information gained by salespeople during the actual call may often cause them to alter their initial objectives or plans. This is called **adaptive selling.**[8]

The Approach

Once the sales rep has the name of a prospect and adequate preapproach information, the next step is the actual **approach.** Making an appointment to see the buyer increases the chances that the salesperson will have the buyer's attention during their meeting.

A good approach makes a favorable impression and establishes some degree of rapport between the salesperson and the buyer. In order to make a favorable impression with customers in the United States, the salesperson should have a firm handshake, be professionally attired, and make good eye contact. Usually each call starts with an introduction (unless the salesperson has called on this customer before) and a limited amount of small talk. Sometimes salespeople will draw attention to their products by handing the buyer a sample or by highlighting some benefit in which the buyer will likely be interested.

The approach usually takes up only the first minute or so of a call, but it can make or break the entire presentation. If the approach fails, the salesperson often does not get a chance to give a presentation. At the end of the approach, the salesperson must gain the buyer's agreement to move into the need assessment stage of the call.

Need Assessment

Companies and consumers purchase products and services to satisfy needs or to solve problems. In a business situation, the company's purchases are always related to the need to improve performance—to become more efficient and effective at fulfilling customer needs. **Need assessment** is the stage in which the *salesperson must discover, clarify, and understand the buyer's needs*. The best way to uncover and understand needs is by asking questions. In fact, research has determined that the more questions salespeople ask, the more likely it is that they will be successful.[9]

There are several types of questions that salespeople can use to encourage their buyers to reveal and discuss their needs:[10]

- **Situational questions.** These are questions that ask for factual information about the buyer's current situation. Salespeople ask situational questions to get ideas about how the customers might be able to use their products. If salespeople do a good job of researching the customer during their precall planning, then they are able to use fewer situational questions. Examples are:
  - a) How often do you change the cutting oil in your drill presses?
  - b) Who is involved in the purchase decision for this product?
  - c) How much inventory of this product do you carry?

- **Problem discovery questions.** These are questions used to uncover potential problems, difficulties, or dissatisfaction that the customer is experiencing that the salesperson's products and services can solve. Salespeople use these questions to uncover customer needs around which they can build their presentation. Examples are:
  - a) Which part of your production process is the most difficult in terms of controlling quality?
  - b) Have you experienced any delays in getting those materials from your current suppliers?
  - c) Have you experienced any problems in servicing your presses?

- **Problem impact questions.** These are questions about the impact that the buyer's problem will have on various aspects of the company's operations. Salespeople ask these questions to make the buyer think about the consequences of *not* solving the problem and to help the buyer see that the seriousness of the problem justifies the time and money it will take to achieve a solution. Examples are:
  - a) What impact do the quality consistency problems have on your production costs?
  - b) What effects do the delays in receiving the materials have on your operations?
  - c) How do these maintenance problems affect your operations?

- **Solution value questions.** These questions ask about the value or the importance of a solution to a problem uncovered earlier in the conversation. Salespeople use these to reinforce the importance of the problem and to help the buyer assess the value of a solution. Examples are:
  - a) If the rejection rate on your quality inspection was reduced to under 1 percent, how much would that save you?
  - b) How much are your production costs increased by material stockouts?
  - c) How important is reducing downtime to minimizing your production costs?

- **Confirmatory questions.** Finally, these questions ask for confirmation from buyers that they are interested in hearing about how your products will help them. Salespeople may use confirmatory questions as transitions into their presentation of product features and benefits. Examples are:
  - a) So you would be interested in a maintenance program that would minimize your downtime, is that correct?

b) If I can provide evidence to you that our products would significantly lower your rejection rate, would you be interested in that?

Salespeople ask these questions in the logical order just presented. The situational questions should be asked first, followed by the problem discovery questions, the problem impact questions, the solution value questions, and then the confirmatory questions. Each type naturally leads to the following type, and each one helps build the buyer's interest in hearing about the solutions the salesperson has to offer. It should be noted that studies by Neil Rackham of 35,000 sales calls demonstrate that the most successful salespeople are those who use fewer situational questions and more problem discovery, impact, and solution value questions.

The Presentation

After assessing the needs and desires of the customer, the salesperson moves into the main body of the sale, the presentation. The **presentation** is primarily a discussion of those product and/or service features, advantages, and benefits that the customer has indicated are important. While most presentations are oral, they often include written proposals and supporting material as well as visual aids. The goal of the presentation is to convince the customer that the product or service being sold will satisfy the customer's needs better than that of a competitor.

Features describe the characteristics of the product or service, **advantages** describe how the feature changes the performance of the product or service, and **benefits** describe how the advantage will help the buyer. For each feature and advantage that a salesperson presents, he or she should also present one or more benefits of that feature to the buyer. In fact, the benefits should be those that address specific needs mentioned by the customer. Listed at the top of page 66 are some examples of products, along with their features, advantages, and benefits:

Shut Up and Listen!

Salespeople have the reputation of being good talkers. What separates the most productive salespeople from the pack, however, is a different communication skill: the ability to listen.

In this age of relationship marketing, salespeople can be successful only if they understand customer needs. This knowledge is gained during need assessment, which should be viewed as an in-depth learning exercise for the salesperson. First, salespeople must get the client to talk by asking open-ended questions. Then they should shut up and listen to the answers!

Some questions for salespeople to try:

- What changes do you see for your industry in the coming year?

- We don't have a magic wand, but if we did, what changes would you make in your company?

- Would it be fair to ask what it is you know about my company?

- Of all the things we've talked about, what do you perceive to be your priorities?

Source: Don Beveridge, "Become a Good Listener," *Industrial Distribution*, March 2000, p. 82.

Product	Feature	Advantage	Benefit
Copy machine	Ten service reps	Fast service	Saves time
Shoes	Inventory control system	Reduces need for inventory	Saves money
Motor oil	Rust inhibitor	Oil and engine have longer life	Saves money
Forklift truck	One-month trial	Ensures product meets needs	Saves money and time

Product Demonstrations

A good sales presentation is built around a forceful product demonstration. Reps should demonstrate everything possible during the presentation. Today a rep can use any of numerous software packages with notebook or laptop computers to make full-color presentations that include sound effects, personalized graphics, and full-motion video testimonials.

American Airlines equips its sales reps worldwide with high-powered notebook computers and presentation software that incorporates graphics, sound, and video. Whereas the company used to spend more than $100,000, using an external production firm, to put together an important presentation, reps can now do it themselves for under $5,000. The new tools are so easy to use that even the

Apple CEO Steve Jobs knows the importance of product demonstration in unveiling his company's latest innovations.
© Reuters NewMedia Inc./CORBIS

most technophobic rep can and will develop professional-looking, cost-effective multimedia presentations.[11] However, there is a danger in forgetting that even the glitziest multimedia presentation cannot take the place of the personal touch and understanding that the rep brings to the presentation.

Internet technology is even allowing sales reps to make effective product demonstrations *remotely*. Such Web-based presentations are becoming increasingly common.[12] Inexpensive services such as Expertcity Inc.'s GoToMyPC enable the customer to access the sales rep's PC from anywhere in the world. The salesperson can then talk to the customer over the phone as they both simultaneously view a detailed product demonstration on their PCs. Showing what the product can do is much more effective than merely describing it.[13]

Prepared Sales Presentations

The advisability of using a prepared sales presentation, better known as a canned sales talk, is debatable. Without doubt, a prepared presentation done poorly and without feeling is a dismal experience. However, many firms do use canned talks successfully. The prepared presentation has several advantages:

- It gives new salespeople confidence.
- It can use tested sales techniques that have proven effective.
- It gives some assurance that the complete story will be told.
- It greatly simplifies sales training.

The use of a prepared presentation does *not* mean that sales reps must use someone else's words. Above all, the salesperson's own feelings and personality should be evident in the presentation.

Developing Effective Presentations

The task of developing a presentation is not an easy one. Some simple advice may be helpful here:

- **Keep the presentation simple.** The temptation to tell everything is overwhelming. Don't do it. The prospect can absorb only a limited amount of information at any one time. Don't overload the system.
- **Talk the prospect's language.** Don't build the presentation around industry jargon or product model numbers. If customers don't understand what the rep is talking about, they seldom say so. That would be an admission of ignorance. They usually pretend to understand and then say, "I'll have to think it over for a while."
- **Stress the application of the product or service to the prospect's situation.** Tailor the presentation to the application or person at hand. Even within the same firm, different individuals place different priorities on what is important about the product. You must adapt your presentation to the situation and person.
- **Above all, seek credibility at every turn.** The entire presentation is nothing if it is not believed. Each statement must be credible. Prove points one by one. A critical point is not complete until the prospect believes it. The real key to successful selling lies in this credibility.

Meeting Objections

Objections are encountered in practically every presentation. They should be welcomed because they indicate that the prospect has some interest in the proposition. A prospect who is not interested in buying seldom raises any objections, silently going along with the presentation but saying at the end, "I'm not interested in your deal." There are several important techniques that should be used in responding to a buyer objection:

- *Listen* to the buyer. It is important that you listen actively. "Learn as much as you can about the objection," says certified professional sales trainer and speaker Rick Grosso. "Encourage your prospect to expand and tell you more."[14] Do not assume that you know what the buyer is going to say, and never interrupt—nothing annoys a buyer more!

- *Clarify* the objection. Repeat and clarify the objection by asking for more information, using questions such as "Let me see if I understand you correctly, [repeating the objection as you understand it]. Is that correct?" The buyer may confirm that you are correct in your understanding or provide additional information. Sometimes this step can uncover a misunderstanding that the buyer has about your product and/or service.

- *Respect* the buyer's concern. Acknowledge that you understand and appreciate the concerns. Remember that the buyer is not attacking you personally, so you should not become defensive.

- *Respond* to the objection. It is important that you respond to the buyer's concern. The specific response to the objection depends on the type of objection it is.

The most common types of objections and specific strategies for handling them are discussed next.

Price or Value Objections

Buyers who say "I don't need it" or "It costs too much" are indicating that they don't think the *value* of solving the problem or meeting the need is *worth the cost*. In this case, the salesperson must convince the buyer of the importance of the problem and of the value of the solution. It may be necessary to go back to the need assessment part of the call to ask some additional problem impact and solution value types of questions to increase the buyer's perception of the seriousness of the problem and the importance of a solution. If the buyer acknowledges the importance of the problem but still feels that the company can't afford the product/service or that it is not a price-competitive solution, then the salesperson can offer some price value comparisons of alternative solutions.

Product/Service Objections

Sometimes the buyer acknowledges the importance of a problem but doubts whether the product or service can solve his problem or improve his operations. The buyer may disagree with the salesperson's assessment or, in some cases, even doubt the genuineness of the salesperson. In this case the salesperson needs to convince the buyer that her product will do what she says. She must demonstrate or prove that the product has the capability to fulfill the need. Some of the proof-providing tactics are to offer the buyer

- case histories
- testimonials
- independent tests
- a demonstration
- trial use
- expert opinion

Some objections relate to needs that your product *cannot satisfy*. In this case, it is best to first acknowledge that your product or service cannot meet the particular need. Then try to increase the perceived value of your product by reemphasizing those important needs your product *can* meet.

Procrastinating Objections

Procrastinating objections can be difficult to overcome. Some such objections are:

- Let me think about it a while.
- I have to talk it over with my boss.
- I have to wait until the next budget cycle.
- I have some other reps to talk to before I make a decision.

Procrastinating prospects use such excuses to avoid acting on a proposition immediately or to avoid admitting that they don't have the authority to make the decision.

In door-to-door selling, a sale that cannot be closed on one call usually has little chance of completion. In many business sales, however, the prospect cannot be pushed into a sale without creating considerable ill will. In fact, businesses are taking more and more time before committing. Customers today are very thorough. They use the Internet to research all options, and are careful not to make a mistake. A survey of purchasers found that only 13 percent tend to buy within three months, while 44 percent require 6 to 12 months to decide. A full 20 percent of purchasers say they require a year or longer before a typical sale is complete.[15] The sales rep must understand this extended buying cycle, and remain a patient and trusted adviser to the customer.

The amount of aggressiveness must be modified to fit the prospect and the situation. Some people will not be pushed or rushed. In these situations, *the best strategy is to ask for a commitment for some future action that will move the sale forward.* For example, the salesperson might ask for a meeting with the buyer and his boss or with whoever else seems to have substantial influence over the decision.

Hidden Objections

Prospects may state their objections to a proposition openly and give the salesperson a chance to answer them. This is an ideal circumstance, because everything is out in the open and the salesperson does not need to read the prospect's mind. Unfortunately, prospects often hide their real reasons for not buying. Further, stated objections may be phony. A prospect may say she does not like the looks of a product, when she really thinks the price is too high. The rep must determine the real barrier to the sale to be able to overcome it.

After gaining commitment and closing the sale, reps follow up in order to assure customer satisfaction and to build long-term relationships.

Some salespeople have developed special methods for getting the prospect to disclose what is blocking the sale. One saleswoman uses what she calls her "appeal for honesty" tactic. She says to the reluctant prospect, "You expect me to be honest with you, as you should. But haven't I the same right—to expect you to be honest with me? Now honestly, what is bothering you about the proposition?" However, *the best technique for discovering hidden objections is to ask questions that keep the prospect talking.*

As we noted in the planning section, it is often necessary for salespeople to change their original objectives and strategies for the sales call. Salespeople must recognize the need and be willing to adapt their presentations when the buyer's objections signal that they may have initially chosen the wrong strategies. Another important principle to remember in handling most objections is to avoid arguments at any cost. The sales rep should ask questions that help clarify the prospect's thinking. This provides insights into the precise obstacles that are hindering the sale. Even if prospects are dead wrong, sales reps should never offend them. A sales rep can win an argument only to lose the sale.

Gaining Commitment

At some point after the salesperson has convinced the buyer that his or her products at least warrant further attention, *the salesperson must ask the buyer to commit to some action that moves the sale forward.* This is called **gaining commitment.** In a relatively simple sale, it is important for the salesperson to get a commitment from the buyer to purchase the product on the first call (usually the only call) or she will have lost the sale. Some of the techniques frequently used to close these transaction sales are highlighted in the box titled "Common Sales Closes."

However, sales of complex business products usually require more than one call. In fact, some large sales may take several years to complete. To get the buyer to agree to some action that moves the buyer closer to the sale, the salesperson may suggest a demonstration, review the specifications, or offer a sample. The keys to obtaining commitment are, first, to *plan realistic objectives for each sales call* and, second, to *ask for a commitment.* If the salesperson doesn't ask, then he or she won't move the sale forward. To ask for an action that in effect finalizes the sale, the salesperson may simply say, "Can I place an order for you today?"

Common Sales Closes

The Assumptive Close

Many salespeople rely on the assumptive close—they merely assume prospects are going to buy and begin taking orders by asking such questions as:

Now, what size do you want?

When can we deliver this—today or tomorrow morning?

Will three dozen be enough, or should I send four?

If the prospect answers such questions, the close is under way.

Special-Offer Close

Some sales managers give their sales force a special customer offer each time around the territory. The 3M Company's Scotch Tape division has used this closing tactic. If the special deal were a billfold, the sales rep might say, "If you put in this specially priced dealer display today, we will include this billfold."

Summary Close

Another frequently used close is to provide a summary of the benefits that the buyer has already acknowledged and then to suggest an action for finalizing the sale. For example, the salesperson could say, "You have agreed that our products will be easier for the consumer to use and that our advertising support will convince the retailers to stock the product, correct? Then I suggest that you place your first order today so that you have it on the retailer's shelves when our advertising campaign kicks off."

Sometimes the buyer may volunteer to take an action that moves the sale forward or even finalizes the sale. For example, the buyer may say, "We've decided that we need to make a change and we think your company is in the best position to serve our needs." But often it does not happen this way, and the salesperson must ask for the commitment.

Follow-Up

Reps must learn that the sale is not over when they get the order. Good sales reps follow up in various ways. They make certain that they have answered all the buyer's questions and that the buyer understands the details of the contract. If the merchandise is delivered at a later date, the reps are present at the time of delivery or call soon afterward to ensure that everything is in order.

The follow-up step of the sales process has become critical to the success of contemporary sales organizations. This is especially true given recent sales management trends toward the concepts of relationship marketing and consultative selling. That is, instead of focusing on one-time, transactional sales, today's salespeople work to build and maintain long-term, mutually beneficial partnerships with their customers. Of course, customers would never form partnerships with organizations whose salespeople forget about them after the sale!

Indeed, the concepts of relationship marketing have made sales organizations rethink the steps of the sales process.[16] Organizations realize that it is much more expensive to acquire new customers than it is to retain existing customers. So, although generating new accounts is still important, salespeople must be careful not to sacrifice effective follow-up for prospecting. Further, effective follow-up essentially consists of asking questions to customers in an ongoing attempt to monitor their needs. Thus, when dealing with loyal customers, salespeople must continually revisit the need assessment step of the sales process.

Meeting Customer Needs—After the Sale

Erica Feidner has been the top salesperson at Steinway & Sons since 1994. "We don't know anyone who has done what Erica has done," says head of sales and marketing Frank Mazurco. "If only we could clone her. How does she do it?" Certainly it does not stem from a high "closing ratio," as there are other Steinway salespeople with a greater percentage of walk-in customers who actually buy a piano. In fact, Erica refuses to sell a piano that she feels is not right for a particular customer. She will often ask a customer to wait for long time periods—months or sometimes even years—until the right piano becomes available.

One key to Erica's success is the large volume of *referrals* that result from her commitment to cus-

tomers *after the sale has been made*. That is, her follow-up is extraordinary, as it includes a steady stream of correspondence regarding sales events, reminders to insure the piano, advice on where to take piano lessons, and even invitations to recitals. Customers are so pleased with this that they tell their friends and relatives about the outstanding customer service they receive from this particular Steinway salesperson. This leads to a large number of customers who ask for Erica by name.

Source: James B. Stewart, "Matchmaker: Erica Feidner Knows the Piano You Want," *The New Yorker*, August 20, 2001, p. 78.

Interestingly, when the buyer and seller form a very close integrative partnership, it sometimes makes sense for someone other than the salesperson to maintain the relationship and perform the follow-up selling tasks. In these cases, an operational-level employee in the selling organization would replace the salesperson.[17] For example, Bose Corporation, a Massachusetts-based manufacturer of high-end stereo equipment, has formed close partnerships with select suppliers. Ultimately, the supplier salesperson who developed the account was replaced by a fellow employee who works full-time at an office within the Bose facility—even though the employee still draws a paycheck from the selling firm. Being part of the customer's social system makes the supplier employee especially effective as he or she places purchase orders and helps design products for the customer firm.

Whether managed by the salesperson or an operational-level employee, good follow-up is the key to building a loyal clientele. Satisfied customers voluntarily provide more business. People truly appreciate being served by good salespeople. Once they locate a person who pleases them, they are not likely to forget that individual in the future.

Summary

As part of their jobs, salespeople perform a wide variety of activities. The majority of their time is spent in selling activities, which revolve around the eight steps of the personal selling process.

The first step is prospecting, which involves identifying and qualifying leads. There are a number of possible methods of generating leads. The most frequent source of leads is existing customers. In order to qualify a prospect—to decide if

the prospect is a good one—it must be determined whether the prospect has a need for the product, can afford to buy the product, and is receptive to being called on by the salesperson.

The second step is preapproach planning. This includes all of the information-gathering activities salespeople perform to learn about their prospective customers. Then, based on this research, salespeople plan their presentations. As a part of their plan, they must decide on the objective for the call as well as on how they are going to approach the buyer and what kind of questions they will ask.

The third step is the approach, during which salespeople meet the buyer, introduce themselves, engage in momentary small talk, and, most important, gain the buyer's agreement to move forward into the need assessment part of the presentation.

During the fourth step, identified as "need assessment," the salesperson must discover, clarify, and understand the buyer's needs. The salesperson uses a variety of questions to encourage buyers to reveal their needs.

The presentation of the product or service and its features and benefits is the next step. The general goal for salespeople is to convince their customers that their company's products and services will satisfy the customers' needs better than those of a competitor. Today many salespeople use computers to help them make effective presentations.

The sixth step is handling the buyer's objections. Buyers often question the price or value of the product, or they may not believe that the product will improve their operations. The salesperson must be able to overcome these objections as well as others. Sometimes salespersons will find it necessary to adapt their presentations in order to move the presentation forward.

At the seventh step, the salesperson must ask the buyer to commit to some action that will move the buyer closer to the sale. Often it takes multiple calls before the buyer is ready to commit to the sale.

The final step of the personal selling process is follow-up, which takes place after the purchase. Given that selling today is consistent with relationship marketing concepts, follow-up is arguably the most important step. To effectively build relationships, the salesperson must ensure customer satisfaction by following through with value-added service after the sale.

Key Terms

Adaptive selling	Gaining commitment	Problem impact questions
Advantages	Identifying leads	Prospecting
Approach	Need assessment	Qualifying leads
Benefits	Personal selling process	Situational questions
Confirmatory questions	Presentation	Solution value questions
Features	Problem discovery questions	

Questions and Problems

1. Which step of the personal selling process has been most impacted by Internet technology?

2. Should marketing or sales be responsible for generating leads?

3. How does the salesperson determine whether the lead is a good prospect?

4. Should the salesperson try to close on every call? Why or why not?

5. Identify what type of question each of the following is:

   a) If your inventory could be reduced by 20 percent, how much would that save you?

   b) Can you tell me how you recruit your new salespeople?

   c) How does the turnover in your sales force affect your operations?

   d) Have you experienced any problems in servicing your office equipment?

6. Identify a feature, an advantage, and a benefit for each of the following products: a camera, a backpack, fat-free ice cream, lawn care service.

7. What are the advantages and disadvantages of using prepared, or canned, sales presentations? Give examples of when using a canned

presentation might be better than using a less structured presentation.

8. If the salesperson doesn't believe that the customer has been honest in giving her opinions about the product, what should he do?

9. If the customer says to the salesperson, "You seem like a nice guy and I would like to buy from you personally, but I don't think your company is worth a nickel!" what should the salesperson say?

10. It has often been said that salespeople are born, not made. Do you agree or disagree? Explain why.

Experiential Exercises

A. Spend a day with a salesperson from two different companies.
   a) Report in itinerary form how you spent each day.
   b) Describe each job, comparing and contrasting both.
   c) Tell which position you would prefer and why.

B. Identify prospects for a new brand of special occasion and novelty cards.

C. Pick a product normally sold by a salesperson. Talk to a customer who has just purchased or has been considering purchasing the product and find out the important characteristics of the salesperson from the customer's point of view.

Internet Exercises

A. Search the Internet to identify a short list of prospects for each of the following types of sales organizations:
   a) Professional beauty/barber instruments—scissors, shears, manicure implements, and so on.
   b) Pharmaceutical sales.
   c) Safety equipment sales—work gloves, safety glasses, hard hats, and so on.
   d) A travel agency specializing in business travel.
   e) Law enforcement supplies—handcuffs, leg irons, mace, and so on.
   f) Payroll services.

B. The box "Common Sales Closes" on p. 71 describes the following three common techniques used to close a sale: assumptive close, special-offer close, and summary close. Sales trainers have taught many other closing techniques over the years, but some of these are of questionable ethics. Use a search engine to find descriptions of some of these other sales closes, such as the "standing-room-only close." Describe the closing techniques that you find, and discuss the extent to which they are consistent with the marketing concept and the principles of relationship marketing.

C. A few organizations now offer sales certification. Visit the two sites listed below, and describe their sales certification processes. What does someone have to do to earn a sales certification? Who is eligible? What are the benefits of a certification?
   a) Sales and Marketing Executives International (www.smei.org).
   b) National Association of Sales Professionals (www.nasp.com).

References

1. Christen P. Heide, *Dartnell's 30th Sales Force Compensation Survey* (Chicago: Dartnell Corporation, 1999). p. 153.

2. Allen Lucas, "Leading Edge," *Sales & Marketing Management*, June 1995, pp. 13–14.

3. "Nine No-Fail Ways to Boost Referrals for Your Business," *American Salesman*, December 2001, pp. 18–24.

4. Lucas, "Leading Edge."

5. Bob Donath, James W. Obermayer, Carolyn K. Dixon, and Richard A. Crocker, "When Your Prospect Calls," *Marketing Management* 3, no. 2 (1994), pp. 27–28.

6. Quoted in Ginger Trumfio, "Opening Doors," *Sales & Marketing Management*, May 1994, p. 81.

7. Heide, *Dartnell's 30th Sales Force Compensation Survey*, p. 162.

8. Rosann L. Spiro and Barton A. Weitz, "Adaptive Selling: Conceptualization, Measurement, and Nomological Validity," *Journal of Marketing Research*, February 1990, pp. 61–69.

9. Neil Rackham, *The Spin Selling Fieldbook* (New York: McGraw-Hill, 1996), pp. 16–20.

10. This discussion is based to a large extent on concepts developed by Neil Rackham, which in turn were based on a research study by the Huthwaite Corporation of 35,000 sales calls. These ideas were originally reported in Rackham's book *The Spin Selling Fieldbook*.

11. Tom Dellecave Jr., "Now Showing," *Sales & Marketing Management*, February 1996, pp. 68–71.

12. Dana James, "Web Conferencing, Talk Eases Salespeople's Fears," *Marketing News*, November 19, 2001, pp. 4–5.

13. Kathleen Cholewka, "Ultimate Access," *Sales & Marketing Management*, October 2001, p. 27.

14. Quoted in Ayo Mseka, "The Right Way to Handle Objections," *Advisor Today*, June 2001, p. 31.

15. John R. Graham, "Successful Selling: Learn the Customer's Buying Cycle," *The American Salesman*, March 2000, pp. 3–9.

16. Nikolaos Tzokas, Michael Saren, and Panayiotis Kyziridis, "Aligning Sales Management and Relationship Marketing in the Services Sector," *Service Industries Journal*, January 2001, pp. 195–210.

17. David T. Wilson, "Deep Relationships: The Case of the Vanishing Salesperson," *Journal of Personal Selling & Sales Management*, Winter 2000, pp. 53–61.

CASE 3-1 OMNICO, INC.

Follow-up on the Golf Course

"Follow-up, follow-up, follow-up! That's the key to success in sales. And there's no better place for follow-up to occur than on the golf course!" These are the words of Buddy Towers, sales manager of Omnico, Inc.

Truly a legendary figure at Omnico, Towers started working there as a salesperson 35 years ago, immediately after graduating from the University of Michigan. He has never worked for any other company. His record at Omnico is outstanding. He's been the top-producing salesperson for 20 of the last 35 years—an especially impressive record given that the Omnico sales force typically averages more than 20 salespeople.

This history of success stemmed from the fierce loyalty that Towers inspired among his customers. Towers sums up the reasons for this loyalty in one word: golf. "I simply could not have succeeded in sales without golf," he says. "Out on the golf course is where my customers and I learn to know and trust each other. That's what kept them coming back to me."

Towers, however, is no longer out in the field. After his long, distinguished selling career, he assumed the administrative position of sales manager at Omnico about one month ago. He had grown tired of all the traveling. He was 55 years old and had just become a grandfather for the first time. He hated to be away from home so much.

When Towers applied for the sales manager position, Omnico's CEO/president felt like he couldn't say no. "Buddy Towers *is* Omnico's sales," the president said. "He's done and made so much for this company over the years. In my opinion, he's earned the right to get what he wants around here."

Upon assuming the job, Towers noticed a market research report that compared industry averages for customer retention. He discovered that Omnico was well below the average for its in dustry. In other words, relative to competitors, Omnico is not as likely to maintain long-term relationships with its clients.

Towers's conclusion is that Omnico salespeople fail to appreciate the importance of relationship selling. His number one goal is to change this. At his first sales meeting as manager, he went over financial data that demonstrated how much more expensive it is to acquire new customers than it is to keep current ones. He told them, "If we keep losing customers at this rate, we'll be out of business in three years!"

He then encouraged his salespeople to go out and cultivate closer, more personal relationships with their key customers. And, of course, he advised them to do this on the golf course. He even offered to pay for golf lessons for those who needed them.

Some of the salespeople were not so thrilled with Towers's idea. Laura Kilburn, a successful rep who had worked for Omnico for five years, strongly objected. She spoke up in the meeting and said, "Buddy, you're still old school. Today's customers don't come back to us because they're our golfing buddy; in fact, many of mine don't even golf. Customers re-buy from Omnico only when our products and service improve their bottom line. Follow-up is important, sure—but it involves a lot more than playing stupid games with the customer."

Questions:

1. Whose side are you on, Buddy Towers's or Laura Kilburn's? Explain.

2. Notice that Omnico, Inc., is not identified with any particular industry. Do you think buddy-buddy relationships (like those cultivated on a golf course) are more critical to the success of salespeople in certain kinds of industries? Discuss.

CASE 3-2   GEM TOOLS, INC.

Evaluating Sales Leads

"It's a jungle out there, where only the savviest operators survive," George likes to tell his troops. As division sales vice president of his company, George is proud of his devoted effort and the reputation he has earned as a "real hands-on guy." He enjoys his regular Friday after-lunch ritual, a relaxed time to phone friends to arrange weekend plans as he sifts the pile of sales lead forms that accumulate during the week.

Passing by in the hallway, Janice, the company's new marketing communications director, stops to watch George at work through his open office door. What she sees alarms her.

With a wastebasket positioned strategically alongside his desk, George plucks forms from the stack before him and squints thoughtfully at each form for a few seconds. He carefully lays some of the forms on another, much smaller pile that he will send to his road warriors in the field, but he flicks most of them disdainfully into the trash. George is screening advertising inquiries, raw leads from trade publication reader service cards indiscriminately passed on by marketing communications to the sales department.

"Those leads cost us 28 bucks apiece!" Janice protests, striding into George's office like cavalry to the rescue. She works hard to run an advertising campaign to excite the marketplace and motivate likely buyers to ask for more information. Brochure requests have skyrocketed. Inquiry counts have soared. It's a numbers game to Janice, and she boasts about her marketing communications program's sizzling scoreboard.

But Janice worries that salespeople, and boss George in particular, view the extra volume as an imposition, possibly even a threat. Not that anyone has said anything; it's just that tone of voice she hears from salespeople on those rare occasions when she travels to the field.

"How can you tell so quickly who's a good lead and who's not—who's going to buy and who's not?" Janice demands. She wants to add, but doesn't, that the sales department is breaking the rules.

Each inquiry should be followed up with a salesperson's phone call, she believes, maybe even a visit. That's the sales department's job. Summarily trashing leads without checking them out defeats her program at the start, Janice seethes.

Janice's anger stems in part from her already-existing anxiety. She had been worrying because she didn't really know what happened to all those names and addresses her department had been shoveling to George's office across the hall. Spending so little time making calls on prospects with salespeople, Janice had never seen how most of the inquiries she has forwarded actually frustrate salespeople, waste their time, and justify their muttering that "the leads are no good."

George has been trying to protect his people with his home-grown lead-qualification system. "It's easy to tell which are which, with my experience," George calmly answers Janice, a parent educating a child. "Sit here and let me show you how it's done."

George slides a lead from the stack and with a flourish offers it for their mutual inspection. "See, this has no phone number; he's obviously not a serious buyer." George flips the lead card into the wastebasket triumphantly.

"Here's another one 600 miles away from our nearest office—so we can't follow it up right away. We'll call on this prospect when one of our people gets up there next month," George promises without conviction.

"This one's for a $200 meter, and we sell $200,000 complete power systems." George holds the lead with two fingers at arm's length as if it were vilely soiled. "Let this guy call back later if he just wants the meter."

On it goes, George's decision rules enraging Janice.

As marketing communications director, Janice frets over the fate of the advertising inquiry database she wants to create so that she can earn recognition upstairs for the inquiry count's rapid growth. Yet she knows she will not win points by arguing with the senior sales executive, so she remains silent.

Questions:

1. Who is right, Janice or George?
2. What would you recommend to Janice and to George?

This case was reprinted with permission from Bob Donath, James W. Obermayer, Carolyn K. Dixon, and Richard A. Crocker, "When Your Prospect Calls," *Marketing Management Magazine*, 1994, pp. 27–28.

CASE 3-3   FLETCHER ELECTRIC, INC.

Partnering Relationship

Molly Stevens, account manager for Fletcher Electric, Inc., was pondering her next move with Tymco, her largest account. Fletcher manufactures a line of pumps, electric motors, and controls that are sold to companies that use Fletcher's parts in manufacturing all kinds of equipment. Tymco, a maker of street sweepers and other specialized industrial products, had purchased Fletcher controls for the last five years but also purchased controls from several small distributors for specific applications when Fletcher's products could not meet the specifications. Stevens originally sold the controls by proving to the engineering department that Fletcher's quality could meet their specifications and demonstrating the controls' accuracy and long life. Then she convinced the purchasing agent that the pricing would be more stable with one major vendor than with multiple distributors. Since then, Stevens has heard no complaints about Fletcher's products. Tymco even allowed a trade magazine to write an article about Tymco's experience with Fletcher controls.

Early last year, Stevens persuaded the purchasing agent for Tymco to switch to Fletcher electric motors for several applications. Although engineering was not involved in this decision, Stevens had to prove to the purchasing agent that the products were as good as the ones they were currently purchasing. Stevens estimated that Fletcher had about 30 percent of the Tymco motor business, 30 percent went to Visa SA from Mexico, and the remainder of the business belonged to Smart & Company, which actually distributed several lines of electric motors imported from the Pacific Rim.

Last month, Stevens received a call from the director of engineering asking for a meeting to discuss some issues with Fletcher motors. She was delighted, because one of the Fletcher engineers had suggested combining Fletcher motors and controls and shipping the units as one assembly. Stevens believed that such a meeting would be a perfect opportunity to present the new idea. She created and presented a proposal to the engineering department that, if accepted, would mean doubling Fletcher's share of the electric motor business. The proposal would require some redesign by Tymco, but the savings over two years would be more than the redesign costs. After that, Tymco could increase profits on those products by about 3 percent. But several engineers pointed out that Fletcher was unwilling to manufacture controls for all of Tymco's needs, and they were reluctant to make such a change with a company that was not willing to work more closely with them. In addition, one engineer seemed very unhappy that the purchasing department had switched to Fletcher motors. That engineer thought the reject rate of 2 percent was too high; all of Tymco's other vendors were achieving fewer than 1 percent rejects. At the conclusion of the meeting, the director of engineering said to Stevens, "Molly, we've enjoyed a long and good relationship with Fletcher. And your idea is a good one. Right now, though, I don't think Fletcher is the company we should do that with. But we'll consider it and let you know."

Questions:

1. In what stage of partnering is the relationship between Fletcher and Tymco?

2. Is there anything Molly Stevens could have done to set the stage for better acceptance of her proposal?

3. What should Molly Stevens do right now? If her visionary objective is to develop a strategic partnership with Tymco, is it still realistic? What should she do to achieve that visionary objective?

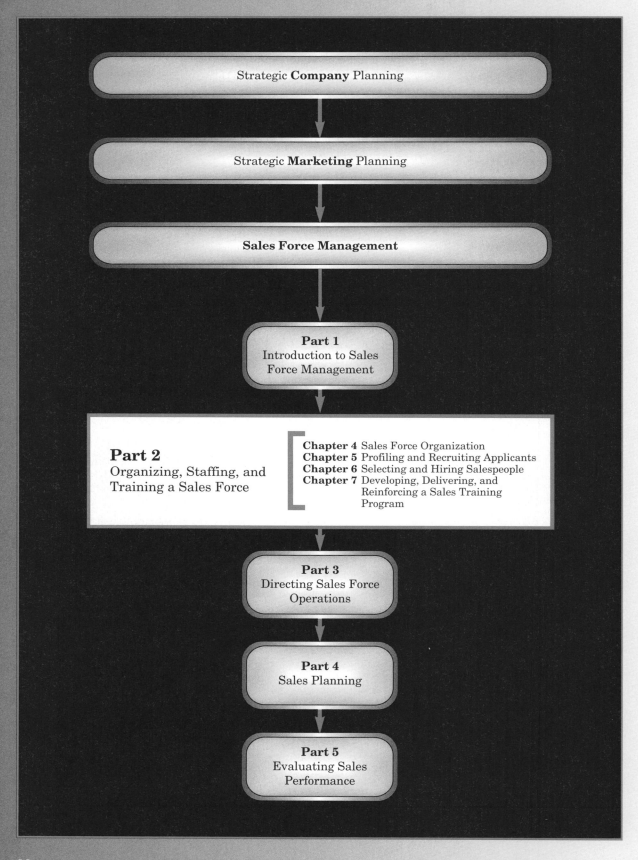

Strategic **Company** Planning

Strategic **Marketing** Planning

Sales Force Management

Part 1
Introduction to Sales Force Management

Part 2
Organizing, Staffing, and Training a Sales Force

Chapter 4 Sales Force Organization
Chapter 5 Profiling and Recruiting Applicants
Chapter 6 Selecting and Hiring Salespeople
Chapter 7 Developing, Delivering, and Reinforcing a Sales Training Program

Part 3
Directing Sales Force Operations

Part 4
Sales Planning

Part 5
Evaluating Sales Performance

Organizing, Staffing, and Training a Sales Force

Most sales executives devote the bulk of their time to organizing, developing, and directing the activities and people involved in operating a sales force. This is the stage in the management process in which the sales organization actually implements the strategic planning designed to help the company reach its sales goals.

Sales operations—the topic of Parts 2 and 3 of this book—include organizing and staffing the sales force and training the salespeople. In addition, sales operations include designing compensation and expense plans for the sales force, motivating the group, and leading field-selling activities.

Part 2 consists of four chapters covering the organization, staffing, and training activities of sales force management. Chapter 4 deals with sales force organization—the characteristics of a good organization, the basic types of organization, the organizational specialization within a sales department, and other organizational options such as national account management, selling teams, and independent sales organizations. Organizational options for international sales are also discussed.

Staffing the sales force—selecting the right people—is the most important activity in the entire management process. Selection involves first determining the types of people wanted and recruiting those types (Chapter 5), and then selecting from the applicants, completing the hiring process, and socializing the newly hired salespeople (Chapter 6). Chapter 7 is devoted to sales training activities. The need for training assessment is discussed first, followed by program design, reinforcement, and evaluation.

4

Sales Force Organization

Listen to the customer and act on what they tell you.

—Pat Nathan, vice president of Dell Computer Corporation—

In the management process, you must decide where you want to go before you can figure out how to get there. In more formal terms, management should first establish its objectives and then plan the appropriate strategies and tactics to reach those goals. To implement this planning, the activities and people must be properly arranged and effectively coordinated. This is where the concept of organization comes in. The fundamentals of organization are essentially the same whether we are talking about organizing a sales force, a production department, a sorority, or any other group involved in a common effort.

Nature of Sales Organizations

An **organization** is simply an arrangement—a working structure—of activities involving a group of people. The goal is to arrange these activities so that the people involved can act better *together* than they can *individually*.

Organizational changes occur in companies' sales and marketing efforts as firms find that their existing structures are inappropriate to implement the marketing concept. As we noted in Chapter 2, one idea underlying the marketing concept is that all marketing activities should be organizationally integrated and coordinated.

In recent years, many firms have restructured their sales organizations to make them more responsive to the changing needs and, in some cases, demands of their customers. Companies are doing this by organizing around their customers. As noted by Carleton S. (Carly) Fiorina, CEO of Hewlett-Packard (HP), "The new business is completely customer-centric, representing a single HP face to corporate and enterprise customers across all geographies and product lines."[1]

The trend is toward flatter organizations in which coordination across activities is more important than top-down control. In these organizations, salespeople are often part of cross-functional teams designed to serve specific customers. These changes are occurring because companies are changing the way they do business with their suppliers. These organizational trends are discussed in detail later in the chapter.

Sales Force Organization and Strategic Planning

A close relationship exists between a company's sales force organizational structure and its strategic marketing and sales force planning. The organizational structure has a direct and significant bearing on the implementation of strategic planning. The key here is to design an organizational structure that will help those who work within it to successfully implement the strategic marketing and sales force planning.

An **organizational structure**—whether it is for a sales force or any other group involved in a joint effort to meet a goal—is a control-and-coordination mechanism. In addition to organizational structure, management has several other mechanisms it can use to direct the efforts of its sales force: its compensation plan, training program, supervisory techniques, and so on. But the organizational structure looms large because it typically is set up before these other mechanisms are established. Consequently, any mistakes in organization can result in reduced efficiencies in selection, compensation, training, and other tools of managerial control and guidance.

Therefore, as a control mechanism, the organizational structure guides the company—or in some cases, the sales force—in carrying out the strategic planning to pursue marketing and sales force goals. Often a sales force fails to reach its goals because the organizational structure hinders the effective implementation of the strategic sales force planning.

To illustrate, assume that a company's sales goal is to increase its market share to 20 percent next year and that its key sales strategy is to increase its sales to large national accounts by 30 percent over last year. However, the company's sales force is structured so that each rep's efforts are spread thinly over accounts of all sizes. No key executives are assigned to sell to national accounts. Under these organizational conditions, it is doubtful that this company will successfully implement its plan.

Characteristics of a Good Organization

Some management generalizations that characterize a good organization are summarized in the box titled "Principles of Organization Design." These features apply to organizations in any field—not just sales management—and they are

Principles of Organization Design

- **Organizational structure should reflect a marketing orientation.** When designing a sales organization, management should focus first on the market and the customer. Executives should consider the selling and marketing tasks necessary to capitalize on the market demand and to serve the firm's customers. From this base, an organizational structure can be built.

- **Organization should be built around activities, not around people.** This goal is sometimes difficult to achieve because it may be almost impossible to avoid some organizing around people—that is, making "people adaptations" in the structure.

- **Responsibility and authority should be related properly.** When you give someone a job to do, also give the person the tools to do it. Responsibility for each activity should be clearly spelled out and assigned to some individual. Then the necessary authority should be delegated to that person.

- **Span of executive control should be reasonable.** By *span of executive control*, we mean the number of subordinates who report directly to one executive. What constitutes a "reasonable" span of control depends on the nature of the subordinates' jobs and the abilities of the executives and subordinates. As a guideline, the span should be small—usually not more than six or eight people. However, there are many exceptions, and the recent trend to fewer organizational levels of management has resulted in broader spans of control at each level.

- **Organization should be stable but flexible.** An organization should be like a tree—firmly rooted but flexible enough so that a strong wind won't break it. *Stability* in an organization means having trained executive replacements available when needed. *Flexibility* refers more to short-run situations such as seasonal fluctuations in the number of workers needed. An organization might subcontract some work during peak seasons or hire a temporary sales force to deliver samples of new products.

- **Activities should be balanced and coordinated.** Balancing activities does not mean making all organizational units equal. Instead, balance means not letting one unit unduly become more important than another. In sports, you don't stress the offense to the neglect of the defense. In sales management, effective *coordination* is needed (1) between sales and nonmarketing departments, and (2) between sales and other marketing units. Some examples:
  a) Sales—production: Sales furnishes accurate sales forecasts; production provides dependable production schedules.
  b) Sales—finance and accounting: These units collaborate in controlling selling costs and setting credit policy.
  c) Sales—advertising: Advertising can generate leads to prospective customers and make them more receptive to sales force calls. Sales reps can tell retailers how the producer's ads will bring people to the store.

useful when designing a new organization or revising an existing one. A company's formal organizational structure may comply with all or most of the desirable characteristics. However, in the real world most firms need an additional element to make the formal structure work well. That key element is an **informal organization.**

Role of an Informal Organization

A healthy organization is a self-adjusting one. Through its own devices, it finds ways to get a job done with minimum effort. A formal organization's well-being is maintained by the system known as the informal organization structure. This structure represents how things actually get done in a company, not how they are supposed to be done according to a formal organization chart.

The following example shows how an informal organization works. A sales manager's secretary opens a letter from a customer complaining about an overcharge on an order. If the lines of the formal organization chart were followed, the secretary would refer the letter to the sales manager. This manager would relay the message up through executive echelons until it reached the administrator in charge of the chief executives in sales and accounting. This top administrator would forward the complaint down through channels to the appropriate person in the billing division. The answer would follow the reverse path up and down through channels until the sales manager's secretary received it and could notify the customer. Such procedures are rather ridiculous, and most organizations would not follow them. Instead, the informal structure would be used. The sales manager's secretary would simply telephone or walk over to see a clerk in the billing department to find out what happened to the customer's order.

Frequently, salespeople do things that are above and beyond their formal job requirements, such as helping another rep prepare a quote or showing a new rep how to search the company's online product catalog. These behaviors, which are known as citizenship behaviors, are also part of the informal organization.[2]

Basic Types of Organizations

Most sales organizations can be classified mainly into one of four basic categories:

- A **line organization.**
- A **line-and-staff organization.**
- A **functional organization.**
- A **horizontal organization.**

Figure 4–1 describes these categories, explains when each is likely to be used, and states their major advantages and limitations. Figures 4–2 and 4–3 depict line-and-staff and functional sales organizations. Finally, Figure 4–4 shows the horizontal organizational form. The horizontal structure has been adopted by some of the biggest companies in the United States—such as AT&T, Du Pont, General Electric, and Motorola—to gain greater efficiencies and customer responsiveness.[3] Kraft Corporation recently restructured into a hybrid organization in which functional staff personnel provide advice to the horizontal customer teams.[4] Usually most medium- and large-sized firms will expand one of the basic structures in some specialized way so that the sales force can be more effective. We discuss specialization in sales organizations in the next section.

Specialization within a Sales Department

In the organizational examples discussed earlier, the sales force has not been divided on any basis. As a sales force grows, the job of the executive managing the sales force becomes more difficult. The number and complexity of a company's products and/or markets may also call for some organizational division if the sales effort is to be effective.

FIGURE 4-1   Basic types of organization—their nature, uses, and merits

Organization Type

	Line	**Line-and-Staff**
Nature	Simplest form of organization. Authority flows from chief executive to first subordinate, then to second subordinate, and so on down.	Take a line organization and add staff assistants who are specialists in various areas—advertising or marketing research, for example. The staff executive is responsible for all planning connected with the specialized activity, but has only an advisory relationship with sales managers and sales reps. The same staff executive—an advertising manager, for example—has line authority over people in the advertising department, but is in a staff-authority (advisory) relationship with the sales force.
When used	In very small firms or within a small department in a larger company.	Probably the most widely used basic form of organization in sales departments today. Likely to be used when any of the following conditions exist: • Sales force is large. • Market is regional or national. • Line of products is varied. • Number of customers is large.
Relative merits	Low-cost operation; quick decision making; highly centralized authority. Lack of managerial specialization and frequently no replacement for top executive, who is the owner of the firm.	Provides benefits of division of labor and executive specialization. Total cost of organization can be high, especially when staff assistants have their own departments. Decision making is slower. A potential problem: Strong staff executives may want to assume line authority instead of staying in an advisory role.

	Functional	**Horizontal**
Nature	A step beyond line-and-staff structure in that each activity specialist—advertising or sales promotion, for example—has line authority over the activity in relations with the sales force. Suppose a credit manager wants the salespeople to make collections on delinquent accounts. A staff executive can only *recommend* to the general manager that the reps do this job. A functional executive has line authority to *order* the assistant sales manager or the salespeople to do the job.	Eliminates both management levels and departmental boundaries. A small group of senior executives at the top overseeing the support functions like human resources, finance, and long-term planning. Everyone else is a member of cross-functional teams which perform core processes such as product development and sales and fulfillment. These teams are self-managed.
When used	Large company with varied product lines and/or markets. The key is to limit the number of executives who may use the functional line authority. The more people giving orders to the sales force, for example, the more opportunity there is for trouble.	By large and small companies seeking greater efficiencies and customer responsiveness. Firms which are establishing long-term partnering relationships with their customers are the most likely to adopt a horizontal structure. Various cross-functional teams work with customers' teams to solve problems and create opportunities for greater productivity and growth.
Relative Merits	Advantages of specialization of labor plus the assurances that functional executives' plans and programs will be carried out because the executives can order that this be done. The major drawback is that line sales executives and the salespeople may get orders from more than one person.	Reduces supervision and eliminates activities that are not necessary for the process. Costs are reduced and customer responsiveness is greatly enhanced.

FIGURE 4-2

Line-and-staff sales organization

FIGURE 4-3

Functional sales organization

The most common way to divide sales responsibilities is to split the sales force on some basis of sales specialization. There is a definite trend toward the use of specialized sales forces in the United States. The key strategic question here is, What should be the basis of the specialization—geography, type of product, market-based divisions, or other criteria? To make this decision, management should carefully analyze many factors, including sales force abilities, market and customer considerations, nature of the product, and demands of the selling job.

Geographic Specialization

Probably the most widely used system for dividing responsibility and line authority over sales operations is the **geographic organization**—the sales force is grouped on the basis of physical territories. In this type of structure, each sales-

FIGURE 4-4

The horizontal corporation

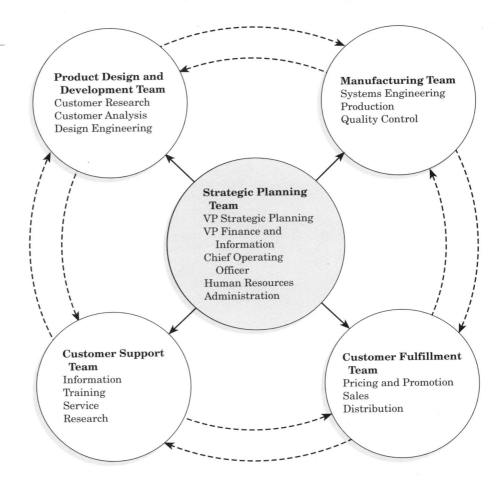

person is assigned a separate geographical area, called a *territory*, in which to sell. A reasonable number of salespeople representing contiguous territories are placed under a territorial executive who reports to the general sales manager. The territorial sales executive is usually called a *regional* or *district sales manager*. Companies with large sales forces often have two or three levels of territorial sales executives, as in Figure 4–5.

A firm can benefit in many ways from territorial specialization in its sales department. For example, this structure usually ensures better coverage of the entire market, as well as better control over the sales force and sales operations. A firm can meet local competition and adjust to local conditions by having an executive responsible for a limited segment of the market. Local management also can act more rapidly in servicing customers and handling their problems.

A drawback in a geographical sales organization is that there is usually no specialization of marketing activities. Each district manager, for example, may have to work in advertising, sales promotion, and marketing research, in addition to managing a sales force.

FIGURE 4-5

Geographical sales organization

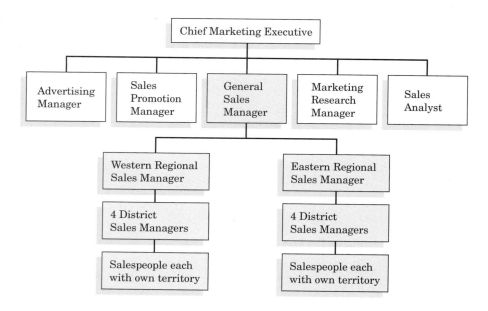

Product Specialization

The type of product sold is another frequently used basis for dividing the responsibilities and activities within a sales department. The two most widely used structures featuring **product specialization organization** are product operating and product staff organizations.

Product Operating Specialization

In the company represented in Figure 4–6, products have been separated into three groups: A, B, and C. Salespeople in each group sell only the products included in that group. All sales reps in group A report directly to the sales manager of product group A, who in turn is responsible to the general sales manager. The three product sales managers are strictly line-operating executives; they have no staff assistants. The staff executives in advertising, for example, are located in the home office and are not specialized by product.

Product operating specialization is likely to be used when a company is selling:

- A variety of complex, technical products, as in the electronics field.
- Many thousands of products—a hardware wholesaler, for example.
- Very dissimilar, unrelated products—a rubber company may use three sales forces to sell (a) truck and auto tires, (b) rubber footwear, and (c) industrial rubber products such as belts, bushings, and insulating materials.

3M Corporation uses separate sales forces to sell its wide product lines. One group of salespeople sells industrial adhesives, and another sells safety equipment.

The major advantage of this form of organization is that the sales force can give specialized attention to each product line. Also, each line gets more executive attention because one person is responsible for a particular product group.

FIGURE 4-6

Sales organization with product-specialized sales force

FIGURE 4-7   Sales organization with product managers as staff specialists

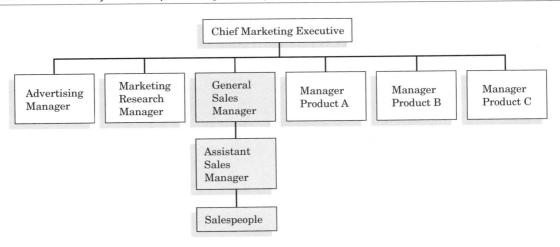

Probably the biggest drawback is that sometimes more than one salesperson from a company calls on the same customer. Such duplication of coverage not only is expensive but also can evoke ill will from the customers. Product operating specialization also has the same weakness as the geographic type in that the product sales managers have no staff assistants in advertising, sales promotion, or other specialized marketing activities.

Product Staff Specialization

Figure 4–7 illustrates **product staff specialization,** which is commonly used when management wants to use staff assistants who specialize by product. The company in Figure 4–7 has three staff executives, called **product managers** (or, in some companies, brand or category managers). Each bears responsibility for planning and developing a marketing program for a separate group of products.

These people have no line authority over the sales force or the sales force managers. They can only advise and make recommendations to the line managers. The sales force is not specialized by product. Instead, each salesperson sells the products of all three product managers.

A company can use this structure when it wants some of the advantages of specialization by product line at the planning level but does not need the specialization at the selling level. Thus, in one stroke the product staff organization corrects two of the weaknesses in a product operating structure: (1) the problems of duplicate calls on a customer and (2) the lack of specialization in planning the functional activities. Of course, a product staff organization loses any advantage of having salespeople specialize in a limited line of products. Product staff specialization is frequently used by consumer product companies such as Procter & Gamble or Quaker Oats.

Market Specialization

Many companies divide the line authority in their sales departments on the basis of type of customer, classed either by industry or by channel of distribution. For example, a division of Kimberly-Clark that sells Huggies diapers, Kleenex tissues, and a variety of feminine products uses separate sales forces to reach mass merchandisers, grocery stores, and military post exchanges (PXs). DoubleClick, a company that sells online advertising, reorganized its salespeople according to industry channels: automotive, business, entertainment and youth, technology, women and health, and travel.[5]

A sales organization featuring **market specialization** is illustrated in Figure 4–8. The sales manager in charge of each industry group is a line-operating executive with authority over one group of salespeople. These executives have no staff assistants under them. Each sales rep sells the full line of products used by the customer group.

The use of market specialization in sales organizational structures has increased in recent years, while product specialization, at least in some industries, has declined. This trend is expected to continue. Certainly market special-

FIGURE 4-8

Sales organization specialized by type of customer

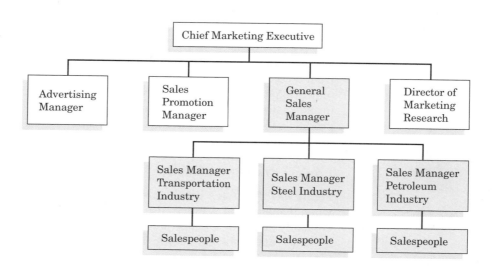

ization is consistent with the customer orientation philosophy that underlies the marketing concept. Among the companies that already have made the market specialization move in their sales organizations are such well-known names as Xerox, IBM, NCR, Hewlett-Packard, General Foods, and General Electric.

Xerox embarked on an ambitious three- to five-year program that eventually had its 4,000 to 5,000 sales reps selling the company's full line of office-automation products. In effect, the company switched from a product-oriented sales organization, consisting of several product sales forces, to a market-oriented structure. The company spent between $10 and $20 million a year in its training program to implement this organizational change.

IBM reconfigured its sales force by industry; that is, reps are now assigned by industry, not necessarily by geography. The reps are industry experts who sell primarily to customers within specific industries. This focus on customers is widely credited for the company's double-digit sales growth. As one IBM client executive noted, "Customers were demanding that we focus our organization more closely on their industries, so IBM changed its organization to meet their demands. Now we have intimate knowledge of their businesses."[6]

Although it overcomes some of the disadvantages of product specialization and conflict of interest between channels, market specialization does have some limitations. It causes overlap in territorial coverage and therefore is costly. Also, unless separating the sales force by markets results in some product specialization, the customer-based organization may include the disadvantages of full-line selling.

Combination of Organizational Bases

In the examples of organizational bases given earlier, we assumed that a company divides its sales force on only one basis, such as territory, product, or market. Actually, many firms use some combination drawn from the structures already discussed. For example, a firm may combine geographical specialization with product staff specialization (through the use of product managers). Or a sales force may combine market specialization with geographical specialization.

As we look at sales management in the 2000s, it is evident that the trend toward specialized sales forces will continue. The basis of specialization—geography, product, market, or a combination—may vary from company to company, but some specialization is needed to remain competitive. In the following section we discuss additional organizational alternatives that can benefit a company's selling effort.

Additional Strategic Organizational Alternatives

In our discussion of organizational structures, we looked at an outside sales force that makes calls *in person* on accounts (customers). We implied that the reps are alone when they make these face-to-face sales calls, and we did not consider the impact of the size of the account on these organizational structures.

FIGURE 4-9

Organizational options for the
2000s

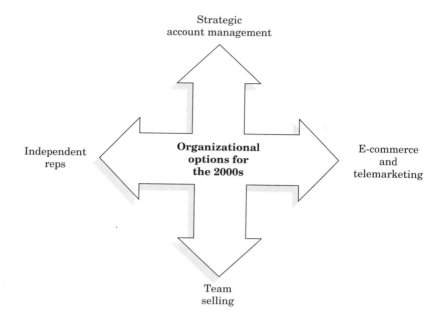

However, there are additional selling strategies with significant organizational implications that do include such factors as (1) account size, (2) team selling, (3) outside selling without in-person sales calls, and (4) the use of independent agents. (See Figure 4–9.) These organizational alternatives, which have attracted increasing managerial attention in recent years, are likely to gain even greater acceptance as we move through the early 2000s.

Strategic Account Management

Many companies have developed separate structures and programs within their organizations for dealing with major accounts—that is, their large-volume customers. Large customers can range from firms with only local or regional markets to multinational corporations. Some firms use the term **strategic account management (SAM)** or **global account management (GAM)** to describe their management of large customers; others use the terms *national, corporate,* or *major account management.* However they are described, large customers are extremely important to a seller because they usually account for a *disproportionately large share* of a seller's sales volume and profit. In addition to their large buying size, major customers are also differentiated by the *complexity of their buying process.*

Several factors contribute to the complexity of the buying–selling process of major accounts. On the buyer's side, people in different geographical locations may be involved in the buying process. Even at one site, several executives, including top management, may influence the buying decision. Price concessions, special services, and custom-made products may be demanded by large buyers. Salespeople in different geographical areas may be calling on the same customer, and many customers do not want the confusion of dealing with a different salesperson and a different contract for each site. Similar conditions on the seller's side add to the complexity and potential confusion. The large dollar volume involved usually attracts executives from other functional areas, and maybe even the company president.

The Virtual Office

With the advent of cell phones, laptops, and the Internet, many companies, such as IBM, AT&T, and Lucent Technologies have eliminated district sales offices. Instead the reps work out of virtual offices. These offices are called virtual because, although they are not "real" locations, reps can use them to do all of the things they once did in the district office or even in a home office. Virtual offices, which sometimes consist of nothing more than a digital cell phone and/or a laptop, and can be set up almost anywhere at almost any time, not only reduce costs but also allow salespeople to respond to customer needs efficiently and effectively. However, sales managers today do not see their reps in person as much as they did in the past. Therefore, managers must be proficient at using the same tools to supervise and provide assistance to their reps.

Obviously there is a dramatic need for close organizational coordination both within the seller's company and between the buyer and seller. Many sales executives believe that the major accounts are too important to be handled only by the average territorial sales rep. Consequently, they are modifying their sales organizations to provide better treatment for these accounts.[7] Three commonly used organizational approaches are:

- **Creating a separate sales force.** In recent years many firms have established separate sales forces to sell to key accounts. A variation is to have the major-account salespeople call on customers' home offices while using the regular sales force to service the customers' branch and field offices. Hewlett-Packard splits its sales force into three groups: the red team, the blue team, and the green team. The red team goes after only strategically important accounts in targeted industries; the green team calls on the wholesalers and distributors that are used to sell to the smaller accounts; and the blue team includes telesales and some other, less important accounts that don't fit in the other categories.[8]

  In contrast, Xerox national account managers work hand-in-hand with the local reps to develop strategies for approaching the customer on both the national and local levels.[9] 3M Corporation also has key account managers who work with local reps around the globe on corporate strategic accounts.[10]

- **Using executives.** Some companies use their top sales and marketing executives or their field sales executives for major-account selling. This approach is an alternative for firms that cannot afford a separate sales force. A company that has only a few large customers may also find this approach useful. Sending top executives to call on key accounts ensures that the salesperson has the authority to make decisions about prices and the allocation of manufacturing facilities. On the other hand, executive time spent on servicing key accounts is time taken away from planning and other management activities.

- **Creating a separate division.** A company may establish a separate division to deal with its key accounts. This option has been used by some apparel manufacturers that produce and sell private-label clothing for the large general-merchandise chains such as Sears and JCPenney. This organizational structure has the advantage of integrating the manufacturing and marketing (including the sales) activities related to the major accounts. On the other hand, this structure is expensive because it duplicates other units in the selling firm.

A DAY-TO-DAY OPERATING PROBLEM

MAJESTIC PLASTICS COMPANY

MAJESTIC
Plastics Company

A Series of Operating Problems Facing a Sales Manager

The Majestics Plastics Company, formerly the Majestic Glass Company, is a manufacturer of bottles, jars, and other containers. Although it originally produced glass containers, over the years management saw the handwriting on the wall as the market demand for its products declined and, concurrently, the demand for plastic packaging increased substantially. Consequently, in 1993 the company's factory in eastern Ohio was completely converted to the production of plastic containers, and the company was renamed. Bottles for cosmetics and toiletries accounted for the bulk of the company's sales volume. However, containers for soft drinks, milk, food products, medicine, and shoe polish were also important in Majestic's product mix.

Clyde D. Brion, the company's general sales manager, directed 18 salespeople, each based in a different city. Each sales rep was paid a commission of 10 percent on all sales in his or her territory. The reps received an additional 5 percent on orders from new customers, provided the order was larger than a specified minimum quantity. In addition, the company paid all reasonable travel and entertainment expenses that were incurred by the reps.

Orders from large and regular customers were shipped directly from the Majestic factory to users' plants by rail. For smaller and infrequent buyers, stocks of standard bottles and jars were maintained in warehouses owned by public warehouse companies. At these warehouses, Brion also rented desk space with basic secretarial and telephone services for each sales rep. This arrangement, in effect, provided Majestic Plastics with regional sales branches and product inventory in 18 cities.

Competition was keen in the container industry. Several large firms produced plastic bottles and jars. Competition also came from containers made of glass, metal, or paper. It was especially important that the Majestic sales force be alert to new business possibilities, that they follow up leads and market tips quickly, and that they offer maximum service. It was Majestic's policy to meet competitors' prices, but not to undercut a competitor willfully in order to steal business.

At the time you are studying this case, Brion is facing several problems in the operation of his sales force. He is anxious to solve each one promptly and correctly. Brion also wants to set up safeguards against recurrence of the problem. At the same time, he wants to establish a policy for dealing with the problem should it arise again.

Twelve of these operating problems facing Brion appear at various places in this text. In each instance, the particular problem is located at a relevant place in the chapter. The first in the series is a problem in organization, and it follows on the next page.

Note: The concept of Majestic Plastics operating problems is based on earlier writings of Professor Phillip McVey, then at the University of Nebraska–Lincoln.

Buying Centers and Team Selling

In Chapter 1 we stated that growing expertise among buyers would continue to challenge strategic sales management during the 21st century and beyond. Many business and government organizations have already developed and implemented the concept of a buying center in their buying process. The **buying center** may be defined as all the individuals involved in the purchasing decision process. Thus, a buying center usually includes people who play any of the following roles:

- *Users* of the product.
- *Influencers* who set the product specifications.
- *Deciders* who make the actual purchasing decision.
- *Gatekeepers* who control the flow of purchasing information.
- *Buyers* (purchasing agents) who process the purchase orders.

In contrast to consumer purchasing, organizational buying is generally based more on economic reasons than on emotional ones. Among the many factors

A DAY-TO-DAY OPERATING PROBLEM

MAJESTIC PLASTICS COMPANY

MAJESTIC
Plastics Company

Location of Authority

Clyde Brion, general sales manager of the Majestic Plastics Company, received the following letter from Centra Wineries, Inc., a San Francisco firm that had bought standard-line Majestic bottles for many years:

April 9
Mr. Clyde D. Brion, General Sales Manager
Majestic Plastics Company
Lancaster, Ohio 43130

Dear Mr. Brion:

We have decided reluctantly that we must remove your company from our list of acceptable container vendors unless you can provide sales service more in keeping with our needs.

Please understand that this action in no way implies dissatisfaction with Majestic bottles or with your San Francisco representative, Mr. Harlow Britt.

As you know, the domestic wine industry is a fiercely competitive, fast-moving, low-margin business. We operate on a system of guaranteed resale prices to our distributors and dealers. Consequently, any competitive price-cutting pressures must be met by trimming our costs. Such a small saving as 3 cents per unfilled bottle may on occasion make the difference between profitable and unprofitable business for us.

Similarly, to escape storage costs we never stock more than our immediate requirements of unfilled bottles. We depend upon bottle manufacturers to provide guaranteed deliveries to us on very short notice—never more than 10 days.

While Mr. Britt is very helpful, we find that he lacks authority to adjust your prices to meet our needs, or to guarantee on-time deliveries to us at your risk. He tells us that he must have your written approval on these questions, and the time required to obtain it may be 24 to 72 hours.

We hope you can give Mr. Britt the authority he needs to retain our patronage.

Yours truly,
V. Collasini
Centra Wineries, Inc.

Brion checked his records on this customer and learned that the average elapsed time from order date to delivery date was 19 days. On orders that Britt had marked "rush" and Brion had expedited, the average elapsed time had been nine days. No deliveries had been guaranteed.

Question: Now what does Clyde Brion do? Answer the letter.

---

buyers consider when choosing a supplier are the quality-price ratio, delivery reliability, reputation of the supplier, information and market services provided by the supplier, and previous experience with the supplier. It should also be noted that purchasing managers will continue to have increased status and authority within the firm as materials management grows in importance. This increased status and authority is reflected by such titles as vice president of materials management or vice president of supply chain management.

Team Selling

As noted in Chapter 2, a growing number of firms are using selling teams to call on the various individuals in the buying center. A **selling team** is a group of people representing the sales department and other functional areas in the firm, such as finance, production, and research and development (R&D).

Organizational Options for Team Selling

The organizational arrangements for team selling are quite flexible. Usually the functional specialists and management levels on the selling team match those from the buying center in any given purchase–sale transaction. Therefore, the functional and executive composition of a selling team varies from company to company, and

This team of sales representatives discusses the call they just made on one of their major accounts.

from one selling situation to another within a given firm. Companies like IBM and Compaq, which sell customized combinations of computer hardware and software, use teams of salespeople and technical experts who work closely with the customer's buying team. At IBM, for example, client executives manage teams, which include product reps, systems engineers, and consultants.[11] On the Monsanto customer team, IBM included research experts in molecular technology to help Monsanto with genetic engineering problems. As a result, IBM won a contract with Monsanto worth $1 billion.[12] At 3M Corporation, cross-functional teams have been formulated from each of the company's regions; these teams include people from logistics, management information systems, and sales.[13]

In recent years, there has been a trend toward including representatives from the customer's organization on the team. In order to serve its important customers, General Electric (GE) creates large teams that are both cross-functional and cross-company. It formed a 140-person cross company-team to help one customer, Southern California Edison, reduce the downtime on its steam turbine generators, which were purchased from GE. The team consisted of 60 people from GE and 80 from Southern California Edison. Medical equipment manufacturer Baxter International has gone even further by jointly setting targets and sharing the savings or the extra costs.[14] In these cases the two companies have entered into a partnership, as described in Chapter 2.

Some companies establish a separate location where sales teams meet with customer buying teams. At these **selling centers,** the selling team presents an integrated program that matches the account's needs. The agenda for the program is usually developed in consultation with the buying team. Xerox has six of these centers, which it calls executive briefing centers, and management believes that they stimulate openness, which improves communication and thus the relationship with the buying team.[15]

Strategic Considerations

A number of factors must be considered if a company chooses to adopt a team-selling approach. The size and the functional diversity of the team must be established. Management must determine how it will reward the individuals on the team as well as the team itself. To a large extent these decisions should be based on the strategic objectives for the team. For example, if one of the primary responsibilities of the team will be to provide a great amount of after-sale support, and if that support will be provided by people other than the salesperson, it is often effective to include the support staff as part of a sales team. This enables the support personnel to develop a better understanding of the customer's support needs relatively quickly. Furthermore, with their expertise, support people can help close the sale.

However, there are some general guidelines that may affect strategic decisions. On the one hand, it has been found that individuals tend to exert less effort as team size increases, so there is some rationale for limiting the size of the team. On the other hand, there is evidence that greater skill diversity is related to increased effort and interaction on the part of the team members. Therefore, it is a good idea to form teams with individuals who are from several different functional areas or departments within the firm.

Team selling is not the best alternative in every situation. It is expensive and consequently is used only when there is potential for high sales volume and profit. For example, companies may use teams to call on their major accounts but not on their low-volume accounts. Even then, team selling is likely to be used only in complex situations involving a large capital expenditure, a long-term contract, customized products and services, or a new account. We call these *new-task* situations. *Routine* selling situations—even for large amounts—are likely to be handled by a sales rep and a purchasing agent working together, with no team involved. The in-between situations—*modified rebuys*, we call them—may involve a selling team, but with fewer members than in new-buy situations.

The overriding consideration in the decision to use sales teams should be whether the approach is consistent with the needs of the buyer. If your important customers or potential customers are using buying teams for their complex purchasing decisions, then your firm should consider using multifunctional sales teams to call on these customers.

Independent Sales Organizations

Most producers use some type of wholesaling or retailing intermediaries to get their products to the final customer. According to the most recent U.S. Census of Retail Trade, less than 5 percent of the dollar volume of products bought by household consumers is purchased directly from producers.[16] In business goods, the dollar volume of direct sales—producer to business user—is very high. But most business-goods producers also use some type of wholesaling intermediary. Most producers, then, rely in part on using someone else's sales force to move the product to market. At the same time, these intermediaries must be sold on representing a certain producer and selling the producer's products. In effect, an intermediary's organization becomes both a customer and a sales force for this producer.

The two major categories of these independent sales forces are merchant intermediaries (wholesalers and retailers) and agents. Additionally, most wholesaling intermediaries (merchant wholesalers and agents) have outside sales forces—sales forces that go to the customer. Therefore, the management of these sales forces is within the scope of this book. However, at this point we are interested only in the sales force organizational relationships between a producer and these intermediary companies.

An Ethical Dilemma

A strong regional manufacturer decided several years ago to expand into a new geographic area. Although the company served all of its current customers with its own sales force, it chose to use a manufacturer's rep to expand into the new territory. The company was not certain how long it would take to build up the business in the new area, and using a rep organization would enable the company to limit its expenses during this developmental period.

During the next several years, the rep did an outstanding job of opening up new accounts for the manufacturer. The rep was well liked by her customers, and the company was very satisfied with the amount of effort that had been devoted by the rep to the company's products. In fact, management readily acknowledged that the rep's knowledge of the customers in her market had clearly been the primary factor that enabled the company to penetrate this market with such rapid success.

Sales in this territory were now at a level large enough to support the company's own rep, and the company was not planning on renewing its contractual arrangement with the rep. Rather, it would replace the rep with one of its own salespeople.

Is this company acting ethically if it replaces the independent rep with one of its own salespeople?

Independent Agents

Many producers, either with or without their own sales forces, rely heavily on the sales forces of independent agents to reach the market. These agents are wholesaling intermediaries that do not take ownership title to the products they sell, and they usually do not carry inventory stocks. Independent agents are paid a commission on the sales they make. Consequently, the commission is a variable expense to a producer—that is, a producer doesn't pay if no sale is made.

The most widely used type of agent is a **manufacturer's representative,** also called a *manufacturer's agent* or simply a *rep.* A single producer usually uses several manufacturers' agents, each having a specified geographical territory. Each agent has its own sales force and generally represents several manufacturers of related, but not directly competing, products. Manufacturer's reps are most often used in the following situations:

- When a manufacturer does not have a sales force. (The rep then does all the selling.)

- When a producer wants to introduce a new product, but for some reason does not want its existing sales force to handle it.

- When a company wants to enter a new market that is not yet sufficiently developed for the seller to use its own sales force.

- When it is not cost-effective for a company to use its own reps to call on certain accounts because the sales potential does not justify the cost.

From a producer's point of view, there are advantages in using the sales forces of manufacturer's agents. These reps know their market and have already established relations with prospective accounts. An individual producer, on the other hand, especially one new in the market, probably will not have the same access to customers.[17] Another benefit of using reps is that it is less expensive in sparsely populated markets, with smaller accounts, or with a limited line of products. For example, Lucent Technologies uses independent reps to sell to its smaller customers. These reps generate 10 percent of the company's revenues.[18]

Brokers, another type of independent agent, are used extensively, at least in some industries. The prime responsibility of brokers is to bring sellers and buyers together. Brokers can also furnish considerable market information regarding prices, products, and market conditions. Brokers may represent either the seller (90 percent of the time) or the buyer (10 percent), but not both parties in the same transaction.

Brokers are used in marketing services as well as products. Hotels, airlines, and resorts, for example, make extensive use of travel agents as a sales force. Brokers play a major role in the sale of stocks, bonds, and other financial services.

Wholesale Distributors

Wholesale distributors are another type of independent sales organization that producers may use to reach their final customers. Wholesalers—also called *jobbers*, *distributors*, or *industrial distributors*, depending on the industry—are intermediaries who take ownership title to the products they sell. They also carry a physical inventory of these products. Wholesalers may represent only one producer, but most often they represent many producers of related and competing products. A large percentage of producers, especially producers of business (industrial) products, use wholesale distributors.

Wholesalers can be very useful in selling situations where (1) individual sales are small, (2) the buying process is not highly specialized, or (3) rapid delivery and local service facilities are important.

Independent versus Company Reps

Whether to use independent or company reps depends on the specific market the firm is trying to serve. As a basis for making the decision, a company must establish clear objectives for each of the markets it is targeting. Then it must develop strategies to achieve those objectives. The strategies will dictate whether the company should use direct salespeople, independent reps, or some combination of both.

Often the decision revolves around three considerations:

1. Which type of rep is most effective in achieving your objectives for the market?
2. Which method is the most economical?
3. Which gives you the necessary amount of control in order to achieve your objectives?

The answer to which method is most effective in achieving your objectives depends directly on what those objectives are. For example, if the primary objective is to quickly achieve wide distribution for a new product, manufacturer's reps may be the best alternative for a company without an established company sales force. If the long-term objective is to develop partnerships with a certain group of customers, then it is probably best to serve those customers directly even though this may be an expensive alternative.

As illustrated in Figure 4–10, the answer to which is the most economical method is a function of (1) the potential volume in the particular market and (2) the cost of sales that is directly related to the number of company salespeople that would be required to serve that market. It can also be seen that the direct sales force has a variable cost-to-sales ratio, and the independents have a

FIGURE 4-10

Captive versus independent sales force

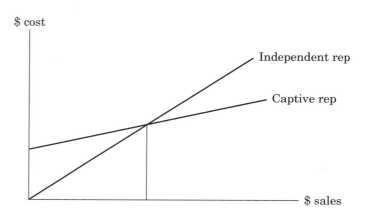

Economic Considerations

fixed cost-to-sales ratio. When sales are low, the direct cost-to-sales ratio will be high, but it decreases as volume rises, whereas the ratio for the independents stays the same regardless of the volume. Because of this, the use of direct salespeople becomes more economical at higher volumes. Generally, the volume in a market must be fairly substantial before a company can cover the costs of serving the customers with direct salespeople.

The question of control should be decided on the basis of how much control is needed to achieve the desired objectives. When a firm uses independent reps, it loses control over the amount of time devoted to its product lines because these reps usually represent more than one company. It also loses control over the approach and attention given to its customers. If the firm's customers each require a specialized approach and a great deal of attention, using independent reps may not be the way to achieve sales objectives. However, control in itself is not an objective; sometimes the objectives may be achieved more efficiently and effectively using independent reps.

Choosing an Independent Agent. It is important to pick the very best agent available. In particular, the agent should be one who best matches the market strategy and the culture of the parent organization. The goals of the two organizations should be compatible, and the selling philosophies of the two should be the same. The product lines that the agent carries should complement those of the manufacturer, and the manufacturer's products should be the primary line for the agent. In order to be compatible, a parent company should devote the same amount of resources (time and money) to the selection of its independent agents as it would to the selection of its own company reps.

Managing the Independent Sales Force. It is difficult enough to run your own sales force, but you face further organizational challenges when you use independent sales reps—whether agents or distributors. The biggest and perhaps most obvious challenge is the one mentioned above—that the producer has very little control over the independent sales force. This factor creates at least two managerial problems. First, a producer must compete with other firms for the selling time of the agent's or distributor's salespeople. This is a particularly tough challenge if the manufacturer and its products are not well known. Second, it is difficult to get manufacturer's reps to service an account and perform nonselling activities because they get no commission for such work.

There is no perfect solution to the second problem because the top independent agents will have their choice of companies to represent. They do not need your company to survive and will not put up with attempts to control their actions. Therefore, the best strategy is to provide your reps with the proper amount of support. This may involve training the salespeople of the agent or distributor. The manufacturer can also provide technical product information and can have a missionary sales force that does promotional work supporting the intermediary's efforts. Providing the appropriate level of support will alleviate the control problems. Furthermore, it is important to work with the reps as partners, making joint decisions on issues that affect the sales of products in the markets the reps serve.

E-Commerce and Telemarketing

In Chapter 1 we said that this book deals with the management of a sales force that goes to the customer. But an increasing number of firms—both large and small—have moved some selling efforts from outside to within the company. Instead of making face-to-face sales calls, salespeople are "going to the customer" by using telephones, fax machines, television, and computers.

Telephone selling is not new. What is new today, however, is the innovative use of communication systems to aid selling efforts and other marketing activities. Generally, **telemarketing** refers to situations in which a customer is contacted by a sales rep via telephone, and **e-commerce** refers to situations in which communication with the customer is carried out through the Internet (often via e-mail). In 2000, business-to-business e-commerce revenues totaled over $200 billion; this figure is expected to grow to over $7 trillion by 2004, representing over 35 percent of the overall business-to-business market.[19] Telemarketing generates sales of over $300 billion and is expected to continue to grow as well.[20]

Two main reasons for the growing use of e-commerce and telemarketing as forms of sales specialization are (1) many buyers prefer them over personal sales calls in certain selling situations and (2) many marketers find that they increase selling efficiency. For a buyer, placing routine reorders or new orders for standardized products by computer or by telephone takes less time than fielding in-person sales calls does. For a seller, keeping salespeople on the road means facing increasingly high costs, so any selling done via the Internet or over the phone reduces such expenses. Also, using e-commerce or telemarketing for routine selling allows the field sales force to devote more time to developmental selling; major-account selling; and other, more profitable selling activities.

In some cases, e-commerce or telemarketing is the primary interface with the customer. For example, Dell Computer Company, with over $500 million in personal computer sales, launched its business through telephone sales and still does the majority of its business through this channel.[21] Owens Corning, the maker of Fiberglas, is another company that relies primarily on a variety of e-commerce platforms for serving its customers.[22] These companies used their reps exclusively to develop customer solutions for their most important accounts. On the other hand, many companies are trying to extend coverage by providing customers a choice of how they wish to do business: via the Internet, over the phone, by fax, or by meeting with a rep. Consolidated Freightways and Automatic Data Processing (ADP) have each extended this strategy even further by allowing customers to switch from making unassisted online transactions to speaking with a rep, either online or by telephone, merely by clicking the appropriate box on the company website.[23]

Some companies, such as Hewlett-Packard and IBM, use telephone reps or e-commerce to handle small or low-priority sales. This allows the direct sales reps to concentrate on bigger potential accounts.[24] In these telemarketing programs, the rep is responsible for qualifying customers as to their sales potential, assessing their needs, recommending products and services, taking orders, and providing customer service.

As noted in Chapter 1, many companies use the Internet and telemarketing to assist the sales force. Estimates of the increases in sales in these situations range anywhere from 10 percent to 400 percent. Shachihata, which sells preinked rubber stamps through independent reps, created a consumer development department whose sole function is to follow up on leads and generate appointments for the reps. This led to an increase in appointments of four to five times the number generated the previous year.[25] Eastman Chemical customers can track orders, obtain account information, and receive technical assistance online 24 hours a day.[26] Other companies use telemarketing to provide after-sale service to customers. General Electric (GE) is famous for its "Answer Center," whose 250 telephone operators answer 3 million inquiries a year concerning GE products that the customers have purchased or are considering purchasing.[27]

The selling activities performed by e-commerce or telemarketing can be summarized as follows:

- Identification of prospective customers.
- Qualification of sales leads (including screening and referral).
- Sales solicitation.
- Order processing.
- Product service support.
- Account management.
- Customer relations management.
- Competitive reporting.
- Expense reporting.

In most companies, telemarketing or e-commerce is not the exclusive method used to generate and service sales. It has not replaced the direct selling effort, but rather it is used to supplement the direct efforts in some way. As we noted in Chapter 2, many companies are using multiple selling channels to reach customers more efficiently; telemarketing or e-commerce is often one of the channels.

Organizing for International Sales

Throughout the 21st century and beyond, increasing numbers of American companies will be engaging in international marketing. Since 1986 the level of U.S. exports has risen at a rate four times that of the increase in gross domes-

An International Perspective

Even when a company chooses to employ its own sales force, it still must decide whether to hire foreign reps or reps from its own country. Foreign nationals are familiar with the local customs and culture but unfamiliar with the product and the company's marketing practices. The company reps, on the other hand, know the product and the company but are unfamiliar with the local customs and culture.

The answer to this question can be found by examining the needs and desires of the customers. Research on similarity in sales has generally demonstrated that, all other things being equal, the customers would rather be served by someone who is similar to themselves. Therefore, it is probably better to hire a national from your target market unless there are some overriding reasons not to. For example, some products are so complex that the salespeople may require extensive training and/or experience before they can sell these products. It may not be economically feasible to provide the amount of in-depth training that would be needed if the company hires inexperienced nationals, or it may not be possible to find enough qualified individuals in the target country.

If a company does hire foreign nationals, it should provide adequate product and company training. Likewise, if a company hires reps from its own country, it should provide extensive training in the cultural norms of the foreign market.

tic product (GDP), and U.S. company investment in foreign operations has doubled during the same period to over $500 billion.[28] Additionally, international trade is being encouraged by a number of trade organizations and agreements that are lessening the trade barriers around the world. The most important of these is the **World Trade Organization (WTO),** which currently has more than 140 members around the globe. For the United States, the **North American Free Trade Agreement (NAFTA),** signed in 1994, is also important because it eliminated many of the trade barriers between the United States, Canada, and Mexico. Increases in foreign investment and exports as well as reductions in trade barriers together mean that more firms are developing global sales operations.

The individual company decides to sell its products overseas for many different reasons: customer requests, home-market saturation, or excess capacity. Whatever the reason, it is important that the company's sales efforts are part of a long-term international strategy that has the full support of senior management. The plan must examine whether there is a need or demand for its products and how the company will sell its products abroad. A company has essentially three options with regard to distributing its products internationally: It can (1) turn over the export of its product to home-country intermediaries, (2) partner with foreign-country intermediaries, or (3) establish its own company sales force in the foreign country.

Home-Country Intermediaries

Depending on the products, there are a number of export intermediaries, located in the producing firm's country, who provide international marketing services from a domestic base. Firms such as export merchants, trading companies, export management companies, agents, brokers, and distributors all

A Peruvian wholesaler calls on an a apparel store. He is representing a U.S. apparel manufacturer.

offer international sales and distribution services for those companies that do not wish to become immediately involved in the complexities of international sales or that want to sell abroad with a minimum financial and management commitment.

Even in the case of minimum involvement, the company must make a number of critical sales management decisions. Sales managers must identify the appropriate agent or distributor and must reach an agreement with that intermediary regarding services and compensation. It may also be necessary to train personnel and to establish a system for monitoring sales results.

Foreign-Country Intermediaries

Many small and midsize firms that decide to establish a sales organization in a foreign country cannot afford to employ their own international sales forces. Therefore, many manufacturers set up a network of manufacturer's agents, distributors (wholesalers), and/or dealers (retailers) in foreign markets. In many cases these independent organizations are already selling other products and services in the target country. In addition to personal selling, these intermediaries perform many services, including advertising products, providing market information, making repairs, collecting invoices, and settling disputes. In return, the American firms usually grant the intermediaries exclusive territorial sales rights and may grant one wholesaler the sole distributorship for an entire country.

In foreign markets without sufficient sales potential to justify establishing a company sales force, such as those in developing countries, distributors are used. Other markets are so large geographically that a company may use independent reps to cover the outlying areas and company salespeople to cover the population centers.

Cultural diversity also affects this decision. Some multilingual, culturally heterogeneous markets require several different reps to deal with customers from the varying cultural groups. This is often the case in the markets in Southeast Asia.

Foreign intermediaries are generally less aggressive and perform fewer marketing activities than their American counterparts, but some of the factors described above often make it difficult for the company to bypass them. If a company decides to use foreign-company intermediaries, it must first identify the prospective candidates. Sources of information for locating foreign distributors include the following:

- The U.S. Department of Commerce.
- Foreign consulates.
- Foreign chambers of commerce.
- Business publications.
- Published directories.
- Intermediary associations.

After identifying candidates, the company begins the selection process. The firm should consider the nature of each prospective distributor's business. In other words, do the company's products fit with the prospective distributor's current products? The company should also consider the distributor's current volume of sales, its financial strength, and its managerial capability and stability.

Company Sales Force Located Abroad

In a country where the volume and profit potential warrants it and government regulations allow it, an American firm may establish its own company sales force. Only the largest companies—those with at least $500 million in sales—should consider the possibility of establishing their own sales force in a foreign market.[29] These sales forces may sell directly to the final customers, or they may sell through local distributors and dealers. Using its own sales force enables a company to (1) promote products more aggressively and (2) control its sales effort more completely. For both of these reasons, Boston Scientific Corporation, a manufacturer of medical devices, shifted from using local distributors to employing its own sales and marketing personnel in 20 international markets.[30]

For products that are technically or chemically complex, the manufacturer may feel that using company-employed salespeople is necessary to ensure that customers receive the proper training and assistance. The company's legal liability with regard to the use of these kinds of products is another factor that may cause the company to use its own salespeople.

Summary

An organization is an arrangement of activities involving a group of people. The goal is to arrange the activities so that the people who are involved can work better *together* than they can *individually*. The sales force organizational structure has a significant influence on the implementation of a company's strategic planning.

The general characteristics of a good organization are: (1) an organizational structure that reflects a market orientation; (2) an organization that is built around activities and not around the people performing these activities; (3) responsibilities that are clearly spelled out, and sufficient authority granted to meet the responsibility; (4) a reasonable span of executive control; (5) stability combined with flexibility; and (6) balanced and coordinated activities both *within* the sales department and *between* sales and nonmarketing departments.

Most sales organizations can be classified into one of three basic categories: a line organization, a line-and-staff organization, or a functional organization. A line organization is the simplest form of organization and is often appropriate for small firms. A line-and-staff organization enables a company to use staff assistants who are specialists in various areas of marketing. A functional organization carries specialization a step further by giving more line authority to the executive specialists. Also, a new horizontal structure being used by a number of firms is a much flatter organization with fewer levels of management.

In most medium- and large-sized companies, the sales forces are divided on some basis of sales specialization. The most frequently used bases are (1) geographical territories, (2) type of product sold, (3) classes of customer, or (4) some combination of these categories.

Giving each sales representative the responsibility for his or her own geographical territory is probably the most widely used form of sales force specialization. Specializing a sales force by type of product sold is often used when a company sells unrelated products, highly technical products, or several thousands of products. Product specialization may also involve the organizational concept of a product manager. Specialization by markets may be done on a channel-of-distribution basis or on an industry basis.

In the organization of an outside sales force, the use of the following four organizational strategies is increasing: strategic account management, team selling, independent sales forces, and e-commerce and telemarketing. For strategic account management, firms may use a separate sales force or executives, or they may establish a separate division. Selling teams comprised of people from several departments are being used to match the needs of customer buying centers. Sometimes a firm cannot afford or does not want to have its own sales force; in that case it will use some type of independent agent. Telemarketing is sometimes used as the primary selling method, but often it is used only to assist the sales force.

Organizing for international sales also presents some difficult challenges for sales management. Companies must decide whether to use independent selling organizations in the home country or in the foreign country, or to employ their own salespeople. Even if the company decides to use its own salespeople, it must still determine whether it will hire reps from its own country or foreign nationals.

Key Terms

Brokers
Buying center
E-commerce
Functional organization
Geographic organization

Global account management (GAM)
Horizontal organization
Independent agent
Informal organization

Line-and-staff organization
Line organization
Manufacturer's representative
Market specialization

North American Free Trade
  Agreement (NAFTA)
Organization
Organizational structure
Product managers
Product operating
  specialization

Product specialization
  organization
Product staff specialization
Selling centers
Selling team
Strategic account management
  (SAM)

Telemarketing
Wholesale distributors
World Trade Organization
  (WTO)

Questions and Problems

1. Explain how coordination can be effectively secured between the sales department and each of the following departments: production, engineering and design, personnel, finance, export sales.

2. What are the reasons for the lack of coordination that sometimes exists between advertising executives and field sales managers? What are some proposals for developing better coordination between these two groups?

3. The choice of organizational structure is influenced by factors such as:
   a) Size of the company.
   b) Nature of the products.
   c) Nature and density of the market.
   d) Ability of executives.
   e) Financial condition of the company.
   Explain how each of these conditions may affect the choice of structure.

4. In your opinion, what are the best policies or procedures for solving the following problems, which are often found in a line-and-staff organization?
   a) A strong-willed staff executive tries to take on line authority instead of remaining an adviser.
   b) A line executive consistently bypasses or ignores advice from staff departments.

5. What type of organizational specialization within the sales department do you recommend in each of the following companies?
   a) Manufacturer of high-quality women's sportswear with 100 salespeople selling to department stores and specialty stores throughout the nation.
   b) Plumbing wholesaler covering the southeastern quarter of the country with 50 salespeople.

   c) Manufacturer of chemicals used in fertilizers with 35 salespeople selling to 500 accounts located throughout the country.
   d) Manufacturer of office machines with 1,000 salespeople.

6. A regional hardware wholesaler in Detroit, Michigan, employed 20 salespeople, each of whom sold the full line of products. It became apparent that the list of products was simply too long for one person to sell effectively. The company felt it had a choice of
   a) reorganizing the sales force by product lines, or
   b) adding more representatives, reducing each person's territory, but still having each carry the full line.
   What do you recommend?

7. A manufacturer of small aircraft designed for executive transportation in large companies has decided to implement the concept of a selling center. What people in this company should be on the selling teams? What problems is this firm likely to encounter when it uses team selling?

8. How does the quote at the beginning of the chapter—"Listen to the customer and act on what they tell you"—relate to the concepts discussed in the first four chapters?

9. a) What courses of action would you propose for a company that wants to get its manufacturer's reps to devote more time to selling its products?
   b) A manufacturer of small motors uses industrial distributors to reach its market. What can this producer do to encourage the distributors to spend more time selling the company's products?

10. A manufacturer of playground equipment now uses its own sales force to sell directly to customer groups such as city park departments, school districts, private day nurseries, and companies that maintain day care centers for employees' children. This producer would like to install a telemarketing system to reduce some of its field-selling costs. What problems is this seller likely to encounter in the telemarketing move? What recommendations do you have for solving these problems?

11. A manufacturer of pharmaceuticals wants to market its products in the European Union (EU). Its sales are currently $400,000. How should the company enter the EU market—with its own sales force or with some type of independent distributor? Support your choice.

12. A U.S. manufacturer of industrial tools wants to market its products overseas. It is considering establishing sales organizations in several different countries. In which of the countries listed below do you think this manufacturer should use an independent selling organization rather than its own sales force?
   a) Switzerland.
   b) Malaysia.
   c) Spain.
   d) China.

Experiential Exercises

A. Obtain an organizational chart for a firm that sells consumer products and a firm that sells industrial products. Compare and contrast the sales organization structure in terms of span of control, centralization, specialization, line-and-staff components, and so on.

B. Contact an executive from any small organization and ask about the formal organizational relationships. Without seeing the firm's organizational chart (if there is one), draw an organizational chart based on the information given to you by the executive. Does this organization violate any of the principles of organizational design? Compare your organizational chart to the firm's official chart.

C. Contact a manufacturer's rep for any type of product. (Such reps are usually listed in the yellow pages for most major cities.) Find out what criteria reps use to select the manufacturers they are willing to represent. Also determine what types of assistance the various manufacturers they represent provide to the manufacturer's rep.

Internet Exercises

A. Visit the websites of the following four companies to determine how their sales forces are organized—for example, by product, by type of customer, by geography or some combination of these factors.
   a) IBM.
   b) Hewlett-Packard.
   c) Eli Lilly.
   d) Procter & Gamble.

References

1. Quoted in Erika Rasmusson, "5 Companies to Watch," *Sales & Marketing Management*, July 2000, p. 85.

2. Phillip M. Podsakoff and Scott B. MacKensie, "Organizational Citizenship Behaviors and Sales Unit Effectiveness," *Journal of Marketing Research*, August 1994, pp. 351–63.

3. John A. Byrne, "The Horizontal Corporation," *Business Week*, December 20, 1993, pp. 76–81.

4. George S. Day, "Aligning the Organization to the Market," Prakash Nedungadi Memorial Lecture, Indiana University School of Business, January 1997.

5. Chad Kaydo, "Reorganizing a Sales Force," *Sales & Marketing Management*, March 2000, p. 90.

6. Geoffrey Brewer, "Brain Power," *Sales & Marketing Management*, May 1997, pp. 39–41.

7. Sanjit Sengupta, Robert E. Krapfel, and Michael A. Pusateri, "An Empirical Investigation of Key Account Salesperson Effectiveness," *Journal of Personal Selling & Sales Management*, Fall 2000, p. 253.

8. Daniel S. Levine, "Justice Served," *Sales & Marketing Management*, May 1995, pp. 53–58.

9. Kerry J. Rottenberger-Murtha, "The Lean and the Green," *Sales & Marketing Management*, February 1993, pp. 68–71.

10. Erika Rasmusson, "3M's Big Strategy for Big Accounts," *Sales & Marketing Management*, September 2000, pp. 92–98.

11. Goeffry Brewer, "Love the Ones You're With," *Sales & Marketing Management*, February 1999, pp. 40–41.

12. Neil Rackham, "The Other Revolution in Sales," *Sales & Marketing Management*, March 2000, p. 36.

13. Rahul Jacob, "Why Some Customers Are More Equal Than Others," *Fortune*, September 19, 1994, pp. 215–20.

14. Ibid.

15. Joseph Conlin, "Teaming Up," *Sales & Marketing Management*, October 1993, pp. 98–104.

16. U.S. Census of Retail Trade, 2000.

17. Kimberly Weisul, "Do You Dare Outsource Sales?" *Business Week Online*, June 18, 2001.

18. Dan Hoover, "Independents Day," *Sales & Marketing Management*, April 2000, pp. 66–67.

19. Melinda Ligos, "Clicks and Misses," *Sales & Marketing Management*, June 2000, p. 69.

20. "Telemarketing Cited as Chief Form of Direct Marketing," *Marketing News*, January 1, 1996, p. 9.

21. Erika Rasmusson, "Best at E-Business," *Sales & Marketing Management*, July 2000, p. 72.

22. Don Peppers and Martha Rogers, "Build Stronger Relationships," *Sales & Marketing Management*, July 2000, p. 50.

23. Danielle Hall, "Get Closer to More Customers," *Sales & Marketing Management*, May 2000, p. 26; and Christine Galea, "Planning a Web Relaunch," *Sales & Marketing Management*, May 2000, p. 118.

24. Tim Clark, "A Sales Force Weaves New Strategies," *Business Marketing*, May 1993, pp. 26, 32.

25. John F. Yarbrough, "Salvaging a Lousy Year," *Sales & Marketing Management*, July 1996, p. 72.

26. Gabrielle Birkner, "Eastman Draws Customers On-line," *Sales & Marketing Management*, June 2000, pp. 41–42.

27. Aimee L. Stern, "Telemarketing Polishes Its Image," *Sales & Marketing Management*, June 1991, pp. 107–10.

28. Rob Norton, "Strategies for the Export Boom," *Fortune*, August 22, 1994, pp. 124–31.

29. Lawrence Richter Quinn, "Global Warning," *Sales & Marketing Management*, April 1997, pp. 54–58.

30. Slade Sohmer, "Emerging as a Global Sales Success," *Sales & Marketing Management*, May 2000, pp. 124–25.

CASE 4-1   TRICON INDUSTRIES*

Organizing the Sales Force

Laura Thompson, the vice president and general manager for the Heavy Duty Products Division of Tricon Industries, was shaken. She had been heading up a task force of Tricon's divisional vice presidents. The committee's charge was to make recommendations with regard to possible changes in the organizational structure of Tricon's three divisions.

Jon Belth, the vice president of the Braking Systems Division, had just left Thompson's office. He had accused Thompson of taking a position on the possible reorganization that was not in the company's best interests but rather served the purpose of consolidating her own power and authority. Thompson felt that this was an unfair accusation, but she also felt that she understood why Belth would make such an accusation. Belth felt threatened. If there was some type of consolidation of the marketing and sales efforts of the three divisions, his position might not exist under the new structure. And if the number of managerial positions was reduced overall, he might be out of a job. Thompson knew that her position was at risk as well, but that she was less likely to be let go than Belth.

Although Thompson recognized that there were a number of problems associated with any reorganization that the committee might recommend, she was committed to move forward with the discussions and subsequent recommendations. If there were disagreements, these would be acknowledged in the report to Peter Gray, the chief executive officer of Tricon, who had created the task force.

Tricon Industries is a diversified company whose products serve the construction and transportation industries as well as numerous other general industrial markets. The Heavy Duty Products Division (HDPD) produces brake linings for on-road trucks, and its primary customers are original equipment manufacturer (OEM) axle manufacturers such as Spicer and Mercedes and trailer manufacturers such as Fruehauf and Monon. HDPD's strategy is to seek approval for its products at the OEM level in order to push them through the channel to the large national trucking fleets such as Consolidated Freightways and Roadway. It also targets the aftermarket sales by convincing the fleets to specify HDP products as replacements when the original brake linings wear out. This division, which has sales of $81.8 million, is the largest and oldest of the three divisions.

In 2002, Tricon purchased the off-highway braking division of an international construction equipment manufacturer and created the Braking Systems Division (BSD). This division designs and manufactures braking system products for construction and mining original equipment manufacturers (OEMs) throughout the world and is a leading supplier of genuine replacement parts to the aftermarket. OEM customers include worldwide companies such as Caterpillar, Komatsu Dresser, and John Deere. BSD is currently establishing a worldwide network of distributors that will provide sales, installation, and service support to the OEM and aftermarket customers. With sales of $50 million, BSD is the most international of the divisions.

The Specialty Products Division (SPD), the smallest of Tricon's divisions, has sales of $20 million. It was acquired in 2001 because of its high growth potential. In addition to braking products, the division's product lines include driving applications, such as clutches, as well as extruded products. The business segments served by the division include industrial drives and motor brakes, light aircraft, lawn and garden, and recreational vehicles. These applications are primarily low-volume specialty applications.

Each division has its own dedicated sales representatives, who are assigned to geographic territories. In the HDPD and the BSD, the sales engineers are assigned to either the OEM or the aftermarket customers. (See Exhibit 4–A for Tricon's organizational chart.) In the OEM market, the sales reps sell directly to the manufacturers; in the aftermarket, the reps call on independent distributors. There are currently 24 sales reps serving the three divisions. Each salesperson is responsible for serving his or her existing customers as well as for finding new customers.

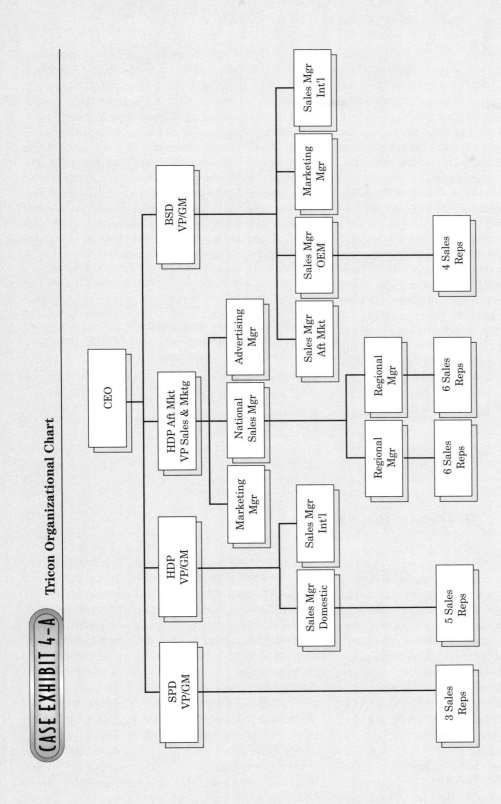

CASE EXHIBIT 4–A Tricon Organizational Chart

CEO

SPD VP/GM

HDP VP/GM

HDP Aft Mkt VP Sales & Mktg

BSD VP/GM

Marketing Mgr

National Sales Mgr

Advertising Mgr

Sales Mgr Aft Mkt

Sales Mgr OEM

Marketing Mgr

Sales Mgr Int'l

Sales Mgr Domestic

Sales Mgr Int'l

Regional Mgr

Regional Mgr

4 Sales Reps

3 Sales Reps

5 Sales Reps

6 Sales Reps

6 Sales Reps

113

Laura Thompson realized that the BSD and the SPD had been purchased because their product lines, technologies, and markets were seen as complementary to the HDPD's existing competencies. However, these acquisitions took place without a formal plan for integration. For the most part, each division continues to operate fairly independently; as a result, Tricon is not taking advantage of the potential synergies which exist between the companies. Thompson felt that consolidation of the sales forces offered the greatest opportunity for achieving some of the synergies.

However, the prevailing philosophy has been that there are sufficient differences between the various product lines and customers to justify separate organizations. Jon Belth had argued, "Our current structure allows our sales engineers to provide specialized attention to our customers." Thompson acknowledged that Belth was correct, but she argued that the negatives of the current structure outweighed the benefits. As she stated in the recent meeting, "Many of our customers are called on by more than one sales engineer from Tricon. This duplication of effort is not only very expensive, but it may be hindering our customer relationships. Some of our customers are confused about which division to call with questions or problems, and some of them just don't want to deal with more than one rep from the same company."

Thompson knew that she must sell the benefits of consolidation over the objections of Belth and possibly others. Although she felt that she could present a convincing case for consolidation, she knew that designing an acceptable structure for the new sales organization would be a challenge. There were clearly a number of options, and she wasn't certain which would best meet the needs of Tricon and its customers.

Questions:

1. Should Tricon consolidate its sales forces?

2. If Tricon were to reorganize its sales forces, what are the options and which structure would you recommend?

*Adapted from a case prepared by John Hiel and Julie Singh under the direction of Rosann L. Spiro.

CASE 4-2   MICROPLASTICS, INC.

Need for Reorganization

"Perhaps a bit of history regarding our sales organization will help you in your coming weeks as our new sales manager," said Don Lopez, president of Microplastics, Inc., to Katie Curry, the firm's new sales manager. The company had been organized in 1988 to manufacture to specification small plastic parts that were sold directly to other manufacturers, particularly high-technology industries.

Lopez continued, "It seems as if our sales force has been in a constant state of upheaval for the past five years. A year hasn't gone by but that we reorganized it some way or another. But nothing seems to work. Let me go back to 1988 and trace our troubles for you. Our growth had been great in the early days of our industry. We had little direct competition and we were making plenty of money, sold everything we could make. Then competition came into the market and we hit a recession. Sales dropped 40 percent and profits turned to losses. At first we thought that it was happening to everyone, but soon we discovered that our competitors were not being hit as hard as we were. Their salespeople seemed to be able to sell into accounts where our people couldn't.

"We became most unhappy with our sales organization, which at the time consisted of 28 people who reported to one sales manager. We fired the sales manager and brought in a man from one of our most successful competitors. It cost some money to get him, but we were willing to pay it. Well, right off the bat this bozo wants to hire three assistant sales managers to supervise the sales force, a sales training director to train them, a sales analyst for the home office, and a home-office sales engineer to back up the field sales force technically."

"That's a lot of money," Katie Curry commented when Lopez paused. "How did he justify it to you?"

"I remember it well because it scared me to death," Lopez said. "He said that if we wanted to be a big-time company we would have to do things the way the big boys do them. He insisted that the key to success was to back up the field people with tremendous support from the home office and supervise them closely in the field."

"Well, how did it work out?"

"Need you ask? Sales stayed about the same but our costs skyrocketed. We lost our shirts. I never saw such confusion. No one seemed to know what they were supposed to do. So we fired the sales manager and promoted one of the sales reps to the job. He immediately cleaned out all of the staff the other fellow had hired, so we were back to square one. But not quite."

"Oh, did the new manager make some changes?" Curry asked.

"He felt that our real problem was that the reps couldn't sell to all types of customers, so he divided them into two groups. The first bunch of 10 reps was to sell to the large manufacturers, where there was a lot of engineering work to be done with the customer's people. The second group was to cover the smaller assemblers, where engineering was not so important and where you dealt with the owner directly," Lopez explained.

"What happened?"

"Mass confusion! The reps didn't want to give up their customers, so they held on to them as long as they could. And it didn't seem to help sales. We didn't sell any more large accounts than we were previously selling. The guy got tired of managing and asked to go back into the field where he felt he knew what to do.

"You can bet that the next sales manager was selected with a lot more care," Lopez continued. "We interviewed more than 20 people until we found this fellow who had a terrific record over at National Plastics. We thought we had a barn burner in him. He came in, surveyed the situation, and wrote a report for me on what had to be done."

"You're shaking your head. What went wrong?" Curry inquired.

"He personally spent a day with each sales representative to diagnose what was wrong with the operation," said Lopez. "On the basis of his judgment, 19 of our reps were incompetent, with no hope of ever becoming the type of salesperson he thought was needed to do the job. He planned to fire them immediately. Then he would call in the remaining nine reps for an intensive training program to teach them how to sell the way he wanted them to. I remember vividly how he leaned over my desk with his fists clenched and sternly said, 'My sales force will sell the way I want them to sell or they won't be around.' Well, we had some words over that report. I just could not let him fire 19 people who had been with us from the beginning and who had helped us build the company. I wanted him to train all of them, but he said it couldn't be done. They just weren't his 'type of people.' That kind of talk really gets my goat. He was putting these people down like they were dirt, and I told him so. Well, one thing led to another, and there went the new sales manager."

"And you had no inkling of this aspect of his personality before hiring him?" Curry asked.

Lopez drew a deep breath and confessed, "I must say that we did. His previous boss described him as one tough, driving guy who was hard to live with but who really got results. I guess all we wanted to hear was that he got results. We didn't stop to think about how he got them."

"And so here we are," Curry summarized. "You want to know what I have discovered and what I intend to do about it."

"That's it!" said Lopez. "Have you anything to report yet?"

"It's a bit premature now to lay out a program for you," she replied, "but the seeds of it are in everything that has happened previously. I'll be ready next Friday for a report on my proposed program."

"Fair enough," said Lopez.

Curry had already made up her mind about what needed to be done, but she did not want to reveal it until she had figured out how to go about it. She had quickly related to everything that had been told her. The sales manager who had wanted to reorganize for some staff support was right. The span of control was ridiculous, and the reps were getting little support from the home office. The second manager had been right in seeing that the reps were not equally effective in selling to all types of customers. The third manager was certainly correct in his appraisal of the reps. The sales force had some people with mediocre talents. For the most part, they constituted a seedy crew that had looked good in the early days of the industry before competition became a factor in the market. But she realized that there would be little she could do about this problem immediately. It would have to be worked on over a lengthy period. For the time being, she had to develop a means for working with these people, and that seemed to call for some sort of reorganization.

Question:

1. What changes should the new sales manager recommend?

CASE 4-3   EXCEL TOOLS, INC.

Sales Organization for New Products and Markets

Excel Tools planned to introduce several new products during the mid-2000s, some for the consumer market and others for industrial users. Both the sales volume and the number of sales calls on industrial users had been declining. Consequently, the field sales manager, Roger Starr, was wondering whether the present organizational structure of the sales force was appropriate for meeting the increasingly difficult competition being encountered from both domestic and international competitors and for exploiting the expanded market opportunities provided by the new product lines.

Excel Tools was a large manufacturer of a wide assortment of products, most of which were sold to the industrial market. Except for power tools, the company had little experience with consumer products. Excel had diversified both by acquiring existing companies and by expanding its own product lines. Sales in 2001 were $950 million. In addition to power tools, the company made and marketed such products as meters and valves for the gas, oil, and water industries; taxi meters; parking meters; iron and steel castings; and sewer cleaning equipment. With its home offices in Cincinnati, Ohio, the company operated manufacturing facilities in 11 states and five foreign countries. Excel marketed electrical and pneumatic power tools, both portable and stationary models. These products were sold to both consumer and industrial markets. Separate Excel-owned brands were used to differentiate the portable tools from the stationary models. In addition, the firm manufactured power tools under retailers' brands, such as Sears's Craftsman label. Sales in the power tool division totaled $190 million in 2001.

Competitive gaps existed in the product assortment offered to each of these markets, but the new product lines were intended to fill these gaps. In the consumer market, a new low-priced line was intended to complement the product group that previously consisted only of upscale, higher-priced units. A new line of portable tools was intended to round out the product assortment designed primarily for industrial users. While sales declined in 1999 and 2000, management's long-range planning projected that the sales volume of power tools would double by the year 2007. Major competition was expected to continue from such companies as Black & Decker, Stanley, Rockwell Manufacturing Company, and the producers of Skil power tools.

As vice president of sales for the power tool division, Starr was responsible for achieving the sales goals set for all power tools, including those sold through distributors (wholesalers) in the United States and abroad and those sold directly to private-brand customers and to large chain-store organizations and discount retailers. Reporting to Starr were 10 regional sales managers in the United States, covering approximately 100 territories. International sales, which had been rising, were under the direction of Pierre Dubnow in the Paris office. The domestic salespeople under each regional manager were divided into two groups on the basis of product line—portable or stationary tools. Both groups of salespeople called on many different types of wholesalers. These included automotive wholesalers, hardware wholesalers, builders' supply houses, machine tool distributors, and any other types of industrial distributors or consumer goods wholesalers whose customers might constitute a reasonably sized market for Excel power tools. Reps in either sales force also might call on retail dealers in a promotional or missionary capacity. The salespeople might perform such assignments as demonstrating the proper tool for a given job, setting up in-store promotions, arranging for the dealers to participate in Excel's cooperative television and newspaper advertising programs, or training dealer salespeople to sell Excel tools more effectively.

Several factors prompted Starr to review the division's organizational structure. With its ambitious new programs to extend its lines, the company was, in effect, expanding both its consumer and industrial markets. The broader product assortment, however, made each member of the sales forces less specialized than before.

This was occurring at the same time that Excel's competitors were moving toward more specialized sales organizations. Excel's biggest competitor—the largest company in the industry—had divided its sales force into four specialized groups. Smaller competitors marketed a more limited line of power tools, so their sales force efforts automatically were more specialized than Excel's.

Moreover, the greatly increased importance of large national accounts, such as Wal-Mart, Sears, and Home Depot, had placed great pressure on the firms selling to them to assign sales reps to service each firm. Excel had not yet altered its structure to accommodate national account selling. Something would have to be done about this organizational need.

The recent decline in sales volume was another factor prompting Starr to review the division's organizational structure, although he recognized that the structure might have had no relation to the decline in sales. Starr also was aware of a common disadvantage to a product-type sales organization—namely, two sales reps, each with a separate product line, may be calling on the same account. In Excel's case there had been instances of conflicts and lack of coordination between the portable tool reps and those who sold the stationary tools in setting up cooperative advertising and other promotional programs.

To get more specialized selling efforts, Starr was considering an organizational structure in which each of the existing sales forces would be divided into two groups, according to class of customer. Thus, the company would have four sales forces, the same as its biggest competitor. Existing and potential accounts would be analyzed to determine whether they served industrial or consumer markets. Then they would be divided accordingly and separate sales forces would be assigned to each customer group. Each industrial account, for example, would be called on by an industrial portable tool sales rep and an industrial stationary tool rep. Starr realized that this four-way division of the sales force would mean adding new people. Such a structure might also entail a different supervisory arrangement at the regional-manager level.

The increased specialization of effort would be a definite plus factor. Interviews with some of the salespeople indicated that most of the reps preferred to work in one market or the other. That is, they preferred to do industrial selling or to do the sales and promotional work involved with the distributors and merchants in the consumer market. Rarely was anyone encountered who liked to sell in both markets equally.

An alternative being considered was to keep the double sales force structure but divide the reps on a customer basis rather than by products. For example, one sales group would sell both portable and stationary power tools, but only to industrial accounts. In this arrangement, Excel would hope to develop account specialists and, at the same time, have only one rep call on a given account. Organizing the sales force by customer group meant that each rep would cease to be a product specialist. A rep now selling only portable tools would have to learn about selling stationary tools. However, often specialization by customer resulted in product specialization because the account bought either only portable or only stationary tools. Starr also was considering other organizational arrangements. One suggestion he was considering was to continue with the existing structure but supplement it with better programs for motivating and supervising the salespeople.

The sales manager in the Chicago regional office, Charles Webster, had a different proposal—that the company abandon its specialized sales forces and, instead, give each rep a smaller geographical territory to sell both portable and stationary tools to all classes of customers in the territory. Webster argued that neither the customer groups nor the product lines were different enough to warrant the costs and problems that resulted from specialization.

Regardless of the organizational structure finally selected—but assuming Excel continued with more than one sales force whether it was specialized by customer, product, or some other basis—there would still be an organizational question involving the regional managers. Starr was wondering whether to continue with one regional manager over all groups of salespeople in a given region or to establish separate managers for each group of reps in a region. If the sales force were further specialized, this would put increased responsibility on the regional managers under the present system. Furthermore, Excel's major competitor was using specialized managers along with its more specialized sales force. The fundamental problem was this: At what level should the organization be divided on whatever basis selected? At the level of the field salespeople only? At the regional manager level? Or conceivably at the field sales manager level, with a separate field sales manager for each major group of sales reps? Starr also was considering the possibility of using product managers or customer-group managers in a staff capacity to plan merchandising and promotional programs, and to otherwise support the field-selling effort.

Questions:

1. What type of sales force organization should Excel Tools, Inc., adopt?
2. Based on your decision, what regional manager structure should the company adopt?

5 Profiling and Recruiting Salespeople

Eagles don't flock. You have to find them one at a time.

—Ross Perot—

Billions of dollars have been spent on research to improve the recruiting and selection of salespeople. Though the process has been improved, selecting those who turn out to be successful remains one of the greatest challenges in sales management today. It is also one of the most costly—it can involve placing ads and using an employment agency; taking time to screen, interview, and assess candidates; and training those who are hired. The costs for these activities are all wasted if the newly hired reps don't perform or don't like the job and leave the company. Additionally, there are the opportunity costs of lost sales. A poorly motivated, ineffective rep can damage a company's reputation and ruin established relationships with customers. These relationships may take years to reestablish, and the costs in terms of lost revenues may be devastating.

Nevertheless, too many managers make hiring decisions based solely on what "feels right" rather than on objectively determined criteria. Additionally, many managers start recruiting only when someone is leaving rather than establishing an ongoing recruiting program. As a result, they often end up settling for someone just to fill the open position.

We believe that staffing—the selection of personnel at any level in an organization—is the most important activity in the management process. We cannot overemphasize how crucial it is for administrators to choose the right people. Obviously, recruiting and selecting salespeople is not a sales

The Growth of Population Diversity

According to the U.S. Census Bureau, significant changes in the composition of the population have occurred over the past 10 years. These changes will impact the sales force of the future. Salespeople will be drawn from an older and more culturally diverse group of candidates. The number of workers of Hispanic origin will grow by 36 percent; those of black, non-Hispanic origin will grow by 17 percent; and those of Asian and other ethnic origins will grow by 37 percent. Meanwhile, the number of white, non-Hispanic workers will grow by only 6 percent. Companies will be challenged to adapt their recruiting and selection procedures to attract individuals of a variety of ethnic backgrounds.

Source: "Charting the Projections: 2000–10," *Occupational Outlook Quarterly*, Winter 2001–2, pp. 2–3.

manager's *only* job, but it is the *most important* one. The hiring process warrants much more thought and preparation than managers usually give it. Ideally, managers should always be recruiting.

Sales Force Selection and Strategic Planning

In most organizations, the sales force is the one group that directly generates the revenues for the organization. Thus, the sales force is the group most directly involved in carrying out the company's strategic marketing plans. How well these plans are implemented depends to a great extent on the choice of salespeople. Certainly the selection process should be consistent with the company's strategic marketing planning and its sales force planning.

Let's look at some practical applications of the relationship between sales force selection and strategic marketing planning. Assume that a company's goal is to maintain its leading market position and its market share. One major marketing strategy may be to provide considerable service to existing accounts. The sales rep's job consists primarily of existing-account maintenance rather than new-account development. This affects selection because the two tasks—maintenance and development—usually call for different types of salespeople.

As another example, the company may adopt a strategy of promoting from within as part of its strategic planning for the development of future executives. Hiring older, experienced sales reps at high salaries probably would not be a sound way to implement such a strategy.

The selection process should also be strategically integrated with all aspects of sales force management. If a company has no sales training program, it should not recruit inexperienced students just graduating from college. If management prefers to hire people right from college, the firm had better institute a training program.

Importance of a Good Selection Program

Good **selection** is vital to the firm because, as noted earlier, it is the sales force that directly generates revenues for the firm. In this section, we further explore the reasons why a good sales selection program is essential.

A DAY-TO-DAY OPERATING PROBLEM

MAJESTIC PLASTICS COMPANY

MAJESTIC
Plastics Company

Adding Minority Reps to the Sales Force

There were seldom any vacancies on the Majestic Plastics Company sales force, and Clyde Brion, general sales manager, was proud of that fact. He had several applications from available recruits on an informal waiting list, and he tried to keep the facts on these applicants up to date. Occasionally unsolicited applications were received, and some were from unusual types of applicants. For example, Brion had once been urged to hire an ex-convict. Currently, Majestic's sales force was composed of 14 men and 4 women, all of whom were white (Caucasian). On more than one occasion, Brion had been asked why the company had no minority sales reps. When such questions were asked by Majestic executives, by customers, or by public officials, Brion believed he could not ignore them.

One afternoon Brion was asked to come to the office of the company president, Boyd Russell. He found himself in a conference with Russell, several other department heads, and two men who were introduced as representatives of the Affirmative Action Program in the U.S. Department of Health and Human Services (HHS).

The visitors explained that the Majestic Plastics Company had been loyally served for many years by minority workers in the factory, on the custodial staff, and in a few cases in clerical jobs. However, no mi-

nority people held supervisory, sales, or managerial jobs. The HHS representatives directly requested that the company place some minorities in each of these categories or suffer censure through national publicity. When asked if qualified minority reps could be found, the visitors displayed well-prepared dossiers on several people. As nearly as Brion could judge during a quick examination of these files, the people easily met the minimum standards he had maintained in sales force recruiting.

The meeting continued after the visitors left. Brion said that a minority salesperson might find "rough sledding" on the sales force, and some customers might be resentful toward the rep. Brion also pointed out that there were no openings on the sales force now or in the near future. To accommodate a new rep, Brion said he would be forced either to discharge a salesperson now at work or create a new and unnecessary territory.

In closing the meeting, Russell said, "We'll have to look at this thing positively. Life could get mighty unpleasant for us if we don't!"

Question: What action should Clyde Brion take in this situation?

Note: See the introduction to this series of problems in Chapter 4 for the necessary background on the company, its market, and its competition.

- **Qualified salespeople are scarce.** For many reasons, good salespeople are hard to find. Selling does not have the high social prestige of some other careers and therefore may not attract the most top-notch candidates from colleges and universities. Indeed, a survey of students in a large introductory marketing class found that most students viewed selling in a negative way, associating it with door-to-door activities or with less-than-desirable personal traits, such as being pushy or obnoxious.[1] Furthermore, many young people are not aware of the opportunities provided by jobs in outside selling. They often equate selling with clerking in a retail store.

- **Good selection improves sales force performance.** The salesperson-recruiting process has a strong impact on profits. When a firm hires a salesperson whose performance is just acceptable rather than outstanding, it is forgoing additional sales revenues and profits that the outstanding rep would have generated. Also, a good selection program is likely to reduce sales force turnover and thus lead to improved sales performance.

- **Good selection promotes cost savings.** A good selection program brings about both direct and indirect cost benefits. Substantial *direct* cost savings are often generated when sales force turnover is reduced. A beginning salesperson may cost a company well over $100,000 before reaching productive status. This figure includes recruiting and selection costs, training and supervision costs, and salary and travel expenses. Well-chosen reps will provide a good return on the investment the company has made in them. The *indirect* cost benefits of good selection don't show up in accounting records, but they include the prevention of lost sales that can result from poor selection.

- **Good selection eases other managerial tasks.** Proper training, compensation, supervision, and motivation are vital to successful management of a sales force. However, if a company selects the right people for the sales job, training is easier, less supervision is required, and motivation is less difficult.

- **Sales managers are no better than their sales force.** No matter how good a manager he or she is, an executive with a poor sales force cannot surpass a competitor who has much better salespeople.

The Law and Sales Force Selection

Increasingly, firms are held responsible for the legality of their recruiting and selection policies. Although certain aspects of the selection process may be performed by the human resources department, the sales manager most often makes the final hiring decisions. Sales managers must therefore understand the complex laws that govern sales force selection policies. Figure 5–1 summarizes the particular laws and other regulations directly related to sales force selection. Federal legislation and related regulatory guidelines emphasize two concepts in employment: nondiscrimination and affirmative action. **Nondiscrimination** requires employers to refrain from discriminating against anyone with regard to age, race, religion, sex, national origin, disability, or status as a veteran—and to eliminate all existing discriminatory conditions, whether intentional or inadvertent. **Affirmative action** requires employers to do more than ensure neutrality—they must *make additional efforts* to recruit, employ, and promote qualified members of groups formerly excluded. These efforts must be made even if that exclusion cannot be traced to discriminatory actions of the employer.

If a qualified applicant suspects that a job rejection is discriminatory, he or she may file a lawsuit against the employer. If the company has as employees a disproportionately low number of people from the group represented by the applicant, that may be enough to establish discrimination.

Discrimination charges can also be filed against a firm that uses recruitment sources with few people from the protected classes. For example, if a firm that employs predominantly white males hires salespeople only from within the firm, then this recruiting practice may be discriminatory even if there wasn't any intent to discriminate. The easiest way the firm can protect itself from these charges is to recruit from multiple sources, some of which clearly include the protected classes. Similarly, in advertising the position, the firm must be very careful not to use any language that could be construed as discriminatory.

The guidelines set by the Equal Employment Opportunity Commission (EEOC) and the Office of Federal Contract Compliance (OFCC) cover the full scope of sales force selection activities—setting hiring specifications and recruiting and processing applicants. They also set prescribed limits regarding the

FIGURE 5-1

Key laws and regulations affecting a sales force

Civil Rights Act of 1964

Prohibits discrimination based on race, color, religion, nationality, or sex.

Federal Contract Compliance, Executive Orders

Ensures that federal contractors and subcontractors with 50 or more employees will comply with federal legislation and submit affirmative action plans.

Age Discrimination in Employment Act (1967)

Prohibits discrimination based on age.

Fair Employment Opportunity Act (1972)

Established the Equal Employment Opportunity Commission (EEOC) to ensure compliance with the Civil Rights Act for firms with 25 workers or more.

Rehabilitation Act of 1973

Requires affirmative action to hire and promote handicapped persons if the firm employs 50 or more workers and is seeking federal contracts in excess of $50,000.

Vietnam Era Veterans Readjustment Act (1974)

Requires affirmative action to hire Vietnam veterans and disabled veterans of any war by firms holding contracts in excess of $10,000.

Uniform Guidelines on Employment Selection Procedures (1978)

The EEOC, the U.S. Civil Service, and the Departments of Justice and Labor jointly issued these guidelines to prevent discriminatory practices in hiring.

Americans with Disabilities Act (1990)

Prohibits discrimination based on handicaps or disabilities (either physical or mental).

use of various tools in the selection procedure, such as application blanks, interviews, and tests. These will be highlighted in Chapter 6.

Probably the greatest problem these agencies pose for sales executives is that the burden of proof to show that a company is complying with the regulations generally rests with the company. That is, the firm must be able to demonstrate (if called on to do so) that its recruiting and selection processes are *not* discriminatory and that all of its selection requirements, sources, and tools are predictive of performance in a given sales job.

Scope of Sales Force Staffing Process

There are five major activities involved in staffing a sales force:

1. *Plan* the recruiting and selection process.
2. *Recruit* an adequate number of applicants.
3. *Select* the most qualified applicants.
4. *Hire* those people who have been selected.
5. *Assimilate* the new hires into the company.

The flowchart in Figure 5–2 illustrates these major activities. You will notice that planning and selecting are broken down into several related steps.

FIGURE 5-2   Sales force staffing process

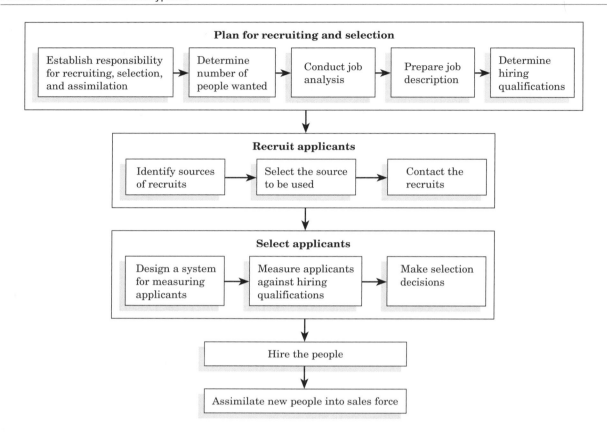

The Planning Phase

As can be seen in Figure 5–2, the first step of the planning phase is to establish responsibility for recruiting and selection. These responsibilities may be assigned to the top sales executive, the field sales manager, the human resources department, or some combination of these positions. Second, the company must determine the number and type of people needed. This involves analyzing the market and the job, and preparing a written job description. Planners must also establish the qualifications necessary to fill the job.

The Recruiting Phase

The recruiting phase includes identifying sources of recruits that are consistent with the type of person desired, selecting the source to be used, and contacting the recruits. Selecting the source entails an evaluation of its potential effectiveness versus its cost.

Job fairs give candidates an opportunity to meet recruiters from many different companies.

The Selection Phase

The selection phase has three steps. First, it is necessary to design a system for measuring the recruits against the standards that were established in the planning phase. Second, the system must be put into effect with those who have become applicants. Making the actual selections is the third step. Selection is covered more thoroughly in Chapter 6.

The Hiring and Assimilation Phases

After the company has made an offer to a recruit, the job is not done. Sometimes the recruits have other job offers and you must convince them that your company offers them the best opportunity. The staffing process is complete when the new salespeople are successfully assimilated into your organization. Hiring and assimilation are also covered more thoroughly in Chapter 6.

Establishing Responsibility for Recruiting, Selection, and Assimilation

Management must decide who will be responsible for making the recruiting and selection decisions and who will be responsible for assimilating the new hires into the organization. How these decisions are made is often related to the size of the firm and to the nature of the selling task. In a small firm, for example, it is usually the top-level sales executive or even the president who makes these decisions. Since the sales force is small, these decisions do not place too much of a burden on any one executive.

In a large firm, however, the large number of territories and the normal turnover in those territories means that the job of recruiting and selecting new salespeople will be a continuous one. It would be very difficult for any one executive to make all of these decisions; therefore, the decisions are usually shifted to lower-level sales managers. Additionally, in large firms the human resources department usually assists managers with their recruiting and selection responsibilities. The human resources department may do all of the recruiting and initial screening of the recruits, but it is usually the sales manager who makes the final hiring decisions.

Determining the Number of People Needed

A company should try to accurately determine how many sales reps it needs and then hire that number. It should not employ more than are needed with the intent of weeding out some as time goes by. Such an action would indicate that the firm has no faith in its selection system and is using performance on the job as an additional selection tool.

Sales personnel needs should be forecast well in advance of the time the people will actually be employed. This policy forces the various sales units to plan systematically. It also allows better programming of recruiting, interviewing, and other steps in the selection procedure.

Additionally, management should first review any changes in the company's strategic marketing plan to determine how the plan will affect the number of salespeople needed. Planned increases and decreases in marketing expenditures lead to changes in the level of forecasted sales. This in turn will probably affect the number of salespeople needed. For example, is the company planning to continue with its present channels-of-distribution structure? A firm now using manufacturer's reps in a certain region may be planning to replace these reps with a company sales force. Is the company planning to cut sales force costs by using the Internet and reducing the size of the outside sales force?

For the specific estimates of the number of new salespeople that must be hired, management should consider the following factors, which are depicted in Figure 5–3:

- Reps needed for changes in the deployment of salespeople: new territories, eliminated territories, realigned territories.
- Promotions out of the sales force.
- Expected retirements from the sales force.
- Expected turnover, including terminations and resignations.

The manager adds the total number for each of these categories to estimate the number of new reps that will have to be hired (see the example in Figure 5–3). The question of how many reps are needed to cover a particular area is discussed in Chapter 13, on sales territories.

FIGURE 5-3   Determining the number of salespeople needed

New territories	−	Eliminate/ combine territories	+	Strategic Plans Promotions	+	Retirements	+	Termination/ resignations	=	Total new reps needed
Expansion into Texas. Reps needed:		MN and RI territories combined. Reps eliminated:		2 promotions expected:		2 retirements expected:		1 termination expected:		
4	−	1	+	2	+	2	+	1	=	8

Developing a Profile of the Type of People Needed

A sales manager needs detailed specifications when selecting salespeople. Otherwise, he or she cannot know what to look for. Certainly, a company should be as careful in buying the services of men and women as it is in buying the products these people use or sell.

There are three tasks associated with developing a profile of the type of people wanted:

- **Job analysis**—the actual task of determining what constitutes a given job.
- **Job description**—the document that sets forth the findings of the job analysis.
- **Job qualifications** (sometimes called *hiring specifications*)—the specific, personal qualifications and characteristics applicants should possess to be selected for the given job.

These tasks are detailed next.

Job Analysis

There are many different types of sales jobs and specific skills associated with each of those jobs that will make someone a success or failure.[2] Therefore, before it develops the selection process, the company should conduct a thorough job analysis. The analysis should clearly identify the specific tasks that salespeople will perform. Additionally, it should provide information on which activities are critical for job success.

Any member of the sales organization or the human resources department may conduct the analysis—or the company can hire an outside specialist. An effective analysis of a sales job usually requires extensive observation and interviewing. The person conducting this analysis should spend time traveling with several salespeople as they make their calls.

The analyst also should interview many of the people who in some way interact with the reps in the sales job. The analyst should start interviewing with the reps themselves and then include sales force managers, customers, and other executives who are directly involved with the personal selling activities of the company. Also, salespeople can complete time and duty sheets on which they record their activities and the specific times they performed the activities for a specified period.

Job Description

Once the job is analyzed, the resultant description should be put in writing. The job analysis and subsequent written description must be done in great detail. It is not enough to say that the salesperson is supposed to sell the product, call on the customers, or build goodwill toward the company.

Scope of Job Description

Most well-prepared job descriptions have similar items of information. The following points are usually covered:

- *Title of job*—a complete description so there is no vagueness, especially in a company that has several different types of sales jobs.
- *Organizational relationship*—to whom do the salespeople report?
- *Types of products and services sold.*
- *Types of customers called on*—purchasing agents, engineers, plant managers, and so on.
- *Duties and responsibilities related to the job*—planning activities, actual selling activities, customer servicing tasks, clerical duties, and self-management responsibilities.
- *Job demands*—the mental and physical demands of the job, such as the amount of travel, autonomy, and stress.
- *Hiring specifications*—the qualifications an applicant needs to be hired for the job. While job qualifications technically are not part of a job analysis, there is merit in presenting the job duties and the job qualifications in one document.

Exhibits 5-A and 5-B (on pages 144–148) are examples of sales job descriptions for two sales positions. Exhibit 5-A is the job description for a Xerox Corporation marketing representative. Exhibit 5-B is called a "Charter of Accountability" and the position is a passenger sales representative for an international airline.

Uses of Job Description

Conducting the job analysis and writing the job description become the first two steps in the selection process. As such, they provide strategic guidance for the steps that follow. Recruiters cannot talk intelligently to prospective applicants if they do not know in detail what the job involves. A firm cannot develop application forms, psychological tests, and other selection tools if it has not first analyzed the job. If hiring criteria and selection tools are developed through job analysis, misplacement and turnover can be reduced.

However, hiring is only part of it. *A job description is probably the most important single tool used in the operation of a sales force.* A job analysis should be the foundation of a sales training program. By studying the description, the executive in charge of sales training knows in detail what the salespeople's duties are and what they must learn. Job descriptions are also used in developing compensation plans. If management does not have a clear idea of what the sales force is supposed to do, it is difficult to design a sound compensation structure. Also, a salesperson's periodic performance ratings will be more meaningful if the company designs an evaluation form that includes many of the detailed aspects of the sales job. Finally, a good job description enables management to determine whether each salesperson has a reasonable workload.

Qualifications Needed to Fill the Job

Most Difficult Part of Selection Function

The next step in a selection program—determining the qualifications needed to fill the job—is probably the most difficult part of the entire selection process.

FIGURE 5-4

Ten traits and abilities of
top salespeople

Trait	Related Ability
Ego strength	To handle rejection
Sense of urgency	To complete the sale
Ego drive	To persuade people
Assertiveness	To be firm in negotiations
Willingness to take risks	To be innovative
Sociability	To build relationships
Abstract reasoning	To sell ideas
Sense of skepticism	To question, to be alert

Source: Erika Rasmusson, "The 10 Traits of Top Salespeople," *Sales & Marketing Management*, August 1999, pp. 34–37.

This is because there is no generally accepted profile for success across selling positions. Each company should establish its own individualized set of hiring requirements for each type of sales job in that firm. Cigna Group Insurance is one company that places great importance on this aspect of recruiting and selection. As noted by Cigna's senior vice president of sales, Al Bowles, "We spend lots of time creating a profile of competencies that we can measure against."[3]

It should be noted that a sales rep who fails in *one* company or territory might not necessarily fail in *all* companies or territories. Many people have become successful with one firm after failing in an earlier environment. Even within a given firm, salespeople sometimes perform poorly in one territory (because of social, ethnic or other environmental factors) but are successful after transferring to another region.

Are There Generally Desirable Characteristics for Salespeople?

Though every selling situation is different, most managers, customers, and salespeople agree that there are some generally desirable characteristics for salespeople.[4] These characteristics are presented in Figure 5–4.

It is also generally acknowledged that the salesperson of the future must be able to work with electronic communications and technology.[4] Salespeople have access to electronic data banks with product, customer, and competitive information. They also have multimedia options for making presentations to their customers. Salespeople need to be comfortable with the technology in order to utilize the information options in a comprehensive manner.

Team selling, which now accounts for 20 to 30 percent of all sales, is expected to grow significantly. This shift is having an important impact on the type of salesperson companies desire. A study of 26 of the leading corporations, including General Electric and AT&T, found that the "ability to work on a team" was a job requirement.[5] The box on the next page titled "Recruiting for the Team" highlights some additional changes.

Even though there are some generally desirable traits, we emphasize again that it is important for each company to develop its own set of criteria for selecting salespeople. The following major categories of traits are those for which specifics should be developed:

- Mental capacities (planning and problem-solving ability).
- Physical characteristics (appearance, neatness).

Recruiting for the Team

In this reengineered business environment, many companies are choosing partners, not products. Customers are demanding more value-added services and more follow-up after the sale than one person can provide. Teaming is essential!

Character traits long associated with salespeople, such as independence, self-sufficiency, and a need to control, are considered a handicap in the new selling order. Companies now seek salespeople who are very *adaptable*, with a *willingness to share* and *the ability to put the group's goal above their own*—in other words, people who show selfless behavior.

- Experience (sales and other business experience).
- Education (number of years, degrees, majors).
- Personality traits (persuasiveness, adaptiveness).
- Skills (communication, interpersonal, technological, job-specific).
- Socioenvironmental factors (interests, activities, memberships in organizations).

When dealing with qualifications in any of the categories listed above, management must be careful to comply with laws regarding nondiscrimination in employment (see again Figure 5–1). Many qualifications that once were used to screen sales force applicants—such as age, marital status, and ethnic background—can no longer be used. Similarly, an arrest (or even a conviction) cannot be used to screen out an applicant. Exceptions exist if the company can show that a requirement related to an otherwise protected group is a bona fide occupational qualification (BFOQ). Chapter 6 discusses BFOQs in more detail.

Methods of Determining Qualifications

There is no single satisfactory method for every company to use in determining the qualifications needed in its sales force. Several different procedures are currently being used. Some are adaptable for companies that have large sales forces and have been in business for some time, and thus have recorded histories of background and performance. Other methods may be used by firms that are large or small, old or new. Some of these methods are discussed in this section.

Study of Job Description

Many hiring specifications can be deduced from a carefully prepared job description. Job description statements about the degree of sales supervision, for instance, indicate that the salesperson should have the resourcefulness to work alone. Statements about the nature of the product, viewed in light of the company's training program, indicate something about the desired technical background or experience qualifications.

Analysis of Personal Histories

A large company in business for several years can determine its job qualifications by analyzing the personal histories of its present and past salespeople. The company must be big enough and old enough for a sample of histories to make the

FIGURE 5-5   A personal-history analysis—the process with examples

The Three-Step Process:

1. List all present and past salespeople; include their (*a*) *selection records* (application blanks and interview results, for example) and (*b*) *performance records* (sales results, quotas, and job evaluations).
2. Divide all salespeople into two or three groups, depending on management's judgment of their sales ability. In our example, the reps are divided into two categories—good and poor. Possible classification criteria include sales volume, percentage of sales quota attained, gross margin, ratio of expenses to sales, and missionary selling activities.
3. List each trait that influences success in selling. Then decide if there is any significant difference in how much of the trait good salespeople possess in contrast to the poor ones. Differences between good and poor performers in such qualifications as age at time of hiring or previous sales experience are easily determined. However, it is much more difficult to measure differences in personality traits in the two groups. This step is time-consuming and must be done carefully.

Now for Our Example:

1. Two characteristics—age at time of hiring and amount of education—are used to illustrate a personal-history analysis.
2. A sample of 600 past and present salespeople was used, 360 of whom were considered good.
3. Age and education brackets were established; then each of the 600 was placed in the correct bracket for the rep's age at time of hiring and amount of education. The results are shown in the following two tables.

A. Age when Hired	Number of Reps				B. Previous Education	Number of Reps			
	Good Reps	Poor Reps	Total	Percent of Good Reps		Good Reps	Poor Reps	Total	Percent of Good Reps
Under 25	30	70	100	30%	Some high school	30	70	100	30%
25–35	180	20	200	90	High school graduate	250	25	275	91
36–45	100	50	150	66%	Some college	20	80	100	20
46–55	40	60	100	40	College graduate	55	45	100	55
Over 55	10	40	50	20	Postgraduate study	5	20	25	20
Total	360	240	600		Total	360	240	600	

4. From Table A, we find that those sales reps most likely to succeed in this company were between 25 and 35 years of age when hired. Ninety percent of these people were good sales reps. Those reps who were under 25 or over 55 when hired seem to perform the most poorly.
5. In Table B, we find that high school graduates seem to have the right amount of education for future sales success. A person who started high school or college but did not graduate seems to be a particularly poor risk.
6. From the findings on the tables, it is probable that some years of business experience are necessary in this company. If 18 is the average age of high school graduates and 25 to 35 is the best hiring-age range, then the years in between have to be accounted for.

findings reasonably reliable. The procedure is to analyze various characteristics of good and poor sales reps to determine whether there are certain traits present in the good reps and absent in the poor ones. The traits of the good sales reps are then used to develop a **job profile** of the kind of person the firm is seeking. Figure 5–5 briefly describes the procedure for making an analysis of personal histories, along with a simple illustration.

In Figure 5–5, two characteristics—age at time of hiring and amount of education—are used to illustrate how personal histories can be studied. Similar analyses may be made for any other trait believed to influence success in selling in a given company. The firm could study environmental and experience factors in much the same manner as age and education. Mental abilities may be quantified by means of intelligence tests. General appearance could be measured by giving a person a rating on neatness and appropriate dress, and test scores can be used to measure personality traits.

This personal-history information can be analyzed using the method demonstrated in Figure 5–5 or by using a more sophisticated statistical technique called *discriminant analysis.* This type of analysis identifies characteristics that vary significantly between the groups. Once these distinguishing characteristics have been identified for a particular sales force, they can be used to develop a profile of the successful salesperson.

Based on an analysis of its current sales consultants, Andersen Consulting (now known as Accenture) totally revised its selection criteria. The company discovered that students with part-time jobs and extracurricular activities were more likely to succeed than those with higher grade-point averages.[6]

Recruiting and Its Importance

After determining the number and type of salespeople wanted, the next major step in selecting a sales force is to recruit applicants for the position to be filled. **Recruiting** includes all activities involved in securing individuals who will apply for the job. The concept does not include the actual selection of people by means of interviews, tests, or other hiring tools. That step is the topic of Chapter 6. A sound selection program cannot exist without a well-planned and well-operated system for recruiting applicants. If recruiting is done haphazardly, a company runs the risk of overlooking good sources of prospective salespeople. Also, there is a risk of hiring unsuitable people simply because the firm must select immediately from the available applicants.

The importance of recruiting grows in relation to increases in the costs of selecting salespeople and maintaining them in the field. Certainly, the direct costs of recruiting—costs such as maintaining recruiting teams and placing recruiting advertisements—are increasing. But more important than the *direct* cost of recruiting is the effect that recruiting may have on the *total* costs of selection and training. It may be desirable to increase the cost of the recruiting activity if it results in finding better-quality applicants.

The costs of having an open sales territory are also great. *If a firm must do a significant amount of recruiting, it should be done continuously.* Even when no immediate need for new salespeople exists, the firm should develop a list of potential recruits. Then when an opening does occur, the time and costs of filling that territory will be relatively low. Sales managers should be proactive in their recruiting efforts. They should anticipate openings, look constantly for potential recruits, and keep a file on those who might be able to fill a future need. As J. Doug Clopton, a regional manager for Hershey's Chocolate, stated, "The best time to recruit is *before* you have an opening."[7]

Need for Many Recruits

A philosophy to follow in recruiting is to get enough qualified applicants to maximize the chances of finding the right person for a job. The shortage of qualified sales representatives makes it imperative for a business to screen several people for each opening. The following is a useful rule of thumb to determine the number of recruits needed to select one salesperson:

- A recruiting effort may reach 20 people who are interested in the job.
- A review of application blanks will eliminate 10.
- The initial interview will eliminate another 6 or 7.
- The 3 or 4 finalists are screened further by interviews, tests, and other selection tools.
- One person is finally hired.

Finding an adequate number of recruits may not be as easy as it sounds. Today's recruits want a lot more than just a high salary. In fact (we'll see in Figure 5–7), candidates for sales positions place a higher value on things other than salary. If companies want to succeed in recruiting salespeople in tight labor markets, then they must offer the advantages that recruits want.[8]

Finding and Maintaining Good Recruiting Sources

Most firms actively recruit sales reps from many sources. To determine the best sources, a recruiter should first find out where the company's best salespeople came from in the past. This assumes that there has been no substantial change in the job description or job qualifications. The evaluation of current sources will be discussed at the end of this chapter.

If the company is recruiting for the first time, or if its current sources are inadequate, then the job description and hiring specifications provide a useful starting point. These documents reveal factors that affect the recruiter's choice of sources. For example, the educational qualifications for the job may indicate whether colleges are a good source for recruits. If industry knowledge is a requirement, the recruiter may consider employees from other departments within the company.

Once satisfactory sources are located, management should maintain a continuing relationship with them, even when the firm is not hiring. Firms that want college graduates should keep in touch with professors who have furnished assistance in the past. Customers who have supplied leads to good people should be reminded periodically of the company's gratitude and be encouraged to suggest more prospects.

Sources for Recruiting Sales Representatives

Some frequently used **recruiting sources** or leads to sources, as shown in Figure 5–6, are:

- Referrals.
- Current employees.
- Other companies (competitors, customers, noncompetitors).
- The Internet.
- Educational institutions.
- Advertisements.

FIGURE 5-6

Sources of sales force recruits

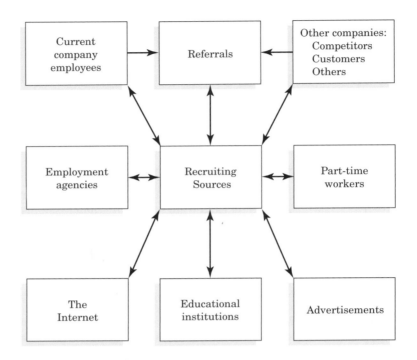

- Employment agencies.
- Part-time workers.

Referrals

A **referral** is a recommendation by one individual that another be hired for a position. Referrals often come from someone included in one of the other sources shown in Figure 5–6, but they may come from other people as well. Because they are the preferred source of sales recruits, we will discuss them separately.

Many managers prefer referrals as a source of recruiting salespeople because of the advantages they offer. Most referrals come from someone who works for the company. They know the job requirements and the recruit. Chances are pretty good that the recommended candidate will have the necessary skills as well as fit within the company culture. The current salespeople, for example, are an excellent source of leads to new recruits. They clearly know the job and the company, and they often meet reps and employees from other companies. Both Microsoft and Dr Pepper/Seven Up, Inc., rely to a great extent on employee referrals as a recruiting source. Dr Pepper/Seven Up makes 40 percent of its new hires from referrals.[9]

The big disadvantage of using referrals is that you may not get enough of them. Both Microsoft and Dr Pepper/Seven Up have found a good way to combat this problem. An employee receives a monetary reward if a person referred is hired and meets initial performance goals. Additionally, managers at Microsoft believe that its strong corporate culture stimulates employee referrals.[10] Again, it should be noted that referrals often come from another recruiting source.

An Ethical Dilemma

Qualified salespeople are hard to find, especially experienced salespeople who are familiar with a recruiter's industry. One way to get such people is to aggressively recruit them from a competitor's sales force. Not only do these reps know the business, but they also might bring along some of their customers. However, competitors object strongly to "pirating," as they call it. They have spent much money training these reps, and now they lose the benefit of the reps' sales productivity. The recruiting companies believe that taking salespeople from competitors is no different from taking customers—that's called competition. Is it ethical for a sales manager to directly approach a competitor's sales rep with a job offer?

Current Employees

Some companies recruit their sales force from workers in their production plants or offices. Management has been able to observe these people and evaluate their potential as sales reps. These workers are acquainted with the product and also have been indoctrinated in company policies and programs. Their values fit with the company culture. Many companies like to recruit within their own organizations because these candidates are the least costly to recruit and train. Hiring salespeople from within the company can also be a great morale booster, because most plant and office workers consider transfer to the sales department to be a promotion. General Motors (GM) believes strongly in recruiting from within the company. In fact, at General Motors University, GM conducts cross-functional training for many different positions. After they "graduate," employees can attain positions in new departments, including sales.[11]

Other Companies: Competitors, Customers, Noncompetitors

A *competitor's* sales force is a major recruiting source for salespeople. However, there are different views about recruiting competitors' salespeople. On the one hand, they know the product and the market very well. They are also experienced sellers and therefore require little training. On the other hand, it may be harder for these people to unlearn old practices and make the adjustment to a new environment. Also, for some managers, recruiting from a competitor's sales force may present an ethical dilemma, as described in the box above.

A firm may seek leads to prospects from its *customers*. Purchasing agents are often good sources of names. They have some knowledge of the abilities of the sales reps who call on them. Customers' employees themselves may be a source of salespeople. Often, retail clerks make good salespeople for wholesalers and manufacturers. These clerks know the product. They also know something of the behavior of the retailers—the market to which the hiring firm sells.

Sales reps working for *noncompeting companies* are another source, particularly if they (1) are selling products related to those sold by the recruiting firm or (2) are selling to the same market. A salesperson working for a supplier of the recruiting firm, for example, is a potential source of recruits. Presumably, recruits from this source have some sales ability and need relatively little training.

Recruiting from other firms raises some questions. Hiring the good employees of a customer obviously has drawbacks. The task must be handled very diplomatically to avoid losing the customer.

A firm that hires from the outside should determine (1) why the applicants are interested in changing jobs and (2) why they want to work for the hiring company. Applicants may figure that the quickest way to success is to move from one company to another. Some people find that a new job is not what they expected, however. A recruiting source many companies may overlook is *former employees*. It is interesting to note that many firms have established Internet "alumni" networks to maintain connections with those who have left. As Agilent Technologies' director of global talent states, "We want to be able to welcome back folks who have left and expanded their skills."[12]

The Internet

Web-Page Recruiting

Many companies are using their own websites to solicit applicants for sales positions. Microsoft's website receives over 500 résumés per week. Eli Lilly is another firm that uses its website to recruit candidates. Johnson & Johnson distributes a CD-ROM at job fairs that links directly to the company's career website, where candidates can learn about job openings and submit their résumés.[13] The most positive aspect of Web-based recruiting is that the cost of obtaining these résumés is very small. Also, voluntary applicants usually know something about the firm and have shown some initiative by submitting their résumés. However the company does bear a significant cost in that it must establish a process for sorting through the large numbers of applicants to find those who qualify for the position.

Internet Recruiting Sites

Many companies are using *Internet recruiting sites* to fill sales positions. The largest such site is Monster.com, a nonprofit recruitment and human resources database that posts job listings from companies such as Sprint, Sony, and Wells Fargo to name just a few. More than 1,600 postings are for sales or marketing positions. Monster.com also contains up to 24,000 résumés at any given time. Sales and Marketing Executives International is another organization that sponsors a recruiting site (www.smei.org). Most of the recruiting sites offer keyword searches by state, locality, industry, company, or title.

Résumé Search Services

Résumé search services are firms that use the computer to sort through thousands of current résumés, looking for specific characteristics. They pass on the selected résumés to the recruiting company. These firms charge far less than employment agencies do, and they guarantee qualified candidates. If there is no match, the company using the service doesn't have to pay anything.

Educational Institutions

Companies frequently use colleges and universities as a source of recruits for sales positions. This is a very cost-effective method of recruiting because col-

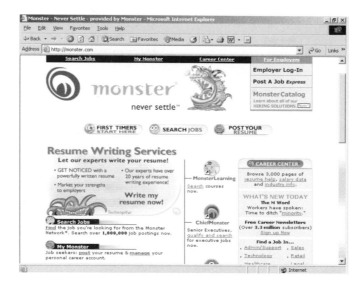

lege campuses provide large numbers of individuals who are educated and look-ing for jobs. Also, there isn't any charge for the recruiting services that univer-sities provide.[14] Companies may also look beyond traditional four-year colleges to recruit from community colleges, vocational–technical schools, or even high schools.

Some companies have developed distinctive identities with students by speaking to classes and student organizations, participating in job fairs or on ad-visory boards to marketing departments, and providing scholarships and sum-mer internship opportunities. Some firms such as IBM and Johnson & Johnson provide diskettes as part of their recruiting materials.[15]

The recruiter who interviews the students also plays a critical role in at-tracting them to sales jobs. Yet too often the recruiter emphasizes aspects of the job that are not the most important to the students (see Figure 5–7). Students say that these recruiters violate a basic principle of selling: Know your customer.[16] Recruiters must be flexible and emphasize such attributes as job satisfaction and company stability as well as advancement opportunities and salary.

Advertisements

Newspapers and trade journals are the most widely used media in which ads for sales jobs are placed. Some companies use advertisements to recruit high-cal-iber salespeople for particularly challenging jobs. However, most firms that use advertising—particularly in newspapers—are trying to fill the less attractive type of sales job, such as in-home selling or clerking in a retail store.

Advertisements ordinarily produce many applicants, but the average quality of the applicants may be questionable. Although the initial cost of reaching re-cruits through ads is low, additional screening may be needed to weed out those who are clearly unqualified.

A company can increase the quality of prospects recruited by advertisements by selecting media carefully and by placing proper information in the ad copy. By buying space in a trade journal rather than in a daily newspaper, for example, a

FIGURE 5-7   Differences in student and recruiter perceptions of important attributes for selecting a sales position

	Attributes as Selected by the:	
Importance Rank	**Student**	**Recruiter**
1	Job satisfaction	Training program
2	Fit with goals	Advancement opportunity
3	Recruiter morale	Recruiter morale
4	Company financial stability	Company reputation
5	Company reputation	Fit with goals
6	Employees voice own views	Job satisfaction
7	Job security	Defined career path
8	Cost-of-living increases	Recruiter friendly
9	Defined hiring process	Company financially friendly
10	Recruiter shows interest	Salary
11	Recruiter friendly	Defined hiring process
12	Advancement opportunity	Recruiter shows interest
13	Employee creativity	Student activities
14	Salary	Job security
15	Training program	Recruiter personality

Source: Dan C. Weilbaker and Nancy J. Merritt, "Attracting Graduates to Sales Positions: The Role of Recruiter Knowledge," *Journal of Personal Selling & Sales Management*, Fall 1992, pp. 49–58.

firm is automatically more selective in its search. The more information given in the notice, the more it serves as a screening device.

To be effective, a recruiting ad must both *attract attention and have credibility.* An advertisement that does not get read, or one that is read but is not considered believable and sincere, is a wasted effort.

Now, what information should be included in a recruiting advertisement? Here are some points to consider.

- **Company name?** The answer is, It all depends. By placing their names in their ads, well-known firms may attract applicants who otherwise would not answer a blind ad. But companies with a poor public image (such as some in-home sellers) often must hide their identities in an ad to attract prospects.

- **Product?** Usually yes, unless it is a product (gravestones and cemetery lots, perhaps) that is likely to turn away prospects who otherwise might be interested once they learned more about the company and the job opportunities.

- **Territory?** Yes, especially if it is not in the area where the ad is run.

- **Hiring qualifications?** Yes, include enough of them so the ad serves as a useful screening device. But keep in mind the legal guidelines (discussed earlier in this chapter) when stating any hiring requirements. As a general rule, all ads should carry the "Equal Opportunity Employer M/F" line.

- **Compensation plan, expense plan, and fringe benefits?** Yes, include some information in these areas, especially if it is a strong point. A company paying straight salary is more likely to mention this point than is one that pays straight commission.

- **How to contact the employer?** The ad must have a phone number or a mailing address. The address in a blind ad is usually a post office box.

Five recruiting ads are shown in Exhibit 5-C at the end of this chapter. Take a look at them and decide which are good, which are poor, and why.

Employment Agencies

Agencies that place salespeople are a frequently used source of recruits. If the agency is carefully selected and good relations are established with it, the dividends can be satisfying. The agency can do some of the initial screening, because presumably it will abide by the job specifications given. Fees usually range from 10 to 40 percent of the new employee's first year's compensation, and they increase as the compensation goes up. Agencies where the employer pays the fee probably attract a better quality of sales recruit. The employer's cost for the agency's fee may be offset by the savings in the advertising and initial screening activities done by the agency.

Part-Time Workers

The use of part-time salespeople in outside selling jobs is increasing. Part-time workers are easy to contact, readily available, and usually can work flexible hours. For example, in-home selling firms such as Mary Kay and Amway frequently use students or homemakers as salespeople.

Diversity

For outside selling jobs, firms can ensure **diversity** in recruiting by using any of the sources that we discussed in the preceding section. In this section, however, we call special attention to minorities and women as recruiting sources for two reasons. First, these groups are underemployed in outside sales jobs. That is, the percentage of minorities and women in outside sales jobs is far below their percentage in the total population. Second, the changing economic, demographic, and legal conditions in this country are bringing major changes to the sales field. As reported earlier in the box titled "The Growth of Population Diversity" the composition of the workforce will change to include a more culturally diverse group of people. The sales force of the future will be drawn from this culturally diverse group of workers, including women, American-born minorities, and immigrants.

Minority Groups

Many executives report only limited success in attracting minority groups to outside sales jobs. In fact, the outside sales force typically has the lowest percentage of minority employees of any department in a company. For example, a recent survey of 200 companies found that 62 percent of the firms had less than 5 percent African Americans employed as salespeople. Many companies cite two reasons for this low percentage: (1) not many African Americans apply and (2) they don't have adequate recruiting sources. But

Lawrence Graham, a professor of African American studies, says, "The truth is, they're just not tapping into the right sources." Groups such as the Urban League and the National Black MBA Association, as well as most business schools, have resource centers with hundreds of résumés on file.[17]

As noted earlier, there are legal reasons to practice diversity. The Equal Employment Opportunity Commission, which strives to ensure that minorities have the same opportunities as whites, investigates as many as 30,000 cases of racial discrimination each year. In many cases companies are forced to pay stiff fines and implement diversity programs. But practicing diversity is also good business. As minorities make up more of the labor force, so too will they be a greater percentage of the purchasing population. For some companies, such as AT&T and Levi Strauss & Co., ensuring sales force diversity is seen not only as the right thing to do but also as a key to success.[18]

Women

Reports on the perceptions and experiences of sales executives concerning women in outside selling jobs are interesting and enlightening. Overall, these experiences and perceptions have been quite favorable. Furthermore, this favorable reaction is not limited to consumer products companies or service industries. Women also are performing well as sales recruits in industrial sales jobs. Many companies that may have originally recruited women as the "politically correct" thing to do have found that women are a vast untapped resource with a significant positive effect on the bottom line.[19]

Yet women are still grossly underrepresented in most outside sales forces. Women account for about 50 percent of the total labor force, yet in few companies do they account for more than 25 percent of the outside sales force. Looking at sales management ranks, the picture is even worse—on average, only 14 percent are women.[20] There are still factors that inhibit the entry and progress of women in outside sales forces.

Nevertheless, the influx of women into outside sales forces will continue to increase. To counter the shortage of qualified salespeople, management must strongly recruit from the population segment that comprises over half of the labor force.

Recruiting Evaluation

To better direct its focus in the management of its recruiting sources, a company should continually evaluate the effectiveness of its recruiting program. To conduct **recruiting evaluation,** management might use some form of matrix approach, such as the one in Figure 5–8. This information should enable management to determine which sources produced the best recruits. This approach lends itself to computer technology, which can aid in the evaluation process. A spin-off benefit of recruiting evaluation is that it can be used in the performance ratings of sales executives who are involved in recruiting. That is, some companies use "recruiting effectiveness" as one factor in evaluating a sales manager's judgment and promotability.

FIGURE 5-8   Recruiting evaluation matrix

Evaluation Criteria

Recruiting Sources	Consistent with Strategic Planning?	Number Recruits	Number Hired	Percent Retained after 3 Years	Cost	Frequency of Use	Rep's Performance after 2 Years
Referrals							
Within company							
Other companies Competitors Customers Noncompetitors							
Educational institutions							
Advertisements							
Employment agencies							
Voluntary applicants							
Computerized databases							

Summary

Selecting the right people (staffing the organization) is one of the most important steps in the management process. Sales force selection should be coordinated with an organization's strategic marketing and sales force planning because the sales force often plays a major role in implementing the plans. Sales executives must understand the various civil rights laws and other government regulations that have a substantial impact on all phases of sales force selection.

Sales selection includes five phases. First, management determines how many and what kind of people are wanted. The second phase involves recruiting a number of applicants. The third phase involves processing these applicants and selecting the most qualified. Then those selected must be hired and assimilated into the organization.

Management can determine the *number* of salespeople to be hired by conducting an analysis based on the company's past experiences and future expectations. To determine the *type* of person wanted, management should first conduct a job analysis and then write a job description for each position to be filled.

Determining the qualifications needed to fill the job is the most difficult part of the sales selection process. As yet, we simply have not been able to isolate the traits that make for success in selling. However, we do know that it is important to develop *individualized* hiring specifications for a given job in a given firm. As a starting point, management should study the job descriptions. They should also analyze the personal histories of their present and past salespeople to identify those characteristics that distinguish the successful reps from the less successful ones.

After determining the number and kind of salespeople wanted, the next major step in sales force selection is to recruit several applicants for the job. A well-planned, well-operated recruiting system is essential for a successful selection program. A company must identify the sources that are likely to produce good recruits and maintain a continuing relationship with these sources, even during periods when the firm is not hiring.

Many managers feel that referrals are the best source of sales recruits. These referrals may come from many places, including from within the company doing the recruiting. Often the present sales force is an excellent source of leads to new recruits. Also, some companies recruit new salespeople from employees in their offices or factories.

Another major source of recruits is other companies—competitors, customers, or noncompetitors. A company may try to hire competitors' salespeople, or a firm's customers may supply recruiting leads. Some companies will hire customers' employees, although this must be done very carefully. Another source is salespeople working for noncompeting firms.

Increasingly, firms are using the Internet to identify candidates. Résumé search services will perform the search for a fee, or managers can access several job banks on the Internet.

Many companies recruit salespeople from educational institutions—universities, community colleges, vocational–technical schools, or high schools. Some firms rely on advertisements to reach prospective applicants. For some types of sales jobs, employment agencies can provide good prospects.

Voluntary (walk-in) applicants can be an excellent source, but usually there are not enough of these people. Part-time workers, such as students or homemakers, are excellent candidates for certain selling jobs.

Increasingly, companies are looking to women and minority groups as sources of applicants for sales jobs. This trend is expected to continue and to intensify. A company should periodically evaluate the effectiveness of its recruiting program to ensure that it is using the best sources available.

Key Terms

Affirmative action	Job profile	Recruiting evaluation
Diversity	Job qualifications	Recruiting sources
Job analysis	Nondiscrimination	Referral
Job description	Recruiting	Selection

Questions and Problems

1. What is the best way for a company to avoid being sued for a lack of affirmative action?

2. Why would a company be willing to rehire someone who had earlier left the firm?

3. Assume that you have just opened a dental supply house that manufactures dentures and other dental correction devices. What criteria would be important in selecting salespeople to sell for your company?

4. If a person wants to be a top-notch professional career sales rep and has no interest in being a manager, is a college education necessary? Discuss. If your answer is no, why do so

many firms recruit salespeople from colleges, and why is a college education so often listed as a qualification for a sales job?

5. Assume that a company wants to hire a sales engineer—that is, fill a position where the major emphasis is on technical product knowledge. Should this firm recruit engineers and train them to sell, or recruit sales reps and teach them the necessary technical information and abilities?

6. Prepare a list of the qualifications you feel are necessary to fill the sales job described in Exhibit 5-B (page 146).

7. Is it ethical for a sales manager to directly approach a competitor's salesperson with an outright offer of a better job?

8. How would the sources and methods of recruiting salespeople *differ* among the following firms?
   a) A company selling precision instruments to the petroleum industry.
   b) A coffee roaster and canner in Denver selling to wholesalers and retailers in the Southwest and the Rocky Mountain regions.
   c) A national firm selling kitchenware by the party-plan method.
   d) A luggage manufacturer selling a high-grade product nationally through selected retail outlets.

9. One manufacturer of dictating machines recruits only experienced people and does no recruiting among graduating college students. A competitor recruits extensively among colleges in its search for salespeople. How do you account for the difference in sources used by firms selling essentially the same products?

10. The following companies are looking for product salespeople and decide to use advertising to recruit applicants. For each firm, you are asked to select the specific advertising media and to write a recruiting advertisement for one of those media. You may supply whatever additional facts you need.
    a) Manufacturer's agent handling lighting fixtures for both the industrial and consumer markets.
    b) Manufacturer of outboard motors.
    c) Wholesaler of lumber and building materials.

11. What sources should be used to recruit sales reps to fill the jobs described in Exhibits 5-A and 5-B?

12. Evaluate the five recruiting advertisements for salespeople shown in Exhibit 5-C (page 149).

Experiential Exercises

A. After interviewing some members of the sales force and/or the appropriate executives in a local firm, prepare a detailed job description on one of the following jobs:
   a) Automobile dealer salesperson.
   b) Driver salesperson for local soft-drink bottler.
   c) Missionary salesperson for manufacturer.
   d) Salesperson for some type of wholesaler.

B. Prepare a list of qualifications needed to fill each job you analyzed and described in the preceding exercise.

Internet Exercises

A. Visit one or more of the following websites, or a specific company site, to find several sales positions in which you think you might be interested. Name the company, describe the job, and the application procedure. Describe what appeals to you about the particular positions that you have selected.
   a) Jobtrack (www.jobtrack.com).
   b) Monster.com (www.monster.com).
   c) Yahoo! (www.com/business/employment).
   d) Sales and Marketing Executives (www.smei.org).

CASE EXHIBIT 5-A   Job Description—Marketing Representative for Xerox Corp.

JOB DESCRIPTION

Primary Function: To achieve assigned sales operating plan objectives in Group III establishments by: prospecting new accounts, developing and maintaining customer rapport, identifying customer requirements for office equipment, matching customer requirements to existing Xerox equipment via written proposals, demonstrating Xerox equipment, signing orders for equipment, resolving customer problems, ensuring proper installation of equipment, training customers on the proper use of equipment, and performing customer care calls to ensure customer satisfaction.

Source of Supervision: Marketing/Sales Manager

JOB DUTIES AND RESPONSIBILITIES

Conducts Customer Prospecting Calls

- Plans, organizes, and prioritizes the following activities on a regular basis: customer prospecting calls, customer appointments, customer care visits, customer follow-up calls, customer training, demonstrations, and internal meetings.
- Performs 15–30 customer prospecting calls (cold calls) per day to identify potential new business or develop customer rapport with previous contacts.
- Asks office personnel questions to identify key decision maker(s) (e.g., office manager).
- Asks probing questions and listens to customers' responses to identify potential office equipment requirements.
- Documents customer information (e.g., customer's name and location, type of existing office equipment, customer requirements for new office equipment) on an account profile form to create a record of all customer prospects.
- Distributes business cards, sales brochures, and promotional information to customer locations to establish contact with potential customers.

Conducts Customer Appointments

- Schedules appointments with customers to further identify customer requirements for office equipment.
- Gathers information to identify customers' requirements for office equipment by asking probing questions (e.g., current copying and/or FAX equipment used, satisfaction with current equipment, lease agreement on current equipment, number of copies per month, type of copying done, the amount of work that is sent out for outside copying, future needs for copying and/or FAX equipment).
- Answers customers' questions about Xerox equipment and service.
- Verbally presents information to customers using brochures and other written materials (e.g., price lists) to inform customers about Xerox equipment and service.
- Documents results of customer calls and necessary actions needed to advance the call through the sales cycle.

Conducts Customer Call Follow-Up

- Seeks information to answer customers' questions from various resources (e.g., written documentation, field support personnel, sales managers, and other sales representatives).
- Returns customer telephone calls to answer questions and provide information.
- Writes follow-up thank you letters to customers summarizing the key points of customer calls.

- Mails information (e.g., flyers, brochures) to customers regarding new office equipment and sales promotions.

Develops Written Sales Proposals

- Discusses customer requirements with sales managers and other sales representatives to obtain information and develop a strategy for meeting customer requirements.
- Inputs information into sale range pricing database to obtain information regarding the cost and financing of office equipment.
- Calculates finance factors using basic mathematics $(+, -, \times, \div)$ and finance principles to obtain cost of ownership information.
- Writes sales proposals that recommend office equipment and provide product, service, and financial information to meet customers' requirements.
- Types sales proposals using a 6085 computer terminal (if necessary).

Performs Product Demonstrations

- Schedules appointments with customers to demonstrate equipment.
- Cleans and checks equipment to ensure equipment performance quality (e.g., copy quality, free from jamming).
- Tailors demonstration to meet identified customer requirements.
- Obtains information about competitors' equipment and integrates this information into demonstration.
- Practices demonstration to ensure that equipment is working properly.
- Performs demonstration for customer by presenting product information, running customer applications on the equipment, answering customer questions, and probing the customer for additional requirements.

Negotiates Close of Sale

- Discusses terms of lease or sale of equipment with customer to clarify all costs of ownership.
- Obtains written commitment from customer to lease or purchase equipment by asking questions to obtain customer information (e.g., desire to purchase equipment, customer location, contact person, billing specifications) needed to complete order form.
- Reviews information on equipment order form with customer to clearly specify the terms of the agreement and ensure information accuracy.
- Answers all customer questions regarding the terms of the lease or sale of the equipment.

Completes Paperwork to Place Customer Orders for Equipment

- Communicates order information to customer administration representatives, billing representatives, and credit representatives to ensure timely processing of customer order for equipment.
- Obtains additional information from customers to clarify any problems with equipment orders.
- Discusses possible dates for equipment installation with scheduler and confirms installation date with customers.
- Initiates follow-up communications with all order-to-install personnel to ensure the accurate and timely processing of customer orders and equipment installation.

Assists in the Installation of Equipment (if necessary)

- Measures space requirements to ensure sufficient space is available for equipment installation.
- Assists Customer Service Engineers (CSEs) with the installation of equipment.

Trains Key Operators and Other Equipment Users

- Presents an overview of equipment features and capabilities to customers.

- Demonstrates proper use of the equipment by running specific customer applications.

- Answers customer questions regarding the operation of equipment, servicing of equipment, ordering of supplies, and trouble-shooting equipment problems.

Maintains Rapport with Customers

- Conducts periodic post-sale customer care visits to answer customer questions, solve customer problems, maintain rapport with customers, and identify any additional office equipment needs.

- Obtains information and contacts the appropriate personnel to resolve customer problems and ensure customer satisfaction.

Participates in Quality Improvement Activities

- Attends planning and review meetings and territory reviews to help forecast sales and develop strategies for closing sales cycles.

- Attends team meetings and participates in developing creative solutions to existing problems.

- Writes and delivers presentations in order to share information with other sales representatives and managers.

- Uses the tools of Leadership Through Quality to improve work processes and solve problems.

JOB PREREQUISITES

Must possess a Bachelors degree or have 2–3 years of relevant sales experience. Must pass all parts of the qualifying test battery for the Marketing Representative position regarding written and verbal communication skills, planning and organization skills, presentation skills, listening ability, problem-solving ability, mathematics/finance skills, and customer relations skills.

The above statements reflect primary activities that are necessary for success in Marketing Representative positions, and shall not be considered a detailed description of all job requirements. The purpose of this job description is to serve only as a basis for developing a new selection process for Marketing Representatives and to provide job applicants with a detailed description of the work requirements.

Source: Used with permission of Xerox Corporation.

 **CASE EXHIBIT 5-B**   Job Description—Sales Representative for an International Airline

CHARTER OF ACCOUNTABILITY

Position: Passenger Sales Representative

Reports to: Regional Passenger Sales Manager

1. Mission

The mission of the Passenger Sales Representative is to generate sales of passenger services and products while optimizing yield and traffic mix levels and achieving the targeted cost/revenue ratio; and to provide professional, prompt, and reliable service to the existing and potential customer base.

2. Policy Guidelines

The activities of the Passenger Sales Representative are governed by the policies, procedures, and guidelines established by the Regional and District management and Headquarters; the corporate Personnel Manual and all other related company manuals; and with DOT, FAA, IATAN, ARC, and all other applicable governmental and industry rules and regulations.

3. Authority

The Passenger Sales Representative is authorized to sell passenger products and services; to identify and develop new sources of traffic; to represent the company in all first level sales contract negotiations; and to perform the activities listed in Section 5.

4. Accountability

The Passenger Sales Representative is accountable for:

- Evaluation of the assigned territory's market potential and competitive influences.
- Preparation of a realistic sales budget.
- Identification and development of new sources of traffic.
- Planning and execution of an effective time and territory management system.
- Achievement of the passenger sales volume/yield targets.
- Negotiation of cost-effective contracts with select agents and corporate/leisure accounts.
- Participation at industry trade shows scheduled within the assigned territory.
- Production of group travel bookings with a high percentage of passenger materialization.
- Accurate and timely presentation of required reports.
- Comprehensive knowledge of all company products and services.
- Quality and professionalism of customer service activities and effectiveness of sales techniques.

5. Responsibilities

The Passenger Sales Representative is responsible to:

- Evaluate the market potential of the assigned territory and prepare an attainable sales budget complete with its applicable cost budget.
- Identify potential opportunities for new sources of traffic through market research data and sales leads; develop and implement appropriate strategies.
- Achieve agreed-upon passenger revenue targets through a planned and systematic sales campaign—targeting high-potential accounts, evaluating actual versus expected production for each account, and taking corrective action when required.
- Negotiate advantageous commission contracts with select agents and corporate/leisure accounts.
- Develop call plans based upon production levels and geographic location of accounts; set account goals and strategies; prepare seasonal analysis of time usage and adjust to optimize available time.
- Prepare call strategies and make presentations to corporate, leisure, and agency sales sources and develop group packages and programs to meet their special needs.
- Attend and participate in industry trade shows scheduled within the assigned territory; set up and man the booth; pack material for next location; and submit report on results for future consideration.
- Generate group travel business; negotiate commission and number of blocked seats; complete precall forms; monitor space confirmation; reduce/adjust block space to ensure high passenger materialization.
- Track and report on the competitive influences and market conditions in the territory and recommend actions to counteract competitive activities.

- Project a positive and professional image when representing the company at appropriate industry functions and associations; establish and maintain cooperative working relationships with industry counterparts.
- Coordinate with other district and regional personnel for the planning and implementation of media projects, agent reward systems, and other marketing activities.
- Maintain all pertinent records and prepare ad hoc and periodic reports for management review and decision-making purposes.

6. Position Scope

No. of Staff	Cost Budget	Sales Budget
0	$100,000	$4,000,000

CASE EXHIBIT 5-C Advertisements for Sales Positions

References

1. Charles Butler, "Why the Bad Rap?" *Sales & Marketing Management*, June 1996, p. 30.

2. Emory Mulling, "Prepare for the Hunt to Hire the Best Sellers," *Washington Business Journal*, April 9, 1999, p. 88.

3. Quoted in Elana Harris, "Hire Power," *Sales & Marketing Management*, October 2000, p. 88.

4. George Avlonitis and Despina A. Karayanni, "The Impact of Internet Use on Business-to-Business Marketing," *Industrial Marketing Management* 29 (2000), pp. 441–59.

5. Geoffrey Brewer, "Brain Power," *Sales & Marketing Management*, May 1997, pp. 39–48.

6. Nina Munk and Suzanne Oliver, "Think Fast," *Forbes*, March 24, 1997, pp. 146–51.

7. J. Doug Clopton, "Becoming Proactive about Recruiting," *Sales & Marketing Management*, September 1992, pp. 93–97.

8. Erin Strout, "How to Win Today's Recruiting War," *Sales & Marketing Management*, March 2000, p. 85.

9. Katharine Kaplan, "Help (Still) Wanted," *Sales & Marketing Management*, February 2002, pp. 38–43.

10. Ibid.

11. Erin Strout, "Finding Your Company's Top Talent," *Sales & Marketing Management*, May 2000, p. 113.

12. Abby Nickenson, "Alma Matters," *Sales & Marketing Management*, February 2002, p. 52.

13. Kaplan, "Help (Still) Wanted."

14. Audrey Bottjen, "The Benefits of College Recruiting," *Sales & Marketing Management*, April 2001, p. 11.

15. Kaplan, "Help (Still) Wanted."

16. Danielle Service, "Poor Marks for Recruiters," *Sales & Marketing Management*, June 1995, p. 77.

17. Allison Lucas and William Duke, "Race Matters," *Sales & Marketing Management*, September 1996, pp. 51–62.

18. Ibid.

19. Christen P. Heide, *Dartnell's 30th Sales Force Compensation Survey* (Chicago: Dartnell Corporation, 1999), pp. 168–71.

20. Ibid.

CASE 5-1 GALACTICA

Recruiting Sources

Brenda Crohn, the recruiting director for a textbook publisher called Galactica, was in the middle of a heated argument with John Stubbins, the vice president of marketing. The argument revolved around where to place the ads to recruit candidates for sales positions. "I know that the quality of the applicants generated off an Internet job site may not be as good as those from our current trade journal ads; but we can reach a lot more candidates through the site, and I need a large pool of people to find qualified candidates. Even if we hire fewer of them, I would rather have a bigger pool to pick from," argued John.

Crohn was frustrated that the only criterion John seemed to be considering was the number of applicants the Internet ad would generate. "John," Crohn interrupted, "you are right about the number of applicants the ads will generate. Our current ads generate an average of 1.2 applicants per ad, and we could expect more than twice that number from an Internet ad. I've got an estimate from one of the job bank sites of 3.9 per ad. But you've got to consider the costs as well as the number of qualified applicants. We like to hire experienced reps, and those who respond to the Internet ads are much less likely to have the experience we prefer."

"So what are the differences in costs?" Stubbins asked.

Crohn replied, "Well the total selection costs for our current ads are $59, and for the Internet ad they would increase to $124. But as you acknowledged a minute ago, the quality of the Internet applicant would be lower, and therefore we would make fewer offers than we usually do. We currently hire 50 percent of the applicants we get per ad; my guess is that this percentage would drop to something less than 33 percent of the Internet applicants."

"So what is the bottom line on all of this?" asked Stubbins. "The Internet ad costs us more, but we get a bigger pool of candidates. Even if we reject a higher number of them, it may actually cost Galactica less per rep hired. You know right now we are batting about 20 percent in terms of the reps we hire becoming successful. That means that I am always looking for new reps. I think that we should give the Internet a try!"

Crohn was not convinced. She told Stubbins, "I do not have a bottom line at this point. So let me put the figures together and get back to you in a couple of days. Then we can make an informed decision about the Internet option."

Questions:

1. What would you recommend to John Stubbins? Should Galactica change from using its current trade journal ads to Internet ads? Explain the reason for your recommendation.

2. If Brenda Crohn's guesstimates and estimates are wrong, how might that change your decision? At what number of applicants is there an economic breakeven between the two types of ads?

3. What other considerations besides costs, number of applicants, and number hired has neither Brenda Crohn nor John Stubbins mentioned?

CASE 5-2   COMPUTER SERVICES CORPORATION

Improving the Recruiting Process

Paul Robbins, national sales manager for Computer Services Corporation (CSC), was frustrated. The company's recruiting efforts this past spring had not yielded the number of recruits CSC needed to fill its open territories. This was not a new problem; it was a repeat of similar problems the company faced the previous year, but this year the need for recruits was even greater and the results had been worse. While some districts did better than others, the recruiting efforts across sales districts had not been as effective as they needed to be. Out of every four offers CSC had made, three had been turned down.

Located in Dallas, Texas, CSC manufactures and markets a full line of business forms, computer hardware and software, machine ribbons, computer accessories, and a host of other office products and services. The entire line—well over 6,000 products—is sold to a broad base of customers. For example, 50 percent of the country's phone bills are printed by CSC; UPS shipping forms are another CSC product. This diverse product line has contributed to the tremendous success of the company. CSC has been in business for 30 years, and management is extremely proud of the company's 15 consecutive years of earnings and sales growth.

CSC considers itself a customer-oriented company. The sales organization is responsible for implementing CSC's strategy of being a full-service, high-quality supplier. Because reorders provide the majority of sales for CSC's primary products, it is imperative that the sales representatives maintain regular and close contact with their customers. To facilitate this close contact, CSC has 105 sales offices throughout the United States. Each office has a district sales manager who reports to one of eight regional managers. The regional managers report to the national sales manager. Most of the sales managers have six or seven salespeople reporting to them.

The salespeople are authorized to sell the entire CSC product line. Each rep is responsible for a specific geographic area. The reps must learn their customers' business and identify ways to help their customers improve their operations and profits. Then they design the forms and sell the products that will improve the customer's operations.

The salespeople are usually compensated on a base salary plus commission. It takes each rep approximately two years to reach the point where the commissions become significant. At that point, the reps can elect to shift their income to a higher proportion of commission. Most of the senior salespeople are on straight commission, and many earn more than $100,000 per year. There is no limit on how much a rep can earn.

The turnover rate at CSC is much lower than the industry average. The reps are well trained and well paid. The low turnover rate suggests that the reps are relatively satisfied with the supportive environment of CSC. As Paul Robbins had noted to one of his sales managers, "CSC does not have any problem in retaining its reps. The problem is just getting recruits to commit to CSC in the first place."

CSC recruits exclusively from business majors at one or two of the universities located in each of the regional areas. For example, in the Houston District Sales Office, the sales managers recruit at the University of Texas and at the University of Houston. The sales managers who have or are anticipating open territories interview 10 to 15 candidates each at one or two campuses. There is no generally agreed-on set of qualifications or format for conducting the interviews. Each manager is free to conduct the interviews in the way that best suits him or her. After the first round of campus interviews, the manager will invite two to four recruits to the district office for a second round of interviews.

During the district office interviews, the recruits meet with several district staff personnel and spend time with one of the sales representatives. If a regional manager is available, the recruits will interview with one of them as well. Then, based on the outcome of the second round of interviews, the sales manager will usually make two to three offers. Currently the average offer is for $22,000, which applies to the salesperson's first six months. At that time, the salary drops to $20,000 and the potential to earn commission becomes available to the rep. Typically, the average first-year rep will make about $24,000 with salary and commission combined.

However, a lot of quality people are not accepting CSC's offers. Instead, they are accepting offers for similar positions with some of the marketing giants like P&G and Johnson & Johnson, which offer higher starting salaries and company cars. Typically these offers amount to $5,000 to $6,000 more per year than those of CSC.

Paul Robbins knows that one logical solution to the company's recruiting problems is to offer starting salaries comparable to those of other companies. However, his boss, Joe Cannon, is not going to support this idea. Cannon has two main reasons: First, the budget for the year has already been set, and raising starting salaries would mean a substantial increase in marketing costs. Second, and even more important, is that CSC wants to maintain its hiring philosophy of "bringing them in hungry." CSC has always tried to hire people who are "money-motivated," who are excited by the unlimited earning potential at CSC. In fact, management has intentionally kept starting salaries below market so that it is the long-term potential and not the starting salary that attracts recruits to CSC.

Robbins had to admit that CSC's hiring philosophy seemed to work well. The low turnover and large commissions earned by the salespeople attest to its success. Yet he was also certain that unless he did something, the company would continue to spend an excessive amount of time and money on recruiting—with dismal results.

Question:

1. Should Paul Robbins be concerned about the recruiting results? If so, what changes should Paul make or recommend to improve the results?

CASE 5-3   PEERLESS GENERATORS, INC.

Developing a Recruiting Program

Jim Shaw, sales manager for Peerless Generators, recognized that he was fortunate to still have his job. Most of the company's top management had been replaced with people from the Multitech Company when the two firms merged operations in March 1998. Roger Konstant, the new president of Peerless Generators, had told Shaw that the only thing that saved him was that Shaw's performance in operating an industrial sales force was far superior to that of anyone in the Multitech sales management organization. Now Shaw was approaching Konstant's office for a meeting that was suddenly called on a Monday morning in early May 2002. Roger Konstant greeted him warmly. "Good morning, Jim! Hope you were able to enjoy the weekend."

"Yeah, wasn't the weather great? Got in a couple of rounds of golf," Shaw replied with a smile.

"Great! Never can tell what the weather is going to be like this time of year here in Cleveland," Konstant observed. He continued, "Jim, I've got to catch a plane to the coast so I'll have to be quick about this."

Jim Shaw's stomach tightened. He thought, Don't tell me . . . not now.

Konstant said quickly, "Seems you've impressed the Multitech people more than we knew. I've been on the phone for two hours with Jane Conover, who heads their marketing organization. It seems that she has been dissatisfied with their field sales operations for some time but has not been able to get their sales force turned around to her liking. She has had a marketing consulting firm, Marketing Associates, study the problems, and they have submitted their report. They believe that Multitech's sales force has not lived up to expectations because the firm has not been hiring the right people. They claim that this poor selection record is the result of a poor recruiting program. The consultants recommend that the firm's recruiting program be overhauled."

He continued, "Now, as for you! The consultants recommended that an outside party be brought in to develop the new recruiting program. I'm sure they had themselves in mind for the job, but Conover recalled the terrific recruiting program you installed here at Peerless and wants you to come in to do it. You're due in New York tomorrow morning. You have a 10 o'clock meeting with Jane Conover. A copy of the consultants' report will be waiting for you at the Plaza. All reservations have been made for you. Pick up your tickets downstairs; you're out of here at 6, so go home for the rest of the day. You'll need the rest. Got to run now."

And Roger Konstant was gone. As he returned to his office to give his people instructions for his unexpected absence, Jim Shaw wondered if this was how the new management always operated.

Shaw did not know Jane Conover, nor did he really know much about Multitech sales operations. He wasn't really sure what all the company sold or to whom they sold it. He would soon find out. Shaw arrived at the Plaza in New York and was getting settled in his room when the telephone rang. Conover had sent her assistant to the hotel to brief Shaw about company operations. The assistant, Stu Jackson, was in the lobby now, loaded down with materials for Shaw's information. Shaw listened carefully for the next two hours while Jackson briefed him on Multitech sales operations and plans. It developed that the firm's problems with its sales operations were far more extensive than Jim had been led to believe.

"Top management is not happy with sales operations in any of its 12 companies. Studies have continually shown that the firm's sales performance in each of its markets is below average for that industry. Evidently, we're just not very good at selling our goods," Stu Jackson stated. "We hire more than 600 sales reps in total for the whole system, but the turnover is killing us. We lose 25 percent a year. Right now we just hire on a catch-as-catch-can basis. The field sales managers hire reps to replace those we lose as best they can. We can discern no pattern, except that they do tend to hire reps from other technically oriented firms and from competitors." Shaw nodded as Jackson continued. "On top of all that mess, top management has launched a strategic expansion program that schedules us to hire a total of 100 new sales reps each year for the whole system."

"Why do you keep speaking of the company as a whole and not of the individual firms? Doesn't each firm have its own distinctive needs?" Shaw asked.

"Not really. They all sell highly technical equipment to the electronics industry. Each company was a successful high-tech start-up that we purchased when the entrepreneur or the investors were ready to cash out. We considered combining all the sales forces, but it proved to be not the thing to do. Each has its own niche in the market and deals with separate technology. And company policy is to allow the firms that we take over to keep their own identity."

When Jackson had completed his briefing, Shaw asked, "Do you know exactly what Conover wants me to do?"

"I think she wants you to tell her what to do. She just wants the problems solved," Jackson replied.

Shaw nodded and thanked Jackson for working so late to help him out. Shaw knew that sleep might be elusive that night—he had much to mull over. He knew he would stall for time by asking Jane Conover to tell him as much as possible about the situation so he could discern her thoughts on the matter.

The next morning Conover quickly took over the meeting once the usual formalities had been observed. "I need a plan. Tell me how to solve this problem, but do it quickly. I'm being pressed hard from the top about our field sales operations, and I am afraid that field sales are not my cup of tea. I came up through marketing and product management at General Electric. You're free to write your own ticket in the deal. Pick your role. Use my budget. Stu Jackson is yours if you want him. He'll handle your budget and arrangements. Can I have your report next week?"

Jim Shaw was silent for a moment, trying to process all this information while looking reasonably intelligent. He finally replied, "I'll do better than that. I'll tell you tomorrow what I propose to do." Jim did not want to stick around New York for a week. He had already made up his mind that he did not want to work separately with each subsidiary; it would involve too much traveling and too much time. He contemplated developing a model recruiting program for each of the firm's sales managers to follow. It would tell each sales manager how to develop a recruiting program for his or her operation. Jane Conover smiled and said, "See you tomorrow at 9."

Questions:

1. Outline what a model recruiting program should cover.

2. What career opportunities does this event provide Jim Shaw?

6 Selecting and Hiring Applicants

The worst mistake a manager can make is to make a bad hire.

—Anonymous—

In our staffing process, we have determined the number and type of salespeople needed, and we have recruited applicants. Now we are ready for the third phase: selection. This phase involves (1) developing a system of tools and procedures for matching the applicants with the predetermined requirements, and (2) actually using this system to select the salespeople. The major selection tools are:

- Application blanks
- Personal interviews
- Psychological tests
- References and credit reports
- Assessment centers

These tools are described in detail in this chapter. Then we turn to the fourth phase of the staffing process: hiring. The chapter finishes with a discussion of the final phase: assimilating new hires into the company.

Selection Tools and Strategic Planning

Selecting applicants is an integral part of implementing the strategic sales force plan. If the selection stage is handled effectively, it can help ensure successful sales performance. Conversely, a poor job of processing applicants can hinder implementation, even though the first two steps in the staffing process—planning and recruiting—were done well. Matching company needs and applicants' potential is very important to the strategic and tactical aspects of sales force management.

The sequence in which companies use the selection tools described in this chapter varies from one to another. Initial screening (beyond that done in recruiting) may start with an application blank, an interview, or some form of test. The purpose of the initial screen is to eliminate undesirable recruits quickly and inexpensively. Therefore, no matter which technique comes first, it is usually brief—a short application blank, a brief interview, or a simple test that can be administered and interpreted quickly. The general idea is that the *least costly selection tools should be used first.*

No single selection tool is adequate by itself. Companies should use a series of tools to carefully determine an applicant's qualifications. In many cases, the information derived from one tool can complement or verify that derived from another. Some pertinent data about an applicant ordinarily come only through an interview, while other traits are revealed only by testing. Also, the tools a company uses to process its sales recruits should fit the particular needs of the firm. Standardized forms (application blanks, interview forms, and so on) prepared for general use are usually less effective than those a company develops itself.

Selection tools and procedures are only *aids* to sound executive judgment and not *substitutes* for it. They can eliminate obviously unqualified candidates and generally help recruiters spot extremely capable individuals. However, for the mass of recruits between these extremes, the tools currently used can only predict those who have the *potential* to be successful in the job. Executive judgment still plays a critical role in making the final choice.

Legal Considerations

The legislation summarized in Chapter 5 protects certain classes of people against discrimination. As a result of these laws and their enforcement by the Equal Employment Opportunity Commission (EEOC) and the Office of Federal Contract Compliance (OFCC), there is certain information that employers should *not* request during the selection process. These inquiries are outlined in Figure 6–1. Additionally, companies should not conduct preemployment medical screening until after a job offer has been extended. The offer should be made contingent on a physical if, and only if, the medical requirements are related to job performance.

Hiring decisions may no longer be made on gut feeling. Title VII of the Civil Rights Act of 1964 provides that companies must base their selection of employees on objective criteria. These criteria must be (1) independently measurable, (2) job related, and (3) predictive of performance. For most sales positions, previous years of sales experience would meet these criteria.

Companies subject to affirmative action guidelines must keep an "applicant flowchart" that lists the processed applicants by sex and ethnic group. If the company finds that it is rejecting a disproportionately high number of women or minority applicants, it should review each step in the hiring process to determine which tool is producing this result. Once identified, the particular tool must undergo a validation procedure if management wants to continue using it.

Validation is the process of statistically measuring the extent to which a given selection tool or hiring qualification is a predictor of, or is related to, job performance. To reduce selection mistakes and possible legal hassles later, companies

FIGURE 6-1   What to ask and what not to ask

Do Not Ask:

- The applicant's age.
- Whether the applicant has children or the ages of the children.
- Who will care for the children if the applicant is hired.
- The applicant's race or a question directly or indirectly indicating race.
- The applicant's height or weight.
- An applicant's citizenship.
- Whether the applicant was ever arrested.
- Whether the applicant is married, single, divorced, or widowed.
- The applicant's religious affiliation.
- What the applicant's spouse does.
- The applicant's maiden name or her father's surname.
- The names and/or addresses of any relative of an adult applicant.
- Whether the applicant belongs to a specific organization, if that would indicate race, religion, or ancestry.
- Whether the applicant owns or rents.
- With whom the applicant lives.
- Whether a woman would be comfortable supervising a man.

Lawful Inquiries:

- How many years of experience do you have?
- Why do you want the job?
- Can you do extensive traveling?
- What languages do you speak?
- Are you a citizen or resident alien of the United States?
- Questions about convictions if they relate to the fitness of the applicant to do the job.
- Do you prefer to be addressed as Mr., Mrs., Ms., or Miss?
- Questions about the applicant's goals.
- Questions regarding specific skills.
- What didn't you like about your former job, and why did you leave?
- Questions regarding education and schools attended.
- Would you be comfortable supervising others?

Source: *Approaches to Affirmative Action*, Bureau of National Affairs, Inc.

should validate their selection tools *before* using them. This increases management's chances of using the best available selection criteria. Moreover, if a company is later charged with discrimination, validation is the best defense possible.

Many questions formerly asked on application blanks and during interviews either are no longer permitted or must be handled very carefully. Sometimes human resource personnel may ask questions in sensitive areas after the person is hired, as in asking about age and marital status for insurance purposes. Interviewers may ask questions in sensitive areas, during the interviews only if they relate to **bona fide occupational qualifications (BFOQs).** Age and sex may be BFOQs, for example, if the sales job calls for a salesman to model the line of men's wear he is selling. If a certain ethnic background and ability to speak a certain foreign language are BFOQs, then of course questions pertaining to these factors are perfectly appropriate. To summarize, any selection question or hiring qualification must be "job relevant"—that is, it must be directly related to the job.

Application Blanks

Reasons for Using Application Blanks

The **application blank,** or personal-history record, as it is sometimes called, is the second most widely used selection tool. (The interview discussed in the next main section of this chapter is the only tool used more often.) Sometimes a firm uses two blanks—a short one and a longer, more detailed one. The short form ordinarily serves only as an initial screening device. A longer blank may be used as an initial screen or for other purposes. The facts stated on the form can be the basis for probing in an interview. For instance, the interviewer can ask several questions about job experiences the applicant listed on the blank. Later the recruiter can use the data on the application to reevaluate the characteristics needed for the job. One national pharmaceutical firm uses data on the application blank to screen for high performers who will stay with the firm. Using an analysis of the application information for its current and past salespeople, the firm weights certain characteristics more heavily than others.[1]

Information Asked for on Application Blanks

A company ordinarily should ask only for information it intends to use, either now or later. Unless a question relates to some standard or job qualification, its presence on a blank may be challenged. However, sometimes a company may ask for personal information so that it can keep records. A seven-part classification of sales job qualifications—mental capacities, physical characteristics, experience, education, personality traits, skills, and socioenvironmental factors—was proposed in Chapter 5. An application blank is an excellent tool for getting significant information in three of those categories—physical characteristics, experience, and socioenvironmental factors.

When a certain *physical condition* is a bona fide occupational qualification, a company might ask questions about it. For example:

- The job requires frequent lifting of 60-pound objects. Can you safely perform such a task?

- The job requires much driving of a car and physical activity when calling on customers. Do you have any physical problem that would interfere with the performance of such activities?

On an application blank, **experience requirements** are usually divided into two groups, educational background and work experience. Companies ask questions about educational background because they believe that applicants' performance in school tells something about their mental abilities and personality traits. Anyone who has graduated from high school or college (depending on the firm's requirements) is presumed to have the necessary basic intelligence. Further, a course of study indicates much about a person's interests. Working one's way, at least partially, through school may indicate self-reliance and industry.

Most application blanks ask for information about the candidate's employment history, including periods of unemployment. If a company has certain experience qualifications, the application blank is a good tool for determining whether a candidate meets these requirements. Companies also usually like to know the reasons why a person left each previous job. If possible, the prospective employer should verify these reasons with someone other than the applicant.

Companies ordinarily are interested in the **socioenvironmental qualifications** of prospective employees. Questions may be asked on topics such as the following:

- Membership in social, service, and business organizations.

- Offices held in organizations.
- Hobbies, athletic endeavors, and other outside interests.

Information on the prospect's socioenvironment can be extremely helpful because it reveals something about his or her interests, capabilities, and personality. Active participation in organizations may indicate an ability to meet and mix with people. Holding office may imply leadership traits and administrative abilities.

Once again, remember that questions about age, marital status, religion, or any of the points discussed above must comply with federal laws and regulations.

Personal Interviews

Nature and Purpose

Virtually no salesperson is ever hired without a **personal interview,** and there are no satisfactory substitutes for this procedure. Much has been written about the use of weighted application blanks, various kinds of tests, and other aids in hiring. But none of these tools completely takes the place of getting to know applicants personally by talking to them.

A personal interview is used basically to determine a person's fitness for a job. Moreover, personal interviews disclose characteristics that are not always observable by other means. An interview is probably the best way to find out about the recruit's conversational ability, speaking voice, and social intelligence. By seeing the applicant in person, an executive can appraise physical characteristics such as general appearance and care given to clothes. As noted in a recent survey of 651 executives, image does matter in hiring decisions.[2] (See the box titled "Image Matters.") The interview may also reveal certain personality traits. The interviewer may note the applicant's poise under the strain of an interview, along with any tendency to dominate or lead a conversation.

Another purpose in interviewing is to get further information about or to interpret facts stated on the application blank. For example, an applicant may have written down that he was a district manager in a previous job. The prospective employer may ask what his responsibilities were and how many employees he supervised.

Fundamentally, all the questions asked during an interview are aimed at learning four points about the applicant:

1. Is this person capable of excelling at this job?
2. How badly does this person want the job?
3. Will the job help this person realize his or her goals?
4. Will this person work to his or her fullest ability?

Image Matters: What Type of Sales Rep Would You Avoid Hiring?

This question was posed by a *Sales & Marketing Management* survey of its readers. Their answers follow.

80%	Anyone who was a sloppy dresser
78%	Anyone who used salty language
77%	Anyone who has visible body piercings or tattoos
51%	Anyone who looked unstylish

Source: Adapted from Melinda Ligos, "Does Image Matter?" *Sales & Marketing Management*, March 2001, p. 55.

These points cover the applicant's past behavior, experiences, environment, and motivation. Another set of questions typically deals with an applicant's future goals. Within these broad categories of past behavior and future goals, each firm must select those inquiries that are pertinent for its sales positions.

Finally, the interview is not only a means by which a company determines an applicant's fitness for a job; it is also a tool for "selling" the position and the company to the recruit. The interviewer can help interest applicants by talking about the nature of the job, the compensation, the type of training and supervision provided, and the opportunities for the future.

Reliability of Personal Interviews as Predictors of Success

Interviews are the most widely used selection tool. Although for many occupations interviews are not good predictors of an applicant's subsequent job performance, studies have found that they can be good predictors of success in the sales job.[3] This is due in part to the fact that the sales job requires skills similar to those on display in the interview. Also, it has been discovered that behavioral/performance-based interviews are better predictors of subsequent success than other types of interviews.[4] (This type of interview is discussed later in this chapter.)

Too often, however, interviews are not as effective as they could be. An inherent weakness is that the interviewing process is heavily dependent on the behavior of the interviewer. Unfortunately, many people do not know how to interview an applicant effectively, nor do they know how to interpret an applicant's responses. An interviewer's reactions, for example, can greatly affect an applicant's performance. It is so important, and yet so difficult, for an interviewer to remain completely neutral and consistent through a series of interviews with several applicants. Another problem is that an interviewer's first impression may be based on gut reaction instead of on an objective evaluation of the candidate's qualifications. This reaction is highly subjective and therefore may not be consistent with the impression that other interviewers have. Still another behavioral consideration is that most interviewers talk too much, listen too little, and ask the wrong questions. These factors tend to lower the value of the interviewing process as a selection tool. Consequently, most interviewers do not accomplish their intended goal of matching applicants with hiring specifications and thus predicting job performance. Yet, despite all of these potential shortcomings, a well-planned, properly conducted interview is a valid predictor of performance and should always be used in the selection process.

Improving the Validity of Interviews

There are ways to offset potential weaknesses and improve the validity of interviews as predictors of job performance. It is important for the recruiter to thoroughly review the applicant's résumé or application before proceeding further in the selection process. Sometimes companies use a telephone interview or a brief in-person interview (such as a campus interview or a job fair interview) as part of the initial screening process. The screening step can weed out obviously unqualified or uninterested candidates. It may also highlight certain aspects of the candidate's background that are in need of further investigation.

It is also important to have more than one interview with each candidate. In general, a company should not depend on a single interview held in a single place with a single interviewer. This advice is based on the assumption that the more time a company spends with prospective recruits and the more people who talk with them, the greater the opportunity to get to know them well. Additionally, interviewers should use standardized rating forms that they fill out after each interview with an applicant. Those in charge of hiring can review the information on these forms, evaluate it, and use it for making comparisons among the applicants.

Another way to improve validity is to train interviewers on how to conduct interviews and how to use rating forms. Training sessions that involve practice interviews with a follow-up group discussion can increase the consistency of applicant ratings by the interviewers. Additional suggestions for improving the interviewing process are discussed below.

Interview Structure

Selection interviews can differ according to the extent to which the questions are detailed in advance and the conversation is guided by the interviewer. At one end of the scale is the totally structured or guided interview, and at the other end is the informal or nondirected type.

Guided Interviews

The procedure in a **guided interview** is highly standardized. All interviewers for a firm use the same guide sheet containing a series of questions. The interviewer asks these questions and makes notations concerning the candidate's responses. The guided interview seeks to overcome common problems encountered in using personal interviews as a selection technique. Many sales executives engaged in selection activities do not know what questions to ask. They may know the qualifications for the job, but they do not know what questions will tell them whether the applicant possesses these characteristics.

Also, because all of the applicants are asked the same questions and their responses are recorded, an interviewer working alone can readily compare and rate the candidates he or she has seen. Furthermore, several interviewers who have seen either the same or a different set of candidates have a good basis for comparing their evaluations. Some people criticize the guided interview as being inflexible. But this is not necessarily the case. Trained interviewers can use their judgment and make slight modifications without detracting from the full value of the guided form.

Nondirected Interviews

At the other end of the structured interview scale is the **nondirected interview.** Ordinarily, the interviewer asks a few questions to get the applicant talking on certain subjects, such as his or her business experiences, home life, or school activities. The interviewer does very little talking—just enough to keep the conversation rolling. The theory is that significant characteristics come to light if the applicant is encouraged to speak freely.

The major problem with the nondirected interview is that much time may be wasted unearthing little information. Some of what an applicant says may be irrelevant or impossible to evaluate. Also, the values of standardization are lost in the nondirected interview. Research has demonstrated that this type of interview is not a very accurate predictor of job performance.[5]

Most firms today use an interview format somewhere between the guided and the nondirected interview, such as those described in the next section.

Interview Focus

Many companies now use interviews that focus on the applicant's behavior. One type poses questions concerning candidates' past or intended behaviors that relate to their sales aptitude. Another allows interviewers to observe candidates' performance on selling-related exercises.

Behavior-Based Interviews

Questions that focus on *past behaviors* are based on the premise that what a person has done in the past is indicative of what he or she will do in the future. Applicants who have performed successfully in the past are expected to be successful in the new job. Rubbermaid is a company that uses this type of interview. Looking for clues that indicate how the potential salesperson deals with other people, Rubbermaid's recruiters ask specific questions about how he or she has handled real situations in the past.[6] The following examples contrast traditional and behavior-based questions:

Traditional	Behavior-Based
• Do you get along with people?	• Tell me about any incident in your last job that caused conflict with a customer. What did you do to work it out?
• What qualities do you think are important for success in this job?	• Give me a specific example of a job situation in which you had to use your problem-solving abilities.
• What is your biggest weakness?	• Tell me about your greatest failure.

Focusing on past behaviors is valid if the new job is similar to the old one. However, if the applicant has not had experiences similar to those in the new job, then exploring past behavior becomes less useful. In this case it may be better to ask about *intended behaviors*—how applicants think they would behave in job-related situations. This type of question is based on the premise that people's behavioral intentions are related to their subsequent behavior.

Performance-Based Interviews

Some companies ask candidates to perform *exercises simulating selling situations.* For example, at Copyrite, Inc., candidates first review the annual report and videotapes on the company. Then they are asked to "sell the interviewer on

---

Hiring for Team Synergy

A candidate for a team selling position should possess a set of characteristics different from those of a sales rep who works individually. One critical dimension is how well the person works with others. Another is how well a person will fit into the existing culture of the team. The best way to answer these kinds of questions is to ask the people who know the team members best—that is, ask the team. Involve the team members in determining qualifications, conducting in-terviews, and providing selection recommendations. Some experts are convinced that this is the best way to ensure that the synergy of an excellent team can continue when one or more team members leave and other people are hired.

Source: Adapted from Paul Ludwick, "Teams by Design: Hiring for Synergy," *Public Management*, September 1995, pp. 9–14.

Brainteasers

- You have 12 balls, and one has a different weight than the others. Using a balance (a two-armed scale) only three times, how would you figure out which ball was different and whether it was lighter or heavier? (McKinsey & Co.)

- How many barbers are there in Chicago? (McKinsey & Co.)

- Why are manhole covers round? (Microsoft)

- You are in a room with three light switches. Each one controls one light in the next room. You must figure out which switch controls which bulb. You may flick only two switches, and you may enter the room only once. (Boston Consulting Group)

the company from what they have learned." The Office Place, an office supply and equipment dealer, gives candidates a product ID number and asks them to be prepared to make a presentation on that product during their interviews.[7] These exercises are valuable in showing how much time, effort, skill, and creativity the candidates bring to their presentations.

Stress Interviews

The stress interview is one in which the interviewer intentionally places the applicant under stress. For example, the applicant may be handed an object such as a pen or a notebook and asked to "sell" it to the interviewer. In recent years, a number of companies have been asking interviewees to solve brainteasers and riddles in order to gauge their ability to think quickly and creatively. The answer isn't as important as how one gets there.[8] (Test yourself on the examples in the box titled "Brainteasers.") In some stress interviews, the interviewer may be intentionally rude, silent, or overly aggressive in questioning just to see how the candidate will react. The ultimate performance-based, stressful exercise in sales is one in which the candidate rides with a rep to observe several cold calls and then is asked to make a cold call on his or her own.

These techniques give the interviewer some idea of how the candidate will behave under the stress encountered in the sales job. However, these methods can also irritate applicants and lessen their interest in the job.

Timing and Method of the Interview

During Initial Screening

Because interviewing takes executives' valuable time, the interviewer should quickly find out whether the recruit is interested and qualified. To do this, the interviewer should, first, give a brief job description and, second, ask a few questions concerning the minimum requirements. Many companies conduct an initial *telephone interview.* Figure 6–2 is the patterned interview form used by the Xerox Corporation when a telephone interview is the initial screening device.

Some companies use a *face-to-face interview* as the initial screening device. For example, when recruiting teams visit college campuses, one or more team members may briefly interview a prospect to determine whether that person should be considered further. Initial screening interviews should last only 15 or 20 minutes. Figure 6–3 is a copy of the form that Xerox uses to evaluate a campus interview.

FIGURE 6-2   Telephone screen evaluation

XEROX

Telephone screen evaluation

Applicant	Interviewer	Date

1 Would you tell me about your current job? (Determine whether the applicant has related experience, training, interest, etc.)

2 Why are you looking for a job at this time? (Determine whether reasons are acceptable.)

3 Why are you looking for this particular job at Xerox? (Determine whether the applicant's perceptions of the job are sufficiently accurate.)

4 What background, qualifications, and abilities do you feel you have which would enable you to be successful on this job? (Determine whether the applicant can sell him/herself and whether these qualifications are beneficial.)

5 What are your salary expectations? (Determine whether the applicant is realistic.)

6 Where do you expect to be five years from now? (Determine whether the applicant has sufficient ambition.)

7 When would you be able to start with Xerox? (Determine whether this fits into manpower needs.)

Summary of Applicant's Qualifications

Apparent Strengths:

Apparent Weaknesses:

Interviewer's Recommendations

A. Recommended for testing: ☐ Yes   ☐ No

B. Areas requiring clarification in additional interviews:

Used with permission of the Xerox Corporation.

FIGURE 6-3   Campus interview—evaluation report

XEROX

Campus Interview — Evaluation Report

| C | | | | | | | | | | |

Social Security Number   Applicant's First Name   MI   Last Name   Major   Interview Date Mo. Day Yr

1   10 11   20 21 22   38 39   41 42   47

1

EEO Code   Sex   Degree   Position Interest   College Code   Graduate Date Mo. Day Yr

48   49   50   51   69 70   73 74   79

Interviewer Name (Print)   Employee No.   Org.(ISG, XBS, RTG, etc.)   School

Interviewer's Recommendation (Circle One)

80
1 Invite   Days Avail _____   To Whom/For What

1.

80   80
2 Write-Off   3 Refe   2.

80
4 Employment Department Use Only   3.

Evaluation Criteria	Evaluation (Circle Level)				
	(Does Not Meet Xerox Standards)		(Meets Xerox Standards)		(Exceeds Xerox Standards)
Aggressiveness and Enthusiasm	1	2	3	4	5
Communication Skills	1	2	3	4	5
Record of Success	1	2	3	4	5
Rational Thought Process	1	2	3	4	5
Maturity	1	2	3	4	5
Overall Evaluation	1	2	3	4	5

Summary of Applicant's Qualifications

Apparent Strengths:

Apparent Weaknesses:

Areas Requiring Clarification:

Major Codes: Col. 39-41

305 Finance Gen.	720 Metallurgy
410 Engr Chem.	803 Economics Gen.
422 Engr Electro	815 Political Sc.
428 Engr Industr.	899 Social Sci.
434 Engr Mchncl.	309 Economic Bus.
312 Marketing	420 Engr Electri.
844 Humanities	704 Chemistry
331 Mgt. General	729 Physics
399 Business Gen.	

See College Major Code Table for additional codes.

EEO Codes: Col. 48

1 - Black
2 - Asian or Pacific Islanders
3 - American Indian or Alaskan Native
4 - Hispanic
5 - White

Degrees: Col. 48

1 - Associate
2 - Bachelor
3 - Master
4 - Doctorate

Sex: Col 49

M - Male
F - Female

College Codes: Col. 70-73

See College Code Table for Alphabetical List of codes.

Used with permission of the Xerox Corporation.

Recently, a number of companies, such as AT&T, Shell Oil, and Nike, have started using videoconferencing to interview candidates.[9] The *videoconference interview* can then be replayed multiple times to all those who will take part in the hiring decision. Some companies use in-house systems, whereas others use an outside firm that provides this service. It is expected that use of videoconferencing will increase due to the savings in time and cost it allows.

At Later Stages

Firms that do a thorough selection job ordinarily interview applicants several times before they are hired. After applicants pass through the initial screen, much remains for the company to learn about them before a final decision can be made. In turn, candidates must be told many things about the job. The more time a company spends with prospective recruits and the more people who talk with them, the greater the opportunity to get to know them well. Although telephone interviews and videoconferencing may be used in the earlier stages, final interviews will generally be conducted in person.

Psychological Testing

Psychological testing—which includes everything from intelligence to personality tests—is another major tool often used in the sales selection process. Typically a company uses a battery of psychological tests rather than a single test. Over the years, psychological testing has undoubtedly been the most controversial of all the selection tools. Today the added burden of complying with legal guidelines has increased the complexity and controversy surrounding such testing. Even so, it is becoming increasingly popular as a selection tool.

The increased use of psychological tests has occurred for several reasons. First, employers have become more knowledgeable about the legal requirements surrounding the use of tests. Second, some studies have shown that testing is a better predictor of job performance than any other selection tool.[10] Finally, as the cost of making a poor selection decision continues to rise, employers are turning to testing as an additional means of improving their selection decisions.

Main Types of Tests Used in Sales Force Selection

- **Mental intelligence tests**—intended to measure a person's intelligence quotient (IQ) and general ability to learn. Some examples of these tests are (1) the Otis Self-Administering Test of Mental Ability and (2) the Wonderlic Personnel Test.

- **Aptitude tests**—designed to measure a person's aptitude for selling. This category also includes tests that measure social aptitude (social intelligence). Some examples are (1) the Sales Aptitude Checklist, (2) the General Sales Aptitude Test, and (3) the Diplomacy Test of Empathy.

- **Interest tests**—designed to measure or compare a person's interests with the interests of successful people in specific occupations. Some examples are (1) the Strong-Campbell Interest Inventory and (2) the Kuder Occupational Interest Survey.

- **Personality tests**—intended to measure various personality traits. These tests are the most risky and difficult to validate because of our inability to identify the traits needed for a particular sales job. Some examples of these tests are (1) the Bernreuter Personality Inventory, (2) the Edwards Personal Preference Schedule, (3) the Multiple Personal Inventory, and (4) the Gordon Personal Profile.

Legal Aspects of Testing

Although federal legislation put restraints on the use of testing in the selection process, *testing is legal*. In fact, a testing and selection order issued by the Office of Federal Contract Compliance says that "properly validated and standardized employee selection procedures can significantly contribute to the implementation of nondiscriminatory personnel policies" and that "professionally developed tests . . . may significantly aid in the development and maintenance of an efficient work force." The key phrases in this quotation are *properly validated* and *professionally developed*. These requirements are discussed below.

A Framework for Testing

Ideally, tests should provide objective information about a candidate's skills and abilities. Companies can and should use this information to support what is discovered in the interview process or to uncover areas to explore during the interview. It is important to remember that no test can predict with 100 percent accuracy. Therefore, the results should *not* be used as the sole acceptance or knockout factor. Accordingly, the test results should not include a hiring recommendation. Rather, it is the responsibility of the hiring manager to decide whether the psychological profile is correct for the job in question.[11]

Selecting and Developing Tests

In building a good testing program, a company should use tests that measure the criteria developed during the planning phase of the hiring process. The firm can develop in-house tests with the aid of company or outside psychologists. Alternatively, it can use tests professionally developed by outside consulting firms such as the Klein Behavioral Science Consultants or the Austin Technology Incubator (ATI) Company. Typically, tests developed outside have a broad usage base, which makes validation less complicated and less costly.

Conditions When Testing Is Most Effective

A program for testing in sales selection is most likely to be effective when any of the following conditions exist:

- The firm hires a relatively large number of salespeople and management wants to improve its success ratio.

- The company is hiring young, inexperienced people about whom little is known. (If experienced reps are being selected, their performance records rather than test results should be the criterion.)

- The executives who interview recruits are not adept at discovering personality traits and selling aptitudes. Normally, executives with a great deal of experience in hiring do a much better job of interviewing than do administrators who are new at the job.

- In companies where the cost of failure is high, the expense of testing may be considered a small investment to ensure that no one slips through the selection screen. If the testing procedure prevents just one failure a year, the costs of the testing may be justified.

- The executives can competently interpret the psychologist's recommendations and feel free to act on their own judgment regardless of the tests.

However, many testing specialists and managers agree that the variable requirements of different sales jobs call for customized tests. Many firms use customized sales aptitude tests to identify behaviors that are critical to a specific sales position.[12]

Companies should validate each test they use as part of the selection process. As discussed earlier in this chapter, this means that the company should be able to demonstrate a relationship between test results and the performance of its salespeople. If the company is using standard tests supplied by an outside consulting firm, the supplier should provide proof of the tests' validity. If the company has developed customized tests, it must validate them.

Problems in Testing[13]

Most testing procedures generate the concept of an average or normal type of employee. The implication is that this person is the best to hire for a given job. The danger is that a potentially successful sales representative may be screened out simply because he or she does not fit the stereotype. Testing may eliminate a truly creative person who does not fall in the average or normal range in testing. The creativity that does not measure well on a standardized test may be the very trait that would make that person an outstanding sales representative.

Another problem with testing is that tests are sometimes used as the sole deciding knockout factor. An applicant may look good based on interviews, the application blanks, and reference checks. But if the test scores are especially low, management may be reluctant to hire that person.

Tests are sometimes misused because executives fail to apply the concept of a *range* of scores. For many kinds of tests, psychologists agree that a range of scores is acceptable. All who fall within that range should be judged as *equally qualified for the job*. Unfortunately, most people tend to feel that a person scoring near the high end of the acceptable range is a better prospect than one scoring in the lower part of that range.

Another factor to watch for in testing is that applicants can fake the answers on some tests, especially on some personality or interest tests. Reasonably intelligent applicants for a sales job know they should indicate a preference for mixing with people, in contrast to staying home and reading a good book. Cultural bias is another situation that can creep into tests. A person may score poorly, not because of a lack of interest, aptitude, or native intelligence, but only because the test included questions that assumed a certain cultural background.

References and Other Outside Sources

When processing applicants for sales jobs, an administrator can get help from two general sources of information outside the company. In the first, the applicant furnishes the leads, name, phone number, e-mail address, or other contact information of a person who is familiar with his or her experience or aptitude; this is called a **reference.** In the other, the company solicits information on its own initiative; this source includes credit and insurance reports, school records, and motor vehicle histories.

A company may check an applicant's references by letter, telephone, or personal visit. Each method has some limitations. A personal visit may take too much time, and it is not practical unless the reference is located near the prospective employer. Using a personal visit or the telephone is advantageous because nothing is in writing. However, some references, especially those at companies with strict policies in this area, will not supply information to a stranger over the telephone. A letter is probably used more frequently than the two other methods, but often it is of very little value. Firms hesitate to put anything derogatory in writing. This leads us to the big problem today with any kind of a reference check. Companies are extremely leery about giving out meaningful information regarding former employees. Reference policies may, in effect, put a tight rein on the employee information they release. This situation has developed because companies fear being sued for defamation of character.

Despite the obstacles, management should not bypass references as a selection tool. If only one significant fact is uncovered, it makes the effort worthwhile. When talking with an applicant's former employer, a key question to ask is: Would you rehire this person? Additional questions that may provide some insights are: In which areas does the applicant need improvement? Why did the applicant leave? Did performance in the applicant's territory go up or down after he or she left? For the reasons noted above, companies generally give very positive references only to those people who deserve them and say little, except to verify information, about those whose performance was inadequate.

Most people list as references only those who are certain to give them a positive reference. In order to get a more balanced picture of the candidate, you can ask the reference for the names of several other people who would be familiar with the applicant's work. Also, if you are hiring salespeople with experience, the best reference source is the candidate's previous customers. They can provide an accurate picture of the salesperson's skills or personality. Questions that should be asked are: How would you rank this person compared to other salespeople who currently call on you? Was this person genuinely interested in serving your needs? Was the candidate efficient and dependable?

Background Checks

A special source of outside information is the **credit report,** or a report from some other investigating agency. These agencies specialize in preemployment investigative interviews with former employers, co-workers, neighbors, and creditors. Reports from local credit bureaus, through their affiliation with their national association, can provide a wealth of information on a prospective salesperson. Often, former employers and other references give information to a credit bureau that they would not divulge to a prospective employer. Several companies—Equifax and Fidelifacts/Metropolitan New York, for example—specialize in providing preemployment data to employers. Using information from several different databases, they provide summaries of the applicant's financial condition, criminal and driving records, and employment history.

Today, reference checks and other forms of background investigation are critical because, sad to say, too many job applicants lie about their backgrounds. Some applicants lie about their educational record, past salaries, and/or past job responsibilities. Career fraud—that's the fancy name for it—often goes undetected, simply because many companies don't take the time and effort needed to do a thorough background check.

Drug Testing and Drug Use

One controversial issue related to the sales selection process today is whether companies should test applicants for drug use before making hiring decisions. If the answer is yes, then the next question is: If an applicant tests positive, is this an automatic knockout factor in the selection process? Or, if the applicant is otherwise highly qualified, will the company proceed with hiring on the condition that the applicant will undergo counseling or other drug treatment? Whatever the answers to these questions, this point seems clear: A company should have a clearly stated policy about drug testing and drug use for its sales force and also its sales managers. Sales managers will continue to face these and other such controversial issues.

Legal Considerations

Essentially any question that is illegal to ask a candidate is also illegal to ask a reference. All inquiries should be job related. One step companies can take to lessen the legal liability that occurs in checking references is to ask the candidate to sign a release form that gives the company permission to contact previous employers, educational institutions, and so on. Employers may run credit checks on applicants without informing them. But if candidates are rejected on the basis of a credit check, they must be informed of this.

Assessment Centers

An **assessment center** is another hiring tool a company can use as part of its sales force selection process. A company sets up an area in which it conducts a lengthy assessment experience. Candidates are given simulated exercises that they must address as if they were in a real organization.[14] Such exercises may involve business games, case analyses, leaderless discussion groups, role-playing, or individual presentations. The assessment is conducted by trained executive observers and usually takes from one to three days. Assessment centers have been used primarily to evaluate people for promotion within a firm and to aid in an individual's professional development. However, they have also been used in selecting new salespeople. AT&T uses assessment centers to evaluate candidates for account management positions. The main factor limiting the use of this tool is probably its high cost.

The Job Offer Decision

When all the steps in the selection process have been completed, one thing remains to be done. A company must decide whether to make a job offer. This decision involves a review of everything known about each applicant. What detailed impressions have the applicants made? What are their qualifications, and what is their potential? What do they want, and what can the firm offer them? This last point is far broader than just the monetary aspects of the job. It involves all the hopes and ambitions of each applicant as matched against the opportunities and rewards offered by the job and the company.

Recruiting reps for foreign assignments, whether they are nationals or internationals, is difficult.

Ranking the Recruits

The hiring company should develop two lists: The first is a list of the recruits in the order of the firm's preference for them; the second is a list of the recruits in the order of their preference for the firm. The second list can be developed by the firm's interviewers according to how interested the recruits seemed in joining the firm during the interviews.

Should the firm make offers to those who top its preference list regardless of their apparent interest? The decision depends on the depth of the list, the decrease in quality as people of lesser rank are considered, the amount of money involved, the time factors faced by both the recruits and the sales managers, and competing offers from other firms. The costly recruiting and selection process can be completely nullified if the person or people selected do not accept the firm's offer.

Communicating with Applicants

At this stage, it is important that the company not leave any applicant dangling. If the firm clearly has decided *not* to hire a certain applicant, an executive should gently, but clearly, tell the person. To those applicants who are still in contention for the job, an executive might say something like this at the close of an interview: "As you know, we have several people applying for this position. My hope is that we will move along in the process and be able to notify you one way or another in two weeks."

If the decision is to hire a certain person, the next step is to make a formal offer and persuade the person to accept it.

The Hiring Phase

A well-designed **hiring** process properly implemented tells the recruit that the firm is well managed and that it really wants the recruit as an employee. Sometimes firms inadvertently send a message of indifference to the recruit: "It's no big deal one way or the other to us if you take the job." Remember that everyone likes to feel important. People seek work environments in which they are made to feel that they somehow make a difference, that they are important to the company.

Extending the Offer

What Will Be Included in the Offer?

The most important part of the offer is, of course, the compensation that the salesperson will be paid. The type and amount of compensation are covered in detail in Chapter 9. The offer should also include the other benefits that will be part of the employment package. These might include any or all of the following: insurance, retirement contributions, vacation pay, educational benefits, profit sharing, a company car. In many cases, to alleviate some of the inconveniences of moving, the new employee's relocation expenses are also paid. Most large companies usually pay for moving expenses when they transfer employees.

A number of firms now also offer to help the potential employee's spouse or significant other find a job. While this may not need to be a part of the formal offer, it may be a very important consideration in the candidate's decision. As more families have come to include two people who are pursuing careers, it has become important that both people are able to find good employment opportunities in the same location. Helping the other person identify job opportunities will certainly create a very positive impression on the candidate—and could be the factor that causes the recruit to accept one firm's offer over another attractive offer.

How Will the Offer Be Extended?

Who will make the offer? How will it be made? Will a contract be written up? Some firms want the sales manager for whom the recruit will be working to make the offer. Other firms leave such matters to professionals in the human resources department. Sometimes high-level executives, even the company president, may make the offer in the hope of impressing the recruit with the importance of the job.

Most job offers are initially made over the telephone. Before picking up the phone, the sales manager must make two important decisions: (1) How much time will be allowed for acceptance? and (2) What concessions will be made if the recruit wants to negotiate some of the terms of the deal? Once on the telephone, the manager will have to make some quick decisions about these matters. Prior consideration greatly facilitates a smooth telephone offer. A formal letter follows only if the candidate accepts the telephone offer. This letter is very important and requires careful wording since it becomes a contract.

Aggressive managers often prefer to make job offers in person. This puts more pressure on the recruit to respond favorably and quickly. It is quite easy for the recruit to avoid giving direct answers over the telephone. Moreover, the telephone does not allow the manager to read the recruit's body language to make additional judgments about the negotiations.

Socialization and Assimilation

Socialization is the process through which the new recruits take on the values and attitudes of the people who are already working for the firm. This process

---

A DAY-TO-DAY OPERATING PROBLEM

MAJESTIC PLASTICS COMPANY

MAJESTIC
Plastics Company

Extending a Job Offer

"I need some time to think about your offer, Mr. Brion. I feel that changing jobs is a serious matter, and I don't want to act precipitously. The job does appeal to me and definitely would be a step up for me. Can I give you an answer March 1?" asked Sharon Axe in her reply to Clyde Brion's job offer over the telephone on a dreary day in early February 2002.

Brion had been under considerable pressure from his boss to hire a woman sales rep for the sales territory that had been vacated when one of the firm's older reps had retired. He had recruited and interviewed four experienced saleswomen, all of whom were qualified for the job. However, Axe stood out as the most promising one.

After consulting with his boss, Brion had called Axe to make her the firm's standard job offer. He was somewhat surprised by her request for time to think

about it; he thought she wanted the job and was eager to get going.

He also was eager to get the position filled because many of the accounts in the territory had voiced some concern about the company's inattention to their needs during the past few weeks. Brion had been trying to cover the territory as best he could, but the time he could spend doing it was limited.

Brion stalled for a few moments, making some pleasant remarks about how happy he was that Axe liked Majestic Plastics, but he had to reply to her request for time *now*.

Question: Exactly what should Clyde Brion say to Sharon Axe?

Note: See the introduction to this series of problems in Chapter 4 for the necessary background on the company, its market, and its competition.

---

begins before recruits go to work for the company and continues until they are fully assimilated into the company's culture. Successful socialization of recruits and new salespeople helps them adjust to their new jobs. More important, it also leads to increased involvement and job satisfaction in the long run.

Pre-entry Socialization

Both before accepting the offer and during the preemployment period, the recruits will start thinking about the experiences they are about to encounter, and they will begin to prepare themselves mentally. It is critical that the candidates be provided with realistic **job previews** that allow them to make informed employment decisions. Having accurate information about the job and the company helps the recruit form realistic expectations about the challenges to be faced and the level of effort and the kinds of skills required to meet these challenges. It also allows recruits to decide whether there is congruence between their values and those of the company. After a recruit accepts the offer, realism at the preemployment stage will lead to greater satisfaction with the job and commitment to the company.[15]

Most firms start indoctrinating the recruit the minute initial contact is made. Booklets describe the operations of the company and its distinctive qualities. These publications are part of the recruiting process described in Chapter 5. Further introductory work is done in the selection interviews, as discussed in this chapter. The sales executive describes the company's operations and answers the recruit's questions. The thoroughness of the interview will tell the recruit something about the organization even before the offer is made.

Many firms go a step further in presenting a realistic picture by asking recruits to view a videotape of the salesperson on the job. Northwestern Mutual Life, IBM, and Deloitte & Touche are among the firms providing the recruits with interactive diskettes that are filled with information on the job and the company. Deloitte & Touche information categories include information on the company's mission and shared values statement, an overview of the firm, details on training, employee benefits, and professional development opportunities.[16] Some firms ask recruits to spend a day making calls with a salesperson so that they will have a more realistic perspective of what the job entails.

Procter & Gamble, Ford Motor Company, American Express, Dow Brands, Nortel Networks, and many other companies that hire college graduates for sales positions offer summer internships for students. These internships allow students to learn about the company before they make a long-term commitment. Likewise, many of these companies are relying more on internships to help them assess whether the potential employees can do the job and whether they fit into the culture of the company.[17]

The more recruits understand about the company and its culture before making a decision, the more effective their self-selection will be. That is, those people who fit in the company's culture are more likely to accept the offer than those who don't. Also, the more information recruits get at this stage, the smoother their assimilation into the organization will be.

Assimilation of New Hires

The second stage in the socialization process—**assimilation**—begins when the recruits accept the position. The newly hired employees must learn how to perform the tasks associated with their jobs, and they must become familiar with the people in various work groups with whom they must interact. In many companies a great deal of this information will be covered in an initial training program. However, assimilation cannot be accomplished exclusively through training. There must be a conscious effort made to provide recruits with information, experience, and the personal attention that will enable them to understand the informal as well as the formal norms and values of the corporate culture.

It is especially difficult to assimilate new sales reps when they are thrust into a sales territory with no home-office training. The new person has little opportunity to become integrated with the work group. For this reason, it is usually advisable to keep new salespeople around the home office long enough to get to know the employees in supporting departments very well.

The first few days are particularly trying, since the new person has not had time to develop communications with the other members of the organization and must look to the manager for answers. The manager should give as much time as possible to starting the trainee in the right direction. A good technique is to confer with the new employee at the beginning of each day, for a time, to answer questions and present new material. The trainee should be encouraged to ask questions about the job and the company.

New sales reps appreciate this attention. It makes them feel wanted and valued by the company—something most individuals earnestly seek. One of the quickest ways to affect people's attitudes adversely is to ignore them. New reps may interpret a lack of attention to mean that the sales manager does not care about them, even if the truth is that the executive is just preoccupied with operational problems. It comes as quite a blow to new workers to encounter such apparent lack of interest, since they were given so much attention while they were

This new rep gets a warm welcome.

being interviewed. If the honeymoon ends abruptly, the new hires may believe their recruitment was just sales talk and they should have known better than to be taken in by it. The wise sales manager will try to prolong the honeymoon until the new people can take their places in the organization with confidence.

Relationships

A new rep needs to know from whom to take orders. The entire organizational plan should be explained so that the rep knows his or her relationship to others, who else reports to the rep's immediate boss, and to whom the boss reports in the department and the company. The support staff must be informed of their relationship to the new person. Those who report to the same boss must become acquainted with their new workmate, and other employees should also be informed about the position the new rep occupies.

Introductions are a two-way street—a new salesperson is eager to meet other employees, and they want to meet him or her. The introductions should be so arranged that those involved have enough time to do more than just say hello. A short chat with each person is helpful. It allows people to form more than a quick impression of each other, and it helps them to remember names. Present employees should be given background information on the new salesperson so that they can converse on some common ground. The new rep should be briefed on the people to be met—who they are, what they do, and what their interests are.

Mentoring New Employees

A **mentor** is someone with knowledge, experience, rank, or power who provides personal counseling and career guidance for younger employees. Many of the nation's major companies, such as Xerox, General Electric, and Pacific Bell, have formal mentoring programs. The goals of these programs are to make the employees feel comfortable in their new jobs, to teach them the corporate culture, to give them someone to whom they can turn when they need support or advice, and in some cases to push them up the corporate ladder.

There are three types of mentoring programs. The first is one in which a senior manager is assigned to each of the new sales reps for a period of a year or sometimes a little longer. This manager advises, teaches, and helps the rep learn the corporate culture. Because this person is supposed to be a friend as well as an adviser, the mentor is never the employee's direct boss. Rather, the mentor should not have the authority to fire or promote the employee.

A second form of mentoring involves co-workers who are chosen to be the new reps' advisers/trainers. Senior salespeople are assigned to the new sales reps and are expected to teach them the ropes. In some cases, especially in small companies, the mentor is also the primary trainer, teaching product knowledge and basic selling skills. Again because of the importance of the personal relationship between the mentor and the employee, companies should take care to assign a mentor who does not or will not have any direct authority over the new rep.

The third type of mentoring is an informal process in which a senior executive selects a younger salesperson or manager and helps him or her climb the corporate ladder. A well-placed mentor inside the company can protect the reps' interests in the company's political arena as well as help them advance if their talents warrant it. The mentor knows the cast of characters and can provide valuable advice.

It is comforting to know that some firms recognize the difficulties encountered by newly hired employees in being integrated into both the company and the community and are *doing* something about it.

Meeting Social and Psychological Needs

An individual's assimilation into the organization involves considerably more than just getting started on the job. He or she should be socially integrated into the new environment. Newly hired salespeople too often are thrust into a strange city, their children are upset, and their new home is not as comfortable as the old one—conditions that hardly foster efficiency at work. The sales manager is in a

An International Perspective

A new job not only affects the person accepting the job; it may affect two, three, or four other people as well. Certainly the person with the new position welcomes the opportunity. However, the spouse may face leaving a good job for a lesser position or, even worse, no job. Their children, too, are affected by the need to leave their schools and friends. When the new position is a foreign one, these problems are compounded by the challenge of facing an unfamiliar culture. If candidates feel that their families will be unhappy, they may not accept the offer. The National Foreign Trade Council reports that 81 percent of relocation candidates turn down the opportunity because of family-related problems.

To attract salespeople to foreign assignments, the company must provide support for the entire family. In some cases, financial support may be less important than helping the spouse find a job or helping the family find schools for the children. It is also important that the company provide the family with predeparture cultural training so that their expectations will be realistic.

Source: Michele Marchetti, "Enticing Families to Move Overseas," *Sales & Marketing Management*, September 1996, pp. 44–45.

position to cushion the shock of social uprooting by providing some social activities and contacts. The manager should take positive steps to see that recruits and their families get into activities in which they are interested. The golfer should be worked into a foursome, and the bridge player invited to join an established group.

The job itself also plays an important social role. Co-workers are an obvious reference group because employees often spend more time with their co-workers than with their families. People often derive a great deal of satisfaction from the personal relationships they develop on the job. The sales manager can help new employees initiate these relationships by bringing them together with their co-workers in social situations.

Summary

The third phase in the sales force selection process involves (1) developing a system of tools and procedures to measure the applicants against the predetermined hiring specifications, and (2) actually using this system to select the salespeople. Processing applicants is a key activity in implementing a company's strategic planning. When using any selection tool, management must make certain that it is complying with all pertinent laws and regulatory guidelines.

The application blank and the personal interview are the two most widely used selection tools. A short application blank may be used as an initial screening device. A longer application blank is a primary source of personal history information that can be used in hiring and in other phases of sales operations. An application blank is an excellent tool for getting information in three major categories of job qualifications—namely, the applicant's physical condition, experience, and socioenvironmental information.

The personal interview, which is the most widely used of all selection tools, is designed to answer four questions regarding an applicant: (1) Is the person capable of excelling at this job? (2) How badly does the person want the job? (3) Will the job help the person realize his or her goals? (4) Will the person work to his or her fullest ability?

Unfortunately, interviews are not always an accurate predictor of job performance, because too many people don't know how to interview. The predictive validity can be improved by using more than one interview, with more than one interviewer, in more than one place. Training the interviewers, providing a reasonable amount of structure to the interview, and using behavior-based interviews can also improve the process.

Interviews may vary according to (1) structure (guided versus nondirected interviews); (2) focus (behavior- versus performance-based interviews, or stress interviews); and (3) timing and method (early or late, telephone or face-to-face). Some companies are using videoconferencing to conduct interviews.

Psychological testing is another major selection tool, and researchers consider it the best tool for predicting job performance. The most commonly used tests cover four areas—mental intelligence, aptitudes, interests, and personality. There are some problems in using tests as part of the hiring process. Also, testing is more likely to be successful when firms are hiring a large number of inexperienced people using inexperienced recruiters, when the cost of failure is high, and when executives are free to use their own judgment.

Reference checks are widely used in the sales selection process. A personal visit or a phone call to a reference usually is a better method than letter writing. A key question to ask is whether the reference would hire the applicant. Credit reports and other outside sources may supplement reference checks. Assessment centers, the final hiring tool discussed briefly in this chapter, allow hiring companies to observe candidates perform simulated exercises.

Once acceptable recruits have been identified, the fourth phase of the staffing process begins: hiring.

During preoffer planning, the acceptable recruits should be ranked. Then the company must decide what will be included in the offer and how it will be extended. The offer should include the compensation and the benefits. Some firms also offer to help the spouse or significant other find a job. Most offers specify a time by which the offer must be accepted.

Much of the sales recruit's long-run success with a company depends on the fifth and final phase of the staffing process: socialization and assimilation. There is much to learn about the company, its people, and how things are done in the organization. The initial socialization begins during the preemployment period as the reps hear and read about the jobs they will soon begin. The second stage is the actual assimilation into the firm. During this period, the reps should become familiar with the firm's operation and employees. Many firms are using mentoring programs to help salespeople feel comfortable in their new jobs.

In order to retain salespeople, companies must integrate them fully into the firm. The desire for social acceptance in the work group is so strong that the recruit who fails to gain it will probably quit. The sales manager can help employees initiate relationships by bringing the new employees together with their co-workers in social situations.

Key Terms

Application blank
Assessment center
Assimilation
Bona fide occupational
   qualifications (BFOQs)
Credit report
Experience requirements

Guided interview
Hiring
Job previews
Mentor
Nondirected interview
Personal interview
Psychological testing

Reference
Socialization
Socioenvironmental
   qualifications
Validation

Questions and Problems

1. In the application form that an aptitude testing firm has prepared for sales positions, the following questions are asked. In each case, what do you think is the purpose of the question?
   a) What is the most monotonous task you ever did?
   b) In people you like, what do you like about them?
   c) What has been the outstanding disappointment in your life?
   d) What is your best friend's strongest criticism of you?

2. How may the limitations of the interview be eliminated, reduced, or counterbalanced?

3. When interviewing an applicant for a sales job, management ordinarily should be vitally interested in complete answers to the following three questions:

   a) How badly does the applicant want or need the job?
   b) Can the job furnish the applicant with the success he or she wants, or offer the applicant the opportunity to realize his or her goals in life?
   c) Will the applicant strive to achieve the level of work his or her capacity will allow?

   Prepare a series of questions an interviewer might ask the applicant so that the company can answer these three questions following the interview.

4. What are the advantages and disadvantages of using videoconferencing to interview sales candidates?

5. What are the potential drawbacks in soliciting references from a candidate's former customers?

6. Can you eliminate the personal biases and prejudices of interviewers so that they will conduct an interview impartially? Explain.

7. Suppose that halfway through your interview for a job in which you are very interested, the interviewer says, "I don't think you are right for this job." How would you respond?

8. What is the point of asking a recruit during an interview, "How many golf balls would it take to fill the swimming pool at the Summer Olympics?"

9. What are some of the problems or dangers in using tests as part of the sales force selection process?

10. Many sales managers claim that the real factor that determines whether people will be successful in selling is their motivation for hard work. Where is this motivational factor measured in psychological testing? How should sales managers determine a person's motivation to do a good job?

11. Some managers believe that the reference is not very helpful as a selection tool. Do you agree with this appraisal? If so, why do you think it continues to be used by virtually every firm that is hiring salespeople or other employees?

12. How could a candidate's ethical standards be evaluated in the interview process?

13. One recruit you want to hire stands out above all the others you interviewed. You make her an offer that is standard throughout your medium-sized company, which has a commissioned sales force of 33 reps. The recruit wants a higher initial salary for the first year before going onto commission. Normally, all trainees are paid $2,500 a month plus expenses for the first year. The recruit demands $3,000. The average commissioned sales rep makes $84,000 a year after four years in the field. What would you do?

14. A sales manager made the following statement: "I don't lose any sleep over it when one of my reps leaves for another position. Generally, it's the people who don't quite fit in who leave." Evaluate this manager's statement.

15. To what extent can members of the peer group facilitate a trainee's assimilation into the work group? How could management encourage such efforts?

Experiential Exercises

A. **Step 1:** Ask 10 of your peers what are or will be the most important considerations in their job search decisions.

Step 2: Develop a brief questionnaire that asks respondents to rank the factors you uncovered in Step 1.

Step 3: Administer the questionnaire to 20 of your peers. Summarize the results in a report.

B. **Step 1:** Change the wording on the questionnaire developed above from "Rank the criteria below according to their importance to you in accepting a job" to "Rank the criteria below according to the importance that you feel that students will place on them in their job searches."

Step 2: Administer the questionnaire to 20 recruiters who visit your campus.

Step 3: Summarize the results in a brief report. Also in your report, compare the responses of the recruiters to the responses of your peers.

C. Interview three recruiters from three different companies. (These should be companies with whom you will *not* have interviews.) Ask them to describe the qualities they are looking for in the candidates they interview. Ask them what questions, exercises, and/or other strategies they use to get at this information.

Internet Exercises

A. There are numerous Internet sites that provide advice on searching for and getting a job. Visit the sites listed below and report on what services (in addition to job listings) each one provides.
  a) CareerBuilder (www.careerbuilder.com)
  b) Monster.com (www.monster.com)
  c) Career Lab (www.careerlab.com)

B. Visit the websites of three Fortune 500 companies and answer the following questions:
  a) What specific information is provided that may be considered part of the preemployment process?
  b) Which of these companies does the best job of preemployment socialization through its website? Why do you think so?

References

1. Myron Gable, Charles Hollow, and Frank Angelo, "Increasing the Utility of the Application Blank: Relationship between Job Application and Turnover of Salespeople," *Journal of Personal Selling & Sales Management* (Summer 1992), pp. 39–55.

2. Melinda Ligos, "Does Image Matter?" *Sales & Marketing Management*, March 2001, pp. 53–56.

3. E. James Randall and Cindy H. Randall, "Review of Salesperson Selection Techniques and Criteria: A Managerial Approach," *International Journal of Research in Marketing* 7 (1990), pp. 81–95.

4. George F. Dreher and Thomas W. Dougherty, *Human Resource Strategy: A Behavioral Perspective for the General Manager* (Boston: McGraw-Hill Higher Education, 2001), p. 107; and Julia Lawler, "Highly Classified," *Sales & Marketing Management*, March 1995, pp. 75–85.

5. Dreher and Dougherty; *Human Resource Strategy*, p. 107.

6. Mark McMaster, "Ask SMM," *Sales & Marketing Management*, December 2001, p. 58.

7. William Keenan Jr., "Who Has the Right Stuff?" *Sales & Marketing Management*, August 1993, pp. 28–29.

8. Nina Munk and Suzanne Oliver, "Think Fast," *Forbes*, March 24, 1997, pp. 146–51.

9. Dan Hanover, "Hiring Gets Cheaper and Faster," *Sales & Marketing Management*, March 2000, p. 87.

10. Richard Nelson, "Maybe It's Time to Take Another Look at Tests as a Selection Tool?" *Journal of Personal Selling & Sales Management*, August 1987, pp. 33–38.

11. Geoffrey Brewer, "Professionally Speaking," *Sales & Marketing Management*, February 1996, p. 27.

12. Elana Harris, "Reducing the Recruiting Risks," *Sales & Marketing Management*, May 2000, p. 18.

13. For additional information on evaluating and using psychological tests in the selection process, see "Standards for Educational and Psychological Testing," from the American Psychological Association, Washington, DC; and "Principles for Validation and Use of Personal Selection Procedures," from the Society

for Industrial and Organizational Psychology Association Inc., a division of the American Psychological Association in Arlington Heights, IL.

14. Dreher and Dougherty, *Human Resource Strategy*, p. 107.

15. David H. Rylander and Philip H. Wilson, "Socialization of Salespersons: Framework for a Dynamic Environment," working paper pre-

pared for American Marketing Association Winter Marketing Educators' Conference, 2002, pp. 6, 12.

16. Ginger Trumifio, "Recruiting Goes High Tech," *Sales & Marketing Management*, April 1995, pp. 42–44.

17. As reported by the Indiana University School of Business Placement Office, 2002.

CASE 6-1   DELTA PRODUCTS COMPANY

Selection of Sales Representation

"We were formerly employed at TRW—Jim was in microelectronics marketing as a salesperson, and I worked inside to provide technical assistance and service to Jim's accounts. We were a team. Our division was directly hit with the defense and aerospace reductions in 1999. We were terminated. They call us displaced workers." Christina Alvarez and her partner Jim Reynolds were explaining their sales proposition to Tom Shilling, marketing manager for the Delta Products Company.

Alvarez continued, "But we have had enough of working for other companies. We decided to form our own marketing company, Pacific Technical Sales. We will do for other companies exactly what we did for TRW. That is, we will sell microelectronic devices, except we will do it for a commission instead of a salary and all the benefits. And we'll do it for several noncompeting companies. We will not sell anything for another company that you are prepared to make. No conflicts of interest!"

Jim Reynolds came in on cue. "We propose to represent your firm in California, Arizona, and Nevada for a commission base of 5 percent. That rate will be renegotiated for significant contracts in which highly competitive bidding is encountered."

Tom Shilling asked, "And what about business that walks through our door in which you played no role?"

Alvarez replied, "Each week we would furnish you a list of the firms that we have contacted, and we would be protected on those accounts for six months. Everything is spelled out in this portfolio, which explains who we are, what we have done, and what we can do for you."

"I know you need time to consider our proposal, for it is a departure from your previous policy of having your own salesperson in the field. However, since your local sales rep no longer is with you and market conditions have changed considerably, we think you should consider retaining our firm instead of hiring another salesperson," Reynolds declared. "Is it convenient for you to see us next Monday morning at 11 for your answer?"

Tom Shilling studied his bulging day book and replied, "Monday is really bad for me. I'm all jammed up. Besides, I need more time to consult with the boss about it. This would be a pretty big change for us to make. I can hire salespeople without talking it over with anyone, but you are another matter. No, I'll have to do a lot of talking with some people before I can give you an answer. Let's make it next Thursday morning at 11."

Alvarez and Reynolds departed as Shilling rose and cordially walked them to the front door. He said, "I'll take your portfolio home tonight and give it a close look, and tomorrow I'll get with Mr. Gross, our president, about it."

Shilling intended to encourage the two people because he faced a serious problem trying to maintain field sales representation in the declining, highly competitive markets being faced.

Delta Products Company designed and manufactured small electronic devices for other manufacturers that incorporated them into whatever products they made. It did business all over the world; international sales accounted for 35 percent of its business. Sales in California, Arizona, and Nevada had accounted for about 10 percent of the company's sales during the 1980s but had dropped to only 4 percent by 1999 because of the firm's historical dependence on sales to firms in the defense and aerospace industries. Shilling had already started strong sales programs to solicit business from new accounts outside the defense/aerospace industry.

However, the cost of the field sales force had become a burden. Shilling had terminated the firm's salesperson, Herb Hawkins, for the California/Arizona/Nevada region. Hawkins's selling costs had soared way out of line because of a significant drop in sales in the region. His total selling costs for 1998 had been $192,466, of which $85,000 had been his salary. No bonuses had been paid, since his performance had been below expectations. The bulk of his expenses had been for automotive and entertainment costs. Hawkins had been with Delta since its inception in 1980. He was its leading producer for years when his territory was the focus of much defense and aerospace activity.

In a rather disturbing meeting with Hawkins, Shilling had reviewed the situation with him and declared that the company could no longer afford $192,000 to cover his territory. He then told Hawkins that the firm could afford to pay only 5 percent of sales for field-selling costs. Based on Hawkins's 1998 sales volume, this meant a total cost of $116,000. Consequently, Shilling had told Hawkins that his 2000 salary would be $50,000 plus some bonuses for meeting quotas, with an expense allowance not to exceed $60,000. No more lavish entertaining and no more paying more than $30,000 for a car. Hawkins had a strong preference for driving vehicles costing well in excess of what could be deducted for income tax purposes.

Herb Hawkins had rejected the offer. He was 63 years old, and since the combination of his company pension plan, his savings, and Social Security would exceed what was being offered him, he decided to take early retirement.

Shilling did not immediately begin a search for Hawkins's replacement. He felt that he could use the savings from not having a salesperson in the area to help meet his budget deficits for the year. He was in no hurry to replace Hawkins since he felt he and the staff could serve the existing accounts from the home office in Redondo Beach, California. However, while attending a trade show, Shilling had occasion to renew acquaintance with Brian Snowcroft, with whom he had worked closely when they both were at Hughes Aircraft in the early 1980s. He thought highly of Snowcroft's talents and knowledge of the industry. He recalled Snowcroft's background: He had graduated from Arizona State with a degree in electrical engineering. After starting to work for Hughes in Tucson, Arizona, on a classified technical project, he had been thrust into contract relationships because of his excellent customer skills. He enjoyed great success with Hughes but was about to be put adrift due to the cutbacks Hughes was making. He had only three more months before he was going to be on the street looking for work.

Shilling told Snowcroft of his situation with Hawkins and asked him if he would be interested in it. Snowcroft did not say no, and he was not indignant when told of the reduced compensation package. He was told he would not have to move to Redondo Beach but could cover the territory from his home in Tucson. It was left that, if Snowcroft was interested in the job and wanted to talk about it some more, he would call Shilling.

Sunday night Tom Shilling settled down in his lounge chair to study the Alvarez–Reynolds proposal. He was impressed with it. Friday afternoon he had called a friend of his at TRW to ask her to investigate the records of both Alverez and Reynolds at TRW. She had reported back within the hour that their records were spotless. They were both well thought of and highly recommended. They had been terminated only because of the cutback of all employees.

As Shilling was thinking about the matter, the telephone rang. It was Brian Snowcroft. He had been laid off that afternoon, much sooner than he had anticipated. He was now interested in the job. However, he said that he would have to have a minimum salary of $65,000 to be able to survive financially. He said that he had been making in excess of $85,000 a year for the past five years. With his high fixed costs plus having two kids in college, he needed more than $65,000 a year to stay financially above water.

The two men talked for more than 30 minutes about the job and the situation. Shilling let Snowcroft know that he was also under great financial pressure and was being forced to make some cutbacks that he was reluctant to make, but such were the times. Shilling signed off by saying that he would get back to Snowcroft the following week.

In a way Shilling was grateful that Snowcroft had called, for it helped him focus his thinking on the problem at hand. The thought crossed his mind that perhaps he should abandon efforts to fill the position with an experienced salesperson and hire a beginner right out of an engineering college, someone he could pay a beginning salary of perhaps $25,000 a year. However, he wondered if the additional delay of having to start a search for a college graduate might upset his boss, who had indicated some apprehension over the firm's lack of a sales rep in the area. Shilling did not want to look indecisive.

He rose from his chair to go to the window to gaze at the blue Pacific below him as he pondered the problem.

Question:

1. What course of action should Tom Shilling follow regarding the vacant position?

CASE 6-2   BAY AUTOMOTIVE PARTS CENTER

Selection of Inside Salesperson

"The job calls for someone with a great telephone voice and an easy way of talking with people. I want someone our customers will really want to talk with," Bill Monk, owner of Bay Automotive Parts Center, declared to Linda Monk, his partner and spouse.

Linda was in charge of office operations, which included handling all incoming sales orders. Bill handled the outside sales operations, and the couple's three children—Ken, Kay, and Kate, ages 25, 27, and 29, respectively—ran the distribution center. Kate was in charge of purchasing and inventory management. Kay managed warehouse operations and order picking. Ken managed the receiving and shipping department. Much to their parents' dismay, none of the Monk offspring had much interest in the sales end of the business.

Each time an opening on the three-person inside sales force came up, Linda had pressured her children to get some experience in sales. She thought that their taking turns on the inside sales desk would be good training. They resisted her overtures. They maintained that it was too important a job for their inexperienced efforts. Moreover, none of the children was blessed with a good speaking voice. Consequently, Bay Automotive was looking for an inside salesperson to fill the vacancy that developed when Sal Nunzio retired.

Bay Automotive Parts Center of Baltimore, Maryland, was a large independent distributor of automotive parts in the Chesapeake Bay area, with sales in excess of $25 million a year. It had an outside sales force of five reps who called on local area garages and parts dealers. Bill Monk handled the significant accounts himself. However, on a day-to-day basis the bulk of the orders came in by telephone to people who took the orders. The three inside salespeople handled the incoming orders, but usually there were times during the day when Linda and/or Bill would have to handle some overload calls.

Linda, resigned to selecting a new inside salesperson, had considered 11 people for the job, 2 people from within the firm and 9 recruited from other sources. From those people, Linda had narrowed her choices to three people, each of whom represented different prototypes for the job.

First, there was Larry, an older man with considerable experience in the automotive business, both in repair and in parts sales. For the previous two years he had worked the inside desk for a parts distributor in Detroit. He quit that job to move to Baltimore to be closer to his children and grandchildren. He knew the auto parts business and was considered by his previous employers to be a reliable employee. He could go to work immediately with little training. The firm's compensation package, which was slightly below the market for such jobs, was satisfactory to him. He was ready to go to work.

The second person under consideration was Dorothy, who was working in a telemarketing "boiler room" selling health insurance. She was good at it, but she disliked what she was selling. She voiced serious concerns about the scripts she had to read to the prospects. She had said in her interview, "I want to sell legitimate products to people who really need them."

Dorothy was a local person who had graduated in 1990 from the University of Maryland, majoring in the dramatic arts. Her speaking voice and stage presence were superb. She was quick-witted and able to handle herself quite well with all sorts of people. While she had shown a slight surprise at Bay Automotive's compensation package, she seemed to accept it. Linda wondered how long Dorothy would stay interested in the job. But she thought that whatever that time would be, it would be well worth it for what she and the other people would learn from her about telemarketing. Linda secretly hoped some of Dorothy's polish would rub off on Kay and Kate.

The third person being considered was Steve, who had worked for Bay Automotive for more than 10 years in various capacities. He was currently filling orders and reported to Kay Monk. When he learned of the vacancy, Steve came to Linda and said he wanted the job. He was sure he could do it, he wanted the higher earnings, and he wanted to get into sales and develop his skills. He had been a loyal worker with good work habits. The Monks held him in high regard and really wanted to help him but were not certain that this was the best way to do it—for either him or the firm. While Steve had helped out on incoming sales calls when things got too busy for the regular crew to handle, he was not famous for having a melodious voice.

Linda assembled what she had developed on each of the candidates for the job and laid the information before the family after an evening meal. An extensive discussion followed. Each candidate had his or her supporters. Ken really liked Dorothy, but for the wrong reasons. Finally Bill said, "As I see it, it comes down to a question of (1) Do we hire an old parts pro who knows what to do and can do it now? (2) Do we go for the modern telemarketing professional who might be able to teach us a thing or two? or (3) Do we reward our loyal employee and friend who wants to improve himself. Is that it?"

They all nodded in agreement and then tried to avoid making a decision.

Question:

1. Who should be selected for the job?

CASE 6-3   UNIVERSAL COMPUTERS

Evaluation of Hiring Procedures

Fran Long, branch sales manager, walked into her office at Universal Computer's southeastern regional headquarters in Atlanta, Georgia. She had spent the previous week in the field working with some of her sales reps who were having trouble with some key accounts. While she had kept in close contact by telephone with her office staff during the week, her paperwork had stacked up. The in-basket was overflowing. She groaned as she surveyed the work ahead of her that morning, but she got to it immediately. She turned the basket upside down and began processing the paper—first in, first dealt with.

After Long had read and processed several intercompany memos, suddenly a letter from Sharon Altman caught her attention. Altman, a marketing major, had graduated from one of the state's universities with an outstanding record while working full-time in the school's computer department. After on-campus interviews, Altman was invited for a series of personal interviews at the company's Atlanta offices. She made an excellent impression on everyone in the company who had interviewed her, and everything on her résumé checked out satisfactorily. Consequently, she was offered a job as a sales trainee at the market rate for such people. She was given two weeks to accept or decline the offer that had been made in a letter sent to her three days after her interview. She had been informed verbally that she would be receiving the offer. She had requested and been granted the two weeks to answer.

After working through all the nice commentary about how great Universal was and how much she was impressed with Fran Long and all the people she had met, Sharon Altman got to the bottom line—she had accepted a sales job with another firm.

Long was displeased. She had made a great effort to recruit Altman and thought that she had been successful. Altman had given no indication that she was considering another job. Long considered calling her immediately to find out what happened, but she looked at the stack of papers to be processed and decided to postpone taking any action that day. She wanted to think about it for a while.

Fifteen documents later, she was looking at another letter rejecting a job offer she had made to a young man from North Carolina. His story was about the same as Altman's. An outstanding prospective sales rep was made an offer when he indicated that he wanted one. Long was puzzled by this rejection because the young man fit the stereotypical person the company was famous for hiring. He was a Universal man from his haircut down to his shoes. What's going on here, Long wondered.

By noon Long had finished with the in-basket and wished she had stayed home. Three more people to whom job offers had been made unexpectedly rejected them to accept other opportunities.

Long knew she had a problem on her hands, because hiring good people was the lifeblood of the business. The firm had been built on its ability to attract, train, and keep a highly effective sales force.

Universal Computers was one of the world's largest computer companies, with offices in every major city around the globe. Its growth and profitability had been the envy of the international business world. Unfortunately, during the previous two years it had encountered financial difficulties as its revenues suffered from competitive intrusions into its markets as well as from a sluggish economy. Management had made massive cutbacks in budgets and personnel. Changes in top management rocked the business world. The price of its stock dropped by more than 50 percent.

The company's sales management program had been copied extensively by its competitors. *Universal* was a household word. Fran Long thought, "You just don't reject an offer from us, particularly in these tough times. And above all, you don't play games with us." She recognized that these recruits had used the Universal offers for bargaining with other firms. She had used the same tactic in reverse when she came to work for Universal 10 years previously.

With five sales trainee positions to fill, Long had interviewed 22 people for the openings. There were eight other recruits who were considered acceptable to hire, but they were not nearly as promising as the recruits who had received the offers. She arranged for a meeting that afternoon with everyone involved in the selection process.

After explaining what had happened to the offers that they had made, Long said, "I want to discuss three things right now: What went wrong? What should we do right now? And how do we keep this same thing from happening in the future?"

The discussion was spirited, with each person having some opinions. The group thought that there was nothing wrong with its selection process. The procedures that had worked so well for years were followed. Those recruits were given the royal treatment. No insincerity had been detected; all of the recruits seemed to be bona fide candidates.

The group wondered if they made a mistake by not putting more pressure on the recruits. Perhaps they should not give them so much time to consider the offer, and maybe they should have gotten a verbal acceptance before making a written offer.

"Good deeds never go unpunished!" observed Long's operations manager. He continued, "We were nice guys. Maybe we should quit being so nice. Competition is getting rough, as we well know, and that holds true for people as well as markets."

Fran's assistant demurred. "Do we really want to hire anyone who really doesn't want to work for us? I think not. I just can't see pressuring anyone to come to work for us. It hasn't come to that, has it?"

Long nodded and asked, "To what extent have our current competitive and financial problems played a role in this matter? Let's face it, we avoided all discussion of it with these people. We pretend it doesn't exist. But it does. Should we get it out on the table and talk about it with these people, or would that be washing our dirty linen in public?" She did not wait for an answer but instead hurried on to the immediate problem: "How do we go about making the next offers? Should we bring them in to Atlanta again and get their acceptance on the spot? If we don't fill these five slots, will we look bad in New York when this year's sales training program begins?" She said the words, but she really wondered if they should be hiring available bodies to fill slots instead of waiting until the right people could be hired. After all, the world wouldn't end if they weren't able to fill their sales trainee positions with college graduates. She knew that there were a lot of good people on the streets looking for jobs.

Questions:

1. Why did the applicants reject Universal's job offer?

2. If Fran Long wants to hire five trainees from those who have already been interviewed, how should she do it?

3. If you were in Fran Long's position, exactly what actions would you take?

CASE 6-4   PACIFIC PAPER PRODUCTS

Indoctrination of New Salespeople

"I'm getting too old for this job. Everything seems to have changed. I don't seem to be able to manage things the same way I used to," Mo Martin complained to his longtime friend Bernie, who was a bit weary of Mo's never-ending complaints about the ways of the modern world.

Mo Martin, vice president of sales for Pacific Paper Products, had started his career in sales with the paper division of Weyerhaeuser, the huge wood products company, when he graduated from college in 1971. After completing the company training program, he was assigned to the firm's Southern California regional office where he enjoyed a stellar sales career through a combination of hard work and a large, fast-growing territory. Weyerhaeuser was known as an excellent company to work for, and Mo was enjoying much success in his sales career. However, he became progressively dissatisfied with his status at Weyerhaeuser, because his peers in his training program were being promoted into various management positions while he was still selling. He kept asking his boss about it, and he was continually told that the company felt that his superior selling skills would best benefit the company if he remained in selling. He was given several large key accounts for which he was solely responsible. One of those accounts was Pacific Paper, a paper wholesaler. Mo eventually became close friends with its owner, who persuaded Mo to work for him as vice president of sales. Starting in 1983, Mo Martin established himself as an excellent sales manager by most indexes one might want to use: sales increases, profit margins, selling costs, turnover, and modernization of the sales system.

Mo's traditional management style was to develop close personal relationships with his people. There was much socializing among the sales force that was located in the Southern California region. Sales meetings were often held in Palm Springs or San Diego, at which golf tournaments were usually featured. The company sponsored several charity celebrity golf tournaments at which the salespeople played significant roles by inviting various key customers to play.

Mo spent much time in the field working closely with the sales reps. He tried to spend at least one day every three months with each of the firm's 33 sales reps. Every birthday, anniversary, wedding, graduation, or other memorable event in a rep's family was recognized with appropriate gifts or cards.

The sales group was diverse, with 10 reps from minority groups and four women. The first woman was hired in 2000. Mo was aware that the women had not assimilated into the sales force very well at all, even though their collective sales performance was good. As he had said when asked why he had hired them, "They were the best of the applicants."

He normally went out of his way to help new sales reps become part of the work group. He kept close daily contact with new reps, helping them with whatever personal problems they were encountering in changing their jobs. He had made personal loans to some new reps who were having financial troubles. Mo said, "They can't sell effectively if they're worried about their family or finances. Anything I can do to help them become effective salespeople and happily accepted in our work group will eventually pay us big dividends."

However, Mo had quickly detected that his management style was not well accepted among the women he had hired. Although they had not come to him as a group, individually they had let him know that they did not play golf and did not like to go to a bar with him to talk over the day's sales calls. Moreover, they were not really interested in socializing that much with the other sales reps, or even having much ado made over their birthdays. Mo had held a surprise birthday party for Ruth Spencer on her 40th birthday. She was not amused, as they say, and she let him know about it.

Since they exchanged confidences almost daily—they were neighbors and socialized extensively—Bernie was well aware of Mo's problems. Bernie kept observing that times had changed and Mo had to change with them. "What worked for you before may not work for you now. Maybe some people only want to work for you; they don't want to be your buddies. They only wanted a job, not a social life," Bernie told him.

"Yeah, I know you're right, but how about me and what I want? I enjoy my job so much because it's so much fun working and playing with my people. If I can't have fun and do it my way, why do it? Maybe I should take early retirement and say to heck with it."

"Hold the phone, Mo. Don't go off the deep end just yet. I know someone who might be able to help you with your problem. I met this woman manage- ment consultant who specializes in advising man- agers on these matters. Talk to her. And talk to some other people, too. I think there are some things you can do to get some perspective on your situation."

Question:

1. What advice would you give Mo Martin?

7

Developing, Delivering, and Reinforcing a Sales Training Program*

Those who seek mentoring will rule the great expanse under heaven.

—Shu Ching, *Chinese Book of History*—

The training program is a vital link in the process of converting the recruit into a productive sales rep. The money spent on recruiting and selecting salespeople may be wasted if their hiring is not followed up with the proper training programs. Additionally, experienced reps may not improve or even maintain their productivity if they are not provided with an adequate amount of continual training.

In this chapter we discuss developing and conducting a sales training program. Successful programs consist of four phases: training assessment, program design, reinforcement, and evaluation. In each phase sales executives must make a number of decisions, as shown in Figure 7–1.

The two basic types of training programs are initial training (or indoctrination) for new hires and continuous training programs (or refreshers) for experienced reps. The decisions the executive makes with regard to training vary with the type of program being considered.

*The authors wish to acknowledge the contributions of Dick Canada, Chairperson of Dartmouth Group Ltd., to this chapter. A former National Sales Training Manager for Xerox, Dick offered his own ideas as well as reviewing and improving those of the authors.

FIGURE 7-1

Phases of developing and conducting sales force training

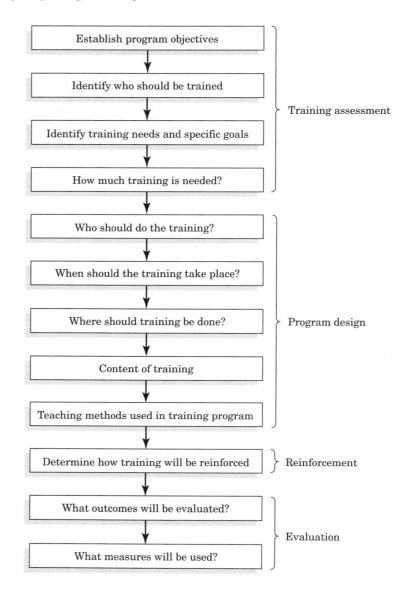

The Value of Sales Training

As product life cycles have become shorter and relationships between companies and their customers have become more complex, training for salespeople has become more important than ever before. Most sales executives agree that training is a critical factor ensuring the salesperson's success. The salesperson's product knowledge, understanding of customer needs, and selling skills are directly related to the amount of training he or she receives. Training may even lead to greater effort. As salespeople develop greater self-confidence through training, they may be encouraged to put their skills to use by trying harder than they did before.

Despite the relationship between sales training and sales productivity, studies report that over one-third of business firms do no sales training, and many other firms provide only on-the-job training.[1] Yet many other companies are investing heavily in sales training programs. Corporations are spending more than $54 billion each year on formal training.[2] On average, companies spend $7,079 per year to train a newly hired sales rep and $4,032 per year to provide ongoing training to each experienced rep.[3] Many companies view training as an essential means of protecting the investments they have made in their sales forces. In fact, the number of hours spent by U.S. corporations on sales training now exceeds the amount spent on training at the executive, senior, and middle-management levels.[4]

Training professionals, however, argue that often companies are not spending their training budgets wisely and, as a result, their training is not very effective. They estimate that, at the average company, 9 out of 10 reps who have been through training have been disappointed with it.[5] Customers, too, often feel that the salespeople who serve them are not very effective. Thus, it is apparent that many sales training programs are not imparting the skills salespeople need to achieve success.

There are three main reasons why this is happening. First, many companies design training programs without thoroughly assessing their training needs.[6] Second, the buyer's preferences for and evaluations of salespeople are typically ignored in the design of most sales training programs.[7] Third, managers and trainers do not continually reinforce the skills learned in the training programs. This lack of skill reinforcement leads to minimal behavioral change by the salesperson.[8] Xerox Corporation has for years been recognized as possessing one of the finest sales training programs in the world, yet the company found an 87 percent loss of skills 30 days after the initial instruction.[9] In other words, even companies that spend a lot of money on training may not be spending those dollars carefully enough to be effective.

It should also be noted that companies frequently try to use training to solve problems it cannot actually solve.[10] For example, reps may be performing poorly because the company is selecting the wrong *type* of person for the job, not because those reps are poorly trained. If sales are low, it may be due to a poor marketing strategy—a problem beyond the scope of sales training. Training is not a panacea, but it can lead to significant improvements in performance if it is properly designed, implemented, and reinforced. In the remainder of this chapter, we discuss how to design, deliver, and reinforce an effective sales training program.

Sales Training and Strategic Planning

Many aspects of sales training are affected by the company's strategic marketing plan. Conversely, the sales training program—when properly coordinated with the firm's marketing objectives and strategies—can help the company implement that plan.

In today's competitive marketplace, customers are demanding more and more from their suppliers in terms of quality and service. In response to these pressures, firms are placing greater strategic emphasis on developing long-term partnerships with their customers. Rather than just selling products and services, salespeople are expected to build relationships and provide solutions to their customers' problems. As a result, the selling process has become ever more interactive and situation-specific. Salespeople have to know more about the product and more about the customer. Many firms have adopted team-selling strategies in order to respond to customers' expectations. In these strategies, the salesperson works much more closely with people from other areas in the firm, such as manufacturing, engineering, and research. As a result, sales training has become much broader in scope, covering topics such as quality management, teamwork, and other interpersonal skills necessary for building relationships.

The firm's marketing strategies and objectives provide the basis for establishing sales training objectives. For example, a marketing objective of increasing market share by 20 percent calls for one kind of training program, and the objective of maintaining market share by providing better service to existing customers calls for a different kind.

If a company makes a major change in its sales organizational structure, an intensive training program for experienced sales reps may be needed. This sort of situation occurred when Xerox embarked on a three- to five-year program to train all 4,000 of its reps to sell the full product line rather than a selected part of the line as they had been doing in the past.

Training Assessment

In the **training assessment** phase, sales executives must ask themselves four questions:

- What are the training program objectives?
- Who should be trained?
- What are the training needs of the individual rep?
- How much training is needed?

The following sections look at each question in turn.

What Are the Training Program Objectives?

Most companies expect to influence the productivity of their field sales organizations through the design and delivery of their training programs. But training programs may have other objectives as well. They include a lower employee turnover rate, better morale, more effective communication, improved customer relations, and better self-management. These objectives are shown in Figure 7–2 and described below.

- **Increased sales productivity.** Companies try to improve their return on sales investment by improving the productivity of their salespeople. This can be done by increasing sales per salesperson or by lowering costs. Training is frequently used to accomplish greater sales per salesperson and sometimes used to lower costs.

- **Lower turnover.** Good training programs lower employee turnover in part because well-trained people are less likely to fail. A well-thought-out training program prepares trainees for the realities of a life in sales—including the fact that discouragement and disappointment are to be

FIGURE 7-2

Objectives of sales training programs

expected early in a sales career. The trainee who can handle the early problems is less likely to become discouraged and quit.

- **Higher morale.** Closely tied to turnover is the matter of morale. People who are thrust into the business world without proper training or preparation are likely to suffer from poor morale. Lack of purpose is another reason for poor morale. Hence, a major objective of a sales training program should be to give trainees some idea of their purpose in the company and in society.

- **Improved communication.** Training is used to ensure that salespeople understand the importance of the information they provide to the company concerning their customers and the marketplace. They need to know how the information will be used and how it affects the performance of the firm.

- **Improved customer relations.** A good training program helps trainees become aware of the importance of establishing and maintaining good customer relations. They should learn how to avoid overselling, how to determine which products are needed, and how to adjust complaints.

- **Improved self-management.** Management has become increasingly interested in how employees use their time. The goal is to learn how to produce more output from the relatively few hours available for working. Salespeople must be organized and allocate their time effectively in order to be successful.

Technological advances in recent years have provided sales reps with great opportunities to improve their productivity. Computers, particularly laptop computers, are playing an increasingly important role in selling during the 21st century.

Providing training online allows a rep to do the "lessons" at his convenience.

They allow the rep to access the company's databases and communicate with the operating sales system. Properly used, they can be of immense benefit. However, the reps must learn how to use the new technology.

Who Should Be Trained?

New Hires

Obviously, newly hired company sales reps require some training. How much they need will be discussed in the next section.

Experienced Reps

The need for training among the existing sales force is not so obvious, but usually at least some salespeople are struggling to achieve their objectives. They need help, and the company can profit by giving it to them.

Of course, things continually change. New products are introduced, markets shift, and buyers come and go. These and other changes require retraining the sales force to handle the new developments. But even without such changes, every salesperson can benefit from appropriate sales training. Even the most experienced or skilled salesperson can benefit from refresher courses. Sales training is most effective with those reps who have a strong desire and commitment to learn coupled with a specific lack of skills or knowledge. Remember that experienced reps need to know how the training will benefit them before they will embrace it.

Generally speaking, a company will achieve its best investment return when it gives priority to training the middle 60 percent of its sales force (see Figure 7–3). People who are in the top 20 percent of a field sales force usually are not going to

A DAY-TO-DAY OPERATING PROBLEM

MAJESTIC PLASTICS COMPANY

MAJESTIC
Plastics Company

Training for an Experienced Sales Rep

Clyde Brion, general sales manager for the Majestic Plastics Company, had a problem. One of the company's veteran sales reps, Bobby Day, had announced his refusal to attend any sales training courses. Majestic had seen sales and customer satisfaction slip in some of its key territories over the last two years. This had prompted Brion to hire an outside training specialist to conduct a five-day sales seminar for the company's 18 sales reps. Brion hoped that through the use of case studies, videotapes, and role-plays, his reps would improve on their interpersonal and overall selling skills.

Bobby Day, however, didn't like the idea. He told Clyde Brion, "I've been one of this company's top salespeople for 23 years. The last thing I need is to leave my territory for a week just to get some silly training. Leave the training to the new kids. I lose commissions when I'm not out there selling. Five days out of the territory is money out of my pocket."

In reviewing Bobby Day's performance over the last several years, Brion had to admit that Day was one of Majestic's better reps. After graduating from a midwestern community college, Day started his sales career in the life insurance industry. In his third year on the job, he sold one of Majestic's executives a term-life policy. The executive was so impressed with Day that he offered him a position in Majestic's growing sales force. Day accepted and began his career in the Washington, D.C., area before being reassigned to the bustling New Jersey territory. He has been there ever since, winning five "Salesperson of the Year" awards. Although many people within Majestic feel that Day is not much of a team player, Majestic's CEO boastfully refers to Day as his "Lone Wolf Superstar."

Question: What should Clyde Brion say to Bobby Day?

Source: This case was prepared by Steven Reed under the direction of Professor R. Spiro.

FIGURE 7-3

Best return on investment in the training of salespeople

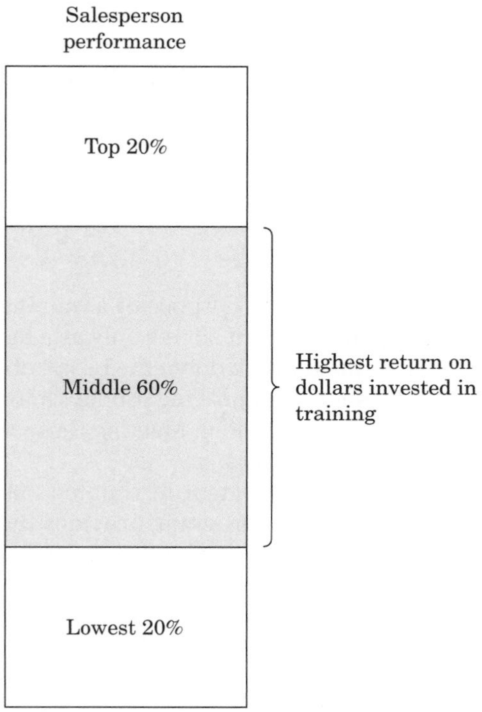

Salesperson performance

Top 20%

Middle 60%

Lowest 20%

Highest return on dollars invested in training

increase their performance substantially above the level they are currently achieving. By the same logic, sales reps who are consistently in the lowest 20 percent of the organization may be in the wrong job, a problem that cannot be helped through training.[11]

Customers

At times it is also important to train people who are not the company's employees: independent manufacturers' representatives, distributors, dealers, and users. For example, manufacturers' representatives promote those products that are easiest to sell or that have the highest commissions. Experience shows that the products that are easiest to sell are those that the rep knows best. Usually the rep is most familiar with the products that are best supported by their manufacturers. Agents and distributors want and expect support from the companies they represent. Firms that give it to them send several valuable messages: We want you to make money with our line; we will support you in the best way we can; and we want you to be part of our organization.

One medical equipment and supply company will not allow any physician to buy or use its products until the physician has gone through the company's training program. This policy is part of the firm's program to lessen medical product liability litigation. It has worked; the company has had no suits to date.

Sales Managers

Although the focus of this chapter is on the training that sales managers should provide to their salespeople, it seems obvious that sales managers need training as well. However, many companies that provide excellent training programs for their salespeople fail to do the same for their managers. It is critical to give the sales management candidates training and experience in management tasks. Genentech, a leading biotech firm, recognizes this need and provides management training in its Talent Development Program. This program, geared to future managers, is designed to develop five competencies: planning and business organization skills, strategic implementation ability, human resources management, leadership and team building, and professional commitment.[12]

What Are the Training Needs of the Individual Rep?

To say that the purpose of a training program is to increase sales productivity is so general that it serves only as a hazy guidepost for making decisions. The manager must break down the broad objectives into *specific goals* for the individual rep, such as improving product knowledge, prospecting methods, probing, or relationship building. Meeting these separate goals should result in achieving the broad objectives.

The assessment of training needs, the most important step in designing a sales training program, provides the starting point for setting training goals and designing the program. The company uses the analysis to identify weaknesses in selling skills and then designs programs to eliminate these weaknesses.

Setting these specific objectives also:

- Helps the trainer and trainee focus on the purpose of the training.
- Guides prioritization and sequencing of training.

- Guides the choice of training methods.
- Provides a standard for measuring training effectiveness.

Naturally, the objectives of any segment of a sales training program will vary depending on the nature of the trainee. The program designed to convert an inexperienced recruit into a professional sales rep will be more comprehensive than a program intended to refresh the selling skills of an experienced rep or update the existing sales force on new products.

Standardization and Customization

Some training programs, such as those for inexperienced reps or those concerning new products or policies, can be provided to all of the salespeople in a *standardized* form. However, a significant portion of the training for experienced reps should be based on identifying the needs of the individual and then *customizing* a curriculum to meet those individual needs. G. D. Searle, now a subsidiary of pharmaceutical company Pharmacia, has improved the effectiveness of its training through customization. Its 1,100 salespeople, in consultation with their sales managers, may select from a variety of courses according to their individual needs.[13]

Sources of Information

Companies can and should use many sources to gather the information concerning their training needs. The most frequently used source is managerial judgment. While managers' assessments may be accurate, it is important for a firm to systematically collect information from a number of other sources as well. Performance measures, such as sales volume, number of calls, selling expenses, and customer complaints, can help managers assess training needs.

Interviews with or surveys of salespeople and customers can also provide valuable insights. For example, executives at Factiva, a joint venture between Dow Jones and Reuters that provides competitive information to businesses, first met with managers to define roles and competencies. Then they asked all members of the 300-person sales force to grade themselves on each of the competencies. This enabled Factiva to identify the areas in which the salespeople felt they needed more training.[14] NBC established a task force of salespeople and trainers to assess training needs and to establish priorities for training.[15]

Some companies use customer questionnaires as the basis for identifying individual training needs. Each salesperson delivers the questionnaires to a selected group of customers, who are asked to assess the importance of a variety of skills to the selling relationship and to rate the salesperson's application of these skills.

Another method of assessing training needs is to conduct a **difficulty analysis** of the sales job. In this analysis the sales manager attempts to discover what difficulties his or her staff encounters in the field. Then the company can devise proper training to help overcome those problems. The manager conducts the difficulty analysis by going into the field and interviewing sales reps about their problems. Frequently, the manager reviews a series of calls in which the reps failed to get orders and attempts to discover just what caused the failure. If the analysis discloses that reps are picking poor prospects, for example, they would be given additional training on prospecting.

How Much Training Is Needed?

The amount of training needed depends on the training objectives. A half-day program might suffice to introduce reps to a new promotional program, whereas two or three days might be needed to teach them the features and benefits of a new product or service. A program with the objective of improving the sales reps' customer orientation may require three or four days, but a program designed to teach basic selling skills to inexperienced recruits may take as long as six months.

Generally, inexperienced recruits need to learn not only about their companies and the products they are selling but also about basic selling techniques. Recruits who have had sales experience may require less basic training but may have inadequate knowledge of specific selling techniques that are most appropriate for their current selling assignment. This situation would call for considerably more training.

Most training programs for new hires last from three to six months, with costs ranging from a low of $1,433 to a high of $16,000 per rep; on average, it costs $16,000 to train a pharmaceutical sales rep. As you might expect, the more technical the products are, the longer the training for new recruits.[16]

In the case of continual training, there is a trade-off between the gains that should result from training and the lost sales that may result from the rep's absence from the field. Of course, the long-term perspective suggests that the benefits from training will eventually outweigh any short-term losses. But there is a limit to how long and how often you can pull a rep out of the field and not affect the level of customer service. Surveys show that the amount of time companies devote to continual training varies from a low of 12.8 hours per year to a high of 86 hours per year for an experienced rep.[17]

Program Design

In the **program design** phase, the following questions must be answered:

- Who should do the training?
- When should the training take place?
- Where should it be done?
- What should the content of the training be?
- What teaching methods should be used?

Who Should Do the Training?

Regular line executives, staff personnel, and outside specialists may all serve as trainers. Any one or a combination of them can be used successfully. It is not uncommon for a firm to use all three, each for different purposes. In choosing trainers, it is very important to remember that the quality of the teaching itself will have a greater impact on what is learned than the content of the training.

Line Personnel

Line personnel who may conduct training include senior sales representatives, field supervisors, territorial managers, and sales managers who are in direct command of the sales force. Some firms have also made effective use of peer training. They set up situations in which inexperienced people are partially trained by their peers on the sales force. It works well if the sales force is skilled and has a vested interest in developing the new person's selling ability.

Advantages The words of line personnel carry much more authority than those of staff people or outside specialists, since the trainees know that the former have had successful sales experience. Having the boss do the training achieves a certain unity of action because afterward there can be no mistaking what the supervisor expects. Furthermore, recruits can be trained to sell the way the manager wants them to sell. Line executives who train their own salespeople can evaluate each person's ability better than administrators who do not participate in the training program can. Also, better rapport can be established between the executive and the sales force, since training affords a wonderful opportunity to become acquainted.

Disadvantages The potential disadvantages of using line personnel are lack of time and lack of teaching ability. The pressures of other activities may force managers to give, at best, only partial attention to the training program. This can be harmful to trainee morale. Also, a line executive may know a great deal about selling but be unable to teach others about it. Neither of these disadvantages is serious, however, since both can be remedied by proper managerial action. Line administrators can be given the necessary time for training. And teachers are not necessarily born; they also can be trained.

Staff Trainers

Staff trainers can be hired specifically to conduct training programs, or staff people who hold other jobs in personnel, production, or office management can take this on. We will focus on the specially hired sales trainer, since use of other staff personnel ordinarily is not recommended. Members of the personnel department are seldom qualified to conduct a sales training program. They may be involved in certain phases of the instruction, such as furnishing company information or handling the physical arrangements of the program. However, entrusting them with the technical details of the training program is generally unwise.

Advantages A trainer specifically hired to handle the training program can attend to the details, prepare the necessary materials, and give trainees the attention they need. Frequently, it is less expensive to hire a specialized staff-training officer than it is to add the additional line executives needed to allow them more time for training activities.

Disadvantages In theory, the staff trainer lacks control over the trainees and does not speak with the authority of a line executive. However, in practice, this is an academic point, since the trainees know that the trainer has the backing of the boss.

Companies incur additional cost in maintaining a separate training department. The median salary of the trainer alone can be $60,000 per year, depending on his or her qualifications. This limits the number of firms that can hire a sales trainer; smaller companies cannot afford the cost.

Outside Training Specialists

A recent survey of firms showed that over 70 percent use outside training specialists to provide at least part of their training.[18] Some small and medium-sized firms often turn the entire training of their sales reps over to outside firms, primarily because they lack the resources to provide the training internally. Raleigh Cycle Company started outsourcing its training several years ago. Subsequently Raleigh doubled the number of dealers and increased sales by 35 percent. Joe Shannon, the director of national sales, attributed these gains to the training program.[19]

Practically every large city has firms that specialize in sales training. Their scope varies widely. Some will establish and administer an entire training program, whereas others specialize in teaching specific sales techniques. Training firms may specialize in a very narrow field. For example, some organizations do nothing but train real estate brokers or pharmaceutical reps or advertising account reps.

The key to successfully using an outside specialist is to select the one that is right for your firm. The following steps can help ensure that you do so:

- Set specific objectives for the training.
- Select a trainer who has sales experience.
- Select a trainer who has expertise in the area of your training need.
- Select only those programs that allow you to customize.
- Get references.
- Preview or audit the program.
- Ask for specifics on what results your company can expect.

Self-development programs are also important in training a sales force. Many firms pay part or all of the cost of approved educational programs or seminars. Sometimes they furnish subscriptions to educational services and newsletters. The basic idea is that the company benefits from having well-educated employees.

When Should the Training Take Place?

There are two basic attitudes toward the timing of training. Some executives believe that everyone placed in the field should be fully trained, not only in product and company knowledge but also in selling techniques. Training programs for new salespeople may last from a few weeks to a year or more before the salespeople are sent into the field. Sales managers may have trainees work for a while in either production or service to acquire product knowledge.

Other managers want recruits to exhibit a desire to sell before investing in training them. Some insurance companies require a new agent to sell a certain amount of life insurance before going to a sales school. The first training program is only a basic course. After that, the agent must again go into the field and sell successfully before attending more advanced schools for underwriters.

This philosophy has considerable educational and managerial merit. From the educational point of view, it is much easier to train people who have had some field experience versus those who have none. People who have experience in facing problems are eager to find solutions to them. If many prospects have said that the price is too high, for example, reps will be eager to find out how to cope with that objection. From a managerial point of view, weak salespeople are usually eliminated if they must sell before being trained. By putting new employees in the field first, the manager can determine how much and what type of training they really need.

The only trouble is that people who might have been successful had they been given proper instruction may be eliminated by the push-them-off-the-dock method. To avoid this trouble, companies should use delayed training only when product knowledge is easily acquired; the prospect does not require a polished selling approach; and customers are sold only once, with each sale being of little importance to total volume. If a sales rep botches a particular sale, the company is not seriously injured.

The need for training does not end with completion of the initial program. Most sales authorities see training as a continual function. It never ceases; it only changes form. Salespeople periodically need refresher courses. The financial services firm Charles Schwab is well known for the continuous training it provides to its reps. The ongoing education program, called Learning for Excellence in Advice and Professionalism (LEAP), includes Web and classroom courses and a series of workshops for salespeople at different stages of their professional development.[20]

Where Should the Training Take Place?

The decision on the training program's location involves the extent to which it should be centralized. Unless there is some reason for centralizing training in one location, it should be decentralized. Compared to training in the field, centralized training is usually more expensive and requires more organizational effort.

Decentralized Training

Decentralized training can take several forms: (1) field sales office instruction, (2) use of senior salespeople, (3) on-the-job training, (4) sales seminars or clinics, or (5) self-guided assignments.

Advantages The advantages of decentralized sales training are many. First and foremost, it is usually less expensive than centralized training. The trainee remains in the field to work while learning, and the company avoids the substantial expense of supporting both the trainee and a central school staff.

Second, there is definite educational merit to decentralized training. Education requires time. Studies prove that cram courses are inefficient since the students quickly forget much of what they learn. A decentralized program can match instruction to the speed at which the trainee can learn the material. The limit on how much effective training can be accomplished in the shorter time frame of a centralized program has caused Xerox, Motorola, ARCO, and many other companies to decentralize training efforts as much as possible.

Third, decentralized training has considerable managerial benefits because the branch manager or an assistant is usually directly responsible. If the branch managers do a good job, trainees gain confidence in their leadership. At the same time, the managers can evaluate each of the trainees through direct observation.

Many companies are turning to self-guided Web-based instruction. Not only are these programs cost effective and self-paced, but they can also be customized to address the training needs of the individual rep. This is particularly useful for continual training. This method will be discussed further in a following section of this chapter.

Questions to Ensure Training Effectiveness

- Is your training aligned with your company's strategic goals?
- Does top management support your training?
- Does it reflect the needs of your customers?
- Is it immediately relevant to your business?
- Are the salespeople empowered to leverage what they learn?

- Is the training reinforced?
- Are the results of the training measurable?

Source: Adapted from Mark McMaster, "Is Your Training a Waste of Money?" *Sales & Marketing Management*, January 2001, p. 47.

Disadvantages First, the major weakness of decentralized training, and it is a big one, is that the branch or field manager may not be able to perform the training role properly. Time demands, combined with lack of training skills or the desire to train, may make the field manager an inept trainer.

Second, if complex or expensive equipment is needed in the training program, it may not be available in the field. For example, an interocular lens company had to set up an operating room to train its reps about eye surgery.

Centralized Training

Centralized training may take place in organized schools or in periodic sales meetings at a central location, often the home office. Some large companies that hire many sales reps each year maintain permanent centralized sales schools. Technology services company NCR's training camp, called Sugar Camp, is an example of such an installation. Xerox's International Training Center in Leesburg, Virginia, is another. Smaller concerns typically conduct one or two sales schools a year in the home office, each lasting three or four weeks.

Advantages In centralized training, highly skilled personnel are usually available to teach. Also, proximity to the plant or the home office allows the trainees to become acquainted with home-office personnel and manufacturing facilities. It is important for them to meet the top executives. Centralized training certainly saves executive time because it eliminates travel. Also, a centralized school normally has more formal facilities for training than are available in the field. The needed equipment and materials are handy for the instructor's use. Another significant advantage is that the trainees can get to know one another. An esprit de corps can develop among the members of the class, and this is conducive to good morale.

From an educational standpoint, housing trainees at a central location, so they are not subject to the distractions of home life, has some merit. They can focus attention on learning how to be better salespeople.

Disadvantages Centralized training has two main weaknesses. First, as noted above, it is expensive to take people out of the field and support them while training. Second, the amount of time a person can be kept at a central training location is limited. Moreover, trainees eventually become bored. When boredom sets in, education stops. Also, some people do not want to be away from their families for extended periods.

Many companies overcome the disadvantages of using either centralized or decentralized by designing a program that incorporates both. Companies usually provide some centralized indoctrination training first and then supplement this with some field training.

What Should the Content of the Training Be?

The primary purpose of most sales training programs is either to teach people to sell or to improve their current selling skills. Therefore, a significant amount of **training content** is devoted to product knowledge and persuasive communication skills. However, several factors other than the mastery of the persuasion process affect success or failure in selling. These are the trainee's attitude toward the selling job and toward training, knowledge of the company, product knowledge and application, knowledge of competitive products, knowledge of customers, knowledge of business principles, selling skills, relationship-building skills, team-selling skills, time-management skills, computer-assisted-selling skills, and knowledge of the legal constraints on selling. All of these factors should be addressed in sales training programs. Not every training program should necessarily cover all of them at one time. Rather, the specific content of the training will vary depending on the objectives of that particular training session. Each of the factors just mentioned is discussed below.

Attitude toward Selling and toward Training

For training to have its greatest impact, it is important first to instill in the trainees a thorough understanding of the nature and importance of the selling job and of their role in achieving the company's overall objectives. Some trainees may hold beliefs about selling and about training that are not accurate, and these beliefs will hinder their learning. For example, some people believe that salespeople are born with sales ability and that sales training for anyone else is largely a waste of time. This is simply not true. Other commonly held myths about selling are shown in Figure 7–4. Salespeople must also understand the importance of their role in the company. They are the primary communication link between the company and its customers. Often they are the only people in the firm directly responsible for generating revenue. Without communication between the firm and its customers and without the revenues generated by the sales reps, the firm would not exist.

Knowledge of the Company

All trainees need a certain amount of information about the company's goals, organization, policies, and procedures. It is also important for the trainee to understand the history and the current mission of the firm. This background information helps the reps develop a sense of pride about their companies. It also helps them to understand and adopt the values of top management as their own.

Trainees need to be shown how to work within the corporate system—whom to contact to get things done and how the system operates. They need to be taught the company policies and procedures—and the reasons for them. When sales reps understand the reasons behind the procedures, they are more likely to adhere to them, and they can do a better job of explaining them to the customers.

FIGURE 7-4   Prevalent myths about the selling process

Myth No. 1.	**Salespeople are born—not made.**
	This simply is not true. Such great sales forces as those of IBM, Xerox, and Procter & Gamble are based on excellent sales training programs. These firms hire young people who are largely without sales experience or skills and teach them how to sell.
Myth No. 2.	**Salespeople must be good talkers.**
	On the contrary: Good salespeople are good listeners. The prospect has the information the sales rep needs; all the rep has to do is learn to ask the right questions, then listen to what the prospect says.
Myth No. 3.	**Selling is a matter of knowing the right techniques or tricks.**
	Unfortunately, there are no magic selling techniques, and methods that work for some reps do not work for others. Success in selling is more than mastering techniques; it is a result of several potent factors such as work habits, attitudes, products sold, and markets covered.
Myth No. 4.	**A good salesperson can sell anything.**
	Not so! A successful sales career results when the individual sells the right product made by the right company to the right people. Any salesperson can prosper in a substantial number of jobs, and it pays handsomely when reps match their talents to prospective jobs.
Myth No. 5.	**A good salesperson can sell ice to an Eskimo.**
	Selling is not a sport in which a sales rep tries to unload unwanted goods on an unwilling buyer who cannot pay for them. Good selling starts by finding someone who needs the product and can afford it. In other words, good salespeople call on good prospects.
Myth No. 6.	**People don't want to buy.**
	Not so! People want new cars, nice houses, new clothing, sports equipment—all sorts of things. Industrial buyers *must* buy all the things their companies need for operations. People wait for the salesperson to show them how his or her proposition will benefit them.

Product Knowledge and Application

A large part of training is usually devoted to providing knowledge about the products and services to be sold and their applications. Ordinarily, the amount of this training varies according to the products' technical complexity.

Trainees must know about the products they sell, and they must understand the varied applications of those products. It is one thing to be familiar with the features of the product and quite another to be able to apply this information in the field to solve customer problems.

Today, much product information is put into a computer database that the sales rep can access directly. Many reps carry portable laptop or notebook computers with them on sales calls. This makes it possible for them to call up whatever product information they need right in the customer's office.

Knowledge of Competitive Products

Salespeople should know about their competitors' products as well as their own because they must sell against them. Detailed knowledge of competitive products allows sales reps to design presentations to stress the advantages of their products over the competitors.

Knowledge of Customers

In today's competitive environment, salespeople must be *customer oriented* in order to be successful. Therefore, the trainees must understand their customers' businesses. Each customer has a different set of priorities and problems, and the salesperson must be able to recognize and respond to all of them. Also, within

An International Perspective

For six months, Steve Waterhouse, a sales representative for Waterhouse Group, had been courting a Japanese company that specialized in planning meetings. Finally, he had a chance to meet with one of the company's representatives to discuss the services her company might buy from Waterhouse. At the beginning of the meeting, she handed him her card in the traditional Japanese way, bowing slightly and holding the card in front of her with two hands. Steve took the card, turned it over, and scribbled something on the back of it. He looked up to see that his potential client was aghast. Even though he apologized, the damage was done and he did not make the sale. It was a $100,000 mistake.

This true story demonstrates how important it is for companies to provide cross-cultural training to their representatives who will have international assignments. Many companies are not providing this type of training, and their representatives are much more likely to return home before they are supposed to due to poor performance and or an inability to adjust.

Source: Betsy Cummings, "Selling Around the World," *Sales & Marketing Management*, May 2001, p. 70.

each account there are usually several different people with whom the salesperson must work. The rep must know the priorities and preferences of all those people who may have some influence on the decision. Furthermore, reps must have a thorough knowledge of the people and businesses to whom their customers are selling.

Knowledge of Business Principles

Many salespeople are held accountable for the profitability of their territories. Also, as noted in earlier chapters, salespeople often serve as consultants to their customers. Therefore, it is important that they understand the basic business practices that underlie the operations of their own companies as well as their customers' companies. Baxter Healthcare, a leading supplier of products for the health care industry, includes business knowledge in its sales training for both salespeople and account managers. The sessions cover such topics as distribution fundamentals, pricing fundamentals, and finance for profit.[21]

Selling Skills

Of course, trainees must develop the selling skills and techniques that enable them to effectively communicate with and persuade their customers. These skills were discussed in detail in Chapter 3.

Relationship-Building Skills

Many companies are focusing on developing long-term relationships with selected accounts. The salesperson must be trained to help identify these accounts and to nurture the relationships with these customers. Managing each account for long-term profitability rather than for the short-term sale requires salespeople to prioritize their activities differently. They must work with customers to anticipate and identify problems and find mutually beneficial solutions. This requires a great degree of mutual openness, trust, and commitment, which is not usually found in transaction selling.

This group of sales reps is participating in boot camp exercises to teach them the skills and attitudes necessary for effective team selling.

Team-Selling Skills

Many salespeople work as part of a team. The skills that are critical to the successful performance of a team are not the same set as those that are critical for reps selling on their own. For example, being sensitive to the needs of others, accepting the shortcomings of others, being willing to cooperate, keeping others informed, being receptive to the ideas of others, and placing team success above individual success are a few of the elements on which training must focus. Many companies incorporate sessions that build sensitivity and trust among fellow teammates.

Time-Management Skills

Most salespeople are given a great amount of autonomy to manage their territories. They must allocate their time not only among their customers but also among the various aspects of their jobs—specifically selling, service, and administrative responsibilities. The primary training objective is to convince the salespeople that ineffective use of their time can significantly reduce their productivity.

Computer-Assisted-Selling Skills

Many companies are training salespeople to use computer programs to help them allocate their time between accounts; to develop their call schedules; and to handle many of the administrative details of their jobs, such as placing orders, submitting call itineraries and reports, and developing specifications and quotations. Laptops are also becoming an integral part of sales presentations. Before AT&T reps approach a customer, they access DealMaker. This software uses key customer information to suggest a negotiation strategy and to help reps handle objections.[22] As the performance of sales activities becomes more dependent on the use of computers, companies are providing training classes that build computer literacy.

Knowledge of the Legal Constraints on Selling

Properly trained salespeople can reduce their companies' exposure to product liability and false promotion litigation and increase the chances of a successful defense if a suit occurs. They can also lessen the chance that charges of price discrimination or unfair competition will be brought against the company.

The number of claims in the area of product liability has been increasing rapidly, and the cost of settling these claims is rising. Many are over $1 million. Salespeople should be instructed to adopt the following practices to protect the company against charges:

- Always make accurate, understandable statements regarding product warnings, characteristics, and use.
- Avoid making exaggerated claims.
- Review sales literature, warnings, and labels to be sure they are accurate and complete.

With regard to price discrimination, the Robinson-Patman Act of 1936 makes it illegal to offer different prices for the same product or service to different customers unless those differences are cost justified or the price is offered to meet a competitive price. It is important that salespeople are taught the circumstances under which they may offer reduced prices to customers and the documentation they must have to substantiate the reason for doing so.

What Teaching Methods Should Be Used?

Several different teaching methods may be used to present material in a sales training program (see Figure 7–5). Keep in mind that not all methods of presentation are

FIGURE 7-5

Presentation techniques in sales training programs

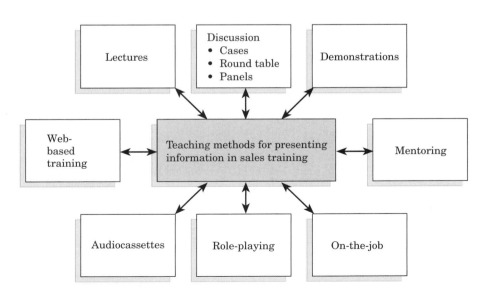

equally effective for all parts of the training. The best format requires blending the topic and the audience.

Lectures

The lecture method can allow trainers to present more information in a shorter time to a larger number of students than any of the other techniques. Selling techniques are best taught by participation methods, but a *limited* number of short lectures introducing students to the underlying problems and principles can be extremely helpful in most sales training programs. Similarly, company information and some product knowledge can be presented in published material, but some lecturing is usually necessary as well. Also, a lecture is frequently the best way to present a basic outline of a subject. Merck's pharmaceuticals reps spend 90 percent of their training in the classroom, where they are taught the scientific principles of medicine. Merck believes that this enables its reps to maintain peer-to-peer discussions with physicians.[23]

Discussion

Discussion should play a large role in any sales training program, since it gives the students an opportunity to work through their own problems. It is the best method for making the experiences of competent salespeople available to trainees. It is also the best method for letting experienced sales reps exchange thoughts and know-how.

Discussions can take several forms. Many are simply open talks on various topics between the teacher and the students, with the teacher controlling the discussion and stimulating it. However, cases, roundtables, and panels can also be used to stimulate and facilitate discussions.

The box labeled "Let's Play Zodiak" presents a very creative method of using board games to teach sales concepts. These games have been used by Motorola, Novartis, and other companies to train their sales reps.[24] Aesop.com, a Web marketing consultancy, uses another novel approach—a book club. Each salesperson is required to read a certain book before meeting for an hour of discussion. Aesop reps have read such selections as Jay Conrad Levinson's *Guerrilla Marketing* and the Chinese classic by Sun Tzu, *The Art of War*. These discussions often leap from the literature to day-to-day business strategies and foster camaraderie as well.[25]

Let's Play Zodiak

Motorola uses a board game called Zodiak to teach its salespeople, who often lack financial experience, how their day-to-day activities affect the finances of the whole company. Each player plays for three "years" (actually six hours), invests money in the company, secures loans and acquires investors to buy a $40 million company, and takes other actions that affect the market success and profitability of the company. In playing the game, salespeople analyze customers' financial and strategic information, perform sensitivity analysis for increased prices and value-added services, and deal with shareholder demands and customer complaints. The game breaks up the usual routine, and salespeople enjoy the creativity and the competition against their fellow salespeople. The reps have fun while learning how their financial decisions affect the bottom line.

Source: www.paradigmlearning.com/Products, March 2002.

Demonstrations

Demonstrations can be used to great advantage in teaching both product knowledge and selling techniques. What better way to teach how a product operates than to actually demonstrate its use? Instead of just telling trainees about the different types of questions that can be used to probe for information, for example, instructors can perform a skit or set up a simulation that demonstrates the questions in a given context. Trainees can be shown how to handle innumerable selling situations that are difficult to describe. Whirlpool Corporation provides its salespeople with a unique type of demonstration. Small groups of newly hired reps live for two months in a house that is equipped with Whirlpool appliances, where they learn by using these appliances in their daily lives.[26]

Role-Playing

In role-playing, the trainee attempts to sell a product to a hypothetical prospect. Often these role-plays are videotaped and critiqued by the trainer and/or peers. This type of learning-by-doing education can be highly effective in teaching selling techniques, particularly in initial training programs. NBC puts its salespeople through a two-day session in which small groups role-play the entire sales process with a new customer, from research to presentation to troubleshooting.[27]

In handling the role-playing sessions, the trainer must explain the importance of taking criticism the right way. Students must be convinced that the critiques will help them become more effective. They must realize that many problems have no cut-and-dried answers and that the suggestions they receive will give them other options to handle problems. The first few presentations are usually poor, but they get better as each trainee takes a turn. The teacher must inform the class that the person chosen to lead off will make more mistakes than will those who follow. Obviously, those who follow will learn from observing the mistakes of the others. The trainer should focus on major problems in the presentation rather than on the details. For example, one of the first questions the instructor should ask the class is: "Just why did Joan fail to make the sale?" or "Just why did Joe get the order?" Students must acquire an ability to see where a sale was made or lost. Frequently, the outcome hinged on only one major reason or event.

A few companies, such as Du Pont High Performance Films, use role-playing on a continual basis to *practice* critical, issue-oriented sales calls just prior to making these calls.[28]

Web-Based Training

Many companies are turning to Web-based training to save money or to reach employees in far-flung global locations. The biggest advantage to Web-based training is cost—not having to bring people together eliminates not only travel, lodging, and meal costs but also instructor salaries. Studies show that online training takes 50 percent less time and costs 30 to 60 percent less than other forms of training.[29] IBM plans to move 35 percent of its training online and estimates that the company has already saved $100 million in its implementation of e-learning programs.[30] However, the push to online training is not just because of the dollar savings; it also is fueled by rapid spread of information and the need for sales-people to keep pace with constant change. It also keeps reps in the field. When they can go online when it is convenient for them and move at their own pace, they don't lose selling time. Experts predict that online training will become a $14 billion industry by 2004, quadrupling in size since the year 2000.[31]

Companies such as IBM and AT&T are using a blend of online training and face-to-face training.[32] Often the online training focuses on basic skills and knowledge, such as introductory tutorials and new product or customer updates. Face-to-face training can then be reserved for teaching and practicing more advanced skills.

There are some pitfalls in using online training. It is easy for the reps to either put it off when they are busy or not do it at all if they feel it is not specific to their needs. However, these problems can be offset by making sure that the information is relevant, by setting time limits for completion, by testing results, and by rewarding progress and completion.[33]

Audiocassettes

Most sales representatives do lots of driving between accounts, and many companies feel that this driving time can be translated into professional development through the use of audiocassettes. Companies such as 3M and Pharmacia provide their sales forces with audiocassettes that cover a wide range of topics.[34] Selling techniques, time management, and motivational speeches are a few of the topics typically covered. Many companies purchase their tapes from outside suppliers, but some companies choose to produce their own.

On-the-Job Training

On-the-job training is the most popular form of sales training. Eighty-four percent of the companies surveyed by Dartnell use on-the-job training.[35] Generally, the procedure is for the trainee to observe a senior rep or sales supervisor making several sales calls. The sales trainee, in turn, makes several calls while the senior rep or supervisor observes and coaches. Then the supervisor and trainee discuss what took place during that call and what the trainee could have done more effectively. This method places the student in a more realistic situation than any of the other techniques do. Usually this method is used as the final stage of the trainee's sales education.

Mentoring is a more informal type of on-the-job training frequently used by companies. A mentor in a training program is usually an experienced rep who is paired with a new trainee. As in the assimilation phase of the staffing (discussed in Chapter 6), the mentor provides advice and support to the new hire. Both Boeing and IBM say they get some of their best training results when they pair a seasoned veteran with a beginner.[36]

Reinforcement

Most salespeople won't change their behaviors as a result of training unless there is some ongoing **reinforcement.** In fact, as noted earlier in the chapter, Xerox found that most of its salespeople retained only 13 percent of the information learned in training after 30 days unless it was reinforced. Yet in many companies reinforcement doesn't occur as frequently as it should, largely because managers don't place a priority on this activity. They don't have time, they are uncomfortable, or they don't know how to provide constructive feedback—and rarely are they recognized or rewarded for their efforts in the skill development area.[37]

There are many ways to reinforce training, including all of the original training methods we have discussed. The most frequently used method is for the sales manager to serve as a coach, reinforcing training efforts during actual calls. Some companies use senior salespeople to coach new reps. Some companies follow up the training session with refresher classes. Boston Scientific Corporation provides follow-up sessions for its five-day training seminar in 13 cities around the globe.[38] Other companies use Web-based methods to reinforce formal training sessions. These methods lower the costs of reinforcing training. Whatever the method, it is important to build some type of reinforcement into the overall training program.

Training Evaluation

Finally, during the **training evaluation** phase, sales executives must assess the effectiveness of their training programs. Evaluation is necessary to determine the value of the training and to improve the design of future programs. In evaluation, executives must decide what outcomes will be evaluated and how these outcomes will be measured. The outcomes must be measured against the objectives for which the training was designed. Outcomes generally fall into one of the following four categories:[39]

- **Reactions.** These outcomes indicate, in a subjective manner, whether those who participated in the training thought it achieved the stated objectives and generally whether it was worthwhile. Reactions may be measured by having participants complete questionnaires or, less formally, by recording verbal comments from the trainees, their supervisors, or the training staff.

- **Learning.** This outcome equates to how much information was absorbed and usually involves giving the trainee some type of test. There may be "before" and "after" tests or just one test taken after the training is completed.

- **Behavior.** This outcome provides an assessment of whether the trainee has changed in substantial ways. The appraisal of behavior is usually conducted by a supervisor who can observe the rep directly. It may also include self-assessment or input from customers.

- **Results.** These are indicators of whether the training is transferring to improved performance results. This is the ultimate test of whether the benefits of training outweigh the costs. Such measures as increased sales and profitability, better customer retention and penetration, and numbers of new accounts can be used to assess bottom-line results.

Although companies are spending billions of dollars on training, most are not taking the time to critically evaluate their training effectiveness. Both financial and nonfinancial effectiveness should be evaluated.[40] Too many companies are overdependent on testing knowledge. It is important to measure factual knowledge as part of a systematic evaluation program, but it is just as important to use other types of measures too. Otherwise, the sales manager will not be able to relate training outcomes to performance in the field. Boston Scientific Corporation tests for product knowledge but evaluates skill mastery as well.[41]

Summary

A successful training program consists of four phases: training assessment, program design, reinforcement, and evaluation. Training is an important factor contributing to the success of salespeople. A good program begins by establishing program objectives and then determining who should be trained. The company must then identify individuals' training needs. This is the key to how much training will be needed.

During the program design phase, the company must decide who will do the training, where and when it will be conducted, what topics will be covered, and what methods will be used. While line personnel have distinctive advantages as sales trainers, they often lack the essential teaching skills. Thus, training is often the responsibility of staff sales trainers. Many companies also use outside training specialists to provide part of their training.

New reps need enough initial training to do a respectable job. However, there are advantages to delaying training until the new person has some experience that can be carried into the classroom. Although initial training is often conducted centrally, most sales training is provided in the field.

Training programs cover a wide range of topics, such as knowledge of the product, company, customer, competitors, and business principles; selling and relationship-building skills; team selling; time management; computer-assisted selling; and legal constraints.

Among the many different methods used to train salespeople are lectures, discussions, demonstrations, role-playing, Web-based training, audiocassettes, and on-the-job training.

It is very important that companies provide a method for systematically reinforcing their training programs. Otherwise, salespeople are unlikely to change their behavior.

Increasingly, top management is demanding that training programs prove their worth. Training outcomes generally fall into four categories: the reactions of the salespeople, their learning, their behavioral change, and their performance results.

Key Terms

Centralized training	On-the-job training	Training assessment
Decentralized training	Program design	Training content
Difficulty analysis	Reinforcement	Training evaluation

Questions and Problems

1. "I don't have any training program. I just hire salespeople who have already proved successful for other companies and turn them loose. I let the big corporations do all my training for me and then just hire away their best people." This was the attitude expressed by the sales manager of one relatively small office-machine firm. Is this a sound policy? What are some of the strengths and weaknesses of this position?

2. "Salespeople are born, not made. It's futile to try to train a person to be a salesperson, so I don't." How would you answer a sales manager who said this to you if you were trying to get him or her to hire you as a sales trainer?

3. "The school of hard knocks is the best training school for salespeople. I just shove them off the dock. Those who have it in them will learn selling on their own, and those who don't have it in them—well, we don't want them around the company anyway." How would you answer a manager who said this?

4. How can the sales manager keep top-notch sales reps interested in continual training programs?

5. You have been made sales trainer for a firm with 125 salespeople. How would you determine their specific training needs?

6. What kind of training is needed for a salesperson who has been promoted to a sales management position?

7. How can the sales manager determine the quality of the various instructors in the firm's training program?

8. You read an article about an outside training specialist and liked what you read. You feel that hiring this specialist may be beneficial to you in your job as sales trainer to Large, Inc. Unfortunately, you know only what this one article said. You want to know much more. Exactly what would you want to learn about this outside specialist?

9. How would you motivate a manager to spend more time reinforcing the skills new reps practiced in the formal training program?

10. How should the sales trainer go about establishing the agenda or curriculum for a refresher course?

11. How could you prove the cost-effectiveness of your sales training program?

Experiential Exercises

A. Identify a business and a position within it that deals with the public. For example, you could choose a loan officer or a teller in a bank; a bagger, meat cutter, or checkout clerk at a grocery store; a sales clerk at a Gap store; or a sales rep for a local beer distributor. Talk to people within and outside the company who deal with the person in that position, and talk to some of the people who currently hold that position. Then prepare a written assessment of the typical training needs of a new person for that position.

B. Describe the training for a field sales position, focusing on the following elements: who and how many participate, what content is covered, who conducts the training, what techniques are used, how long it lasts, where it is conducted, what costs are associated with the training, whether there is any reinforcement after the training, and how the training is evaluated.

Internet Exercises

A. Assume that you are a sales manager for a medium-sized company that wants to contract with an outside supplier to provide sales training in the area of selling skills for new reps. Using one of the Internet search engines, such as Yahoo!, Google, or Infoseek, identify suppliers of such sales training. List the Web addresses of these suppliers, and describe the programs they provide.

References

1. Christen P. Heide, *Dartnell's 30th Sales Force Compensation Survey* (Chicago: Dartnell, 1999), p. 143; and S. Joe Puri, "Where Industrial Sales Training Is Weak," *Industrial Marketing Management*, May 1993, pp. 101–8.

2. Kevin Dobbs, "Training on the Fly," *Sales & Marketing Management*, November 2000, p. 93.

3. Heide, *Dartnell's 30th Sales Force Compensation Survey*, p. 143.

4. Puri, "Where Industrial Sales Training Is Weak," pp. 101–8.

5. Mark McMaster, "Is Your Training a Waste of Money?" *Sales & Marketing Management*, January 2001, pp. 42–48.

6. Ibid.

7. Puri, "Where Industrial Sales Training Is Weak."

8. McMaster, "Is Your Training a Waste of Money?" pp. 42–48; and Mike Zaruba, "Why Most Sales Training Doesn't Work," *Sales & Marketing Executive Report*, April 16, 1997, p. 6.

9. Neil Rackham and Richard Ruff, *Managing Major Sales* (New York: Harper Business, 1991), p. 130.

10. McMaster, "Is Your Training a Waste of Money?" p. 43.

11. Conversation with Dick Canada, Director of the Institute for Global Sales Studies, Kelley School of Business, Indiana University, 2002.

12. Mark McMaster, "Grow Your Own Managers," *Sales & Marketing Management*, December 2000, p. 90.

13. Andy Cohen, "Ending School Daze," *Sales & Marketing Management*, November 1996, p. 32.

14. Andy Cohen, "From the Ground Up," *Sales & Marketing Management*, November 2000, p. 23.

15. Chad Kaydo, "Training: A Complete Regimen for Making Your Salespeople Smarter," *Sales & Marketing Management*, December 1998, p. 33.

16. Heide, *Dartnell's 30th Sales Force Compensation Survey*, p. 43.

17. Ibid., p. 145.

18. Ibid., p. 141.

19. Erika Rasmusson, "Getting Schooled in Outsourcing," *Sales & Marketing Management*, January 1999, pp. 50–51.

20. Elana Harris, "Best at Sales Training," *Sales & Marketing Management*, July 2000, p. 68.

21. Mark Vuturo, "Teams: It's Process Alignment, Not Functional Alignment," presentation at the New Horizons in Personal Selling and Sales Management Conference, American Marketing Association Selling and Sales Management Strategic Interest Group, Lake Buena Vista, FL, July 1996.

22. Mark McMaster, "Training Places," *Sales & Marketing Management*, October 2001, p. 43.

23. Harris, "Best at Sales Training," p. 68.

24. Paradigm Learning, www.paradigmlearning.com/Products, March 20, 2002.

25. McMaster, "Training Places," pp. 44–45.

26. Betsy Cummings, "Welcome to the Real Whirled," *Sales & Marketing Management*, February 2001, pp. 88–89.

27. Kaydo, "Training," p. 33.

28. Jay Kennedy, "Practicing Sales Excellence," *Sales & Marketing Management Executive Report*, March 5, 1997, p. 6.

29. Malcom Fleschner, "Business Class," *Selling Power*, September 2001, p. 133.

30. McMaster, "Is Your Training a Waste of Money?" pp. 42–48.

31. Dobbs, "Training on the Fly," pp. 96–98.

32. McMaster, "Is Your Training a Waste of Money?" pp. 42–48.

33. Kevin Brass, "Pushing E-Learning," *Sales & Marketing Management*, March 2002, p. 56.

34. Cohen, "Ending School Daze," p. 32.

35. Heide, *Dartnell's 30th Sales Force Compensation Survey*, p. 141.

36. Dobbs, "Training on the Fly," p. 96.

37. Rackham and Ruff, *Managing Major Sales*, p. 130.

38. Slade Sohmer, "Emerging as a Global Success," *Sales & Marketing Management*, May 2000, p. 125.

39. Donald Kirkpatrick, *Evaluating Training Programs: The Four Levels* (New York: Berrett-Koehler, 1992).

40. Earl D. Honeycutt Jr., Kiran Karande, Ashraf Attia, and Steven D. Maurer, "A Utility Based Framework for Evaluating the Financial Impact of Sales Force Training," *Journal of Personal Selling & Sales Management*, Summer 2001, pp. 229–38.

41. Sohmer, "Emerging as a Global Success," p. 125.

CASE 7-1   SUNRISE CLEANERS

To Train or Not to Train

Sunrise Cleaner Company's sales have been expanding rapidly in the past several years and are expected to continue increasing throughout the next decade. In order to meet this demand, Mickie Parsons, Sunrise's sales manager, has hired a number of sales representatives and expects to hire 6 to 10 salespeople in the coming year and more the following year. In the past, Sunrise hired only experienced reps, but lately the company has been hiring recent marketing graduates. While the new grads don't have experience, they often have a high level of motivation and a good understanding of overall marketing planning. However, the less experienced reps need more training—both on company policies and sales procedures—before they are effective in making sales calls. Parsons is trying to design a training program that will provide the necessary training at the lowest possible cost.

Currently, Sunrise does not have a training program. The new hires just spend a week in a territory with an experienced rep, and then they are given their own territory. While this system was satisfactory with experienced people, it is not adequate for the inexperienced people the company is now hiring.

Mickie Parsons has suggested to the president of Sunrise, Keat Markley, that the company institute a one- or two-week training program at company headquarters. Parsons has suggested two options. The first option is to hire a staff recruiter/trainer who would spend half of his or her time on recruiting and the other half on training. The new staff specialist would be paid a salary of about $60,000 a year—so the added cost with respect to the training responsibilities would be $30,000 a year. The second option is to contract with an outside company that specializes in sales force training. That company would provide a specialist to set up and conduct a training program at a cost of approximately $20,000 per week.

Parsons was just concluding her presentation to Keat Markley. "I feel that a training program would increase the average annual sales per rep a minimum of 5 percent—to $1,050,000 per rep."

Markley replied, "I am not convinced that the training would improve performance enough to justify the costs. You know it isn't just the cost of the trainer. We would also have to bring these reps into headquarters and pay their expenses while they are here. There would be some equipment and materials involved . . . all for a 5 percent increase in sales! I want to be sure that the 5 percent would more than cover these costs. What about using computer training software to train the new reps? Everything I read says that all of the top companies are using online programs to do a lot of their training and that they are saving bundles in the process."

"I've have checked into that option," Parsons said, "but I don't think that a basic off-the-shelf program would be very effective for training inexperienced graduates and the initial cost of developing a customized program would be excessive—a minimum of $300,000, with each additional week module costing $50,000. Besides, I think an online program works best for refresher training or for introducing new product information, not for teaching basic selling skills—that should be face-to-face training."

"OK," said Markley, "you put together an analysis that considers all the costs of these training options, and then make a recommendation to me. Be sure that you look at the increase in sales that will be necessary to cover these additional costs."

Parsons left the meeting already calculating the costs in her head. She knew that bringing a rep into headquarters would cost $250 per rep for travel and $750 per rep per week for lodging and meals. Materials for any of the programs would likely add an extra $100 per rep and the audiovisual equipment for the face-to-face training would be approximately $300 per training session. She headed for her office, where she could put all of these costs together in order to make a reasoned recommendation to Markley as soon as possible.

Question:

1. What type of training program should Mickie Parsons recommend to Keat Markley? What is your reasoning for your recommendation?

CASE 7-2   IMAGINATIVE STAFFING, INC. (A)

Training Program for a Selling Team

"I'm not sure what's going on around me right now, but it seems as if somebody is trying to tell me something." Angie Roberts, CEO of Imaginative Staffing, Inc., of New York City, was expressing her thoughts to her assistant, Nicole Gamin. Roberts didn't wait for an answer but continued, "I met some marketing professor at a party the other night, and he seemed to think he was holding a class about what's new in selling. He kept babbling something about team selling. I wasn't sure what he was talking about at first. Maybe he had some professional ball team he wanted to sell to someone with more dollars than sense. But then I caught the drift that he was talking about a way to make sales presentations.

"Then last night I read an article in one of the trade journals about team selling. To top it off, my daughter informed me that she was forming a team with some of her Girl Scout friends to sell their cookies this year. Is there some kind of message for us in all this?" Roberts asked Gamin.

Gamin smiled and answered innocuously, "Maybe so!" She had a long list of daily agenda items to go over with her boss and really didn't want to get involved with a discussion about the merits of team selling. "Now let's go over what must be done today."

"You're putting me off because you don't like me to mess up your plans for the day. Well, it won't work. I want to know more about team selling, so put it on the agenda somewhere for today," Roberts insisted.

"All right, you're having lunch with your executive committee. Let's put it on the agenda for that meeting." Gamin evidently had said the right thing because her boss immediately got down to the business at hand, planning the day. Mondays were always busy. Not only did all departments start each Monday with a short meeting to plan the week, but the head of each department met with the CEO for lunch, during which company-wide matters were discussed. Roberts felt strongly that these Monday lunches were important. They allowed her not only to learn what was going on in the company but also to foster communications between her and the other managers in the organization.

Imaginative Staffing, Inc., was a temporary-services firm in New York City. Formed in 1990, it had grown to $17 million in revenues. Besides herself and her assistant, Nicole Gamin, the company had a chief financial officer, a sales director, four sales reps, an operations manager, 10 account managers, five administrative assistants, and a receptionist.

One reason Roberts had perceived the team-selling messages was that for some time she had been frustrated by the length of time it took to close a sale with a good prospect. On average, it took about six months of hard work to make a sale to a major customer. One of the sales reps would make the contact and do all of the selling, sometimes with the help of the sales director if the situation seemed to warrant it.

Large and small corporations made extensive use of temporary help for one or more of several reasons: (1) to fill in for workers who, for some reason, were unable to work; (2) to handle overload conditions; or (3) to take care of seasonal peak workloads. In the current legal environment, many organizations were reluctant to hire permanent employees until there was a clear-cut, long-run need for them. Such factors as benefit packages, insurance, unemployment claims, and termination difficulties made management think seriously about hiring people as employees.

The lunch meeting proceeded smoothly as the group ate and disposed of the agenda items in order. When the last item, team selling, came up, members of the group looked at each other with puzzlement. What was it about? Only Susan Borland, the sales director, knew what team selling was. She was not eager to take the lead in the discussion, preferring instead to sit back to find out what was on Roberts's mind. She did not have long to wait.

The CEO began, "You may wonder why I have put this item on the agenda, so I'll not keep you wondering. For some time I have not been satisfied with our selling effort. It seems to take too much time to gain the confidence of prospective accounts to the extent that they feel comfortable with us. We are relatively new in this market. They don't know us. I've heard and read about team selling as a system that might be of use to us. I want to know exactly what it is and if it is something we should be using."

"It's interesting that you bring this up today because I just had a breakfast meeting with a sales team for Colony Cablevision," Susan Borland said. She continued, "As you know, I'm on the board of directors of my homeowners' association. We have more than 1,000 homes in our planned development, most of whose owners individually subscribe to a cable television system at an average cost of about $45 a month. Now we have been approached by Colony to enter into a bulk billing deal in which all the homeowners will be billed by the association at an attractive price, less than $20 a month for the package. Well, they flew in one of the top managers from their home office to join with the local manager, the local technical engineer, the local marketing manager, and the person who would be our account manager. Each of them made a presentation, and I must say it was effective. I think the board bought it. Anyway, at the time I wondered if this was something we should be doing."

The meeting was interrupted by the receptionist informing several of the managers that their 1:30 appointments were waiting. As they stood up to leave, Roberts asked Borland to prepare a plan for developing and training a sales team for the group to consider at some meeting in the near future.

Susan Borland had been with the company from its beginning. In the early days she did whatever needed to be done, but as the firm grew and was able to hire people to do specific jobs, she devoted more and more of her time to sales. At first she was the firm's only salesperson, but as the company grew she was able to hire more sales reps and she spent increasingly more time in the office, yet she still helped the sales reps whenever they needed it. She was interested in her assignment and intended to get on it that afternoon with the help of her assistant, Judy Morgan.

After briefing Morgan about the team-selling assignment, Borland told her to go to the library and research the subject. "Find out everything you can about it and who is using it."

That evening, Borland was talking about the day with a friend and the conversation drifted into team selling. The friend, a sales rep for a leading software company, was familiar with the concept since his firm used it to sell to important accounts. He advised, "Don't put too many people on the team, or things can get confusing to the prospect. On one of our first team sales calls, we had seven people in there pitching. It was a disaster. The prospect was overwhelmed with information, much of which was useless. Our people weren't trained. We had some of the programming people in there, and you can imagine their selling skills. They just wouldn't talk about what the prospect wanted to hear; they just talked in their lingo."

Susan Borland listened. She had already decided who should be on the sales team, but now she realized that some of these people would require training.

Questions:

1. Should Imaginative Staffing, Inc., adopt a team-selling system for selling to important accounts?

2. If so, who should be on the team?

3. What training would be needed by the team? To what extent should the team's presentation be planned?

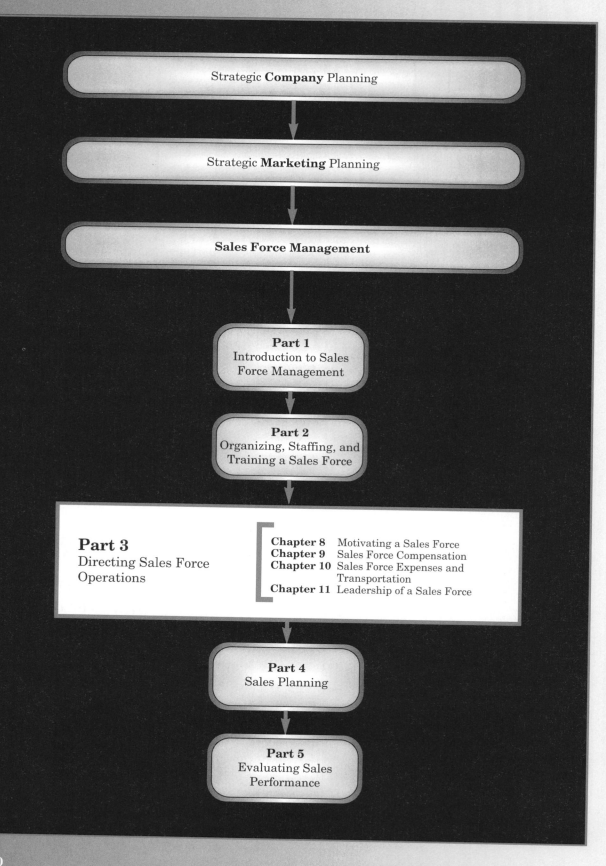

Strategic **Company** Planning

Strategic **Marketing** Planning

Sales Force Management

Part 1
Introduction to Sales
Force Management

Part 2
Organizing, Staffing, and
Training a Sales Force

Part 3
Directing Sales Force
Operations

Chapter 8 Motivating a Sales Force
Chapter 9 Sales Force Compensation
Chapter 10 Sales Force Expenses and
Transportation
Chapter 11 Leadership of a Sales Force

Part 4
Sales Planning

Part 5
Evaluating Sales
Performance

Directing Sales Force Operations

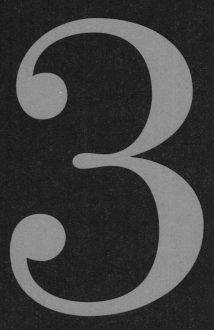

In Part 2 we dealt with organizing, staffing, and training a sales force as the first group of activities involved in *operating* a sales force. Part 3 continues with operational activities that are part of *implementing* a company's strategic sales force planning. Part 3 consists of four chapters involving *directing* sales force operations.

Chapter 8 deals with sales force motivation—behavioral concepts in motivation and motivational tools, including sales meetings and contests. In Chapter 9 we present the topic of sales force compensation—the objectives and requirements of a compensation plan, the steps in designing a plan, the question of compensation *level*, and the *methods* of compensating a sales force. Sales reps' expense plans and transportation are covered in Chapter 10. The final chapter in Part 3 is devoted to the leadership of a sales force—leadership characteristics and styles.

8 Motivating a Sales Force

*To love what you do and feel that it matters—how could anything
be more fun!*

—Katherine Graham—

All motivation is self-motivation. Salespeople cannot be motivated unless they want to be. The challenge for management is to identify, understand, and channel the motivation that their salespeople possess. A sales manager acts as a catalyst, providing both the stimulation for salespeople to feel motivated and the proper rewards so that they continue to feel motivated.

Motivation—What Is It?

To better understand the behavioral concept of motivation, let's first ask: Why do people act as they do? Or: Why do people act at all? The answer: People seek, consciously or unconsciously, to fulfill some physiological or psychological need. All behavior starts with an aroused, or stimulated, need. Hunger, security, or a desire for prestige are examples of needs.

These needs may originate within the person, or they may be stimulated by an external force. You may simply become hungry, for example, or you may see an ad for food that makes you hungry. In either case, once the need is aroused you will be motivated—you will want to take some action. *The desire to expend effort to fulfill a need* is what we call **motivation.** In terms of the sales job, motivation is the effort salespeople want to make to complete various aspects of their jobs.

FIGURE 8-1

Motivational effort

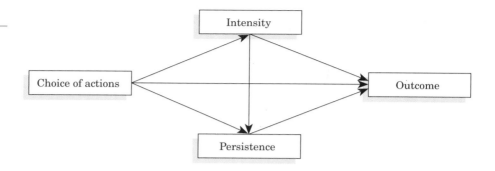

Dimensions of Sales Motivation

Motivational effort is generally thought to include three dimensions: intensity, persistence, and choice.[1] *Intensity* refers to the amount of effort the salesperson expends on a given task; *persistence* refers to how long the salesperson will continue to put forth effort; and *choice* refers to the salesperson's choice of specific actions to accomplish job-related tasks. For example, a salesperson may decide to focus on a particular customer (choice). She may increase the number of calls she makes on this customer (intensity) until she gets the first order (persistence). As noted in Figure 8–1, the choice of a specific action may affect the intensity and persistence. Likewise, intensity may affect how long a salesperson persists at a specific task.

The sales job consists of a large variety of complex and diverse tasks. Because of this, it is important that the sales rep's efforts be channeled in a direction consistent with the company's strategic plan. Therefore, the *direction* of the salesperson's effort is as important as the intensity and persistence of that effort.

Motivation and Strategic Planning

A sales manager concerned with motivating salespeople finds that the most complex task is getting them to expend effort on activities consistent with the strategic planning of the firm. Many salespeople don't need external stimulation to work hard and long; their internal needs motivate them to do so. However, every sales rep must be externally motivated to perform actions that support the strategic objectives of the firm. For example, if a company's strategic plan calls for changing its customer mix, a sales staff must be motivated to change its allocation of calls in a way that is consistent with the strategic change.

Importance of Motivation

The nature of the sales job, the individuality of salespeople, the diversity of company goals, and the continuing changes in the marketplace make motivating sales reps a particularly difficult and important task.

Unique Nature of the Sales Job

Salespeople experience a wonderful sense of exhilaration when they make a sale. But they must also frequently deal with the frustration and rejection of not making the sale. Even very good reps don't make every sale. Also, while many customers are gracious, courteous, and thoughtful in their dealings with salespeople, some are rude, demanding, and even threatening.

Salespeople spend a large amount of time by themselves calling on customers and traveling between accounts. This means that most of the time they are away from any kind of support from their peers or leaders, and they often feel isolated and detached from their companies. Consequently, they usually require more motivation than other workers do to reach the performance level management desires.

Individuality of Salespeople

Sales reps have their own personal goals, problems, strengths, and weaknesses. Each rep may respond differently to a given motivating force. Ideally, the company should develop a separate motivational package for each sales rep; but a totally tailor-made approach poses major practical problems. In reality, management must develop a motivational mix that appeals to a whole group but also has the flexibility to appeal to the varying individual needs.

A related point is that the sales reps themselves may not know why they react as they do to a given motivator, or they may be unwilling to admit what these reasons are. For example, a salesperson may engage in a certain selling task because it satisfies her ego. Rather than admit this, however, she will say that she is motivated by a desire to serve her customers.

Diversity in Company Goals

A company usually has many diverse sales goals, and these goals may even conflict. One goal may be to correct an imbalanced inventory and another may be to have the sales force do missionary selling to strengthen long-term customer relations. These two goals conflict somewhat and require different motivating forces. With diverse goals such as these, developing an effective combination of motivators is difficult.

Changes in Market Environment

Changes in the market environment can make it difficult for management to develop the right mix of sales force motivational methods. What motivates reps today may not work next month because of changes in market conditions. Conversely, sales executives can face motivational problems when market conditions remain stable for an extended time. In this situation, the same motivators may lose their effectiveness.

Behavioral Concepts in Motivation

Finding an effective combination of motivators may be easier if a sales executive understands some of the behavioral factors that affect sales force motivation.

The motivational process begins with an aroused need, but, as depicted in Figure 8–2, three conditions must exist before an unfulfilled need leads to enhanced sales performance.[2] First, salespeople must feel that the rewards are

FIGURE 8-2

Motivational conditions

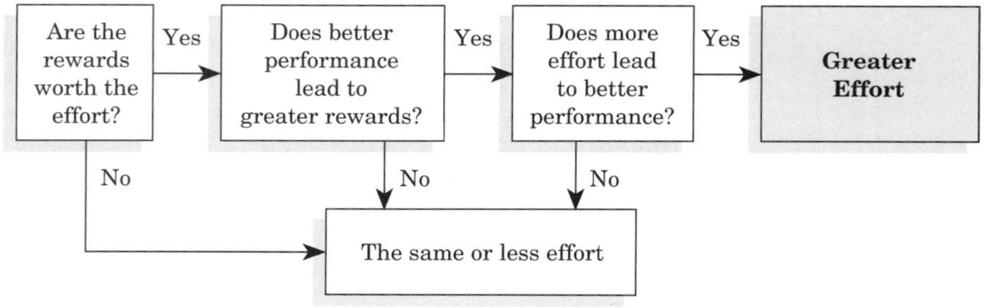

desirable—that is, they will satisfy some need. Second, they must believe that the rewards are tied to performance, and they must understand exactly what performance is required to get the rewards. Finally, sales reps must believe that the performance goals on which the rewards are based are attainable. In other words, the reps must feel that if they expend effort, they can achieve the goals that have been set for them.

The behavioral factors that relate to individuals' needs, and to the conditional links between performance and rewards as well as between effort and performance, are discussed below.

Understanding Individual Needs

Managers must know what salespeople's needs are before developing motivational programs. Such programs often fail because they appeal to the wrong needs. Four motivational theories offer classification systems that can help managers recognize and understand different kinds of needs: Maslow's hierarchy of needs theory, Hertzberg's dual-factor theory, expectancy theory, and role theory.

Hierarchy of Needs Theory

In his hierarchy of needs theory, Abraham H. Maslow proposed five levels of needs that every individual seeks to satisfy.[3] These basic needs, presented in Figure 8–3, can be satisfied with extrinsic and intrinsic rewards.

Extrinsic rewards (such as pay and recognition) are provided by others. **Intrinsic rewards** come from performing the task itself. For example, a salesperson's feeling of accomplishment that comes from landing a big account is an intrinsic reward. The bonus the salesperson receives for landing that account is an extrinsic reward.

Potential sales management actions or rewards that can help satisfy the needs described by Maslow are also presented in Figure 8–3. Some of these needs are considered more basic than others. For example, physiological and safety needs are the most basic needs; social needs are more basic than esteem and self-actualization needs. Thus, the needs form a hierarchy, as shown in Figure 8–3. Until the more basic needs of safety and security are fairly well satisfied, the higher-order needs will not be aroused. A recent survey of 555 salespeople found that those who earn the most are those who least prefer cash as an incentive and those who earn the least prefer cash over other incentives.[4] Occasionally, a previously satisfied need (e.g., job security) may become unfulfilled (loss of job); that need will then take precedence again over the higher-level needs.

FIGURE 8-3   Maslow's hierarchy of needs and possible sales managers' actions

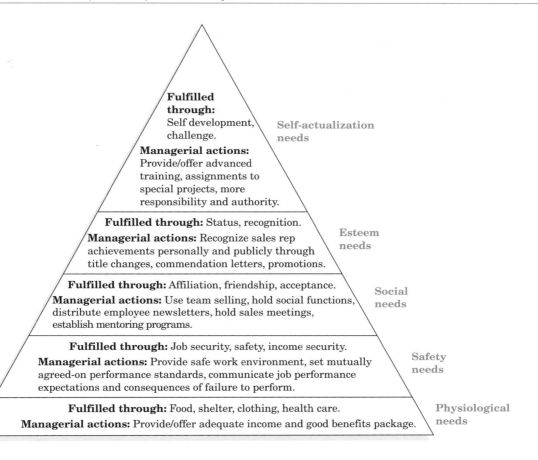

Fulfilled through: Self development, challenge.
Managerial actions: Provide/offer advanced training, assignments to special projects, more responsibility and authority.

Self-actualization needs

Fulfilled through: Status, recognition.
Managerial actions: Recognize sales rep achievements personally and publicly through title changes, commendation letters, promotions.

Esteem needs

Fulfilled through: Affiliation, friendship, acceptance.
Managerial actions: Use team selling, hold social functions, distribute employee newsletters, hold sales meetings, establish mentoring programs.

Social needs

Fulfilled through: Job security, safety, income security.
Managerial actions: Provide safe work environment, set mutually agreed-on performance standards, communicate job performance expectations and consequences of failure to perform.

Safety needs

Fulfilled through: Food, shelter, clothing, health care.
Managerial actions: Provide/offer adequate income and good benefits package.

Physiological needs

Dual-Factor Theory

Another theory of motivation, developed by Frederick Hertzberg, is also based on the idea that people have needs that they will seek to satisfy through their behavior.[5] However, Hertzberg's dual-factor theory groups sources of satisfaction and dissatisfaction into only two groups, **hygiene factors** and **motivation factors.** Examples of hygiene factors (which correspond to Maslow's lower-order needs) are company policies, supervision, and working conditions. They are called hygiene factors because they deal with the condition of the work environment rather than the work itself. Examples of motivation factors (which correspond to Maslow's higher-order needs) are recognition, responsibility, challenge, and opportunities for growth. These factors are part of the job itself and are called motivation factors because they must be present for the person to feel motivated.

Pay can be both a hygiene and a motivation factor. Adequate and competitive salary levels overall are considered a hygiene factor, whereas commissions or raises directly related to performance are viewed as a form of recognition—part of motivation.

Inadequate levels of hygiene factors will cause a sales force to be dissatisfied. And, while adequate levels of these factors will lead to the absence of (or less) dissatisfaction, they will not serve to motivate the reps. Only the higher-order factors lead to motivation.

Expectancy Theory

Expectancy theory builds on the idea that needs provide the starting point for understanding an individual's motivation. However, it goes several steps further by explaining all three of the conditional links described above—reward/effort, performance/reward, and effort/performance—that transform a need into the desire to expend effort to satisfy the need. Below, each of the conditional links is explained in detail.

Reward/Effort Evaluation

Understanding how to appeal to a salesperson's needs is a complex task. Each rep is unique and has a different combination of needs. Therefore, company rewards and incentives valued by one rep may not be valued by another. As shown in Figure 8–4, sales managers often do not know the relative value placed on various incentives by their salespeople. Several factors detailed below help illustrate how sales reps evaluate rewards.

Are the Rewards Worth the Effort? For company rewards and incentives to have an impact on motivation, salespeople must *value* those rewards. In other words, they must feel that the rewards are worth the effort.

Assume that a given sales rep, working under a straight salary compensation plan, has reached her sales goal. Suppose the reward is a congratulatory pat on the back from management and a formal recognition award for the best sales performance of the period. This rep may say to herself, "This honor award would be fine if I were bucking for a promotion or if I wanted to boost my status with management or my co-workers, but what I really want is more money—a nice bonus or a salary increase for my outstanding performance." At the end of this thought process, the rep decides that the reward for reaching her goal is not worth the effort. Management in this case should consider establishing monetary rewards for those reps on straight salary who meet their sales goals.

FIGURE 8-4

What motivates your employees?

Ranked by Employees	Ranked by Managers
1. Interesting work	1. Compensation
2. Appreciation of work done	2. Job security
3. Being well-informed	3. Growth and promotion opportunities
4. Job security	4. Good working conditions
5. Compensation	5. Interesting work
6. Growth and promotion opportunities	6. Personal loyalty to employees
7. Good working conditions	7. Tactful discipline
8. Personal loyalty to employees	8. Appreciation of work done
9. Tactful discipline	9. Help with personal problems
10. Help with personal problems	10. Being well-informed

Source: Kenneth A. Kovack, "Employee Motivation, Addressing a Crucial Factor in Your Organization's Performance," working paper, George Mason University, Fairfax, Virginia, 1997. This study involved 1,000 employees and their managers.

It is also important for the manager to realize that different people value different rewards. The more closely the manager can match the assignment and the rewards with what the individual rep values, the more motivated the rep will be.

Are the Rewards Equitable? A significant factor in salespeople's evaluation of rewards is whether or not they feel the rewards are equitable. Reps compare their performance and rewards with those of their fellow salespeople and ask themselves whether they are being treated fairly. Equity theory suggests that if a salesperson feels that reps whose efforts and performance are not as good as his are receiving greater rewards, he may decrease his efforts. Rewards perceived to be inequitable are unlikely to be a motivating force. And there is a strong possibility that where significant inequities are perceived to exist, salespeople will leave rather than continue to be treated unfairly.

Performance/Reward: A Conditional Link

Not only must sales reps value rewards; they must also feel that attaining them is conditional on performance. If the rewards are pretty much the same regardless of how good or bad a rep's performance is, then these rewards will not be effective motivators. Also salespeople must understand exactly what they must accomplish in order to get a particular reward.

Performance Evaluation. Sales managers must design a reward structure in which greater rewards are tied to better performance. The evaluation process should be linked to the reward system, and sales managers should make every effort to keep the process as objective as possible. The goals should be clear, concise, and measurable. Every sales rep should be made aware of the criteria and the process that will be used to evaluate them.

Sales managers must work with each rep individually to make sure that she or he has accurate understanding of what is expected and what the rewards are. Many companies use a supervisory technique called **management by objectives (MBO)** to increase the sales staff's understanding and acceptance of the criteria by which they will be evaluated. In MBO, the manager and salesperson set mutually agreed-on performance goals. Sales reps who participate in an MBO program are more likely to know what is expected of them and to feel that their goals are attainable and equitable than those who do not take part in such a program. To be motivated, salespeople must believe that improved performance will lead to greater rewards.

Effort/Performance: A Conditional Link

Salespeople must believe that greater effort will lead to improved performance. If they believe this, they will be motivated to try harder. If they don't believe their additional efforts will make a difference, they won't try, regardless of the potential for reward. The accuracy of the sales staff's perceptions concerning effort and performance determines whether motivation can lead to improved performance.

Suppose, for example, a salesperson believes that making a greater number of calls will lead to improved performance, when in fact what the rep really needs to do is to improve the quality of the calls or to call on a different mix of customers. This rep may be motivated to make the additional calls, but such effort will not lead to significantly improved performance. Salespeople must have accurate perceptions of which activities will lead to improved performance.

FIGURE 8–5 Salespeople's perceived reasons for failure and their motivational impact

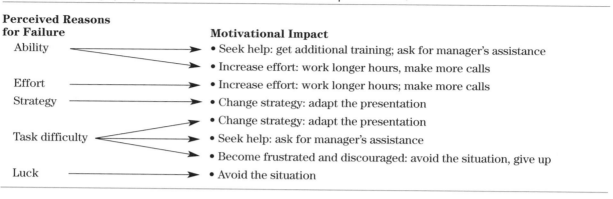

Similarly, they must correctly understand the reasons for their successes and failures. Otherwise, it is likely that they will also have inaccurate perceptions of the effort/performance link.

Perceived Reasons for Success and Failure. Salespeople usually attribute their successes and failures to one or more of the following reasons: ability, effort, strategy (or tactics), luck, or the difficulty of the task.[6] Sales reps will be motivated to do different things, depending on the **attributions** for success or failure they have made. For example, if a salesperson feels that he did not reach his goals because he did not put forth enough effort, he will be motivated to work harder—to work more hours and/or to call on more accounts. However, if he feels that he lost sales because of the particular presentation he was using, he will change his strategy by adapting his presentation. Changing strategies is sometimes called "working smarter."

If sales reps feel their failures are due to lack of ability, they should be motivated to seek advice or help. But sometimes they will instead increase their effort to compensate for their lack of ability. If they feel that the difficulty of the task contributed to their failure, they may be motivated to work harder and/or smarter. However, if they feel that the task is impossible, or that the goal is unreasonable, they will be frustrated and less motivated. Figure 8–5 summarizes these attributes and their impact on selling behavior.

Through training, counseling, and day-to-day coaching, sales managers can help their people both recognize which activities lead to improved performance and make correct attributions for success and failure. They can also set attainable goals. More important, sales managers themselves must understand that encouraging their salespeople to work harder is not the only path to success, nor necessarily the best one. Motivating sales reps to understand customer differences, think about alternative sales strategies, and be adaptive when the situation calls for it may lead to better results than will simply telling them to try harder.[7]

Role Theory

Role theory concerns the social roles people occupy and the various behaviors that are appropriate to those roles. As noted above, salespeople must understand exactly what they must do in order to improve their performance. However, this is often difficult because much of their job activity involves dealing with people outside the company (namely, customers) and because they usually work with little or no direct supervision. As a result, there can be considerable role ambiguity and role conflict in the salesperson's role.

Role Ambiguity

Role ambiguity results when sales reps are not sure what is expected of them. For example, reps may be uncertain of whether or not they have the authority to meet price competition or to grant credit. They may be unclear about their organizational relationship with staff executives. A marketing research manager may ask the reps to perform some duties in the field; the reps may not know how much time and energy to devote to such requests.

Role Conflict

Role conflict stems from two sources. One source is that a sales rep is trying to serve two masters—the company and the customer. Because these two often have different and conflicting interests, a rep can get caught in the middle. For example, a customer wants lenient credit terms, but the credit manager wants to deal in short-term credit with stringent terms. Or a customer expects gifts and lavish entertainment, but the rep's management, fearful of bribery accusations, wants to cut back on these items.

Another potential source of conflict lies in the varying demands placed on the sales reps by different groups within their own companies. For example, the marketing department may push the reps to follow up on the leads generated by the return of the trade publication reader interest cards, but the sales department wants the reps to concentrate on existing customers.

Sales managers must make sure that all salespeople understand what is expected in their respective roles. Writing clear and detailed job descriptions and letting the sales force participate in setting their own goals are ways of decreasing role ambiguity and conflict.

The importance of having the sales force know what is expected of them and how to handle various situations goes beyond improved performance. Research has demonstrated that when salespeople have a clear understanding of their roles, not only is their performance higher; their job satisfaction is also higher and their propensity to leave is lower.[8]

Salesperson Characteristics

Salespeople's needs, their evaluation of rewards, and their perceptions of the conditional links described above are influenced by the personal characteristics described below.

Demographics

Age, family size, income, and education all affect the value that salespeople place on various rewards. For example, sales reps relatively satisfied with their current income level may be more interested in such things as status, freedom, and self-development than in pay and benefits. Others, less satisfied, may be very concerned about their income levels. Salespeople with greater education may place a higher value on opportunities for training and advancement than others.

Psychological Traits

Some psychological traits are linked to how the sales rep evaluates rewards. For example, a rep with a high need for achievement will be motivated by greater responsibility and challenge. Other traits affect the person's perceptions of the effort/performance link. Salespeople with high levels of self-esteem, for example, will feel confident about their efforts to improve performance.

Experience

Another factor that affects salespeople's perceptions is experience. The more experience they have in sales, the more understanding reps will have about what kind of effort leads to improved performance and about what performance levels are necessary to attain the rewards they desire.

Career Stages

Studies have shown that salespeople's needs change as they progress through their careers.[9] The career stages are related to demographic changes. In the **exploration stage** of their careers, sales reps are very achievement oriented and are particularly interested in advancement and growth opportunities. During the **establishment stage** of the career cycle, sales reps usually become committed to their occupations, striving to succeed, to get ahead. Typically this is also the time when family responsibilities become greater. Money and fringe benefits become much more important during this stage, but status, recognition, and intrinsic job satisfaction are important as well.

In the **maintenance stage,** sales reps are valuable to the company because they generally account for a large volume of their company's sales. Yet they are at a stage where their performance may begin to level off, and motivating them becomes particularly important. Salespeople in the maintenance stage are often motivated by job security, job enrichment, and status enhancement.

Team Selling

The success or lack of success of team selling can often be explained by the willingness of the individuals on the team to cooperate with the team efforts. What motivates an individual to cooperate in team-selling efforts?

- **Belief in the goal.** The individual must think that the goals of the team are worthwhile. A person who does not believe in the goal probably won't work very hard to achieve it.

- **Belief that cooperation will lead to the goal.** The person must feel that the group has the ability to carry out the goal and that cooperation is necessary in order to be successful. If the salesperson feels that the team has been given an impossible task or unrealistic goals, motivation will be low.

- **Belief that the benefits to the individual of cooperating will outweigh the costs.** The individual must feel that the rewards, both extrinsic and intrinsic, outweigh the personal costs of participating. If the salesperson feels that she is not being compensated fairly, then her commitment to the team will be low. The salesperson may attempt to free-ride, letting others do her share of the work. The individual must also feel that he or she will have an influence on the team's actions and that his or her participation will make a difference to the team's success.

Source: Adapted from Thomas W. Porter, "Marketing Teams," working paper, Kelley School of Business, Indiana University, 2001.

In the **disengagement stage,** salespeople are mentally preparing for retirement. While reps in this stage have adequate knowledge to perform their jobs, they may have lost the desire to sell. They are withdrawing psychologically. This attitude may overwhelm their ability to sell. That is, as they lose interest in their jobs, their performance will slip. It is difficult to motivate reps who have reached the disengagement stage. The best thing the manager can do is to give them some reason for staying involved and committed. Assignment to special projects and/or problems is one way to recognize and use their skills and knowledge.

Selecting Effective Combinations of Motivational Tools

The preceding section indicated that it is difficult to predict how any given salesperson will respond to a motivational package. But sales managers should begin by getting to know each rep as an individual in order to understand his or her specific needs. Only then will the sales manager design an effective motivational program. Some companies feel that personal goals are such an important motivator that they tie the achievement of bonuses to both sales goals and personal goals.[10] *Every motivational program should have some elements within it that can be tailored to the individual's needs.* The starting point for a successful motivational program is to establish specific performance objectives that have been agreed on and can be measured by both the manager and the rep.

Given a set of performance objectives, managers must determine the most effective combination of motivation methods for their salespeople. Motivational tools may be divided into two categories: **financial rewards** and **nonfinancial rewards.** Each type is outlined in Figure 8–6. Notice that the basic sales management tasks of leadership, training, planning, and evaluating are also considered part of the

---

FIGURE 8–6   Specific elements in the motivational mix

Financial Rewards

- Basic compensation plan
  Salary
  Commissions
  Bonus payments
  Fringe benefits
- Sales contests

Nonfinancial Rewards

- Recognition awards, such as pins, trophies, certificates
- Praise and encouragement from management
- Job enrichment
- Opportunity for promotion (this may also be a financial reward)
- Sales meetings and conventions

Other Elements

- Leadership and supervision
- Sales training programs—induction and continuation
- Sales mentoring
- Sales planning elements
  Forecasts
  Budgets
  Quotas
  Territories
- Evaluation of salesperson's performance
- General management elements
  Organizational structure
  Management's leadership style
  Channels of communication
  Corporate culture

motivational mix. Because each of these is discussed in separate chapters, the discussion that follows focuses primarily on the financial and nonfinancial rewards.

Financial Rewards

Compensation

Money is often used as an incentive for salespeople. A recent study found that 69 percent of the companies surveyed use cash as an incentive and that salespeople like to receive cash. Surveys show that salespeople *prefer* pay raises and cash incentives over any other type of motivational program. Yet only 15 percent of salespeople surveyed say that they are *motivated* by the expectation of financial reward.[11] Therefore relying on additional compensation to motivate your salespeople may not always be effective. The design of sales force compensation plans is discussed in Chapter 9.

Other Financial Rewards

Many companies offer their salespeople performance incentives that are not in the form of cash but that would cost the reps a significant amount of money if they were to buy these things for themselves. Companies such as Lexmark, Grainger Industrial, and Panasonic use merchandise and travel to encourage their reps to improve their performance. In order to appeal to varying preferences, Lexmark and other companies have individualized their incentives. They use a points-based program in which salespeople earn points toward merchandise they may select from a catalog.[12]

Increasingly popular are a category of incentives called *experience-based incentives*. Shred-it, a document destruction company headquartered in Toronto, Canada, gave 14 reps a trip to a NASA space camp, where the reps learned to pilot the shuttle and experienced weightlessness. Ford Motor Credit sent three salespeople from each of its top 15 dealerships to fly T-6 fighter planes, pairing each rep with an experienced pilot.[13] Many of the incentives described here are used in conjunction with sales contests, described next.

Sales Contests

Sales force contests are short-term incentive programs that use prizes and awards to motivate sales reps to achieve goals specified by management. Contests are a popular motivational device.

A contest should have a clear-cut purpose, such as something management wants the sales force to do that it isn't doing. Contests are best used to achieve such specific goals as getting new accounts, selling specific products, or relieving certain overstocked inventory positions.

In planning and conducting a successful contest, managers must design the contest, select the prizes, and promote the contest.

Contest Design

The contest should be designed so that each person has an equal opportunity to win. If the average or poor reps learn that the top producers win all the prizes, they will silently withdraw from the competition. Opportunity to win may be equalized through the use of quotas or by allowing for differences in territories and selling abilities. The rep who makes the greatest improvement relative to others is the winner. In this way, even the poorest salesperson has a chance to win.

A variation of the design described above is an **open-ended contest,** in which there is no limit to the number of people who can win by meeting their preset goals. In this way, people are competing only with themselves. This is in contrast to a **closed-ended contest,** in which there are a limited number of winners. Northern Telecom has successfully used an open program, whereas IBM recently used a closed program, which is described on page 241 in the International Perspective box.[14]

Another method of broadening the opportunity to win is to use a **tiered contest.** In this type of program, two or more levels of prizes are awarded. If salespeople perform at or above a certain level, they get a certain prize—say, a trip to Europe. If they achieve at a lower level, they get a different prize—maybe a trip to the Bahamas. This can be used in conjunction with an open-ended contest in which everyone can win. Tissues Technology, a company that sells and leases surgical lasers, has an incentive program in which there are eight levels of prizes, with choices at each level.[15]

Prizes

Contest success depends to a great extent on the attractiveness of the prizes. Cash prizes, merchandise, and travel are frequently used as incentives. Cash prizes have the advantage of giving the rep the greatest choice in how to use the prize. On the other hand, travel and merchandise are more visible and interesting to promote and publicize. Also, as noted above, some studies have found non-cash prizes to be more effective than cash prizes for motivating sales reps.[16] In the Tissue Technology contest described above, one of the top prizes is a two-week African safari. As noted earlier, one way to increase the choice associated with merchandise is to use a point system in which the winners earn points toward merchandise they may select from a catalog.

Promotion

The sales contest and the prizes that will be given out should be widely and continually publicized throughout the duration of the contest. At least 10 percent of

Cyberspace Incentives

Many companies are now conducting their sales contest and other incentive programs online. In the case of contests, participants can access the contest rules, their up-to-the-minute standings, and an electronic catalog of prizes online. CTC Communication Corporation recently tested an online contest. As noted by one of the company's regional managers, because the online contest provides real-time results instantaneously, it really "gets the competitive juices going!" The salesperson gets instant recognition of his or her success and immediate redemption of prizes.

Instant tracking and updating is the primary advantage of putting incentive programs online. Another advantage is the ease with which managers can make adjustments to the program—boost award points, change the rules, update the electronic awards catalog. Also, the costs of promoting and administering an online program are significantly less than for an offline program. As a result of these advantages, experts predict that in three years 50 percent of sales incentive programs will be online.

Source: Dana James, "Incentive Programs Move to Cyberspace," *Marketing News,* December 4, 2000, p. 4.

the budget for the contest should be spent on promotion. The goal is to keep everyone excited.

Objections to Contests

While contests can increase sales and boost morale, they may also have some unintended effects. Frequently, sales contests lead to undesirable selling methods, such as overstocking, overselling, and various pressure tactics. In the short run, such tactics may enable a sales rep to win the contest, but in the long run they can cause trouble. Many executives object to contests on the grounds that they create morale problems. To some extent, the open-ended and tiered programs can alleviate the possible morale problems.

One of the biggest objections to sales contests is that a decline in sales almost inevitably occurs afterward. The sales force cannot keep up the high level of activity indefinitely. Also, some crafty sales reps "stockpile" orders by getting customers to delay orders in the period just before the contest begins. Many questions have been raised about the long-run benefits of a contest. If a contest has achieved wider distribution and new dealerships, a long-run benefit should occur. But if the contest has focused mainly on sales volume, its long-range value is questionable. Lack of permanent accomplishment is not necessarily bad, however. For instance, many contests are designed for short-run purposes such as selling out on overstocked inventory.

In summary, then, contests can be effective motivators, but they must be carefully and thoroughly designed to encourage participation by the greatest number of people.

Nonfinancial Rewards

Managers often assume that financial incentives are the best motivators and that developing a good compensation package is the only thing they must do to motivate their sales force. However, evidence suggests that sales reps are motivated by both financial and nonfinancial incentives. A variety of factors—including job enrichment, recognition, promotion, encouragement, and praise—motivate performance. These factors are discussed below.

Job Enrichment and Support

Salespeople thrive on challenge. One way managers can challenge reps is to give them greater responsibility, authority, and control over their jobs. Also, most people like to have variety in their job-related tasks. Doing the same things over and over again quickly becomes boring to someone who is seeking challenge. Varying some aspects of the sales job can provide a stimulus for increased levels of motivation. Together, increases in responsibility and variety are known as **job enrichment.** Additionally, like everyone else, salespeople want to feel that they are performing a meaningful task that will make a significant contribution to their companies and/or to those around them. Managers must make sure that each salesperson understands the importance of his or her contribution to the company's performance. Finally, salespeople must also be given adequate support in the areas of training, technology, and information to be able to compete in today's high-tech market.

Public recognition of a job well done is a good motivational tool.

Recognition and Honor Awards

A fundamental principle of good human relations is that individuals who deserve commendation must be given full recognition. Most salespeople enjoy public recognition of their accomplishments. Plaques, pins, or certificates can be used to recognize accomplishment levels. It is really difficult to give too much recognition to anyone. This is exemplified by the following quote from Joe Rice, a Belden-Stark Brick Corporation sales manager:

> The last trip I qualified for was a trip to Istanbul to meet the president of our parent company. I can afford a trip to Istanbul on my own, but a chance to be recognized as one of the top American salespeople is something you can't put a price on.[17]

Recognition programs are most effective when they include approximately half of the company's salespeople. If too many people receive them, the awards lose their value; if too few receive them, the awards may be viewed as too hard to achieve. The awards should be publicized and presented in a public ceremony or banquet. Involvement by top management adds significance and prestige to the award.

Many companies develop clubs for outstanding producers or those who meet certain goals. Membership in such clubs usually bestows on high achievers the right to various recreational diversions in addition to the ego-gratifying recognition connected with just being in the select group. The life insurance industry has long had its Million Dollar Round Table to recognize agents who sell that amount of life insurance each year. Stroh's has a Top Performers Club into which 4 out of the top 88 performers are inducted each year. Bausch & Lomb has its Pinnacle Club for the top 10 percent of its sales force.[18] Membership in such clubs is valued highly by most reps, who consider it a major career accomplishment.

Promotions

Title changes can be another source of motivation. Changing a rep's title from sales representative to senior sales representative, for example, can indicate the rep's accomplishment. Dow Chemical Company recognizes eight levels of achievement for career salespeople, from sales representative to corporate account executive. Each level entails a major increase in responsibility.[19] Of course, the possibility of being promoted into management is a motivating factor for many salespeople.

Encouragement and Praise

The easiest and least expensive form of motivation is personal encouragement and praise from the manager. Small things such as a personal note, a pat on the back, or a thank-you for a job well done go a long way. Most reps like to feel that someone knows and cares about how much extra effort went into heading off the competitive threat to the company's largest account or how hard they tried, even though they didn't get that new account. As Xavier Williams, an area sales vice president for AT&T Business Services, stated so aptly, "Sustained performance comes from day-to-day motivation—and that has to come from me."[20]

Corporate Culture

Some companies have very supportive corporate cultures in which they provide support to their employees that goes beyond the training and technology directly related to their jobs. Dun & Bradstreet, for example, recognizes the need for reps to balance their careers with their family needs and allows their salespeople to work flexible schedules.[21] Medtronics goes above and beyond to provide a healthy work environment—it provides its salespeople flextime scheduling, on-site fitness centers, free health screenings, adoption assistance, massage therapy rooms, and even meditation rooms. These perquisites motivate Medtronics reps to work hard for the company that has treated them so well, and to stay loyal. The company's earnings for 2001 were a "healthy" 15 percent.[22]

Sales Meetings

Sales meetings are one of the most commonly used methods of motivating salespeople. Most companies have one or more sales meetings a year, and some have them as frequently as once a week. The most important aspect of the sales meeting is communication. Being able to interact with management and with fellow reps makes reps feel like part of a team. More important, increased communication between salespeople and their managers leads to improved performance.[23]

Purposes of Sales Meetings

Management can use sales meetings to communicate the company's long-term goals and strategic objectives and to explain how important the salesperson's role is in achieving these goals. This instills self-esteem and pride in the reps and helps

During this sales meeting, these reps are learning about a new marketing program.

them identify with the company. This kind of communication is particularly important for salespeople who are often physically isolated from their companies. In many companies, the reps rarely see each other except at sales meetings. Thus, the meetings enable them to develop friendships and build team spirit and solidarity.

Sales meetings are also used to inform reps about product changes and new products, to explain new advertising and marketing programs, to provide training, and to inspire the sales staff to work harder and smarter. Meetings such as these can help the sales staff understand what is expected, improve their knowledge and skills, and build confidence in their efforts to succeed. Some meetings are held primarily for the purpose of recognizing and rewarding salespeople's performance.

Planning for Sales Meetings

A poorly planned sales meeting is probably worse than no meeting at all. A boring, tedious meeting in which salespeople have no opportunity to interact and participate can be demoralizing. This problem can be avoided by careful planning, by using speakers who are effective communicators, and by using a variety of communication formats. Videotapes, small-group discussions, role-playing, demonstrations, and question-and-answer sessions can all be effective communication methods. Soliciting input from the reps about what they think should be covered in the meeting can help as well. Follow-up to ensure that the key points of the meeting are reinforced is important as well. Xerox uses its intranet site to post all of the material presented in its sales meetings. The salespeople can access the material as soon as the meeting is over.[24]

Challenges and Changes in Sales Force Motivation

One of the most pervasive motivational challenges facing sales force managers is the plateaued salesperson. Another motivational issue, somewhat related to the first, is whether or not to segment the sales force for the purposes of motivation, communication, and administration.

Plateaued Salespeople

A **plateaued salesperson** is one who has stopped improving and developing. Often these people (usually but not always in the 40 to 50 age bracket) have performed well in the past, but they reach a point where they seem to lose the drive to sell or even the interest in striving for new goals. This is a significant problem for most sales managers.

Plateaued salespeople are not performing up to expectations, and it is very difficult to get them to do so. Yet managers are hesitant to terminate them because these reps are likely to have developed very strong relationships with a few important customers, and they may still generate a large number of sales with these customers without trying very hard. Causes of plateauing, symptoms, and possible solutions are presented below.

Causes of Plateauing

The lack of upward mobility is the number one cause of plateauing. Salespeople faced with limited opportunities for promotion see their careers coming to a standstill. Other reasons are boredom, perceptions of unfair treatment, burnout, and satisfaction with income levels.

Symptoms of Plateauing

There are early signs of plateauing. Sales reps who have done so in the past may no longer prospect hard enough or follow through. They seem to be sick or absent more than they used to be, and they work fewer hours. They seem to lack energy, time, enthusiasm, creativity, and a sense of humor. Their paperwork may become sloppy, and the sales manager may get more complaints from these reps' customers. Usually these reps are not keeping abreast of new products and technologies. They relish the past and resist changes.

Possible Solutions for Plateauing

The first step for a good solution is to recognize the symptoms early. Then it is important for the sales manager to discuss the situation with the rep. The manager must identify the problem and set clear performance expectations. If the rep does not improve his or her performance, then more creative solutions may be necessary. One solution is to give the salesperson a new assignment, such as coaching new salespeople, gathering competitive intelligence, surveying customers for new product ideas, or developing a new territory. The new responsibilities may relieve the boredom and/or provide a challenge that would excite and motivate the rep. Another alternative is to shift accounts, which forces the sales rep out of a comfortable territory that requires little to maintain into one where he or she must start over. It is the manager's responsibility to take action to get these people out of their ruts. Their experience and skills are too great to waste.

Sales Force Segmentation

Throughout the chapter, we have stressed the importance of recognizing individual differences. It's true that using one program to try to motivate all reps may not be very effective, yet it is impractical to design totally different motivational programs for each salesperson. **Sales force segmentation** offers a balance between the extremes of individual motivation and blanket motivation.[25]

In this approach, the sales force is first segmented, or divided, into several groups. Sales reps can be grouped according to their career stages or their sales

An International Perspective

IBM recently conducted a global sales contest called "You Sell, You Sail." The contestants—from 140 countries—were 2,000 IBM reps and 5,000 independent distributors. Both the reps and the distributors sell IBM's midsized computers to small and medium-sized businesses. The prize? A Caribbean cruise.

The overall goal of the contest was year-to-year revenue growth, and the winning slots were allocated to IBM's global regions based on their contribution to total sales. But because each of the geographic terri-

tories has different ways of doing business, the specific criteria for winning were set by the regions themselves and thus varied somewhat across regions. As a result, 200 IBM salespeople (and their guests) from the regions of Europe, Canada, Africa, Asia-Pacific, and the United States set sail together from Miami on a Caribbean cruise.

Source: Melanie Berger, "IBM's Global Sails Program," *Sales & Marketing Management*, February 1997, p. 34.

expertise, for example. Then an appropriate motivational mix can be designed for each. Compensation, communication, supervision, and recognition incentive programs can all be tailored to the specific needs of the group.

Another approach is for the company to offer several alternative compensation and benefit packages and let each rep choose which program he or she wants. The company can even offer a menu of incentives and benefits, letting reps choose from the list and, in effect, design their own programs. Segmentation is a means through which managers can provide rewards that appeal to all of the salespeople rather than to just some.

Motivation and Performance

It is important to remember that motivation—the desire to expend effort—is not the only requirement for successful sales performance. Salespeople must have the *ability* to perform as well as the motivation to do so.

The ability to perform sales tasks can be acquired or learned through training and experience. Some companies hire only experienced, proven salespeople who already have the necessary skills. But when companies hire inexperienced people, management must provide the training for them to gain the necessary skills. It is not enough for the reps to be motivated; they must also know how to do what is expected of them.

Recruiting and selection procedures are also important. In hiring *inexperienced* people, companies must be careful to select those with an aptitude for learning sales skills. In hiring *experienced* people, they must be certain that those selected have the desired set of skills. It is also important in both cases to select people whose needs are consistent with the demands or rewards of the particular sales job.

The motivational program must be integrated with the entire sales management program. A good motivational program will not compensate for poor recruiting, selection, and training. Motivational policies must be a part of a well-planned and well-executed sales management program.

A DAY-TO-DAY OPERATING PROBLEM

MAJESTIC PLASTICS COMPANY

MAJESTIC
Plastics Company

The Sales Contest

Bud Cowan, the Majestic sales rep in Dallas, was angry. He wanted to know what Clyde Brion planned to do about the sales contest. Although the $15,000 award had already been delivered to another Majestic rep, Cowan felt the prize was actually his.

It had been only a year ago that Clyde Brion had dreamed up the idea of a $15,000 contest for the Majestic sales force. Having just introduced the new ROYAL line of plastic containers, the company was interested in seeing sales for the new product get off to a quick start. Brion had suggested a sales contest, the company's first, whereby the rep selling the most from the ROYAL line would receive a check for $15,000 hand-delivered by the Majestic president.

Having developed the guidelines, Brion then informed the sales force of the contest, which would last for nine months. The reaction from the reps was quite enthusiastic; in the first month alone, the ROYAL line's sales exceeded company projections.

With one month to go in the contest, Bud Cowan appeared to be well on his way to winning the prize. He had worked extremely hard introducing the ROYAL line to all his customers in the Dallas area, even going as far as holding product seminars on weekends. His efforts appeared to be paying off when, out of the blue, Wally Thomas, Majestic's rep in Milwaukee, delivered a huge order to his largest account, Badger Foods.

With that order, Thomas was able to secure the contest and one month ago had received the $15,000

check in a ceremony at company headquarters. This week, however, came a startling development. It seemed that Badger Foods had decided to cancel plans for a new product line and no longer needed the shipment of ROYAL line plastic containers. Having neither opened nor used any of the shipment, Badger was expecting a full refund on the returned goods. This practice was in line with Majestic customer policy and, although disappointed, Majestic did not want to get into any kind of legal battle with one of its best customers.

When asked by Clyde Brion about the lost sale, Wally Thomas expressed shock and disappointment but still felt the $15,000 prize belonged to him. "I sold that order within the contest time frame, fair and square! It's not my problem if a customer changes its mind after I've delivered the product. The boys in headquarters should deal with that! I worked hard and won that contest," Thomas said.

Bud Cowan, however, disagreed. "Thomas played this contest like a fiddle! I'll bet he set up that bogus order with Badger Foods on the first day of the contest. Heck, he's been buddies with those guys for over 20 years. I want that $15,000 and a handshake from the president," demanded Cowan.

Question: What should Clyde Brion do to resolve this dilemma?

Note: This case was prepared by Steven Reed, under the direction of Rosann Spiro.

Summary

All human behavior starts with motivation. That is, the reason people act in a certain way is that they are motivated to do so. Motivation is the desire to expend effort to fulfill an aroused need. Sales managers are interested in the effort salespeople desire to expend on various activities or tasks associated with the sales job.

Sales executives generally agree that effective motivation of a sales force is essential to the success of any sales organization. The problem lies in finding the right combination of motivators for any given group of salespeople. Motivating a sales force is difficult because of the unique nature of the sales job. Also, each rep is an individual who responds in his or her own way to a given motivator.

Another motivational difficulty occurs when there is a conflict in management's sales goals. Finally, changes in the market or selling environment pose motivational problems.

To motivate salespeople, managers must first understand their needs. Both Maslow's hierarchy of needs theory and Hertzberg's dual-factor theory help managers understand the kinds of needs salespeople have. Managers must also understand how their sales reps evaluate rewards. Salespeople will ask themselves: Are the rewards worth the effort? Are they equitable? Salespeople must also believe that rewards are based on performance.

Managers must make sure that salespeople not only know what is expected but also understand what kinds of activities will lead to better performance. Role theory helps managers understand that salespeople often experience role ambiguity and role conflict due to the nature of their jobs. This can make it difficult for the reps to understand management's priorities for sales performance.

Management's task is to select the right combination of motivators—the right motivational mix for a given sales force. Motivational tools fall into two categories: financial rewards, such as compensation, travel, merchandise, and sales contests; and nonfinancial rewards. Nonfinancial rewards include job enrichment, recognition and honors, promotions, encouragement and praise, and support from the corporate culture. Sales meetings are another method commonly used to motivate salespeople.

In the future, the problem of plateaued salespeople will continue to challenge managers. It is important that managers recognize the symptoms of plateauing and work with their plateaued reps to overcome these problems. Sales force segmentation—a system in which people are grouped according to their motivational needs and different rewards are offered to each group—provides an innovative approach to the challenge of motivating salespeople.

It is important to remember that motivation is only one component of successful sales performance. Motivational policies must be incorporated into a well-planned and well-executed sales management program.

Key Terms

Attributions
Closed-ended contest
Disengagement stage
Establishment stage
Exploration stage
Extrinsic rewards
Financial rewards
Hygiene factors

Intrinsic rewards
Job enrichment
Maintenance stage
Management by objectives
   (MBO)
Motivation
Motivation factors
Nonfinancial rewards

Open-ended contest
Plateaued salesperson
Role ambiguity
Role conflict
Sales force segmentation
Sales meetings
Tiered contest

Questions and Problems

1. Define motivation and explain why it is particularly important for salespeople.

2. Which is more important, the *strength* of a salesperson's beliefs about the effort/performance link or the *accuracy* of those beliefs?

3. a) List several roles that a sales rep is likely to play.
   b) List several different role partners with whom sales reps are typically involved.

4. What types of role conflicts are sales reps likely to experience?

5. What can management do to reduce a salesperson's
   a) Role ambiguity?
   b) Role conflicts?

6. Explain why persistence is an important dimension of motivation for the sales position.

7. Would providing salespeople with flextime and/or on-site child care be a motivational factor for a rep who has young children or would it just make the rep feel committed to the organization? Explain your answer.

8. Explain what kind of behavioral changes can be expected if a salesperson attributes failures to luck, effort, strategy, ability, or task difficulty.

9. Explain how the sales manager should handle a rep who is one of the company's best performers but is constantly driving all of the other reps crazy with her combative, haughty attitude.

10. "If you pay a salesperson enough, you will have a well-motivated salesperson." Do you agree? Explain.

11. Explain how motivation is related to each of the following aspects of managing a sales force:
    a) Supervising the sales force.
    b) Setting sales quotas.
    c) Recruiting and selecting salespeople.
    d) Designing the expense-payment plan.

12. If you were a district sales manager, how would you motivate the following sales reps?
    a) An older sales rep who is satisfied with his present earnings level. He plans to remain as a career sales rep and retire in six years.

    b) An excellent sales rep whose morale is shot because he did not receive an expected promotion. He has been with the company five years.

13. A sales manager once said, "Motivating salespeople is the same as babying them. I am careful to hire only motivated people. This way I don't have to worry about motivating them. Good sales reps don't need any motivation from me—they motivate themselves." What do you think about this philosophy?

Experiential Exercises

A. Interview a sales manager, asking what motivates three or four individual reps under his or her supervision. Then interview these same reps (one at a time) and ask them what motivates them. Compare the reps' responses with those of the manager.

B. Design a sales contest for the salespeople who sell advertising for your local school paper, for a local copying service, for a local beverage supplier, for a telemarketing firm, for your school's telemarketing fund-raising group, or for a school organization.

Internet Exercises

A. Assume that you have just been promoted into a sales management position and (because you sold your sales management text after graduation) need some information on how to motivate the sales reps who are reporting to you. Search the Web for such information and report on what you find.

B. Assuming you are still in the sales management role described above, search the Web for sales training seminars that address motivational issues. Describe these programs and give your assessment of whether they would help motivate your sales reps.

References

1. Ruth Kanfer, "Motivation Theory and Industrial Organizational Psychology," in *Handbook of Industrial and Organizational Psychology*, ed. M. D. Dunnette and Leaetta M. Hough (Palo Alto, CA: Consulting Psychologists Press, 1990), pp. 75–170.

2. These conditions are based on expectancy theory concepts developed by Victor H. Vroom, *Work and Motivation* (New York: John Wiley & Sons, 1964), and others; Edward C. Tolman, *Purposive Behavior in Animals and Men* (New York: Appleton-Century-Crofts, 1932); and Kurt Lewin, *The Conceptual Representation and the Measurement of Psychological Forces* (Durham, NC: Duke University Press, 1938). Expectancy theory as a framework for explaining salesperson motivation was popularized by Orville C. Walker, Gilbert A. Churchill Jr., and Neil M. Ford, "Motivation and Performance in Industrial Selling: Present Knowledge and Needed Research," *Journal of Marketing Research*, May 1977, pp. 156–68.

3. Abraham H. Maslow, *Motivation and Personality*, 2nd ed. (New York: Harper & Row, 1970), chapters 3–7.

4. Vincent Alonzo, "Money Isn't Everything," *Sales & Marketing Management*, January 1999, p. 28.

5. Frederick Hertzberg, Bernard Mausner, and Barbara B. Snyderman, *Motivation to Work*, 2nd ed. (New York: John Wiley & Sons, 1959).

6. Andrea Dixon, Rosann Spiro, and Maqbul Jamil, "Successful and Unsuccessful Sales Calls: Measuring Salesperson Attributions and Behavioral Intentions," *Journal of Marketing*, July 2001, pp. 64–78.

7. Jaap Vink and Willem Verbeke, "Adaptive Selling and Organizational Characteristics: Suggestions for Future Research," *Journal of Personal Selling & Sales Management*, Winter 1993, pp. 15–23.

8. Jagdip Singh, "Striking a Balance in Boundary-Spanning Positions: An Investigation of Some Unconventional Influences of Role Stressors and Job Characteristics on Job Outctomes of Salespeople," *Journal of Marketing*, July 1998, pp. 69–86

9. William L. Cron, Alan Dubinsky, and Ronald Michaels, "The Influence of Career Stages on Components of Salesperson Motivation," *Journal of Marketing*, January 1988, pp. 78–92.

10. Melanie Berger, "Setting Personal Goals for Employees," *Sales & Marketing Management*, February 1997, pp. 35–36.

11. Libby Estell, "Economic Incentives," *Sales & Marketing Management*, October 2001, p. S4; and Vincent Alonzo, "Motivating Matters," *Sales & Marketing Management*, January 1999, p. 28.

12. Mark McMaster, "Personalized Motivation," *Sales & Marketing Management*, May 2002, p. 16.

13. Mark McMaster, "Wowing the Sales Force, *Sales & Marketing Management*, June 2001, p. 67.

14. Melanie Berger, "When Their Ship Comes In," *Sales & Marketing Management*, April 1997, pp. 61–65.

15. Jeff Baectold and Andrew Osman, "Tissue Technologies," working paper, Kelley School of Business, Bloomington, Indiana, 1997.

16. Libby Estell, "Economic Incentives," *Sales & Marketing Management*, October 2001, p. S4; and Vince Alonzo, "Cash Isn't King," *Sales & Marketing Management*, July 1997, pp. 26–28.

17. Vincent Alonzo, "Recognition? Who Needs It?" *Sales & Marketing Management*, February 1997, pp. 26–27.

18. Ibid.; and Elana Harris, "Stars in the Making," *Sales & Marketing Management*, March 2001, p. 62.

19. "Up the Ladder," *Sales Manager's Bulletin*, January 1993, pp. 1–2.

20. Audrey Bottjen and Eduardo Canto, "Pep Talks That Inspire Reps," *Sales & Marketing Management*, June 2001, p. 66.

21. Ibid.

22. "Best Corporate Culture," *Sales & Marketing Management*, September 2001, p. 31.

23. Mark C. Johlke, Dale F. Duhan, Roy D. Howell, and Robert Wilkes, "An Integrated Model of Sales Managers' Communication Practices," *Journal of the Academy of Marketing Science*, Spring 2000, pp. 263–77.

24. Erin Strout, "Masterful Meetings," *Sales & Marketing Management*, May 2000, p. 76.

25. Thomas N. Ingram and Danny N. Bellinger, "Motivational Segments in the Sales Force," *California Management Review* 24 (Spring 1982), pp. 81–88.

CASE 8-1   DIAMOND HOUSEWARES

Problems with a Mature Sales Rep

"It's time to talk about old Dan. He's not cutting it, not getting the job done these days. You've been protecting him, but I had accounting send up his numbers. He hasn't met a quota for two years. He serves some of our most important accounts. Why haven't you done something about it before this?" Kurt Diamond, CEO of Diamond Housewares, demanded of Dave Mitchell, the company's sales manager.

Diamond Housewares had been formed in 1960 by Kurt Diamond's father to sell a line of imported products, all designed to be used in operating a home. As the years passed, the company began to develop its own products and have them manufactured by subcontractors. As plastic and rubberized goods increasingly displaced metal products in the housewares industry, the company purchased a financially distressed, local plastic injection molding company in Chicago, Illinois. It began making some of its own products. Kurt Diamond spent most of his time in production creating and making new products. Sales were left in the hands of Dave Mitchell.

Diamond Housewares was financially sound and highly profitable due to the steady introduction of new products that found ready market acceptance. The company did little advertising, preferring instead to spend its promotional money at the houseware industry's trade shows. It maintained sales offices and showrooms in the major trade marts. Dan Ricker was the sales rep working from the Dallas Trade Mart, an important market for the company. One of his key accounts was the JCPenney Company, headquartered in Dallas.

Dan Ricker had been hired in 1963 when he graduated from the University of Oklahoma as a marketing major. Ricker's father and Diamond's father had been close friends, so Ricker and Diamond had known each other most of their lives, but they were not considered close since they had contrasting personalities. Diamond was an introvert and socialized little, whereas Ricker had an outgoing personality and many friends. Ricker developed a highly profitable business for the company in the southwestern territory by working long and hard developing the department stores and the emerging mass distributing firms as accounts.

Dave Mitchell was more than a little surprised at Kurt Diamond's sudden interest in Dan Ricker. It was the first time Diamond had taken any interest in the sales force for a long time. Usually he had something to say only when sales were down, which fortunately they seldom were, or when one of the company's new products flopped. Of course, any product failure was the fault of the sales force and had nothing to do with the product. Mitchell understood how that game was played, which was one reason he had kept his job for so long. He had joined the company in 1966 and was promoted to sales manager in the Chicago home office in 1987 after spending 20 years working out of Pittsburgh, Pennsylvania. He later learned that Kurt Diamond had offered the sales managership to Dan Ricker but Ricker had turned it down for two reasons: He didn't want to take the pay cut, and he didn't want to move to Chicago. Being paid on a straight commission, Ricker had earned substantially more than the sales manager did. However, that had changed. His earnings had declined with his sales volume.

Mitchell paused after Diamond stopped talking and then said, "Do you want an answer, or was that just some therapy we went through?" He didn't wait for a verbal answer. One was written on Diamond's face. "OK, no need to give you the Dan Ricker history. We both know how much he has done for us. He's been a top producer for years. And he has been loyal to us. Time and again, some competitor has tried to lure him away from us but he's been one of us all the way. So don't you think we should cut him a little slack, give him time to work out his problems?"

Diamond replied, "I recall a punch line that went 'What have you done for me lately?'" Then he asked, "What do you mean problems? What's going on?"

"Evidently, more things than Dan can handle all at once. First, you remember his daughter Kay and that guy she married. Well, he lost his job at IBM and hasn't been able to find another one. He's been out of work for a year. They had to sell their home and have moved in with Dan, two kids and all. So now Dan is out about $40,000 a year trying to keep Kay's family intact. If that wasn't enough, his son Matt has gotten into some serious legal trouble with substance abuse and that's also costing Dan a lot of money and worry. To top that off, I'm not so sure about his health. He won't say anything, but he's dragging a bit and doesn't look too good to me."

Mitchell shook his head as he continued, "I've talked with him about his problems, but what can I say? I haven't got any solutions for them except to let him work them out. It'll take some time, but these things will work themselves out. Dan's no fool, and he's working on them. Then he'll be back with us full-time."

Diamond responded, "Come on, give me a break. Dan Ricker is over the hill. He's a tired old man. Tired of working. Tired of hustling—and for what? For a few more bucks for us? Get real!" He continued, "If you don't do something, we'll be losing some key accounts. Lose the Penney account and . . . well, never mind."

The discussion was suddenly interrupted by a telephone call for Dave Mitchell. It was from the buyer at JCPenney.

Questions:

1. What should Dave Mitchell do about Dan Ricker?

2. Pretend you're Dan Ricker. What would you do in response to what was recommended in the first question?

CASE 8-2   BIOLAB PHARMACEUTICAL COMPANY

A Quest for Motivational Skills

"How did your interview go today? Are you going to get that promotion you want?" Hobie Dobbs asked his spouse, Kathryn. Although they had been married less than a year, Hobie had been paying close attention and had learned when silence was a definitive answer to one of his questions. This was clearly one of those times. Nothing was said, but nothing had to be said, for anger and frustration were etched in Kathryn's face. She dropped her briefcase on the floor rather loudly as she headed for the refrigerator in search of some moral support. Hobie followed and ventured a suggestion, "The Ben & Jerry's ice cream is at the bottom of the freezer."

It worked. After the second spoonful, Kathryn said, I couldn't believe it. There he sat telling me that I'm not properly motivating my reps. That I cannot be promoted until I learn how to motivate people better. Me, Katie O'Brien." My career is being threatened by a bozo who tells me I can't motivate people well enough to suit him."

Kathryn O'Brien, a senior sales rep for Biolab Pharmaceutical Company, supervised five junior sales reps in her St. Louis, Missouri, territory. She had worked for the company for three years and had an excellent record. Each year she was one of the company's top producers. She was well liked by her peers and subordinates. It seemed to everyone that Kathryn was well on her way to a great management career with Biolab.

Biolab Pharmaceutical Company was a huge, international manufacturer of ethical drugs most noted for its biological and blood-related products. Kathryn reported to Ed Simpson, district manager, who also worked out of the St. Louis office. Thus, Simpson had more opportunity to observe Kathryn at work than was the case in the relationships between most district managers and their senior salespeople.

Hobie also worked for the company in customer service; he was a pharmacist who could be called on an inbound 800 number by any physician, druggist, or sales rep for product and application information. He and Kathryn became good telephone buddies in her early days with the firm because she relied on him for information.

"Gee, that's kind of general, isn't it? Exactly what does he mean when he says you can't motivate people? You sure don't have any trouble motivating me." Hobie paused and then continued, "Did you try to pin him down? Ask him what he was talking about? Get some specifics?"

"Yeah, it was like pulling teeth. He squirmed and had trouble looking me in the eye. He really didn't want to get into it with me, but I wouldn't leave until I understood what he was talking about. He kept saying that my five sales reps were not performing well enough to suit him. He thought they should be producing more results and that the reason they weren't was that I was not motivating them to work harder. He said that they just were not making the calls and making the efforts that they should be."

"And that's your fault, is that it?" Hobie asked. "Who hired them, who trained them, who sets all the compensation policies? But since they made you the senior rep over them, everything is your fault, I suppose. Can you get rid of reps who aren't performing up to expectations?"

Kathryn responded, "No, I can only write them up, give them a bad evaluation."

"Have you done that?" Hobie asked.

Kathryn explained, "No, and I won't. It's true they aren't setting the world on fire, but they're doing all right, about average for trainees. They are busy learning the business right now at their stage of development and I don't see why I should put more pressure on them than they have right now. First, learn the business, then when they know what they are doing they can start working harder."

"Seems reasonable to me. Did you tell Simpson that?"

"Are you kidding? I was so mad I couldn't think, let alone speak. Besides I don't agree with his ideas of motivation. He keeps giving us those Bubba stories about how his old football coach used to motivate him and those other players to go out and die for dear old Mizzou. Then he starts talking about his Marine Corps days and how they motivate people—pride, don't let your buddy down, and all that. He's from another world. Well, we sell drugs to physicians for about 40 hours a week. We're not fighting for our lives and we sure aren't trying to beat the brains out of the competition."

"You seem to know how *not* to motivate your reps. Now, what do you think *will* motivate them?" Hobie asked.

"I don't want to talk about it anymore tonight. I want to think about it. I'll tell you tomorrow morning what I am going to do." And with that, Kathryn declared the meeting over.

The next day began much earlier than usual because Kathryn was eager to get her conflict with Simpson behind her. Confrontation was to be the order of the day. She had decided to attack Simpson's evaluation of her motivational skills directly with him instead of appealing it to his superior, as she had a right to do under company policy. She was not interested in getting embroiled in the company's cumbersome bureaucratic processes. She would attack this threat right at its source—and if her effort failed, she would resign. She had good reason to believe that she could get a similar job with a competitor, so she was not worried about being unemployed.

She laid out her plans to Hobie, who listened carefully, saying nothing until she was through talking. Then he asked, "And what are you going to tell Simpson about your motivational philosophies and skills that will change his evaluation of you? What makes you think he is really interested in what you think about how to motivate your people? He seemed to be focused on your reps' input efforts. Hard facts! From what you tell me about him, what reason do you have for thinking that he can change his mind about anything? And by the way, what are you going to say about your motivational philosophies?"

Kathryn responded, "First, I am going to insist that the sales reps' basic motivational structure is pretty well set when we hire them. If they're lazy, we're not going to be able to change it. Furthermore, all sales management literature indicates that a firm's basic compensation plan provides the bulk of its motivational thrust. Add the training program to the mix, and I maintain that, as a senior salesperson, sort of a bargain-basement supervisor, I have little power to really motivate the reps. Consequently, he is evaluating me on something over which I have little control.

"Next, I know how the game is played. I may win something on appeal, but that will be the real end of my future with the firm. I would have dirtied the nest, made waves, or whatever you call it. I would be tagged a militant, and that would be that. So if my career is not to be with Biolab, so be it. The quicker I get out, the better. It would be foolish to stay around and let this guy do a job on me. I don't need it, and I don't have to take it. So that's the way it's going to be."

Hobie smiled. He knew it was going to be an interesting day.

Questions:

1. Do you approve of Kathryn's plan of action? If so, why? If not, what changes would you suggest she consider making?

2. Do you agree with Kathryn's philosophies of motivation? If so, why? If not, what are your philosophies of motivation?

CASE 8-3   INTERNATIONAL CHEMICAL INDUSTRIES

Use of Motivational Funds

The following memo from George McCall, vice president of sales operations at International Chemical Industries, was distributed to all regional and district managers:

> Each manager should be prepared to give a short presentation to the group during our national sales meeting next week about how the motivational fund for his or her area was spent in 2002. Being new to the organization, I want to familiarize myself with what we are doing in this important area. Moreover, it seems to me that many of you may be doing some things that would be of interest to the other managers.

Underlying McCall's memo was a hidden agenda: McCall was suspicious that much of the firm's motivational fund was being squandered on ineffectual motivational tactics. He wanted to open up the subject not only to discover what was going on but also perhaps to develop some uniformity to what everyone was doing.

International Chemical Industries produced and distributed basic chemicals, such as nitrates, sulfur, and potassium, around the globe. It was one of the world's largest chemical concerns. Its U.S. operations were directed from offices in Houston, Texas. The U.S. sales operations were divided into five regions, each of which contained five districts. Thus, there were to be five regional managers and 25 district managers at the meeting the following week.

Historically, management budgeted 3 percent of its sales volume of $722 million for the costs of managing sales operations. Of that amount, 83.3 percent was allotted to field-selling costs, which included the salaries and expenses of both the field sales reps and their field managers. The costs of the regional and district sales offices were covered by the remainder of the sales budget. From that amount, area managers were allotted a small fund of approximately 0.02 percent of sales that could be used for motivational purposes in any manner they desired. For example, the district manager for Chicago spent $70,000 in 2002 on a special motivational program for the area's five reps. (Chicago accounted for 5 percent of the company's U.S. sales volume, or about $36 million.) Each rep who achieved quota for the year received a free trip for two people, all expenses paid, to St. Thomas in the Virgin Islands. All reps won and went together with their spouses for a most successful holiday. The manager planned to institute another such program for 2003. The response to McCall's memo was good. The managers seemed to take delight in relating how they spent their motivational fund. It seemed to McCall that they were in competition with each other to see who could come up with the most innovative plan. McCall was pleased to learn that they had been putting their motivational funds to good use. He was also pleased with the attitudes of the managers. Morale seemed to be high. The managers seemed to relate to each other exceptionally well, except for two isolated cases about which McCall had been made aware by his predecessor and for which he was taking steps to remedy.

In summarizing what he learned from the managers' presentations, he categorized the managers' programs into three groups. Twelve of the district managers had developed some sort of program to reward the sales reps' total effort for the year much along the lines of the Chicago district's program. Seven of the managers used the money for shorter special-purpose programs such as contests to encourage certain desired behavior such as pushing certain products or getting new accounts.

One such program stood out in McCall's mind since it particularly impressed him at the time. The manager of the New York office had become concerned with the tendency of the reps to concentrate on the firm's established accounts. He wanted them to make more calls on potentially new accounts. To that end, he designed a contest to reward those reps who not only called on prospective accounts but also managed to make them new customers. Since it usually took many calls on a prospective account before a sale was made, the contest had been conducted over a two-year period.

Six of the managers used the money for doing several smaller, short-run, action-oriented, one-shot deals. For example, the manager of the Charlotte, North Carolina, district walked into the office one midsummer day waving two season tickets for the city's professional basketball team. She announced, "These go to the person who brings in the first new account this month." That resulted in a flurry of new account activity and a dispute between two reps over who brought in the first new account. The manager settled the argument by giving both of them two season tickets. She made two reps happy. McCall was impressed with her savvy in handling what could have been a sticky situation. On another occasion, she walked in and announced that if the district met its quotas for the quarter, all reps and their families would be treated to a long weekend outing on a chartered boat out of Wilmington. The district sales volume had not been up to plan, but that quickly changed as everyone started working hard for their boat rides.

McCall was not sure which of these models was best for the company, in either the short run or the long run. He had heard some of the managers talking about how much they liked learning about what the other managers were doing with their motivational money. He wondered if such information should be included in the company's monthly newsletter. How would such information be used? Would a rep in Chicago pressure the manager for a contest that provided season tickets to the Bulls or Bears games after learning of the Charlotte program?

After due consideration, McCall felt that the money was being well spent and wondered if it should be increased. He had several questions: What returns were being realized from those expenditures? How could he build a case to his superiors for increasing the motivational funds budget? Should he do it across the board or test it by giving an increased budget to a district manager representative of each of the three types of programs that were evidenced?

Questions:

1. What should George McCall do about the firm's motivational fund?

2. What policies should George McCall establish regarding the motivational fund?

9 Sales Force Compensation

How little you know about the age you live in if you fancy that honey is sweeter than cash in hand.

—Ovid—

As we indicated in Chapter 8, compensation is the most widely used method of motivating a sales force. It is the key to changing salespeople's behavior. Yet over the years numerous studies, interviews with executives, and other reports have consistently indicated that many companies are dissatisfied with their sales force compensation plan. Often the problem is that the environment in which these firms are operating is constantly changing. Companies reformulate their strategies to take advantage of changing opportunities, but frequently they do *not* change their compensation plans to match the changes in their strategies. According to a survey by *Sales & Marketing Management*, companies with sales of $20 million to $99 million had changed their compensation plans only 1.8 times in the previous 10 years.[1] The clearest signal that your compensation plan isn't working is that you are missing your sales objectives. Companies should review their compensation plans once a year to ensure that they are consistent with the organization's direction. In this chapter, we study sales force compensation, suggesting ways in which sales executives can design effective compensation plans.

The structure for sales force compensation looks something like this:

- Financial compensation.
  a) *Direct* payment of money.

    b) *Indirect* payment—paid vacations or company-financed insurance programs, for example.

- Nonfinancial compensation.
  a) *Opportunity* to advance in the job.
  b) *Recognition* inside and outside the firm.
  c) *Enjoyment* of the job.

Most of our discussion in this chapter will deal with *direct* payments of *financial* compensation.

The compensation problem is twofold. A company must determine both the level of earnings and the method of paying its sales force. By **level of earnings** we mean the total dollar income paid to each sales representative for a given period of time. The **method of compensation** is the plan by which the reps earn or reach the intended level. One company may use a straight salary method of payment, for instance, whereas another may choose to pay a salary plus a commission.

Sales Force Compensation and Strategic Planning

A close relationship exists between a company's strategic marketing planning and its sales force compensation plan. The compensation plan has a direct bearing on the successful *implementation* of the marketing plan. As an example of this relationship, assume that a manufacturer of industrial machinery is planning to enter a new geographic market to increase the firm's overall market share. On the one hand, a straight salary compensation plan probably would help to implement this strategy. On the other hand, a stronger incentive—perhaps a large commission—might be necessary when the strategy calls for aggressive selling to liquidate excess inventories.

To get salespeople to aid in successfully implementing the company's strategic marketing plan, management needs to coordinate its sales compensation plans with the company's goals. But it is surprising how often a firm has a sales compensation system that is at odds with management's stated goals. Many firms, for example, say they want a sales compensation plan that "emphasizes profitability," yet they maintain a commission component based on sales volume rather than on gross margin or some other measure of profit.[2]

Management also should recognize that companies and their market positions change over time. Consequently, a sales compensation plan also should change to reflect the company's evolution in its business environment. One type of pay plan is needed when a firm is just getting started and it wants to reach and maintain a certain level of sales revenue. Another type of plan will be required later when the company is realigning territories, introducing new products, and adding new channels of distribution or new types of intermediaries.[3]

As we noted in Chapter 2, companies are changing the way they do business. Successful companies in the 21st century will focus on developing long-term relationships with their customers. Sales efforts must shift to reflect these changes; and because sales efforts must change, compensation plans must be revised as well. Instead of being rewarded for selling as much as possible and winning market share, salespeople will be rewarded for building relationships with customers, keeping customers longer, and increasing the value of each one.[4]

FIGURE 9-1

What a good sales compensation plan should do

FIGURE 9-1

What a good sales compensation plan should do

Correlate efforts and results with rewards

Control salespeople's activities

Ensure proper treatment of customers

Attract and keep competent salespeople

Motivate salespeople

Good sales compensation plan

Be economical yet competitive

Be fair

Be simple

Give salespeople both security and incentives

Be flexible yet stable

Objectives of a Compensation Plan

The objectives of a good compensation plan, which are shown in Figure 9–1, may be viewed from the perspective of the company as well as from the perspective of the individual salesperson. None of these objectives are mutually exclusive. In some situations, one goal may conflict with another. All, however, are valuable guidelines for a sales executive to recognize and follow.

The Company's Perspective

We begin by considering objectives from the company perspective.

To Motivate Salespeople

Companies want to encourage salespeople to reach and exceed their goals. Thus, compensation plans are designed to motivate salespeople to perform. According to a survey of sales and marketing executives, most companies do a relatively good job of using the sales compensation plan to motivate their salespeople. Seventy percent of those surveyed reported that their plans were effective or very effective. However, the remaining 30 percent reported that their plans are not effective or at best only somewhat effective.[5] Clearly, designing a plan that motivates salespeople to meet or exceed their goals is not an easy task.

To Correlate Efforts and Results with Rewards

Correlating efforts and results with rewards is an ideal that most companies constantly seek yet seldom achieve. In the United States, in practically any situation—whether it be in business, politics, athletics, or social life—we usually pay off on *results*, not on *efforts*. It is nice, of course, if the results are

This salesperson is receiving a bonus check for achieving her quota.

commensurate with the efforts. But the key to receiving rewards in most cases is getting results—also called performance or productivity.

This situation can be very problematic. A person can work very hard (expending much effort) but get few results—and therefore little reward. This can happen even when the minimal results are due to factors beyond the control of the salesperson. In reverse, we all know of situations where seemingly little effort has brought big results and consequently big rewards.

One problem in sales management is that it is frequently hard to equate efforts with results. Another is that sometimes it is difficult even to measure results. For example, a given amount of effort on the part of salesperson Bill Garner may result in $50,000 of sales. The same amount and quality of work put forth by Sue Anderson may not result in any sales but may build the foundation for profitable future business with a customer. However, this relationship may not be reflected in sales until months or even years later.

To Control Salespeople's Activities

A good pay plan should act as an unseen supervisor of a sales force by enabling management to control and direct the sales reps' activities. Today, this usually means motivating the reps to ensure a fully balanced selling effort, that is, a *total* selling job. The compensation plan must offer incentives flexible enough to cover such varied tasks as full-time selling, missionary work (defined in Chapter 1 as building goodwill or offering information rather than soliciting orders), or controlling selling expenses. Compaq Computer's sales managers base 20 to 40 percent of their reps' compensation on individualized sales objectives, such as directing a rep to work with a specific new account, increasing sales of a specific product line, or improving customer satisfaction.[6]

To Ensure Proper Treatment of Customers

Companies will be increasingly competing on the basis of customer service. A seller's ability to maintain strong, long-term relationships with customers depends largely on providing customer service that results in a high level of customer satisfaction. A good compensation plan is one that motivates salespeople to treat customers properly, thus providing customer satisfaction. Many companies, such as AT&T, Siebel Systems, and IBM are using customer satisfaction metrics as one factor in compensation determination.[7]

To Attract and Keep Competent Salespeople

A good pay plan helps a company *build the quality* of its sales force. It should also *assist in attracting* high-caliber reps. Finally, a sound plan should *help to keep* desirable people.

To Be Economical Yet Competitive

From management's standpoint, a compensation plan should be economical to administer. A firm whose compensation expenses are disproportional to its revenues will have to increase the price of its product or suffer decreased profit margins. Most firms, however, want to keep their sales force expenses in line with those of competitors. It is not always easy to balance being economical with being competitive.

To Be Flexible Yet Stable

A compensation plan should be sufficiently flexible to meet the needs of individual territories, products, and salespeople. Not all territories present the same opportunity. A representative in a territory where the company is the leader should ordinarily not be compensated by the same method as a rep in a newly entered district. Some companies, such as FleetBoston Financial Corporation, are using individualized pay plans, in which each salesperson is allowed to choose what percentage of his or her compensation should be straight salary and what percentage should be incentive based.[8] Flexibility also is needed to adjust for differences in products. Some products are staples and can be sold by taking orders for frequent repeat sales. Others are sold one to a customer and thus require much creative selling.

At the same time, the basic plan should possess stability. The basic pay plan should contain features that enable a company to meet changing conditions without having to change the basic plan. For example, the basic plan may include three categories of commission rates—high, medium, and low percentages—to reflect differences in profitability among products. However, a product category may be changed from time to time as competition and other external factors affect its profitability. These category reassignments can be made without changing the basic pay plan at all.

The Salesperson's Perspective

The salesperson's perspective may differ from the company's perspective.

A Secure Income and an Incentive Income

Every plan should provide a regular income, at least at a minimum level. The principle behind this point is that sales reps should not have to worry about how to meet living expenses. If they have a bad month, if they are in seasonal doldrums, or if they are sick and cannot work for a period, they should have some income. However, this steady income should not be so high that it lessens the desire for incentive pay.

In addition to a regular income, a good pay plan should furnish an incentive to elicit above-minimum performance. Most people do better when offered a reward for some specific action than when no incentive is involved. It should be noted that it is not possible to design a workable system that offers the greatest degree of both security and incentives. The concepts are mutually incompatible. In practice, the company must develop a compromise structure.

Simplicity

Simplicity is a hallmark of a good compensation plan. Sometimes simplicity and flexibility are conflicting goals—that is, a plan that is simple may not be sufficiently flexible, and a plan with adequate flexibility may achieve that goal at the expense of simplicity. However, the plan should be simple enough for salespeople to understand readily; they should be able to figure out what their incomes will be. In general, there should be *no more than three measures* combined to calculate the reps' compensation.

Fairness

A good compensation plan must treat all salespeople fairly. Nothing will destroy salespeople's morale faster than feeling that their pay is inequitable. One way to ensure fairness in a plan is to strive to base it as much as possible on measurable factors that are controllable by the sales force. The next section covers this point further.

Designing a Sales Compensation Plan

The steps in designing a pay plan for a sales force are shown in Figure 9–2. However, before designing a new pay plan or revising an existing one, a sales executive should review a few fundamental points. These are presented below, followed by a discussion of the first three steps of designing the plan—reviewing job descriptions, identifying the plan's specific objectives, and establishing the level of compensation.

FIGURE 9–2

Steps in designing a sales compensation plan

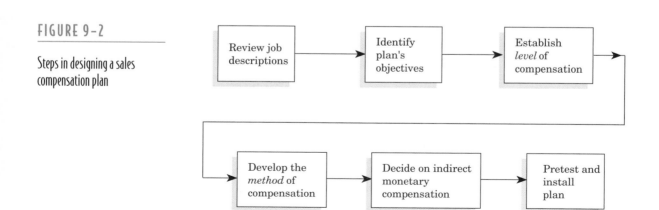

Some Useful Generalizations

- **There are inherent conflicts in the objectives of most compensation plans.** Sales executives want a plan that maximizes the sales reps' income and at the same time minimizes the company's outlay. Or they want one plan to give the sales force security and stability of income as well as incentive. In each situation, the desires are diametrically opposite. The best a manager can do is to adjust the pay plan until a reasonably satisfactory compromise is reached.

- **No single plan fits all situations.** Consequently, a firm should have a plan tailor-made for its own specific objectives. There may be considerable similarity in the general features of plans used by several firms, but the details should reflect the individual objectives of each company. Many companies also need more than one compensation plan because of differences in types of sales jobs, territories, or products.

- **It is very important to achieve external parity in salespeople's earnings.** Management should pay its sales force at a level competitive with salespeople in other firms. An excellent source of information on this point is the Dartnell Corporation's annual *Survey of Sales Force Compensation*. This survey reports average annual pay levels (1) by industry and by company sales size, and (2) by different levels of salespeople.

- **Management should solicit suggestions from the sales force regarding the compensation plan.** Salespeople are more likely to accept a plan if they were consulted about it during its design and development.

Review Job Descriptions

The first step in the design of a new compensation plan, or the revision of an established one, is to carefully review the detailed job descriptions. This should disclose the exact nature, scope, and probable difficulty of each job. A separate description should be included for each selling position, such as sales engineer, missionary salesperson, or sales trainee. The job descriptions indicate the services and abilities for which the business is paying.

Identify Specific Objectives

Part of the job of designing a compensation plan is deciding *specifically* what it is intended to accomplish. It is not enough to say that the goal is to get an honest day's work for a day's pay or to attract good people. These are examples of the broad, general type of objective referred to earlier—objectives *every* plan should attempt to accomplish. The following are examples of specific objectives:

- Increase profits by 10 percent.
- Increase sales volume of a certain class of products by 10 percent.
- Increase volume at existing accounts.
- Improve customer satisfaction.
- Stimulate missionary work.
- Develop a new territory.

Compensation should be based primarily on factors (1) that salespeople can *control* and (2) that the company can *measure*. However, most factors contributing to sales success are only partially or not at all controllable by the sales force. Salespeople have some control over their sales volume, for instance, but this control is limited by product attributes and company pricing policies. The point is that a firm should try to base most of each salesperson's compensation on factors over which the rep has a maximum of control.

The next step is to give as much consideration as possible to the elements that the company can measure. Sales, selling expenses, calls made, new accounts brought in, displays set up, or gross margin contributed are all easily measured. In contrast, such activities as improving customer satisfaction or training dealer salespeople are not as easily evaluated. Even so, companies should develop some kind of measurement for activities that contribute to long-term relationships with customers.

Establishing the Level of Compensation

One of the two key tasks in designing a pay plan is to determine the *level* of compensation. (The other—to develop the *method*—is discussed in the next section of this chapter.) The level of pay means the average earnings of the salespeople over a given period. In many respects, the level is more important than the method. People usually are more interested in *how much* they've earned than in *how* they earned it. To the company, the level of income is the direct sales cost. Management is interested in the compensation level because that is what attracts most salespeople. If reps believe that they will not be able to earn enough, they probably won't be attracted to the job regardless of the method used. Conversely, they may take a job that pays well, even though the firm does not offer the combination of salary and commission they prefer.

There is no clearly prevailing pay rate for sales jobs, as there is for certain office or factory jobs. However, compensation levels for salespeople can be compared among different industries. Figure 9–3 shows some examples of this spread. In the banking industry, the median earnings of senior sales reps (five or more years of experience) were $177,400 in 1999. At the lower end of the scale, median earnings were $49,100 in hotel and lodging and $59,800 in the wholesal-

FIGURE 9-3   Median compensation levels for senior salespeople, selected industries, 1999

Industry	Median Compensation*	Industry	Median Compensation*
Banking	$177,400	Manufacturing	$67,400
Pharmaceuticals	108,300	Fabricated metals	66,100
Educational services	99,800	Transportation equipment	64,600
Electronic components	72,400	Chemicals	62,900
Business services	71,500	Insurance	62,800
Printing and publishing	71,400	Wholesaling (consumer goods)	59,800
Office equipment	69,100	Hotels and lodging	49,100

*Does not include average benefits of $7,614 in 1999.

Source: Christen P. Heide, *Dartnell's 30th Sales Force Compensation Survey* (Chicago: Dartnell Corporation, 1999), p. 49.

ing of consumer goods. None of these figures include benefits (insurance and pension, for example), which averaged $7,614 per sales rep across all industries.

The *method* of compensation has a bearing on the *level* of compensation. Salespeople who work under a straight salary plan typically earn less than reps who are paid a straight commission or some combination of salary and commission.

The level of sales compensation is also closely related to the *experience* of the salesperson. This is understandable because the more experienced representatives have usually developed more skills. As a result, their productivity should be higher.

Developing the Method of Compensation

The other key task in designing a sales compensation plan (besides setting the pay *level*) is to develop the *method* by which the reps will be paid. The building blocks available to management when constructing a sales compensation plan include the following elements:

- Salaries
- Commissions
- Bonuses
- Indirect monetary benefits (e.g., vacation and insurance)
- Expenses

Some of these components are incentives for the sales force; others offer stability and security in earnings; still others may help the firm control sales costs. The more elements used in building a plan, the more complex it is, as shown in Figure 9–4. *Although there is a box for expenses in the figure, ordinarily reimbursement for travel and other business expenses incurred by salespeople should be kept separate from their compensation.* The two elements usually cause enough problems on their own without combining them. Sales force expenses are covered in Chapter 10.

FIGURE 9-4

Building blocks for a sales compensation plan

Security	Incentives	Benefits	Expenses
Salary	Commission	Paid vacation	Travel
	Bonus	Insurance	Lodging
	Profit sharing	Moving expenses	Company car
		Pension	Entertainment
		Profit sharing	Others
		Others	

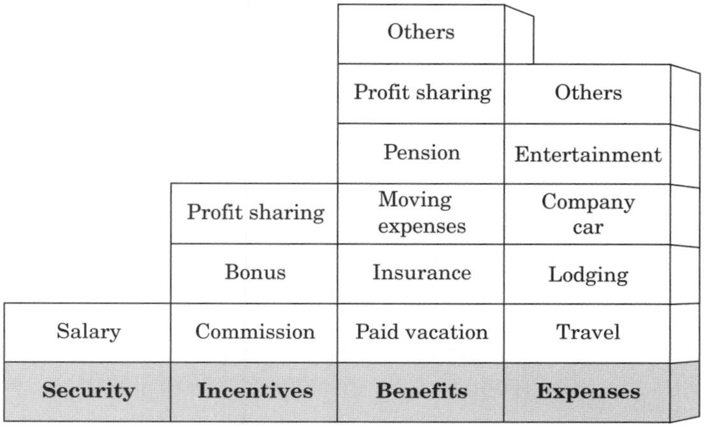

Basic Types of Compensation Plans

Fundamentally, there are only three widely used methods of compensating a sales force:

1. **A straight salary**—a fixed element related to a unit of time during which the salesperson is working.
2. **A straight commission**—a variable element related to the performance of a specific unit of work.
3. **Some combination of compensation elements.**

Over the past 45 years, there has been significant growth in plans that combine salary with an incentive feature. This trend has been primarily at the expense of straight salary and straight commission plans. Today about 68 percent of all companies use some form of combination plan to pay their sales forces.[9]

These generalized statements do not reveal the wide variations among different industries. Primary metals firms, for example, tend to prefer straight salary plans. At the other extreme, companies marketing financial services, especially securities brokers, are heavy users of straight commission plans. Surveys of salespeople indicate that the reps themselves strongly endorse some form of combination plan.

Emphasis Shifting from Volume to Profits and Customer Satisfaction

Traditionally, sales compensation plans have been geared to generate sales volume. Today, however, there has been a shift away from sales volume *alone* and toward *profitable* sales volume. Over 51 percent of all firms provide an incentive to their salespeople that specifically rewards profitable sales.[10] These firms realize that sales volume alone is a poor indicator of a salesperson's value to the firm.

When designing incentive plans that stress profits, many firms adopt the gross-margin approach. That is, the commission or other incentive is based on the gross margin (net sales less cost of goods sold) resulting from a sales rep's total sales. Many other firms still base their commission payments on sales volume. However, these commission plans are often structured to stress the sales of profitable products.

Customer satisfaction is an important objective for sales organizations. IBM, Xerox, and Saturn are among the firms that now include in their compensation plans a component that measures *customer satisfaction*.[11] Firms using this measure of performance must be sure that the salesperson—rather than the product, its distribution, or some other dimension—is the primary factor influencing customer satisfaction ratings.

Straight Salary Plans

A **salary** is a direct monetary reward paid for performing certain duties over a *period of time*. The amount of payment is related to a unit of time rather than to the work accomplished. A salary is a fixed element in a pay plan. That is, in each pay period, the same amount of money is paid to a sales rep, regardless of that person's sales, missionary efforts, or other measures of productivity.

A DAY-TO-DAY OPERATING PROBLEM

MAJESTIC PLASTICS COMPANY

MAJESTIC
Plastics Company

Reps Selling Too Many Low-Profit Products

Over the past several days the top executives in the Majestic Plastics Company had been conducting their annual performance review of the company's operations. The company president, Boyd Russell, sat in on most of these sessions and periodically became quite involved in some of the departmental reviews. The sales department was the one currently under discussion, and Clyde Brion, the general sales manager, was the focus of attention. Overall, the sales and profit results were satisfactory, but the executives noted what they thought was a problem in two sales territories. One was centered in Boston, where Louise Shannon was the rep, and the other was in Chicago, which was Henry Sadowski's territory.

In each of these territories, the sales reps' total sales volume was satisfactory. The problem was that the bulk of their sales volume was in low-profit products—that is, products whose gross margin was well below the company's desired average. Then the chief financial officer, Oliver Twombly, recalled that this same situation had been brought up at last year's performance review. Clyde Brion realized he was on the spot with his fellow executives, including the president.

Top management really did not want to change the basic compensation plan (straight commission on sales volume) because, over the company as a whole, it apparently had been working okay. And Brion concurred in this decision. He pointed out that Shannon and Sadowski consistently met their total sales quotas and that each had won a sales contest designed to stimulate total sales. But their performance was not balanced. They went way over quota on low-margin products and generally failed to meet quota on high-margin goods. They were not selling a desirable mix of products, nor were they generating their share of new accounts. Basically they were getting large repeat orders from a few established accounts. And Shannon and Sadowski generally were neglecting the newer products that were the foundation of the company's future growth.

Brion had been aware of this situation for some time, but he had never given it the attention it deserved, partly because the two reps' total sales volume was satisfactory and partly because he had other brushfires to put out. Now he was convinced that he had better do something—and do it quickly.

Question: What should Clyde Brion do to remedy the imbalanced sales performance of Louise Shannon and Henry Sadowski?

Note: See the introduction to this series of problems in Chapter 4 for background information on the company, its market, and its competition.

Strengths of Straight Salary Plans

A regular income gives the salesperson a considerable degree of security. A salary plan also provides stability of earnings, without the wide fluctuations often found in commission plans.

The assurance of a regular, stable income can do much to develop loyal, well-satisfied salespeople. Sales forces on straight salary usually have lower turnover rates than those on commission. Also, management can direct the sales force into various activities more easily under a salary plan than under any other method of compensation.

Because people on salary are less likely to be concerned with immediate sales volume, they can give proper consideration to the customers' interests. Also, customers often react more favorably to a salesperson if they know he or she is on straight salary.

Limitations of Straight Salary

A frequent objection to the straight salary plan is that it provides no direct incentive to the sales force. True, a salary plan does not offer the strong, direct incentive that a commission or bonus plan does. However, salary adjustments can provide incentives. Theoretically, salaries could be revised daily or weekly in relation to the salesperson's performance, but this is not practical. The problem is finding a *frequency* of salary adjustment that is practical and that works as an incentive. Companies sometimes do not make adjustments often enough.

Another reason many salary plans fail to provide adequate incentive is that the *bases* of adjustment are not sound. Often there is no clear-cut understanding among managers of what constitutes satisfactory performance. Another disadvantage of a straight salary is that it is a fixed cost. There is no direct relationship between salary expense and sales volume. When sales are down, the fixed cost of compensation can be a burden on the firm.

When a Straight Salary Plan Is Best

Generally speaking, a salary plan is best used when management (1) wants a well-balanced sales job and (2) can supervise and motivate the reps properly. Specific situations suited to a straight salary include the following:

- Sales recruits are in training or are still so new on the job that they cannot sell enough under a commission to earn a decent income.
- The company wants to enter a new geographical territory or sell a new line of products.
- The job entails only missionary sales activities.

Straight Commission Plans

A **commission** is a regular payment for the performance of a *unit of work*. A commission is related to a unit of accomplishment, in contrast to the salary method, which is a fixed payment for a unit of time. Salespeople usually receive commissions according to factors that are largely under their control. Commission plans generally consist of three items:

1. A *base* on which performance is measured and payment is made—for example, sales in dollars or units of the product.
2. A *rate*, which is the amount paid for each unit of accomplishment—for example, if a firm pays a nickel in commission for each dollar of sales, the rate is 5 percent.
3. A *starting point* for the commission payments.

The straight commission method may or may not include a provision for advances against future earnings (a drawing account). Essentially, straight commission plans and straight salary plans are diametrical opposites. That is, the strong points of one generally are the weak points of the other.

Advantages of Straight Commission Plans

Probably the major advantage of the straight commission method of sales compensation is the terrific incentive it gives to the sales force. Many firms have no ceiling on sales reps' commission earnings, so their income opportunities are unlimited. Commission payments also are a strong motivating factor to get the reps to work hard.

A commission plan probably is the best type of pay plan for weeding out ineffective sales reps. Another big advantage to the company is that a commission is a direct expense—that is, an expense is incurred only when a sale is made or some other activity is performed.

Disadvantages of the Plans

The limitations of the commission method mentioned most often can be summed up under one point: It is difficult to supervise and direct the activities of salespeople because their overriding concern is to sell more merchandise, without regard for the interests of the company or the customer. The reps may concentrate on easy-to-sell items and ignore slow-moving ones. Customers may be sold more items, or more expensive items, than necessary. Sales reps on commission often disregard any thought of a fully balanced sales job, and management cannot expect them to do missionary work.

Management is not totally helpless to combat some of these problems. In fact, it can exercise considerable control by judiciously modifying commission rates and bases. For example, to deter a focus on easy-to-sell, low-margin items, the company can pay a commission on gross profit, thus lowering the rates on such products.

When a Straight Commission Plan Is Best

Conditions under which the straight commission method is the best choice include the following:

- A company is in a weak financial position and therefore selling costs must be related directly to sales.
- Salespeople need great incentive to achieve adequate sales.
- Very little missionary work is needed.
- Developing long-term relationships with customers is not required.
- A firm uses part-time salespeople or independent contractors such as manufacturers' agents.

Commission Bases and Rates

When a firm uses the commission method, it must make decisions about commission bases, commission rates, split commissions, and limits on earnings.

Commission Bases. Management must determine what **commission base** to use—that is, what measurement of performance to use in figuring payment. Most bases are related to sales volume or gross margin. A company can focus its reps' attention on *profitable* sales volume by basing the commissions on gross margin.

Rates of Commission. Management also must determine the **commission rate**—that is, the amount paid for each unit of accomplishment. Rates vary among companies. Even within a given firm, there may be rate differentials among the products or territories. The choice of rates is affected by factors such as (1) the level of income desired for the sales force, (2) the profitability of given products, (3) difficulty in selling a product, or (4) classes of customers.

By establishing different rates for different product lines, the company, in effect, is stressing the profit feature. That is, higher commission rates are paid on the high-margin products to encourage their sales. Conversely, low rates are paid on sales of low-margin products.

Rates may be *constant* throughout all stages of sales volume, or they may be on a sliding scale, going up or down as sales volume increases. A *progressive* rate increases as the volume increases. For example, each quarter (three-month period), a business may pay 5 percent on sales up to $20,000; 7 percent on the next $80,000 (sales from $20,000 to $100,000); and 10 percent on everything over $100,000. A salesperson who had sales of $130,000 for the quarter would receive a commission of $9,600, computed as follows:

5% on first $20,000	$1,000
7% on next $80,000 ($20,000 to $100,000)	$5,600
10% on $30,000 (amount over $100,000)	$3,000
	$9,600

A progressive rate is intended to offer reps a great incentive in that the more they sell, the more they make on each sale. The company usually can afford to step up the rate because only the variable costs increase with each dollar of sales. The larger the sales total, the less the overhead charged to each unit of volume. A progressive rate requires careful administration to prevent reps from taking advantage of the system. Reps may postdate or predate orders so that all fall in one period. Thus, they artfully boost their volume during a given period and consequently qualify for a higher rate on the last orders turned in.

A *regressive* rate works in reverse (see Figure 9–5). A firm may pay 7 percent on the first $20,000 of sales in a given period, 5 percent on the next $20,000, and 3 percent on all sales over $40,000. This type of commission plan has some merit if it is hard to get the first order but reorders come frequently and automatically. A regressive rate also may be used to even out the earnings of all salespeople or to reduce the effect of windfall sales. Managers using a regressive rate must plan carefully to discourage a salesperson from (1) withholding orders at the end of a commission period when they would command a lower rate and then (2) turning them in at the start of the next period.

Split Commissions. When two or more salespeople work together on a sale, provision must be made to split any commission or other credit given. Various sit-

FIGURE 9-5

Example of progressive and regressive commission rates

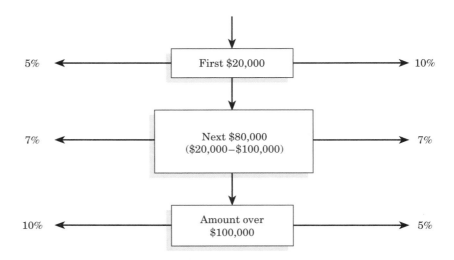

Compensating Cross-Functional Selling Teams

Team selling is gaining in both prevalence and importance. It requires the joint selling effort of several people, often from different functional areas within the firm. For example, Hallmark's selling teams include members from marketing, sales, finance, logistics, operations, information systems, and customer service. As a result, designing a compensation plan for a selling team can be a truly challenging assignment.

Several principles should be followed in designing a team-based compensation system:

- **Shared reward.** Some form of shared reward is always necessary. That is, some significant portion of the team members' pay should be variable, based on the team's operating success. But there should be a balance between individually based and team-based compensation.

- **Role–reward congruence.** Each team member contributes in a different way to the team. There-

fore, not all of the team members must be measured and paid in the same manner. The specific performance measures used and the percentage that is team based should be chosen in accordance with the tasks performed by the individuals on the team.

- **Team-member input.** For teams to succeed, all of the team members must be committed to the team goals and satisfied with the compensation structure. Therefore, it is important to gather input early in the process from those who will be affected by the pay program.

- **Peer evaluations.** Part of the evaluation of performance should be based on team members' evaluations of their fellow members' contributions to the overall performance of the team. This helps the company recognize individual performance and pinpoint freeloaders.

uations may call for a decision on the issue. It may take a team of three people to complete a sale of, say, a large technical product. One may be the territorial sales rep, the second a sales engineer or service rep from the home office, and the third the district manager. If a commission or bonus is part of the compensation plan for each of these people, distribution of the credit is a problem. (See the box labeled "Compensating Cross-Functional Selling Teams" for a discussion of other compensation considerations surrounding team selling.)

Geographical location can also complicate the commission division. For example, a salesperson in the Birmingham, Alabama, district may make a sale, but the order is placed through the buyer's home office in Atlanta, Georgia. To further complicate matters, delivery may be made to plants in Nashville, Tennessee, and New Orleans, Louisiana, as well as to Birmingham. If each of the four cities is covered by separate sales reps, the sales manager has a real problem in splitting any commission involved.

No simple or generally accepted method exists for handling split credits. Instead, each firm must feel its own way, using executive judgment to arrive at a policy.

Limits on Earnings. Should management place a limit (commonly called a ceiling or a cap) on the earnings of its salespeople? This question will most likely arise when part or all of the compensation plan is based on commission. Actually, earnings limits for salespeople are quite common among American businesses.

Executives who favor caps on salespeople's earnings put forth some compelling arguments. For example, no sales reps—even star performers—should earn more than their bosses. One reason for this is that top-performing sales reps may turn down a promotion into management if it means taking a cut in pay. Another argument is that reps should not benefit from windfall sales—particularly large single orders—especially when they made no significant contributions, put forth no special effort, or had no influence or control over those sales.

However, the reasons against ceilings or limitations on sales earnings seem to outweigh the arguments favoring them. The more a salesperson earns, the more the company makes, particularly if the earnings are in the form of a bonus or commission. The idea of a ceiling seems totally alien to the philosophy of selling. A firm ordinarily does not limit sales of its products to x dollars a year, yet placing limits on sales reps' incomes has the same effect.

If management does decide to curb the earnings of its salespeople, it can use any of several methods besides establishing a ceiling. One approach is to reduce commissions or bonus payments on all sales. A second is to establish a system of regressive commission rates, whereby successively lower commission rates are paid as sales volume increases beyond a given level. Third, windfall accounts may be classified as house accounts. These accounts are turned over to the territorial sales manager, and the salesperson receives no earnings credit for sales to them. Finally, management may even change its basic compensation plan to place less emphasis on the incentive features and more on the fixed element of salary.

Combination Plans

As noted earlier, some form of combination pay plan is used to compensate about 68 percent of all sales forces.[12] Broadly speaking, the purpose of any combination plan is to overcome the weaknesses of a single method while at the same time keeping its strong points. Most of the combined plans fall within the following three categories:

- Salary plus commission
- Salary plus bonus
- Salary plus commission and bonus

In a combination pay plan, what portion should be incentive and what portion salary? The answer depends on the nature of the selling tasks and the company's marketing goals. The incentive portion should be larger when a company is trying to increase its sales or gross margin, especially in the short run. The salary element should be larger when management wants to emphasize customer servicing, a fully balanced selling effort, or team selling. The incentive portion in combination plans is most often in the 40 percent range. It has been increasing over the past two decades and will probably continue to increase slightly in the next decade.[13]

Combination plans introduce a component that we have not yet discussed—namely, a bonus. The word *bonus* is probably the most loosely used word in the compensation vocabulary. As a result, it is sometimes difficult to accurately assess the extent to which it is used in pay plans. A **bonus** is a lump-sum payment for an above-normal performance. Because of its nature, a bonus cannot be used alone but instead must always be combined with another element such as a salary or commission. Strictly speaking, management need not announce in advance either the amount of the bonus or the basis for distributing it. However, most companies devise sales bonuses to stimulate the sales force to perform certain tasks. Unless they explain the plan in advance, managers will gain nothing

An Ethical Dilemma

Many companies have a sales force compensation plan that is a salary plus a bonus for reaching a sales volume quota. Other firms employ a performance evaluation system that rates salespeople according to their ability to reach their sales quotas. In order to reach his or her quota—whether it be for compensation, performance evaluation, or some other purpose—sometimes a rep will predate or postdate some orders.

To illustrate, let's assume that the reps in our company are assigned quarterly (three-month) sales volume quotas. One salesperson has done well during the first quarter, reaching his quota by mid-March. That rep then generates additional orders during the last half of March. But he either arranges with the customers to delay delivery until early April or simply dates the orders as of early April. Or he may tell the

customers that the company is temporarily out of stock in late March and the product will be available in early April. In any event, since the postdated orders show up on his sales record in April, he gets a running start on meeting his quota for the second quarter.

In another situation, a rep may predate orders. Suppose this rep, in contrast to the one described above, is having difficulty meeting her quota for the first quarter. She knows she is going to get some orders from regular customers in early April, though, so she arranges with the customers to have these orders placed or dated in late March, but for April delivery. Thus, these orders are counted toward her January–March quota period.

Is it ethical for sales reps to predate or postdate their orders so they can meet their quotas for a certain period?

by giving a bonus. Thirty-nine percent of the firms participating in Dartnell's annual compensation survey use some type of bonus in their compensation.[14]

The most commonly used basis for paying a bonus is the measure of a salesperson's performance against a quota—another aspect of compensation that has not been discussed yet. A **sales quota** is a performance goal assigned to a marketing unit for a specific period of time. The marketing unit may be a salesperson, a branch office, a district or region, or a dealer or distributor. The performance goal may be stated in dollars, product units, or selling activities. For example, each sales rep might be assigned a sales volume, gross-margin, or customer satisfaction goal for the coming three-month period. Quotas may also be established for individual products or types of customers. The specified time period usually is a month, a quarter, six months, or a year. When salespeople achieve their quotas, they often receive some sort of reward or bonus for their performance. For example, a sales rep may get a cash bonus of x dollars for going 10 percent over a sales volume quota.

Salary Plus Commission

The salary-plus-commission plan is used more than any other type of compensation method. Although there is no generally agreed-on percentage split between the fixed and the variable elements, on average the variable portion accounts for 40 percent of the total compensation.[15] The salary-plus-commission plan provides the advantages of a salary plus the incentive and flexibility features of a commission. KMC Telecom pays its reps a base salary plus commissions that start at 50 percent and run as high as 225 percent depending on the product sold.[16] Such plans, however, are costly to operate because of the number and complexity of elements involved. Also, the addition of incentive features at the expense of the salary can reduce managerial control over the sales force. In the final analysis, the success of a salary-plus-commission plan—or of any combination plan, for that matter—depends largely on the balance achieved among the elements.

Salary Plus Bonus

For the company that wants to control its sales force at all times and still offer some incentive, a salary-plus-bonus plan may be the answer. Usually, the salary element constitutes the major part of the total earnings—much more so than in a salary-plus-commission plan. The salary-plus-bonus arrangement is excellent for encouraging some activity for a short time. For example, a company may want to generate new accounts, encourage repeat business, or push missionary work for one product line. Some companies are using bonuses to help the sales force focus on long-term objectives such as improving customer satisfaction. Outer Circle Products, a maker of insulated storage containers, bases its bonuses on the accomplishment of personal performance objectives.[17]

Many companies are using bonuses to reward team performance. If the team achieves its goals, then all of the team members receive a bonus. A few companies even tie bonuses to the accomplishment of personal goals such as losing weight or learning a foreign language.[18]

Salary Plus Commission and Bonus

A number of companies use all three components—salary, commission, and bonus—in their compensation plans. This allows them to have a certain degree of control and to provide an incentive as well as offer a bonus for the accomplishment of a specific goal. For example, Siebel Systems pays a base salary plus commissions plus a quarterly bonus based on customer satisfaction surveys for each rep.[19]

Linking the Method to the Objective

As we noted earlier in the chapter, it is very important that the compensation plan be linked to the achievement of specific objectives. The choice of which methods to use depends on the specific objectives that have been chosen. To provide examples, we list the specific objectives that were presented earlier and suggest the best methods to achieve them:

- *Increase profits by 10 percent.* Some form of incentive is usually necessary, such as a commission or a bonus.
- *Increase sales volume of a certain class of products by 10 percent.* A higher rate of commission may be paid on sales of the high-margin items or on whichever line of goods the company is pushing.
- *Increase volume at existing accounts.* A bonus may be paid for increasing business at existing accounts by a certain percentage. The bonus could be tied to a quota for repeat business. Alternatively, higher commissions could be paid for repeat business.
- *Improve customer satisfaction.* A bonus is the best way to accomplish this objective, although increases in salary may be used as well.
- *Stimulate missionary work.* Missionary activities may include training dealer salespeople, making demonstrations, or building displays. Some of these efforts can be individually measured, and a bonus can be given for

their accomplishment. Efforts that cannot be measured easily may be rewarded by having salary form the bulk of the total compensation.

- *Develop a new territory.* Probably all income should be in the form of salary, at least in the earliest stages of territorial development.

Indirect Monetary Compensation

Today, most salespeople enjoy the same employee benefits as production and office workers in a company. Young people going into selling are more security conscious than they were years ago, and management is more sensitive to its social responsibility. Sales executives are realizing that rewards are due in two other general areas. One is **nonfinancial compensation** in the form of honors, recognition, and opportunities for promotion. These features help salespeople develop a sense of self-worth and a feeling of belonging to a group.

The other type of reward is an **indirect monetary benefit:** an item that has the same effect as money, though payment is less direct than a salary or commission. Indirect monetary benefits, which are also referred to as *fringe benefits* or just *benefits*, include such things as retirement plans, paid vacation days, and insurance. Indeed, what were once considered "fringe" benefits are now better considered to be an integral part of the compensation package. As noted earlier, these benefits averaged $7,614 per salesperson in 1999. This figure is in addition to the average earnings of $68,000 for senior salespeople and $46,400 for intermediate reps.[20] Figure 9–6 shows the most widely used sales force benefits that are paid in part or in total by the company.

FIGURE 9-6   Company-paid fringe benefits for salespeople

Benefit	Percentage of Companies
Medical insurance	96%
Group life insurance	71%
Dental insurance	69%
Long-term disability	56%
Pension plan	55%
Short-term disability	49%
Profit sharing	44%
Thrift savings plan	22%
Employee stock purchase plan	21%

Source: Christen P. Heide, *Dartnell's 30th Sales Force Compensation Survey* (Chicago: Dartnell Corporation, 1999), p. 137.

Firms also give their salespeople paid holidays and provide paid vacation time that varies according to the employees' length of service. Paid vacations present a managerial problem in connection with salespeople who work substantially or entirely on commission. These reps usually do not receive vacation pay that equals their commissions. Firms often allow these reps to draw against their future earnings and repay the amount following the vacation. Also, most companies pay a commission to the reps on any sales that come in from their territories while they are on vacation.

Indirect monetary benefits are important in attracting desirable sales applicants. These benefits probably give salespeople a degree of security and make them more loyal and more cooperative than they would be otherwise. Such characteristics undoubtedly have some bearing on a reduction in the turnover rate.

Final Steps in Development of the Plan

Pretest the Plan

Once management has tentatively selected the method of compensation, the next step is to pretest the entire compensation plan. This involves determining how the proposed plan would have operated if it had been in effect during the previous few years. Management can estimate what the company's cost would have been and what income would have been earned by the salespeople. Pretesting a compensation plan is a simulation exercise that can easily be done on a computer. No amount of pretesting will answer all questions, however. If the new plan had been in effect, sales might have been quite different.

The commission features of a plan are easier to pretest than the salary elements are. If the base salary is increased 20 percent, it is hard to say how much more effective the missionary work will be or how much harder the sales force will work. However, managers can make several calculations regarding the commission elements. By assuming various levels of sales for each line of products, management can compute what the compensation cost will be.

Introduce the Plan to the Sales Force

A change in a compensation plan—especially a major one—can create a real culture shock for the sales force. Often in the wake of such a change, salespeople believe that management is simply trying to reduce selling costs. Thus, they look on any changes in the pay plan as a way to lower the sales reps' earnings.

Consequently, management should develop and introduce any new plan the same way porcupines kiss each other—very carefully. If the plan has been carefully developed, then the salespeople already have been asked for suggestions and criticisms. However, even though the reasons for changing the previous plan may have been thoroughly and candidly discussed, managers should announce the plan well in advance of when it is to take effect. AlliedSignal (before it merged with Honeywell in 1999) implemented compensation changes over a two-year period. For the first six months, there were no changes in pay, but the salespeople's pay statements indicated how much they would have made under the new plan, and Allied pay them the difference if they would have earned more under the new plan. During the next six months the company used the new plan but made up the difference if sales reps earned less under it. Then in the third phase, Allied still made up the difference but worked with the reps to figure out how they could repay the company if they underperformed. The final stage was full implementation.[21]

Install the Plan and Evaluate It Periodically

A compensation plan may be installed throughout the entire sales force, or it may be tested in only one or two territories. If a company cannot conduct a realistic pretest, then it may field-test the plan in a few districts under actual selling conditions. Sometimes a company will phase in a new plan over a period of time—three or six months or even a year. This phasing-in period gives the salespeople a chance to adjust to the new plan—that is, to buy into the new system.

Because companies have been changing their incentive systems more frequently and because incentive systems have become more complex than ever before, some companies such as Hewlett-Packard, Lexmark, and Johnson & Johnson are outsourcing the administration of their incentive plans. Companies that provide these services include Oracle, Synergy, and Trilogy.[22]

The final step is to make certain the entire plan will be evaluated frequently to prevent it from becoming outmoded. A common mistake is to spend much time and money developing a good compensation system (or selection or training program) and then allowing the system to become outdated. As noted at the beginning of this chapter, companies should audit their compensation plans annually. This is a sound management practice that ensures that a compensation plan aligns with changes in the strategic direction of the firm.

Summary

Compensation is the most widely used method for motivating a sales force. Most of our discussion in this chapter involved direct payments of financial compensation. When building a compensation plan, management must determine both the level of earnings and the method of paying the sales force. The sales force pay plan has a significant influence on the implementation of a company's strategic marketing plan.

From the company's perspective, the general goals of a good compensation plan are (1) to motivate salespeople, (2) to correlate a salesperson's efforts and results with rewards, (3) to control salespeople's activities, (4) to ensure proper treatment of customers, (5) to attract and keep competent salespeople, (6) to be economical yet competitive, and (7) to be flexible yet stable. From the salesperson's perspective, a good compensation

plan (1) provides both a steady income and an incentive income, (2) is easy for the sales rep to understand and simple for the company to administer, and (3) is fair.

When designing a pay plan, a company should first review its job descriptions to see what the reps are being paid to do. Then management should set specific goals for the pay plan. Compensation ideally should be based on items (1) that the sales force can control, and (2) that the company can measure objectively.

A major step in building a compensation plan is to establish the *level* of pay for the salespeople. Another major step in designing a compensation plan is to determine the *method* of compensation. Fundamentally, there are only three methods for compensating a sales force: (1) a straight salary, (2) a straight commission, and (3) some combination of compensation elements (salary, commission, bonus). Some form of a combination plan is used in about 68 percent of all sales forces.

A straight salary plan ensures a regular, stable income for the sales force. It enables management to direct the sales force into a variety of activities. The main drawback to a straight salary plan is that it does not provide any direct incentive to the sales force. It is also a fixed cost to the company. Generally speaking, a straight salary plan is best used (1) when management wants a fully balanced sales job, and (2) when management can supervise the salespeople so that they are properly motivated.

The main advantage of a straight commission plan is the tremendous incentive it gives the sales force to do what the commission is based on. To management, a straight commission plan is a variable expense. Under a straight commission plan, it may be difficult to direct the activities of the sales-

people. There are several situations in which a straight commission plan is best. With a straight commission pay plan, management must decide on the base and rates for paying the commission. Also, policies are needed regarding split commissions and drawing accounts. Management must also decide whether it will limit its sales reps' earnings.

Combination pay plans typically are a compromise designed to retain as much as possible the strong points and to overcome the weaknesses of straight salary or straight commission. Combination plans include some type of bonus paid for above normal performance. These bonuses are often tied to quotas, which are performance goals.

Most sales compensation plans also include indirect monetary benefits such as paid vacation time and company insurance plans. The final steps in designing a pay plan involve pretesting the plan, introducing it to the sales force, installing the plan, and evaluating it periodically.

Key Terms

Bonus
Commission
Commission base
Commission rate

Indirect monetary benefit
Level of earnings
Method of compensation
Nonfinancial compensation

Salary
Sales quota

Questions and Problems

1. As stated in this chapter, two broad goals of a sound compensation plan are (*a*) to control and direct sales force activities and (*b*) to ensure proper treatment of customers. Can these goals be reached by use of any managerial tool or activity other than a good pay plan?

2. Rank the following types of sales jobs by total earnings, showing which type you feel should have the highest level of compensation, which is second, and so on. Justify your rankings.
   a) Missionary sales for a large soap company.
   b) Sales for a steel manufacturer.
   c) Pharmaceutical sales.

   d) Sales by appliance wholesalers to retail stores.
   e) Life insurance sales.
   f) Sales for a software manufacturer.
   g) Sales for a manufacturer of children's clothes, calling on retail department stores and other clothing stores.
   h) Sales for a firm selling conveyor systems.

3. What might be some of the difficulties of letting salespeople develop their own goals for their sales volume (i.e., their own quotas)?

4. In 1998, a firm hired several college graduates for sales jobs at a yearly salary of $32,000 plus

travel expenses. By 2002, most of these people were making a salary of $36,500 to $37,000 a year, plus travel expenses. In 2002, the same company hired more graduates and paid them $35,500 a year, plus travel expenses. This was the salary being offered to qualified college grads for entry-level sales jobs in this company's industry in 2002. Thus, the people with no experience received almost the same pay as those with four years' experience. Discuss the problems involved in this situation and suggest remedies.

5. Assume that salespeople's earnings in a certain firm have no limit, and that a good sales rep can earn more than some of the company's sales managers. What incentive do these salespeople have to move into management? Especially consider those for whom a promotion means a decrease in income.

6. Give some specific examples of how each of the following factors can influence a company's choice of a sales force compensation plan:
   a) Caliber of the salespeople.
   b) Nature of the job.
   c) Financial condition of the company.

7. The following are three problems often faced by sales managers:
   a) Salespeople tend to overemphasize the easy-to-sell parts of multiple product lines in an effort to build sales volume; other, more profitable lines are forced into the background.
   b) Salespeople are not taking time to develop new accounts.
   c) To improve a company's long-term position, salespeople should be doing more missionary work and developing long-term customers to meet expected competition.

   Suggest a specific type of compensation plan that may be used to solve each of these problems.

8. What is the economic justification underlying the progressive commission rate? Is there any economic justification for a regressive rate? Which of the two rates is better for stimulating a sales force?

9. What plan would you recommend for each of the following companies in handling split commissions?
   a) A manufacturer of sheets, pillowcases, towels, and related items sells to a department store chain. The order is placed through the chain's buying offices in New York. Delivery is made to stores throughout the country on an order from the department manager in each store. The manufacturer's salespeople call on the units of the chain located in their territories.
   b) A manufacturer of oil-well-drilling equipment sells to main offices and drilling locations. Salespeople in the area where the product is delivered must service the item.

10. What do you think would be some potential problems in having team members rate each other as part of their performance evaluation?

11. A luggage manufacturer uses volume quotas for its sales force.
    a) What measures may this firm take to encourage its salespeople to do nonselling tasks such as prospecting for new accounts or setting up dealer displays?
    b) How can the customers be protected against high-pressure selling and other, similar activities by this manufacturer's sales force?

12. In what respects would a compensation plan differ among salespeople for the following firms?
    a) A manufacturer of small airplanes used by executives.
    b) A wholesaler of office equipment and supplies.
    c) An automobile dealer.

Experiential Exercises

A. Call 10 different firms and ask them to identify the methods they use to compensate their salespeople.

B. Ask 20 of your friends what portion of their compensation they would like to be salary (a fixed component) and what portion they would like to be some type of incentive (commission or bonus), assuming that they were in a sales position. Try to determine why different people have different preferences in this regard.

Internet Exercises

A. Visit the following sites and compile data on current salary levels for salespeople in different industries and different parts of the country.

a) Career Journal from The Wall Street Journal (www.careers.wsj.com)

b) Wageweb (www.wageweb.com)

c) Monster.com (www.monster.com)

B. The Wall Street Journal's career page includes a comparable wage calculator for different parts of the country. Assume your current salary is $50,000 in your hometown, and then calculate the equivalent salary in three different parts of the country.

References

1. Erin Strout, "Growing Pains," *Sales & Marketing Management*, November 1999, pp. 79–82.

2. Paul R. Dorff, "Designing Compensation Plans to Boost Sales Performance," *National Productivity Review*, Summer 2000, pp. 73–77.

3. Strout, "Growing Pains," p. 81.

4. Don Peppers and Martha Rogers, "The Money Trap," *Sales & Marketing Management*, May 1997, pp. 58–60.

5. "Does Your Sales Compensation Plan Motivate Your Salespeople?" *Sales & Marketing Executive Report*, March 5, 1997, p. 1.

6. Michelle Marchetti, "Pay Changes Are on the Way," *Sales & Marketing Management*, August 2000, p. 101.

7. Eilene Zimmerman, "Quota Busters," *Sales & Marketing Management*, January 2001, pp. 59–60.

8. Andy Cohen, "What Keeps You Up at Night?" *Sales & Marketing Management*, February 2000, pp. 46–47.

9. Christen P. Heide, *Dartnell's 30th Sales Force Compensation Survey* (Chicago: Dartnell Corporation, 1999), pp. 42–43.

10. Ibid., pp. 154–55.

11. Arun Sharma, "Customer Satisfaction–Based Incentive Systems: Some Managerial and Salesperson Considerations," *Journal of Personal Selling & Sales Management*, Spring 1997, pp. 61–70.

12. Heide, *Dartnell's 30th Sales Force Compensation Survey*, pp. 36–37.

13. Ibid., pp. 40–41.

14. Ibid., p. 43.

15. Ibid., pp. 40–43.

16. Betsy Cummings. "The Perfect Plan," *Sales & Marketing Management*, February 2002, p. 53.

17. Michelle Marchetti, "No Commissions? Are You Crazy?" *Sales & Marketing Management*, May 1998, p. 83.

18. Melanie Berger, "Setting Personal Goals for Employees," *Sales & Marketing Management*, February 1997, pp. 35–36.

19. Eilene Zimmerman, "Quota Busters," *Sales & Marketing Management*, January 2001, p. 59.

20. Heide, *Dartnell's 30th Sales Force Compensation Survey*, pp. 119, 49.

21. Michelle Marchetti, "Compensation Is Kid Stuff," *Sales & Marketing Management*, February 1999, p. 70.

22. Peter Kurlander and Jan Blackburn, "Sales Compensation Software: A Practical Guide," *Compensation & Benefits Review*, September/October 1999, pp. 54–62.

CASE 9-1   ID SYSTEMS, INC.

Directing Salespeople's Efforts through a Compensation System

"Today, world crime escalates daily, with terrorism and hijackings almost commonplace. Bombing, kidnapping, and electronic fraud dominate both national and international news. Add to that the less dramatic, but damaging, cost of white-collar crime, and the conclusion is clear: Never before has absolute identification been so important."

That is the theme of ID Systems, Inc., manufacturer of personal identification systems. The three main product areas are cardkey systems, proximity reader systems, and retina-scanning devices. The cardkey security systems control who is permitted to enter a defined area and during what time of day they may enter. Each card is coded by means of a microchip within the card. The cards cannot be duplicated, as some with magnetic strips can. The proximity reader systems are based on a concept similar to the cardkey systems. However, instead of carrying a card that must be inserted into a system, the user simply carries a plastic plate, about one inch by two inches, that activates the lock at a certain distance from the door. The retina-scanning device is based on the fact that every pair of eyes has a unique pattern of blood vessels. The identification system compares the retinal scan with a template of characteristics stored in a memory bank. When the template is matched with an acceptable degree of accuracy, access is granted.

The average cardkey or proximity system sells for about $3,000 per door, and the retina scan is around $25,000. The average sale for the company is $60,000 to $75,000. In 2002, ID Systems, with sales of $72 million, controlled 30 percent of the U.S. security market. Its two closest competitors are Schlage (with 20 percent of the market) and Boye (with 15 percent). Seventy-five additional companies each have 3 to 4 percent; and another 200 companies, which are not Underwriter's Laboratory (UL) approved, have approximately 5 percent of the market. The demand for security identification systems is exploding, and the market is expected to have sales of $4.4 billion by the year 2006. ID Systems, whose products are becoming more and more high tech with each new design or improvement, is in an excellent position to compete in the changing marketplace. Its product line is the trend of the future, and its potential for sales is enormous.

ID Systems' sales force consists of 24 sales representatives divided into six districts across the United States. Each district has a sales manager, an electrical engineer, and a sales support engineer. There is also an international sales zone. International sales, all through an independent distributor network, comprise 73 percent of ID's sales.

Each sales rep is expected to make 16 calls and to quote four jobs in a week. The sales rep makes the initial call and determines what the customer needs and what will satisfy those needs. Then the sales engineer does a "walk-through" with the rep to make sure the design is technically feasible.

The territories are designed to equalize potential, and each rep has a quota of $1.5 million per year. The compensation is a base salary of $34,000 plus a graduated commission based on gross sales. For sales of $800,000 and under, the reps receive a 5 percent commission; for sales above $800,000 to $1.2 million, they receive 6 percent; for sales above $1.2 million to $1.5 million, they receive 8 percent; and for everything over $1.5 million, they get 10 percent.

Cheryl Sites is the vice president of sales for ID Systems. She began her career with the company as a sales rep, progressing through the positions of district manager and regional manager. She has been the vice president for several years and is well respected for her market knowledge and sense of fairness in dealing with employees.

Recently, Sites has been struggling with a serious problem of how to implement a new marketing and sales strategy. ID Systems has been growing at a healthy rate for the past 10 years. This growth has come primarily from skimming the more profitable and larger accounts on the market. Management realized that there is a tremendous amount of untapped business, and that much of it is located in areas of relatively low population that the sales force does not heavily penetrate. On the one hand, realistically, it would be difficult for the existing salespeople to cover the more densely populated parts of their territories as well as the outlying areas. On the other hand, these areas by themselves do not have enough volume to support a full-time rep. Therefore, the company decided to establish a distributor network to supplement the direct sales by the reps.

The salespeople have been given the task of identifying and supporting the distributors for their own territories. The reps are each supposed to have sales of $300,000 each year through their distributor networks. They must locate the distributors, get them set up, support them with their service, and maintain a working relationship with them. They are also expected to help train the distributors' employees.

Cheryl Sites agreed with the new strategy. She felt that it made sense from an overall strategic perspective. She also felt that, in the long run, ID's salespeople would benefit from the opportunity to develop a greater sales base through the distributor network. However, her salespeople seem to view the new strategy from a short-term commission perspective. While the sales reps received the same commissions from sales through their distributors, the prices to the distributors are generally discounted by 40 percent off the normal selling prices. As the reps see it, they are getting significantly less for selling the same amount of product. Furthermore, they know that it takes a lot of additional effort initially to get the distributor set up and that the ongoing support requirements are going to be greater. They do not want to spend time with distributors when they feel they can continue to do well without them.

The reps also do not want the distributors stealing sales from them. Even though the distributors would be selling in areas that the ID reps have not had time to cover, the reps would technically be giving up some of the potential in their territories. If these concerns were not enough, one of the reps said to Sites yesterday, "Why should I help find my own replacement?" Apparently, many of the reps are threatened by the establishment of a dealer network. They envision ID eventually selling exclusively through distributors, and having reps who merely service these distributors. Sites is also concerned that if she pushes the reps into setting up some distributors, they may set them up, but they won't support them very well. This could give ID a bad name, making it difficult to establish additional distributors.

Sites is considering her options. Her preference is to find some way of motivating the current reps to support the establishment of the distributor network. One way is to change their compensation to provide some short-term incentive to establish and support the distributors. She is not certain what that incentive should be, and she is not certain, given the reps' attitude, whether it would work. Another alternative is to hire several new reps whose only responsibility would be to set up and sell through the distributors. Of course, the current reps wouldn't like this idea either. Finally, she could recommend to management that ID change its strategy of establishing a distributor network at this time.

Question:

1. Should Cheryl Sites recommend a change in strategy? If not, what steps should she take to implement the new strategy?

CASE 9-2   IMAGINATIVE STAFFING, INC. (B)

Compensating a Sales Team

Susan Borland, sales director, and her assistant, Judy Morgan, had been assigned the task of developing a program for team-selling the company's services to prospective accounts. As they dug into their task, they encountered particular difficulty with the matter of how to pay the team.

Imaginative Staffing, Inc., is a temporary-services firm in New York City that supplies temporary workers to firms located in the five boroughs. Formed in 1998, it had grown to $17 million in revenues in 2002. Besides Angie Roberts, the president, and her assistant, Nicole Gamin, the company had a chief financial officer, a sales director, four sales reps, an operations manager, 10 account managers, five administrative assistants, and a receptionist.

One reason Roberts had become aware of the team-selling concept was that for some time she had been frustrated by how long it took to close a sale with a good prospect. On average, it took about six months of hard work to make a sale to a major customer. One of the sales reps would make the contact and do all of the selling, sometimes with the help of the sales director if the situation seemed to warrant it.

Large and small corporations made extensive use of temporary help for any of several reasons: (1) to fill in for workers who, for some reason, were unable to work; (2) to handle overload conditions; or (3) to take care of seasonal peak workloads. In the current legal environment, many organizations were reluctant to hire permanent employees until there was a clear-cut, long-run need for them. Such factors as benefit packages, insurance, unemployment claims, and termination difficulties made management think seriously about hiring people as permanent employees.

Susan Borland and Judy Morgan had decided that a selling team should usually consist of at least three people: a sales rep, the person who would be the account's manager, and one person from top management. There was considerable debate on two issues: Should someone from the sales director's office be on the team (Borland or Morgan)? and who in top management should be involved? In particular, much consideration was given to Angie Roberts's role. Should the president be part of a sales team on an important sale, or would that undermine the development of the company's salespeople?

In any event, the matter of paying the people became an issue. Borland thought that there should be no special compensation plan for the selling team. "After all," she said, "they are paid a salary for their work and they all get substantial bonuses at the end of the year depending on how much profit we have made. If they sell more, they'll get paid in their year-end bonus."

Morgan demurred. "Two problems here: Delayed payment provides little immediate incentive, and the impact on a person's bonus by any one sale would be slight. I think we need to build some push

into this team-selling concept by giving the victors some of the spoils."

Under the existing system, a sales rep who brought in a new account was paid a commission of 10 percent of that account's billings for the first year. The commission was paid at the end of the month in which the money was received from the account. Thereafter, the sales rep received 1 percent of the account's billings. The account manager who took over the managing of the new account was paid a salary plus 1 percent of her account's billings. The company would not accept any account with billings less than $10,000 a year. It had slightly more than 500 active accounts, of which about 100 had billings totaling approximately $11 million. The typical new account started out with billings of about $12,000 for the first year, and it grew as it gained experience with the company.

It was part of the account manager's job to develop each account's use of the firm's services. This usually involved getting to know the account's special needs and problems, and then developing programs for using temporary employees to solve them. It often involved recruiting people with special skills who could work as needed for different accounts. For example, one client required people with the ability to read music. Another required people fluent in Russian.

The reps and the account managers had been receiving earnings based on customer billings. Consequently, both Susan Borland and Judy Morgan anticipated problems with them if those earnings were threatened by the team-selling concept. Why would they want to adopt a new selling system that would threaten their earnings? Clearly, they would have to see the system as a way to increase their earnings.

Another problem automatically arose. If the reps and the account managers received incentive compensation based on account billings, how would that affect the attitudes of the other team members? Wouldn't they also want some pay based on the productivity of their work? If that was to be, then how much?

Questions:

1. Should the president be part of the selling team when appropriate?

2. Should the team receive compensation for its productivity, or should the teamwork be considered part of the job?

3. If you feel that a productivity compensation plan for the sales team is called for, design one.

CASE 9-3   WORLD WIDE SECURITY AND PROTECTION SYSTEMS, INC.

Setting Quotas

World Wide Security and Protection Systems, Inc., manufactures and distributes a line of security and protection systems to consumers, businesses, and the government throughout the United States and in some European countries. A 49-person company sales force sells products in the United States; the company's international sales are handled by an export management company.

Prior to the end of each fiscal year in June, the sales managers in the United States sit down with each sales rep to establish his or her quota for the upcoming year. During these discussions, the two people go over the rep's performance for that year. The sales manager brings along the sales records for the previous year for each of the rep's accounts, as well as various forecasts of industry sales and general business conditions. They go over each account and review past accomplishments and plans for moving forward. They also identify new accounts that should be targeted for the coming year.

In the Phoenix territory, the district manager, Gino Brancolini, was preparing to meet with Rick Gimbert, who was one of the district's top salespeople, to set Gimbert's quota for the upcoming year. Gimbert's sales for the previous three years were as follows:

2000	$1,050,000
2001	1,118,000
2002	1,240,000

Brancolini opened the meeting by saying, "Rick, we want you to know how pleased we are with your development and with your contribution to Security and Protection's growth. You have exceeded your quota every year since you began with us. You have a great future with this company."

Gimbert acknowledged the compliment with a "Thanks." He was pleased with the praise, but he had heard these words before as a prelude to Brancolini's raising his quota by a large percentage. So he added, "I've been lucky in that the Phoenix area has seen some significant growth over the past few years."

Brancolini smiled at Gimbert's comment, recognizing it as a bargaining tactic. "Rick, you are much too humble. I am sure that you will continue to exceed expectations. Here is your quota for next year." He handed Gimbert a letter that specified the upcoming quota.

Gimbert looked at the letter and scowled. "There is no way that I am going to be able sell $1.4 million next year. The 9/11 terrorist attack in 2001 helped everyone's sales that year and this year; but the fear caused by 9/11 has receded. Anyone who beefed up security because of the attacks has done so by now. It is the slow economy that is going to be the biggest driver next year."

Brancolini countered, "You may be right about the receding fear associated with 9/11, but you're in one of the fastest-growing areas in the nation. Also, don't forget that there will be a 10 percent across-the-board increase in prices next year."

"Yeah," said Gimbert, "that is just one more reason why I won't be able to meet this quota. When prices go up, demand generally goes down. As I see it, the higher prices will make our products harder to sell. The economy is down, construction is down, and prices are up. How can you expect me to sell more?"

"Well, Rick, just how much do you think you can sell?" Brancolini asked.

Gimbert replied, "$1.25 million."

"Come on, Rick, you are sandbagging me. You did just about that much last year."

Brancolini's use of the word *sandbagging* referred to the financial importance of salespeople reaching their quotas. Security and Protection's salespeople make a 5 percent commission on their sales, out of which they pay their own expenses. But once they reach quota, they get a 1 percent bonus on the quota amount as well as an additional 1 percent commission on all sales over quota. Because there is a lot of money involved in meeting quota, where the quota is set is important to each rep and their managers.

"Look, Gino, if I don't make quota, I lose money. Five percent of $1.25 million is $62,000. My expenses run about $15,000. I need the extra money. Set my quota too high and I will just go somewhere else. This job isn't worth it!"

"Calm down, Rick. I know this is important to you; but you have always made your quotas, so you can't say that we have been setting them too high."

"That's not the way I see it," said Gimbert. "Each year, I have had to bust my tail to make quota. Then, when I do, you think it's too low and raise it. I'm damned if I do and damned if I don't. Well, I am tired of it and I'm not going to do it anymore. I won't accept any quota higher than $1.25 million."

Gino Brancolini did not like being given an ultimatum, but Rick Gimbert was such a good sales rep that he did not want this to escalate any further, so he said, "OK, Rick, let me think this over and get back to you tomorrow."

Questions:

1. What actions would you advise Gino Brancolini to take in this matter?

2. What are the problems in this case?

10 Sales Force Expenses and Transportation

Our men give their talent to the company and their genius to their expense accounts.

—*Life*—

One sales manager observed that, even when properly managed, sales force expense accounts are a nuisance and, when improperly managed, they can amount to grand larceny. This may be an unusually sour view of the situation. However, it points up the problem of establishing and administering a plan for controlling travel and other business expenses incurred by the sales force.

Sales reps are among the few company employees who are allowed to spend the company's money—and the amount they spend can be quite substantial. As of April 2002 the cost per sales rep for *meals and lodging alone* averaged about $236 per day in a typical metropolitan area, such as Atlanta.[1] If a salesperson who does not live in Atlanta works there for a week, the expenses will add up to $1,180. Remember, too, this figure does not include everything. Management often spends another 5 to 6 percent of sales on transportation and entertainment to bring in an account. For many companies, when we talk about sales force travel and entertainment expenses, we are talking about big money.

Sales Force Expenses and Strategic Planning

Expense account policy is one element in a firm's strategic marketing plan. New enterprises are often financially unable to bear the fixed costs of their reps' selling expenses. Entrepreneurs want all costs to be variable—that is, related to sales volume. Thus, as a matter of strategy, start-up companies will likely offer reps a deal in which the reps pay all their own selling costs in exchange for a higher rate of commission. Reps who accept this deal hope it will allow them to make more money than they could make if the company paid selling expenses. One fact is certain: If the reps pay their own expenses, there will be little waste.

In contrast, some firms hope to woo customers by treating them lavishly. The adroit use of entertainment can lure a customer into the company's fold to stay. Other firms want to develop an image of prosperity. They require their reps to go first class in their travel and in relationships with accounts.

Often firms use expense account policy as a strategic tool for recruiting salespeople. A generous expense account and a company car will attract many financially strapped college graduates. One of the most recent strategic trends is the willingness of companies to pay for items that can lead to increases in salesperson productivity. Figure 10–1 shows an increase in firms willing to pay 100 percent of the cost for such things as laptops, car phones, home fax machines, and home photocopiers. The numbers in every category except entertainment show a sharp increase from 1994 to 1998. This trend is expected to continue as more and more firms adopt sales automation.

Internal Revenue Service Regulations

Income tax laws significantly affect how much salespeople spend on travel, entertainment, and gifts to customers. Congress and the Internal Revenue Service (IRS) have progressively tightened the regulations on the deductibility of such expenses on income tax returns. For many years the government has strictly limited the deductibility of business entertainment expenses. Since 1994, only 50 percent of legitimate business entertainment expenses and only 50 percent of business meal expenses can be deducted when computing a firm's income tax.

FIGURE 10-1 Percentage of companies paying 100 percent of selected selling expenses

Item	1994	1998
Auto co-owned	16%	35%
Auto leased	30	31
Car phone	38	61
Entertainment	81	75
Home fax machine	25	53
Home photocopier	16	47
Laptop	28	65
Lodging	80	86
Mileage	37	63

Source: Christen P. Heide, *Dartnell's 30th Sales Force Compensation Survey* (Chicago: Dartnell Corporation, 1999), p. 121.

Furthermore, the tax deductibility of business gifts is limited to $25 per year for each recipient.

Moreover, tax auditors often scrutinize travel and entertainment (T&E) expenses closely because experience has shown that there is a high probability of error in T&E expenses. Thus, salespeople should keep careful records of all such expenses to support the deductions on their companies' tax returns (or on their personal returns, if they pay their own expenses).

Legitimate Travel and Business Expenses

Management should specify in writing the expenses for which the company will pay—not only the broad expense categories, such as transportation or lodging, but also the details within each category. For example, management may reimburse sales reps only for coach fare in the case of air travel or for only the cheapest lease on a rental car. *All* items relating to travel should be clarified beforehand.

There is no unanimous agreement on what constitutes a legitimate expense for reimbursement, but we can generalize about major categories of expenses. With regard to allowable items, a good general policy is that the salesperson should be reimbursed (1) for *business expenses* incurred in connection with work and (2) for *personal expenditures* that would not have been necessary otherwise. Telephone, faxing, and other *communication* costs are considered legitimate business expenses, as are *office supplies* and *stenographic services*. *Transportation* costs incurred on the job are also considered business expenses and are usually covered in full. Personal expenses include all *lodging* costs incurred while the rep is away from home overnight on business. Companies also usually cover the cost of out-of-town *meals*, but they frequently limit the amount per meal. The average **per diem cost** in the United States is $215.[2] This is the average amount the salesperson spends per day on a car, hotel, and meals. Figure 10–2 shows the percentage breakdown of U.S. per diem costs between lodging, car, and food.

FIGURE 10-2

U.S. salesperson pier diem costs
Source: *Sales & Marketing Management*, April 2001, p. 11.

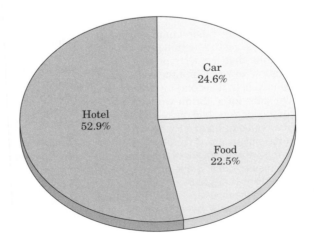

Undoubtedly, the most controversial of all expense categories are *entertainment* and *gifts*. The prevailing practice seems to be to allow all necessary and reasonable entertainment expenses. There may be limits in the form of per person maximums on allowable items, such as meals and theater tickets. Or the entertainment may be restricted to lunches or dinners. Taking a client to dinner at a restaurant is the most popular method of entertainment.[3]

The advent of the 50 percent IRS limit on the deductibility of entertainment expenses has dampened management's enthusiasm for entertaining. Additionally, the soaring costs of entertainment have made most companies reappraise their entertainment policies. Giving business gifts is a long-standing practice, but limits on the tax deductibility of business gifts has altered the gift-giving practices of many companies. Surveys show opinions divided on gift giving. Some firms do it because they like to. Other organizations would like to end the practice but feel they would suffer competitively. Many firms limit their gifts to the Christmas season. Also, some organizations do not allow their buyers to accept any gifts—even small ones. For example, Wal-Mart strictly forbids its buyers to accept a gift—even a can of Coke—from a supplier.[4]

A DAY-TO-DAY OPERATING PROBLEM

MAJESTIC PLASTICS COMPANY

MAJESTIC
Plastics Company

Reduction in Travel Expenses

Clyde Brion had just finished reading a memo from the president's office, instructing all department managers to reduce their travel expenses. No percentage reductions were specified, nor were the managers given any details as to how reductions were to be achieved. Brion realized that his sales force accounted for a substantial share of the company's total travel expenses, so he recognized the major responsibility being placed on his shoulders. His problem was how to achieve a significant cost reduction without unduly hurting sales force morale.

Brion knew that many other companies were struggling with this same cost-reduction problem. For example, several firms that formerly provided first-class air transportation now required their personnel, including the executives, to fly economy class (coach fare). For his own sales force, Brion wondered if he could use some of the ideas he had picked up in an article in the international edition of *USA Today*.

One substantial cut in air-travel costs could be made if the sales reps were to stay over Saturday night on their out-of-town sales calls. Some airlines' weekday fares are two or three times higher than those that include a Saturday-night stayover. Some companies now *require* their reps to stay over Saturday night;

other firms put this on a *voluntary* basis. Either way, however, poses morale problems. Reps may resent the requirement if it means giving up personal or family time, and volunteers may incur the ill will of those who think they look bad because they do not volunteer to stay over.

Some airlines offer half-price fares to those who leave very early in the morning or very late at night. For transportation in town or to the airport, some companies are shifting from taxis to buses. Hotel bills are reduced by having salespeople stay at Holiday Inns rather than at Marriott or Hyatt hotels. On food, one company saved 19 percent by requiring receipts for expenses as low as $15 instead of $25, because employees had been padding their food expense accounts.

Brion was seriously considering these various alternatives for cost cutting, especially the Saturday-night stayover. He also was wondering what other options he should explore.

Question: What specific steps should Clyde Brion take to reduce his sales force travel expenses?

Note: See the introduction to this series of problems in Chapter 4 for the necessary background on the company, its market, and its competition.

This sales team returns home after a successful call on an important customer.

Characteristics of a Sound Expense Plan

A well-conceived and well-executed expense plan has certain general characteristics. Naturally, no perfect plan exists. Every plan has inherent limitations.

No Net Gain or Loss for the Reps

The expense plan should be designed so that employees neither profit nor lose. A sales rep should net the same income working on the road as at home—an ideal difficult to achieve in practice.

Some firms give sales reps expense allowances in lieu of compensation. Employees often prefer an increase in a nontaxable expense account to a raise in taxable salary or commissions. However, this practice is unwise for at least two reasons. First, it tends to nullify the control feature of a good compensation plan. Second, it encourages people to violate tax laws. An expense account is nontaxable only to the extent that it reimburses the employee for legitimate business expenses. If a salesperson receives reimbursement for bogus expenses, that reimbursement should be treated as income and taxed.

Equitable Treatment of the Reps

Sales reps should be able to maintain approximately the same standard of living on the road as at home. They should not have to sacrifice comfort to stay within expense limits. To ensure equitable treatment, sales managers should recognize differences in travel expenses among the different territories. Costs may be higher in an Atlantic Seaboard territory than in the Great Plains, for example.

No Curtailment of Beneficial Activities

A good expense plan should not hamper the performance of selling duties, nor should it curtail activities beneficial to the company. A plan that attempts to set selling expenses as a percentage of sales may discourage a rep from developing a new territory. If all expenses are limited to 1 percent of sales, for instance, no one would be eager to go into new territories, where expenses often are abnormally high in relation to early volume.

Minimal Detail and Administrative Expense

A sound expense control plan should be simple and economical to administer. Clerical and administrative expenses should be minimized. Often, expense reports either require too much unnecessary detail or duplicate information requested elsewhere.

Clarity

A good expense plan should be clear enough to prevent misunderstandings between management and the sales force. One way for managers to reach this goal is to consult the sales force when establishing or revising an expense-control plan. Management should explain the plan to the sales force in detail and in writing before putting it into effect. The plan should be especially clear about the timing of reimbursement. The company should pay promptly or, better yet, make an advance payment available to those who need it.

Company Control of Expenses and Elimination of Padding

A good plan controls expenses and curtails padding. However, *control* is not synonymous with *stinginess*. A sales manager should be able to get all the benefits of control without damaging sales force morale by adopting a Scrooge-like approach.

Expense account padding is a problem most sales managers face at one time or another. A recent survey of sales managers by *Sales & Marketing Management* found that 15 percent of them had caught a rep padding his or her expense accounts within the past year.[5] Padding is often a *symptom* of a problem in another area. Managers' good judgment in other areas will prevent sales reps from abusing their expense accounts. Recognition of achievement, a good training program, and an adequate compensation plan are practices that help eliminate expense account padding.

Methods of Controlling Expenses

First, management must decide whether the company will pay for sales reps' field-selling costs or have the reps pay their own expenses out of their earnings. Almost all firms pay for travel and business expenses if salary is an element in the compensation plan. If the sales reps pay all their own expenses, chances are that they are compensated by the straight commission method.

Salespeople Pay Own Expenses

Salespeople who are compensated by straight commission usually pay their own selling expenses. Management usually figures into the commission a certain percentage of sales for the field sales function. It offers the total amount to the sales rep and says, in effect, "What's left over after you pay your costs is yours." The main reason for this is that some people paid a straight commission might be tempted to cheat on an expense account during periods of lean sales. Also, from management's standpoint, the plan is simple and costs nothing to operate.

There are also at least two reasons reps themselves prefer to pay their own expenses. First, such a plan gives them freedom of operation—they don't have to explain their expenses to management. Second, many reps gain income tax advantages when paying their own expenses. They can deduct more expenses than if their earnings and expenses are separated by the company.

When salespeople pay their own expenses, however, the results may not be what management wants. A company loses considerable control over its reps' activities. For example, the reps are not likely to travel long distances to call on and entertain prospective new accounts who do not offer immediate sales potential.

Unlimited-Payment Plans

The most widely used method of expense control is the **unlimited-payment plan,** in which the company reimburses sales representatives for all legitimate business and travel costs they incur while on company business. There is no limit on total expenses or individual items, but reps are required to submit itemized accounts of their expenditures.

The main advantage of the unlimited-payment method of expense control is its flexibility. Cost differentials between territories, jobs, or products present few problems under this plan. Flexibility also makes the plan fair for both salespeople and management, assuming that reps report their expenditures honestly and accurately. Furthermore, this plan gives management considerable control over the sales reps' activities. If sales executives want a new territory developed or new accounts called on in out-of-the-way places, the expense plan is no deterrent.

However, an unlimited-payment plan may not allow management to accurately forecast its direct selling costs. The unlimited feature is an open invitation for some people to be extravagant or to pad their expense accounts with unjustifiable items. The plan offers no incentive for a salesperson to economize.

It is debatable whether the unlimited-payment method leads to more or fewer disputes between management and the sales force than other expense-control systems. The unlimited feature should reduce the number of disagreements, but friction may arise if management questions items on the expense reports. Probably a manager's greatest need in an unlimited-payment plan is to establish a successful method of controlling the expenses. Certainly a sales manager should analyze the reps' expense reports to determine what is reasonable and practicable.

Limited-Payment Plans

A **limited-payment plan** may take either of two forms. In one form, the plan places a limit on the amount to be reimbursed *for each expense item*. For example, a company may pay a maximum of $140 a day for lodging, $7 for breakfast, $12 for lunch, and $25 for dinner (or $44 each day for food). In the other form, the plan provides a *flat sum for a period of time*, such as a day or week. One company may allow $180 a day; another firm may set its flat sum at $900 a week. Management may set the same limits in all its territories, or it may establish different limits to account for territorial cost differentials.

Setting limits on expense payments has some advantages. Limited-payment plans are especially suitable when sales reps' activities are routine and travel routes are repetitive. Then the expenses can be more accurately forecast. These maximum expense forecasts then aid in budget planning. Also, knowing in advance what the limits are should reduce expense-account disputes between management and the sales reps, particularly if both parties perceive the limits to be fair.

The manager's major problem in administering a limited-payment plan probably is establishing the limits for each item or time period. Management may study past reports to determine the mileage sales reps typically cover each day. It may examine hotel and motel directories to establish limits on lodging. A separate

An Ethical Dilemma

Many companies control their sales reps' travel and other business expenses by using some form of limited-payment plan. That is, management will set a maximum amount that the company will reimburse for specific items such as lodging, meals, entertainment, and laundry. Typically, reps do not have to furnish receipts for certain kinds of items—local transportation, for example—or for items under the maximum limit.

Sometimes under these limited-payment expense control plans, the salespeople's expense accounts do not record what *really* happened. A rep may overspend the dinner limit by $10 and then make it up on the report by adding to an inexpensive breakfast or lunch. One rep padded his taxi expenses (where no receipts were required) to make up what he overspent on food. He claimed that there was no way he could eat properly in that city on the limited amount set by the company. In other cases, reps may underspend the limit on meals or entertainment, but their expense accounts state that they spent the maximum allowed. The reps claim that they should be allowed to economize in order to earn extra money, so long as their job performance and customer service do not suffer.

As a means of getting around the controls built into limited-payment expense plans, are any or all of the above-described practices ethical?

study should be conducted for each territory to ensure that the plan reflects regional cost differentials. Also, management should monitor the program to ensure that the limits reflect a territory's current structure. Sales reps should be included in these various deliberations, because limited-pay plans are good only if the sales force believes the limits are equitable.

Companies typically encounter several other problems in limited-payment plans. High-caliber salespeople may object to limits on expenses because they feel that the company does not trust them. Also, the system can be inflexible. A sales rep may have some unusual expense, such as an entertainment item he or she could not escape without losing the account. If entertainment is not an allowable expense, the rep may not be reimbursed. Some companies avoid such inflexibility by allowing these unusual expenses if they are reported separately with an explanatory note.

When management sets limits for each item, the plan may be hard to control. Reps may switch expenditures among expense items—that is, they may attempt to recoup money spent in excess of the limit for one item by padding the claim for some other item. Also, the plan cannot prevent a cheater from economizing on some expenses and then padding the account up to the allowable limits.

Combination Plans

The advantages of both the limited and unlimited plans can sometimes be realized by developing a control method that combines the two. Management may set limits on items such as food and lodging, for example, but place no ceiling on transportation. Another combination method is an **expense-quota plan.** Under this system, management sets a limit on the total allowable expense, but the ceiling is related to some other item on the operating statement, such as net sales. For example, a quota of $2,000 may be set for a month because monthly sales are expected to be $40,000. Expenses can be tied to sales even more directly by allowing sales representatives a monthly expense account not to exceed 5 percent of their net sales. The compensation plan can play some part in this expense-control system by paying a bonus if the rep keeps expenses at an amount under quota.

Expense-quota plans do have the advantage of enabling management to relate sales force expenses to net sales. In this method, management has some control over this direct selling cost. Furthermore, the reps have some operating flexibility within the total expense budget. Reps who have been made expense-conscious are not likely to be wasteful.

Control of Sales Force Transportation

One significant selling expense with little room for discretion is the cost of transportation. Transportation expense decisions are usually clear-cut because they are based on the costs and the nature of the selling environment. The rep who covers Manhattan must use taxis, buses, and the subway; a car would be next to useless. Without a car in Los Angeles, however, the rep goes nowhere. The situation largely dictates the transportation required. Some aspects are open to managerial control, however.

An International Perspective

As they say south of the border and also in Madrid, *las diferencias culturas* (cultural differences) pose problems for American companies that manage a sales force in foreign countries. And these differences are not limited to areas of selecting, training, and motivating salespeople. Other areas—renting cars in Europe for sales force transportation, for example—also can be a whole different ball game.

Unless they are forewarned, sales managers may be surprised by the high costs in Europe—especially the steep prices for fuel and sales taxes. Gasoline runs $4 to $5 for a U.S. gallon. (The last time one of this book's authors rented a car in Italy, regular unleaded gas—not superpremium—came to $5.35 a gallon, after converting lire to dollars and liters to U.S. gallons.) On auto rentals, the value-added tax—a form of sales tax—in various European countries is as follows:

Great Britain	17.5%	Norway	22%
France	18.6%	Sweden	25%
Holland	17.5%	Denmark	25%
Germany	15%	Spain	15%
Austria	21.2%	Italy	19%

Most cars of the size that sales reps are likely to rent have standard (not automatic) transmissions and no air conditioning, even in Italy, Spain, and Portugal.

Besides the costs and car equipment, sales reps should be alert for other potential surprises. In Italy, for example, retail stores, including nonairport rental agencies, typically close for three hours at lunchtime. Obviously, this cultural feature must influence a rep's planning for an auto pickup or dropoff. Sometimes the rental location is difficult to find. One major company's location in Rome is tucked away in an underground garage.

The question of whether to purchase additional insurance to cover collision and other damage can be a bone of contention for renters. Some rental agencies require this added insurance, even though the driver is covered by his or her U.S. insurance policy or credit card company.

Customer service overseas may be of a different level than that in the United States. Car rental executives say that the level of their customer service in Europe is uniformly high. But impartial industry observers do not agree. An American Express Company executive, whose department has to reconcile billing disputes between drivers and rental companies, says that the level of customer service in Europe is below what it should be. As one executive who has lived abroad said regarding the familiar-looking rental locations, "It's an illusion. You walk in and see the same uniforms and smiling people, and you think you are dealing with home boys, but you're not."

Source: James S. Hirsh, "Renting Cars Abroad Can Drive You Nuts," *The Wall Street Journal*, December 10, 1993, p. B1.

Ownership or Leasing of Automobiles

Since most sales travel is done by automobile, a car has become almost standard equipment. Management may provide company-owned cars or leased vehicles, or salespeople may use their own cars. No one policy for car ownership is best under all conditions. The final decision rests on a consideration of the following factors:

- **Size of sales force.** With a small sales force, a company achieves simplicity and economy either by having salespeople use their own cars or by leasing cars for them. Only when its sales force is large does a company generally find it advantageous to own the cars.

- **Availability of centralized maintenance and storage facilities.** If a company maintains centralized vehicle storage and repair facilities, it is in a good position to furnish the sales force with cars.

- **Unusual design required.** Some companies require that the cars used by their salespeople be a special color, have a specially constructed body, or carry some form of company advertising. Sometimes the vehicle must double as a sales car and a delivery truck. In these situations, the company should furnish the cars.

- **Control of car's operating condition.** If the company furnishes the car, management is in a better position to demand that it be kept presentable. The company probably can provide cars that are newer than the average salesperson's own car. However, sales reps may take better care of their own cars than they do of company-owned or leased vehicles.

- **Personal preferences.** Some people are financially able and willing to furnish their own cars for work. When sales reps *must* provide the cars, however, management runs the risk of losing good applicants. Some reps may not want to drive their own cars for company business, or they may not have suitable cars.

- **Annual mileage.** A rep's average annual mileage influences the automobile ownership decision. The more miles driven, the more advantageous it becomes for the company to own the cars. The point of indifference varies depending on the cars used and the company's auto-expense allowances. Suppose the company pays a flat 30 cents per mile auto allowance and that management has calculated the cost of owning the preferred model to be $4,000 a year, plus 10 cents a mile. Under these circumstances, the point of indifference would be 20,000 miles. If the salespeople covered less than this mileage, management would probably encourage them to own the cars.

- **Operating cost.** It is hard to say definitively which of the three alternatives—employee-owned, company-owned, or company-leased— offers the lowest operating cost. It depends to a great extent on rental costs, number of miles driven, and method of reimbursing the sales force. It also is difficult to measure some indirect costs of company ownership, such as the administrative expense of operating the system.

- **Investments.** If the company is not in a strong financial position or does not want to make the investment, it can lease cars or have the salespeople provide their own.

- **Administrative problems.** One major administrative question that comes up when the company furnishes cars is whether they should be available for the reps' personal use and, if so, to what extent. Most companies allow reps to use company cars for personal transportation. Management may or may not suggest some limits. If a company adopts a no-limit policy, reps may choose not to buy their own cars, or they may use the company car as a second family car.

  Use of a company car for private purposes is another indirect monetary payment, the same as group insurance or a paid vacation. Some businesses ask the rep to pay for the gas when driving the car for personal use. Others pay all expenses for both business and private use. Some ask that operating expenses be paid only on long personal trips such as vacations.

Leasing is the easiest way to put the sales force on wheels. The sales executive does not have to be a transportation expert, and the firm avoids the problems of buying the car, maintaining it, and later reselling it. Marko Foam Products, a California firm that leases a fleet of 45 automobiles, says that the company has saved $2,000 to $3,000 per automobile since it started leasing.[6]

The IRS's policy greatly encourages companies to lease automobiles, particularly the more expensive models. Whereas lease payments are deductible, almost without question, the IRS often contests (in audits) depreciation deductions for expensive company-owned cars. Leasing also minimizes a company's record-keeping chores.

Reimbursement Plans for Employee-Owned Cars

Salespeople who use their own cars on company business are often reimbursed for the cost. Three separate types of expenditures are involved in owning and operating a car. One type is *variable costs*, which are generally related directly to the number of miles driven. Examples of variable-cost items are gasoline, oil, lubrication, tires, and normal service maintenance. A second class of expenditures is *fixed costs*, which tend to be related to time rather than miles driven. Fixed costs include depreciation, license fees, and insurance. The third group, *miscellaneous expenses*, is difficult to standardize. Typical items are tolls, parking, and major repairs. Usually miscellaneous costs are not incorporated into one of the ordinary automobile expense-control plans. These items are listed separately on the expense account.

Salespeople may be reimbursed for using their cars on company business by some kind of a fixed-allowance plan or by a flexible-payment method.

Fixed-Allowance Plans

One general type of **fixed-allowance plan** is based on *mileage*, and another is based on a period of *time*. Under the first, the employee is paid the same amount for each mile driven on company business. The flat rate per mile is used by more companies than any other major plan, although there is a trend toward more flexible methods. Under the other type of fixed-allowance plan, a flat sum is paid for each period of time, such as a week or a month, regardless of the number of miles driven. The reimbursements cover both fixed and variable automobile costs.

Fixed-allowance plans have several advantages. They are generally simple and economical to administer. Salespeople know in advance what they will be paid. Also, if payment is based on a flat allowance for a given period of time, the company can budget this expense in advance. People who drive few miles (5,000–10,000 per year) prefer it because they can generally make money under such a plan.

The criticisms of fixed-allowance plans are so severe, however, that we wonder why they remain popular. Generally speaking, the plans are inflexible and may be unfair—some salespeople may benefit, while others lose. The fixed sum for a given time period can be reasonably good only if everyone travels in a routine fashion and costs are the same in each territory. Similarly, the flat-mileage allowance is equitable only if all reps travel about the same number of miles in the same type of cars under the same operating conditions. These conditions are highly unlikely and unrealistic.

Consider the inequities introduced, for example, by variations in the number of miles driven. In the operation of a car, some costs are fixed regardless of the number of miles driven. Therefore, the greater amount of driving, the more miles over which to amortize the fixed costs. In other words, the fixed costs per mile decrease as the total mileage increases. Under a fixed allowance per mile, every

FIGURE 10-3   Example of results of flat-rate-per-mile plan under varying annual mileages

Annual Mileage	Fixed Cost	Variable Costs at 12 Cents per Mile	Total Costs	Per Mile Costs	Payment to Representatives at 25 Cents per Mile	Gain or Loss to Representatives
5,000	$3,000	$ 600	$3,600	$.72	$ 1,250	−$2,350
10,000	3,000	1,200	4,200	.42	2,500	−1,700
20,000	3,000	2,400	5,400	.27	5,000	−400
30,000	3,000	3,600	6,600	.22	7,500	+900
40,000	3,000	4,800	7,800	.195	10,000	+2,200

additional mile works to the financial benefit of the sales reps. An example is outlined in Figure 10–3. Assuming annual fixed costs of $3,000, variable costs of 12 cents per mile, and a mileage allowance of 25 cents, the results are shown for various annual mileages. A sales representative who drives 5,000 miles per year receives $1,250, when the total costs are $3,600. Thus, the rep's earnings are reduced by $2,350. At the other extreme, a representative who drives 40,000 miles gets $10,000, which is a gain of $2,200 over actual costs. If the representative were paid a fixed sum per month, similar inequities would result but in reverse. That is, a payment of $400 a month would benefit the low-mileage traveler at the expense of the person who drove many miles in a year.

Flexible-Allowance Plans

To avoid the inherent weaknesses in a fixed-allowance system, companies have developed several **flexible-allowance plans.**

A *graduated-mileage* rate plan pays a different allowance per mile depending on the total miles driven in a time period. For example, one firm pays 30 cents a mile for the first 15,000 miles driven in a year and 20 cents for every mile over 15,000. Mileage allowances are graduated downward to reflect the fact that total costs per mile decrease as mileage goes up. Although a graduated plan corrects some of the faults of a flat-rate method, it usually does not consider differences in territorial costs and types of cars.

Under a plan that *combines an allowance per time period with a mileage rate*, management figures automobile allowances in two parts. Thus, the differences between fixed and variable costs of owning and operating a car are reflected in the payment. To cover fixed costs, the company makes a flat payment for each given time period, such as a week or a month. In addition, variable costs are reimbursed by mileage allowances, which usually are flat rates although they could be graduated. For example, one company pays $300 a month plus 12 cents a mile; another pays $350 a month plus 20 cents a mile over 750 miles a month.

A widely recognized and respected plan was developed more than 50 years ago by the founder of Runzheimer International, a management consulting firm that specializes in employee mobility issues, headquartered in Rochester, Wisconsin. This company typically divides the United States into several geographic regions and then computes the total annual costs, which include ownership and operating expenses for cars in each of these regions. As an example, Figure 10–4 shows the cost allowances for a midsized car in Dallas, Texas, as of April 2002.

FIGURE 10-4   Runzheimer annual vehicle costs for a midsized four-door car in Dallas, Texas

Annual Fixed Costs

1. Annual vehicle costs	$4,950
2. Insurance	1,159
3. License and registration	101
4. Personal property tax	398
5. Total fixed costs	6,608
6. 71.4% of fixed costs	4,718

Operating Costs Per Mile

7. Miles per gallon	19
8. Fuel price per gallon	$1.118
9. Fuel and oil per mile	$0.0606
10. Maintenance per mile	$0.0521
11. Tires per mile	$0.0193

Standard Cost Reimbursement

A. Fixed cost per month	$398.18
B. Operating cost per mile	$0.1320

Source: Runzheimer International website, www.runzheimer.com/bvsc/html/usvssprint.htm, April 10, 2002.

In some respects, the **Runzheimer plan** gives the same results as the graduated mileage system in that the more miles driven, the smaller the per mile allowance. However, the Runzheimer plan is much more accurate because payments reflect variations in types of cars, miles driven, and territorial operating costs. For a midsized car in April 2002, for instance, the annual fixed costs varied from $9,003 in Los Angeles, California, down to $6,282 in Sioux Falls, South Dakota. In summary, a Runzheimer plan seems to be the most equitable and accurate method available for paying salespeople for the use of their cars.[7]

Other Methods of Expense Control

Selling costs loom large in the expenses of most firms. Top executives may worry about the cost of sales force compensation, but they are even more concerned about their reps' field-selling expenses. At this point we shall note briefly a few additional methods of controlling field-selling expenses besides the expense account and automobile-allowance plans we have already discussed.

Training and Enforcement

Right from the start, management should teach sales reps how the company expects them to spend its money. Any violators of company expense policy should be subject to immediate reprimand or something stronger. Otherwise, the reps will assume that management will overlook expense account abuse.

Some firms make it quite clear from the beginning that expense account fraud will be a basis for dismissal. Moreover, these firms include a section in their job performance evaluations appraising how wisely a rep spends company money. A rep who wants a position in management should develop a reputation as an honest person who is careful with company money. Management may tolerate some character flaws in its people, but dishonesty is not one of them.

Credit Cards

Many firms use credit cards to control various expense items. By accepting credit card charges only from a designated list of hotels and restaurants, for example, a company can control where its reps sleep and eat. Also, reps who use company credit cards need to carry less money when they travel, thus reducing the risk of loss or theft.

The Expense Bank Account

In some instances companies place an undue burden on representatives who have to pay their expenses and then wait for reimbursement. Reps may have to finance three or four weeks of expenses—that is, $2,000 to $4,000. To avoid this, some firms place a certain sum, say $2,000, in a checking account for each representative. The rep pays expenses by drawing on that account. When the account needs replenishment, or at regular intervals, the rep files an expense report. Upon approval of the report, the company deposits enough in the checking account to bring it back up to the initial sum.

Change in Nature of Entertainment

The costs of entertaining customers have skyrocketed to ridiculous levels in many areas. It is easy to spend $1,000 entertaining a client for one evening in New York City or Los Angeles.

Consequently, home entertainment, quiet dinners, or small parties offer attractive alternatives to the manager or rep seeking lower entertainment costs. The rep will include out-of-pocket costs directly associated with the party in the normal expense account. Some firms have simply stopped taking clients to Broadway shows or treating them to an expensive night on the town.

Internet Selling and Telemarketing

High field-selling costs are one reason for the rapid expansion of Internet selling and telemarketing. Maintaining a website and making long-distance telephone calls can substantially reduce a firm's field-selling expenses.

In many companies, salespeople are pushing their smaller customers to make purchases through the company's Web page because the transaction costs are lower. Similarly, a telephone call can substitute for a personal sales visit. Both buyer and seller can benefit because many buyers would much rather spend a few minutes placing an order on the Internet or over the telephone than spend an hour listening to the rep's in-person sales pitch. Both parties seek transactional efficiency.

Controlling Expenses: A Five-Step Process

One of the authors of this book was in Chicago, visiting the sales manager of a major publisher while the manager was reviewing some sales rep expense reports. The manager moaned, "OK, you're supposed to be the expert on selling expenses. Here's one for you: How can I devise an expense account that will keep this guy from spending $20 parking in a Wabash Street garage when he could park much cheaper in Grant Park? How do you get reps to treat the company's money as they would their own?"

The author replied, "You don't have an expense account problem in your hand. You have a training and supervision problem. Teach your salespeople how you want the company's money spent, and then see that they do it."

The author continued, "Controlling selling expenses can be seen as a five-step process. First, make up your mind that you really want to control the expenses. Some managers like to gripe about how much their sales reps spend, but really don't want to do anything about the system for fear it might affect their own expense account behavior.

"Second, establish selling expense budgets. Some hard facts about field-selling costs must be developed. Often management is simply unaware of how much it costs to operate in the field these days. It's too easy to unfairly judge some sales rep who is honestly trying to operate in the field when you do not know the facts about the matter.

"Third, communicate management's expense standards and practices to the sales force in writing. Leave no room for doubt about what is expected, but allow room for unexpected costs and unusual situations.

"Fourth, set up a routine, automatic auditing system for the expense reports. Most sales managers prefer to control this function rather than have the accounting department do the job.

"Finally, departures from company policy must be recognized and dealt with. In cases where the rep is abusing the expense account or is openly defrauding the company, dismissal is appropriate. Remember that filing false expense reports is fraud. Sometimes a few reps lose sight of this fact."

Careful Travel Planning

Many large companies have a *travel manager* whose job it is to minimize travel expenses by careful advanced planning. With the help of a travel manager, sales reps and managers can coordinate their routes to accomplish as much business as possible on each trip, and to reduce travel costs.

Some firms whose people must travel extensively by air have developed in-house travel agencies to help lower travel costs. These firms also carefully study the costs of flying from different airports under different conditions. Prices vary greatly, even from day to day, depending on when one travels, how far in advance reservations are made, how long the traveler stays, which airline and route are selected, and what the competitive situation is at the time.

Some firms have also established the position of *fleet manager*, whose responsibility it is to purchase cars, fuel, and maintenance services. Other companies outsource their fleet management. GE Capital Fleet Services is a well-known outsourcing provider that offers support 24 hours a day.

Summary

The handling and control of expense accounts is one of the most sensitive areas in sales management. Expense accounts are strictly regulated by the Internal Revenue Service, which stipulates in some detail what is and is not tax deductible. Management should identify in writing, and in detail, what expenses it will cover for reps. Normally, sales reps are reimbursed for their business expenses plus some personal costs that would not have been necessary if the reps were at home. A sound expense plan should be simple to administer, neither enrich nor impoverish the reps, and control the level of selling expenses.

Management must decide if the company will pay for the sales force's field-selling costs or if the reps should pay their own expenses. Salespeople working on a straight commission usually pay their own expenses. Under any other compensation plan, however, the company should pay the rep's expenses as an item separate from the compensation plan.

In the most widely used expense-control plan—the unlimited-payment plan—reps are reimbursed for all legitimate expenses, but they must itemize expenses and document certain large expenditures. Under a limited-payment plan, management either sets limits for certain items (such as food, lodging, and entertainment) or else provides a fixed total allowance for some time period.

A company should develop a plan for controlling the sales force's transportation costs. When reps travel by car, management must decide whether to own or lease the cars, or to have the reps use their own cars. If reps use their own vehicles, the company should formulate a program to reimburse them. Often some form of fixed allowance per mile or per time period is used. However, the preferred method is to develop some system of flexible allowances that considers the variation in the miles each rep drives and the costs of driving in the rep's area.

The greatly increased costs of travel and entertainment have encouraged most companies to attack such expenses aggressively by several means. In many cases, entertainment has been curtailed. The Internet and telemarketing have entered the picture because they are less expensive for contacting customers than field sales calls. Travel plans are now more carefully monitored to limit costs than was previously the case.

Key Terms

Expense-quota plan
Fixed-allowance plan
Flexible-allowance plans

Limited-payment plan
Per diem cost

Runzheimer plan
Unlimited-payment plan

Questions and Problems

1. "The expense-control plan should enable our representatives to maintain (at no extra cost to them) the same standard of living while on the road that they enjoy at home," said the sales manager of a metal products manufacturer. Discuss the implications in this statement.

2. When recruiting salespeople, some firms offer the opportunity for additional net income through the expense plan. Evaluate this policy on economic, human relations, and ethical bases.

3. What factors should management consider when deciding what method to use for controlling and reimbursing sales reps' expenses? Give some examples of how each factor might influence the decision.

4. "I don't make any money when my reps are home. I want them on the road all the time. I want them to live in luxury. Our present gross margin allows us to spend a lot of money so we can make even more money. I don't care what the reps spend just so they are happy and keep selling. All I care about is how much they sell." Comment on this entrepreneur's statement.

5. A company's dire need of a replacement part had shut down its production line. A sales rep in the supplier's office was told to deliver the part as quickly as possible. She did so in record time, but in the process she received a ticket for speeding. On her expense account, the rep applied for reimbursement of the $150 fine. As sales manager with responsibility for the rep, what would you do?

6. A petroleum firm with a sales force of 300 people planned to sell its fleet of company-owned automobiles and have the salespeople furnish their own cars instead. What problems are involved in this change?

7. The petroleum firm noted in Question 6 was trying to decide which method to use to reimburse the sales reps for the use of their cars on business. Each rep traveled about 15,000 miles a year. The company was computing the costs on the assumption that the reps drove mid-sized cars. The following payment methods were under consideration. What would be the total annual cost to the firm under each of the three proposals?
   a) A straight 40 cents a mile.
   b) $300 a month plus 18 cents a mile.
   c) The Runzheimer plan. (Use Figure 10–4 and information in the text.) Assume that the 300-rep sales force was equally divided among territories based around Dallas and Los Angeles.

8. In lieu of a salary increase last year, a television manufacturer granted its sales force the privilege of using company cars for any personal purposes, and the company paid all expenses. Previously, the firm had strictly prohibited any personal use of these cars. Discuss all aspects of this policy decision.

9. A publishing company was considering leasing small Chevrolet or Dodge cars instead of paying its present 30 cents per mile to sales reps for using their personal cars. Several of the reps were driving economy cars and were willing to take less than 30 cents per mile in order to keep from changing cars. What should the company do?

10. The major U.S. airlines have frequent-flyer plans, which offer awards (free flights or upgraded seats) after a person has accumulated a certain number of miles flying on a given airline. In the case of sales reps who accumulate miles on business travel, who should get these awards—the reps who did the traveling or their companies who paid for the trips? If you give the awards to the reps, should the awards be considered taxable income to the salespeople?

Experiential Exercises

A. Contact a local car dealer to compare the costs of leasing or buying a fleet of 10 cars. Assume that the cars will be midsize American cars and that the salespeople will average 30,000 miles per year.

B. Contact sales managers from five different companies. Ask them to explain the expense reimbursement plan for their salespeople.

Internet Exercises

Runzheimer International's website (www.runzheimer.com) provides sample information for most of the company's reports.

A. Visit this site and report on how much it would cost a company to pay the food, lodging, and car rental expenses for a sales representative for two days in Atlanta, Georgia. (Note that Atlanta was the example provided on this site as this book went to press. The exact city for the examples may have changed; if so, use the city provided in the current example.)

B. Visit the Runzheimer site and report on the cost-of-living differential between Columbus, Ohio, and Chicago, Illinois. (The exact cities for the example may have changed. If so, use the current cities provided in the example.)

References

1. Runzheimer International website, www.runzheimer.com/tmc/Images/atljan02dtp.pdf, April 10, 2002.

2. *Sales & Marketing Management*, April 2001, p. 11.

3. Chad Kaydo, "Road Rules," *Sales & Marketing Management*, September 2000, p. 84.

4. Melinda Ligos, "Gimme," *Sales & Marketing Management*, March 2002, p. 40.

5. Kaydo, "Road Rules," p. 84.

6. Christine Galea, "Driving Down Costs," *Sales & Marketing Management*, May 2000, p. 106.

7. Peter Packer, Communications Director at Runzheimer International, provided this information.

CASE 10-1   PAN PACIFIC TRADING COMPANY

Expense Account Auditing Policy

Kate Cook, sales manager for Pan Pacific Trading Company, wondered what was bothering Larry Cheng, the company's controller. He had asked for a meeting with her concerning sales department expense accounts.

The Pan Pacific Trading Company of San Francisco imported a wide range of consumer products, gift items, apparel, and jewelry from the Pacific Rim nations. Its customers were department stores, gift shops, chain specialty stores, and any other merchant who found the goods attractive. The company's product policies had been most aggressive. It would import anything that management felt would make a good profit. Some of the items defied classification. One profitable item for the Christmas season of 2002 was a novelty from Taiwan—a plastic flower that danced to music.

Since the markets for the firm's imports were so diverse, the company had to encourage buyers for smaller operations to come to Pan Pacific's sales offices. Consequently, the company maintained sales offices at the home office in San Francisco and at the major marts in such cities as New York, Chicago, Dallas, Los Angeles, and Atlanta. Each office was under the direction of a regional sales manager who had the major responsibility of developing that region's markets. The regional managers were paid a modest salary supplemented with a strong incentive system of bonuses that resulted in average earnings in excess of $150,000 a year. Each sales office also had an in-house salesperson who kept the office open each day. There were usually two or three other sales reps who worked large accounts in addition to the regional manager.

Everyone was in the office on "market days." While the apparel trades held a few market weeks during the year, usually six, the gift trades were different. For example, in Dallas every Friday was market day for gift buyers. In addition, several well-attended gift market weeks were held each year. Moreover, the daily traffic that stopped by the sales offices was surprisingly large. Many different merchants who sold the kinds of things imported by the company visited the sales offices.

Larry Cheng had requested a two o'clock meeting, and Kate Cook noted that he was prompt as usual. He marched into her office with his large brown attaché case firmly in hand. After the perfunctory greetings, he asked, "Can I spread my papers on your table?" Cook nodded while wondering what this was all about. She resented Cheng's failure to tell her the subject of the meeting. Cook had nearly said so when Cheng made the appointment, but she had decided she would be better off not knowing what was to be discussed. That way, she could always stall and divert Cheng by saying, "Hey, you just sprung this on me. I'll need some time to study it." Cook took pride in her tactical skills, which had served her well as she rose in the company.

Cheng began, "I don't know where to start. Your sales department expense accounts are not only way out of line, but they're illegal. If the IRS audits us, they'll disallow a lot of your expenses. And I mean yours and your department's."

Cook interrupted, "Does Mr. Tsai know of this meeting and your concern with our expense accounts?" Tsai was the founder and president of the company. Cook wanted to discover Cheng's power base and find out how much clout he was carrying in his crusade for lower and cleaner expense accounts. This was not a new issue with him. Cook and Cheng had this same conversation every year near tax time.

Cheng answered, "No, this is my area of responsibility. I don't run to the boss every time there's a problem. You know he doesn't want to hear about our problems. He only wants to hear about our solutions to them."

Cook knew that Tsai was not too sympathetic to Cheng's close adherence to the Internal Revenue Code. When Cook had brought the expense account issues to Tsai before, he had told her, "In some ways, it is an advantage to have Cheng the way he is; it keeps us on our toes. He will make certain we know what we are doing. On the other hand, he may be of less use than he could be, because he does not believe in our cause. We'll wait and see if he becomes a problem." Cook then understood that Tsai would not appreciate any expense account problems being dumped into his lap. Thereafter, she handled issues as they arose.

"Come on, Larry, you're talking generalities. Get down to specifics. I can't make decisions on such generalities."

"There are so many specifics."

"I don't care how many there are. If you want me to do something about each one of them, you'll have to list them. Get me a document that itemizes each of your concerns so I can start to deal with them." Cook smiled to herself. She had just bought some time to think about the problems that would be on that list. She knew exactly the things that were bothering Cheng. She knew the law and IRS policy. She had even gone out of her way to take a seminar on handling expense account deductions for income tax purposes. She knew it was an important part of her job and she was not about to let any accountant push her anywhere she did not absolutely have to go.

Cook also understood the company's tax compliance philosophies. While Tsai insisted on absolute compliance with all laws of the lands in which the company did business, he also recognized that there were many gray areas in which the laws were subject to great differences of interpretation and administration. He saw no reason to penalize his company by attempting to interpret any law in favor of whatever government was involved. He pushed the law to the limit when necessary and then backed off or compromised if the government forced him to do so. Neither he nor Pan Pacific Trading had ever been charged with any misdeeds. He had told Cook, "Tax audits are inevitable. Count on them! Play the game as tough as you can, but keep good documentation. If a dispute arises, our professional people will settle it as best as they can depending on the documentation we provide them."

Cheng persisted, "Fine. You'll have your itemized list tomorrow. But now I want to tell you the areas that are going to cause us some real problems down the line. First, there's the matter of the cars that everyone drives and deducts. It is quite clear in the law that the government does not want to subsidize the driving of luxury cars. The IRS doesn't feel you need to be driving a Cadillac to do business. Now, you and all of the regional managers and sales reps are driving luxury cars, and the end result is that the company is paying for

them. Get our automotive expense account policy within the law!"

Cook did not like Cheng's tone or attitude. She coolly replied, "What we do is not illegal. As I recall, when we began our present policy, no one questioned its legality." She wondered what was bothering Cheng so much about the cars they were driving. She really liked her BMW. Then she recalled that Cheng drove a Ford. She also realized that perhaps the biggest danger to the company in the matter was Cheng's attitude toward the company's policy. Just after Congress altered the tax code to limit the deductions for the depreciation of automobiles, the company changed its method for handling auto expenses. It started giving each sales manager and rep a flat expense allowance per year generous enough to allow them to drive luxury cars. She knew that several reps rented their cars. She did not know how they handled their tax treatment since such matters were the private, personal concern of each person. The allowance varied depending on the person and the territory. The New York rep's allowance was much lower than the Los Angeles rep's because the New York rep did not even own a car. She either used public transportation or rented a car when she needed one. Cook was given a $15,000 annual allowance. It was treated as income and reported to the IRS on her W-2 form. She then had to take the deductions for its business use. She preferred this system, as did all the other managers and reps. Some members of top management had similar car allowances. Larry Cheng did not.

Cheng continued, "And then there is the matter of your entertainment costs. They are excessive. Any auditor will scream at some of your claims. The New York rep's last expense account claimed that she spent $950 entertaining one customer one evening in New York. That's nonsense! And, Kate, I didn't intend to say anything, but those expense reports of yours on that trip you and Mr. Tsai took to Japan . . . well."

Cook knew he was referring to that $4,500 meal they reported when they entertained several of their Japanese suppliers one evening at a fancy Tokyo restaurant on the Ginza. She said nothing about it to Cheng, however, because she knew she could beat him on that one if he even so much as mentioned it in the itemized list of grievances. Then Cheng launched into the subject of the limitations that had been placed on entertainment expenses by the 1993 tax legislation.

"We need to reexamine our attitudes toward entertainment now that we can only deduct 50 percent of its costs. We are now having to absorb half of our already outrageous entertainment expenses as nondeductible expenses."

Cook dismissed Cheng by saying, "I've got to run to a meeting now. I'm eager to see your list."

Questions:

1. How should Kate Cook handle this problem with Larry Cheng?

2. Is the company's auto expense policy in violation of the IRS code?

3. Evaluate Larry Cheng's concern with the seemingly high costs for entertainment. What would you do to avoid such high entertainment costs?

CASE 10-2　　LUTZ INTERNATIONAL

Tactical Problems in Managing Expense Accounts

Jim Gomez picked up the large stack of mail and memos that had accumulated over the last 10 days while he had been out of town. He quickly glanced through it to see if there was anything urgent or negotiable. A memo from his boss, Mr. Bannon, grabbed his attention. Almost without thinking, he knew it would be his next assignment. The memo asked Gomez to see Bannon as soon as he returned from High Point, North Carolina.

Jim Gomez was a senior consultant for Bannon & Associates, which had offices in New York, Chicago, and Los Angeles. The firm was a partnership of marketing consultants whose reputation over the past two decades had attracted many large firms as steady clients. Gomez worked out of the Chicago office.

Gomez, age 35, started his career as a sales rep for Xerox after graduating from business school. Within five years, he was a regional sales manager. A company program had allowed him to study for his MBA while working. One of his classmates was doing some work for Bannon and needed help; he talked Gomez into moonlighting for Bannon. The firm was impressed with his work and soon made him an offer of a senior consultant position. Gomez liked the variety of tasks encountered in consulting, so he accepted the offer.

As it worked out, Gomez developed a reputation in the field of sales compensation and expenses. His work had been well regarded; he was on the verge of becoming one of the associates, a partner. As he walked down the hall to find out when Bannon would be free to talk, Bannon, who preferred direct action, pulled him into Ann Woodward's office. "Jim, Ann has some expense account problems with the Lutz people. She is bogged down making a marketing audit for their board and can't really take the time to handle it. She uncovered some real bombs ready to explode while doing her audit. They won't wait until the audit is finished. Will you talk with Ann now? She will fill you in on the mess. I have to run for O'Hare. See you next week at the partners' party."

Gomez smiled at that last thought as he made the appropriate noises bidding the boss a safe trip. He knew that the Lutz account was important to the firm. Lutz had been a good client for 10 years. The firm paid its bills on time and did not challenge the time charges at every turn. He said to Woodward, "And how can I help keep the Lutz people happy with us?"

"By heading off a real revolt in their sales department over the reps' expense accounts," Woodward replied. "Let me fill you in on the gory details."

Gomez made himself comfortable on the office sofa as Woodward began. "For years, the Lutz sales reps have significantly enriched themselves with tax-free money by generously padding their expense accounts with the tacit approval of the sales managers, who were doing the same thing. The whole sales department has played fast and loose with their expense accounts."

"So what's new?" Gomez snickered.

"The company controller is what's new. She is as straight as they come. Right by the book, no nonsense. She took one look at the expense sheets, and how they were signed by all the sales managers, and she wants their hides on her barn door. *Fired*—I think that was one of the words she used. I think I also heard such words as *jail*, *tax fraud*, and *IRS*. Oh, yes, did I forget to tell you that she is an ex-IRS special agent?"

"Whee! Ain't consulting a barrel of fun!" Gomez laughed. "Why in blue blazes did the old man hire her? He knows the company's dirty."

Gomez also knew several other facts from previous experience with the Lutz organization. First, it was a highly profitable organization that made and distributed worldwide a line of electro-optical devices that were well regarded in the industry.

Its success was a dual function of its technology and aggressive selling by 47 sales engineers. Gomez had often wondered about the firm's compensation policies because the reps were not really being paid that well. The plan was largely salary combined with performance bonuses at the end of each year. The bonuses were more related to how much profit the firm made that year than to the performance of the rep. Gomez knew that the reps' expense accounts were huge because they traveled extensively and did much entertaining. Moreover, certain liberties with the law were known to occur in some foreign lands when the situation required that money be given to influential people if business was to be done. Thus, management over the years had not wanted to look into the reps' expense accounts too closely. No sales rep had ever been questioned about an expense account.

Gomez said, "The controller can wreck that sales organization if we're not careful. Those reps are highly marketable. All sorts of firms would love to have them, particularly the offshore operators. They know where the business is and how to get it.

Again, why did old man Lutz hire this woman? He had to know. He isn't senile."

Woodward answered, "I asked him just that question. He's scared to death of jail. All that publicity on the Helmsley tax evasion case, with her getting nailed and jailed, has him petrified. He wants to clean up his act before he gets into trouble. And he has a new tax accountant who has been scaring him to boot."

"OK, I guess we'll have to bail him out again. That's what they pay us all that money to do," Gomez responded. "Call your person at Lutz and find out whom I should contact first. In the meantime, I'll figure out how I am going to approach this mess. Got to be real careful here. Some real damage could be done if we don't get all the parties satisfied. How much time have I got before the lady blows the whistle?"

"Not much! I'll call her and tell her that you are on the problem with the sales department and that it would be most helpful to the company if she could give us some time to get matters resolved without losing some valuable people," Woodward promised.

Gomez finished his coffee and returned to his office to do some thinking. This was not going to be easy. He wondered how he should approach the problem. Should he try to develop some legal way that the sales force could continue with their expense account practices, or should he develop a program for making the company squeaky clean?

Questions:

1. What approach should Jim Gomez take in this matter? What should his attitude be?
2. Develop a step-by-step plan for Jim Gomez to propose to the Lutz sales manager and sales force.
3. How should Jim Gomez handle the new controller?

Leadership of a Sales Force

11

The first thing that you have to do to turn around a team is to envision the process.

—Bill Parcells, NFL football coach—

One hallmark of excellent leaders is their ability to motivate people to give their best efforts each day. It's not an easy task—especially in a sales organization. First, salespeople can easily become discouraged; they work alone and face continual rejection from customers. Second, sales managers often do not have daily face-to-face contact with their salespeople. It is difficult to be an effective leader of subordinates who live hundreds of miles away! Yet given the stressful nature of the job, salespeople have a genuine need for interaction with a competent leader who can provide guidance and support. A sales organization bereft of leadership will accomplish little.

Thus, sales managers must not only supervise but also lead. In fact, we think leadership is essential to a sales manager's effectiveness. Someone must be in charge of each organizational unit and provide the leadership necessary for accomplishing the organization's goals. Strong leaders can motivate people to achieve more than they would on their own.

Contrary to what some might believe, research indicates that leadership ability can be learned.[1] But first, sales managers must understand what leadership is. **Leadership** is a process in which one person influences other people's behavior toward the accomplishment of specific goals. Central to this process is **vision**—the identification of where the organization should be headed. Successful leaders tend to have specific characteristics and skills,

FIGURE 11–1

Leadership effectiveness

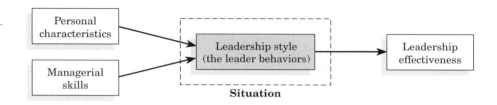

and to exhibit a certain leadership style (or combination of leader behaviors). Gaining insight into leadership is key to the ultimate success of a sales manager.

Leadership Characteristics and Skills

Identifying potential leaders is not easy. An individual's leadership qualities aren't always indicated by the performance of his or her administrative unit. As depicted in Figure 11–1, leadership effectiveness is based on a combination of personal characteristics, managerial skills and behaviors, and the situation. Personal characteristics and managerial skills that affect leadership potential are discussed below, and situational factors are discussed in the next main section of the chapter.

Personal Characteristics

Self-Confidence

Leaders must believe in themselves. To inspire confidence in others, they must set an example. In a sales organization, they must have confidence in their abilities and beliefs in order to face the challenges and problems inherent in the sales manager's position.

Initiative

Leaders are independent self-starters who take initiative. They take charge. Leaders welcome change and create change. They are willing and eager to take the risks associated with change.

Energy

Leaders usually have high energy levels. They are industrious, stepping forward when something needs to be done. Leaders must manage a wide variety of activities and relationships among people—such management takes a lot of energy. Also, a very energetic person is perceived by others as highly motivated and enthusiastic. This behavior is contagious and spreads to those surrounding the leader.

Creativity

Leaders need creativity and imagination. The organization looks to its leaders for solutions to problems—a challenge that often entails creativity and new approaches.

Maturity

Effective leaders must be more interested in the well-being of their organization and the development of their people than in their own self-importance or domination of others. Such an interest is a sign of maturity.

Managerial Skills

Problem-Solving Skills

Most managers spend a significant amount of time resolving problems. Effective leaders identify specific problems and their causes; they formulate and implement solutions. Such leaders must anticipate, analyze, and make decisions.

Interpersonal Skills

Interpersonal skills bear heavily on leadership capabilities. Leaders must discover what best motivates each salesperson. To do this, leaders establish good working relationships with their people. They know and treat each salesperson as an individual. This does not mean that leaders necessarily become good friends with every sales rep—often they cannot and should not. Instead, leaders develop good business relationships. Leaders must also establish good working relationships with superiors.

Communication Skills

Communication skills are a critical component of effective leadership. Setting goals, organizing, forecasting, staffing, training, motivating, supervising, evaluating, and controlling the sales force all involve communication. The sales manager continuously transmits information from upper management to the sales force and from the sales force to upper management. This information must be accurate, clear, concise, and timely. An effective leader must have good oral and written communication skills.

Persuasive Skills

Good leaders rely more on persuasion than on power. They persuade people to do what they want instead of threatening or coercing them. Their ability to persuade is based on the fact that their subordinates admire and respect them.

Leadership Style[2]

Possessing certain characteristics and skills gives the manager the potential to be an effective leader, but more is needed for that potential to become a reality. Ultimately, the measure of good leadership is how the manager behaves. In other words, what the leader does is more important than who she or he is. Good leaders use a wide variety of managerial or leader behaviors. The combination of behaviors that a manager typically uses is known as that manager's **leadership style.** Most behaviors tend to be consistent with one of two distinct styles of leadership: transactional leadership and transformational leadership.

Transactional Leadership

In a sales context, **transactional leadership** *generally refers to those supervisory activities regarding the day-to-day operation and control of the sales force.* In other words, transactional leadership equates to supervision. It is a reactive style of leadership that centers on the exchange—or the give-and-take—between the sales manager and salesperson. Sales managers who are effective transactional leaders appropriately provide **verbal feedback** in the form of rewards and punishments to their salespeople. For example, when a salesperson makes a big sale, the sales manager praises her (gives her a verbal reward). When a salesperson shows up late for a meeting, the sales manager points out his mistake (gives him a verbal punishment).

Transactional leaders exhibit **task orientation**—a short-term focus on getting the job done. This orientation generally involves one-way communication; the leader tells salespeople what to do and how, when, and where to do it. That is, transactional sales managers know the right way to do things and are excellent supervisors. They inform, monitor, and clarify company rules, policies, and procedures to their sales force.

The transactional leadership style relates to the working relationship between the sales manager and salesperson. The sales manager who checks with his or her salespeople each morning to see what their plans are for the day is *directly* supervising their activities. Many other managerial actions constitute *indirect* supervision, such as auditing expense accounts or appraising sales performance.

Transformational Leadership

Transformational leadership *transforms the basic values, beliefs, and attitudes of followers such that they are willing to perform at levels above and beyond expectations.* Individuals exhibiting this style are usually referred to as **charismatic leaders.**[3] These are exceptional leaders who make a meaningful difference in the performance levels of their followers. Whereas transactional leaders focus primarily on short-term problems, transformational leaders take proactive steps in anticipation of the future. In other words, they don't just know the right way to do things; they also know the right things to do. Furthermore, they genuinely care about those they lead. They use two-way communication, and they are always open to listening to the concerns of each follower.

Described below are four transformational leader behaviors that are especially relevant for sales managers.

Articulate a Vision

Transformational leaders create a common, compelling vision for guiding the future of their companies. They describe to subordinates an exciting, challenging future for them and the company. They get people to work toward a common end, even sometimes at the expense of their personal goals.

Of course, the vision for the sales organization typically stems from the company's overall mission as described by the president or chief executive officer. This does not mean, however, that articulating a vision is not the sales manager's responsibility. The sales manager breaks down the overall mission statement into

Management versus Leadership

Sales managers must be more than *managers;* they must also be *leaders* of their sales force. The following table outlines the key differences in terms of the behaviors associated with the two roles—*both of which are important.*

Managers . . .	Leaders . . .
React to what has just happened	Take proactive steps to avoid future problems
Focus on short-term issues, putting out fires one at a time	Build a team that works together toward a long-term vision
Provide reps with feedback, such as praise for a job well done	Are role models who lead by example—they don't just bark orders
Use one-way communication to explain policies and procedures	Listen/respond to the concerns of each rep via two-way communication
Do things right	Do the right thing
Use transactional leadership style	Use transformational leadership style

usable sales tools and objectives for the salespeople. In other words, the sales manager should communicate the big picture to salespeople in ways that make sense for them. This is not easy to do. One estimate is that only about 20 percent of companies have a clearly identifiable mission statement that sales managers understand and effectively articulate to their sales teams.[4]

Foster Group Goals

Fostering group goals means promoting cooperation—encouraging followers to work together toward a common goal. An organization greatly benefits when leaders successfully persuade followers to sacrifice their own personal goals for the sake of the team.

In this era of team selling, it is especially critical for sales managers to build teamwork through identifying the goal of the group. Transformational leaders must convince each salesperson that she or he cannot operate as a lone wolf. Salespeople must help each other. The strong performers, for example, should be asked to help the inexperienced, low-performing reps. In addition, sales managers must encourage their salespeople to recognize the importance of nonsales personnel. Customers have come to expect salespeople to provide solutions to their business problems, but this can only be done when salespeople work closely with engineers, manufacturing specialists, and other co-workers.

Provide a Role Model

Transformational leaders do not merely bark orders—they practice **role modeling,** or leading by example. They behave in a manner that is consistent with the values they espouse and with the goals of the organization. Leaders who demonstrate high levels of honesty can expect their salespeople to be honest, too. Similarly, those who exhibit a strong work ethic inspire their subordinates also to work hard.

In a sales context, there are many specific ways in which sales managers can be effective role models for their salespeople. Because they want their salespeople to listen to customers, sales managers themselves listen to the thoughts and concerns of their salespeople. For similar reasons, sales managers present a professional image through appropriate dress and grooming, and prompt arrival to meetings and appointments. Perhaps the most important way in which managers can serve as role models is to personally demonstrate proper selling techniques so that salespeople see how sales calls should be handled.

Provide Individualized Support

Finally, transformational leaders genuinely care about and respect their subordinates. They oversee their individual development and are concerned about their personal feelings and needs. As we noted in Chapter 8, on motivation, each person tends to have a unique set of needs and capabilities. Thus, providing **individualized support** is a difficult, time-consuming task for any leader. At the same time, it is an important task—especially in a sales context. Sales managers should take the time to learn about each salesperson's background, family, hobbies, and so on. This information may help the manager know how to address specific problems that arise. Because salespeople are under heavy emotional demands due to the inevitable ups and downs associated with selling, most of them greatly appreciate and respond to a sales manager who shows true concern for their individual needs.

Situational Leadership

Obviously, a sales manager cannot use all behaviors, all the time, with all salespeople. What makes a sales manager an excellent leader is **situational leadership**—that is, the ability to tailor leadership style—transformational or transactional—to the needs of the current situation and the individual salesperson.

Figure 11–2 lists four different situations and indicates appropriate leader behaviors for each. For a newly hired, inexperienced sales rep, the sales manager must first engage in a heavy dose of transactional leadership. New reps need to learn a great deal about the rules and procedures associated with the job; thus, the sales manager must engage in extensive one-way communication focused on informing and clarifying. Verbal feedback in the form of both praise and constructive criticism is also essential in this situation. At the same time, elements of transformational leadership are critical for these new reps. In particular, the sales manager should be a role model by accompanying the rep on sales calls and demonstrating proper selling technique; and the manager should provide individualized support to show genuine care and concern for these reps, who might be overwhelmed by the many challenges of a new job.

A burned-out veteran sales rep whose performance has plateaued or dropped also responds to the subtle encouragement associated with individualized support. In addition, this rep should be made to feel like part of a team striving to achieve a specific goal or vision. Ideally, the sales manager describes the process in a way that makes the veteran rep excited again about working toward a common goal with fellow reps. The manager should make a point to praise the rep for what he or she does well, but too much verbal feedback can

FIGURE 11-2   Critical leader behaviors for different situations

Situation	Transactional Leader Behaviors		Transformational Leader Behaviors			
	Informing Basic Rules	Verbal Feedback	Articulating a Vision	Fostering Group Goals	Providing a Role Model	Individualized Support
Newly hired, inexperienced rep	✔	✔			✔	✔
Veteran rep; low performance due to burnout		✔	✔	✔		✔
Unstable situation; crisis environment			✔		✔	
High-performing rep; like autonomy (no team selling)			✔			

sound condescending. After all, this is an experienced rep who already knows the basics of the selling process and the rules of the company; so, this situation requires only minimal amounts of transactional leadership.

Figure 11–2 also refers to an unstable, crisis environment, which is the norm for certain industries such as computer software. In this situation, it is critical for the sales manager to communicate the seemingly ever-changing vision to the salespeople in a way that makes sense for them. Further, the manager should serve as a calm, hard-working role model who readily accepts and adapts to the inevitable changes.

Finally, in some situations the absence of leadership might be most appropriate. Many individuals seek sales jobs because they like the autonomy. That is, they like being their own boss. When these reps perform at high levels, smart leadership may involve only an occasional update of the vision or overall goals of the organization. Of course, this hands-off approach would not be effective for team-selling situations, in which salespeople must be encouraged to work together (i.e., through fostering group goals).

Leadership and Strategic Planning

We believe that the leadership ability of sales managers is critical to the success of sales organizations, but not everybody shares this view. Many firms, particularly smaller ones with limited resources, provide little guidance and supervision for their sales force. The strategic marketing plan for these firms calls for the recruitment of experienced, proven performers who are essentially left alone to do their jobs.

An important factor in this strategic planning with regard to leadership is the importance of any one sale to the firm's welfare. If each sale is vitally important to the firm (as it is for Boeing Aircraft), leadership is critical and thus each rep will be closely supervised. If a single sale or even a single territory is not so important to total corporate well-being, then top management is not likely to spend much money hiring and developing accomplished leaders as sales managers. The leadership decision is a portion of the overall strategic decision as to how important the sales force is in accomplishing the firm's goals.

Tools and Techniques of Leadership

Compared to other business executives, sales managers face unique challenges in providing leadership to their subordinates. Perhaps the best method of leading a sales force is to provide one-on-one personal contact, but this is not always feasible. A sales rep might work out of his or her home in a territory that is hundreds of miles away from the closest co-worker. To be an effective leader, a sales manager must therefore use a combination of tools and techniques to interact with salespeople. These include personal contact, sales reports, telecommunications, sales meetings, printed aids, and other indirect supervisory aids.

Personal Contact

Typically, the sales manager visits sales reps on the job and tries to help them with whatever problems are evident. The manager's objectives and activities when traveling with a rep vary, but generally they include assisting in selling difficult customers or settling grievances, training, and evaluating. It is important to remember that when the sales manager or supervisor accompanies the sales rep on a sales call, the rep should still take the lead in directing the conversation and in moving from one agenda item to another.

When riding with their reps in order to train and evaluate them, managers should take care to observe a variety of things. The following questions should be kept in mind:

- Is the salesperson prepared for the call?
- Does the salesperson understand the customer's business and specific needs?
- Does the salesperson treat customers respectfully and honestly?
- Does the salesperson know the competition?
- Is the salesperson skillful at gaining commitment?

Managers should take notes as they observe the rep, indicating his or her strengths and weaknesses. These should be discussed with the rep as soon as possible after the call.[5]

Sales Reports

Sales reports provide records for monitoring and evaluating sales reps' activity. These reports usually include the number of calls made, number of orders taken, miles traveled, days worked, new prospects called on, and new accounts sold. As

An Ethical Dilemma

Karee McBride is a sales manager for Precision Tools Inc. in the northeastern district. She has been with the company for seven years and has been progressing rapidly up the sales ladder. Originally, her sales territories and her first supervisory assignments were in the eastern district and the north midwestern district, respectively. Six months ago, she was promoted to the northeastern district as a sales manager. She replaced a manager who had been there for 10 years. The district's performance in the last 3 of those 10 years had been steadily declining, so the decision was made to replace the district manager.

Shortly after her promotion, Karee McBride spent a great deal of time analyzing the sales results for the district and realized that there were some performance problems that would have to be resolved if the district's overall performance was to improve. One of these problems involved Bob Chay, who had been with the company for 24 years. Although Chay's sales were down slightly this year from the previous year, his sales for the past four years had been flat. At one time Chay had been one of the top producers, gaining new customers each year and cultivating more business at his existing accounts. Now, however, it appeared that Chay was riding on his relationships with his oldest and best accounts. But even the sales to those accounts seemed to be slipping. McBride guessed that these customers would continue to give Chay some of their business out of a sense of obligation based on their long friendship with him. But some of the new business at these accounts was obviously going to other vendors.

Karee McBride had discussed the lack of sales growth with Bob Chay, but he just said that he was no longer a hot-shot kid, that he was pretty content with his compensation, and that he didn't see the need to work that hard anymore. He also pointed out that his sales were not the lowest in the district. McBride was convinced that there was not a whole lot she was going to be able to do to motivate Chay to do more than he was doing now. She also felt strongly that a new rep could get a lot more growth out of that territory than Chay would or even could.

Chay was eligible for early retirement, but McBride knew that he was not interested in retiring at this time. He was 58. McBride knew that her decision with regard to Chay was complicated by the fact that he was an old friend of her family's. In fact, he was the one who had first given her name to the national sales manager and recommended her for the sales job.

What would you do if you were in Karee McBride's situation?

---

a supervisory tool, the sales report is a silent enforcer of company policy. Reps who know they must account for all their activities will feel more secure and comfortable if they stay within company policy.

Frequently reps are required to submit a **call plan,** which reports their itinerary for the upcoming period. The call plan forces reps to organize their activities. These plans show, for example, whether the reps are routing themselves properly, calling on the various classes of customers in the right ratio, and/or developing appropriate objectives for their calls.

Sales reports are used not only as a supervisory tool but also as data for the company's marketing information system. These reports contain in-depth information on customer problems and needs as well as on competitive activity. Sales managers must ensure that salespeople place a priority on providing timely and accurate information in their sales reports. This reporting activity should be evaluated and rewarded as one of the salesperson's primary responsibilities.

Telecommunications

To supplement their personal contact with sales reps, most sales executives use telecommunications—the telephone, fax messages, voice mail, electronic mail, and computer-based support systems. Computerized support systems assist the sales force in performing its many responsibilities. Companies such as IBM, Hewlett-Packard, and Procter & Gamble give each of their salespeople a laptop computer, which is useful in the following areas:

- **Better customer and industry information.** Laptops allow salespeople and their managers to access complete customer histories and industry information anywhere, at any time.
- **Selling assistance.** Laptops provide electronic libraries of product information and enhanced capabilities for analyzing customer problems. Price quotes, bids, proposals for service, and installation agreements can be generated automatically.
- **Sales support.** Laptops allow salespeople to enter and track orders very accurately. They also allow reps to handle correspondence with customers efficiently.
- **Reporting responsibilities.** Salespeople can submit their call plans and reports, expense reports, and other market intelligence using their laptops.
- **Communication.** The electronic-mail capability of laptop systems enables companies to be in constant communication with their reps regardless of where they are.

At Hewlett-Packard, for example, each of the 900 sales reps has a laptop computer.[6] These computers are programmed to quote prices, write contracts, track orders, and provide product and marketing information.

Portable computer systems provide a way to minimize the time spent on report writing. Yet at the same time, they improve the accuracy of the marketing information reps collect. Companies that have computerized support systems report significant improvements in sales force productivity and management effectiveness. IBM reports that its revenue per rep has increased by 30 percent since its sales force began relying on computerized support systems.

Printed Aids

Sales manuals, bulletins, company newsletters, and other printed aids allow leaders to interact with the sales force. A good sales manual tells sales reps what to do in various circumstances. Some questions can be answered just as effectively in a publication as they can through personal contact.

Meetings

Sales meetings, which were discussed in Chapter 8, are another means used to provide leadership. During sales meetings, managers often explain new procedures, policies, and programs to the sales reps.

Indirect Supervisory Aids

Several other leadership tools can be called **indirect supervisory techniques.** They have inherent supervisory powers and work automatically toward company goals—and they can be exceptionally effective. Unlike the other supervi-

Virtual Leadership

Increasingly, salespeople work out of a **virtual office.** That is, rather than having an office and desk at company headquarters (close to the sales manager), many reps carry their "offices" around with them in their laptops. This trend presents leadership challenges, because it means that sales managers have less face-to-face time with their salespeople.

The high-tech boom that has made virtual offices possible has in turn created a number of new high-tech ways to communicate with—or *lead*—a remote sales force. Options include cell phones, teleconferences, Web conferences, groupware, e-mail, voice mail, and chat.

Virtual communication will never completely replace in-person communication. However, the two can be used together. For example, the sales manager can use e-mail or teleconferencing to identify critical issues and thus craft the agenda of a face-to-face meeting scheduled for the near future. After the meeting, the sales manager can use an online bulletin board to continue a more in-depth discussion of issues initiated in the meeting.

Source: Mary Boone, "The E-vangelist: Face Time," *Sales & Marketing Management*, June 2001, p. 29.

sory methods, these indirect techniques travel with the reps everywhere, every minute of the day, and on every call they make. They include:

- **Compensation plans.** By far the most important automatic leadership tool, the compensation plan encourages reps to do those things that will maximize their earnings.
- **Territories.** Establishment of specific sales territories tells reps what areas they are responsible for.
- **Quotas.** By setting quotas for various product lines or for certain classes of customers, the sales manager can guide sales force activities into desired channels.
- **Expense accounts.** Policies on expenses automatically guide sales force behavior by limiting the amount reps can spend on certain activities.
- **Sales analysis procedures.** Using sales analysis procedures (discussed in Part 4 of this book), management can evaluate the performance of each salesperson and then guide or assist the reps who need help on certain points.

Outcomes of Effective Leadership

The right combination and amount of leadership can result in a number of positive **leadership outcomes** for the sales organization: well-trained salespeople, trust among salespeople, citizenship behaviors, better performance, and sales force morale.

Well-Trained Salespeople

As an effective leader, the sales manager provides a vision that should clarify what the reps are expected to do. Further, verbal feedback and role modeling by the sales manager show reps how to do it. In other words, the right combination of leader behaviors can do much to develop an inexperienced recruit into a productive salesperson. As we noted in Chapter 7, the most helpful sales training

Coaching Sales Reps

The quote at the beginning of the chapter comes from former National Football League coach Bill Parcells—a successful leader of championship football teams. Interestingly, there's a lot about **coaching** on the sports field that applies to a sales context. Many books and articles have been written about the importance of coaching salespeople, which is argued to be the best way to enhance performance. What coaching comes down to is good leadership. The following three elements of leadership are most often used to describe coaching:

- **Verbal feedback.** In the role of a coach, the sales manager provides continued feedback to each rep. It is critical to praise salespeople when they do well. Everyone needs to feel appreciated and recognized.

- **Leading by example.** Coaches are role models. They don't just tell reps how to sell—they *show* them. Sales managers who model professional attitudes and behaviors will inspire their salespeople to emulate them.

- **Mutual trust and respect.** Finally, sales managers trust and respect their reps, who are equally committed to their managers in turn. This environment of mutual trust and respect is created through two-way communication, which allows the manager to help identify and solve problems.

Source: Gregory A. Rich, "The Constructs of Sales Coaching: Supervisory Feedback, Role Modeling and Trust," *Journal of Personal Selling & Sales Management*, Winter 1998, pp. 53–63.

takes place over a period of time and is best done in the field while sales reps are actually facing day-to-day problems. Thus, great leaders are great trainers, and the first important outcome of effective leadership is a highly trained sales force.

Trust among Salespeople

Excellent leaders genuinely care about their subordinates and effectively persuade them to work together as a team. This leads to an environment of **trust** among salespeople and managers alike. Such an environment is critical for the success of any organization. Only when salespeople trust and respect each other can they successfully work together toward a common goal. A renowned leadership expert has written: "Trust is the lubrication that makes it possible for organizations to work."[7]

Citizenship Behaviors

Salespeople managed by great leaders are likely to engage in **citizenship behaviors,** which are voluntary behaviors that are not part of a formal job description yet that are important to the success of the firm. The following are examples of key citizenship behaviors that sales reps might exhibit:

- Offering tips and encouragement to a struggling new rep.
- Showing up to work on time and never missing a meeting.
- Tolerating problems without complaining.
- Volunteering to serve on a community service committee.
- Being courteous and respectful of the rights of others.

These are activities that salespeople are generally not trained—or even asked—to do. Further, the sales manager would not punish salespeople for failing to do

In sports or sales, effective leadership consists of many of the same basic elements.

these activities. At the same time, citizenship behaviors have been shown to be related to overall sales force productivity.

Better Performance

Some sales managers believe that direct supervision stimulates salespeople to do better work. However, there is a limit to how much an employee can be prodded without becoming resentful. For some reps, just knowing that management is aware of their efforts can be beneficial. Conversely, performance seems to suffer when sales reps know that management has no means of knowing what they are really doing.

It is important to most sales reps to know that someone in the organization cares about and recognizes the work they do. If the supervisor is adept, just the fact that he or she is in personal contact should have a good effect on performance.

Sales Force Morale

Effective leadership results in a well-trained, higher-performing sales group whose members trust and help each other as they work together toward a common goal. This combination of positive outcomes equates to higher **group morale** throughout the sales force. Group morale involves a sense of common purpose and a belief among members that group goals can be attained.

Group attitudes toward work are important for both economic and social reasons. From the economic standpoint, productivity is likely to be higher in groups whose members have relatively good morale. It does not always follow that high morale results in high productivity, however. A group may have a good attitude but poor results. Nevertheless, productivity is usually higher for employees who have good mental attitudes toward their jobs. From a social point of view, people who develop negative attitudes toward work can make life miserable not only for themselves but also for those around them. Life is too short to be spent working in an unpleasant environment. The proposition that leaders should promote good morale for its own sake certainly has merit.

In order for group morale to be high, each individual in the group must first be satisfied with his or her job. **Job satisfaction**—sometimes called *individual morale*—is the individual salesperson's *emotional* and *evaluative* feelings toward various dimensions of the job. These dimensions include pay, promotions, security, benefits, and co-workers. In other words, a salesperson will not be generally satisfied with his job if he is unhappy with one or more of these dimensions. At the same time, individual job satisfaction is hardly sufficient for group morale. In a situation where salespeople hate each other but get paid a high salary for doing very little work, job satisfaction could be quite high throughout the sales force. This group, however, could not be said to have high group morale.

Some job satisfaction dimensions might be outside the sales manager's control. For example, in many firms, a mid-level sales manager has very limited input into the overall compensation levels of salespeople. Nevertheless, effective leadership by the manager can go a long way toward increasing individual job satisfaction and, ultimately, group morale.

Problems Encountered in Leadership

Certain leadership and supervisory problems are commonly encountered when managing salespeople. They include poor performance, substance abuse, expense account abuse, other unethical behavior, and sexual harassment.

Poor Performance

When salespeople are not performing up to standards, the best solution is not to fire them but rather to help them become productive employees. Often these reps have received extensive training, so correcting the problem is less expensive than replacing them. Also, because of possible discrimination suits, prudent managers will make sure that they have done everything within reason to help failing employees—firing them should be a last resort.

Although many managers find it difficult to criticize their subordinates, it is often possible to correct a problem just by giving immediate feedback about the problem behavior. This constructive feedback should take place as soon as the manager notices the problem. Managers should be very specific about what the problem is and what the rep must do to correct it. The following steps should be followed in providing effective feedback:[8]

1. State the problem.
2. Get the salesperson's agreement on the problem.
3. Listen to the salesperson's assessment of the problem.
4. Consider extenuating circumstances.
5. Design an action plan for improvement.
6. Get the salesperson's agreement on the action plan.

If the rep's performance does not improve as a result of immediate feedback, the manager should review the problem in a formal performance appraisal; then the manager and rep should agree on a plan for improvement. The manager must make it very clear that poor performance is not acceptable. Each step should be documented with written memos detailing what took place. If the problem continues, the manager should set up a counseling session to review all the previous attempts to encourage improvement. The rep should be given a specified time period to show improvement. If the rep has not improved by the specified time, then the manager, with all of the appropriate documentation, must demote or terminate the rep.

Substance Abuse

One of the most difficult personnel problems sales managers encounter is the salesperson with a **substance abuse** problem. Unfortunately, some sales jobs lead to excessive drinking because they constantly put the reps in social situations where drinking is expected. Such jobs are terrible risks for people who cannot handle the temptations of alcohol.

Surveys indicate that the problems of drug and alcohol abuse among workers are pervasive and costly. A U.S. government study found illicit drug use among 7.7 percent of the nation's workforce, and among 9.1 percent of salespeople. The same study reported heavy alcohol use among 7.5 percent of the nation's workforce—but just 4.1 percent of salespeople.[9] The fact that heavy alcohol use among salespeople is significantly below the national average is surprising. Nevertheless, even if it affects only a few reps, substance abuse can still represent a big problem for sales managers. The performance of sales representatives who are alcoholics or drug abusers almost always suffers. Their work habits are usually poor, and the quality of their work is often unacceptable.

Detection

The signs of alcohol abuse (the odor, for example) can be more obvious than drug abuse, but both may be difficult to detect. If sales supervisors do not have day-to-day contact with their salespeople, the problem may go undetected for some time. Still, there are warning signs: alcohol on the breath, slurred speech, missed appointments, missed work, and declining performance. Excessive use of alcohol or drugs may also exhibit itself in certain behaviors at company functions and conventions.[10]

Some firms (Intel and Exxon, for example) make job offers to applicants contingent on their passing a drug test. Regardless of whether or not a firm uses substance abuse testing, sales supervisors should become familiar with the signs and symptoms of abuse so that they can detect any problems as early as possible.[11]

Dealing with Abuse

The use of illegal drugs on the job is, of course, never allowed; the consumption of alcohol, which is a legal substance, may be allowed in certain situations, such as entertaining customers. However, the abusive use of either alcohol or drugs almost invariably leads to performance deficiencies. It is the performance deficiency, not the abuse itself, that the supervisor should address first.

Entertaining clients in social settings can lead to substance abuse problems among salespeople.

The sales rep should be told that he or she must rectify the performance deficiency or be subject to termination. Then the supervisor can explore the reasons for the deficiency with the rep. When it is possible to get an admission of an abuse problem, the sales manager can recommend that the salesperson seek assistance from a professional substance abuse program. Sales managers should not attempt to provide counseling—they are rarely trained to deal with these problems. If salespeople refuse treatment or do not make satisfactory progress in the treatment, and if their performance does not improve, termination may be appropriate.

Some companies have formal policies for dealing with alcohol and drug abuse, but many do not. If there is no company policy, sales managers should develop their own formal, written policies. These policies should be clearly communicated to the sales force.

Expense Accounts

As noted in Chapter 10, expense accounts can lead to costly problems for management. The folklore of selling is full of fictional sales expense accounts. Expense account policies should be clearly set forth when salespeople are hired. Companies that expect the sales force to be honest make it clear that cheating on an expense account is grounds for dismissal. Then they consistently back up that policy with action.

A sales manager who discovers discrepancies in a rep's expense accounts should review the situation with the rep to be certain there is not simply an error or a misunderstanding of allowable expenses. Some managers simply disallow expenses they feel are not in order. Others go over the expense report with the

A DAY-TO-DAY OPERATING PROBLEM

MAJESTIC PLASTICS COMPANY

MAJESTIC
Plastics Company

A Sales Rep Objects to Harassment

Lisa Brannigan, Majestic's sales rep for the Kansas City area, had called her boss, Clyde Brion, requesting an urgent meeting. Brannigan was having problems at American Pharmaceuticals (AP), one of Majestic's largest customers. Although she had been named Majestic's top salesperson last year, Brannigan's current troubles did not come as a total surprise to Brion. As he prepared for the meeting, Brion reviewed the account history at AP.

As a long-time producer of generic drugs, AP represented the type of customer Majestic craved. It was only four years ago, however, that Majestic sales rep Nancy Sloan had been able to convince Charles "Chuck" Spencer, AP's president, of the value of doing business with Majestic. Within one month of replacing Earl Warner as sales rep on the account, Sloan delivered the largest order in Majestic's history. For the next year and a half, Majestic's business with AP grew tremendously.

After breaking all company sales records, however, Nancy Sloan abruptly resigned from Majestic. Citing "personal and family matters," she left to take a job in banking. Although Clyde Brion sensed something more was involved, he quickly replaced Sloan with one of Majestic's brightest stars, Matt Carson.

Carson had graduated with honors from the University of Missouri before joining a national paper supply company. Bright, articulate, and personable, he quickly became his firm's leading sales rep. Deciding to switch industries, he had joined Majestic with flawless credentials. He seemed the ideal choice to replace Nancy Sloan.

Six months later, however, Matt Carson felt something was terribly wrong at the AP account. Although he had increased sales throughout the territory, AP had stopped placing any significant orders with Majestic. Chuck Spencer seemed apathetic toward the new rep and Majestic. For the next three months, Carson solicited the advice of Clyde Brion on how to deal with Spencer and the erosion of one of Majestic's biggest accounts. When all attempts failed, Carson finally approached an AP purchasing manager who told him, "Chuck likes lady reps. I guess he feels more comfortable buying from a woman."

It was then that Clyde Brion, under pressure from top management to save the AP account, decided to have Lisa Brannigan switch territories with Matt Carson. Carson adapted well to his new territory in St. Louis, while Brannigan began to make significant progress in Kansas City, particularly at AP, where she brought in five large orders within three months. But that was over a year ago, and now Clyde Brion had to deal with a troubled Lisa Brannigan.

"Chuck Spencer keeps making passes at me, and yesterday asked me to join him for the weekend at his lake house. He's a 48-year-old rich and powerful bachelor who expects all the women he meets to fall madly in love with him. I've been totally professional with him since the day I joined the account, but I can't take any more of his antics. Either tell him to cool it with the harassment, or I'm not calling on AP," Brannigan said.

Question: Given that Chuck Spencer has no superior at AP and makes all the large buying decisions, what should Clyde Brion do in response to Lisa Brannigan's request?

Note: This case was prepared by Steven Reed under the direction of Rosann Spiro.

rep, putting the rep on notice that the expense reports are being watched. But such matters are sensitive, and the sales manager must deal with each case as the situation warrants.

Unethical Behavior

Padding expense accounts is one type of unethical behavior. But there are others—for example, recommending unnecessarily high product quality levels or inventory levels, selling out-of-production items without informing the customer, or providing misleading information on competitors. Sales managers who overlook such unethical practices are asking for trouble. While the immediate conse-

Dangers of Dating the Boss

Dating the boss is surprisingly common in sales. More than half of salespeople say they have known of a romantic relationship between their sales manager and a fellow salesperson on their team. Sales executives should understand that this creates the potential for significant problems.

First, such relationships can hurt the morale of the sales team—particularly if the manager shows favoritism to the salesperson he or she is dating. Worse, if the relationship ends bitterly, the company may be open to sexual harassment charges. Such lawsuits can not only cost millions in legal and settlement fees but

also result in negative publicity that tarnishes the company's reputation.

Many legal experts strongly urge sales executives to prohibit romances among colleagues—especially those between a supervisor and a subordinate. Yet only 15 percent of companies have a written policy regarding workplace relationships. What do you think? Should such policies exist in sales organizations? If so, what exactly should be banned?

Source: Betsy Cummings, "An Affair to Remember," *Sales & Marketing Management*, August 2001, pp. 50–57.

quences of allowing such behavior may not seem too great, this practice will likely result in more serious long-term consequences such as lawsuits and negative publicity.

Managers must take immediate action to put an end to unethical behavior. The same steps suggested earlier for problematic performance should be followed in correcting unethical behavior.

Sexual Harassment[12]

In 1980, the Equal Employment Opportunity Commission (EEOC) issued guidelines that interpret **sexual harassment** as a form of discrimination. Since that time, the number of sexual harassment cases filed has been steadily increasing. A typical Fortune 500 company spends millions of dollars a year dealing with sexual harassment. The costs stem from a variety of factors, including the investigation of sexual harassment claims; reduced productivity; increased turnover and absenteeism; and, of course, payments of monetary compensation to victims. It is important that sales managers take proactive steps not only to recognize and put a stop to harassment that does occur but also, and perhaps more important, to prevent it from occurring.

The EEOC defines sexual harassment as follows.

Unwelcome sexual advances, requests for sexual favors, and other verbal or physical conduct of a sexual nature constitute sexual harassment when any of the following criteria are met:

1. submission to such conduct is made either explicitly or implicitly a term or condition of an individual's employment;
2. submission to or rejection of such conduct by an individual is used as a basis for employment decisions affecting that individual;
3. such conduct has the purpose or effect of unreasonably interfering with an individual's work performance or creating an intimidating, hostile, or offensive working environment.

Typically, sexual harassment involves two people who work for the same firm—for example, a male supervisor harassing a female subordinate. Sexual harassment in sales organizations, however, is more commonly **third-party harassment,** which means that the harassment is done by someone *outside the firm.* That "someone" is most often a customer.

Sales managers have a responsibility for taking immediate corrective actions in response to all such incidents. These actions may include reassigning the salesperson to a new customer or territory; requesting that the customer stop the inappropriate behaviors; and, if the customer will not commit to refraining from such behaviors, closing the account. Sales managers must be proactive in creating an environment that does not tolerate harassment. In fact, the selling firm may still be liable even if the sales manager did not know about the sexual harassment—but *should have known about it.*

Beyond the individual managers' actions, the company should develop comprehensive policies against sexual harassment. These policies should include statements about the behaviors that are prohibited; the penalties for misconduct; the procedures for making, investigating, and resolving complaints; and procedures for education and training. Sales managers should understand these policies and ensure that they are followed.

Summary

Leadership—a process in which one person influences other people's behavior toward the accomplishment of specific goals—is essential for a sales manager to be effective. Effective leaders tend to possess similar personal characteristics, such as high levels of self-confidence, initiative, energy, creativity, and maturity. In addition, effective leaders possess advanced managerial skills, including the ability to solve problems, communicate, persuade, and understand what motivates each salesperson.

Leadership style refers to the specific set of leader behaviors that sales managers put forth in a given situation. There are two distinct styles: transactional leadership and transformational leadership. *Transactional leadership* involves those supervisory activities regarding the day-to-day operation and control of the sales force. It presents a short-term, task-oriented focus on getting the job done. Transactional leaders provide one-way communication to salespeople in the form of verbal feedback, letting them know what they are doing right and wrong.

Transformational leadership changes (transforms) the basic values, beliefs, and attitudes of followers such that they are willing to perform at levels above and beyond expectations. Those who use this style are outstanding leaders—usually referred to as charismatic. The primary transformational leader behaviors are articulating a vision of the future, fostering group goals, being a role model, and providing individualized support.

Both transactional and transformational leadership can be an effective way to lead salespeople. The situation determines the appropriate style or combination of styles. The best sales managers instinctively know the right mix of leader behaviors to use for any given situation.

The best way to lead a sales force is through face-to-face, personal contact. Due to lack of time or to distance, however, sales managers must supplement personal contact with other tools and techniques of leadership. These include sales reports, telecommunications, sales meetings, printed aids, and indirect supervisory aids.

A number of positive outcomes result from the right combination and amount of leadership. First, the salespeople are generally better trained and the work environment is characterized by mutual respect and trust among all employees. This in turn leads to higher performing salespeople who are more likely to engage in citizenship behaviors. Finally, the right leadership leads to a sales force with high group morale.

Some frequent problems encountered by leaders include poor performance, substance abuse, expense misappropriation, other unethical behavior, and sexual harassment. Each problem needs to be dealt with proactively to avoid potentially serious consequences.

Key Terms

Call plan
Charismatic leaders
Citizenship behaviors
Coaching
Fostering group goals
Group morale
Indirect supervisory techniques
Individualized support
Job satisfaction

Leadership
Leadership outcomes
Leadership style
Role modeling
Sales reports
Sexual harassment
Situational leadership
Substance abuse
Task orientation

Third-party harassment
Transactional leadership
Transformational leadership
Trust
Verbal feedback
Virtual office
Vision

Questions and Problems

1. What are the personal characteristics necessary for an effective leader? Will possessing these characteristics alone ensure success as a manager? If not, what other elements need to be considered?

2. What specific leader behaviors (from the two leadership styles) would you use in the following situations? Why?
   a) Terry is one of your best sales representatives. She has eight years of experience and has proved her abilities many times.
   b) Diane graduated with a marketing degree within the past year, but she has limited sales experience.
   c) John is a veteran employee. In recent months, however, you notice his performance stagnating.

3. How has the revolution in technology (high-speed computers, e-mail, the Internet, etc.) affected the way sales managers lead their salespeople?

4. Bill Jolton, a salesman for a large national soap company, informs his immediate supervisor that he is quitting at the end of the month. The supervisor is surprised to learn this, since she thought that Jolton was doing a good job and was happy with his work. The supervisor would like to keep Jolton with the firm, for she thinks he shows exceptional promise. How should the supervisor handle the situation?

5. As a sales manager for ABC Company, Rocky Farlow oversees 15 sales reps. Farlow is an outstanding transactional leader, but he is hopelessly ineffective as a transformational leader. Is this a problem? Why or why not?

6. A sales manager of a large metropolitan automobile dealership required his sales force of eight people to meet each morning at 9:00 A.M. for about 30 minutes to plan their activities for the day. During this meeting, he asked each rep to tell what he or she intended to accomplish

that day. Were these meetings sound? What was the manager's goal in setting up such meetings?

7. What are some specific ways in which sales managers can be role models to their salespeople? List several distinct ways.

8. What is the difference between job satisfaction and morale? Is it possible to have high job satisfaction but low morale?

9. You notice that Mike, one of your sales representatives, has been consistently unproductive for the past two months. You have heard rumors indicating that Mike may be abusing alcohol or drugs; however, no proof is available. What actions should you take? Why?

10. One of your sales reps, Nancy, claims that one of your other reps, Bill, has been sexually harassing her and she has asked you to do something about it. You have talked to Bill, but he denies it. What should you do now?

Experiential Exercises

A. Pick a classmate and describe what personal characteristics, skills, and/or behaviors this person exhibits that would make him or her an effective leader. Also describe any characteristics and/or behaviors that would make this classmate less effective.

B. Interview two business managers whom you know to determine whether each is more of a transactional leader or a transformational leader. (Hint: It might be useful to ask them how frequently they use certain behaviors to direct the efforts of their salespeople.) Describe the differences and similarities between the two managers.

Internet Exercises

A. Can a sales manager learn how to be a leader? A variety of consulting/training companies say "Yes, and we can teach them!" Use a search engine to find the websites of a few companies that have programs to teach leadership skills. (Recommended search terms include "leadership training," "coaching," and "sales management.") Describe the program and comment on whether or not you think it would be effective.

B. Visit the websites of the National Institute on Drug Abuse (www.drugabuse.gov) and the National Institute on Alcohol Abuse and Alcoholism (www.niaaa.nih.gov). What are the signs that a person has a substance abuse problem? What do these sites tell you about how a sales manager can detect and deal with drug and alcohol abuse?

References

1. Paul Hunting, "Developing Natural Leadership," *British Journal of Administrative Management*, May/June 2001, pp. 28–29.

2. The leadership style section is based to a large extent on Scott B. MacKenzie, Philip M. Podsakoff, and Gregory A. Rich, "Transformational and Transactional Leadership and Salesperson Performance," *Journal of the Academy of Marketing Science*, Spring 2001, pp. 115–34.

3. Channoch Jacobsen and Robert J. House, "Dynamics of Charismatic Leadership: A Process Theory, Simulation Model, and Tests," *Leadership Quarterly*, Spring 2001, pp. 75–112.

4. Betsy Cummings, "Getting Reps to Live Your Mission," *Sales & Marketing Management*, October 2001, p. 15.

5. Rex C. Houze, "Effective Sales Management," *American Salesman*, May 1995, pp. 3–5.

6. Edmund O. Lawler, "Sales Force Rearms with Portables," *Business Marketing*, July 1993, p. 46.

7. Warren G. Bennis, *Managing the Dream: Reflections on Leadership and Change* (Cambridge, MA: Perseus, 2000).

8. Tom Quick, *Making Your Sales Team No. 1* (New York: AMACOM, 1992).

9. U.S. Department of Health and Human Services Substance Abuse and Mental Health Services Administration, *Worker Drug Use and Workplace Policies and Programs: Results from the 1994 and 1997 NHSDA* (Rockville, MD: U.S. Department of Health and Human Services, 1999).

10. Wayne Friedman, "That Demon Alcohol," *Sales & Marketing Management*, December 1996, pp. 42–47.

11. A number of nonprofit and/or government-sponsored organizations provide extensive information on issues surrounding substance abuse problems. For example, visit the websites of the National Institute on Drug Abuse (www.drugabuse.gov) and the National Institute on Alcohol Abuse and Alcoholism (www.niaaa.nih.gov).

12. This discussion is based to a large extent on the following two articles: Cathy Owens Swift and Russell L. Kent, "Sexual Harassment: Ramifications for Sales Managers," *Journal of Personal Selling & Sales Management*, Winter 1994, pp. 77–88; and Leslie M. Fine, C. David Shepherd, and Susan L. Josephs, "Insights into Sexual Harassment of Salespeople by Customers: The Role of Gender and Customer Power," *Journal of Personal Selling & Sales Management*, Spring 1999, pp. 19–34.

CASE 11-1   SPECTRUM HEALTH, INC.

Leadership in a Crisis Situation

"Okay, we are now officially in a crisis," Cara Bakelin said out loud to herself. She knew she was about to face the toughest leadership challenge of her career—but she was not sure how she would handle it.

After a successful seven-year career in the field, Cara now has been district manager for Spectrum Health for just over two years. She supervises 10 territory reps across her district, the state of Maine. But this is new, because just last week she was the supervisor of 12 reps. Two were laid off by Spectrum as part of its initiative of reducing its U.S. sales force by 24 percent. According to Jack Lord, Spectrum's new CEO, the layoffs were necessary to stay competitive. "This will make us a leaner, more efficient organization," Jack wrote in a memo. Cara knew that other factors contributed to the decision to eliminate salespeople. These included a downturn in the economy, specific government cutbacks of health care funding for most of Spectrum's customers, and the emergence of a tough foreign competitor.

Spectrum Health, Inc., is a $3.2 billion medical equipment manufacturer. The company produces a wide range of medical supplies and devices for health care providers such as physicians, hospitals, and health maintenance organizations. Products range from expensive heart-lung machines to inexpensive stethoscopes, thermometers, and wound closure products.

Cara Bakelin felt that the morale of her sales force was never especially high. The reps were unique individuals who did not seem to interact much with each other. They were each motivated by different goals. She never sensed any animosity among them and had been hopeful that somehow she could make them more of a team. But in her first two years on the job, she has focused primarily on learning her administrative duties, such as quantitative analysis, forecasting, and budgeting.

In fact, the sales executive who performed her recent evaluation told Cara that she needed to do a better job communicating with her salespeople—especially through coaching and individual contact. She had told the executive, "I've never been good with that touchy-feely stuff, but I'll try to do better!"

Cara had also been told that her unit's overall sales levels were disappointing. Market research indicated that Spectrum held a 5.2 percent share of the market in Maine. This was well below the company's current national average of 8.5 percent market share.

What stood out more than anything else was Cara's unit's lack of success in selling the more expensive health care products, such as the heart-lung machine. To effectively sell such complex devices, team selling is required. That is, Spectrum reps must coordinate the efforts of engineers, cardiopulmonary experts, and other high-tech colleagues.

Cara knows she is in a very difficult situation. She needs to try to improve the morale of an underachieving group of people who have a long history of not being committed to anything other than their own individual goals. Further, she has to do this in a tough business climate in which the company is laying off her salespeople. Commitment to the organization is clearly at an all-time low among reps. How can she get these reps excited about working toward a common company goal when they do not trust the company?

Even before the announced layoffs, Cara had taken the advice of superiors and booked more of her work time for individual contact with her reps. In fact, she has devoted next week exclusively to this. She will address all 10 reps first thing Monday morning in a one-hour sales meeting. She then plans to spend the rest of the week, through Friday, coaching them individually. She plans on accompanying at least some of them on sales calls.

Her first challenge is to decide what kind of leadership to provide to—and how much time to spend with—each of her 10 reps. After reviewing her reps' unique needs and talents, Cara feels that they can be categorized into five distinct groups:

1. Two reps, Kristi and Kraig, are high-performing and experienced. They sell all Spectrum products the way that they should be sold. In fact, they are the only two reps who consis-

tently sell the big items such as the heart-lung machine. This success stems in part from the close bonds that the two have formed with some of the nonsales (technical) people at Spectrum.

2. Four reps, Allen, Ashley, Andrew and Art, are solid performers but lone wolves. The performance is average to above average across these four reps. Cara appreciates much of what they do, but she is disappointed in their sales of big-ticket items such as the heart-lung machine. These reps love their jobs, especially the autonomy. They generally have little interaction with others at Spectrum, including both sales and nonsales personnel.

3. Two reps, Daniel and Debra, are low-performing rookies. Actually, these two reps have been with Spectrum for almost one year now. They are the only two reps left that Cara personally hired (two other reps she hired were laid off). They are bright and energetic, but they still lack experience. Cara feels that they could be much better performers if they improve their selling technique.

4. One rep, Erin, is a mediocre-performing misfit. To Cara, Erin stands out as being a loner among loners. The reps are generally not very close to each other, but Erin seems to be the least interactive. Her sales levels are a bit higher than those of the rookies, but they should be since she has been with Spectrum for almost five years. Erin never seems happy. Cara suspects that this stems from the fact that she was born and raised on the West coast, over 3,000 miles away.

5. Finally, the one remaining rep, Robert, is a low-performing, burned-out veteran. Now approaching 60 years old, Robert was a solid performer in years past. Since Cara became sales manager, however, Robert's performance has dropped significantly. Cara gets the sense that Robert is looking forward to his retirement; and, in fact, she is, too.

Cara wants to develop a strategy for effective leadership of her sales force. She understands there are different styles of leadership, and that most leader behaviors are either transactional or transformational. She also understands that her leadership style should be appropriate for the current crisis situation. Cara wants to develop a specific plan of action for each of the five groups of salespeople, but she needs your help.

Questions:

1. What is the general message that Cara Bakelin should give all the reps in the Monday-morning meeting?

2. What are the specific leader behaviors that Cara Bakelin should exhibit toward each of the five different categories of reps? Be specific.

CASE 11-2   JUPITER SPECIALTIES

Developing a Sales Information System

Mike Bachman, the vice president of sales for Jupiter Specialties, recalled his earlier conversation with Pete Poorman, the company's chairperson and CEO. Bachman had told his boss that the sales information system was a mess and that he felt it would be best if they designed a new system from scratch. Poorman reminded him that the company spent a lot of money designing this system just a few years ago; he went on to inform Bachman that the system was providing all the information he thought they could possibly use, and it was doing so in a timely manner. "We know everything about how our products are performing, and we have a great deal of specific information about each customer."

He ended by asking, "What more could you possibly want?"

"That is just the problem," Bachman had told his boss. "We have an overload of information, and because of that the reps either aren't using it at all or are spending too much time trying to use it."

His boss again told him that he was not in favor of scrapping the present system, but he asked Bachman to prepare a report detailing the problems and said he would consider it.

Jupiter Specialties is a national distributor of gifts and novelties. Jupiter's customer base is composed of 30,000 retail stores, primarily in the gift and bookstore trades, located throughout the United States. The company is a primary vendor for such department stores as Neiman Marcus, Saks Fifth Avenue, Dayton-Hudson, Marshall Fields, and Lord & Taylor. Jupiter, whose sales growth has been averaging 8 to 10 percent a year, currently has sales of $30 million and is expecting its growth to continue over the next decade.

Pete Poorman is one of the company's founders. Reporting to him are the vice presidents for sales, administration, accounting, manufacturing, and marketing. These managers are responsible for understanding specific corporate strategies, raising questions concerning potential problems, and helping to establish schedules for projects. They are also accountable for planning the implementation of decisions involving the employees under their direction and maintaining communication between departments. Mike Bachman is the newest of the vice presidents, having been with the company nine months.

Reporting to the vice president of sales are four regional managers who oversee the district managers and key account activity in four U.S. sales regions: East, Midwest, South, and West. The company's 15 district managers are responsible for training new sales representatives and maintaining ongoing support of the field sales personnel. The district managers, who are responsible for maintaining the quota requirements of the field staff, report to the regional managers, but Mike Bachman frequently communicates directly with the district managers.

Jupiter currently has 75 field sales representatives, called sales consultants. The consultants are responsible for selling Jupiter's product line to various independent and chain retailers. They are paid a salary plus commission plus group bonus. On average, the individual consultant is responsible for a territory quota of $400,000.

Administrative personnel at corporate headquarters in Asheville, North Carolina, are responsible for field sales force support. The staff collects information from its operations in the field and uses it to generate a series of reports that track the performance of individual sales representatives, customer accounts, and products. These reports have been designed to be used directly by the sales force to improve their ability to service customers and organize their selling effort.

The reports can be classified into three distinct categories. (See Table 11-2A for a listing of the reports.) The first category contains information related to the sales in each territory. The reps can use this information to track sales quotas by county on a monthly, year-to-date, and product basis. They can also compare this year's performance with the previous year's. The reps also receive quarterly reports on their sales ranking compared to other reps and on their region's ranking compared to other regions as well as reports on their commissions and regional bonuses to date.

The second category of information tracks the performance of individual accounts. These reports are intended to help the salespeople improve the service rendered to specific accounts and to pinpoint where selling effort is needed or might be most productive. For example, one report contains overall sales, turnover, and margin information for a specific account; another report provides the same information by product and product categories; and others detail specific suggestions for periodic changeover of the customer's inventory.

The third category of reports contains information on the credit status of individual accounts. These reports are used for determining how reliable customers have been in their dealings with Jupiter and whether the customer qualifies for larger inventories of product.

Mike Bachman recognized that some of the reports were in fact useful to the reps. The "Retail Product Analysis" report enabled the rep to show the customer precisely how much Jupiter's products contribute to their gross profit, and the "Sales by Category" report can help the rep develop effective selling strategies. However, many of the salespeople complained that there were too many reports and that there was too much information in most of them. One rep stated that she received much more data than she was capable of absorbing and analyzing. Another described stacks of old reports that he could not examine in a timely manner, if at all.

Question:

1. What should Mike Bachman recommend to Pete Poorman concerning Jupiter's sales information system?

TABLE 11-2A   Jupiter Specialties Sales Reports

Sales by Territory

Sales Summary—monthly sales by the rep
YTD Sales Summary—YTD sales vs. previous year by the rep
Sales by Product Category—monthly sales by product category by the rep
Sales by Region—monthly sales by region
Quota Summary—percentage of quota achieved by the rep
Quota by County—percentage quota achieved by county by the rep
YTD Rep Ranking—sales rank based on YTD sales for all reps
Rep Commission Statement—monthly commissions earned
Regional Bonus Statement—group bonus earned by region
Incentive Summary—summary of incentive monies earned by the rep
Gross Sales Comparison—gross sales by reps
Net Territory Comparison—net sales by reps

Individual Accounts

Merchant Inventory Plans—plans for periodic changeover of customer's inventory
Qualified/Nonqualified Quarterly Report—information regarding timing for inventory changeovers at qualified and nonqualified accounts
Retail Product Analysis—account performance information which details product contribution to customer gross profit
Product Category Summary—performance information on specific product categories by account
Account Action Report—suggested merchandising actions based on inventory turnover data by account
Account Activity Report—monthly sales activity by account
Region Account Ranking—account ranking by sales for the region
Region Account Ranking by Rep—account ranking by rep for the region

Credit Status

Accounts to Collection—accounts that have been turned over to collection for late payment
Accounts in Previous Collection—accounts previously turned over to collection
Cost of sales

CASE 11-3   KAPFER EQUIPMENT COMPANY

Declining Performance of Good Sales Rep

"Johnny's been one of our outstanding reps for the past 10 years. I can't believe what I've just learned," Tom Grant, sales manager, said to Jackie Kapfer, partner and co-manager of the Kapfer Equipment Company of Lincoln, Nebraska.

"And what is that?" Jackie asked.

"He's been moonlighting on us for the past six months. He's a partner in an apartment construction project over in Sioux City with an old buddy of his. That's why his sales have been so bad these past few months. He's not working full-time for us anymore."

Kapfer Equipment distributed a wide line of heavy-duty equipment, machines, and tools to the construction trades, governments, mining companies, and the oil industry in a five-state area around Nebraska. Its customers were anyone who had a large-scale construction project to build. The company had a long and good relationship with the 15 manufacturers it represented. Its lines included such items as crawler tractors, excavator–shovels, motor graders, cranes, backhoes, off-highway trucks, loaders, rollers, compactors, conveyors, pavers, and asphalt equipment.

The company had been founded by Otto Kapfer in 1920 and passed to his son, Max, in 1945. Max's two children, Dirk and Jacklyn, had taken over the enterprise in 1985 upon Max's retirement. Dirk worked with the suppliers and the service side of the business while Jacklyn, who was called Jackie by everyone but her mother, ran daily operations.

Each person on the 22-member sales force sold the entire line of products and services to every type of customer in his or her assigned territory. It was a difficult job because it included many different types of products and customers.

John Knight had joined the company in 1990 after five years as a salesperson for Caterpillar. Prior to that he had worked as an engineer in heavy construction, mostly building the interstate highway system. He had graduated from Iowa State University in 1976 with a degree in civil engineering.

Since John had developed many valuable contacts in the Omaha area from his work for one of the area's largest construction companies, he was assigned that territory. He met his quotas the first year and exceeded them by 23 percent the second. He became the company's second most productive sales rep, consistently exceeding his sales quotas. Tom Grant had considered him managerial timber. It was thought that he might become sales manager if Tom ever left the company or was promoted to a higher position in the company.

Jacklyn asked, "How did you find out about John's apartment project?"

"Well, six months ago his sales fell 30 percent below quota. He blamed the economy but said that things would pick up soon, that I shouldn't worry. Well, when somebody tells me not to worry, that's when I really start worrying. I pulled out his activity reports. He wasn't making the calls as he used to make them. Something was wrong. And you know we require a report on every situation in which we don't get the order but some other company does. I knew of some business that John Deere had sold that we bid on, so I looked for the report on it. No reports! So I go see him."

Jackie asked, "Why didn't you call him in? Why waste your time going over to Omaha?"

"Because all the evidence would be in Omaha. It's easy for a guy to lie to you in the office. In the field where the bodies are buried it's easier to get to the truth. I went to his house unannounced. No one was there, but a neighbor told me that John was probably at his apartment project. She gave me the address. I went over and caught him red-handed, working on the roof with his partner. Did he ever look sheepish!"

Tom paused for effect and then continued, "He came down and we had a long, very frank talk. I was so mad I wanted to fire him on the spot. If he wasn't so big, I might have decked him. I kept my cool, but he knew I was mad.

"His story was that he got caught in the apartment project by the real estate recession. Initially, he was only an investor in the deal his friend had put together, but they ran into trouble. Their permanent financing collapsed when the bank got into some trouble with the Feds. Also, the insurance company that was furnishing the construction money was about to pull the plug on them, so they had to get the project finished fast for what little money they had. So John and his partner had been working to complete the project to save themselves. He insisted that it would be done in a month and that he would then be back at work at full speed. He pleaded for his job. He said he really liked to work for us. He also said he would continue to do an outstanding job for us if we would just give him a little room right now to get out of the mess he was in."

"What did you say to that?" Jackie asked.

"I told him how I felt about how he had treated us and that I thought he had used very bad judgment in how he handled his problem. However, I said that I would think about it and let him know my decision tonight."

"And what have you decided?"

"I decided to talk it over with you and Dirk first. After all, he has been one of the company's valuable earning assets. You wouldn't like it if I sold the warehouse out from under you without you knowing it, would you?"

Jackie replied, "Look, I know you have made up your mind what you want to do. So tell me and I'll put in my two cents' worth if I feel like it."

Questions:

1. Should John Knight be fired?

2. If not, what should Tom Grant do about the situation?

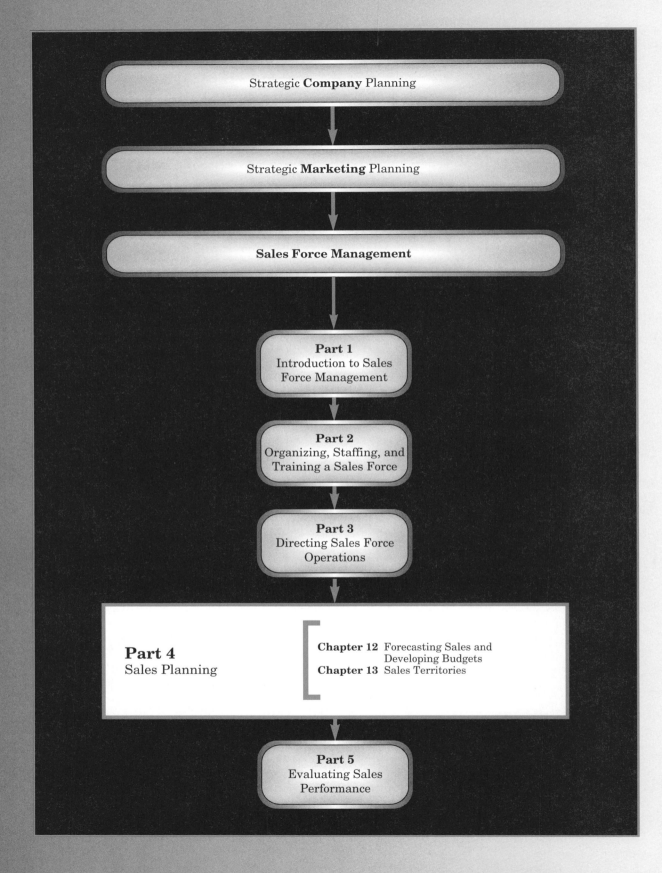

Strategic **Company** Planning

Strategic **Marketing** Planning

Sales Force Management

Part 1
Introduction to Sales Force Management

Part 2
Organizing, Staffing, and Training a Sales Force

Part 3
Directing Sales Force Operations

Part 4
Sales Planning

Chapter 12 Forecasting Sales and Developing Budgets
Chapter 13 Sales Territories

Part 5
Evaluating Sales Performance

Sales Planning

The first stage in the sales management process is planning. This is followed by implementing the plans through sales operations. The process ends with an evaluation of the sales performance. Sales planning involves establishing sales goals and then deciding which strategies and tactics to use to reach them.

However, a company manages its sales force within the context of its total marketing program. Therefore, the path taken in *sales force* planning depends on the company's strategic *marketing* planning. The strategic marketing planning, in turn, depends on the *overall company* planning. Thus, sales executives take their sales planning cues from the firm's strategic marketing planning and corporate planning.

Our coverage of sales planning starts with determining the sales forecast and developing budgets in Chapter 12. In Chapter 13, we deal with designing sales territories, assigning sales reps to these territories, and routing the salespeople.

12 Forecasting Sales and Developing Budgets

Salespeople underestimate how much they spend and overestimate how much they sell.

—Andy Cohen, *Sales & Marketing Management*, October 1996—

The foundation of the planning efforts of most companies is a sales forecast. The importance of sales forecasting is clearly shown at Otis Elevator Company, a world leader in the development and marketing of elevators and moving stairway systems. According to Heinz Dickens, Sales Manager of International Operations at Otis, sales forecasting at the International Division of Otis begins with estimates of sales for the coming year. These are provided by salespeople and sales managers in the company's territories. Many of the sales territories include whole foreign countries.

Otis, like many large companies, uses its sales forecasts to allocate resources across different functional areas. Production uses sales forecasts to develop production schedules and quantity requirements, and to regulate inventories; finance uses them to set operating budgets and to project cash flows; human resources uses them to establish hiring levels; and marketing uses them to allocate resources across different marketing activities.

Sales forecasting at Otis is not an exact science, says Dickens. The International Division often makes adjustments to the forecast for elevators and moving stairways as unforeseen events surface, such as wars and changes in governments. These events can dampen or stimulate sales of the company's products. Otis tries to improve forecasting accuracy by including many different types of information in the sales forecasts. For example, the company compiles monthly reports on the progress of negotiations with its potential customers. "Though we may be off-target sometimes," says Dickens, "our manufacturing operation would come to a standstill if we did not produce a reasonably good sales forecast."

The problem confronting Otis Elevator year after year is how to develop an accurate sales forecast that helps managers make sound business decisions. In this chapter, we will help you understand the importance of forecasting, illustrate types of forecasting methods firms use, and discuss several guidelines on the selection of a sales forecasting method.

Sales Forecasting and Strategic and Operational Planning

A company must establish its marketing goals and strategies—the core of a marketing plan—before it makes a sales forecast. The sales forecasts will differ according to whether the marketing goal is to liquidate inventory or to expand the firm's market share by aggressive advertising or some other goal.

Once the sales forecast is prepared, it becomes the key factor in all *operational* planning throughout the company. Forecasting is the basis of sound budgeting. Financial planning for working capital requirements, plant utilization, and other needs is based on anticipated sales. The scheduling of all production resources and facilities, such as setting labor needs and purchasing raw materials, depends on the sales forecast. The sales forecast also plays a critical role in sales force planning. The sales forecast helps sales executives determine the budget for the department, and it also influences sales quotas and compensation of salespeople.

If the forecast is in error, the plans based on it will also be in error. For example, if it is overly optimistic, the organization can suffer great losses because of overexpenditure in anticipation of revenues that are not forthcoming. If the sales forecast is too low, the firm may not be prepared to provide what the market demands. This means that the company will be forgoing profits and giving its competitors a bigger market share. Clearly, valid sales forecasts can play a major role in the success of the company.

Explanation of Basic Terms

Before we discuss the methods used in forecasting, we need to define and explain some of the basic terms used in forecasting sales. Because the terms are closely related and used loosely in business, they frequently cause misunderstandings among managers.

Market Potential and Sales Potential

What do we mean when we speak of a "potential" market for a product? **Market potential** is the total expected sales of a given product or service for the *entire industry* in a specific market over a stated period of time. To be complete and meaningful, the definition of market potential (and sales potential and the sales forecast, which we will discuss next) must include four elements:

1. The item being marketed (the product, service, idea, person, or location).

2. Sales for the entire industry in dollars or product units.

3. A specific time period.

4. A specific market delineated either geographically, by type of customer, or both.

For example, the market potential for beer in the United States in the year 2003 is expected to be 194 million barrels. Note that this statement about the market potential of beer includes information on each of the four points discussed above. Market potential for beer also could be stated for blue-collar men, white-collar women, men and women ages 21 to 25 in the state of Indiana, and so on.

Sales potential refers to the maximum share (or percentage) of market potential that an *individual firm* can reasonably expect to achieve. For example, Budweiser brand accounted for 40 percent of the approximately 180 million barrels of beer consumed in the United States in 2002. It is reasonable to argue that Budweiser beer's sales potential is close to 40 percent of the market in the coming years. When we speak of a company's sales potential, we must again specify the product, market, and time period.

Market potential is a total-industry concept, whereas sales potential refers to an individual firm. Thus, we may speak of the "market potential" for beer, and the "sales potential" (or market share) for Budweiser beer. Market potential and sales potential are equal in the case of a monopoly. In most industries, however, market potential and sales potential are different, since there are many firms competing in the market. As discussed in Chapter 13, it is sales potential that provides the basis for designing sales territories.

Sales Forecast

A **sales forecast** is an estimate of sales (in dollars or units) that an individual firm expects to achieve during a specified forthcoming time period, in a stated market, and under a proposed marketing plan. A company may make a forecast for an entire product line or for individual items within the line. Sales may be forecast for a company's total market or for individual market segments.

At first glance, the company's sales potential and sales forecast may appear to be the same. But usually that is not the case. The sales potential is what would be achieved under ideal conditions. The sales forecast typically is less than the sales potential for many different reasons. The company's production facilities may be too limited to allow the firm to reach its full sales potential. Also, the firm's financial resources may not be adequate enough to allow it to realize the full sales potential in the current period.

Estimating Market and Sales Potentials

Under conditions of great uncertainty, such as those that exist when a firm is trying to market an innovation, it is very difficult to develop accurate forecasts. Estimates are often inaccurate. If the innovation hits a market favorably, the projections will probably prove to be too low; if it misses the market, the sales projections will prove to be insufficiently conservative.

The three fundamental techniques for estimating market and sales potentials for a product are market-factor derivation, surveys of buyer intentions, and test

An International Perspective

The western European countries formed the European Union in the 1990s. As a result, many of the trade barriers that had existed between countries in Europe were eliminated. The reduction of trade barriers also made it easier for U.S. companies to enter the European market. Potential for U.S. products in these markets is very large. However, viewing this European market as a single entity would be shortsighted.

The demand for products across the European Union will continue to vary significantly due to differences in preferences, habits, culture, climate, and incomes. Understanding these differences is critical to estimating the potential for sales of U.S. products in Europe. Researchers Ryans and Rau have developed a taxonomy of emerging Euro-consumer clusters. The descriptions of these clusters provide a basis for understanding differences in European buying preferences and patterns.

Euro-Consumer Clusters

- **Cluster 1:** United Kingdom and Ireland
  a) Northeastern Europe
  b) Average income
  c) Age profile—average of EC
  d) Common language—English
- **Cluster 2:** Central and northern France, southern Belgium, central Germany, and Luxembourg
  a) North Central Europe—average income
  b) Low proportion of middle-aged people and high proportion of older people
  c) French and German languages

- **Cluster 3:** Spain and Portugal
  a) Southwestern Europe
  b) Young population
  c) Lower-than-average income
  d) Spanish and Portuguese languages
- **Cluster 5:** Greece and southern Italy
  a) Southeastern Europe
  b) Lower-than-average income
  c) Young population
  d) Greek and Italian languages
- **Cluster 4:** Southern Germany, northern Italy, southeastern France
  a) South Central Europe
  b) High proportion of middle-aged people
  c) Higher than average income
  d) German, French, Italian languages
- **Cluster 6:** Denmark, northern Germany, the Netherlands, and northern Belgium
  a) Northern Europe and Switzerland
  b) Very high income
  c) High proportion of middle-aged people
  d) Multilingual—Scandinavian, French, Italian, and German languages

Source: John K. Ryans and Pradeep A. Rau, *Marketing Strategies for the New Europe: A North American Perspective in 1992* (Chicago: American Marketing Association, 1990).

---

markets. Each of these methods is based on an analysis of the customer. Therefore, we will first describe the customer analysis and then discuss each method.

Customer Analysis

The starting points in any **customer analysis** are to determine who will use the product and to identify all possible characteristics of those users. A distinction must be made between the person who *buys* the product and the individual who actually *uses* it. The market potential is based on the individual or firm for which the product is intended. Although many women buy shirts for men, the market potential for men's shirts is determined by the number of men users, not by the number of women buyers.

Are the users household consumers, industrial users, or both? If they are household consumers, the seller may want to classify them further by demographics such as age, sex, marital status, area of residence, income, occupation, religion, and education. Lifestyle information may also be used, such as the types of exercise and recreation in which the user is interested. In the case of businesses selling to businesses, the seller must collect information on the types and quantities of products potential buyers manufacture and sell to their end users. Managers must gather the names and positions of the persons influencing the purchase decision, as well as information about the company's competitors. Most companies have compiled such information through periodic contact with their customers or through the use of marketing research.

Performing a customer analysis also requires a determination of why customers are buying the product and what their buying habits are. Most products are purchased to fulfill some need. Understanding these needs can improve the accuracy of a company's market potential estimates and sales forecasts. For example, consumer sensitivity to the prices of grocery products has resulted in greater sales of private-label (i.e., store-brand) products, and in response to consumers' concerns about price, consumer product giants, such as Philip Morris and Procter & Gamble, routinely chop prices of their products to stay competitive. Price also plays a major role in forecasting demand in areas outside of grocery products. For example, AT&T uses price and customer income to forecast demand for new telecommunications services.[1] The forecasters at AT&T believe—and their results support this belief—that price and income are important determinants of sales of products and services. In all these cases, the understanding that price plays an important role in purchase decisions will help the companies produce accurate forecasts.

Market-Factor Derivation

The **market-factor derivation** method for determining the size of a potential market begins with a market factor. A **market factor** is an item or element in a market that (1) causes the demand for a product or service or (2) is otherwise related to that demand. To illustrate, the annual birthrate is a market factor underlying the demand for playpens. That is, this element is related to the number of playpens that a manufacturer can sell. Using the birthrate as a market factor, a manufacturer of playpens would estimate the sales potential for playpens as follows:

Estimated number of births, 2003:	4,000,000
Times: Percent who buy playpens	× 0.33
Market potential	1,320,000
Times: Potential market share	× 0.30
Sales potential	396,000

An independent supermarket operator in Denver, Colorado, computed the store's sales potential by using *Sales & Marketing Management*'s estimate of food and beverage sales in the Denver metropolitan area (about $4.158 billion) as the market factor.[2] The store did not sell to the entire area but rather appealed only to a region in which about 15 percent of the population resided. So the operator estimated the market potential to be about $623.7 million. Since three other large supermarkets plus some smaller stores competed in that same area,

the operator set 20 percent as the store's probable share of the market. Therefore, the sales potential was $124.7 million for the year.

Denver food sales	$4,158,287,000
Times: Percent of market covered	× 0.15
Market potential	$ 623,743,050
Times: Potential market share	× 0.20
Sales potential	$ 124,748,610

This market-factor derivation technique for determining market and sales potentials has several advantages. First, the validity of the method is high. The method is usually founded on some valid statistics that have relatively little error. Other favorable aspects of this technique are that it is fairly simple, requires little statistical analysis, and is relatively inexpensive to use.

It should be noted that the market-factor method, like the other methods of estimating potentials, can be used as the basis of the sales forecast. In order to forecast sales, the company must estimate what portion of its sales potential it can reasonably expect to achieve in a given period.

Surveys of Buyer Intentions

The **survey of buyer intentions** technique for determining potentials consists of contacting potential customers and questioning them about whether or not they would purchase the product or service at the price asked.

One manufacturer contemplating the production of an aluminum playpen for babies used this technique. The playpen was to be made exactly like the ordinary wooden playpens on the market, except that aluminum tubing would be used instead of the wooden bars. The manufacturer established that it would be satisfied if it sold 5,000 aluminum playpen units per year. Since the cost of the unit would be higher than that of the wooden units, the manufacturer wanted to know two things. First, how many people would buy such a product if it were placed on the market at the retail price of $59.95? Second, what did customers think the price of such a product should be?

The manufacturer conducted a survey through personal interviews with 240 parents of infants. The results showed that 170 of the 240 (approximately 71 percent) were interested in such a product. However, they also indicated that the price would have to be $39.95 to capture that size of market. The average (mean) price quoted ($45) would eliminate half of the respondents who showed interest in the product. Still, 10 people (4 percent of the market) said they would be interested in purchasing the product at the retail price of $59.95.

The survey indicated that only about one-third of all families with infants purchase playpens. Thus, the total market potential for the $59.95 aluminum playpens would be approximately 52,800 units. This figure was derived by multiplying the total number of births per year (4 million) by one-third (0.33) and taking 4 percent of the result. This simple calculation showed the manufacturer that market interest in the playpen well exceeded the goal of selling 5,000 units and was therefore sufficient to warrant further investigation.

The primary advantage of surveys of buyer intention is that the method is based on information obtained directly from the people who will ultimately purchase or not purchase the product or service. Major disadvantages of this method are its cost and its time-consuming execution. For the sales manager who needs a quick idea of the market potential of a product, the survey method is not suitable. If a manufacturer intends to distribute nationally, consumer surveys can easily run into thousands of dollars and take three to six months to complete. Furthermore, surveys of buying intentions are hazardous undertakings. It is easy for the respondents to say that they would buy a certain product, but the acid test is whether or not they actually do.

Test Markets

Test marketing involves introducing and marketing a new product in a market that is similar to the company's other markets. For example, Indianapolis, Indiana, and Columbus, Ohio, are often used as test markets by companies because their socioeconomic and demographic profiles are similar to the profiles of many other cities in the United States. The demand for the product in the test market will then be used to forecast sales of the product in other markets.

Although test marketing takes considerable time and money, it is probably the most accurate method of estimating the sales potential for certain products. The reason is that a test market actually requires the buyers to spend their money. The other methods discussed require an estimate of what share of the market the product will achieve. Frequently, these estimates are merely guesses. The test market eliminates this guessing.

In the world of new ventures, venture capitalists view the first stage of development in which the product or service is initially offered for sale as a test market. Jerry Zimmer started ZDC, a computerized system for managing and measuring the energy used in master-metered apartment houses, in Boulder, Colorado, with a $60,000 initial investment. He sold about $1 million worth of his systems in the Denver market area during ZDC's first year of operation. On the basis of that test, the company was able to raise an additional $500,000 to expand market coverage. The first several years of the life of many new products is essentially a test market that proves that people will buy the product and that it is profitable.

The one obvious advantage of the test-marketing technique is that it results directly in a sales potential for products under consideration. However, test marketing requires a considerable amount of effort and time before results are known. Products that require extensive investment in fixed assets before they are introduced to the market cannot be evaluated by this method. Similarly, test markets provide poor evaluations of products that require time to gain acceptance or have a low rate of consumption. Test marketing is used mainly when a relatively small number of units can be produced at a minimum cost.

Territory Potentials

Once the company has determined total sales potential, the sales manager usually wants to divide that potential among the various territorial divisions. This allows the manager to allocate selling efforts properly and to evaluate the relative performance of each district. The usual method for this is to use some pertinent market factor or index broken down by small areas.

A **market index** is a market factor, expressed as a percentage, or in some other quantitative form, relative to some base figure. A market index may be

FIGURE 12-1

Division of sales potential among territories using retail sales as a market index

Territory	Percentage of Total Retail Sales*	Territorial Sales Potential $25M × Col. 1 × 100
New England	5.6	$1,400,000
Middle Atlantic	12.1	3,025,000
East North Central	16.5	4,125,000
West North Central	7.5	1,875,000
South Atlantic	19.0	4,750,000
East South Central	5.6	1,400,000
West South Central	11.5	2,875,000
Mountain	6.7	1,675,000
Pacific	15.5	3,875,000

*From "Survey of Buying Power," *Sales & Marketing Management*, September 2000, p. 54.

based on two or more market factors. For example, the **buying power index** developed by *Sales & Marketing Management* is based on three factors—population, effective buying income, and retail sales. This index, like many other published indexes, provides information broken down in many ways: regions of the country, states, cities, counties, and metropolitan areas. This index is primarily designed to aid the executive in allocating activities among areas.

Figure 12–1 provides an example of how the buying power index is used to allocate total sales potential among territories. A manufacturer of men's suits determined that national sales potential for its suits was $25 million for the next year. Management then determined the percentage of national retail sales that occur in each of the manufacturer's nine sales territories and multiplied the percentage by $25 million to yield sales potential on a territory-by-territory basis.

In forecasting sales for industrial products or business-to-business goods or services, companies often use the **North American Industry Classification System (NAICS)** developed jointly by the United States, Canada, and Mexico to replace the former U.S. Standard Industrial Classification (SIC) system. Under NAICS, businesses are divided into numerically ordered categories. Each firm is assigned a four-digit number on the basis of its main line of business. Then data collected by most government agencies are classified and published by those numbers. For example, as shown in Figure 12–2, NAICS 325 contains all firms in the chemical manufacturing industry. The pharmaceutical and medicine segment of that industry carries the four-digit number 3254. The pharmaceutical preparations companies are numbered 325411. By referring to 3254 in NAICS, companies selling products to pharmaceutical firms can discover how many firms (potential customers) are included in that category, where they are located, what their sales volumes are, how many employees they have, and much more. Much of the information can be used to help estimate potentials. Anyone doing research in industrial marketing should become familiar with NAICS data.

Firms also can use experts to meet their data needs. A large number of commercial data supply and marketing research companies provide businesses with information that can help them with their forecasting needs.

FIGURE 12-2   The North American Industry Classification System (NAICS)

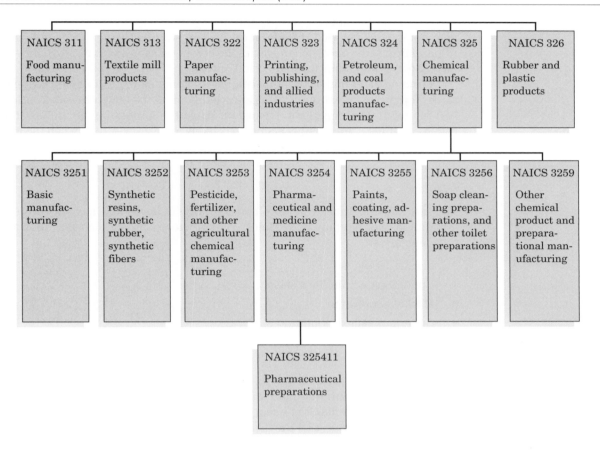

Sales Forecasting

After determining the market or sales potential for a product or service, management can make a sales forecast. This is an essential step in sales planning.

Difficulty of Sales Forecasting

The difficulty of developing an accurate sales forecast varies from situation to situation. When sales of a product are very stable from one period to the next, a sales forecast for an upcoming period is not difficult to perform. When sales of a product fluctuate dramatically from period to period, accurate sales forecasts are difficult to develop. Accurate sales forecasts are also difficult to attain for new products, since a historical sales record is lacking. Developing a sales forecast for an existing product is less difficult, since managers have some historical data to guide them.

Sales Forecasting Periods

Sales forecasts are commonly made for periods of three months (quarterly), six months, or one year. Usually the sales forecasting period coincides with the firm's fiscal year since the fiscal year is used as a basis for planning expenditures.

However, some firms find that their operations cycle is considerably shorter than a year and prefer to forecast for that cycle. For example, four cycles or seasons are present in the apparel trades. The firms produce goods for one season and then completely sell out of those goods before starting the next season's work. Apparel firms are concerned only with the coming season's activity since they are buying goods and labor for that period only.

Firms usually undertake long-run sales estimates to plan capital expenditures. Top management often seeks knowledge about the long-term sales outlook before undertaking any plant expansion. When the forecasting horizon is short (one year or less), forecasting accuracy is likely to be greater than when the forecasting period is long.

Factors Influencing the Sales Forecast

The sales forecast must take into consideration changes that have occurred or are anticipated that may affect sales. These changes can be placed in four general categories:

- Marketing plans.
- Conditions within the industry.
- Market conditions.
- General business conditions.

Marketing Plans

Any changes in the price structure, channels of distribution, promotional plans, products, or other internal marketing policies may influence future sales. The forecaster must estimate the quantitative extent of these influences. He or she may know, for example, that the firm will soon have to raise prices. Although this action will reduce unit volume, total dollar volume might go up or down, depending on the product's price elasticity. Thus, formulating a realistic sales forecast is impossible without taking price changes into consideration. If the firm planned to alter its channels of distribution or its advertising expenditures, these actions would also influence future sales.

Conditions within the Industry

A firm obtains its sales volume from total industry sales. Therefore, any change within the industry has an impact on the firm. Whatever volume new producers in an industry gain must come from existing companies. Thus, the sales forecast for those companies may have to be revised downward. If a competitor is planning to redesign its line of products, the firm must consider the possibility that the competitor may obtain a larger share of the market during the coming period.

Market Conditions

If basic demand factors are in a slump, the future sales of the firm will be affected. The firm's manager must be aware of any basic changes in the primary demand for the industry's output. An analysis of future market conditions is particularly important if the concern sells to relatively few industries.

Mor-Flo, a manufacturer of solar water heaters, saw its sales potential suddenly multiply several times when the nation suffered shortages of natural gas. And, as the price of gasoline soared, the sales potentials for the makers of compact cars expanded significantly. As gasoline prices dropped in 1986, sales of large cars increased.

General Business Conditions

A major influencing factor in future sales development is the general state of the economy. Basically, many of the methods of sales forecasting are simply reflections of overall opinion of what the general economy will be like during the coming period.

Sales Forecasting Methods

The following methods may be used to forecast the sales of a product or service. The methods can be placed in three general categories. Survey methods rely on the opinions of experts, such as sales reps, sales executives, and the customers who will be making purchase decisions. Mathematical methods apply mathematical and statistical techniques to historical data to forecast sales. Operational methods take information about the company's capacity and financial requirements to derive a sales forecast.

- Survey methods:
  a) Executive opinion.
  b) Sales force composite.
  c) Buyers' intentions.

- Mathematical methods:
  a) Moving average models.
  b) Exponential smoothing models.
  c) Regression models.

- Operational methods:
  a) Test markets.
  b) "Must-do" calculations.
  c) Capacity-based calculations.

Figure 12–3 shows the sources of the data for the various methods. Surveys of buyer intentions and test markets were discussed earlier in the chapter, as they are methods that are used both for estimating potentials and for forecasting sales. They will not be discussed again, but each of the other methods is explained below.

Executive Opinion

The **executive opinion** method of forecasting is the oldest and simplest technique known. It consists of obtaining the views of top executives regarding future sales—views that may or may not be supported by facts. Some executives

FIGURE 12-3

Sales forecasting methods

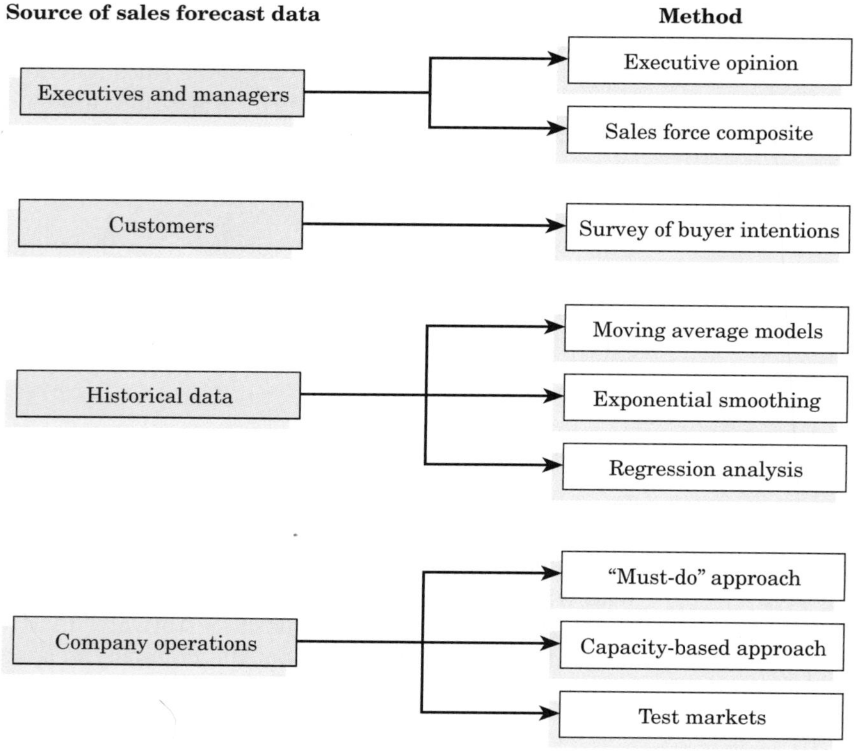

Source of sales forecast data   **Method**

| Executives and managers | → | Executive opinion |
| | | Sales force composite |

| Customers | → | Survey of buyer intentions |

Historical data	→	Moving average models
		Exponential smoothing
		Regression analysis

Company operations	→	"Must-do" approach
		Capacity-based approach
		Test markets

may have used forecasting methods, such as those we will discuss soon, to arrive at their opinions. Others may have formed their estimates largely by observation, experience, and intuition.

The forecasts made by the executives are averaged to yield one forecast for all executives, or the differences are reconciled through discussions among executives. For example, executives at Wyeth, a large pharmaceutical firm, use this approach in geographical areas and for products where forecasting software does not exist. Executives review monthly shipments and orders to arrive at sales forecasts for the geographic areas and products. The final forecast is then used to develop a financial plan for the coming year.[3]

The major advantage cited for this technique is that it is quick and easy to do. A survey of 150 firms found that 86 percent used the executive opinion approach to forecast sales.[4] Perhaps because it is easy to use, the executive opinion method is especially popular among small- and medium-sized companies.

Despite its popularity, the executive opinion approach has several disadvantages. Many managers consider this method to be highly unscientific, little more than educated guesses. Many managers also argue that the executive opinion method requires too much management time since differing forecasts must be reconciled before a final forecast is made. Finally, the opinions of highly placed executives and executives with strong feelings may influence the final forecast more than executives who are more knowledgeable about the company's products.

The Delphi Technique

A highly publicized technique developed by the Rand Corporation for predicting the future and for forecasting sales is the **Delphi technique.** In administering a Delphi forecast, a company selects a panel of experts, who are typically managers. Each expert is asked to make a prediction on some matter. The resulting set of forecasts is fed back to the whole panel. The experts are then asked to make another prediction on the same matter, with the knowledge of the forecasts of the others on the panel. This process is repeated until the experts arrive at some consensus.

Sales Force Composite

The **sales force composite** method is based on collecting an estimate from each salesperson of the products and/or services they expect to sell in the forecast period. The estimate may be made in consultation with sales executives and customers and/or based on the salesperson's intuition and experience. The individual forecasts are then aggregated to yield an overall forecast for the firm. This method places the responsibility for making the forecast in the hands of those who have to make it happen and who are closest to the market. Sales quotas and compensation that are based on sales force composite forecasts are likely to be regarded as fair by the reps.

However, salespeople are often poor forecasters. They tend to be either overly optimistic or pessimistic. Unfortunately, the sales reps may be not only motivated to understate the forecast if their goals are based on it but also unaware of broader economic and company forces at work. Finally, the process takes much time from both management and the reps. To correct these problems managers and sales representatives are urged to minimize any padding of sales figures that might arise from overly optimist estimates of demand, and minimize the practice of "low-balling" sales forecasts so that quotas can be obtained. The sales forecasting process should also be as simple as possible.[5]

Sales managers often work with their salespeople to develop accurate forecasts.

Moving Average Technique

The simplest way to forecast sales is to predict that sales in the coming period will be equal to sales in the last period. Such a forecast assumes that the conditions in the last period will be the same as the conditions in the coming period. It is likely, however, that the factors affecting sales change from period to period. Hence, it makes sense to take an average of sales from several periods to construct the sales forecast for the coming period. This approach is called the **moving average technique.** The moving average technique takes the following form:

$$\text{Sales}_{t+1} = 1/n(\text{sales}_t + \text{sales}_{t-1} + \ldots + \text{sales}_{t-n})$$

where sales_{t+1} is forecasted sales, sales_t is sales in the present period, sales_{t-1} is sales in the period immediately past, and so on. The sales of the designated periods are summed and then divided by the number of periods to yield the average. When a forecast is developed for the next period, the sales total in the oldest period is dropped from the average and is replaced by actual sales in the newest period, hence the name *moving average*. The forecaster determines how many periods will be included in the average.

An example of the moving average technique is shown in Figure 12–4 for a toy manufacturer. Deseasonalized data from the past nine periods were employed. Most companies have historical data to which a moving average model can be applied. A two-period moving average was determined by averaging sales in the present period and the previous period. The first period for which a forecast can be developed was the third period, and forecasted sales were $52,000. Sales in period 4 were forecasted to be $63,000. A three-period moving average model is also shown. Note the slight difference in forecasted sales between the two averages, which is to be expected given that an additional period was used to calculate the three-period model.

The most significant advantage of the moving average approach is that it is easy to compute. Moving average models provide accurate forecasts for products with stable sales histories; but the forecasts are less accurate for products that experience dramatic changes in sales, since the sales forecast is based on an av-

FIGURE 12–4   Forecasting toy sales using the moving average method

	Quarter/Year									
	3/00	4/00	1/01	2/01	3/01	4/01	1/02	2/02	3/02	4/02
Actual $ sales in thousands (deseasonalized)	52	52	74	55	64	66	83	76	78	
Two-period moving average			52*	63	65	60	65	75	80	77
Three-period moving average				59†	60	64	62	71	75	79

*$\dfrac{52 + 52}{2} = 52$

†$\dfrac{52 + 52 + 74}{3} = 59.3$

Seasonality in Sales

To improve the accuracy of sales forecasts, the influence of seasonality on sales must be eliminated. The word *seasonality* refers to changes in sales that occur repeatedly in identifiable periods, such as changes that occur in specific months or quarters of the year. For example, sales of pumpkins, turkeys, and stuffing rise every October and November in anticipation of Thanksgiving, whereas sales of sunscreens and charcoal increase every spring and summer.

Seasonal influences can obscure the impact (or lack of impact) of company actions and can lead to less accurate sales forecasts. For example, a toy company runs a promotion in the third and fourth quarters of each year. Toy sales always increase in the fourth quarter of every year in response to the holidays. Thus, the company cannot determine whether the increase in sales in the fourth quarter is the result of the promotion, the natural increase in sales due to the holidays, or both. By correcting for seasonality, the company can ascertain the true effect of its actions on sales, which can lead to a more accurate sales forecast.

To correct for seasonality, the forecaster must develop seasonal indexes based on historical data. The charts below provide an example of how an index is developed and applied to data for a small toy manufacturer. In chart A, the average sales totals of each quarter were found and then divided by the average sales for all quarters to produce a seasonal index. The index is then used to seasonally adjust the actual sales figures, as shown in chart B. Note the differences in sales after the deseasonalization has occurred. For example, sales in the first quarter of the first year are now $48,000 compared to $26,000 if no seasonal adjustment had been made.

A. Determining seasonality of toy sales*

Quarter	1998	1999	2000	2001	2002	Quarterly Average	Seasonal Index
1	26	30	23	40	45	33	0.54†
2	40	31	42	36	50	40	0.66
3	38	50	40	49	60	47	0.77
4	110	124	106	135	150	125	2.05

Overall quarterly average = 61

*In thousands of dollars.
†Quarterly average/Overall average: 33/61 = 0.54, 40/61 = 0.66, etc.

B. Deseasonalized toy sales

Quarter	1998	1999	2000	2001	2002
1	48*	56	43	74	83
2	61	47	64	55	76
3	49	65	52	64	78
4	54	60	52	66	73

*Actual quarterly sales/Seasonal index: 26/0.54 = 48, etc.

erage of sales from several different periods. Moving average models are also unable to reflect the impact of factors that arise in the forecasted period that were not present in previous periods. For example, the moving average model could not predict a significant decrease in sales for the toy manufacturer due to the unexpected entry of a strong competitor into the market.

Exponential Smoothing Models

The **exponential smoothing model** is closely related to the moving average technique for sales forecasting. In moving average models, the sales total in each of the past periods has the same impact on the sales forecast. Using an exponential smoothing model, the forecaster can allow sales in certain periods to influence the forecast more than sales in other periods.

The general form of the exponential smoothing model is

$$\text{Sales}_{t+1} = (L) \text{ Actual sales}_t + (1 - L)\text{Forecasted sales}_t$$

The exponential smoothing model argues that forecasted sales (Sales_{t+1}) are equal to actual sales in the present period times a smoothing constant (L) plus (1 − L) times forecasted sales in the present period. The key difference between the exponential smoothing model and the moving average technique lies in the application of the smoothing constant (L). A smoothing constant with a high value (0.8) allows more recent periods (represented by actual sales in the present period) to influence the sales forecast more than sales in earlier periods (represented by forecasted sales in the present period), whereas a constant with a low value (0.2) allows earlier periods to influence forecasted sales more than sales in later periods. The forecaster determines the value of the constant based on a review of the data and on his or her intuition and knowledge about the similarity between conditions in the forecasted period and conditions in previous periods.

Returning to the toy manufacturer, the forecaster decides that more weight should be placed on sales from earlier periods and so selects a smoothing constant of 0.3 (see Figure 12–5). Forecasted sales in 4/00 were made equal to actual sales in 3/00 to help start the forecasting process. To calculate forecasted sales in 4/02, 0.3 is multiplied by 78 (actual sales in the present period) and added to 0.7 times 70 (forecasted sales in the present period) to yield 72. If the forecaster had decided that more weight should be placed on sales from later periods, a smoothing constant of 0.7, for example, could have been used. Note the differences in forecasted sales in Figure 12–5 when a smoothing constant of 0.7 is used.

One significant advantage associated with the exponential smoothing model over the moving average technique is that the forecaster can determine the degree to which a particular period can affect forecasted sales. A significant disadvantage associated with the exponential smoothing model is that the selection of

FIGURE 12-5   Forecasting with an exponential smoothing model

	Quarter/Year									
	3/00	4/00	1/01	2/01	3/01	4/01	1/02	2/02	3/02	4/02
Actual sales	52	52	74	55	64	66	83	76	78	
Forecasted sales ($L = 0.3$)		52	52	59	58	60	62	68	70	72*
Actual sales	52	52	74	55	64	66	83	76	78	
Forecasted sales ($L = 0.7$)		52	52	67†	59	63	65	78	76	77

*0.3(78) + 0.7(70) = 72.4
†0.7(74) + 0.3(52) = 67

the smoothing constant is somewhat arbitrary. Despite this limitation, exponential smoothing models are used by a large number of companies to forecast sales.

Regression Analysis

The final mathematical forecasting technique that we will discuss is called **regression analysis.** This technique is often used to project sales trends into the future. In this case, sales totals are plotted for each past time period. For example, in Figure 12-6 sales for 2000 and 2001 (on the x axis) are plotted at $7.2 and $9.6 million, respectively (on the y axis). Then, between the points, the analyst can draw a straight trend line that minimizes the distances of all the points from the line. This straight trend line can then be extended to project sales in future periods (see Figure 12–6). One way to estimate this line is to draw it freehand on the plot of points. A more accurate method of estimating this line is to use a mathematical **least squares procedure,** which minimizes the errors between actual and predicted sales.

In simple linear regression, the relationship between sales (Y), the dependent variable, and time (X), the independent variable, is represented by a straight line. The equation for this line is $Y = a + bX$, where a represents the intercept of the line on the y axis and b equals the rate at which Y changes for every unit change in X. When several different variables seem to be important for projecting sales, they can be used simultaneously to project sales. This procedure is called **multiple regression analysis.**

The mathematical complexity of these techniques limits their application in some companies. Yet many firms employ highly trained personnel to use regression models to forecast sales. Also, the availability of software programs designed for nontechnical users has enhanced usage of regression analysis in many companies.

"Must-Do" Forecasts

Often management forecasts what volume of sales it needs to accomplish certain goals. For example, sales forecasts for new products are difficult to

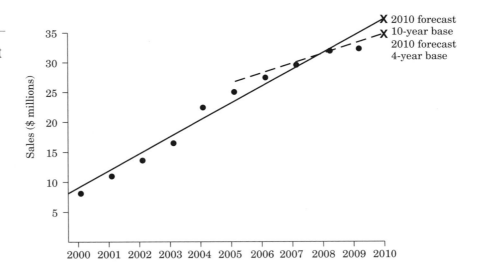

FIGURE 12–6

Projection of sales trend by least squares procedure

develop because historical sales data do not exist. Hence, firms often decide that a reasonable forecast is the sales that must be achieved for the firm to reach its break-even point. In other words, a **"must-do" forecast** is based on the sales volume needed to generate sufficient cash to cover fixed and variable costs. At other times management may forecast a level of sales volume that will allow it to achieve some profit goal.

For example, one new service enterprise budgeted its total overhead costs at $165,000 for the first year. The entrepreneur desired a profit of $60,000, which would represent her salary. Thus, she projected sales at $225,000 for the year and proceeded to plan on that basis.

Capacity-Based Forecasts

Sometimes a firm's market is such that it can sell everything it can make or buy. Thus, its capacity becomes its sales forecast. For example, the owner of a highly acclaimed restaurant developed a **capacity-based forecast** of sales according to how many seats the restaurant had: 120 seats at 30 tables. The restaurant had a dinner-only format in which only two seatings per evening were planned. Thus, a total of 240 people could be served in each of the 300 nights a year the restaurant was open. There was a waiting list to eat at the restaurant during each night, so empty seats would not be encountered. The average ticket with drinks was forecast at $30. Hence, sales for the year were projected at $2,160,000 ($30 times 240 people times 300 nights).

Some Guiding Principles for Forecasting

Sales forecasting is a very difficult task. There are some guidelines available to managers that can enhance the accuracy of the sales forecast. They are summarized in Figure 12–7.

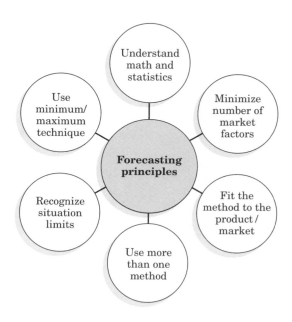

Fit the Method to the Product/Market

Some forecasting techniques work better than others for some products and in some markets. To develop accurate forecasts, it is important to use the most appropriate method. Ocean Spray Cranberries provides a good example of this. The company serves consumers using supermarket chains in the United States and Canada. All of Ocean Spray's product sales are captured in retailer scanning data, so the company has ample historical data from which to build a sales forecast. Forecasters at Ocean Spray employ quantitative techniques, like moving average models, to achieve forecasts for more than 300 different products. The company knows demand for cranberries can be seasonal, so it takes steps to account for seasonality. The forecast is used for procurement purposes and for supply, replenishment, and revenue planning.[6] It is important when choosing a forecasting method that sound logic be the basis of the decision.

Use More than One Method

One way to improve the accuracy of a sales forecast is to use multiple forecasting techniques. For example, the Lockheed Martin Aircraft and Logistics Center (LM) uses times series techniques (like exponential smoothing models) (regression analysis) to forecast sales. The regression analysis is used because of the need to predict demand more accurately. For example, LM employs environmental, industry, and economic factors into its forecasts to enhance accuracy.[7] Similarly, executive opinion could be combined with a mathematical method, such as exponential smoothing, to develop a forecast.

Minimize the Number of Market Factors

In market analysis, simplicity has great virtue. The more factors on which an analysis is based, the more difficult it is to determine exactly what affects the demand for a product. Often the inclusion of many factors in a market index results only in the duplication of a few basic forces. One drug manufacturer computed a market index from the following factors: (1) number of drugstores, (2) population, (3) number of physicians, (4) income, (5) number of hospital beds, and (6) number of people older than 65. Actually, this market index essentially was based on two elements—population and income. Several of the supposed market factors were merely surface indicators of these two basic forces. The number of physicians in an area is a reflection of the population and income of that area. Similarly, the number of drugstores and the number of hospital beds usually depend on population.

Additionally, a large regression analysis model presents the forecaster with many statistical problems and, because of its size, actually can inhibit an understanding of the factors that build sales of the product. A good approach is for the forecaster to discuss the factors that affect sales of the company's products with sales reps, executives, and customers and then to develop a model consisting of a relatively small set of factors believed to affect sales.

Recognize the Limitations of Forecasting

Managers must be comfortable with the limitations of forecasting. As noted earlier, forecasts will be more accurate for some products than for others, and in some situations than in others. For example, forecasts are very difficult when the product is innovative and few similar products exist in the market or when the demand for the product is highly variable from period to period. Furthermore, a company can develop a good forecast for the period but fall short of forecasted sales because the company did not implement the marketing plan very well.

Use the Minimum/Maximum Technique

Sound research strategy dictates the use of both minimum and maximum estimates in all computations in order to obtain a range of variations. Analysts should work up one set of estimates that assumes the worst possible developments in each of the calculations. In doing this, they compute the lowest probable potential market for the product. At the same time, they should estimate what the market potential would be should all things be favorable. They also may prepare other estimates, each based on varying assumptions between the two extremes.

Understand Mathematics and Statistics

The development of a sales forecast typically involves the use of statistics and mathematics. A sales manager should be sufficiently acquainted with statistical techniques to recognize any serious errors in the material presented.

A DAY-TO-DAY OPERATING PROBLEM

MAJESTIC PLASTICS COMPANY

MAJESTIC
Plastics Company

Sales Reps Underestimate Sales Forecasts

On November 15 each year Clyde Brion was required to submit to top management a forecast of sales for the coming year. To that end, on September 30 each sales rep received a kit containing forms to be used in compiling a forecast of sales for the coming year in the rep's territory along with detailed instructions for their use. The company's sales forecast was then a composite of the sales reps' forecasts. Since the company sold to relatively large industrial concerns and the reps were generally well aware of the conditions in each customer's markets, Brion thought the system had worked rather well. Actual sales each year were within plus or minus 10 percent of the sales forecast.

All company planning, including setting sales quotas, was then based on those sales forecasts. These sales quotas became important because sales force bonuses were awarded according to how well the reps performed in relationship to their quotas. Thus, each sales rep's forecast was carefully appraised by management. If it appeared to be off-base, Brion would go over it with the rep and the two would come to some agreement about what the sales from the rep's territory would be.

As the two top sales reps stepped up to receive their awards at the company Christmas party, where year-end bonuses were distributed, an unidentified rep from the back of the room yelled, "Sandbaggers!" There was some laughter and some embarrassment.

Clyde Brion said nothing at the time. Later he inquired of a rep with whom he had close rapport, "What was that sandbagging business all about?"

"Come on, Clyde," the rep replied. "Don't play innocent with me. Everyone knows the game and how to play it. Those two guys are just better than others at selling you their forecasts." Brion let the matter drop without comment. But he was deeply bothered by the implication that he was being conned by these two sales reps.

Question: What should Clyde Brion do about this matter?

Note: See the introduction to this series of problems in Chapter 4 for the necessary background on the company, its market, and its competition.

Review the Forecasting Process

The company should review the forecasting process periodically. The first step in the review is to determine the accuracy of past forecasts to learn if changes are needed in the way forecasts are made. If the company finds that sales forecasts are significantly different from actual sales in the period, it should undertake a review of the sales forecasting process before making any more forecasts.

The evaluation process then should review the data used in sales forecasting. Poor data collection methods can decrease the quality of the data used for forecasting, or the data may be inappropriate for forecasting sales of the product. For example, a large farm-implements company forecast sales according to data provided by sales executives; over the years, it found the forecasts to be very inaccurate. After a review of the situation, the company decided to collect data from its customers instead of its executives and found that the accuracy of its sales forecasts improved significantly.

It should be noted that the *determination of the sales forecasts and sales budgets should be an iterative process.* As mentioned at the beginning of this chapter, the sales forecast provides the basis for preparing detailed sales budgets. However, the amount that the company plans to spend on marketing has a significant impact on the amount of sales the company will be able to achieve. Therefore, changes in marketing expenditures must be incorporated into the preparation of the sales forecasts. In the remainder of this chapter we discuss the procedures for estimating potential and forecasting sales.

Developing Budgets

The budgetary process and its offspring, the budget, are the very core of the planning-control structure of most large companies. At the end of each year at most firms, top management requires the organization to prepare a plan for operations during the coming year. Each operating unit (marketing, sales, production, finance, research, etc.) develops its operational plans according to the basic sales and profit targets for the year provided by top management. Each department head then develops a detailed plan of what the unit must do to achieve these goals. The plan also includes a detailed itemization of the costs of doing those things—the projected costs. The projected costs ultimately are the basis for the unit's budget. The budgetary process is a complex, time-consuming managerial task. It is not much fun. But it must be done!

The sales forecast provides the basis for developing company operating plans. Everything is keyed to the level of expected sales activity. The budgets are essentially based on the sales forecast. If the forecast is wrong, the resulting budgets will have to be revised often to reflect actual sales results.

A *budget* is simply a tool, a financial plan that an administrator uses to plan for profits by anticipating revenues and expenditures. By using various planning procedures, management hopes to guide operations to a given level of profit on a certain volume of operations.

Purposes of Budgeting

The budget is very important for the successful operation of the sales force. It serves several purposes, including planning, coordination, and evaluation—each of which is discussed in this section.

Planning

Companies formulate marketing and sales objectives. The budget determines how these objectives will be met. The budget is both a *plan of action* and a *standard of performance* for the various departments. Once the budget is established, the department can begin organizing to realize that plan. This is especially important to salespeople. It is through a detailed breakdown of the sales budget among products, territories, and customers that sales reps learn what management expects of them.

Coordination

Maintaining the desired relationship between expenditures and revenues is important in operating a business. We might say that the objective of a business is to "buy revenues" at a reasonable cost, and a budget establishes what this cost should be. If sales of $5 million are forecast, management can establish how much it can afford to pay for that revenue. If the company wants a profit of 10 percent on sales, then $4.5 million can be paid to buy the $5 million in revenue. Part of the $4.5 million would go to the production and administrative departments, and another portion would be available to operate the sales department. Thus, the budget enables sales executives to coordinate expenses with sales and with the budgets of the other departments. The budget also restricts the sales executives from spending more than their share of the funds available for the purchase of revenues. In sum, the budget helps to prevent expenses from getting out of control.

Evaluation

Any goal, once established, becomes a tool for evaluation of performance. If the organization meets its goals, management can consider the performance successful. Hence, the sales department budgets become tools to evaluate the department's performance. By meeting the sales and cost goals set forth in the budget, a sales manager is presenting strong evidence of his or her success as an executive. The manager who is unable to meet budgetary requirements is usually less well regarded.

Determining the Sales Budget

Determining expenditure levels for each category of selling expense is very difficult. Two methods for determining budget levels are discussed below: the percentage-of-sales method and the objective-and-task method.

Budgeting by the Percentage-of-Sales Method

Many businesspeople plan and control their enterprises by percentages. Using this method, the manager multiplies the sales forecast by various percentages for each category of expense. The products of these calculations then become the dollar amounts budgeted for the respective categories.

The manager might derive the percentages used for each category from his or her experience and/or feelings about what portion of the sales dollar can or must be spent on each business function to achieve the desired profit. The percentages might also be based on published industry averages for expense categories. Sales managers should use these published averages only as guidelines that must be adjusted to reflect the unique aspects of the particular organization. However they are derived, the percentages are then used in controlling sales and their costs.

Of course there are no guarantees that the percentage-of-sales method will lead to optimal performance. In fact, the expense allocations determined by this method will follow the direction of change in sales. If sales are forecasted to decline, for example, then the budget allocations for all expense categories will decrease as well—yet this may or may not be the optimal allocation to counter the sales decline. Additionally, the effectiveness of this method is dependent on the firm's having accurate sales forecasts. Despite the limitations of the method, the manager knows that if expenses are kept within their percentage budgets, final operations will come out as planned.

Budgeting by the Objective-and-Task Method

In the objective-and-task method of budgeting, the manager starts with the sales objectives, which are specified in the sales forecast. Then the manager determines the task that must be accomplished in order to achieve the objectives and estimates the costs of performing those tasks. These costs will be reviewed in light of the company's overall profit objective. If the costs are too high, the manager may be asked either to find a different way of achieving the objective or to adjust the original objective. This iterative process continues until management is satisfied with both the objectives and the means of achieving them. Many firms use some variation of the objective-and-task method.

The American Marketing Association, a nonprofit association of marketing professionals and academics, uses an objective-and-task method to develop its budget. Its budgeting process starts with forecasts of membership revenue and publication sales. Then the senior managers estimate the costs of the programs designed to achieve the forecasted revenues. If the projected expenses exceed revenues, the managers make adjustments in costs, programs, and revenues until the budget is balanced.

Budgets for Sales Department Activities

Sales executives are responsible for formulating three basic budgets: the sales budget, the selling-expense budget, and the sales department administrative budget.

The Sales Budget

The **sales budget** is the revenue or unit volume anticipated from sales of the firm's products. This is the key budget. It is the basis of all operating activities in the sales department and in the production and finance areas. The validity of the entire budgetary process depends on the accuracy of this one sales budget. If it is in error, all others will also be in error.

The sales budget is based on the sales forecast but calls for extreme detail. It must account for every single product sold by the firm. Little good comes from telling production planners that $100,000 worth of small parts will be needed. The planners must be told specifically what small parts will be needed, in what quantities, and when.

Managers estimate the sales of each product and often make separate forecasts for each class of customer and each territorial division. Budgets for territories and classes of customers usually are of interest only to sales executives. Other departments normally need only the sales budget for product divisions.

To some extent a sales budget can become a self-fulfilling prophecy. You predict that 100 units of Model 101 will be sold in January, so 100 units are produced to be sold in January. Sales of that item may then fall short of the goal, but they cannot exceed it, for that's all there is to sell. Moreover, there is considerable pressure to make the planned sales figure a reality. Thus, once the sales budget is set, management digs in to make it become fact.

The Selling-Expense Budget

The **selling-expense budget** anticipates the various expenditures for personal-selling activities. These are the salaries, commissions, and expenses for the sales force. This is not a difficult budget to develop. If the salespeople are on a straight commission, the amount of the revenue allotted for compensation expense will be determined by the commission rate. Experience usually indicates how much money must be set aside for expenses. If sales reps are paid a salary, the process merely requires compiling the amounts, taking into consideration any raises or promotions to be made during the coming period. Any plans for sales force expansion also should be anticipated in this budget.

The selling-expense budget must be closely coordinated with the sales budget. Suppose the sales budget calls for the introduction of a new product line that requires considerable retraining of the sales force and the addition of a new service department. The expense budgets must reflect those needs. What will it cost to accomplish each line in the sales budget? That is essentially the question the sales manager must answer in preparing the selling-expense budgets that will accompany the sales budget.

The Administrative Budget

In addition to having direct control over management of the sales force, the typical sales executive is also an office manager. Ordinarily, the staff includes sales department secretaries and office workers; the total staff can be large. There may be several assistant sales managers, sales supervisors, and sales trainers under the sales manager. Managers must make budgetary provisions for their salaries and their staffs. They must also budget for such operating expenses as supplies, rent, heat, power and light, office equipment, and general overhead. These costs constitute the **administrative budget.**

The Budgeting Process for the Firm

The first step in the budgetary process is to translate the sales forecasts into the work that must be done to achieve the forecasts. This is no easy task. The firm may want to introduce a new line of whoozits, since widgets are now obsolete. What does that mean in terms of the people needed (staff requirements)? What will it do to office expenses, field-selling costs, trade show commitments, and so on?

Each administrative unit must determine how much money it will need to meet the performance goals set for it. This is usually done by (1) surveying each of the activities the unit must perform, (2) determining how many people will be required to accomplish the job, and (3) figuring what materials and supplies will be needed for those people to do the job properly.

Many sales managers use the previous year's budget as a starting point. Then they take into account any changes in sales strategies and what those will cost to implement. They also get as much information as possible from their salespeople about changes in their territories that may necessitate changes in the budget.[8] The various sales department budgets are compiled into one major budget that is forwarded to the financial executive, who disseminates the information to the other departments.

As described earlier, everything starts with the sales budget. From it, data flow in five directions. Figure 12–8 shows the flow of information from one budget to another. In addition to providing the basis for the various sales department budgets—such as advertising, selling expenses, and sales office expenses—sales budget figures also flow directly to the production department. Here the total production budget is established, and from that the various materials and labor budgets are determined. The financial officer also uses anticipated sales figures from the sales budget to prepare the cash and the profit-and-loss budgets. The cash budget is a tool used to determine how many dollars will flow into and out of the firm each month. This budget is necessary because of the time lag between expenditure and receipt of funds. It is necessary to lay out money for materials, labor, advertising, and selling expenses many months prior to selling the merchandise. Then, after sales of the goods, it may be several months before the firm receives cash. The financial officer must ensure that the firm has sufficient cash to enable it to finance the lag between the expenditure and receipt of funds.

The financial officer also uses the anticipated net sales figure as the beginning of the profit-and-loss budget. The budgets for sales department expenses, production, and general administrative expenses all flow into the profit-and-loss and cash budgets to determine the expected costs of operation. Thus, all budgets are summarized in the profit-and-loss and cash budgets. Errors in the sales department budgets have a twofold effect on the financial plan. First, revenues will not be correct. Second, expenses will be out of line because the sales budget determines the production and administrative expenses.

The due dates on various budgets must be staggered if the budgeting program is to be a success. The sales department budget must be in the hands of the financial officer before final preparation of the production budget, since the production budget is completely dependent on the sales budget. Compiling all the

FIGURE 12-8   Flow of information from sales budget to other budgets

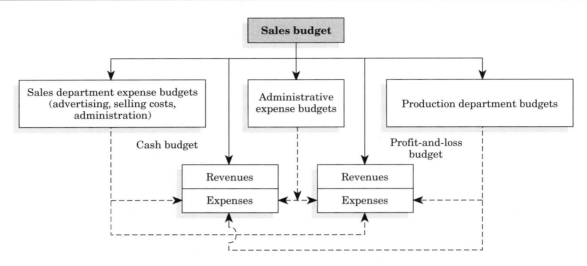

budgets into the overall cash and profit-and-loss budgets can be done only after all other work on the plans of the organization has been completed.

Meetings, compromises, and much hand-wringing are all part of the budgeting process. This give-and-take process can be seen in the comments of the sales manager for American Paging in Minnesota: "Our senior corporate managers meet for an entire week to hammer out our budget. Generally, we'll fight for what's necessary and they deliver the objectives they expect."[9]

Administrative heads tend to be overly generous in their estimates of funds they will need for the coming year. Few managers relish working on tight budgets, yet in well-managed organizations all budgets are tight. As noted by Bill Thorne, president of Morris Paper Company, "If you have a limited budget, it forces you to pay closer attention to the value of your dollar and the quality you expect in return."[10]

Every aspect of this process has become more efficient with the use of computers. With computer spreadsheets, it is possible to make changes in one part of the budget and see the impact of those changes on all other parts of the budget immediately.

Finally, sound planning procedures dictate that all administrative heads sign off on all plans and budgets. That is, they must all agree that they will make it happen.

Budget Periods

Budgets are commonly created for yearly, semiannual, and quarterly periods. Some firms prepare budgets for all three periods; others prefer to operate on an annual basis, thereby reducing the amount of paperwork.

The quarterly budget forces a reappraisal of the firm's position four times a year, thereby decreasing the likelihood that operations will get out of control. Many companies find a quarterly system advisable because it coordinates roughly with their operations conversion cycle. Garment makers usually have four conversion cycles per year. That is, they put out four different lines of goods, one for each season, and find it convenient to budget for each selling season. The main advantage of a short planning period is that it is more likely to be accurate than a long one. The shorter the forecasting period, the less likelihood there is that the estimate will be disturbed by unforeseen developments. In deciding which period to use, a firm must balance the degree of control with the costs of compiling the budgets.

Managing with Budgets

Once prepared and in operation, the budget becomes one of the manager's regularly used tools. The previous month's actual sales and expenses come back from the accounting department by the middle of the present month. All figures that are over budget are marked for attention. Some of the accounts may be over budget for understandable reasons; the manager knows those reasons and either accepts them or expects them to be corrected in the near future. If the manager does not know why an account is significantly over budget, he or she will investigate the overage and take corrective action if necessary.

Summary

The sales forecast is the basis of most corporate planning. From the forecast, the company plans activities and determines production levels. Should the forecast be in error, management may face serious consequences.

The company sales forecast is closely related to the market potential of the products or services it sells. Thus, the forecasting process begins with understanding the firm's market and sales potentials. The basic techniques for determining market potentials are market-factor estimations, surveys of buyer intentions, and test markets. Territory potentials are determined by using a market index to approximate the total sales potential among the territories.

Good forecasting rests on a careful analysis of the factors that affect sales of the product. A perceptive analysis of buyers or end users and their reasons for purchase or use should play a significant role in the sales forecasting process. The impact of changes in the firm's marketing plans must also be incorporated into the forecast.

Many different sales forecasting methods are available to managers. One group relies on surveys of executives, customers, and the sales force to derive the forecast. A second group applies mathematical methods to company records or historical data to yield a sales forecast. A third group employs methods linked to the operation of the company to forecast sales. Each of the forecasting methods possesses several advantages and disadvantages, which both the forecaster and the firm should clearly understand before the forecasting process begins.

The budget is a financial plan that the manager uses to plan for profits by anticipating revenues and expenditures. Budgeting serves several purposes: planning, coordination and control, and evaluation. There are primarily two methods of budgeting. First is the percentage-of-sales method, whereby expenses are estimated as a percentage of sales. Second is the objective-and-task method, where the manager determines the tasks necessary to achieve the objectives and then estimates the costs of performing these tasks. Both methods rely on developing an accurate sales forecast.

There are three basic budgets for the sales department. These are the sales budget, the selling-expense budget, and the administrative budget.

The budgetary process begins in the sales department with the formulation of a sales forecast. From that figure, a detailed sales budget is developed that contains the expected sales of each item in the product line. The production budgets and the selling-expense budgets are developed from the sales budget.

Once the sales forecast and budgets are developed, they become the standard by which the manager judges performance.

Key Terms

Administrative budget
Buying power index
Capacity-based forecast
Customer analysis
Delphi technique
Executive opinion
Exponential smoothing model
Least squares procedure
Market factor

Market-factor derivation
Market index
Market potential
Moving average technique
"Must-do" forecast
Multiple regression analysis
North American Industry
   Classification System
   (NAICS)

Regression analysis
Sales budget
Sales force composite
Sales forecast
Sales potential
Selling-expense budget
Survey of buyer intentions
Test marketing

Questions and Problems

1. Indicate what market factor or factors you would use to estimate the market potentials for each of the following products: Tiger Shark golf clubs, Scott's fertilizer, Chrysler automatic swimming-pool cleaner, Mohawk carpeting, Smith's ski goggles, and McGraw-Hill economics textbooks.

2. After one year of market testing, the manufacturer of a new food product had sold 4,800 packages in the test city of Louisville, Kentucky. Assuming that the test market is representative of the whole nation, determine national sales of the product.

3. In general, how do sales forecasts based on surveys differ from forecasts based on mathematical methods?

4. Use exponential smoothing with a smoothing constant of 0.8 to predict sales based on the data below. Then forecast sales with a smoothing constant of 0.2.

Period

1	2	3	4	5	6
24	32	44	24	30	42

5. In exponential smoothing, when should the smoothing constant be large? When should it be small?

6. What are some of the pitfalls in conducting test markets?

7. The following regression model was developed by a professor to help the owner of a restaurant predict sales:

$$\text{Sales} = 70.0 + 46.5X_1 + 208.5X_2$$

where

$$\begin{aligned}
\text{Sales} &= \$ \text{ sales per month} \\
X_1 &= \text{Advertising expenditure per} \\
&\quad\text{month} \\
X_2 &= \$ \text{ value of coupon}
\end{aligned}$$

Forecast sales if the owner decides to spend $500 on advertising and offers a coupon for $5 off one meal for parties of two or more in a month. Forecast sales if the owner decides to spend $400 on advertising and offers a coupon for $10 off one meal for parties of two or more in a month.

8. A university professor developed a model for predicting the sales of windmills to supply power for businesses and homes. Describe at least five factors that could be in the model.

9. A company's best-selling product line possesses a highly variable sales pattern according to company records. Which sales forecasting technique should be used to provide an accurate sales forecast for the product in the coming period?

10. How can an executive avoid having subordinates ask for more funds than are needed?

11. If total expenses must be reduced by 10 percent, should an across-the-board cut or a selective reduction be used? If selective, how should the selection be made?

12. You feel your sales reps are underpaid. You requested a large increase in the budget for them but it was denied in a conference with the other vice presidents, who all wanted pay increases for their people. You still feel strongly that more money is needed if the sales force is to be kept effective. What would you do about the situation?

13. Your CEO demands that you sign off on an operational plan and budget that you feel is totally unrealistic. What would you do?

Experiential Exercises

A. Develop an estimate of the market potential for a business in your community using one of the methods described in the chapter.

B. Develop an idea for a new consumer product. Develop an estimate of the market potential for this using census data.

C. Using *Sales & Marketing Management*'s "Survey of Selling Costs," estimate the sales budget for a sales force of 10 located in the midwestern states of Ohio, Illinois, Michigan, and Indiana, who spend two nights a week out of town.

Internet Exercises

A. Assume that you are the national sales manager for a company that sells heavy-duty mining equipment to the mining industry in Minnesota, Wisconsin, and North and South Dakota. This company wishes to expand its operations into other parts of the country, and the CEO has asked you to develop potential estimates for the remaining states. Assume that typically a firm would spend $100,000 per $1 million in sales on the type of equipment you sell. Visit the U.S. Census Bureau website (www.census.gov) to develop these estimates. Look for the most recent economic census.

References

1. Zahide Ahu Ozturkman, "Forecasting in the Rapidly Changing Telecommunications Industry: AT&T's Experience," *Journal of Business Forecasting*, Fall 2000, pp. 3–4.

2. "2000 Survey of Buying Power," *Sales & Marketing Management*, September 2000, p. 74.

3. Daniel Kiely, "Forecasting Process at Wyeth-Ayerst Global Pharmaceuticals," *Journal of Business Forecasting*, Winter 2001, pp. 7–9.

4. Paul Herbig, John Milewichz, and Jim Golden, "Forecasting: Who, What, When, Where, and How," *Journal of Business Forecasting*, Summer 1993, pp. 16–21.

5. Mark Moon and John Mentzler, "Improving Sales Force Forecasting," *Journal of Business Forecasting*, Summer 1999, pp. 7–12.

6. Sean Reece, "Forecasting at Ocean Spray Cranberries," *Journal of Business Forecasting*, Summer 2001, pp. 6–8.

7. Dan Carter, "Forecasting at Lockheed Martin Aircraft and Logistics Center," *Journal of Business Forecasting*, Fall 2001, pp. 9–10.

8. Andy Cohen, "Can You Prepare a Budget?" *Sales & Marketing Management*, October 1996, p. 44.

9. Kenny Rottenberger, "How Do You Balance the Sales Budget?" *Sales & Marketing Management*, September 1992, pp. 24–26.

10. Ibid.

| CASE 12-1 | ANDROS INTERCOM |

Revising a Sales Forecasting Approach

"I am very concerned about the accuracy of our sales forecasts in recent years. Last year, for example, we underestimated sales by 16 percent. Based on the faulty sales forecast, we ordered less material from our suppliers and scheduled less production early in the year, causing us to miss many sales opportunities. I wouldn't be so concerned, but the year before we underestimated sales by 21 percent! I realize sales forecasting is a complex exercise and events can pop up that can dramatically affect a company's sales during the year, but we should be doing a better job in this area. Fay, I want to see some improvement in the coming year." Dinos Andros, founder and president of Andros Intercom, was speaking to Fay Philmus, vice president of sales for Andros. Fay had been in her position only three months, but Dinos was the second person at Andros Intercom to complain to her about the poor forecasts. The first person, John Richman, vice president of finance, was equally blunt in his desire to see the company's sales forecasts improve. He had said, "A new salesperson, a new forecaster: good."

Dinos now continued, "Let's meet in two weeks, say on Tuesday the 25th, at 10, to discuss how you plan to forecast sales for the coming year. I'll have John Richman and Ray Forge from production attend as well, to hear what you have to say."

Andros Intercom has been in existence for 20 years, manufacturing and marketing internal wall-based communications systems for new homes throughout the states of Maine and New Hampshire. The communications systems are designed so that people in one room can easily talk to people in other rooms or talk to people outside the home. Andros offers its customers a variety of systems, depending on the type of home and the needs of the homeowner. The company, headquartered in Bangor, Maine, prides itself on making the highest quality internal communication systems while offering customers competitive prices. Through clever marketing of its top-quality but affordable systems, Andros has become the market leader in

the Northeast and has enjoyed record profits in each of the last three years.

In response to the president's request, Fay spent a good part of the next week working with her assistant, David Moss, on examining the old forecasting techniques used by the company to forecast company sales over the past 14 years or so. The two managers then worked on developing a new forecasting system for Andros in the week before the meeting. To make a convincing argument on how Andros should forecast in the future, Fay and David assembled a PowerPoint presentation for the meeting.

The 25th finally arrived. Fay and David walked into a crowded conference room for the 10:00 presentation. "Good morning, Fay," Dinos said. A few other people in the room mumbled their hellos.

"Good morning. I brought my assistant, David Moss, with me for today's meeting. David helped develop forecasts for Spancom and AT&T before joining us about six months ago, and he has helped develop today's presentation." After several people greeted David, Fay started the presentation.

"I would like to begin by reviewing how we have performed our sales forecasts in the past few years. Three methods were employed to develop the final forecast. One involved obtaining information from top executives in the company, based on their intuition, experience, and observations of the business environment. I believe this method was a favorite of my predecessor, who sought to have top management partially responsible for the sales forecast." Several people in the crowd snorted with amusement. "Another method involved obtaining information from each of the company's sales representatives. The sales reps' forecasts were then aggregated to yield an overall forecast for the company. Finally, we had our sales reps survey our customers to determine their purchase intentions for the coming year. The three independent forecasts were combined to yield an overall sales forecast for the year.

"In light of our poor forecasting performance at Andros in recent years, we would like to propose another approach, called regression analysis.

Regression analysis is a mathematical technique in which sales, the variable we are trying to forecast, is related to one or more causes of sales, say, price and advertising. Applying regression analysis to a database will produce a regression line, captured by an equation, which represents all of the data points. The equation is as follows:

$$y = a + b_1x_1 + b_2x_2 + b_3x_3$$

where y is the effect (the number of systems sold, for example); x_1, x_2, and x_3 are actual values or the causes of sales (say prices of our systems and our dollar expenditure on advertising); a is the y-intercept, or where the regression line passes through the y-axis; and b_1, b_2, and b_3 are coefficients that measure the change in y or sales associated with a unit change in x_1 or x_2 or x_3, assuming that all of the other causes remain constant. To forecast, you just plug in the values for x_1, x_2, and x_3 and multiply them by their respective coefficients, sum them, and then add (or subtract) the y-intercept to generate a sales forecast. For example, forecasting with a regression model that looks like $y = 10 + 20x_1 + 30x_2$ requires the forecaster to plug in values for x_1 and x_2, say 40 and 50, to yield a forecast of 240. We will then combine the results of our regression model and the survey of our customers by our sales reps to develop a final forecast."

Fay paused for a moment and then continued. "Please note that this approach recommends dropping sales forecasts developed by the individual sales rep and company executives and eliminating purchase intention data from our customers in the forecasting process. After speaking with a variety of people on this issue, it seems the sales reps were being less than candid about their sales forecasts and those of their customers by underestimating demand for our products to help them meet their quotas."

"Wait!" cried one manager. "You are recommending that we move away from using the input of our customers and our sales force who know the business very well, and our executives, people who also know the business from top to bottom, and move toward a more mathematical approach that is untested and hard for most of us to understand?"

Another manager said, "I understand it. By using regression analysis, you're just saying that the future is going to be like the past. But I question

that! My salespeople may be overly pessimistic about sales prospects sometimes, but they do provide us with some valuable information on future sales."

Fay replied patiently, "We are not recommending this approach. We are offering it as an alternative to existing sales forecasting approaches. We feel using regression analysis is a much simpler sales forecasting approach and one that will produce an accurate forecast. Hear me out on this for a minute." Fay then posted a PowerPoint slide containing the data shown in Table 12–1A. "The regression model we developed using data from company records and the U.S. government argues that sales are affected by the dollar amount spent on advertising by Andros, the average price for our products after discounts have been taken by our customers, and the number of housing starts in Maine and New Hampshire. Advertising and price are variables that we manipulate to build sales, while housing starts is a good variable to use because our systems are placed almost exclusively in new homes. To develop a forecast, we ran the regression model using a program called Excel, which is contained in the latest version of Windows."

"This approach can forecast better than we have been forecasting in the past?" asked one manager.

"If the regression analysis is well conceived, we believe error can be cut significantly," Fay stated. "Here is the database we are using to develop the regression model. After entering the data in the format shown above, the model produced a sales forecast that is very close to the actual sales levels obtained by Andros in 1995 and 1996."

Fay stopped a minute to let the audience absorb her presentation. "So there it is. My team and I have given you one approach for forecasting sales. Please let us know which approach you think Andros should take. We can either try the old approach again this year or go with something different, like the approach we have presented to you today. We will support your decision either way," Fay concluded.

"Wait a second," John Richman exclaimed. "You and your team are supposed to be the experts, yet you are telling us, the nonforecasting crowd, that we are the decision makers? I think you should make the forecasting decision and we'll live

TABLE 12-1A   **Andros Intercom: Forecasted Sales**

Year	Unit Sales	Advertising ($ millions)	Price	New Hampshire and Maine Housing Starts (thousands)
	y	x_1	x_2	x_3
1988	559	.2	3,005	11.0
1989	648	.3	2,985	11.0
1990	661	.32	2,878	11.1
1991	682	.33	3,013	12.5
1992	870	.4	2,799	13.0
1993	885	.41	3,100	13.0
1994	849	.51	2,913	14.2
1995	1,045	.5	2,888	16.4
1996	1,115	.51	2,999	19.5
1997	1,251	.57	2,794	20.7
1998	1,302	.59	2,819	22.2
1999	1,444	.60	2,883	22.1
2000	1,542	.60	2,851	23.0
2001	1,443	.59	3,082	32.4
2002	1,990	.80	3,003	32.3

with it, at least until we can determine the accuracy of the forecast."

"I agree," said Dinos Andros. "Why don't you prepare a document for us by this time next week, showing which forecasting approach you recommend and why you selected the approach. We must put this baby to bed in a hurry, given that our planning period is coming up soon. Sound OK, Fay?"

"Our recommendation will be on your desk in one week," Fay said.

After she returned to her office, Fay thought about the meeting and wondered which forecasting approach she would recommend. Many of the managers in the meeting seemed leery of a mathematical approach to sales forecasting. "Should I just plow ahead with regression analysis, which I think will work, even though it includes a technique that seems to scare people, or should I use an approach that is familiar and understandable to management?" she thought.

Questions:

1. Describe the advantages and disadvantages associated with the old approach to sales forecasting and the new approach to forecasting presented by Fay and her team. Based on your analysis, which approach do you recommend?

2. Run a regression analysis on the database presented in the case. The data can easily be analyzed using a spreadsheet program, like Excel.

3. Report and interpret your results. Then test the accuracy of the sales forecast for Andros by plugging in the values for advertising, price, and housing starts for the years 2001 and 2002. How accurate is the regression model? What are forecasted sales if the company decides to spend $1.1 million on advertising, sells its products for an average price of $3,300, and has 36,000 housing starts in 2003?

CASE 12-2   PRECISION TOOLS, INC.

Revision of Sales Forecasting Model

"It seems to me that our forecasting system, which we have been so proud of for so many years, has sprung a leak. Our forecasts used to be right on the money. Now suddenly we missed by 18 percent in 2000 and 22 percent in 2001. Business was better than we thought it would be, so we missed a lot of sales by underplanning production. Something seems to be wrong and it's causing us to lose market share because we don't have enough inventory to supply the demand. What are we doing about it, Pat?" David Haeppner, president of Precision Tools, Inc., of Salt Lake City, Utah, was talking to Pat Michaels, the company's vice president of sales operations.

Precision Tools, Inc., designed, made, and distributed a wide line of specialized machine tools used in light manufacturing operations. Most of the firm's products were computer driven; thus, the firm was also involved in developing the software needed for operating the machines.

In 1994 the firm's market analyst had developed a relatively simple model for forecasting the demand for the firm's products based on the payroll and employment statistics of the firms included in the SIC categories of the company's target markets. Management became increasingly comfortable with its forecasting model, which provided excellent forecasts for the years of 1996, 1997, 1998, and 1999. However, the model underestimated sales for 2000 by at least 18 percent. It was not known how much more the company could have sold had it been prepared for the unexpected demand.

One sales rep was heard to say, "If this is a recession, let's have more of it." While the firm's customers had reduced their payrolls and employment, their manufacturing activities were increasing. Their increased profits were encouraging their purchase of machine tools. Thus, business was good for Precision Tools, contrary to what its forecasting model had predicted.

In response to the president's question, Pat Michaels replied, "I have asked Cori Newman to develop a new forecasting system for us since it has become obvious that the previous relationship between employment and our sales has changed."

"Call her in! I want to know where we now are and where she is in her thinking." David Haeppner handed the phone to Pat Michaels as he dialed the extension.

Cori Newman had joined the company as market analyst in 1999 after working for Microsoft, a software developer in Orem, Utah, for four years in its marketing research group. She had graduated from Brigham Young University's MBA program in 1994. She quickly responded to the request for her presence in the executive conference room and took with her the portfolio of work she had already done on the forecasting problem.

After observing the usual courtesies, Newman began. "As we have suspected, the relationship between employment and machine tool demand has changed. This is a common problem encountered in all forecasting models based on an analysis of historical relationships. Relationships change! We can easily reformulate our existing forecasting equation to determine whatever new relationship evolves between employment and machine tool demand, but probably that new equation would have to be repeatedly revised.

"I would also like to point out that sales forecasts tend to become self-fulfilling prophecies. If the forecast is low, that is what the company will likely sell. A high forecast likely increases sales through the combined forces of more inventory and more marketing pressure." Newman noted that her audience was receptive so far to her thoughts. She continued, "We have some alternatives. We could ask our customers about their plans for buying our tools the coming year. Academics call it surveying buyers' intentions. We could do it since our total number of customers is not large. The sales reps would contact all of their accounts to find out what they plan to buy for the next budget. Then the reps summarize what they discovered and make a forecast of their sales. We then summarize all of the reps' forecasts to come up with our own. One advantage of this procedure is that we can develop forecasts in more detail, by product lines."

"Then you're recommending that we abandon our mathematical approach to forecasting and go to a survey method. Is that right?" the president asked.

"Not necessarily. I am trying to give you an idea of the different approaches we can use and let you make the decision," Newman replied.

"Whoa! I have trouble with that. You're supposed to be the expert in market analysis, not us. We hired you to tell us what you think we should do. I want a recommendation from you without any equivocation." Pat Michaels firmly told Cori Newman what was expected of her.

Newman was inwardly shaken by Michaels's aggressive position but tried to maintain her composure. She replied, "Very well, you'll have my recommendation in writing Monday morning." After exchanging the usual parting words, she returned to her office to begin what would be a hectic weekend.

She mulled over the other forecasting alternative that she had not been allowed to present at the meeting. She had been about to tell her bosses that she could develop another mathematical model based on data other than employment. She would have to do a lot of statistical work to locate and validate such a series of information, but, after all, that was her job.

Cori Newman wondered if she should recommend continued use of a forecasting method with which management was familiar or if she should recommend switching to the survey of customers' buying intentions system.

Question:

1. What forecasting method should Cori Newman recommend that Precision Tools adopt?

CASE 12-3   AEROSPACE SYSTEMS, INC. (A)

Budget Reduction Policy

As Ted Sowinski, the chief executive officer of Aerospace Systems, Inc., stood before the fax machine, his face noticeably hardened as he read the message from NASA being emitted from the contraption's innards. Everyone in the room was aware of the subject of the incoming message, and all fell silent. They knew from Sowinski's face that the news was bad. Their contract for building a new space probe vehicle had been canceled, a victim of the budget cutbacks by the federal government.

This serious setback to the company's future was not unexpected. The board of directors had discussed the matter thoroughly at its last meeting and had directed management to institute immediate budget reductions throughout the company that would offset the revenues that would be lost because of the potential contract cancellation. Management was ordered to submit to the board its plan for those budget reductions at the next board meeting, which was to be held the first Wednesday of the following month, 22 days away.

As Sowinski took the message from the machine, he directed his assistant to assemble all of the company's divisional vice presidents for a

meeting the next morning. The sole agenda was to be the execution of the budget reductions.

Bill Rooney, vice president of the company's electronics division, returned to his office after the budget meeting with the president and the other vice presidents. Despite his highly emotional protest, he had been firmly directed to reduce the budgets for his division by approximately 20 percent. He had contended that it was totally irrational to cut the budgets of the company's one division that was still profitable and whose revenues were growing. The other executives had been in no mood to hear his case. Some had even told him that he could cut costs without hurting revenues. It struck Rooney that everyone in the room seemed to think they knew more about his division than he did. Nevertheless, he was stuck with the order and knew that any appeal to higher echelons would be not only ineffective but also career suicide.

Rooney directed his assistant to call a meeting of all the division's department heads. The agenda: cutting their budgets.

Michiko Takanaga, manager of sales operations for small consumer electronics, returned from the meeting furious. She had been ordered to reduce costs for her department by $12 million. The method by which she was to do it was left largely to her.

Most of the meeting had been devoted to how best to accomplish the reductions while doing as little damage as possible to ongoing profitable operations. Some of the department heads thought that they would concentrate on getting rid of marginal workers. Everyone agreed that the key to meeting the budget mandates was cutting payroll costs and the resultant lowering of the costs of the benefit package, payroll taxes, and workers' compensation insurance. The total benefit package offered by the company to all employees amounted to 32 percent of payroll. FICA taxes plus workers' compensation cost 17 percent of payroll. The department generated revenue of $85 million in 2000, with a total budget of $76 million. Total payroll was $18 million. The department had 331 employees, 91 of whom were sales reps. The sales reps' average compensation was $76,000 a year. Field-selling expenses for 2000 were $2.9 million, of which travel, lodging, and meals accounted for about $2 million, with the rest going for entertaining customers.

Takanaga decided to confer with her assistants about how the budget reductions should be done. She could just slice everything 20 percent across the board, but that seemed irresponsible to her. She believed that it was her job as manager to make some difficult decisions, and this one was certainly going to fall into that classification.

Since being ordered to do it, she had thought of little else but how she could make the budget reduction. She realized that just about all of the reductions would have to come out of payroll and the resulting savings in the benefit and tax package. Previous budget squeezes had reduced administrative overhead items to bare bones.

One alternative Takanaga was contemplating was terminating enough sales reps so that the entire $12 million reduction would be from payroll

costs and benefit packages. Naturally, she thought of trying to keep the best producers and letting the marginal ones go, but she suspected that she would be cutting into some reps who were good, solid performers even though their records placed them in the lowest quartile of profit producers.

Another alternative was to try to get the sales reps to accept a pay cut sufficient to allow everyone to keep his or her job. She knew that would be a difficult selling job. How could she get a rep who was making $100,000 a year to accept $80,000 just so she wouldn't have to fire anyone? But then she realized that strange things do happen. One offshoot of this thought was to offer to keep the reps who would otherwise be fired if they would accept, say, a 40 percent pay cut. A rep who was making only $60,000 a year might work for $40,000 if it meant keeping his job and benefits package.

The problem weighed so heavily on Takanaga's mind that she talked of little else that evening as she dined with a friend who was a sales manager for a large business machines manufacturer in Japan. He was of the opinion that she would have to redesign the entire sales force so that the sales job could be accomplished with fewer reps. "You'll have to redesign the territories, replan your call patterns, stop calling on some people, use the telephone a lot more, hire some cheaper help for inside selling, get rid of your expensive sales reps, and hire new ones for a lot less money. You're going to have to work like the devil to find a cheaper way to cover your customers."

Takanaga was not sure that her friend's plan could be done. A flat across-the-board reduction of all budgets appealed to her. After all, any damage done could easily be blamed on top management's mandate to cut the budgets.

Question:

1. What advice would you give Michiko Takanaga on how she should reduce her departmental budgets?

13 Sales Territories

You have to recognize when the right place and the right time fuse and take advantage of that opportunity. There are plenty of opportunities out there.

—Ellen Metcalf—

To help the members of the sales force be in the right place at the right time, firms typically assign each salesperson to a unique geographic territory. This assures effective and efficient coverage of all customers, which of course is a key part of the sales manager's strategic planning task. Organizing and appropriately revising sales territories enables management to bring other aspects of planning—such as sales forecasting and sales budgeting—down to limited geographical areas. Ordinarily, it is not practical to plan, direct, and evaluate salespeople's performances without having sales territories. The total market for most firms is simply too large to be managed efficiently without a territorial structure.

Once such a structure is established, management can then set up a system for covering each territory. This step includes scheduling a rep's territorial coverage—that is, determining which accounts will be called on, in what order, and how frequently. Sometimes this step also involves determining the route that each sales rep will follow in covering his or her territory. Planning territorial coverage has become increasingly important, because sales organizations cannot afford to have poorly designed, unbalanced territories. Indeed, research demonstrates that organizations with properly designed sales territories have more productive salespeople—ultimately leading to greater sales volume, market share, profits, and even more satisfied customers for the entire sales organization.[1]

Nature and Benefits of Territories

A **sales territory** comprises a number of present and potential customers, located within a given geographical area and assigned to a salesperson, branch, or intermediary (retailer or wholesaling intermediary).

In this definition, the keyword is *customers* rather than *geographical*. To understand the concept of a sales territory, we must recognize that a market is made up of people, not places—people with money to spend and the willingness to spend it. A market is measured by people times their purchasing power rather than in square miles.

A company, especially a medium- or large-sized one, can derive several benefits from a carefully designed territorial structure (see the accompanying box). In fact, experts predict that many companies could gain millions of dollars a year through better territory design.[2] However, formal territories may not be needed in a small company with a few people selling only in a local market. In this case, management can plan and control sales operations without the aid of territories and still enjoy many benefits of a formal structure.

Lack of territories may be justified when personal friendships play a large part in the market transaction. This is one reason automobile dealers and commodity and security brokers usually do not district their sales forces. Highly specialized sales engineers also may serve in troubleshooting assignments or be called in anywhere to help close an important sale.

Benefits of Good Territory Design

1. **Enhances customer coverage.**
   When a sales territory is too large, potentially important customers are overlooked. The rep simply does not have enough time to call on all customers. Creating territories is a way for management to *control* sales reps activities such that all customers are served in a more efficient manner.

2. **Reduces travel time and selling costs.**
   With no geographic territories, reps inevitably crisscross each other as they traveled to and from their accounts. The result? Reps spend more time traveling and less time selling; and the firm spends too much money in automobile/fuel expenses.

3. **Provides more equitable rewards.**
   Imagine two sales reps who are equal in both ability and motivation. Yet one rep would earn much more commission than the other if assigned to a territory with significantly higher potential. Hardly fair! Sales organizations should reward the salesperson and not just the territory.

4. **Aids evaluation of sales force.**
   With well-designed territories that are equal with respect to both sales potential and workload, sales managers can more easily and fairly evaluate their sales reps' performance. Each rep's actual performance is typically compared to a territorial potential or quota.

5. **Increases sales for the sales organization.**
   Many firms have some territories that are too big and others that are too small. These firms should redesign their territories to be equal. Sales will go down for reps with previously big territories. These lost sales, however, will be more than offset by the sales increases of the other reps.

6. **Increases morale.**
   In general, good territory design results in productive salespeople who efficiently serve satisfied customers and who are being evaluated and rewarded in a fair manner. This in turn leads to increased morale, which benefits the sales organization in many ways—not the least of which is through reduced turnover.

Source: Andris Z. Zoltners and Sally E. Lorimer, "Sales Territory Alignment: An Overlooked Productivity Tool," *Journal of Personal Selling & Sales Management*, Summer 2000, pp. 139–50.

FIGURE 13-1   Procedure for designing sales territories

FIGURE 13-1   Procedure for designing sales territories

Designing Territories

The ideal goal in territorial design is to have all districts equal in both sales potential and the sales reps' workload. When sales potentials are equal, it is easier to evaluate and compare sales reps' performances. Equal opportunities also reduce disputes between management and the sales force and generally tend to improve workers' morale. To achieve both objectives is an ideal, but usually unattainable, goal. However, this should not deter an executive from constantly striving to reach it.

Changing market conditions put continuing pressure on companies to adjust their territories. Different procedures may be used to design the districts. However, a company's territorial structure is influenced by the potential business in the firm's market and by the workload required or sales expected of its sales force. One plan for establishing or redesigning territories includes the following six steps, as seen in Figure 13–1:

1. Select a control unit for territorial boundaries.
2. Determine location and potential of customers.
3. Determine basic territories.
4. Assign salespeople to territories.
5. Set up territorial coverage plans for the sales force.
6. Evaluate the effectiveness of the design on a continuing basis. (We discuss this step in Chapters 14 and 15.)

Determine Basic Control Unit for Territorial Boundaries

When designing territories, the first step is to select a geographical **control unit** as a territorial base. Commonly used units are states, counties, cities, zip-code areas, and metropolitan areas (see Figure 13–2). A typical territory may comprise several individual units. One person's district may consist of four metropolitan

FIGURE 13-2

Territorial control units

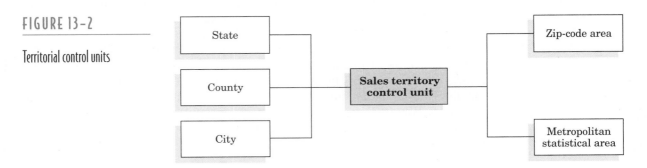

Frequent air travel is the only way this representative can adequately cover her sales territory, which consists of 10 western states.

areas; another's may be three states. The unit should be small for at least two reasons. First, a small unit helps management realize one of the basic values of territories—the geographic pinpointing of potential. Second, the use of small control units makes it easier for management to adjust the territories. If an organization wants to add to one person's district and reduce another's, a county unit facilitates the adjustment better than a state unit.

States

Territorial systems built around states are simple, inexpensive, and convenient. Territories may be built around states if a firm has a small sales force covering a national market and uses a selective distribution policy. A luggage manufacturer on the West Coast that sells directly to a limited number of selected retail accounts, for example, uses the state unit with apparent success.

However, for most companies, states do not serve well as bases for territories because customers often ignore state lines. An Oregon–Washington boundary ignores the fact that many consumers and retailers in southern Washington buy in Portland, Oregon. Trade from Alton and East St. Louis, Illinois, gravitates to St. Louis, Missouri, rather than to any Illinois city.

Counties

For companies that prefer to use a political subdivision as a territorial base, the *county* may be the answer. In the United States there are almost 3,100 counties but only 50 states. Smaller control units help management to design territories that are equal in potential and to pinpoint problem areas. Many kinds of statistical market data (population, retail and wholesale sales, income, employment, and manufacturing information) are available on a county basis.

The only serious drawback to the county unit is that it is still too large for some companies. A manufacturer or a wholesaler may want to assign several reps to cover one county because the potential is far too much for one person to handle. This situation may prevail in such counties as Los Angeles, Cook (Chicago), Wayne (Detroit), or Cuyahoga (Cleveland). It then becomes necessary to divide the county into a series of territories, and some smaller control unit is needed.

Cities and Zip-Code Areas

In the past, such firms as wholesalers of food, drugs, and tobacco often used a *city* as a control unit, because most of the market lay within urban limits. In fact, in many instances even the city was too large, and firms used several sales reps within a single city. Then some subcity unit was needed, and precincts, wards, or census tracts were used.

Postal zip-code areas are one particular subcity unit widely used when an entire city is too large to use as a basic control unit. By using zip-code areas, a company works with geographical areas that ordinarily have a high degree of economic, social, and cultural homogeneity. However, it is difficult to get much statistical market data for geographical units smaller than a county or city.

Metropolitan Statistical Areas

Many companies have found that a significant share of their market has shifted to suburban and satellite cities outside the major central city. These firms have been aided tremendously by the delineation of *metropolitan statistical areas (MSAs)*. The federal government has identified and established the boundaries for about 325 of these areas. An MSA is an economically and socially integrated unit with a large population center. An urban area can qualify in one of two ways to be classed officially as a metropolitan statistical area; it can be a county or group of contiguous counties that (1) has a central city with a population of at least 50,000 or (2) has a general urban area of 50,000, with a total metropolitan area population of at least 100,000. The bulk of the workers in an MSA must be nonagricultural employees, and an MSA may cross state lines.

Because an MSA is defined in terms of counties, a vast amount of market data is available.[3] Although small in total land area, the MSAs account for 75 to 80 percent of the nation's population, effective buying income, and retail sales. Thus MSAs constitute lush, concentrated markets for many consumer and industrial products. Because of this market potential, some firms assign territories that consist of a number of metropolitan areas. They encourage their salespeople to work in those areas only and to skip the regions outside or between them.

Determine Location and Potential of Customers

Management should determine the location and potential of both present and prospective customers within each selected control unit. Sales records should indicate the location of *present* customers in each control unit. *Prospective* customers can be identified with the aid of company sales reps plus outside sources such as (1) trade directories (e.g., Thomas's Register); (2) publishers of mailing lists (e.g., R. H. Donnelley Corporation); (3) subscription lists from trade journals; (4) trade association offices; (5) classified telephone directories; or (6) credit rating firms (e.g., Dun & Bradstreet, Inc.).

Once the customers are identified, management should assess the potential business it expects from each account. Management then can classify these accounts into several categories based on their potential profitability to the seller. This step furnishes some of the necessary background for determining the basic territories.

Determine Basic Territories

The third general step in designing sales districts is to establish a fundamental territory based on statistical measures. This can be accomplished by using either the buildup or the breakdown method. Under the **buildup method** territories are formed by combining small geographical areas based on the number of calls a salesperson is expected to make. This method *equalizes the workload* of salespeople.

The **breakdown method** involves division of the whole market into approximately equal segments based on sales potential. Thus this method *equalizes sales potential.* The buildup method is particularly suited for manufacturers of consumer products or for companies that want intensive distribution. The breakdown method is more popular among manufacturers of industrial products or organizations that want selective distribution.

Buildup Method

Several variations are possible in establishing territories by building up from the basic control unit. Usually, however, these variations depend on some type of customer analysis and study of the salespeople's **workload capacity.** A suggested procedure is outlined in the following paragraphs (see Figure 13–3).

1. **Determine optimal call frequencies.** Management should establish optimal **call frequencies** for each account. In other words, management must determine how many times per year an account should be visited. The call frequency is affected by the sales potential, the nature of the product, customer buying habits, the nature of competition, and the cost of calling on a customer. Thus, the call frequency is primarily determined by the profitability of the account. The optimal call frequencies can be determined using several different computer models or estimated using managerial judgment. Figure 13–4 is an example of how management might divide its customers into three classes based on profitability. Class A accounts are the most profitable and are called on twice a month. Class B accounts are visited monthly, and Class C accounts bimonthly.

FIGURE 13-3   Buildup method of territorial design

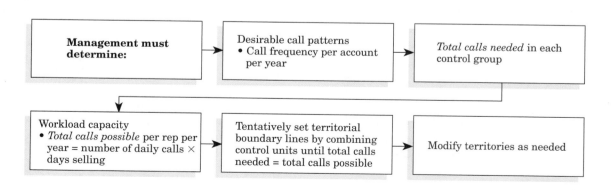

2. **Determine the total number of calls needed in each control unit.** By multiplying the number of each type of account in the control unit by the number of calls that type of account requires, we can determine the total number of calls needed in each control unit. Assuming that metropolitan areas are the control unit, and using the call frequencies shown in Figure 13-4, it can be seen that metropolitan area X requires 630 calls per year and metropolitan area Y requires 660.

3. **Determine workload capacity.** A salesperson's workload capacity is *the average number of calls a salesperson can make in a day times the number of days in a year that the salesperson will make calls.* The number of calls a rep can effectively make in one day depends on several factors. One is the average length of time required for a call. This is influenced by the number of people to be seen on each call and the amount of missionary work to be done. Another factor is the amount of travel time between customers. For example, if a rep works eight hours per day and the average length of a call is an hour and the average travel time is 15 minutes, then the rep can make six calls per day. If the rep makes calls 250 days per year, the annual total that the rep can make is 1,500 calls.

   Continuing with the example in Figure 13-4, a salesperson who can make 1,500 calls per year could call on both area X and area Y and still have time for accounts that require a total of about 210 calls a year $(1,500 - [630 + 660] = 210)$. A salesperson could cover any number of customers who, in total, required 1,500 calls a year.

   The box labeled "Salespeople's Workloads" presents a number of factors that influence either the number of calls a salesperson can make or the optimal call frequency.

4. **Draw tentative territorial boundary lines.** The final step is to accumulate enough contiguous territorial control units until the yearly number of calls needed in those control units equals the total number of calls a salesperson can make (the workload for one salesperson). A company has a choice of places from which to start this grouping. On a national scale, a firm that groups contiguous metropolitan areas into territories may start in Maine and work south to Florida, then go back to Ohio and again work south to the Gulf of Mexico. Another firm, using county control units, may start each territory with a county that includes a major city and then complete a given territory by fanning out in all directions until the necessary number of con-

FIGURE 13-4   Example of call frequency for different customer classes

Customer Class	Call Frequency	Metropolitan Area X		Metropolitan Area Y	
		No. of Accounts	No. of Calls per Year	No. of Accounts	No. of Calls per Year
A	2 per month	10	240	5	120
B	1 per month	25	300	15	180
C	1 every 2 months	15	90	60	360
		50	630	80	660

Salespeople's Workloads

Territorial design depends basically on the company's sales potential and the workload of its sales force. Consequently, management should identify and measure the factors influencing these workloads. Two companies, each selling in markets of comparable potential and geographical size, may have quite different territorial structures simply because of a difference in the sales reps' workloads.

Nature of the job. A sales rep's call patterns are influenced by the nature of the job. A rep who only sells can make more calls per day than the rep who must do a considerable amount of missionary work along with selling.

Nature of the product. The nature of the product can also affect a salesperson's call pattern. A staple convenience good (canned foods) with a rapid turnover rate may require more frequent calls than would an industrial product (conveyor belts) with very limited repeat-sale business. Similarly, a complex technical product may require long calls and numerous presale and postsale calls.

Stage of market development. When a company enters a new market, its territories typically are larger than those in markets where the firm is well entrenched—even though the market potential is comparable in the old and new regions. A large geographical district is needed initially to yield an adequate volume of business.

Intensity of market coverage. If a firm wants mass distribution, it will need smaller territories than if it follows a selective or exclusive distribution policy.

Competition. No general statement can be made about the net effect competition has on the size of the territory. If management decides to make an all-out effort to meet competition, then territorial borders will probably be contracted. Salespeople will be instructed to intensify their efforts by increasing the frequency of calls and the length of time spent with each account. However, competition may be so fierce, or the territorial markets so overdeveloped, that the company is not going to make much profit in the district. It may therefore decide to expand the geographical limits of the district and have the sales rep call only on selected accounts.

Ethnic factors. A company may adjust its territorial boundaries in large cities because of the market concentration of certain racial, national, or religious groups. One part of a city may have a heavy ethnic concentration. Retailers may also be predominantly of the same ethnic group, and use of the group's native language may be widespread in the area. A firm selling to these retailers may alter its territorial boundaries so that the particular nationality group comprises one district. In Chicago, a firm may establish separate territories in some parts of the city to cater to the African-American, Hispanic, Italian, Polish, Jewish, or Vietnamese markets. The person covering each of these districts is from the corresponding ethnic group and often can speak the group's language.

---

tiguous counties are included. Other organizations group counties or metropolitan areas around a branch office or plant.

Often, unless it splits a control unit, a company is unable to group contiguous control units so that the number of calls needed equals the number one salesperson can make. In our earlier example, metropolitan areas X and Y together required 1,290 calls. However, no metropolitan area may be contiguous to X or Y that can be covered with approximately 210 calls, the number needed to create a normal load of 1,500 visits per year.

In most cases like this, it is best not to split the control unit. Rather, the territory can be made a little smaller or bigger than the rest. However, sometimes this may cause significant sales potential inequities among territories. If this is the case, splitting the control unit may be the best option. This is a matter of managerial judgment.

5. **Modify the tentative territories as needed.** The tentatively drawn boundary lines of a given territory may need to be adjusted due to special considerations. For example, the competition may be particularly strong in

FIGURE 13-5   Breakdown method of territorial design

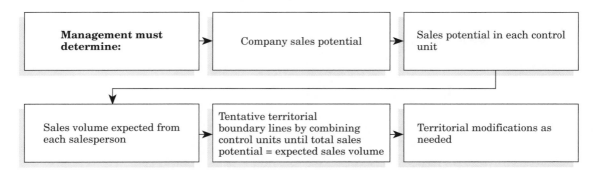

one control unit and require more intense effort from the salesperson than in other control units. The salesperson in this area may need to have a smaller territory so that he or she can make more calls on fewer customers.

Breakdown Method

The breakdown method is often used by firms that want exclusive distribution or that sell some type of industrial products. The steps for this procedure are depicted in Figure 13–5 and are explained below.

1. **Determine sales potential.** The first step is to determine what sales volume the company can expect in its entire market. This is done using one of the forecasting procedures described in Chapter 12.

2. **Determine sales potential in each control unit.** To obtain the sales potential in each control unit, a market index (as described in Chapter 12) is multiplied by total sales potential to allocate it among the various control units.

3. **Determine the sales volume expected from each salesperson.** In this step management must estimate how much each sales rep must sell to have a profitable business. A study of past sales experience and a cost analysis are often used to determine this information. For example, assume that the cost of goods sold and distribution costs are estimated to equal 70 percent of sales; direct selling costs are $30,000; and management wants to earn a profit of 10 percent of sales. Then it can be shown that each salesperson must sell a minimum of $150,000.[4] Of course, based on experience, management may feel that each salesperson can and should sell twice this much. Therefore, expected sales volume is set at $300,000.

4. **Draw tentative territorial boundaries.** The final stage in the statistical phase of the breakdown method is to divide the entire market so that each sales rep has about the same potential. The potential has already been established for each of the basic territorial control units. Therefore, management needs to assign enough contiguous units to each salesperson so that he or she has at least $300,000 of sales potential. In other words, the sales potential of the territory should be equal to or greater than the sales volume expected from each salesperson. The boundaries of each territory should coincide with the borders of the control units.

Sales Territories for Pharmaceutical Sales Reps

In the United States, sales territories for the pharmaceutical industry are typically organized using the following terminology and structure:

- The 48 contiguous states are divided into 5 to 10 geographic *regions*, similar to those shown on the map. Each region is supervised by a regional manager.

- Every region is then divided into several *districts*, each supervised by a district manager. Less populated states, such as Maine, may represent one entire district. More populated states, such as Massachusetts, are likely to be split into several

districts. (Boston alone might consist of two or three districts.)

- The districts are then divided into 8 to 12 *territories*, each typically covered by a single pharmaceutical sales representative. Larger pharmaceutical companies might assign two or more reps to a territory with each one specializing in a specific product or customer group. For example, one rep might call on doctor's offices in the territory, while the other calls on hospitals.

Source: David Currier and Jay Frost, "On the Right Path: Sales Careers in Pharma," *Pharmaceutical Executive*, July 2001, pp. 16–19.

5. **Modify tentative territories as needed.** As in the buildup method, the tentatively drawn boundary lines may need to be adjusted due to special considerations with regard to that geographic area.

Using Computers in Territory Design[5]

Sales managers are increasingly using computers and mapping software to design and realign their sales territories. This is much faster and more comprehen-

Global Positioning System Devices

To help salespeople navigate their territories, some sales organizations are equipping reps with global positioning system (GPS) devices. These are products that communicate with satellites to pinpoint and give directions to specific geographic locations.

GPS provides numerous benefits for salespeople who travel, especially those with large, unfamiliar territories. Most obviously, the technology essentially prevents reps from ever again being lost. By simply entering the address of a prospective customer, a sales rep is provided with step-by-step directions on how to get there—including which highway lane to drive in. Some GPS devices can even identify the fastest route around unexpected road construction.

In addition, company managers can use GPS devices to track their salespeople. That is, information on the specific geographic location can be automatically communicated to the central office in real time. This can be analyzed to determine whether or not salespeople are covering their territories in the most efficient manner.

Prices and features vary significantly. Handheld devices start for as low as $100, while complete navigation systems with automated computer voice can cost several thousand dollars.

Discuss: For what kinds of salespeople are GPS devices likely to be most beneficial? What are the drawbacks?

Source: "Gadget of the Month," *Financial Management*, September 2001, p. 53.

sive than cranking out the breakdown or buildup method by hand. The computer technology is known as a **geographic information system (GIS).** GIS provides an in-depth understanding of a sales territory by combining multiple layers of information about that territory, and then presenting it in an easy-to-comprehend graphic or map. A complete GIS consists of the following four elements:

1. **Software.** GIS requires software that can store, analyze, and graphically display information about the sales territory. Features and prices vary greatly. Low-end business mapping programs are practically free, while high-end software capable of running simulations and optimizing territories can cost more than $20,000.

2. **Hardware.** A standard desktop computer, running on a Windows operating system, is typically sufficient. A quality color printer is also necessary.

3. **Data.** Generally speaking, the GIS output will be more valuable as the amount of inputted data about the territory (i.e., the layers of information) increases. The data include image data, such as aerial photographs or satellite images, as well as data about customer locations, call frequencies, sales, potentials, and so on.

4. **Trained people.** Finally, an individual with training—or at least practical experience—with GIS must operate the system. Training ranges from formal university GIS programs to self-paced learning via a workbook, CD-ROM, or website. GIS has become such a critical part of strategic planning that some companies have created a new position: geographic information officer.

In the late 1990s, Budget Rent a Car Corporation started using GIS business mapping software to realign and analyze the several sales territories in its western U.S. region, which consists of a 75-person sales force covering 10 states. Information about the locations and sales revenues of current and potential customers is inputted from various internal and external databases. The computer analysis of the data results in territories defined with pinpoint accuracy. With

GIS, Budget's salespeople are more efficient and prospective new accounts are easier to find. Further, the whole process is done in considerably fewer worker-hours compared to the previous method. Budget has no plans to go back to plotting and analyzing territories manually.

Assigning Salespeople to Territories

Once the sales territories have been established, management can assign individual salespeople to each district. Up to this point, we have implicitly assumed that the salespeople have equal selling abilities, and that each person would perform equally well in any territory. Obviously, this is not a realistic assumption.

In any given sales force, the reps may differ in selling effectiveness. They also vary in experience, age, physical condition, initiative, and creativity, as well as in selling skills. A sales rep may succeed in one territory and fail in another, even though the sales potential and workload are the same in both districts. For example, in a territory where a large number of the customers are engineers, a salesperson with a technical background may be highly effective. Sales performance also may be influenced by differences in local customs, religion, and ethnic background.

Many companies intentionally design some sales territories so that they are *unequal* in size, as measured by the rep's workload or the territorial sales potential. These unequally sized territories accomplish two purposes. One is to accommodate some of the above-noted differences among salespeople. The other is to give executives some flexibility in managing their sales forces. For example, many firms intentionally design a small territory for beginners or sales trainees. Then, as a rep progresses in skill and performance, he or she is moved (or promoted) to progressively larger and more lucrative territories. Similarly, some companies may initially assign reps to territories out in the hinterland. Later, these reps can be promoted to better territories closer to their homes or offices.

Revising Sales Territories

As companies and markets change, territorial structures may become outdated and need revision. In fact, studies indicate that over half (55 percent) of all sales territories need to be realigned because they are either too large or too small.[6] Sales executives should review their territories at least once a year to see if they need to be realigned. Some sales organizations, such as AT&T, review territories every three months.[7] However, before making any boundary adjustments, management should be certain that the danger signals noted below are the result of poor territorial design, and not of poor administration in other areas. The problem may lie in the compensation plan, inadequate supervision, or a poor quota system.

Indications of Need for Adjustment

Frequently, sales potential outgrows a territory, and as a result the salesperson skims the district rather than covering it intensively. When out-of-date measures of potential are used, the performance results from a district can be quite misleading. In a fast-growing region, for instance, one salesperson's volume may have increased 100 percent over a four-year period, the largest increase of any rep in the firm. Management praises that person highly as the model of a good sales rep. Actually, that rep may have been doing a very poor job because the territorial potential increased 200 or 300 percent during that time. The company really was losing its former share of market because the districts were not small enough to encourage thorough coverage.

Sometimes the selling task changes. Anheuser-Busch found that its customers were demanding more and more value-added services, leaving the company's salespeople with less time to sell. So the company made the territories smaller and hired new reps, giving each rep more time to sell.[8]

At the other end of the scale, territories may need revising because they are too *small*. They may have been set up that way, or changing market conditions may have caused the situation. Overlapping territories are a structural weakness that should be corrected. This problem generally stems from previous boundary revisions. To illustrate, sales rep Carter originally had as a territory the three West Coast states: California, Oregon, and Washington. As its sales potential grew, this territory was divided into two districts. Carter kept California, and a new rep, McNeil, was assigned Washington and Oregon. However, Carter was also allowed to keep certain preferred accounts in what is now McNeil's territory. The reason for this decision was that Carter had spent much time developing the accounts. The customers like Carter, and they might switch to a competitor if Carter does not call on them. Management therefore allowed the overlap to develop in the territories. However, the company planted the seeds for future morale problems because, eventually, McNeil is likely to chafe under the arrangement. Also, overlapping territories generally result in higher costs and selling inefficiencies.

Territorial adjustments are necessary when **claim jumping** is practiced. Say that the company has established territories with definite boundaries but that management has tolerated a person in one district going outside that district's borders and selling in another person's district. On the one hand, if each territory has an adequate potential, and one sales rep jumps another's claim, then the first one obviously is not satisfactorily developing his or her own area. On the other hand, let's assume that one person has done a thorough job in his or her own region and still has the time to go into the next district. Then some adjustment is needed, because the first territory is too small. The increasing costs, inefficiencies, and friction among the reps that can develop when one cuts into another's region should be obvious.

Claim jumping can cause hard feelings between salespeople.

A DAY-TO-DAY OPERATING PROBLEM

MAJESTIC PLASTICS COMPANY

MAJESTIC
Plastics Company

Claim Jumping by Sales Rep Formerly in a Territory

Clyde Brion, the general sales manager for Majestic Plastics Company, had just finished a telephone call from Lucille Koll, the Majestic sales rep in New Orleans. This was the third call in six months that Brion had received from Koll concerning the same problem. She was upset because of what she called claim jumping by James Wiggins, the Majestic rep in an adjoining territory. That is, Wiggins was selling to some Majestic customers in Koll's territory. Koll's territory covered the states of Louisiana, Oklahoma, and Arkansas, plus Memphis, Tennessee. Wiggins's territory was the state of Texas, and he was based in Dallas.

Prior to two years ago, both of these territories constituted one large unit that was covered by Wiggins. But the territory had grown too large in potential for one rep to cover. Wiggins was skimming the market, relying on established accounts, rather than intensively developing the growing potential. The territory was split and Wiggins took the new Texas district. Koll was hired to cover the other newly formed territory.

Wiggins had been with the company for 12 years and consistently ranked in the top third of the sales reps, based on total sales volume. His accounts generally spoke well of him, and Brion rarely received any customer complaints about Wiggins. Koll also had done well since she joined Majestic Plastics. She had a good record in opening new accounts and retaining the old accounts that Wiggins had established. Customer feedback reported that she generally did a fine job providing needed services.

Over the past couple of years, however, Wiggins occasionally sold to one of his old accounts in Louisiana or Oklahoma (now Koll's territory). He claimed that an old customer would telephone him to place an order. In a few cases the customer asked Wiggins to drop by on a personal sales call. Wiggins claimed that Majestic Plastics might well lose those accounts if he did not service them. Two of these customers were firms with manufacturing plants in Texas, but the home offices were in Louisiana. Wiggins continued to call on the Texas plants, but he also was in contact with and making sales to the home offices in Louisiana.

It was these incursions into her territory that were infuriating Lucille Koll. She also claimed that Wiggins was undermining her in the eyes of some of his old customers. She told Brion that Wiggins was simply a claim jumper and that he was using his good-old-boy network to take business away from her. She reminded Brion that she was being paid a straight commission, so Wiggins's activities were taking money out of her pocket. She was particularly upset that Brion apparently had done nothing in response to her previous two phone calls about the same issue.

Question: How should Clyde Brion respond to Lucille Koll's charges?

Note: See the introduction to this series of problems in Chapter 4 for background information on the company, its market, and its competition.

Effect of Revision on Sales Force

Although high morale was identified as a key benefit of good territory design, many salespeople are opposed to their management making any changes in territory alignment. As a result, management may hesitate to make needed adjustments in territorial boundaries for fear of hurting sales force morale. In fact, many territorial problems—overlapping districts, for instance—are a result of management's trying to avoid friction.

Morale problems are most likely to occur with reps whose territories are reduced in size. These reps may suspect that management is trying to curtail their earnings. In addition, the reps are reluctant to lose accounts that they have cultivated over a period of time. Nevertheless, it is important for firms to continue to realign territories for the sake of what's best for the sales force as a whole. The motivation levels of individual reps can be better maintained by demonstrating that the process is fair. Specifically, the sales manager should ask salespeople for input in the realignment process, assure salespeople that they are being treated the same as everyone else, and provide salespeople with transitional funding so that their total compensation does not significantly drop.[9]

Losing accounts through territory realignment will be of most concern to salespeople who are being paid on a commission basis. If the territory revision has been done properly, however, the reduced territory ultimately offers a better sales volume opportunity and the chance to cover the area more intensively. Until the sales rep can fully develop the smaller territory, he or she probably will need some compensation help during the transition period. One procedure is to guarantee the salespeople their previous level of income during a stated adjustment period (perhaps six months). Many firms make no adjustment whatsoever in a person's pay. Instead, management tries to sell the reps on the idea that intensive development of their remaining territory will quickly bring their income to its former level or higher. Understandably, it is usually quite difficult for a rep to accept this line of reasoning.

Territorial Coverage—Managing a Sales Rep's Time

After designing territories and assigning salespeople to their separate districts, management then should plan how each rep will cover his or her territory. In effect, managing territorial coverage is an exercise in managing the sales reps' time. Time management is becoming increasingly important as companies continue looking for ways to control their field-selling costs.

The management of territorial coverage involves two main tasks—routing salespeople and scheduling their time. Computer technology can be used effectively in both of these activities.

Routing the Sales Force

Routing is the managerial activity that establishes a formal pattern for sales reps to follow as they go through their territories. This pattern is usually indicated on a map or list that shows the order in which each segment of the territory is to be covered. Although routing is referred to as a managerial activity, it is not done only at some executive level. Often a firm asks its salespeople to prepare their own route schedules as part of their job.

Reasons for Routing by Management

Managerial routing of the sales force should reduce travel expenses by ensuring an orderly, thorough coverage of the market. Studies indicate that it is not at all unusual for reps to spend one-third of their daily working hours traveling. At that rate, a sales rep is not even inside a customer's office for four months out of a year.

Proponents of management's handling of routing believe the typical salesperson is unable to do the job satisfactorily. They feel that salespeople will look for the easiest, most pleasant way to do their jobs, although this may not be the most effective way. Left to their own routing devices, they will backtrack and crisscross their territory in order to be home several nights a week.

The following diagram illustrates a problem that often occurs when management allows salespeople to route themselves:

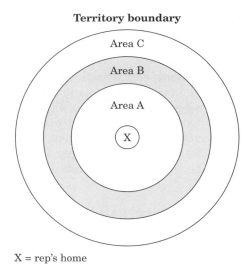

Territory boundary

Area C

Area B

Area A

X

X = rep's home

In area A, the rep can do a full selling job and still easily get home at night. Actual sales in A approximate the area's potential. Sales to accounts in area C also approximate the potential. In this outlying area, a rep is resigned to being away overnight and thus concentrates on doing a creditable selling job. Area B is the problem area; a rep selling here can get home at night only by working less than a full day. Sales in area B are well below potential.

Objections to Routing

Many sales executives feel that routing reduces people's initiative and straitjackets them in an inflexible plan of territorial coverage. They believe that a sales rep in the field is in the best position to decide the order in which accounts should be visited. Market conditions often are very fluid. Therefore, it would be a mistake to set up a route plan and prevent a salesperson from making expedient changes to meet some situation. High-caliber reps usually do not need to be routed, and they may resent it if a plan is forced on them.

Factors Conducive to Routing

Before deciding to route its sales force, management should consider the nature of the product and the job. If the call frequencies are regular and if the job activities are reasonably routine, planning a person's route is easier than if visits are irregular. Salespeople for drug, grocery, tobacco, or hardware wholesalers can be routed without serious difficulty. In fact, to attempt an irregular call pattern with a given customer can result in loss of the account. A grocery or hardware retailer, for instance, plans his buying on the basis of a sales rep's call, say, every Tuesday morning. If this retailer cannot depend on the sales rep's regular call, the buyer may seek another supplier.

Procedure for Establishing a Routing Plan

In order to establish a routing plan, the present and prospective accounts should be spotted on a map of the territory. Then the daily call rates and the desired call frequency must be determined for each account. This information may have already been determined during the territory design process. With all this information available, the actual establishment of routes is reasonably mechanical. Some of the most commonly used route patterns are circular, straight line, cloverleaf, and hopscotch.[10] When call frequencies differ among the accounts, management may employ a skip-stop routing pattern. On one trip, a salesperson may visit every account, but on the next trip this rep may call on only a third of the accounts—the most profitable third.

Routing salespeople effectively is another sales operational area that is ideal for computer application. A number of computer models have been designed to help management determine the one route through a territory that will minimize either total travel time or travel cost.[11]

Time Management and Computer Support Systems

Increasingly, companies are setting up computer-based sales support systems to aid in planning, executing, and reporting on sales calls. In many companies, the salespeople have laptop computers that they carry as they travel around their territories. The primary objective of these systems is to help salespeople make more efficient use of their time.

Computerized support systems are being used to assist the rep in choosing the most promising prospects, selecting the best approaches, and gaining some knowledge of the prospect's needs before the call.[12]

Many salespeople are now entering and transmitting their call reports on personal computers. Use of a well-designed program can save the salesperson time and produce reports that are generally more thorough, accurate, and timely than those done by hand. For example, the 90 sales managers at Mail Boxes Etc., the world's largest franchisor of postal service centers, use their laptops to provide daily information on all customer contacts and follow-ups. This information is used to automatically update the centralized database.[13] In *Sales & Marketing Management*'s annual technology survey, 60 percent of the managers surveyed reported that their salespeople use some type of contact management software. Eighty-one percent report that their salespeople use e-mail to communicate with them.[14]

Another area where computerized support systems are gaining wide acceptance is in the entering, checking, and scheduling of orders. Use of computers in submitting orders significantly improves the accuracy of the orders and decreases the order processing time. W. W. Grainger, an Illinois distributor of maintenance and operating supplies, uses the Internet to provide its customers with information about Grainger's inventories, estimated delivery times, and new product information. Grainger's reps report that because their customers are more knowledgeable about Grainger's products, their sales calls are quicker and more meaningful.[15]

This sales support technology also can be used *during* sales calls. Salespeople can telephone (via computer) for up-to-the-minute information on inventory and delivery conditions. Price quotations can be made, and altered if necessary, during a sales call. As described in Chapter 3, computer graphics can also be used in sales presentations.

Summary

A sales territory is comprised of a number of present and potential customers located within a geographical area. This area is assigned to a salesperson or to an intermediary. There are several benefits to be derived from establishing sales territories. However, formal territories may not be needed in a small company with a few salespeople selling in a local market.

Different procedures are available for designing sales territories, and some of these approaches involve sophisticated mathematical models. Basically, however, a company's territorial structure depends on (1) the potential business in the company's market and (2) the workload required from the sales force. The plan we propose includes three broad steps: The first step is to select a geographical control unit to serve as a territorial base. Commonly used control units are states, counties, cities, zip-code areas, and metropolitan statistical areas (MSAs). The second step is to determine the location and potential of each customer. The third step is to determine the basic territories, which can be accomplished manually by either the buildup or the breakdown method.

Using the *buildup* method, management determines the desirable call frequencies for each customer and the daily call rate for the sales rep. Contiguous control units are then combined until the total annual calls needed in the control unit equal the total number of calls the rep can make in a year.

Under the *breakdown* method, we start with sales forecasted for the total market and allocate it to the control units based on some type of market index. Then the sales volume expected from each salesperson is determined. With this input, management can set its basic territories by combining control units until the total potential in those units at least equals the expected sales from each rep.

Alternatively, the basic territories can be determined by a computerized process, such as GIS. A complete GIS system requires software, hardware, territory data, and trained personnel. Note that whatever method is used for step three, the territories' boundaries may have to be modified to account for special circumstances in that geographic area.

After the territories have been established, management must assign individual salespeople to each district. As companies and markets change over time, the territorial structures may become outdated and need revision. Revising boundaries is usually a very difficult job. A key principle that management should follow is to avoid overlapping territories.

Once sales territories are designed and reps are assigned to them, management should turn its attention to planning how each rep will cover his or her territory. The management of territorial coverage involves two main tasks—routing the salespeople and managing their time.

Key Terms

Breakdown method	Control unit	Routing
Buildup method	Geographic information system	Sales territory
Call frequencies	(GIS)	Workload capacity
Claim jumping		

Questions and Problems

1. What control unit would you recommend in establishing sales territories for the following companies? Support your recommendation.
   a) Manufacturer of laptops.
   b) Food broker.
   c) Appliance wholesaler.
   d) Manufacturer of textile machinery.
   e) Manufacturer of outboard motors.
   f) Lumber wholesaler.

2. The text discussed several qualitative factors that may affect a territory's sales potential and thus necessitate a change in the statistically determined boundaries. How can variations in competition or ability of the sales force be reflected in square miles, trading areas, or other geographical measurements of territories?

3. Is it discriminatory to consider ethnic factors when assigning sales reps to territories?

4. Since it is impossible to equate territories perfectly, should the manager use them to provide promotions for good people? For example, should the best reps be given the choice areas?

5. What are some of the signals indicating that a company's territorial structure may need revising?

6. Assume that a territory's potential has increased to the point where the district should be realigned to form two territories. Properly developed, each of the two new units should bring an income equal to what was previously earned in the one large district. Should management assign the same salesperson, who formerly had the combined territory, to one of the new districts? Or should the rep be transferred to an entirely different area before the division is attempted?

7. Salespeople normally are prohibited from going outside their territorial boundaries in search of business. Sometimes, however, a customer located in one district will voluntarily seek out a sales rep or branch office located in another district. Perhaps this customer can realize a price advantage by buying outside his or her home area. What should be the position of the seller in these situations? Should it reject such business? Should it insist the order be placed in the territory where the customer is located? If the order is placed in the foreign territory, should the salesperson in the customer's home territory be given any commission or other credit?

8. If a company has several branches and insists that each of its suppliers send the same salesperson to all branches, what problems are involved? What course of action do you recommend for firms that sell to the company in question?

9. In the process of redistricting, many firms do not allow a salesperson to keep any former accounts if they are outside his or her new district. One hardware wholesaler realigned its territories. Then the company found that it faced the loss of some good customers because they said they would do business only with the wholesaler's sales rep who had been calling on them for years. Should the wholesaler make an exception and allow this rep to keep these accounts outside the new district, and thus have overlapping territories? Is the loss of these good accounts the only other alternative?

10. "Routing is a managerial device for planning and controlling the activities of the sales force." Explain the function of routing in relation to each of the concepts in this statement.

11. Under what conditions is a firm most likely to establish route plans for its sales force?

12. Under what circumstance should a customer be allowed to access the supplier's internal database?

Experiential Exercises

A. Assuming that Hallmark has 150 U.S. sales reps, provide your recommendations for the allocation of these reps across sales territories. Be sure to base your recommendation on a relevant market factor or factors.

B. Call 10 companies and ask the sales manager (1) when the company last revised its sales territories and (2) what the catalyst or reasons were for the action.

Internet Exercises

A. Assume you are the national sales manager for a brand-new pharmaceutical company that specializes in the manufacturing and marketing of arthritis drugs. Your first job is to create 25 sales territories across the United States (you are in the process of hiring 25 sales representatives). The sales potential of a given market closely parallels the number of senior citizens in that market. Go to the website for the U.S. Census Bureau (www.census.gov) to find the relevant information—using the 48 contiguous U.S. states as the control units. In other words, create 25 sales territories in the United States that have an approximately equal amount of potential based on the number of people in the state(s) who are 65 years old and above. Explain which territories are the best and which are the worst.

B. Visit GIS.com (www.gis.com) to learn more about how a geographic information system can help a sales organization create, realign, and manage its sales territories. Follow the link to the company that sponsors the website, and identify the specific GIS software products that are available for purchase. Finally, search the Internet for other, competing software products. Which one do you recommend? Explain your answer.

References

1. Artur Baldauf, David W. Cravens, and Nigel F. Piercy, "Examining Business Strategy, Sales Management, and Salesperson Antecedents of Sales Organization Effectiveness," *Journal of Personal Selling & Sales Management*, Spring 2001, pp. 109–22.

2. Andris A. Zoltners and Sally E. Lorimer, "Sales Territory Alignment: An Overlooked Productivity Tool," *Journal of Personal Selling & Sales Management*, Summer 2000, pp. 139–50.

3. For a wealth of market information on MSAs, see "Survey of Buying Power," *Sales & Mar-keting Management*, published annually in September.

4. The equation is as follows: Sales − Cost of goods sold − Direct costs = Profit. Algebraically it is: $(1x - 0.7x) - \$30,000 = 0.1x$, which is solved as $x = \$150,000$.

5. This section was largely based on information from the website GIS.com, Your Internet Guide to Geographic Information Systems (www.gis.com), accessed January 2002.

6. Prabhakant Sinha and Andris A. Zoltners, "Sales-Force Decision Models: Insights from

25 Years of Implementation," *Interfaces*, May/June 2001, pp. S8–S44.

7. Erika Rasmussen, "Protecting Your Turf," *Sales & Marketing Management*, March 1998, p. 90.

8. Sarah Lorge, "Marking Their Time," *Sales & Marketing Management*, September 1997, p. 105.

9. Kirk Smith, Eli Jones, and Edward Blair, "Managing Salesperson Motivation in a Territory Realignment," *Journal of Personal Selling & Sales Management*, Fall 2000, pp. 215–26.

10. In a hopscotch pattern, sales reps start one trip at the farthest point, say north, of their home and work back toward home. Then on the next trip, they go to the most distant point in another direction, say south, and again work toward home.

11. "The DCI-SFA Show Preview Guide," a supplement to *Sales & Marketing Management*, March 1998, pp. 1–41.

12. Ibid.

13. Ester Shein, "Answering Machines," *Sales & Marketing Management*, March 1998, pp. 74–78.

14. Andy Cohen, "Out of the Loop," *Sales & Marketing Management*, December 1997, pp. 79–83.

15. Ibid.

CASE 13-1   VILLAGE BEDS

Realigning Sales Territories

Lee Flicker was the newly hired national sales manager for Village Beds. It was his first day on the job, and he was a bit overwhelmed by all he had to do. One significant problem, however, jumped out at him as a high priority: His new company's sales territories were seriously out of balance, and realignment was long overdue.

A relatively small company in the health care equipment industry, Village Beds manufactured a line of beds especially designed for nursing homes. Village Beds was started just 20 years ago in Toledo, Ohio, by its current president, Steve Moser. Before founding the company, Moser had been a nursing home administrator for more than 20 years. This gave him insight into the many problems that both patients and staff had with standard nursing home beds. He developed his new line of beds with these problems in mind. Although expensive, Village Beds have an excellent reputation in the industry for durability, quality and value.

Moser was not, however, an expert at designing a sales and marketing team. The initial sales territories were developed arbitrarily and were changed only by necessity as Village Beds grew and hired more salespeople. Currently, the company has a sales force of just seven reps, who call directly on nursing home companies across the United States. Compensation, which is a combination salary plus commission, varies greatly across the seven reps.

Table 13–1A outlines the current situation, including key statistics for the seven sales territories and reps. The sales territories were clearly out of balance. Not only could Lee Flicker quickly discern this from looking at the statistics, but he had already heard complaints. During his first phone call to her, Mary Jones, sales rep in the Central District, had told him that the inequity of the sales territories was causing morale problems for her and others. Flicker already had a lead on three experienced salespeople he could hire. He decided that

TABLE 13-1A   Selected Statistics for Current Sales Territories

Territory	Salesperson	Total Population	Population 65 Years & Older	Number of Nursing Homes	Last Year's Sales	Square Miles
T1: New England (NY,NJ, MA,CT,ME,RI,NH,VT)	Alice Myers	41,313,324	5,446,964	2,142	$11,928,455	123,409
T2: Mid-Atlantic (PA,MD,WV, DE)	John Kiel	20,169,484	2,892,892	1,205	$4,507,086	82,022
T3: Midwest (OH,IL,MI, MO,IN,WI,MN,KY,IA,KS)	Max Harris	65,326,238	8,341,166	5,396	$41,204,566	581,589
T4: Southeast (FL,NC,VA, GA,TN,AL,LA,SC,AK,MS)	Susan Killeen	63,432,088	8,363,438	3,332	$6,256,858	483,920
T5: Southwest (TX,OK,NM)	Dwayne Fox	26,121,520	2,732,645	1,643	$3,227,755	458,376
T6: Central (CO,NE,UT, ID,MT,SD,ND,WY)	Mary Jones	12,332,667	1,367,003	972	$4,660,451	742,629
T7: West (CA,AR,WA,OR,NV)	Sara Penny	50,316,057	5,575,266	1,942	$7,390,888	548,400
Total		279,011,378	34,719,373	16,632	$79,176,059	3,020,345

moving from 7 to 10 territories was a logical, manageable first step. The problem was how to draw the boundary lines. Village Beds had always used states as control units, and he saw no reason not to continue doing that.

Flicker was concerned about his sales reps' reaction to any realignment plan. Many of the reps had close ties to certain customers whom they would hate to leave behind. Also, it was inevitable that he would reduce the territory size for some reps. He was especially worried about the reaction from Max Harris, who had sold Village Beds in the Midwest territory for over 15 years. The Midwest not only had potential that far exceeded any other territory, it was also the territory in which Village Beds was best known given its Ohio headquarters. Harris also happened to be a close personal friend of Steve Moser, the company president.

Flicker had a spreadsheet file containing the various statistics for each state or control unit (see Table 13–1B on p. 394). He sat down at his computer and began the task of realigning territories. He wanted to do it right. His goal was to create 10 territories that were as equal as possible with regard to sales potential and workload. In addition, he wanted to minimize the changes to the existing territories in order to keep the current seven reps happy.

Questions:

1. What is the best way to realign the existing seven territories into 10 new territories? (Use of a spreadsheet is strongly advised.)

2. Should the current seven salespeople be consulted for the realignment plan? Or, should the new territories be created without their input?

3. To which of the new territories should the seven current reps be assigned? To which of the new territories should the three new reps be assigned? Explain your reasoning.

TABLE 13-1B   Exhibit 13-1b Selected Statistics For The Forty-Eight Continental United States

Sales Territory	State (control unit)	Total Population	Population 65 Years & Older	Number of Nursing Homes	Last Year's Sales	Square Miles
1	New York	18,976,457	2,447,963	669	$3,663,807	49,112
1	New Jersey	8,414,350	1,110,694	364	$2,021,557	7,790
1	Massachusetts	6,349,097	857,128	505	$2,756,465	8,262
1	Connecticut	3,405,565	469,968	254	$1,443,459	5,006
1	Maine	1,274,923	183,589	126	$752,734	33,128
1	Rhode Island	1,048,319	152,006	97	$577,578	1,213
1	New Hampshire	1,235,786	148,294	83	$449,781	9,283
1	Vermont	608,827	77,321	44	$263,074	9,615
2	Pennsylvania	12,281,054	1,915,844	771	$2,812,552	45,310
2	Maryland	5,296,486	598,503	251	$998,299	10,455
2	West Virginia	1,808,344	276,677	141	$537,602	24,231
2	Delaware	783,600	101,868	42	$158,633	2,026
3	Ohio	11,353,140	1,509,968	999	$7,631,590	41,328
3	Illinois	12,419,293	1,502,734	858	$6,379,888	56,343
3	Michigan	9,938,444	1,222,429	436	$3,164,047	58,513
3	Missouri	5,595,211	755,353	545	$4,172,142	69,709
3	Indiana	6,080,485	753,980	561	$4,286,717	36,185
3	Wisconsin	5,363,675	702,641	420	$3,247,697	56,145
3	Minnesota	4,919,479	595,257	427	$3,348,955	84,397
3	Kentucky	4,041,769	505,221	304	$2,422,933	40,411
3	Iowa	2,926,324	436,022	466	$3,603,715	56,276
3	Kansas	2,688,418	357,560	380	$2,946,882	82,282
4	Florida	15,982,378	2,812,899	728	$1,319,299	58,681
4	North Carolina	8,049,313	965,918	413	$783,635	52,672
4	Virginia	7,078,515	792,794	289	$527,526	40,598
4	Georgia	8,186,453	785,899	364	$724,878	58,390
4	Tennessee	5,689,283	705,471	349	$631,836	42,146
4	Alabama	4,447,100	578,123	228	$449,421	51,718
4	Louisiana	4,468,976	518,401	332	$618,187	47,720
4	South Carolina	4,012,012	485,453	179	$327,695	31,117
4	Arkansas	2,673,400	374,276	250	$489,341	53,183
4	Mississippi	2,844,658	344,204	200	$385,039	47,695
5	Texas	20,851,820	2,064,330	1,179	$2,313,575	266,874
5	Oklahoma	3,450,654	455,486	383	$759,958	69,903
5	New Mexico	1,819,046	212,828	81	$154,222	121,599
6	Colorado	4,301,261	417,222	223	$1,107,862	104,100
6	Nebraska	1,711,263	232,732	232	$1,100,870	77,359
6	Utah	2,233,169	189,819	92	$416,221	84,905
6	Idaho	1,293,953	146,217	84	$394,800	83,574
6	Montana	902,195	120,894	103	$500,924	147,047
6	South Dakota	754,844	107,943	112	$559,037	77,122
6	North Dakota	642,200	94,403	87	$405,000	70,704
6	Wyoming	493,782	57,772	39	$175,737	97,818
7	California	33,871,648	3,590,395	1,344	$5,131,090	158,648
7	Arizona	5,130,632	666,982	139	$507,877	114,007
7	Washington	5,894,121	660,142	268	$1,060,689	68,126
7	Oregon	3,421,399	437,939	145	$522,767	97,052
7	Nevada	1,998,257	219,808	46	$168,464	110,567
	SUM TOTAL	279,011,378	34,719,373	16,632	$79,176,059	3,020,345

*Sources of data: 2000 U.S. Census (www.census.gov)

Centers for Medicare and Medicaid Services (www.medicare.gov)

CASE 13-2   ATHENIAN PRESS, INC.

Redesigning Sales Territories

Steve Womble, the sales manager for the Athenian Press, was reviewing the quarterly summary for advertising sales and was concerned by the results, which showed a slight decrease from the previous quarter. More important, ad revenues for the past two years were showing a disturbing trend. Not only had the company not made its targeted growth of 2 percent, but sales were down over the past two years by 7 percent. While Womble felt that a small part of this trend might be attributed to more intense competition in recent years, he felt that most of the decrease in sales was due to the need for change in the sales organization. The market had been changing in terms of both rapid growth and increased customer expectations. Womble, who had recently been promoted to his current position, felt that Athenian Press had not responded to these changes.

Athenian Press, Inc., founded in 1945, publishes a daily newspaper and a Sunday paper that serve the community of Athens, Tennessee, home of the company's main office. The target market contains the central Tennessee counties of McMinn and Meigs plus major portions of Monroe and Hamilton counties. These counties comprise a market of more than 300,000 people.

The *Athenian Daily* has a circulation of 49,582 subscribers. In an average day, more than 60 percent of the adults in the area read this paper. The *Athenian Sunday Journal* has a circulation of 83,621 and is read by approximately 89 percent of the market adults at least once per month.

As with most newspaper publishers, a major source of Athenian's revenue is the amount of advertising sold. Generally, advertisements comprise more than 60 percent of any newspaper, and the size of the paper is determined by the number of advertisements it includes. Most of these advertisements are purchased by retail store merchants to increase customer awareness and to advertise special promotions. The Athenian Press has 800 active accounts and employs eight retail salespeople to call on these merchants. The salespeople report directly to the sales manager. Each salesperson is assigned to a specific territory. Within their territories, salespeople are given a great deal of independence and freedom. Athenian also employs three inside salespeople who are responsible for serving those who place ads in the classified section. These salespeople also report to the sales manager.

Competition for retail advertisements is strong in this area. The Athenian papers compete with several other papers for the advertisements. The *Knoxville Journal* currently holds about 8 percent of the market, while the *Chattanooga Free Press* has 4 percent, and the *Tennessean*, published in Nashville, has 2 percent. The paper also competes against local radio and television stations for the ads of the retail stores. However, its greatest competitor is ADCO Mailing. ADCO is a company that produces advertising fliers distributed by mail. To compete with these fliers, the *Athenian Daily* prints a weekly newspaper insert that contains coupons from the local merchants.

A salesperson for the Athenian Press has three main responsibilities. The first and most important is to meet with the customers on a regular basis to solicit their advertising. Each salesperson is expected to make 10 to 15 calls a day and to spend 30 to 60 minutes per call. For the very active accounts (approximately 50 percent of the accounts), the salespeople are supposed to schedule regular weekly meeting times to discuss the weekly order. For the less active accounts, the salespeople are expected to stay in regular contact by making appointments once or twice per month. Each salesperson is responsible for approximately 100 of these active accounts. For accounts that advertise only infrequently, salespeople are directed to make unscheduled calls when they have time available. The sales reps' second responsibility is to make all of their customers aware of upcoming promotions. If the newspaper is running a special section on dining out, the sales force is responsible for contacting all local restaurant owners to suggest that they may want to be included. The reps' third responsibility is to look for new accounts in their territories. The salespeople must meet with the owners and/or managers of any new stores as soon as they are under construction to inform them of Athenian's services and encourage them to advertise.

Once an order has been taken by a salesperson, the salesperson is in charge of making preliminary sketches of the ad according to the specifications of the customer. These sketches are then sent to the art department, which develops the final copy. The business department is responsible for all billing and accounting; but if a problem arises with bill collection, the salesperson contacts the customer to try to resolve the issue.

The compensation for the salespeople consists of salary and commission plus a yearly bonus based on performance. Salary makes up 60 percent of their total income, and commissions account for the remaining 40 percent; the bonuses are added to this base. The average compensation of $32,000 is considered competitive for this size newspaper, and the salespeople are relatively satisfied with their compensation levels. Sales trainees are paid a straight salary. New reps are given a brief indoctrination to the company before being assigned to "shadow" an experienced sales rep for two weeks. After this period of observing an experienced rep, they are assigned to a territory.

Steve Womble establishes yearly quotas for the salespeople and conducts their annual evaluations. On a continuing basis, he monitors their call reports and meets with each salesperson at least once a month to discuss his or her progress. Each week, the entire sales force has a breakfast at which they share problems and ideas.

Recently Womble had completed a careful analysis of the salespeople's current activities. He concluded that the sales force was not spending enough time with its customers. First of all, each salesperson can spend only about 60 percent of his or her time in the field because of the reps' responsibility of creating the preliminary sketches of the ads. Second, because of the number of accounts salespeople must service, they are not spending as much time as they should with each customer. Additionally, the 15 or 20 minutes it

takes to travel between each account also limits the amount of time they can spend with each customer. As a result, most customer calls are brief and less frequent than they should be, and very little time is devoted to calling on new accounts.

Convinced of the need for change, Womble came up with several options that he discussed with his boss, Linda Gruhn, and with his salespeople. One alternative was to assign the task of creating preliminary sketches to someone other than the salesperson, thus freeing up a significant amount of the salesperson's time. Specifically, art department personnel could perform this task. However, the salespeople felt strongly that the sketches were often needed to close the sale, and they wanted to keep that part of the sale under their control. They also worried about the necessity for increased coordination between themselves and the artists. Finally, as one rep said to Womble, "I really enjoy that part of my job because it requires creativity and imagination. Take that away and it won't be as much fun."

Another possibility was to hire additional salespeople and realign the territories so that each salesperson would be responsible for fewer accounts. The salespeople's reaction to this option was not surprising: They all felt that this was a threat to their sales volumes and thus to their commissions as well. Additionally, Linda Gruhn told Womble that he must be able to justify hiring any additional salespeople before she would approve it.

A final possibility was for Womble to take over selling to several of the largest accounts, thus giving the salespeople more time with the remaining accounts. This would decrease the time Womble could spend on his managerial duties, but he felt he could handle 8 to 10 of these accounts and still provide the salespeople with an adequate amount of supervision. Needless to say, the reps were not in favor of this option, which they saw as a threat to their commissions.

Question:

1. What action should Steve Womble take? Be sure to support the decision you recommend with the appropriate analysis.

Strategic **Company** Planning

Strategic **Marketing** Planning

Sales Force Management

Part 1
Introduction to Sales
Force Management

Part 2
Organizing, Staffing, and
Training a Sales Force

Part 3
Directing Sales Force
Operations

Part 4
Sales Planning

Part 5
Evaluating Sales
Performance

Evaluating Sales Performance

Up to this point, the major parts of this book (after the introductory section) have been devoted to sales planning and sales operations. Part 5 deals with the final major stage in the sales management process—evaluating the performance results of the field-selling effort.

Performance evaluation involves both looking backward and looking ahead. In looking backward, management analyzes its operating results in relation to its objectives and strategic plans. These findings can then be used in forward planning for the next operating period. To illustrate, say that upon looking back, management finds that too much sales volume is in low-margin products. This evaluation result can then influence management's future plans for sales force training, supervision, and compensation.

In the first part of Chapter 14, we introduce some general concepts in performance evaluation and misdirected marketing effort. The balance of the chapter is devoted to the analysis of sales volume. Chapter 15 is a survey of marketing cost analysis. Chapters 14 and 15 together constitute a marketing profitability analysis. Evaluating the performance of individual salespeople is discussed in Chapter 16. In the final chapter, Chapter 17, we step back and take a broad look at evaluation as we discuss the ethical and social responsibilities of sales managers.

14 Analysis of Sales Volume

It is only through evaluation that value exists: and without evaluation the nut of existence would be hollow.

—Friedrich Nietzsche—

Up to this point, this textbook has covered the first two stages of the sales force management process: *planning* and then *implementing* the plans through sales operations. We now focus on the third and final stage: *evaluation* of the sales force performance. Although presented separately, these three activities—planning, implementation, and evaluation—are typically conducted in an interrelated, continuous fashion, as shown in Figure 14–1. Plans are made; they are put into operation (that is, implemented); and the results are evaluated. Then new plans for the next cycle are prepared, based in part on the preceding evaluation findings.

Strategic Relationship between Planning and Evaluation

Planning and performance evaluation are particularly interdependent activities in the sales force management process. Planning sets forth what *should be* done, and evaluation shows what *really was* done. Either of these activities is virtually worthless without the other. To illustrate, let's assume that an organization has done a good job of strategic sales force planning. But without an effective evaluation, management cannot tell (1) whether its plan has worked, (2) to what degree it has been successful, or (3) what the reasons are for the plan's success or failure. In effect, the lack of adequate evaluation can

FIGURE 14-1

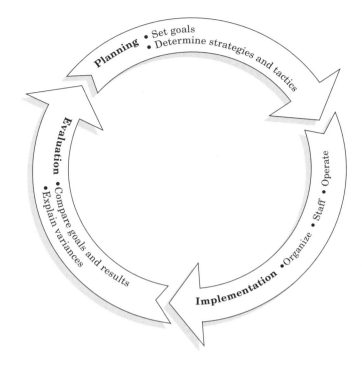

virtually cancel out the value of strategic planning. It's like deciding to go someplace but never knowing when, or if, you arrived there.

A performance evaluation without prior strategic planning is equally useless—and may even be dangerously misleading. Without planning guidelines, a sales rep may think that he or she is doing well by stressing the sale of high-margin products. However, management may prefer that this rep concentrate on opening new accounts or performing more missionary selling activities. If management does not set goals for its salespeople (planning), then what bases can it use for evaluating the reps' performance? Without a par for the course (i.e., a standard of performance), how can management know whether a salesperson is doing a satisfactory job?

Truly, planning and performance evaluation are strategically interrelated and interdependent. Evaluation both follows and precedes planning. Evaluation *follows* the planning and operations of the *current* period of company activity. Actual performance is measured against predetermined standards. Then evaluation *precedes* and influences the planning for the *next* period's operations. To illustrate, let's say that evaluations show the company's gross margin declined because of a heavy sales volume in low-margin products, or there was a decline in the share of total sales coming from new accounts. These evaluation results can influence management when it prepares the next period's plans for sales force training, supervision, and compensation.

Relation of Performance Evaluation to Sales Control

Many writers and business executives refer to the subject of this chapter as *sales control* or *control of sales operations.* We do not use such a label because we believe it is a misleading and unrealistic use of the term *control.* Control is not an isolated managerial function. It permeates virtually all other managerial activities. For example, management controls its sales force by means of the compensation plan, quota system, territorial structure, and expense-payment plan. Control is also exercised through the training program, sales contests, supervision, and other devices.

Introduction to Sales Force Performance Evaluation

Evaluation of sales force performance is a broad term that covers (1) the analysis of sales volume—the topic of this chapter, (2) marketing cost analysis and profitability analysis—the topics of Chapter 15, and (3) various analytical measures used to evaluate an individual salesperson's performance—the topic of Chapter 16.

As established in earlier chapters, a trend toward relationship selling exists in today's sales organizations. In other words, sales organizations work toward developing long-term relationships with existing customers and growing those relationships into major accounts. The end result is that, relative to 20 years ago, a given firm's customers tend to be fewer in number but larger in sales volume. In fact, firms are sometimes better off eliminating direct business contact with small, low-volume customers.[1] Performance evaluations help sales organizations identify (and then focus on) those customers with the greatest potential. Clearly, companies must have the ability to effectively evaluate performance if they are to remain competitive in the 2000s.

A Marketing Audit: A Total Evaluation Program

An audit is a review and evaluation of some activity. Therefore, a **marketing audit** is a comprehensive, periodic review and evaluation of the marketing function in an organization—its marketing goals, strategies, and performance. This audit includes an appraisal of the organization, personnel, and tactics employed to implement the strategies and reach the goals.

A complete marketing audit must include *all* the marketing areas referred to in the above definition—goals, strategies, performance, organization, personnel, and tactics. A fragmented evaluation of some marketing activities may be useful, but it is not a marketing audit. It is only part of such an audit.

A complete marketing audit is an extensive project that provides an ideal for management to work toward. It is expensive, time-consuming, and difficult. But the rewards can be great. Management can identify its problem areas in marketing. By reviewing its strategies and tactics, the firm can keep abreast of its changing marketing environment. Any marketing successes should also be analyzed so that the company can capitalize on its strong points.

Traditionally, an audit is an after-the-fact review. In marketing, an audit is also used to evaluate the effects of alternatives *before* a decision is reached. Thus, the audit becomes an aid in decision making. Further, an audit should anticipate future situations as well as review past ones.

A Sales Management Audit

A marketing audit covers an organization's entire marketing system. A company can also apply the audit concept to major divisions *within* the marketing system. Thus, for example, a company might conduct a physical distribution audit or an

FIGURE 14–2

The evaluation process

To Find Out:

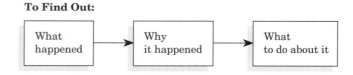

advertising audit. Or, as is pertinent to this book, management can audit the personal selling and sales management activities in a company's marketing system. Thus, like a marketing audit, a **sales management audit** evaluates a firm's *sales* objectives, strategies, and tactics. The *sales* organization and its policies, personnel, and performance are appraised.[2]

The Evaluation Process

The evaluation process—whether it is a complete marketing audit or only an appraisal of individual components of the marketing program—is essentially a three-stage task, as seen in Figure 14–2. Management's job is to:

1. Find out *what* happened—get the facts by comparing actual results with budgeted goals to determine the variations.
2. Find out *why* it happened—determine what specific factors in the marketing program accounted for the variations.
3. Decide *what to do* about it—plan the next period's activities to improve on unsatisfactory conditions and capitalize on favorable ones.

Much of our discussion in Chapters 14 and 15 is devoted to the first step—that is, explaining the techniques for determining *what* happened. Yet the task in the second step—finding out *why* variances occurred between plans and actual results—is much more difficult and time-consuming. It is relatively easy to discover that sales of product A declined 10 percent last year in the western region when management had forecast a 5 percent increase. The real problem is to identify *why* this variation between actual and forecasted sales occurred. Was the forecast in error? Or does the reason lie in the countless possibilities among the elements of the marketing mix or the myriad aspects of sales planning and operations?

Our reason for devoting significant space to the first step is that you cannot decide *why* something occurred if you first don't know *what* occurred. Many companies don't know *what* happened. That is, they have not analyzed their sales and cost performance results in any significant detail. This is surprising because the first step in the evaluation process is actually the easiest, especially with the availability of computer technology and other information-processing equipment.

Components of Performance Evaluation

Because of the time, cost, and difficulty involved in a full marketing audit, sometimes it is more reasonable to evaluate the separate components of the marketing mix. An evaluation of field-selling efforts involves an appraisal of sales volume results, related marketing expenses, and the performance of individual salespeople. These components are sufficiently independent so that management can conduct one or two evaluations without the need to do all of them. One company may decide to analyze its sales volume but not its marketing costs. Another firm may study various ratios involving sales force activities without making any detailed sales or cost analyses.

A **sales volume analysis** is a careful study of a company's records as summarized in the net sales section of its profit-and-loss statement. It is a detailed study of the dollar or the unit sales volume by product lines, territories, key accounts, and general classes of customers. A sales volume analysis may be expanded to include a corresponding study of cost of goods sold. The result is an analysis of its gross margin, also broken down into such segments as products or territories. A **marketing cost analysis** continues from the analysis of sales volume. It is a study of the marketing expenses to determine the profitability of various marketing segments in the organization.

In a general sense, the two types of analyses are component parts of a detailed study of a company's operating statement. In effect, a sales volume analysis (SVA) and a marketing cost analysis (MCA) together constitute a marketing profitability analysis (MPA). Or, look at it this way:

$$SVA + MCA = MPA$$

Performance Evaluation and Misdirected Marketing Effort

A marketing profitability analysis is one step that may be taken to correct the misdirected marketing effort found in many companies today.

Nature of Misdirected Marketing Effort: The 80–20 Principle

A company does not enjoy the same rate of net profit on every sale. In most firms, a large proportion of the orders (or customers, or territories, or products) accounts for a small share of the profits. This relationship between selling units and profits has been characterized as the 80–20 principle. That is, 80 percent of the orders, customers, territories, or products contributes only 20 percent of the sales volume or profit. Conversely, the other 20 percent of these marketing units accounts for 80 percent of the volume or profit. The 80–20 figure is used to epitomize the misplacement of marketing efforts. Actually, of course, the percentage split varies from one situation to another.

Some companies recognize this problem and adjust their strategies accordingly. For example, LivHome, a Los Angeles–based home health care provider, calculates the lifetime value of each customer by collecting and evaluating information about recency, frequency and monetary value of customer purchasing patterns. This information is used to create distinct segments of various customer profiles. LivHome then directs its salespeople to call on those segments most representative of loyal, deep-pocketed customers likely to generate the significant sales volume over the long haul.[3] Many companies, however, are not as focused as LivHome.

The 80–20 situation stems from the fact that marketing efforts and costs are to some extent related to the *number* of marketing units (territories, products, customers) rather than their *actual* or *potential sales volume and profit.* A firm may have one salesperson and one branch office in each territory, with all the attendant expense, regardless of the volume obtained from these districts. For every order received, the seller must process a purchase order, invoice, and a payment check—whether the order is for $10 or $1,000.

Reasons for Misdirected Effort

Because they lack sufficiently detailed information, many executives are unaware of the misdirected marketing effort in their firms. They do not know what percentage of total sales and profits comes from a given product line or customer group.

Total sales or costs on an operating statement are often inconclusive and misleading (see Figure 14–3). More than one company has shown satisfactory overall sales and profit figures, but when these totals were subdivided by territory or products, serious weaknesses were discovered. A manufacturer of plastic products showed an overall annual increase of 12 percent in sales and 9 percent in net profit on one of its product lines one year. But when management analyzed these figures, the sales change within each territory ranged from an increase of 19 percent to a decrease of 3 percent. In some territories, profit increased as much as 14 percent; in others it was down 20 percent.

There is a more fundamental reason for misplaced marketing effort. Sales executives must make decisions even though their knowledge of the exact nature of marketing costs is inadequate. In other words, management lacks:

1. Knowledge of the disproportionate spread of marketing effort.
2. Standards for determining:
   a) What should have been spent on marketing.
   b) What results should have been obtained from these expenditures.

As an example, a sales executive really does not know exactly how much to spend on sales training, marketing research, or sales supervision. Even more troublesome is that management has no yardstick to determine whether the results of these expenditures are satisfactory. If a firm adds 10 missionary salespeople or employs field supervisors where none existed before, the executives

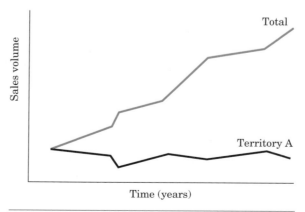

FIGURE 14-3

Total sales figures may hide significant problems

This company may be headed for real trouble. The impressive totals may be hiding some problems that ultimately can destroy the company.

ordinarily cannot say how much the volume or profit should increase. Nor can they compare the value of two expenditures. Assume that a company spends $200,000 on a contest for the sales force. No one can say how much additional volume this expenditure will bring, as compared with spending the same amount on advertising or on sales training, for example.

The Need for Detailed Data

Sales administrators who want to analyze sales volume may find they lack detailed data. The sales department works largely with figures supplied by the accounting department. But these records are rarely itemized sufficiently for the sales managers. Before managers can make a worthwhile analysis, they must establish a system to supply the sales department with the necessary facts.

The possible classifications of sales data and the combinations of these breakdowns have almost no limit. The following are some widely used subdivisions for reporting and analyzing sales:

- **Sales territories.**
- **Salespeople.** If each representative has a district, an analysis of sales volume by territory also serves for individual sales reps.
- **Products.** Reports may be in dollars and/or physical units for individual products or lines of products.
- **Customers.** Management may classify the volume by the individual customers, key accounts, industrial groups of customers, or channels of distribution.
- **Size of order.**

Bases for Analyzing Sales Volume

Total Sales Volume

A reasonable place to begin a sales analysis is with the *total sales volume*—the combined sales of all products in all territories for all customers. This readily available figure gives an overall picture of how the company is faring. However, the *trend* in sales is usually far more important to administrators than the volume for any given year. Two trends—the trend of the company's sales over a period of years and the trend of the company's share of the total industry market—are especially important.

A study of total sales volume is probably the easiest of all types of analyses. The only data needed are (1) the annual sales figures for the company over the past several years and (2) the annual industry sales in the geographic market covered by the firm. From these figures analysts can determine the company's share of the market.

Figure 14–4 shows the sort of information developed in a total sales volume analysis for the Colorado Ski Company. This concern carries two basic product lines, ski equipment (skis and accessories) and a limited line of ski clothes (ski pants and parkas). The company manufactures some of these items and purchases others from outside sources to sell under Colorado Ski's brand. The firm sells to two classes of customers—sporting good stores and specialty ski shops—in some of the major ski markets in the nation. Annual sales in 2002 were $27 million.

FIGURE 14-4

Information used in analysis of total sales volume, Colorado Ski Company

Year	Company Volume (in millions)	Industry Volume (in millions)	Company's Share of Market
2002	$27.0	$360	7.5%
2001	25.2	390	6.4
2000	23.4	360	6.5
1999	20.4	312	7.0
1998	21.0	300	8.2
1997	19.2	234	8.3
1996	19.8	240	8.9
1995	19.2	216	8.9
1994	18.0	180	10.0
1993	15.0	150	10.0

An analysis of the company's volume shows that sales have generally increased each year since 1993, with the exceptions of 1997 and 1999. So far, the picture looks encouraging. However, industry figures shed a different light on the situation. The industry's sales also have increased since 1993, but at a more rapid rate than Colorado's volume. As a result, the company's share of the market has steadily declined. Looking at the 10-year picture, management finds that its sales have increased 80 percent, but its share of the market has declined 25 percent.

After management has uncovered the facts as shown in Figure 14–4, the next step is to determine the reasons for the decline in the company's market position. The possible weaknesses in Colorado Ski's operation are almost limitless. On the one hand, something may be wrong with the product line itself, such as styling, construction, or color. Some aspects of the pricing structure may be the problem. The weakness may lie in some phase of advertising, such as the choice of media or the ads themselves. Then the entire area of sales force management can be examined. On the other hand, it may be that all of Colorado Ski's operations are as good as ever but that the competitors have made improvements. Possibly there are more competitors. Or some of these firms may have significantly improved their product, distribution, or promotional effectiveness.

Sales by Territories

Companies usually can do an analysis of *total* sales volume easily and inexpensively. However, its value to management is limited because it tells so little about the details of a firm's marketing progress. Only the aggregate picture emerges and the separate parts remain submerged. One step toward uncovering these parts is the common practice of analyzing sales by territories. Management wants to identify which territories are strong and which are weak in relation to potential. A company must find out *which* territories are weak before it can determine *why* they are weak.

One reasonably simple, inexpensive procedure for analyzing sales volume by territories involves the following four steps:

1. Select a market index that indicates with reasonable accuracy what percentage of total sales should be obtained from each sales territory. For example, one firm may use retail sales as an index. If 10 percent of the total

national retail sales were in the midwestern district, then 10 percent of the company's sales should also come from that district. Or, if the firm sells in only eight southeastern states, then the total retail sales in the eight-state area would be equated to 100 percent. If 22 percent of retail sales in the eight states were tallied in Alabama, then 22 percent of the sales in the company should also come from Alabama. (Market indexes and their use in determining territorial sales and market potentials were explained in Chapter 12.)

2. Determine the company's actual total sales in dollars or units during the period being studied.

3. Multiply the territorial index by the total sales figure to determine the goal in each district.

4. Compare actual regional sales with the regional goals to see how much variation has occurred.

An example of this procedure is developed in Figure 14–5. The five territories in the western division of the Colorado Ski Company are being analyzed. Colorado Ski's total sales in the western division were $13.5 million distributed among five territories, as shown in the column headed Actual Sales. Sales were $2,700,000 in territory A, $3,690,000 in territory B, and so forth. Next we apply a pertinent market index to the western division's total sales. We find that 27 percent, or $3,645,000 of the total sales in the five-territory market, *should* have been made in territory A. The goal in territory B was 22 percent, or $2,970,000, and so on.

A performance percentage is computed by dividing actual sales by the territorial goal. A rating of 100 percent in the district means that the area turned in its predetermined share of the company's business. Figure 14–5 shows that territories B and C did much better than expected. Districts E and D were a shade below par, and A fell considerably short of expectations.

It is not enough to study the *percentage* by which an area's sales are over or under the goals. The more important measure is usually the *dollar volume*. It is possible that the district may be only a few percentage points under par. However, because the territorial potential is very large, these few percentage points may represent a significant sum of money.

A market segment that is below par—its actual performance does not reach its goal—may be called a *soft spot*. In sales management, the **soft-spot principle** states that an administrator reaps the largest possible gain by working with

FIGURE 14–5

Analysis of territorial sales volume in five-territory western division, Colorado Ski Company, 2002

Territory	Market Index (percent)	Sales Goals ($000)	Actual Sales ($000)	Performance Percentage	Dollar Variation ($000)
A	27%	$3,645	$2,700	74	$−945
B	22	2,970	3,690	124	+720
C	15	2,025	2,484	123	+459
D	20	2,700	2,556	95	−144
E	16	2,160	2,070	96	−90
Total	100%	$13,500	$13,500		

According to the soft-spot principle, sales managers should pay special attention to those sales reps with the greatest need for improvement.

the weakest segments of the organization. Thus, a sales manager in the Colorado Ski Company should devote the most attention to territory A because it has the greatest need for improvement. By the same token, it is doubtful that even considerable attention could improve B and C very much. Already they are far above their goals. Probably the main benefits from a study of B and C would be to determine (1) why they apparently are so successful and (2) whether this information can be used to improve A.

Once management has identified the strong and weak territories, the next task is to determine the reasons for the relative performances. Territory A may be doing poorly because competition is particularly effective or because some aspects of Colorado Ski's operation are especially weak. Assuming that industry sales volume figures for each territory are obtainable with reasonable effort, then company sales percentages in each district may be compared with industry percentages. A sales manager may find, for example, that 15 percent of the *industry's* sales are made in territory A and 10 percent in B. In comparison, 12 percent of the *company's* sales are in A and 20 percent in B. Thus, the company is below average in A, but it is doing far better than the industry average in B.

Sales by Products

The 80–20 principle applies to products as well as to territories in many companies. Very often, most of the products in a company's line account for a small percentage of total volume or profit. Conversely, a few products may bring most of the volume. There is no relation between volume and profit. Products that account for a large proportion of the volume may or may not contribute a corresponding percentage of the net profits.

Several types of volume analyses by product lines may be helpful to management. The first is simply a summary of present and past total sales divided

Product	Territory A ($000)			Territory B ($000)		
	Goal	**Actual**	**Variation**	**Goal**	**Actual**	**Variation**
Skis	$1,629	$1,710	$ +81	$1,263	$1,620	$+357
Accessories	270	234	−36	222	360	+138
Pants	900	360	−540	765	1,080	+315
Parkas	846	396	−450	720	630	−90
Total	$3,645	$2,700	$−945	$2,970	$3,690	$+720

into individual products or groups of products. An appliance manufacturer may want to study the sales trend for each individual product. A hardware wholesaler, however, would be content to group thousands of products into divisions such as housewares, plumbing goods, and electrical equipment.

If industry figures are available for each product line, they may provide a yardstick for a company to measure its own sales performance by products. For example, assume that the sales of product A are decreasing in one firm. Its management need not be too concerned if, over the same period, the industry's sales have decreased at about the same rate.

A further refinement is to study the sales of each product line in each territory. In this way, management can determine the geographical market in which each product is strong or weak. Product A's *total* sales may be up 10 percent over last year, but in the southwestern region, A's volume is down 14 percent. Once these facts are known, an administrator can try to determine the reasons for the variations and then make the necessary corrections.

An analysis of sales by product lines can also be used to refine the territorial analysis discussed in the preceding section. Figure 14–5 showed that territory A was 26 percent under par. Territories B and C were 24 percent and 23 percent above par, respectively. By investigating the product sales in these districts, management can better isolate the reasons for these variations.

In Figure 14–6, market indexes were applied to Colorado Ski's actual volume of $13.5 million to establish targets for products in the five western territories.* For instance, let's assume that the western division's sales had been distributed in relation to potential. Then sales in territory A would have been $3,645,000, with skis contributing $1,629,000; ski accessories accounting for $270,000; and so on.

In Figure 14–5, we found that the company was short of its sales goal in territory A by $945,000, or 26 percent. However, this shortage was not distributed equally among all four products. Further analysis by product lines showed that the sales of ski pants and parkas were the primary sources of the shortages. The

---

*Ideally, a separate index should be used for each product or line of products. To use the same index on all items means that the percentage share of the national market set as a target in the territory is the same for all products. In Figure 14–5, 27 percent of the company's total western division sales should have been contributed by territory A. If the same index is used for all four products, then 27 percent of the sales of each product should be obtained from territory A. Such situations are unusual. Ordinarily, a company selling many different products should not expect that a given territory would contribute the same percentage of the total sales for each product.

company failed to reach its target by $540,000 and $450,000, respectively, for those two products. Sales of skis actually were $81,000 over the performance standard.

Territory B as a whole was $720,000 over its goal figure. However, sales of parkas fell $90,000 (about 12 percent) short of the goal. Volume in skis, accessories, and ski pants was above the target figure in each of these product categories.

As part of its sales volume analysis by products, management must decide what to do about low-volume products and products that did not meet their sales goals. Figure 14–6 suggests that ski pants and parkas in territory A and parkas in territory B seem to be soft spots in terms of sales goals. Thus, these products seem to provide the best opportunity for improvement.

Management's initial thought may be to drop low-volume products. But before taking such a drastic step, the company should consider other factors. A cost analysis will aid in these decisions. If the product is a losing proposition for the company, this would be a strong point in favor of dropping the item. In some cases, however, a low-volume product must be kept whether or not it is profitable. It may be needed to round out a line, and customers may expect the company to carry the item.

Sales by Customer Classifications

A company is even more likely to find the 80–20 principle in operation when sales are analyzed by customer groups. It is not unusual to find that a small percentage of customers accounts for a major share of total volume. Typically, a firm sells to many accounts on a marginal or even unprofitable basis.

A firm can analyze its volume by customer groups in several ways. It may classify accounts on an industry basis. An oil company may group its customers into *industry divisions*, such as service stations or marine, farm, transportation, industrial, and governmental agencies. Another basis of classification is by *channels of distribution*. A sporting goods manufacturer may group its accounts by sporting goods wholesalers, department stores, and discount houses. A third classification is on the basis of *accounts*, or just the key accounts. Any of these three groups may be cross-classified. An oil company may want to analyze its sales to key accounts in the service-station industry group, for example.

Customer classifications usually should be analyzed for each territory and for each line of products. In one company, it may be that sales to wholesalers are satisfactory on an overall basis, although sales to wholesalers may be particularly poor in one territory. An oil company may assume that a given industry market that accounts for 10 percent of total sales also contributes about 10 percent of the volume of each product line. However, an analysis may disclose that this industry accounts for 18 percent of the volume in product A, but only 5 percent in product B.

The Insufficiency of Sales Volume Analysis

A sales volume analysis alone usually does not furnish enough information to the sales department. Furthermore, the data produced may be misleading. A study may show, for example, that the dollar *volume* of product A is 20 percent greater than the sales of product B. Yet, if the company were to determine the gross mar-

Using sales force automation software, sales reps can download the most up-to-date customer information.

gin or net profit of the two products, management would find that B's dollar *profit* is 10 percent higher than A's. A full-scale sales and cost study—a marketing profitability analysis—is ideal, but it is also likely to be difficult and costly. Further, while an analysis of volume alone has its limitations, it is far better than no analysis at all. In spite of the acknowledged value of a marketing cost and profitability analysis, the most widely used measure of sales performance continues to be sales volume.

A compromise between a volume analysis and a full-scale marketing cost study is to expand the volume analysis to include the cost of the merchandise sold. Thus, management ends up with a gross margin analysis by territories, products, or customer groups with relatively little additional expense.

Sales Force Automation and Performance Evaluation

In recent years, sales organizations increasingly have relied on computers and **sales force automation (SFA)** software to manage information, which makes performance evaluation much easier and faster. SFA is typically a single part of an overall customer relationship management system, and thus analyzes information from a variety of the firm's different business functions (e.g., sales, marketing, accounting, purchasing, manufacturing). Siebel Systems is the leading provider of such systems. Key competitors include Oracle, Epiphany, PeopleSoft, Kana Software, WebTone Technologies, and Vignette.[4]

Research shows that company executives are generally satisfied with recent implementations of SFA—although the amount of training required for salespeople to learn the system has tended to be underestimated.[5] Salespeople, however, are sometimes resistant to SFA initiatives. To gain their reps' acceptance, sales managers must first explain and demonstrate how SFA will help improve sales productivity. In addition, management should exhibit a definite commitment to the technology and should be sure to involve reps in designing a program for implementation. These are important managerial actions, because sales force acceptance is necessary for the success of any SFA initiative. The value of the SFA analysis to the sales organization absolutely depends on the reps' ability and willingness to regularly enter data about customers, orders, and expenses.[6]

The sales organization of Hitachi Construction Machinery (HCM) represents one of many SFA success stories. HCM, which has about 100 sales offices throughout the world, sells hydraulic excavators and mining shovels to a wide variety of construction companies. When demand for HCM equipment slumped due to Japan's long-term recession, the company looked for a better way to analyze customer needs and identify opportunities. SFA from Siebel Systems was what they found. The system allowed salespeople to enter unique data about each customer, including personalized comments and responses. This information became instantly accessible to the 1,000 members of HCM's sales force. This allowed each member of the sales team to monitor the sales transaction, and to step in when needed. Further, the central repository of information, accessible to everyone, led to a marketing strategy that was much more customer-oriented than before.[7]

Summary

A particularly interdependent strategic relationship exists between planning and performance evaluation in the sales force management process. In this management process, a marketing audit ideally should play a key role. A marketing audit is a *total* evaluation program. As such, it is a comprehensive periodic review and evaluation of the marketing system in an organization. A sales management audit evaluates sales objectives, strategies, and tactics.

The evaluation process is essentially a three-stage task. First, find out *what* happened—actual results are compared with budgeted goals. Second, find out *why* it happened—what factors accounted for the variation between goals and results. Third, decide *what to do* about the situation—that is, plan next period's activities.

Because of the time and cost needed for a full-scale marketing audit, many companies evaluate only the major components of their marketing programs. One such performance evaluation includes an analysis of (1) sales volume, (2) marketing costs, and (3) salespeople's performance. A sales volume analysis combined with a marketing cost analysis constitutes a marketing profitability analysis.

Performance evaluation is a key tool in reducing the misdirected marketing effort in an organization. Misdirected marketing effort means that a company is expending much effort but getting relatively few results. The 80–20 principle illustrates misdirected marketing effort. That is, marketing efforts (costs) are related to the *number* of marketing units (territories, products, customers), rather than the *sales volume* or *profit* derived from these marketing units.

The basic reasons for misdirected marketing efforts are that management lacks (1) knowledge of the disproportionate spread of marketing effort and (2) reliable standards for determining (*a*) what should be spent on marketing and (*b*) what results should be derived from these expenditures.

A sales volume analysis is a study of a company's actual sales volume compared with the budgeted sales goals. This volume analysis should be done in great detail. That is, the company's sales should be analyzed in total and also by territory, products, customer groups, salespeople, and order size. In each of these subdivisions, the company's performance should be compared with industry figures. In this way, management can measure its performance against the competition.

Detailed sales performance analysis has been improved immeasurably by advances in computer and Internet-related technology. Sales force automation (SFA) software, for example, helps sales organizations manage information efficiently. This technology makes performance evaluation much easier and faster than ever before.

Key Terms

Marketing audit
Marketing cost analysis

Sales force automation (SFA)
Sales management audit

Sales volume analysis
Soft-spot principle

Questions and Problems

1. Explain the relationship between planning and evaluation in the management process.

2. Explain the concept of a marketing profitability analysis.

3. What is the 80–20 principle, and how does it apply to sales performance evaluation?

4. If a firm's volume is increasing each year by a satisfactory percentage, is there any reason for the firm to go to the expense of a volume analysis?

5. As a result of sales volume analysis, many firms have eliminated some of their products or customers. Yet in several of these cases the sales volume has *increased* after the market cutback. How do you account for this result?

6. A territorial volume analysis indicated that a firm's sales had increased at about a 10 percent rate for the past three years in a given district. Is this conclusive evidence that the company's performance is satisfactory as far as sales volume is concerned in the given territory?

7. A company with 15 territories found that product A accounted for 40 percent to 50 percent of the sales in 13 of the districts. But this product brought in only about 20 percent of the volume in the remaining two territories. What factors might account for the relatively low standing of product A in the two territories?

8. Is it possible for a product, territory, or class of customer to be far below par but still not deserve much executive attention? Give examples.

9. Should salespeople be furnished with complete statistics, not only on their own performances but on the performance of other salespeople as well?

10. If a company made a *territorial* volume analysis and found some subpar territories, how might these facts affect the following activities relating to salespeople?
    a) Supervision.
    b) Compensation.
    c) Training.

11. If a firm analyzed its sales volume by *customer classes*, how might the results affect the supervision, compensation, and training of the sales force?

12. What can sales managers do to ensure that their salespeople readily accept and properly use sales force automation (SFA) software?

Experiential Exercises

A. Ask a local store manager to discuss with you (and possibly show you) the reports that he or she uses to track the store's performance as well as the performance of various product categories and salespeople.

B. Contact a field sales representative and discuss the product and customer data reports that he or she uses to plan selling strategies and evaluate performance effectiveness.

Internet Exercises

A. Visit ManagementLearning.com and register for a free membership. Read the online article entitled "Sales Management Audit" (http://management learning.com/art/salesaud/index.html) and do the Sales Audit exercise as you assume the identity of a sales manager.

B. Explore Salesforce.com (www.salesforce.com/us), which is a sales force automation (SFA) website. How do sales managers benefit from using this Internet service? How do salespeople benefit? Using "sales force automation" as a search phrase, find other, similar websites and software products devoted to this application.

References

1. Paul Smith, "Only Some Customers Are King," *New Zealand Management*, April 2000, pp. 24–26.

2. For an excellent explanation of a sales management audit, including a detailed outline of its elements, see Alan J. Dubinsky and Richard W. Hansen, "The Sales Force Management Audit," *California Management Review*, Winter 1981, pp. 86–95.

3. Mark McMaster, "A Lifetime of Sales," *Sales & Marketing Management*, September 2001, p. 55.

4. John Evan Frook, "Selling Skeptical Sales Forces on Automation," *B to B*, October 1, 2001, p. 20.

5. Robert C. Erffmeyer and Dale A. Johnson, "An Exploratory Study of Sales Force Automation Practices: Expectation and Realities," *Journal of Personal Selling & Sales Management*, Spring 2001, pp. 167–75.

6. Amy J. Morgan and Scott A. Inks, "Technology and the Sales Force: Increasing Acceptance of Sales Force Automation," *Industrial Marketing Management*, July 2001, pp. 463–72.

7. The Hitachi Construction Machinery example was taken from the "Customers and Case Studies" section of the company website of Siebel Systems, Inc. (www.siebel.com/about/customer_case_studies), accessed January 3, 2002.

CASE 14-1   SEAL RITE ENVELOPE COMPANY (A)

Analysis of Sales Volume

"You're drowning in data. Haven't you anything better to do around here than reading those reports? You're wasting so much paper, the next thing I know the environmentalists will be picketing the place," exclaimed Max Chernak, Seal Rite Envelope Company's new president. He had stopped by the office of Rose Douglas, the firm's sales manager for the past seven years, to visit with her. His opening remarks were a reaction to the two-foot-high stack of computer printouts spread out in front of Douglas on her desk. She stopped scanning them and looked up as Chernak walked in.

Chernak was smiling as he commented on the pile of paper before her, but Douglas had been warned previously by an acquaintance who had worked for Chernak in another company that he was not a big believer in paperwork. She recalled the words, "He likes to keep things simple. He doesn't spend much time in his office. He always seems to be around. Delegation is not one of his favorite concepts."

The Seal Rite Envelope Company of St. Louis, Missouri, manufactured and distributed a wide line of paper envelopes of all weights, sizes, and paper stock. Its sales force sold to printers, paper wholesalers, and large organizations with their own operations throughout the midwestern states.

Douglas was rather proud of the sales analysis system she had developed. All sales orders were classified by the stock numbers of the products bought, who bought them, who sold them, when they were bought, and how much gross margin was realized from the order. The data were for the previous week and previous month, all compared with sales for the same periods the previous year. Any significant changes in performance were automatically highlighted for her attention by the program. A printout of each week's sales orders and shipments was delivered to her home each Sunday morning so she could study it in preparation for the Monday-morning sales meeting. The reports were generated on Saturday by Sharon Hamilton in accounting in response to Douglas's demand for them. The additional costs ($250) incurred for the reports came from Douglas's budget.

Douglas felt obliged to defend her system for analyzing sales. "I find it helpful to have the facts about what has happened before I go into my weekly sales meeting every Monday morning. I know who is selling and who isn't. I know what is selling and what isn't. And I know how much we're making on everything we sell and on every order."

"I see. Knowledge is power. Is that it?" Chernak asked.

Douglas nodded slightly; she understood she was under attack. Had she been too aggressive in defending her system, considering that she hardly knew Chernak? she wondered.

The new president was not a person who avoided confrontation. He rose to the challenge. "OK! I see that something is highlighted on that page you're looking at. What is it?"

"Well, it seems that the sales of item number 2510 are down significantly for the month compared to last year. We sold hardly any of it last week. Let's see, 2510 is our heavy-duty, brown, 12-inch by 18-inch mailing envelope," Douglas said as she read from the reports.

"So what?"

"What do you mean, so what?"

Chernak said, "I mean, so what? So what is the significance of that information? So what are you going to do about it?"

Douglas knew she was in a bit of trouble, but she could not back down. "I'll make inquiries of the sales force to see if any of them has an explanation. Is something wrong with our product or its pricing? Is it just a random event? Does it reflect a change in market requirements? I'll keep my eye on it to see if anything develops that warrants taking some action."

Chernak replied, "That's what I call micromanagement. How many of such items are there in that report that will require you to do something? Don't answer that! I'm afraid of the answer. We seem to be on different wavelengths. I only want to know a few things, such as our gross margins by broad product lines and sales rep. And, of course, I want to know total dollar sales, gross margins, and expenses. But I would lose all perspective if I had to deal with that volume of information you are processing each week. And what about the costs? Are they worth it? Well, as long as the profit performance of your operation keeps doing as well as it has, you can stare at that paper as long as you like if that's the way you get your kicks."

As Chernak left her office, Douglas was a bit upset by the president's attitude toward her sales analysis system. She had been taught that if she took care of the details, the totals would take care of themselves. She had found that by having good, recent information about all aspects of sales, she gained power in the organization. Her people had learned not to challenge her since she could always pull out data to support her position. She wanted people to know that she was on top of her job.

Douglas decided to think about the matter for a while and ask some other people about her system before doing anything about it. As she looked at the stack of paper in front of her, a troubling thought crossed her mind. Was she spending too much time analyzing these sales reports? Was it all worth it?

Questions:

1. How should Rose Douglas evaluate the effectiveness of her sales analysis system?

2. What would you recommend she do in response to the situation in which her boss obviously disagrees with her attitudes toward information systems?

15 Marketing Cost and Profitability Analysis

Business prophets tell us what should *happen—but business profits tell us what* did *happen.*

—Earl Wilson—

While an analysis of sales volume is useful, it tells us nothing about the *profitability* of territories, products, or customer groups. To determine the profitability of any of these sales control units, we need a marketing cost analysis. Sales executives are particularly interested in a marketing cost analysis because this information can significantly affect the management of a sales force. The discovery of an unprofitable territory may necessitate a shift in territorial boundaries or a different call schedule. The discovery of unprofitable products may lead to a change in the commission rate paid for sales of those items.

Nature and Scope of Marketing Cost Analysis

A marketing cost analysis, as noted in Chapter 14, is a detailed study of a firm's marketing costs. It is used to discover unprofitable segments and inefficiently performed functions of the company's marketing program. It goes beyond a sales volume analysis to determine the profitability of various aspects of the marketing operation. Thus, it becomes an important part of an overall sales performance analysis.

Various sales department budgets are frequently an integral part of cost analyses. Management often wants to establish a standard of performance (a budget) for some selling expense and then to determine the causes of variation between the actual and budgeted expense.

Marketing Cost Analysis and the Accounting System

Marketing cost analysis differs somewhat in purpose and scope from the usual accounting system in a firm. Accounting seeks to maintain a complete *historical* record of company events that in any way have a financial flavor. Thus, the system provides management with the story of merchandise sales, materials purchased, equipment depreciation, salaries paid, and all other activities relating to finances. Marketing cost analysis is a managerial tool designed more for use in the planning and control of a firm's *future* operations. Of course, an analysis of past financial events often serves as a guide for future operations.

A marketing cost study is *not* usually a part of a company's regular accounting system. It takes up where the accounting system stops. A study of costs is largely analytical and statistical. It is not concerned with the routine accounting practices. The regular accounting system, however, provides virtually all the data necessary to conduct a marketing cost analysis. Therefore, to do an effective cost analysis, the company must maintain a detailed system of account classification. For instance, one account for sales commissions is not at all sufficient to analyze the commissions paid (1) on sales of a given product (2) to selected customers (3) in a certain territory.

Marketing Cost Analysis Compared with Production Cost Accounting

Marketing cost analysis and production cost accounting help to control costs in their respective areas. Beyond this general similarity, however, the two concepts are markedly different, as the comparison in Figure 15–1 shows.

To summarize this comparison, sales executives want to know the marketing costs by product in addition to the costs for other marketing units. Moreover, these costs are incurred by salespeople who are not under direct supervision and whose job is not totally routine, in contrast to production workers and their ma-

---

FIGURE 15–1   A comparison of marketing cost analysis and production cost accounting

Comparison Factors	Marketing Cost Analysis	Production Cost Accounting
Bases for computing costs	Marketing unit: territory, customer group, order size, as well as product	Unit of product
	More complex ⟷ *Relatively simple*	
Source of cost incurred	Salespeople in the field	Machines and closely supervised workers
	Less exact ⟷ *More precise*	
Cost–volume relationship	Volume is a function of cost $V = (f)C$	Cost is a function of volume $C = f(V)$
	Difficult to measure ⟷ *Relatively easy to measure*	

chines. Finally, production managers usually know the exact cost–volume relationship between an increase in output and a decrease in cost. A sales manager, on the other hand, wants to know what the effect on volume will be if a given cost is changed. For example, what change in volume would occur if two salespeople were added to the eight now operating in the Dallas district? Sales executives typically cannot determine answers to these questions with nearly the degree of accuracy that production managers can.

Types of Marketing Cost Analysis

A company's marketing costs may be analyzed in three ways:

1. As they appear in the ledger accounts and on the income and expense statement.
2. After they are grouped into functional (also called activity) categories.
3. After they have been allocated to territories, products, or other marketing units.

Analysis of Ledger Expenses

The simplest and least expensive marketing cost analysis is based on studying object-of-expenditure costs as they are recorded in the company's accounting ledgers. The procedure is simply to take the totals for each cost item (sales force salaries, branch office rent, office supplies) from the ledger accounts and then analyze these figures in some detail. Totals for this period can be compared with similar figures for past periods to determine trends. Management can compare actual expenses with budgeted expense goals. When trade associations disseminate cost information, a company can compare its figures with the industry's averages.

An analysis of ledger-cost items is of limited value because it provides only general information. A study may show, for instance, that sales compensation costs are 4.7 percent of sales, whereas the industry's average for firms of similar size is 6.1 percent. Findings of this nature are of some help in guiding management and controlling the sales force. However, a more detailed analysis is needed to pinpoint the reasons for the trends observed in the company's costs and the variations from industry norms.

In Chapter 14 we introduced the Colorado Ski Company as part of our discussion of sales volume analysis. At this point, in Figure 15–2, we show that firm's 2002 income and expense statement, sometimes called an *operating statement* or a *profit-and-loss statement*. This statement includes the company's operating expenses as drawn from the firm's ledger accounts.

Analysis of Activity Expenses

In typical accounting records, expenses are classified according to the immediate object of the expenditure. Thus, ledger accounts may be found for such marketing expenses as sales salaries, branch office rent, and advertising costs. However, for a more effective marketing cost analysis, sales executives usually regroup these ledger expenses into various activity classifications. All the expenses related to a given marketing function, such as warehousing or advertising, are grouped together.[1]

FIGURE 15-2

Income and expense statement, 2002, Colorado Ski Company ($000)

Net sales		$27,000
Less cost of goods sold		18,900
Gross margin		8,100
Less operating expenses:		
Sales salaries and commissions	$3,240	
Sales force travel	372	
Supplies and telephone	178	
Media space	870	
Advertising salaries	218	
Property taxes	120	
Heat and light	168	
Insurance	84	
Administrative salaries	930	
Other expenses	120	
Total operating expenses		6,300
Net profit		$1,800

An activity-related expense analysis is a two-step procedure. The first step involves selecting the appropriate activity categories. Each firm should list the major activities that are relevant to its own marketing program. A retail chain, for instance, ordinarily performs activities different from those of a manufacturer of electric generators. A typical list, however, usually includes many of the following expense categories:

- Personal selling expenses: sales force compensation and travel expenses as well as all costs connected with branch sales offices.
- Advertising and sales promotion expenses.
- Warehousing and shipping expenses.
- Order processing expenses: costs of processing sales and purchase orders, billing, and receiving payments.
- Administration expenses: all costs of sales offices, including executives' salaries and travel expenses; marketing's share of company's general administration expenses.

In the second step of an activity-expense analysis, we take each ledger expense and allocate it among the various activity categories. Many of the ledger expenses listed in accounting records cut across several activity groups. Consequently, management must *allocate* a given ledger expense among the appropriate activities. For instance, the ledger account for office supplies must be allocated to each activity group (such as personal selling, advertising, and warehousing) that incurs this expense. A useful tool here is an expense distribution sheet such as the one pictured in Figure 15–3. All the ledger costs are listed vertically in the left-hand column. (Note that these ledger expenses are the same ones shown in Figure 15–2, the company's income and expense statement.) The activity categories are listed at the top of the columns across the sheet.

Some ledger expenses are easy to apportion because they are direct expenses. That is, the entire amount can be allocated to one activity. In Figure 15–3,

FIGURE 15-3 Expense distribution sheet, Colorado Ski Company, 2002 (showing allocation of ledger expense items to activity categories)

				Activity Cost Categories		
Ledger Expenses	Totals	Personal Selling	Advertising	Warehousing and Shipping	Order Processing	Administration
Sales salaries and commissions	$3,240,000	$3,240,000	—	—	—	—
Sales force travel	372,000	372,000	—	—	—	—
Supplies and telephone	178,000	43,200	22,200	40,900	43,500	28,200
Media space	870,000	—	870,000	—	—	—
Advertising salaries	218,000	—	218,000	—	—	—
Property taxes	120,000	10,000	14,500	66,000	14,000	15,500
Heat and light	168,000	15,300	17,400	100,500	16,200	18,600
Insurance	84,000	12,000	4,200	46,300	14,000	7,500
Administrative salaries	930,000	144,000	62,000	168,000	126,000	430,000
Other expenses	120,000	10,500	11,700	58,300	26,300	13,200
Totals	$6,300,000	3,847,000	1,220,000	480,000	240,000	513,000

advertising salaries of $218,000 were apportioned entirely to the advertising activity. Sales force travel expenses of $372,000 were apportioned entirely to the personal-selling category.

Other expenses are indirect. Thus, they must be apportioned among several activity groups. The main problem in dealing with each indirect expense is to select a basis for its allocation. For example, property taxes may be distributed on the basis of square feet used for each activity. In the Colorado Ski Company example, about 55 percent of the total floor space was in the warehousing and shipping department. Consequently, $66,000 of the property tax expense (55 percent of $120,000) was allocated to this physical distribution activity.

After all individual ledger expenses are allocated, the columns are totaled, and the resultant figures are the activity expenses. In Figure 15–3 the expenses totaled $6.3 million. The total for personal selling alone was $3,847,000. From this type of analysis, the total cost of each activity can be determined accurately. Moreover, a study of an expense distribution sheet each year shows not only which *ledger* costs have increased or decreased, but also the *activities* responsible for these changes. An analysis of activity expenses also provides an excellent starting point for analyzing marketing costs by territories, products, or other marketing units.

Analysis of Activity Costs by Market Segments

The third and most beneficial type of marketing cost analysis is a study of the costs and profitability of each segment of the market. The most common practice in this type of analysis is to divide the market by territories, products, customer groups, or order sizes. A cost analysis by market segment enables management to pinpoint trouble spots or areas of satisfactory performance much more effectively than with an analysis of either ledger expenses or total activity costs.

By combining a sales volume analysis with a marketing cost analysis, a profit-and-loss statement may be prepared for each of the products or market segments. These individual income and expense statements then can be analyzed to determine the effectiveness of the marketing program in each of those segments.

A complete marketing cost analysis by sales territories or some other marketing unit involves the same three-step evaluation procedure outlined in Chapter 14. That is, we determine what happened, why it happened, and what we are going to do about the situation.

To determine *what happened*, the procedure in a cost analysis by market segments is quite similar to the method used to analyze activity expenses. The total of each activity cost (the bottom line in Figure 15–3) is prorated on some basis among each product or market segment being studied. Let's walk through an example of a marketing cost analysis in the three geographic sales regions of the Colorado Ski Company, as shown in Figures 15–4 and 15–5. First, for each of the five Colorado Ski activities, we select an allocation basis for distributing the cost of that activity among the three regions. These bases are shown in the top part of Figure 15–4. Then we determine the number of allocation "units" that make up each activity cost, and we find the cost per unit. This completes

FIGURE 15-4   Allocation of activity costs to sales regions, Colorado Ski Company, 2002

Activity	Personal Selling	Advertising	Warehousing and Shipping	Order Processing	Administration
Allocation Scheme					
Allocation basis	Direct expense to each region	Number of pages of advertising	Number of orders shipped	Number of invoice lines	Equally among regions
Total activity cost	$3,847,000	$1,220,000	$480,000	$240,000	$513,000
Number of allocation units	—	61 pages	9,600 orders	120,000 lines	3 regions
Cost per allocation unit	—	$20,000 per page	$50 per order	$2 per line	$171,000 per region

Region		Allocation of Costs				
Eastern	units	—	21 pages	3,800 orders	39,500 lines	1
	cost	$1,070,000	$420,000	$190,000	$79,000	$171,000
Midwestern	units	—	11 pages	2,500 orders	28,000 lines	1
	cost	$747,000	$220,000	$125,000	$56,000	$171,000
Western	units	—	29 pages	3,300 orders	52,500 lines	1
	cost	$2,030,000	$580,000	$165,000	$105,000	$171,000

FIGURE 15-5   Income and expense statement, by sales region, Colorado Ski Company, 2002 (in $000)

	Total	Eastern	Midwestern	Western
Net sales	$27,000	$9,000	$4,500	$13,500
Less cost of goods sold	18,900	6,300	3,150	9,450
Gross margin	8,100	2,700	1,350	4,050
Less operating expenses:				
Personal selling	3,847	1,070	802	1,975
Advertising	1,220	420	220	580
Warehousing/shipping	480	190	125	165
Order processing	240	79	56	105
Administration	513	171	171	171
Total operating expenses	6,300	1,930	1,374	2,996
Net profit (loss)	$ 1,800	$ 770	($24)	$ 1,054
Net profit (loss) as percentage of sales	6.7%	8.6%	(0.53%)	7.8%

the allocation scheme, which tells us how to allocate costs to the three regions. To illustrate further:

- Personal-selling activity expenses pose no problem because they are direct expenses, chargeable entirely to the region in which they were incurred.

- Advertising expenses are allocated on the basis of the number of pages of advertising run in each region. The ski company purchased the equivalent of 61 pages of advertising during the year at an average cost of $20,000 per page ($1,220,000/61).

- Warehousing and shipping expenses are allocated on the basis of the number of orders shipped. Since 9,600 orders were shipped during the year at a total activity cost of $480,000, the cost per order was $50. Order-processing expenses are allocated according to the number of invoice lines typed during the year. Since there were 120,000 invoice lines processed on the computer, the cost per line was $2 (120,000 × $2 = $240,000 total cost).

- The administration expense of $513,000—a totally indirect cost—is arbitrarily divided equally among the three regions, at a cost of $171,000 per region.

The final step is to calculate the amount of each activity expense that is to be allocated to each region. The results appear in the bottom part of Figure 15–4. We see that $1,070,000 of *personal-selling* expenses were incurred in the eastern region, $747,000 was charged to the midwestern region, and $2,030,000 to the western region. In the case of *advertising*, 21 pages of advertising were run in the eastern region, so that region was charged with $420,000 (21 pages at $20,000 per page). In similar calculations, the midwestern region was charged $220,000 for advertising, and the charge to the western region was $580,000. Regarding *warehousing and shipping* expenses, 3,800 orders were shipped to customers in the eastern region. At a unit allocation cost of $50, eastern's total allocated cost was $190,000. Midwestern's allocated shipping cost was $125,000, and the western region was charged $165,000. For *order-processing* expenses, management found that 39,500 invoice lines went to customers in the eastern region. At $2 a line, this expense came to $79,000. In the case of the *administration* expenses of $513,000, each region was charged $171,000. After the five activity expenses have been allocated among the three sales regions, we can prepare a profit-and-loss statement for each region, as shown in Figure 15–5. The sales volume for each region was determined in our volume analysis in Chapter 14. The cost of goods sold and the gross margin for each region were determined by assuming that the companywide gross margin of 30 percent ($8,100,000/$27,000,000) was maintained in each region.

In summary, Figure 15–5 shows the operating results for each region in the same way that Figure 15–2 reported the income and expense picture for the company as a whole. For example, we see that the eastern region's net profit was 8.6 percent of sales ($770,000/$9,000,000). In sharp contrast, the midwestern region did rather poorly, actually losing $24,000, or 0.53 percent of sales ($24,000/$4,500,000 = 0.53%).

At this point in our performance evaluation, we have completed the *what happened* stage. The next step is to determine *why* the results are as shown in Figure 15–5. As mentioned earlier, it is extremely difficult to answer this question. In the midwestern region, for example, the sales force obtained only about two-thirds as many orders as in the eastern region (2,500 versus 3,800). Was this because Colorado did about half as much advertising in the Midwest as in the East? Or does the reason lie in poor selling ability or poor sales training in the Midwest? Or is competition simply much stronger in the Midwest?

After a profitability analysis has determined *why* the regional results came out as they did, management can move to the third stage in its performance evaluation process. That final stage is to determine *what management should do* about the situation. We shall discuss this third stage briefly after we have reviewed some major problem areas in marketing cost analysis.

Problems in Marketing Cost Analysis

Marketing cost analyses can be expensive in time, money, and personnel. Today, however, the use of computerized information systems enables management to generate data that are more current, more detailed, and lower in cost than was true in the past. But even the computers so far have not overcome the problems related to cost allocation and the contribution-margin versus full-cost controversy.

Allocating Costs

As a foundation for our discussion of cost allocation, let's first distinguish between direct and indirect expenses.

Direct versus Indirect Expenses

Direct costs are incurred in connection with a single unit of sales operations. Therefore, they can readily be allocated in total to a specific marketing unit, whether it is a territory, product, or customer group. If the company dropped a given territory or product, all direct expenses tied to that marketing unit would be eliminated. These are expenses that can be separated from other costs. **Indirect costs** are those shared by more than one market segment. In general, most marketing costs are totally or partially indirect.

Whether a given cost is classed as common or separable depends on the market segment being analyzed. The cost never remains permanently in one or the other category. Assume that each salesperson in a company has a separate territory, is paid a straight salary, and sells the entire line of products. Sales force salaries would be a *direct* expense if the cost analysis were being made by territories. But the salary expense would be an *indirect* cost if the cost were being studied for each product. They cannot be separated by product. Sales force travel expenses would be a *direct* territorial cost but an *indirect* product cost.

The term **overhead costs** is frequently used to describe a body of expenses that cannot be identified solely with individual product lines, territories, or other market segments. Sometimes, overhead costs are referred to as *fixed costs*. However, it is preferable to think of these items as *indirect* rather than fixed expenses. They are fixed only in the sense that they are not *directly* allocable among territories, product lines, or some other group of market segments. The point is that these costs cannot be attached solely to individual market units.

Difficulty of Allocating Costs

A major problem in a marketing cost analysis is that of allocating marketing costs to individual territories, products, or whatever segment of the market is being studied. Actually, the problem of prorating arises at two levels: (1) when accounting ledger expenses are being allocated to activity groups and (2) when the resultant activity costs are apportioned to the separate territories, products, or markets.

A *direct* cost can be allocated in its entirety to the market segment being analyzed. This phase of allocation is reasonably simple. For example, assume that a territorial cost analysis is being made and each salesperson has a territory. Then all of a given rep's expenses—salary, commission, travel, supplies, and so on—can be prorated directly to that rep's territory. Some of the advertising expense, such as the cost of ads in local newspapers and the expense of point-of-purchase advertising materials, can also be charged directly to a given territory.

However, the majority of costs are *common (indirect)* rather than separable, and real allocation problems occur with these expenses. For some costs, the basis of allocation may be the same regardless of the type of analysis made. Billing expenses are often allocated on the basis of number of "invoice lines," whether the cost analysis is by territory, product, or customer group. An invoice line is one item (6 dozen widgets, model 1412, for example) listed on the bill (invoice) sent to a customer. Assume that 22 percent of all invoice lines last year related to orders billed to customers in territory A. Then 22 percent of total billing costs would be allocated to that territory. A cost analysis by product line or customer group would use this same allocation basis—number of invoice lines—when apportioning billing costs.

For other costs, however, the basis of allocation would vary according to whether a firm analyzes its costs by territory, product, or customer group. Consider sales force salaries as an example. In a territorial cost study, these salaries may be allocated directly to the district where the people work. In a product cost analysis, the expense probably is prorated on the proportionate amount of working hours a rep spends with each product. In a cost analysis by customer classes,

Entertaining clients is a direct cost in a territorial cost analysis, but indirect in a product cost analysis.

the salaries may be apportioned in relation to the number of sales calls on each customer group.

Allocating Totally Indirect Costs

The last big allocation problem discussed here concerns costs that are *totally* indirect. Within the broad category of indirect expenses, some costs are *partially* indirect, and some are *totally* indirect. Many expenses do carry some degree of direct relationship to the territory or other marketing unit being analyzed. Order-filling and shipping expenses, for example, are partially indirect costs. They would *decrease* to some extent if a territory or product were eliminated. They would *increase* if new products or territories were added.

However, other cost items, such as sales administrative or general administrative expenses, are *totally* indirect costs. The cost of maintaining the chief sales executive (salary, staff, and office) remains about the same, whether or not the number of territories or products changes.

Many administrators question whether it is reasonably possible to allocate totally indirect costs. Consider, for example, the problem of allocating general sales manager Cruz's expense to territories. Part of the year, Cruz travels in these districts. The costs of transportation, food, and lodging on the road probably can be allocated directly to the territory involved. However, how should Cruz's salary and office expenses be apportioned among sales districts? If Cruz spends a month in territory A and two months in B, then presumably one-twelfth of these expenses may be allocated to A and one-sixth to B. At the same time, this method may be unfair to territory A. During the month's stay in A, Cruz spent much time on the telephone discussing unforeseen difficulties in territory F. Moreover, how would the company apportion the expenses incurred while Cruz is in the home office and not dealing with the affairs of any one particular territory?

Three methods frequently used to allocate indirect costs are shown in Figure 15–6. Each method reflects a different philosophy and each has obvious drawbacks.

FIGURE 15–6

Methods used to allocate indirect costs

Method	Evaluation
Divide cost equally among territories or whatever market segments are being analyzed.	Easy to do, but inaccurate and usually unfair to some market segments.
Allocate costs in proportion to sales volume obtained from each territory (or product or customer group).	Underlying philosophy: apply cost burden where it can best be borne. That is, charge a high-volume market segment with a large share of the indirect cost. This method is simple and easy to do, but may be very inaccurate. Tells very little about a segment's profitability, and may even be misleading.
Allocate indirect costs in same proportion as the total direct costs. Thus if product A accounted for 25 percent of the total *direct* costs, then A would also be charged with 25 percent of the *indirect* expenses.	Again, easy to do but can be inaccurate and misleading. Falsely assumes a close relationship between direct and indirect expenses.

The Contribution-Margin versus Full-Cost Controversy

In a marketing cost analysis, two ways of handling the allocation of indirect expenses are the contribution-margin (also called contribution-to-overhead) method and the full-cost method. A real controversy exists regarding which of these two approaches is the best for managerial control purposes.

In the **contribution-margin method,** only the direct expenses are allocated to each marketing unit (territory, product) being analyzed. These are the costs that presumably would be eliminated if the corresponding marketing unit were eliminated. After deducting these direct costs from the gross margin, the remainder is the amount that unit is contributing to cover total overhead (indirect expenses).

In the **full-cost method,** all expenses—direct and indirect—are allocated among the marketing units under study. By allocating all costs, management is trying to determine the net profit of each territory, product, or other marketing unit.

For any given marketing unit, these two methods may be summarized as follows:

	Contribution-Margin Method		**Full-Cost Method**
	$ Sales		$ Sales
less	Cost of goods sold	*less*	Cost of goods sold
equals	Gross margin	*equals*	Gross margin
less	Direct expenses	*less*	Direct expenses
equals	Contribution margin (the amount available to cover overhead expenses plus a profit)	*less*	Indirect expenses
		equals	Net profit

An example of the contribution-margin method is shown in Figure 15–7. The net sales, cost of goods sold, and gross margin are shown for each of the three geographic regions in the Colorado Ski Company. The direct operating costs of

FIGURE 15–7   Income and expense statement by sales region, Colorado Ski Company, 2002, in $000, using contribution-margin approach

	Total	Eastern	Midwestern	Western
Net sales	$27,000	$9,000	$4,500	$13,500
Less cost of goods sold	18,900	6,300	3,150	9,450
Gross margin	8,100	2,700	1,350	4,050
Less *direct* operating expenses:				
Personal selling	3,082	845	595	1,642
Advertising	732	254	127	351
Warehousing/shipping	160	64	42	54
Order processing	130	43	30	57
Total *direct* expenses	4,104	1,206	794	2,104
Contribution margin	$ 3,996	$1,494	$ 556	$ 1,946
Less *indirect* operating expenses:				
Personal selling	765			
Advertising	488			
Warehousing/shipping	320			
Order processing	110			
Administration	513			
Total *indirect* expenses	$ 2,196			
Net profit	$ 1,800			

the company are allocated among the three regions. These expenses are then deducted from the region's gross margin. The result is each region's contribution to the remaining $2,196,000 of indirect (overhead) costs. The midwestern region, for instance, incurred $794,000 in direct costs and contributed $556,000 to the overhead expenses and net profit. If the company eliminated the midwestern region, presumably management would save $794,000 in direct expenses. However, the region's $556,000 contribution to overhead would then have to be absorbed by the remaining two regions, assuming the indirect costs still totaled $2,196,000. Figure 15–5 illustrated the full-cost approach to cost allocation. Note the situation the Colorado Ski Company faced in its midwestern region. That region showed a contribution margin of $556,000. But using the full-cost method, the region reported a net loss of $24,000, after the indirect expenses were allocated.

There is considerable argument over the relative merits of the contribution-margin and full-cost methods. *Proponents of the full-cost method* contend that the purpose of a marketing cost study is to determine the net profitability of the units being studied. They feel that the contribution-margin approach does not fulfill this purpose. Furthermore, full-cost advocates believe that a contribution-margin analysis may be misleading. A given territory or product may show a contribution to overhead; yet, after the indirect costs are allocated, this product or territory may actually have a net loss (as seen in the midwestern region of the Colorado Ski Company).

Contribution-margin supporters contend that it is not possible to accurately apportion the indirect costs among market segments. Furthermore, items such as administrative costs are not related at all to any single territory or product. Therefore, the unit should not bear any of these costs. These advocates also point out that a full-cost analysis may show that a product or territory has a net loss, whereas this unit may be contributing something to overhead (again, the situation in the midwestern region). Some executives might recommend that the losing region be eliminated. But they overlook the fact that the unit's contribution to overhead would then have to be borne by other units. Under the contribution-margin approach, the company would keep this unit, at least until a better alternative could be found.

An Ethical Dilemma

One of the problems typically encountered in a marketing cost analysis is the difficulty of allocating total indirect cost. These costs include such items as the salaries and office expense of the top sales executives in a firm. In Figure 15–6, we noted some commonly used methods for allocating these expenses.

One such method is to allocate indirect expenses in proportion to the sales volume or gross margin generated in each territory. Assume that a midwestern territory generated $1 million in sales last year and an eastern district's sales were $2 million. Then the eastern territory's allocation of indirect expenses would be twice that of the midwestern unit. The underlying rationale for this expense-allocation basis is that the

cost burden should be placed where it can best be borne. That is, the biggest volume (or gross margin) territories should absorb the largest share of indirect costs.

The salespeople and sales managers in these big territories understandably object to this cost-allocation system. The objections increase especially when the reps' or the district managers' compensation includes a profit-sharing element. Those people also object when their performance evaluations include a review of the district's net profitability.

Is it ethical to allocate indirect expenses to territories on the basis of where these costs can best be carried?

Actually, both approaches have a place in marketing cost analysis. The full-cost method is especially suited for the systematic reporting of historical costs as a basis for future marketing planning. A full-cost analysis is useful when making long-range studies of the profitability of various market segments. This type of analysis can also be helpful when establishing *long-range* policies on product lines, distribution channels, pricing structures, or promotional programs.

The contribution-margin approach is especially useful as an aid to decision making in *short-run* marketing situations. Also, when cost responsibility is directly assignable to particular market segments, management has an effective tool for controlling and evaluating the sales force.

Use of Findings from Profitability Analysis

So far in our discussion of marketing cost analysis, we have dealt generally with the first stage in the evaluation process. That is, we have been finding out *what happened*. Now let's look at some examples of how management might use the combined findings from both sales volume and marketing cost analyses—the profitability analysis.

Territorial Decisions

Once management has completed its volume and cost analyses, it may decide to adjust territorial boundaries to match their current potential. Possibly the district is too small. That is, the potential volume is not adequate to support the expense of covering the territory. Or it may be too large, forcing the salesperson to spend too much time and expense in traveling.

Management may also consider a change in selling methods or channels in an unprofitable area. Possibly mail or telephone selling should be used instead of incurring the expense of personal-selling visits. A company that sells directly to retailers or industrial users may consider using wholesaling intermediaries instead.

A weak territory sometimes can be made profitable by an increase in advertising and sales promotion. Possibly, the salespeople are not getting adequate support. Or competition may have grown so strong that management must be resigned to a smaller market share than formerly.

The problems in poor territories may lie with the activities of the salespeople. They may need closer supervision, or perhaps too large a percentage of their sales comes from low-margin items. They also may simply be poor sales reps.

As a last resort, it may be necessary to abandon a territory entirely, not even using the facilities provided by mail, telephone, or middlemen. Possibly the potential once present no longer exists. However, before dropping a territory from its market, a company should consider the cost repercussions. The territory presumably has carried some share of indirect, inescapable expenses, such as marketing and general administrative costs. If the district is abandoned, these expenses must be absorbed by the remaining areas.

Products

When a cost analysis by products shows significant differences in the profitability of the product line, the executives should determine the reasons for the differences. It may be that these profit variations stem from factors (typical order size or packaging requirements, for example) that are firmly set. That is, management has very little opportunity for profit improvement. On the other hand, many low-profit items often do present opportunities for administrative action. A firm may simplify its line by eliminating some models or colors for which there is little demand. Also, simplification allows the sales force to concentrate on fewer items and probably increases the sales of the remaining products.

Sometimes a product's profitability can be increased by redesigning or repackaging the item. Packaging the product in multiple rather than single units may increase the average order size. This will cut the unit costs of order filling, shipping, and packaging. Another possibility is to alter (increase or decrease) the amount of advertising and other promotional help appropriated for the product. Possibly, a change in sales force compensation is needed (1) to increase the sales of profitable items or (2) to discourage the sales of low-margin goods.

A low-volume item cannot always be dropped from the line. Nor can a company always drop an item even though it shows an irreducible net loss. The product may be necessary to round out a line, and the customers may expect the seller to carry it.

Customer/Size of Order

As suggested in Chapter 14 by the 80–20 principle, some customers are much more important to the firm than other customers. In fact, a **profitability analysis** can reveal that selling to and servicing certain customers actually loses money for the sales organization. Surprisingly, many companies never bother to do such an analysis, and thus have no clue about the relative profitability of their customers.[2]

A key step in this regard is to calculate how much money is spent to get the orders of each customer. A common situation plaguing many companies is the **small-order problem.** That is, often orders are so small that they result in a loss to the company. Many costs such as direct selling or billing are often the same for each order, whether it is for $10 or $10,000. A cost analysis by customer groups is closely related to an analysis by order size. Frequently, a customer class that generates a below-average profit also presents a small-order problem. Sometimes large-volume purchasers build up their volume by giving the seller many

To reduce small-order marketing costs, companies must consider servicing low-volume customers by telephone as opposed to in-person visits.

small individual orders. Management should review both their customer and order-size analyses before making policy decisions in these areas.

Some firms find that certain customers are costing them too much, and thus they end the business relationship.[3] Firing unprofitable customers, however, is not always the right choice. Management first should determine *why* the accounts are unprofitable and *why* the average orders are small, and then consider ways to improve these situations. Several reasons may account for a customer's small orders or unprofitableness. For instance:

- An account buys a large amount in total over a period of a year, but the customer buys in small amounts from several suppliers.

- A company buys a large amount in total and all from one supplier. But this customer purchases frequently, so the average order is small. The increasingly popular just-in-time (JIT) inventory control systems typically involve the frequent delivery of small orders. However, a JIT delivery system is usually a part of a profitable, long-term purchasing commitment. Consequently, both the buyer and seller can benefit from a JIT inventory control strategy.

- An account is small but growing, and a seller caters to it in hope of future benefits.

- A customer is small and, as far as can be projected into the future, will remain small.

There are many practical suggestions for increasing the average size of an order or for reducing the marketing costs of small orders. See Figure 15–8 for examples.

FIGURE 15-8

Ways to increase order size and reduce small-order marketing costs

- Educate customers who buy from several different suppliers. Stress the advantages of purchasing from one supplier.

- For customers who purchase large total quantities in frequent small orders, stress the advantages of ordering once a month instead of once a week. Point out that the buyer eliminates all handling, billing, and accounting expenses connected with three of the four orders. Note further that the buyer writes only one check and one purchase order. In addition, stress that there will be only one bill to process and one shipment to put into inventory instead of three or four.

- Educate the sales force as well as customers. In fact, it may be necessary to change the compensation plan to discourage acceptance of smaller orders.

- Substitute direct mail or telephone selling for sales calls on unprofitable or small-order accounts. Or continue to call on these accounts, but less frequently.

- Shift an account to a wholesaler or some other type of intermediary rather than dealing directly, even by mail or telephone.

- Drop a mass-distribution policy and adopt a selective one. This new policy may actually increase sales because sales reps can spend more time with profitable accounts.

- Establish a minimum order size.

- Establish a minimum charge or a service charge to combat small orders.

Return on Investment—An Evaluation Tool

The concept of **return on investment (ROI)** is another useful managerial aid in evaluating sales performance and in making marketing decisions. The following formula can be used to calculate return on investment:

$$\text{ROI} = \frac{\text{Net profit}}{\text{Sales}} \times \frac{\text{Sales}}{\text{Investment}}$$

The first fraction expresses the rate of profit on sales. The second fraction indicates the number of times the total investment (assets employed) was turned over. By multiplying the investment turnover by the rate of profit on sales, the ROI is determined.

Two questions may quickly come to mind. First, what do we mean by *investment?* Second, why do we need two fractions? It would seem that the sales component in each fraction would cancel out, leaving net profit divided by investment as the meaningful ratio.

To answer the first query, consider a firm whose operating statement shows annual sales of $1 million and a net profit of $50,000. At the end of the year, the balance sheet reports

Assets	$600,000	Liabilities		$200,000
		Capital stock	$300,000	
		Retained earnings	100,000	400,000
			$400,000	$600,000

Now, is the investment $400,000 or $600,000? Certainly the ROI will depend on which figure we use. The answer depends on whether we are talking to the stockholders or to the company executives. The stockholders are more interested in the return on what they have invested—in this case, $400,000. The ROI calculation then is

$$\text{ROI} = \frac{\text{Net profit } \$50,000}{\text{Sales } \$1,000,000} \times \frac{\text{Sales } \$1,000,000}{\text{Investment } \$400,000} = 12.5\%$$

Management, on the other hand, is more concerned with the total investment, as represented by the total assets ($600,000). This is the amount that the executives must manage, regardless of whether the assets were acquired by stockholders' investment, retained earnings, or loans from outside sources. Within this context, the ROI computation becomes:

$$\text{ROI} = \frac{\text{Net profit } \$50,000}{\text{Sales } \$1,000,000} \times \frac{\text{Sales } \$1,000,000}{\text{Investment } \$600,000} = 8.33\%$$

Regarding the second question, we use two fractions because we are dealing with two separate elements—the rate of profit on sales and the rate of capital turnover. Management really should determine each rate separately and then multiply the two. The rate of profit on sales is influenced by marketing considerations—sales volume, price, product mix, advertising effort. The capital turnover is a financial consideration not directly involved with costs or profit—only with sales volume and assets managed.

To illustrate, assume that our company's profit doubled with the same sales volume and investment because management operated an excellent marketing program this year. In effect, we doubled our profit rate with the same capital turnover:

$$\text{ROI} = \frac{\text{Net profit } \$100,000}{\text{Sales } \$1,000,000} \times \frac{\text{Sales } \$1,000,000}{\text{Investment } \$600,000} = 16.66\%$$

$$10\% \quad \times \quad 1.67 \quad = 16.66\%$$

As expected, this 16.66 percent is twice the ROI calculated earlier.

Now assume that we earned our original profit of $50,000 but that we did it with an investment reduced to $500,000. We cut the size of our average inventory and closed some branch offices. By increasing our capital turnover from 1.67 to 2, we raise the ROI from 8 percent to 10 percent, even though sales volume and profits remain unchanged:

$$\text{ROI} = \frac{\$50,000}{\$1,000,000} \times \frac{\$1,000,000}{\$500,000} = 10\%$$

$$5\% \quad \times \quad 2 \quad = 10\%$$

Assume now that we increase our sales volume—let us say we double it—but do not increase our profit or investment. That is, the cost-profit squeeze is bringing us profitless prosperity. The following interesting results occur:

$$\text{ROI} = \frac{\$50,000}{\$2,000,000} \times \frac{\$2,000,000}{\$600,000} = 8\%$$

$$2.5\% \quad \times \quad 3.3 \quad = 8.25\%$$

The profit rate was cut in half, but this was offset by a doubling of the capital-turnover rate, leaving the ROI unchanged.

Use of Return on Assets Managed to Evaluate Field Sales Managers

A variation of the ROI concept is the concept of **return on assets managed (ROAM).** The ROAM concept is particularly useful for evaluating the performance of district sales managers, branch managers, or other managerial segments of a field sales organization. ROAM modifies the factors in the traditional ROI equation to make them appropriate for the organizational segment being analyzed. If management is evaluating sales district performance, for instance, presumably the sales volume in each district is readily available. For the profit figure in the equation, management can determine the contribution margin in each district. That is, from a given district's sales, we deduct the cost of goods sold and all operating expenses directly chargeable to a district. In the "investment" section of the ROI equation, we substitute the assets employed—that is, the "assets managed"—hence the acronym ROAM instead of ROI. In a sales district, the assets managed consist of the average accounts receivable and the inventory carried to serve that district. The net result of these changes is the following equation:

$$\text{ROAM} = \frac{\text{Contribution margin}}{\text{District sales volume}} \times \frac{\text{District sales volume}}{\text{Average accounts receivable} + \text{Inventory}}$$

The usefulness of the ROAM concept as an executive evaluation tool depends on whether the assets in the equation are controllable by the executive being evaluated. If a district sales manager has little or no control over the assets employed in a district, it is not valid to hold the executive accountable for the return earned on those assets. The lack of asset control by individual salespeople is a reason that ROAM should *not* be used to measure the performance of individual reps.

With asset control, however, district sales executives and other field sales managers can improve their ROAM percentage by influencing sales volume, contribution margin, or district asset investment. Thus field sales managers can use the ROAM concept when considering the addition of new customers or products in their districts. In effect, return on assets managed is an analytical tool that facilitates the delegation of profit responsibility to territorial sales managers.[4]

Summary

A marketing cost analysis is a detailed study of a company's distribution costs. It is undertaken to discover which segments (territories, products, customers) of the company's marketing program are profitable and which are not. A marketing cost analysis is a part of a company's evaluation of its marketing performance.

In marketing cost analysis, we need to understand the differences between accounting-ledger costs and activity-category costs. Another useful distinction is the one between direct and indirect expenses. In a marketing cost analysis, one of the major problems is the difficulty of allocating costs. Management must allocate ledger accounts into activity categories. Then each total activity cost must be allocated to the marketing segment (territory, product, customer group) being analyzed. Cost allocation is especially difficult in the case of indirect expenses.

The difficulty of allocating indirect costs leads to the contribution-margin versus full-cost controversy. In the contribution-margin approach to marketing cost analysis, only the direct costs incurred by the marketing unit (territory or product, for example) are allocated to that unit. The unit's gross margin minus its direct costs equals the amount the unit contributes to pay the company's overhead (indirect expense). In the full-cost approach, all costs (direct and indirect) are allocated to the various marketing units being studied. In this way, management tries to determine the unit's net profit.

The company's marketing costs can be analyzed in three ways. One way is to analyze the costs as they appear in the accounting ledgers and on the company's income and expense (profit-and-loss) statement. A second approach is to analyze the marketing costs after they have been allocated to activity categories. The third type occurs after each activity cost has been allocated to the sales territories, products, or other marketing units being studied.

The types of analyses we have summarized tell management *what happened*. Then the executives must try to determine *why* these results occurred. Finally, management must decide *what changes* are needed in the marketing program to correct the misdirected effort.

A marketing cost analysis can be especially useful in identifying and remedying the small-order problem that occurs in so many firms.

Return on investment (ROI) is another tool that management can use in evaluating sales performance and in making marketing decisions. A variation of the ROI concept is ROAM, return on assets managed. The ROAM concept is especially useful for evaluating the performance of field sales managers.

Key Terms

Contribution-margin method
Direct costs
Full-cost method
Indirect costs

Overhead costs
Profitability analysis
Return on assets managed
(ROAM)

Return on investment (ROI)
Small-order problem

Questions and Problems

1. Explain the similarities and differences between marketing cost analysis and production cost accounting.

2. Is an analysis of expenses as recorded in a company's accounting ledgers better than no cost analysis at all? What specific policies or operating plans may stem from an analysis of ledger expenses alone?

3. A national manufacturer of roofing and siding materials has 40 salespeople. Each has his or her own territory and sells all three of the firm's product lines. They sell primarily to wholesalers and large retailers in the lumber and building materials field. The company wants to make a *territorial analysis* of marketing costs. What bases do you recommend it should use to allocate among the territories each of the following costs?
   a) Sales force salaries.
   b) Sales force travel expenses.
   c) Sales force commissions paid on gross margin.
   d) Salaries and expenses of three regional sales managers.
   e) Sales training expenses.
   f) Television advertising (local and national).
   g) Newspaper advertising.
   h) Billing.
   i) Shipping from three regional factories.
   j) Marketing research.
   k) General sales manager's salary and office expenses.
   l) Advertising overhead.

4. The company in the preceding problem wants to analyze its marketing cost by *product lines*. Suggest appropriate bases for allocating the above-listed cost items to the three product groups.

5. What supporting points could be brought out by the proponents of each side in the full-cost

versus contribution-margin controversy over allocation of indirect marketing costs? Which of the two concepts do you advocate? Why?

6. In an analysis of expenses grouped by activities, a manufacturer noted that last year the firm's direct selling expenses (sales force compensation, travel expenses, branch office expenses, etc.) increased significantly over the preceding year. Is this trend necessarily an indication of weaknesses in the management of the sales force?

7. Each of the following firms made a territorial cost analysis and discovered it had some districts that were showing a net loss. What actions involving the sales force do you recommend each company take to improve its situation?
   a) Hardware wholesaler, covering six southeastern states.
   b) Paint and varnish manufacturer.
   c) National business machines manufacturer.

8. What actions involving its sales force can each of the following firms take if they discover unprofitable products in their lines?
   a) Distributor of electrical goods.
   b) Flower seed producer.
   c) Manufacturer of small power tools.

9. "Large-annual-volume customers never present a small-order problem, while low-annual-volume customers always create small-order problems." Do you agree?

10. To determine return on investment, we multiply two fractions: net profit/sales and sales/investment. Why can't we cancel out the sales factor in each fraction and simply divide net profit by investment?

11. Explain how the ROAM concept may be used to evaluate the profit performance of a territorial sales manager.

Experiential Exercises

A. Call sales managers from 10 different companies. Ask them how the performance of their sales districts are evaluated; that is, ask what measures—such as total sales, gross profit margin, ROI, or ROAM—are used.

B. Call sales managers from three companies to determine the process by which they develop their sales budget (sales and selling expenses).

Internet Exercise

A. A company's website can be used as a strategic tool to increase order size and, thus, reduce small-order problems. Search the websites of several companies and explain how this is done. Start with the following sites and programs: American Airlines (http://aa.com) and AAdvantage; Dell Computer (http://dell.com) and Premier Customers; and Sun Microsystems (http://sun.com) and My Sun.

References

1. For an excellent report on the usefulness and effectiveness of analyzing expenses by activity groupings, see Thomas H. Stevenson, Frank C. Barnes, and Sharon A. Stevenson, "Activity-Based Costing: An Emerging Tool for Industrial Marketing Decision Makers," *Journal of Business & Industrial Marketing* 8, no. 2 (1993), pp. 40–52.

2. Erika Rasmusson, "Wanted: Profitable Customers," *Sales & Marketing Management*, May 1999, pp. 28–34.

3. Paul Smith, "Only Some Customers Are King," *New Zealand Management*, April 2000, pp. 24–26.

4. For a discussion of the limitations of the ROAM concept that may influence its applicability and a proposal for an alternative evaluation tool, see William L. Cron and Michael Levy, "Sales Management Performance Evaluation: A Residual Income Perspective," *Journal of Personal Selling & Sales Management*, August 1987, pp. 57–66.

CASE 15-1   SEAL RITE ENVELOPE COMPANY (B)

Profitability Analysis

As Rose Douglas, Seal Rite Envelope Company's sales manager, scanned a computer printout of a profitability analysis of the company's customers, she had in mind that a previous analysis had indicated that the firm's direct selling costs per call were $110 for the company's $22 million sales volume in 2002. Since the firm's average gross margin was about 25 percent, the sales reps had to get an average order of $440 for each sales call they made. Even then, a $440 average order just covered the direct selling expenses. That still left the overhead expenses uncovered. She could quickly see from the data in front of her that she had some problems.

Wanting more data on the profitability of customers by their size, she turned to the computer on her desk and extracted the information shown in Table 15–1A from the firm's customer database. She did not like what she saw. She recalled a lecture in college given by an old marketing professor who loved to talk about misdirected marketing efforts. At the time she thought that he was hopelessly out of date. No firm in modern times could possibly allow such situations to develop. Now she wished she had paid more attention to the lecture, for she suspected that she had a problem with just such misdirected marketing efforts.

Questions:

1. What problems are indicated from the data in Table 15–1A?

2. What should Rose Douglas do about those problems?

TABLE 15-1A   Seal Rite Envelope Company, 2002

Annual Customer Volume ($000)	Number of Accounts	Number of Calls	Sales (% of total)	Gross Profit (% of sales)	Selling Expense (% of sales)	Operating Profit (% of sales)
$200	4	256	10.9	15.9	4.0	11.9
$100–$200	4	274	2.9	23.6	9.5	14.1
$50–$99.9	32	1,344	11.7	19.8	10.2	9.6
$40–$49.9	24	1,011	5.4	18.4	10.2	8.2
$30–$39.9	25	1,158	4.0	21.8	9.6	12.2
$20–$29.9	63	3,114	8.5	22.8	10.9	11.9
$10–$19.9	157	4,725	13.2	23.9	13.4	10.5
$5–$9.9	349	7,021	15.7	25.9	16.8	9.1
$4–$4.9	235	2,639	5.0	29.0	19.3	10.3
$3–$3.9	309	3,233	5.2	31.6	21.9	9.7
$2–$2.9	569	4,212	7.1	31.2	25.3	5.9
$1–$1.9	842	6,360	6.9	30.4	34.3	−3.6
$1	871	6,345	3.5	30.9	75.3	−44.4
No sales	688	2,001	0.0	0.0	0.0	0.0
Total or average	4,172	43,693	100	25.0	20.1	5.0

16

Evaluating a Salesperson's Performance

Why should our endeavour be so loved, and the performance so loathed?

—William Shakespeare—

One of the most critical responsibilities for sales managers is to regularly evaluate the performance of their salespeople. In short, evaluation of salespeople identifies their strengths and weaknesses in order to improve their performance. This is important for the entire organization because improving sales performance has a direct, immediate impact on the company's bottom line.

It is not, however, easy. Performance evaluation is a time-consuming and sometimes unpleasant activity. Especially difficult is dealing with low-performing reps who must be told how and why their performance is unacceptable. To do this well, the manager must put into practice many of the processes that we have discussed in various chapters of this book—including training, motivation, and leadership.

Many organizations are unhappy with their system of evaluating performance.[1] Sales managers frequently make evaluations that are too general and too subjective. Such evaluations may be based on personal observation, managers' attitudes, or a global measure of performance, such as total sales. The problem with these measures is that they do not pinpoint strengths and weaknesses. The evaluation should be detailed enough to give salespeople specific feedback that helps guide and develop them toward their full potential.

This chapter presents the methods and measures that sales managers should use to systematically and objectively assess the performance of their individual salespeople. After examining the nature and purposes of this managerial activity, we outline a complete program for evaluating sales performance. The last section of the chapter is a case example of how one sales manager interpreted the performance data he assembled.

Nature and Importance of Performance Evaluation

Appraising a salesperson's performance is a part of the managerial function of evaluation. It is part of a marketing audit. Management compares the results of a person's efforts with the goals set for that person. The purpose is to determine what happened in the past and to use this information to improve performance in the future either by taking corrective actions or by rewarding good performance. The evaluation system also is one of the means by which managers *direct* the activities of their salespeople.

Concept of Evaluation and Development

Evaluation has an added dimension when viewed from the perspective of evaluation and *development* of individual salespeople. Within this wider context, management engages in a counseling activity rather than in a cold statistical analysis. Certainly management wants to measure past performance against standards to identify strengths and weaknesses in the firm's marketing system, particularly as a basis for planning. But this activity is optimized only if it is also brought to the personal level of the salesperson. It should serve as a basis for the person's self-development and as a basis for a sound company program to guide and develop the personnel.

Concept of Evaluation and Direction

If salespeople are aware of the criteria by which they will be evaluated, they will try to do things to improve their performance on these criteria. For example, if one of the goals of the company's strategy is to improve customer satisfaction, then this goal should be included in the evaluation process. This will serve to *direct* the efforts of the reps toward this goal. If the reps are aware that customer satisfaction will be an important dimension of their evaluation, then they will try to improve their customers' satisfaction.

Importance of Performance Evaluation

A good performance review can be a major aid in other sales force management tasks. Promotions and pay increases can be based on objective performance data rather than on favoritism, subjective observations, or opinions. Weaknesses in field-selling efforts, once identified, may be forestalled by incorporating corrective measures in training programs. On the other hand, management can identify the sales techniques of the outstanding performers with an eye toward having other salespeople adopt them. Performance evaluations may also uncover the need for improvements in the compensation plan. For instance, the existing plan may focus too much effort on low-margin items or too little attention on non-selling (missionary) activities.

Performance analysis especially helps in sales supervision. It is difficult to effectively supervise someone without knowing what the person is doing correctly or incorrectly, and why. If a rep's sales volume is unsatisfactory, for instance, a performance review will show it. Moreover, the evaluation may help identify the cause—whether the rep has a low daily call rate, does not work enough days per month, calls on the wrong prospects, has trouble with the sales presentation, and so on.

An effective procedure for appraising the work of an individual can also help morale. Any person who knows what he or she is expected to do and has some benchmarks for measuring accomplishments feels more secure. A performance evaluation should ensure that reps who deserve favorable recognition receive it, and those who deserve criticism are handled appropriately. The salesperson with the highest sales volume is not necessarily the best one and may not even be doing a good all-around job. To reward this person on the basis of sales volume alone can hurt the morale of others in the sales force. Similarly, morale suffers if management criticizes a rep for low volume when the contributing factor was low territorial potential or unusually stiff competition. A performance-appraisal system should forestall and help correct such situations.

By evaluating the salespeople's achievements, management helps them discover their own strengths and weaknesses. This should motivate them to raise their levels of performance. Like most people, sales reps seldom can make an effective self-evaluation. They may know they are doing something wrong if their output is low, but they may be unable to determine the reasons for this poor productivity.

Difficulties Involved in Evaluating Performance

Many duties assigned to salespeople cannot be measured objectively, and some tasks are difficult to evaluate even on a subjective basis. A manufacturer's representative is supposed to service the firm's accounts; a wholesaler's sales rep is told to avoid high-pressure selling; all salespeople are supposed to build goodwill with customers. Even with close field supervision of the sales force, these tasks can be evaluated only subjectively. And, if management does not closely supervise the salespeople in the field, it may be virtually impossible to measure results from some of these duties.

By the same token, however, many tasks of a seemingly subjective nature can actually be quantified. A salesperson's tendency to pressure or oversell customers, for instance, might be measured by tallying canceled orders, lost accounts, and reorders.

The wide variety of conditions sales reps work under makes it difficult for management to compare their productivity. There is no satisfactory method for equating territorial differences in potential, competition, or working conditions. It is difficult to compare the performance of city salespeople with rural salespeople, for example. Even if the districts are equal in potential, they are not comparable in other ways.

Sometimes performance evaluation is difficult because the results of a salesperson's efforts may not be evident for some time. A district's improved position may show up only after a rep has been working there for a year or more. Furthermore, when two or more people are involved in making a sale or in servicing a customer, it usually is difficult to give individual credit for results.

Technology and Performance Appraisal

Mack W. Sorrells Company, Inc., uses a sales force automation (SFA) and customer relationship marketing (CRM) system to help manage its sales force, which represents manufacturers in the metalworking and woodworking industries. Reps spend about 20 minutes per day inputting their activities and sales numbers. The system then aggregates all information from all reps in a central database.

"[T]he latest information is always available to the sales team, whether they are in the office or on the road," says Sorrells's company president in describing a key benefit of this high-tech system. As explained in previous chapters, reps can readily access this infor-

mation for on-the-spot analysis and evaluation of customer problems.

Of course, sale managers also can readily access this information, which they in turn use to provide analysis and evaluation of the performance of the sales rep. SFA/CRM systems allow for easy tracking and managing of both input and output measures. By reviewing reps' activity logs, for example, managers can offer specific feedback and support to help guide their sales force in the right direction. Yet another way in which technology impacts sales!

Source: Anonymous, "A Successful Sales Force Automation Switch," *Agency Sales*, March 2002, pp. 30–31.

Importance of a Good Job Description

In the task of sales force evaluation, as we have seen for so many other sales force management activities, a good job description is critical. Evaluators must work from the reference point of a statement about *what* a salesperson is supposed to do. Otherwise, they are not in a good position to determine *whether* or *how effectively* the job was done.

Program for Evaluating Performance

This section suggests a five-step procedural system for evaluating sales force performance (see Figure 16–1). The program is complete, but it is also expensive and time-consuming.

Establish Some Basic Policies

Step 1: Preliminary to the actual evaluation, management should set some ground rules. One question that calls for a decision is: Who will participate in the evaluation? Several executives normally are involved. One of the most likely is the salesperson's immediate superior—perhaps a field supervisor, a district manager, or a branch manager. The boss of the immediate supervisor is also likely to be involved. Over 25 percent of companies today use an employee assessment known as 360-degree feedback, which is especially effective in team environments.[2] This technique involves getting evaluative feedback from an employee's peers, subordinates, and clients, as well as superiors.

FIGURE 16–1   Procedure for evaluating salespeople

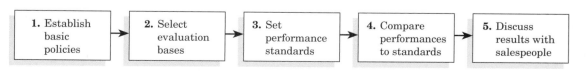

Certainly, the salesperson being evaluated should participate actively, usually with some form of self-evaluation. Involving salespeople in the development of their objectives creates a greater sense of responsibility and commitment on the part of the salespeople. In some firms, the manager and salesperson identify and negotiate specific goals for the upcoming period. Then the rep and manager sign a performance agreement that specifies these goals as the performance standards. This ensures that there will be no misunderstandings about what is expected. This process is often called **management by objectives.**

Another policy decision concerns the frequency of evaluation. While many companies conduct complete performance evaluations only once a year, some prefer that evaluations take place more frequently—quarterly, monthly, or even weekly. Synygy Inc., a software company, makes a point to have dozens of performance reviews with its salespeople every year. According to Synygy's vice president of sales, "If you don't communicate frequently, they don't know where they stand, or how well they're doing on performance improvement."[3] Although the time and costs required to conduct more frequent evaluations must be balanced against the benefits, the improvements in performance generally outweigh the costs.

Select Bases for Evaluation

Step 2: One key to a successful evaluation program is to appraise a sales rep's performance on as many different bases as possible. To do otherwise is to run the risk of being misled. Let's assume that we are rating a sales rep, Ryan, on the basis of the ratio of selling expenses to sales volume. If this percentage is very low compared to the average for the entire sales force, Ryan probably will be commended. Yet Ryan actually may have achieved that low ratio by failing to prospect for new accounts or by otherwise covering the territory inadequately. Knowing the average number of daily calls Ryan made, even in relation to the average call rate for the entire sales force, does not help us very much. By measuring Ryan's ratio of orders per call (batting average) we learn a little more, but we still can be misled. Each additional piece of information—sales volume, plus average order size, plus presentation quality, and so on—helps give a clearer picture of Ryan's performance.

When selecting the bases on which to evaluate salespeople, it is important to remember that the evaluation serves two purposes. One is to recognize and reward people for a job well done; the other is to develop a clear understanding of the salesperson's performance in order to help him or her improve. Salespeople are more likely to respond to and learn from the evaluation when they perceive it to be fair. Consequently, it is important for sales managers to clearly communicate the bases on which salespeople will be evaluated. Some even feel that salespeople should be involved in selecting the bases. Studies show that when salespeople buy into the evaluation process, their satisfaction toward all aspects of the job tends to be higher.[4]

Bases of evaluation fall into two general categories: output measures and input measures. Both types of measures should be used to get a complete picture of the salesperson's performance.

Output Measures

Output measures relate to the salesperson's results—sales volume, gross margin, number of orders, and so on. A list of some output factors ordinarily used as

FIGURE 16-2

Output factors used as evaluation bases

- Sales volume
  a) In dollars and in units
  b) By products and customers (or customer groups)
  c) By mail, telephone, and personal sales calls
- Sales volume as a percentage of:
  a) Quota
  b) Market potential (i.e., market share)
- Gross margin by product line, customer group, and order size
- Orders
  a) Number of orders
  b) Average size (dollar volume) of order
  c) Batting average (orders ÷ calls)
  d) Number of canceled orders
- Accounts
  a) Percentage of accounts sold
  b) Number of new accounts
  c) Number of lost accounts
  d) Number of accounts with overdue payment

evaluation bases is shown in Figure 16–2. These measures are often used to make some meaningful comparisons. One rep may be compared to another, performance this year may be compared to performance for last year, performance may be compared to a goal or target, the rep's share of the market may be compared to that of competitors, and so on.

Each of these measures can be further broken down by type of product, customer type, or channel of distribution, and similar comparisons can be made. Breaking the information down by various subcategories may provide some insights into the rep's performance that would otherwise be overlooked. If the salesperson's performance is below average, it may be that the problem can be isolated to one type of selling situation or to one category of product. If a manager can pinpoint the cause of a performance problem, it becomes much easier to find a solution to alleviate that problem.

All of the output bases are *quantitative* measures. To a large extent, the use of these quantitative measures minimizes the subjectivity and biases of the evaluator. Quantitative properties are also relatively easy to measure. However, since they consider results *only*, these measures may not provide an equitable base on which to compare the performance of one salesperson to another.

Problem of Data Comparability

Ideally, a salesperson should be judged only on factors he or she can control. Management should identify the uncontrollable factors and take them into consideration when appraising an individual's performance.

The sales potential in a territory, especially in relation to size and number of customers, is a good example of an uncontrollable factor. The greater sales potential in one territory versus another may make it easier for the rep in the first territory to reach his or her goals while the rep in the second territory struggles to meet the same goals. Differences in competitive activity or physical conditions among territories must also be considered when comparing performances. Usually, there are territorial variations in the amount of advertising, sales promotional support, or home-office technical service available to customers. These and several other factors make it difficult to compare performance data. This is one of the reasons for considering information on inputs or efforts as well as results.

Input Measures

Two types of **input measures** are used in the evaluation process. The *quantitative* measures focus on the salesperson's efforts or activities. The number of calls a salesperson makes in a day and the number of e-mails sent to prospects are examples of quantitative input measures. Figure 16–3 lists the more commonly used factors. Tracking these factors is considered so important by Bell South Cellular that 25 percent of its sales managers' quarterly bonus is based on how closely they monitor their reps' activities.[5]

The second group of input measures is the *qualitative* factors. These factors measure such things as the quality of the sales rep's presentation, product knowledge, customer relations, and the salesperson's attitude. Figure 16–4 lists other qualitative factors that are often used in the evaluation process.

FIGURE 16-3

Quantitative input factors used as evaluation bases

- Calls per day (call rate)
- Days worked
- Selling time versus nonselling time
- Direct selling expense
  - a) In total
  - b) As percentage of sales volume
  - c) As percentage of quota
- Nonselling activities
  - a) Advertising displays set up
  - b) E-mails/letters written to prospects
  - c) Telephone calls made to prospects
  - d) Number of meetings held with dealers and/or distributors
  - e) Number of service calls made
  - f) Collections made
  - g) Number of customer complaints received

FIGURE 16-4

Qualitative input factors used as evaluation bases

- Personal efforts of the sales reps
  - a) Management of their time
  - b) Planning and preparation for calls
  - c) Quality of sales presentations
  - d) Ability to handle objections and to close sales
- Knowledge
  - a) Product
  - b) Company and company policies
  - c) Competitor's products and strategies
  - d) Customers
- Customer relations
- Personal appearance and health
- Personality and attitudinal factors
  - a) Cooperativeness
  - b) Resourcefulness
  - c) Acceptance of responsibility
  - d) Ability to analyze logically and make decisions

The number of e-mails sent to customers is a quantitative input factor that might be used as a base of evaluation.

Both the quantitative and the qualitative input factors are based on behaviors that are usually under the salesperson's control. Therefore, they are less subject to criticisms concerning inequities among the reps. But the most important value in using these measures is that they are usually critical in locating trouble spots. Assume that a salesperson's output performance (average order size, gross margin, and so on) is unsatisfactory. Very often the cause lies in the certain behaviors over which the rep has control.

Research has demonstrated that an evaluation system that emphasizes behaviors more than outcomes has a number of positive effects on the salesperson's overall performance.[6] For example, the more behavior-based the evaluation system, the more the salesperson is willing to cooperate as part of the sales team and the more the salesperson is committed to the organization. With such a system, the salesperson places a greater emphasis on implementing adaptive strategies. However, it has also been shown that evaluation systems that measure both inputs and outputs lead to higher sales and profits.[7]

Ratio Measures

Most of the quantitative measures discussed above can be combined to create **ratio measures** that can be used for evaluative and comparative purposes. Orders/calls, expenses/sales, and sales/orders are some of the more common ratios managers use to evaluate and compare the performance of salespeople.

A quantitative evaluation of a sales rep's performance can involve the following equations:

$$\text{Sales} = \text{Days worked} \times \frac{\text{Calls}}{\text{Days worked}} \times \frac{\text{Orders}}{\text{Calls}} \times \frac{\text{Sales}}{\text{Orders}}$$

$$\text{Sales} = \text{Days worked} \times \text{Call rate} \times \text{Batting average} \times \text{Average order}$$

If the sales volume for a representative is unsatisfactory, the basic cause must rest in one or more of these four factors. An analysis such as that done in Figure 16–6 on pages 457–58 can help focus the manager's attention on the trouble spot so that additional detailed investigation can pinpoint the rep's exact difficulties.

Sources of Information

When choosing factors to use as bases for a performance evaluation, management should select only those for which data are available at a reasonable cost. The four main sources of information are company records, the sales reps themselves, field sales managers, and customers.

Company records are the main source for data on most of the quantitative *output* factors. By studying sales invoices, customers' orders, and accounting records, management can discover much about a sales rep's volume, gross margin, average order size, and so on. Most firms fail to make optimum use of their records for evaluation purposes. In the past, the information often was not recorded in usable form for a performance evaluation. Firms found it was too expensive and time-consuming to tabulate and present the data in usable form. However, most companies today use computers in collecting, analyzing, and reporting data in a form useful for evaluation.

Reports submitted by the sales force are an important source of information, particularly for performance *input* factors. The regular use of call reports, activity reports, and expense reports can provide the necessary data on the salespeople's work. The Achilles' heel in using sales reps' reports for evaluation is that the information is only as good as the accuracy, completeness, and punctuality of the reps' reporting efforts. This is often a serious problem.

As a rule, sales supervisors and other sales executives regularly travel with the sales reps in the field. The managers observe the reps during sales calls on customers. This allows executives to make a firsthand appraisal of a salesperson's performance with customers.

Customers can be used as a source of evaluation information in one of two ways. The more common method is to gather information submitted by customers on a voluntary, informal basis. Unfortunately, this usually takes the form of complaints, because customers rarely report commendatory performance by sales reps. Increasingly companies are actively soliciting opinions from customers on a regular basis. Some companies ask their customers such questions as *How well does the salesperson analyze your needs?* and *How well does the salesperson build trust?* The customer is certainly in the best position to answer these kinds of questions.[8] However, some firms don't use customers as a source of data. They feel that customers often give excessively good reviews to protect the salespeople they like.[9]

Set Performance Standards

Step 3: Setting standards is one of the most difficult phases of performance evaluation. The standards serve as a benchmark, or a par for the course, against which a sales rep's performance can be measured. Also, standards let a salesperson know what is expected, and they serve as a guide in planning work. Standards must be equitable and reasonable; otherwise, salespeople may lose interest in their work and confidence in management, and morale may decline. If the standards are too high or too low, using them to evaluate performance will be worthless or even harmful.

Standards for many of the output (results) factors can be tied to company goals for territories, product lines, or customer groups. Such performance measures as sales volume, gross margin, or market share probably have already been set.

It is more difficult to set performance standards for the effort (input) factors. A careful time-and-duty analysis of sales jobs should give management some basis for determining satisfactory performance for daily call rates, displays arranged, and other factors. Another approach is to use executive judgment based on the personal observations of those who work with the salespeople in the field.

To measure the efficiency of a company's selling effort, management must balance the output against the input. Consequently, a firm should develop standards for such output/input ratios as sales volume/calls, orders/calls, gross margin/order, and sales volume/expenses.

Once the standards have been set, it is critical that these standards be communicated to the salespeople. Even if the salespeople were involved in establishing the standards, they should be formally communicated to the rep. This ensures that there are no misunderstandings about the benchmarks against which the rep's performance will be judged.

Compare Performance with Standards

Step 4: The accumulated information must be interpreted. This step involves comparing an individual's performance—both efforts and results—with the predetermined standards.

Interpreting Quantitative Data

Some factors ordinarily used as bases for performance appraisal were shown in Figures 16–2 and 16–3. The following discussion shows how these factors can be used with the performance standards in step 3 to evaluate a rep's performance.

Sales Volume and Market Share. The first criterion most sales managers use to judge the relative performance of salespeople is their **sales volume.** Some executives believe that the rep who sells the most merchandise is the best salesperson, regardless of other considerations. Unfortunately, sales volume alone may be a poor indicator of a rep's worth because it tells the firm nothing about the rep's contribution to profit or customer relations.

Sales volume can be a useful indicator of performance, however, if it is analyzed in sufficient detail and with discretion. For evaluation purposes, a rep's total volume may be studied by product line, by some form of customer grouping, or by order size. Even then, the volume figures are not very meaningful unless they can be related to some predetermined standard of acceptable performance, volume quota for each product line or customer group, for example.

A DAY-TO-DAY OPERATING PROBLEM

MAJESTIC PLASTICS COMPANY

MAJESTIC
Plastics Company

A Sales Rep Objects to Her Evaluation

In December each year Clyde Brion compiled information from the firm's sales analysis files on each sales rep, added to it qualitative or subjective information he had about the person's performance, and wrote a letter to each rep summarizing how well the rep had done during the year and what that rep should endeavor to do during the coming year.

It was not one of Brion's favorite jobs, but the company's top management was committed to formal evaluation programs. He knew there would be repercussions from his letter to Margaret Badger, a Los Angeles area sales rep. Neither her numbers nor Brion's observation of her performance would allow her much praise. He was considering how to replace her but was constrained because of company policies.

About 32 seconds after opening Brion's evaluation letter, Margaret Badger phoned him angrily.

"This is a bunch of garbage you cooked up to justify getting rid of me. If you want to fire me, then do it, but don't insult my intelligence by expecting me to buy this rubbish!" Badger challenged.

"I rather expected that you would be coming in to see me. Let's sit down and go over the items you disagree with one by one. We do have excellent records and statistics on what you have done and sold in comparison with the other sales reps," Brion said calmly.

"I'm not talking numbers. I know the numbers stink and I'm not happy about them either. I am talking about comparing noncomparables. It is patently unfair to compare me with the other sales reps. Being the new kid on the block, I was handed a bad territory. Why was it open? The guy in it before me told me why he quit, and I am fighting the same lack of potential and competitive conditions," Badger said.

Brion was well aware that one particular competitor was extremely aggressive because its plant was located there. Stalling for time, he asked, "What do you want me to do?"

"I want some understanding of my situation and consideration in my treatment. This evaluation in my file is the kiss of death for any future here. It says I stink. It says I can't plan my work or penetrate the market. It says I can't sell. And that isn't so!" Badger fumed.

Questions

1. What should Clyde Brion say and/or do in response to Margaret Badger's request?
2. What changes in the evaluation procedure might help?

Note: See the introduction to this series of problems in Chapter 4 for the necessary background on the company, its market, and its competition.

Another important evaluation factor is the salesperson's **market share.** Firms compute this figure by dividing the rep's sales volume by the territorial market potential. Here again the data are more useful if share of market can be determined for each product line or customer group.

Management must be cautious when comparing market-share performance of one person with another. Sales rep A may get 20 percent of the market in his district, while sales rep B captures only 10 percent of her market. Yet B may be doing a better job. Competition may be far more severe in B's district. Or the company may be giving A considerably more advertising support.

Gross Profit. In most firms, a sales manager is (or should be) more concerned with the amount of **gross profit** the salespeople generate than with their dollar sales volume. Gross margin in dollars is a much better measure of a salesperson's effectiveness because it gives some indication of the rep's ability to sell high-margin items. Since the prime objective of most businesses is to earn a targeted return on investment, a person's direct contribution to profit is a logical yardstick for evaluating performance.

Management can reflect its gross margin goals by setting volume quotas for each product line. In this way, the company can motivate the sales force to achieve a desirable balance of sales among the various lines. Then, even though the reps are later evaluated on the basis of sales volume, this evaluation will automatically include gross margin considerations.

As an evaluative yardstick, gross margin has some limitations, however. When management ignores selling expenses, there is no way of knowing how much it costs to generate gross margin. Thus, sales rep A may have a higher dollar gross margin than sales rep B. But A's selling expenses may be proportionately so much higher than B's that A actually shows a lower contribution margin. Furthermore, a salesperson does not fully control the product mix represented in his or her total sales volume. Territorial market potential and intensity of competition vary from one district to another, and these factors can influence the sales of the various product lines.

Number and Size of Orders. Another performance measure combines the **number of orders** and the **size of orders** obtained by each sales rep. The average sale is computed by dividing a rep's total number of orders into his or her total sales volume. This calculation may be made for each class of customer to determine how the rep's average order varies among them. This analysis discloses which reps are getting too many small, unprofitable orders, even though their total volume appears satisfactory because of a few large orders. The analysis also may show that some reps find it difficult to obtain orders from certain classes of customers but make up for this deficiency by superior performance with their other accounts.

Call Rate. A key factor in sales performance is the **call rate**—the number of calls made per day. A salesperson ordinarily cannot sell merchandise without calling on customers; generally, the more calls, the more sales. Sales rep A makes three calls a day, but the company average is four for sales reps who work under reasonably comparable conditions. If management can raise A's call rate up to the company average of four, his sales should increase about 33 percent.

For evaluation purposes, a salesperson's daily (or weekly) call rate can be measured against the company average or some other predetermined standard. Discretion must be exercised in interpreting a rep's call rate, however. Call rates are influenced by the number of miles reps must travel and by the number of customers per square mile in the territory.

Usually, in a given business a certain desired call rate yields the best results. If the rep falls below this rate, sales decline because the rep is not seeing enough prospects. If the rep calls on too many prospects, sales may also decline, since he or she probably does not spend sufficient time with each one to get the job done.

Batting Average. A salesperson's **batting average** is calculated by dividing the number of orders received by the number of calls made (*O/C*). The number of calls made is equivalent to times at bat; the number of orders written is equivalent to the hits made. As a performance index, the batting average discloses ability to locate and call on good prospects and ability to close a sale. A salesperson's batting average should be computed for each class of customers called on. Often, a rep varies in ability to close a sale with different types of customers.

Analysis of the call rate in relation to the order rate can be quite meaningful. If the call rate is above average but the number of orders is below normal, perhaps the rep does not spend enough time with each customer. Or suppose the call rate and batting average are both above standard but the average order is small. Then a field supervisor may work with the salesperson to show the rep how to make fewer but more productive calls. The idea here is to raise the size of the average order by spending more time and talking about more products with each account.

Direct-Selling Expenses. Direct-selling expense is the sum of travel expenses, other business expenses, and compensation (salary, commission, bonus) for each salesperson. These total expenses may be expressed as a percentage of sales. Also, the expense-to-sales ratios for the various salespeople can be compared. Or management can compute the cost per call for each salesperson by dividing total expenses by the number of calls made.

In a performance evaluation, these various cost indexes may indicate the relative efficiency of the salespeople in the field. However, management must interpret these ratios carefully and in detail. An expense-to-sales ratio, for instance, may be above average because the salesperson (1) is doing a poor job, (2) is working in a marginal territory, (3) is working in a new territory doing a lot of prospecting and building a solid base for the future, or (4) is working a territory that covers far more square miles than the average district. A rep with a low batting average usually has a high cost per order. Similarly, the one who makes few calls per day has a high ratio of costs per call.

Routing Efficiency. Dividing the miles traveled by the number of calls made gives the average miles per call. This figure either indicates the density of the sales rep's territory or measures **routing efficiency.** If a group of salespeople all have approximately the same size and density of territories, then miles per call is a significant figure for indicating each one's routing efficiency. Suppose five salespeople selling for an office machines firm in a metropolitan area vary considerably in the number of miles traveled per call. Then the sales manager may have reason to control the routing of those who are out of line.

Evaluating Qualitative Factors

When the evaluation is based on qualitative factors, the personal, subjective element comes into full play. This can be good or bad. With qualitative measures, sales managers can give considerable weight to factors not easy to capture quantitatively. These factors include, for example, civic virtue, sportsmanship, and other citizenship behaviors that are not part of the formal evaluation process.[10] Because these are important behaviors for the sales force, the sales manager is not wrong to take them into account. So in certain cases, some might argue that qualitative measures of performance are better at capturing all aspects of a salesperson's performance.

In other situations, subjective evaluations are less accurate than quantitative assessments. Problems can stem from either the manager's personal bias or the type of evaluation form used. There is an almost limitless variety of evaluation forms. Often each manager develops whatever form seems appropriate for the situation. Most such subjective forms suffer from three major defects.

First is the **halo effect.** Evaluators may be biased by a generalized overall impression or image of the person they are evaluating. If the manager does not like the way a rep dresses, for instance, that attitude may bias all aspects of the manager's evaluation. Similarly, the manager who is impressed with a person's sales ability is also likely to rate other aspects of the person's performance highly.

Second, some rating forms generally overvalue inconsequential factors and undervalue truly important ones. The sales manager should be interested in the salesperson's ability to make money for the firm, not whether the individual is socially adept or impressively dressed. In evaluations, it is essential for the manager to keep in mind what is important and what is not. Often when a former employee files a legal case involving discrimination in hiring, firing, and promotion, the key point is that the manager based evaluations on unimportant factors.

Third, most subjective evaluation forms force the evaluator to make judgments on some factors without a valid basis for doing so. Lacking valid information on the factor, the evaluator allows the halo effect to take over.

In addition, firms face two even more serious problems. First, many raters refuse to give poor ratings to reps who deserve them because of fear of reprisal. As one executive put it, "Who knows what the future holds? The person I downgrade today may be my boss tomorrow." Such managers fail to see any personal advantage in giving accurate ratings. Yet, in any good management evaluation program, a manager's ability and willingness to accurately appraise people is a key factor in that executive's rise in management. A second serious problem is that some people just don't get along. In these cases, evaluators have difficulty being fair.

Management writers have extolled the virtues of behaviorally anchored rating scales (BARS) as superior instruments for subjectively evaluating people. A BARS instrument contains detailed descriptions of the subject's behavior to guide the evaluator's numerical rating of that person. A sample of one question is shown in Figure 16–5. It is important to remember, however, that no amount of instrument sophistication can overcome the basic weaknesses inherent in subjective rating systems.

FIGURE 16-5

A behaviorally anchored rating scale for evaluating team participation

Rating Description	Numeric Rating	Behaviors
Outstanding	10	Can be expected to go beyond what is normally expected to help the team achieve its goals
Above average	8	Can be expected always to cooperate and contribute to the team objectives. Tries hard to help make the team successful.
Average	5	Usually willing to cooperate and participate in team efforts.
Below average	2	Can be expected to participate in team efforts only to the extent required. Shows no initiative with regard to team efforts.
Poor	0	Unwilling to participate. At times may work against team goals.

Step 5 of evaluating sales force performance is to discuss the evaluation with the salesperson.

Discuss the Evaluation with the Salesperson

Step 5: Once the salesperson's performance has been evaluated, the results should be reviewed in a conference with the sales manager. This discussion should be viewed as a counseling interview, in which the manager explains the person's achievements on each evaluation factor and points out how the results compared with the standards. Then the manager and the salesperson together may try to determine the reasons for the performance variations above or below the standards. It is essential to discuss the manager's ratings on the qualitative factors and to compare them with the salesperson's self-evaluation on these points. Based on their review of all evaluation factors, the manager and the salesperson can then establish goals and an operating plan for the coming period.

The performance-evaluation interview can be a very sensitive occasion. It is not easy to point out a person's shortcomings face-to-face. People dislike being criticized and may become quite defensive in this situation. Some sales executives resist evaluation interviews because they feel these discussions can only injure morale. The concern is real and valid. They reason, "Why stir up trouble when you are basically happy with the person's performance?" On the other extreme, some sales managers make a point to rank all salespeople from best to worst. (See the box titled "Ranking Salespeople from First to Last.")

Ranking Salespeople from First to Last

Some of the largest and most respected sales organizations in the United States are experimenting with ranking their salespeople, including Ford, General Electric, and Microsoft. As part of the evaluation process at these companies, sales managers are required to rank order their salespeople—from the best to the worst.

At GE, for example, sales managers must identify the top 20 percent of salespeople, as well as the bottom 10 percent. The top group gets significant bonuses; but those at the bottom typically are fired.

Sales professionals are split on whether or not ranking salespeople is appropriate. Some say this is a heartless, cold-blooded management tactic that destroys teamwork. Others feel that it is a strong motivator. In fact, some even argue that weeding out the poor performers is an act of kindness. "Not removing the bottom 10 percent early in their years is not only a management failure, but false kindness as well—a form of cruelty," says a top GE executive in a letter to shareholders.

Question: As a sales manager, would you rank your salespeople? Why or why not?

Source: "Should You Rank Your Salespeople?" *Sales & Marketing Management,* August 2001, p. 13.

Unperceptive managers often lose sight of subordinates' virtues and strengths and criticize unimportant factors. One key factor in management is learning to use people's virtues to the best advantage while not allowing their weaknesses to hurt the firm.

Using Evaluation Data: An Example

The case example in this section illustrates the computations, interpretation, and use of several quantitative evaluation factors, both input (efforts) and output (results).

The Colorado Ski Company distributes four lines of products nationally—skis, ski accessories, ski pants, and ski parkas (the latter two lines are limited). The firm sells to two basic classes of customers—sporting goods stores and specialty ski shops. The company uses its own sales force to reach these customers directly. Salespeople are paid travel expenses plus a straight commission of 5 percent on sales volume.

For purposes of a performance evaluation, the sales manager of the Colorado Ski Company has divided the products into two basic lines: skis and ski accessories (equipment) and ski pants and parkas (clothing). The retailers' usual initial markup on these products is 50 percent of the retail selling price. There are no significant variations among products in the gross margin percentages realized by the Colorado Ski Company.

The sales manager is especially interested in the performance of three of the sales reps: Joe, who sells in the Rocky Mountain region (a huge territory); Gus, selling in the Pacific Northwest; and Paula, who covers the New England market. Much of the quantitative performance data for these three sales reps is summarized in Figure 16–6. Based on an analysis of these data, the sales manager is trying to decide (1) which of the three did the best job and (2) which particular points should be discussed with each person to improve performance.

If the sales manager of the Colorado Ski Company looked just at the sales production of these three people, he would have to conclude that Joe was best by far. He might even consider replacing Paula, since her volume looks weak in comparison. However, after comparing each rep's volume against the market potential, it is evident that Paula sold a larger share of her market than did either Joe or Gus.

Joe's Sales Performance

The sales manager could see that Joe had worked the fewest number of days (220), made the fewest calls (700), and took the fewest orders (500). He also spent more money than the others ($48,000) and traveled far more miles (60,000). The sales manager can make some allowance for this because Joe's territory, the Rocky Mountain region, is more sparsely settled than either Gus's or Paula's territory.

Joe's batting average (0.714) is certainly adequate, and his average order ($2,400) is more than satisfactory. In fact, it is astonishingly high in comparison with the others ($1,133 and $612). The sales manager can justify this. The tremendous market potential ($6 million) in Joe's territory, in comparison with the number of customers evidently located there, would naturally result in a high average sale. Joe evidently has done a satisfactory job of covering potential prospects. It appears that the market potential per dealer in the Rocky Mountain region is far higher than in the other areas in the country. This would explain why he could take such large orders. Joe makes a little over three calls per day, which is relatively low in comparison to the others (3.75 and 4.8). However, it is not sufficiently out of line to cause any action to be taken, in light of his territory. The large number of miles per call is again indicative of the territory.

Considering expense per sales dollar, it *appears* that Joe is the most efficient sales rep, since he spends only 4 percent of sales for expenses. The reps are paid a straight commission of 5 percent of sales, which brings Joe's total cost of selling to

FIGURE 16-6   Evaluation of sales representatives' performance

	Joe Jackson			Gus Dean		
	Equipment	**Clothing**	**Total**	**Equipment**	**Clothing**	**Total**
Total sales (000)	$ 480	$ 720	$ 1,200	$ 220	$ 460	$ 680
Sporting goods stores	320	440	760	160	320	480
Ski shops	160	280	440	60	140	200
Total calls made			700			900
Sporting goods stores			300			500
Ski shops			400			400
Total orders taken			500			600
Sporting goods stores			150			450
Ski shops			350			150
Days worked			220			240
Expenses			$48,000			$40,000
Miles traveled			60,000			45,000
Total market potential (millions)	$2.00	$4.00	$ 6.00	$1.20	$2.40	$ 3.60
Sporting goods stores	1.60	2.40	4.00	0.80	1.60	2.40
Ski shops	0.40	1.60	2.00	0.40	0.80	1.20

	Sporting Goods Stores	Ski Shops	Total	Sporting Goods Stores	Ski Shops	Total
Average order	$5,087	$1,257	$2,400	$1,067	$1,333	$1,133
Batting average	0.500	0.875	0.714	0.900	0.375	0.666
Calls per day			3.18			3.75
Miles per call			86			50
Expense per sales dollar			4.0%			5.9%
Cost per call, excluding commission			$68.57			$44.44
Cost per order, excluding commission			$96.00			$66.67

	Equipment	Clothing	Total	Equipment	Clothing	Total
Total percent of market	24.0%	18.0%	20.0%	18.3%	19.0%	19.0%
Sporting good stores	20.0%	18.0%	19.0%	20.0%	20.0%	20.0%
Ski shops	40.0%	17.5%	22.0%	15.0%	17.5%	16.7%

(continued)

FIGURE 16–6 (continued)

	Paula Burns			Total		
	Equipment	**Clothing**	**Total**	**Equipment**	**Clothing**	**Total**
Total sales (000)	$ 240	$ 280	$ 520	$940	$1,460	$ 2,400
Sporting goods stores	100	160	260	580	920	1,500
Ski shops	140	120	260	360	540	900
Total calls made			1,100			2,700
Sporting goods stores			500			1,300
Ski shops			600			1,400
Total orders taken		850			1,950	
Sporting goods stores		400			1,000	
Ski shops			450			950
Days worked			230			690
Expenses			$36,000			$124,000
Miles traveled			35,000			140,000
Total market potential (millions)	$1.20	$1.20	$ 2.40	$4.40	$ 7.60	$ 12.00
Sporting goods stores	0.72	0.64	1.36	3.12	4.64	7.76
Ski shops	0.48	0.56	1.04	1.28	2.96	4.24

	Sporting Goods Stores	Ski Shops	Total	Sporting Goods Stores	Ski Shops	Total
Average order	$ 650	$ 578	$ 612	$1,500.00	$947.00	$1,231.00
Batting average	0.800	0.750	0.773	0.679	0.769	0.722
Calls per day			4.8			3.90
Miles per call			32			52.00
Expense per sales dollar			6.9%			5.2%
Cost per call, excluding commission			$32.72			$ 45.92
Cost per order, excluding commission			$42.23			$ 63.59

	Equipment	Clothing	Total	Equipment	Clothing	Total
Total percent of market	20.0%	23.3%	21.7%	21.4%	19.2%	20.0%
Sporting goods stores	13.9%	25.0%	19.1%	18.6%	19.8%	19.3%
Ski shops	29.2%	21.4%	25.0%	28.1%	18.2%	21.2%

9 percent. However, the sales manager can see that this low expense ratio is simply a function of his abnormally high sales, which, in turn, are a result of his large market potential.

Joe's cost per call ($68.57) and cost per order ($96) seemed exceedingly high in comparison with those for the other reps. He worked 20 fewer days than Gus and 10 fewer than Paula. Granted that he traveled 15,000 miles more than Gus, the cost of those miles at 26 cents a mile would be about $3,900, which leaves something to be explained. The sales manager probably should investigate Joe's expense accounts. Expenses are usually related to the number of days worked and miles traveled. They are not related directly to sales volume; it costs as much to take an order for $100 as one for $600. A large market potential that results in large sales can cause the expense-to-sales ratio to be misleading. Thus Joe's high sales volume caused his expense ratio to appear low, when in reality he was spending too much money making calls.

Let's analyze Joe's selling effort with regard to products and customers. He has a more difficult time getting orders from a sporting goods store (0.500) than from a ski shop (0.875) even though his average sale to sporting goods stores ($5,087) is fantastically high. The sales manager may wonder if this is part of Joe's batting average problem. Possibly in attempting to sell sporting goods stores so much merchandise he simply scares some of them away. However, the sales manager should be cautious here. In total, it is better that Joe continue to sell a high average order to sporting goods stores and settle for fewer orders than to bring both figures to average.

The sales manager may want to investigate Joe's high average order to sporting goods stores. It may be that a few large discount sporting goods stores in the territory are placing huge orders with Joe. This may be no reflection at all on his ability to build up an order. Therefore, if his batting average could be raised in the sporting goods field, possibly no loss would occur at all to the average order. Then the result would be higher sales volume. It is something to investigate.

Another thing the sales manager may notice: Joe seems able to sell equipment (24 percent of potential) better than he sells clothing (18 percent of potential). He is well above average in his ability to sell skis, particularly to ski specialty shops (40 percent of potential), but he is below average in attention to clothing (17.5 percent). This may be just a reflection of his basic interest. He may prefer to talk about skis, bindings, and poles rather than about pants and parkas. The sales manager should mention to Joe that he should be doing a bit better in his sales of clothing. However, Joe is not sufficiently below par in any category for the sales manager to be unduly concerned.

Gus's Sales Performance

Probably the first thing the sales manager would note about Gus's sales performance is his apparent inability to sell to ski shops. He is closing only 37.5 percent of these calls, whereas the company average is 76.9 percent. On the other hand, he has an extremely high batting average in getting orders from sporting goods stores (90 percent). The sales manager may conclude that Gus speaks the language of the nonskiing owner of a sporting goods store but does not communicate well with a ski expert. The sales manager may consider a conference with Gus to talk over the needs or problems of the ski shop owner and how they differ from those of the sports shop. Gus may not be sufficiently trained in the technical aspects of skiing to answer the questions and gain the confidence of the ski professional. Gus's expenses seem to be in line with the company average, and his calls per day are satisfactory. While Gus is not achieving par with regard to market share, the deviation is not significant enough to warrant any conference on the matter.

Paula's Sales Performance

Paula seems to do fairly well in getting orders from both sporting goods stores and ski shops. But her average order ($612) is significantly below the company average ($1,231). This indicates a problem area. The sales manager probably wants to determine first if these low average orders are a function of the size of

Paula's customers or whether this truly reflects her inability to sell merchandise. The fact that Paula made 1,100 calls with the smallest market potential indicates that her average customer is considerably smaller than those of the other reps. The sales manager may become alarmed at Paula's relatively high expense of sales. However, he should realize that this is caused by the limited sales potential. Paula's cost per call and cost per order are the lowest of the three reps, indicating that her expense accounts are not out of line with her efforts.

It should be obvious to the sales manager that Paula works hard; she makes almost five calls per day. This factor helps to explain several of the others. Her high call rate probably explains her low cost per call and the relatively large number of calls she makes. It also may explain why she does not sell much per order. Perhaps she does not spend sufficient time with each customer. On the other hand, the number of miles per call (32) indicates that her territory is relatively dense, and this alone may be the reason she can make almost five calls per day. She spends less time traveling between calls than the other two reps.

While a sales manager might at first consider discharging Paula, a detailed analysis shows that she is doing as well as, if not better than, the other two reps. Her costs for efforts undertaken are lower. Also, she achieves a larger percentage of the business available to her. Her only problem seems to be that her territory has limited market potential.

The Sales Manager's Decisions

In conclusion, the sales manager probably will undertake several different projects. First, he may try to get Joe to work a few more days in the year. It is understandable that this rep is tempted to do a little loafing. He has an annual income of $60,000 and leads the sales force in sales. However, Joe's territory has a tremendous sales potential. If he does not want to service it properly, the company can cut it in half, giving each rep a $3 million potential to work with. This would still result in two territories of larger potential than that worked by Paula. Also, the sales manager may investigate why Joe does not sell to more sporting goods stores.

With Gus, the sales manager probably will focus his entire attention on why ski shops are such an obstacle. He probably needs additional instruction on the technical aspects of skiing. The sales manager may want to ask Paula why she does not sell more skis to sporting goods stores. That is about her only real weakness, outside of her low average order. Certainly, the sales manager should investigate the reasons for Paula's low average order. However, as previously noted, this may not be the result of poor selling ability.

Summary

A fair and accurate evaluation of the company's sales force is a critical and difficult task. The manager's appraisal of the salespeople is important not only because pay and promotions should be based on such rating, but also because good supervision and training should be based on an objective evaluation of the sales rep's performance. However, the task is difficult. Subjective methods leave much to be desired, as managerial biases may distort the ratings.

The factors affecting a person's performance are many and varied. Moreover, many of those factors are beyond the person's control. It is critical that a person be evaluated only on factors over which he or she has control.

First, management should set some basic policies on the evaluation of the sales personnel. It should establish who will do the rating, when and how often it will be done, how the results will be used, and on what bases people will be rated. Both output and input factors should be measured in the process. Output factors include measures such as sales, orders taken, gross margins realized, new accounts, and lost accounts. They are all quantitative. The input factors are both quantitative and qualitative.

Calls per day and days worked are examples of quantitative measures. Sales presentation quality, product knowledge, and customer relations are examples of qualitative factors.

By comparing the quantitative input and output measures, various efficiency ratings can be developed. The basic performance equation is

$$\text{Sales} = \text{Days worked} \times \text{Call rate} \times \text{Batting average} \times \text{Average order}$$

By factoring each element in the equation, the sales manager can obtain a good picture of what each rep is doing and why he or she is successful or unsuccessful. Company records are the basic source of information needed for such evaluations.

The qualitative factors are more difficult to measure. The evaluator's subjective biases may influence his or her ratings of these factors. The use of a well-designed merit rating form can help in the measurement of these factors.

Next, some standards must be developed. Relative standards such as what other groups are doing are widely used. However, there is a place for some absolute standards such as total selling costs and days worked.

Finally, performance must be compared with the standards and the evaluation must be discussed with the salesperson.

Key Terms

Batting average	Input measures	Ratio measures
Call rate	Management by objectives	Routing efficiency
Direct-selling expense	Market share	Sales volume
Gross profit	Number of orders	Size of orders
Halo effect	Output measures	

Questions and Problems

1. How can a sales manager determine the accuracy of salespeople's reports?

2. How can a sales manager determine the differences the reps encounter in the severity of competition in each territory?

3. How should a manager decide what weights to place on the quantitative versus the qualitative factors in an evaluation?

4. What are some of the indexes a sales manager can use to evaluate the degree to which each salesperson is covering the assigned territory?

5. As sales manager for a baby food concern, you want to evaluate the ability of your reps to attain good shelf space in grocery stores. How would you do this?

6. How can a sales executive determine the ability of each rep to regain lost customers?

7. An owner-manager of a medium-sized apparel manufacturing company proclaimed, "Don't bother me with all that evaluation hogwash. Just give me sales volume and a good bottom line and I'm as happy as a horse in clover. I am

making so much money now that I can't spend it all. So why should I waste my time and effort massaging such numbers?" How would you reply to this owner?

8. How can an evaluation system be used to direct the efforts of salespeople?

9. "The importance of sales force evaluation increases with the size of the sales force and management's distance from it." Comment.

10. Should citizenship behaviors play a role in the evaluation of salespeople? If so, how much?

Experiential Exercises

A. Ask the sales managers from three different companies how they evaluate the performance of their salespeople. Copy any forms they use. Compare the procedures and provide your evaluation of which sales manager is doing the best job of evaluation.

B. Contact salespeople from three different companies. Ask them to explain how their performance is evaluated and whether these evaluations are tied to their compensation. Also ask them whether they think their evaluations help them improve their performance and whether or not they think the evaluations are fair.

Note: If both A and B are undertaken, you may contact sales managers and salespeople from the same three companies.

Internet Exercises

A. Search the Internet until you find an evaluation form designed to assess the performance of an outside salesperson. What are the strengths and the weaknesses of the form?

B. Go to Zoomerang.com (www.zoomerang.com) and register for the free (basic) service. Create an online performance evaluation survey for a salesperson. You might want to start by choosing the template for Human Resources: Performance Evaluation. Is this online service of Zoomerang.com useful for sales organizations? If so, how might it be used?

References

1. Betsy Cummings, "Tell It Like It Is," *Sales & Marketing Management*, August 2001, pp. 59–60.

2. Brent Green, "Listening to Leaders: Feedback on 360-Degree Feedback One Year Later," *Organization Development Journal*, Spring 2002, pp. 8–16.

3. Cummings, "Tell It Like It Is," p. 59.

4. Charles E. Pettijohn, Linda S. Pettijohn, and Michael d'Amico, "Characteristics of Performance Appraisals and Their Impact on Sales Force Satisfaction," *Human Resource Development Quarterly*, Summer 2001, pp. 127–46.

5. Michele Marchetti, "Board Games," *Sales & Marketing Management*, January 1996, pp. 43–46.

6. Richard L. Oliver and Erin Anderson, "Behavior- and Outcome-Based Sales Control Systems: Evidence and Consequences of Pure-Form and Hybrid Governance," *Journal of Personal Selling & Sales Management*, Fall 1995, pp. 1–16.

7. Ibid.

8. "What the Numbers May Not Tell You," *Nation's Business*, January 1996, p. 21.

9. "Work Week: Customers Rating," *The Wall Street Journal*, May 6, 1997, p. A1.

10. Gregory A. Rich, William H. Bommer, Scott B. MacKenzie, Philip M. Podsakoff, and Jonathan L. Johnson, "Methods in Sales Research: Apples and Apples or Apples and Oranges? A Meta-Analysis of Objective and Subjective Measures of Salesperson Performance," *Journal of Personal Selling & Sales Management*, Fall 1999, pp. 41–52.

CASE 16-1   LORRIE FOODS, INC.

Designing an Evaluation System

Lorrie Foods, Inc., is a privately owned wholesale food distributor that has served the Gainesville, Florida, market since 1943. It commands a 60 percent share of the Gainesville market, with annual sales of $6 million and profits of approximately $1 million. It is a small, loosely structured firm that employs 20 people. Top management consists of the general manager, Tom Adair; a marketing manager, Jennifer Walters; and a sales manager, Warren Gottlieb. Recently the company changed ownership. Both Adair and Walters are new to the firm. Gottlieb has been with the firm for 17 years and remains under the new management as the top-ranking sales executive.

Lorrie Foods has three main product lines: food, paper, and chemicals. Food products include packaged goods, canned foods, and drinks. They represent 70 percent of Lorrie's business. Paper products, which include disposable items such as paper plates, cups, and napkins, account for 25 percent of sales. The remaining 5 percent comes from sales of chemicals such as floor cleaning solutions and kitchen and bathroom supplies.

At the current time, Lorrie has approximately 800 active, major accounts. This customer base, which is very stable, consists of institutions such as hospitals and educational facilities, restaurants, churches, fraternities, sororities, and other organizational groups such as the Scouts. These accounts are served by six outside salespeople. There are another 200 to 300 accounts that are not considered major accounts. Many of these accounts are offices that purchase only paper products and chemicals. Their business is solicited by six telephone salespeople.

Although Lorrie has significant market share, there is strong competition in the Gainesville market. Most of the competition is based in Jacksonville, but there are several national competitors as well, such as Continental Food Services and Kraft. Lorrie is currently the only wholesaler with a warehouse operation in the immediate area. However, Lorrie soon will not be the only local service supplier. The third largest independent food distributor in the nation, Bower Foods, headquartered in Georgia, is planning to enter the market as a full-service warehouse wholesaler. Bower's anticipated entry is the primary driving force behind the reorganization at Lorrie.

Tom Adair, Jennifer Walters, and Warren Gottlieb have worked together to establish a set of strategic objectives for the marketing and sales operations. In order of importance, they are: (1) greater profitability through deeper penetration of the existing market and new product introductions; (2) greater cooperation between the field sales reps and the telemarketing reps; (3) increased market feedback from the reps; and (4) greater nonprice competition. Walters and Gottlieb have both been charged with the responsibility of improving the efficiency and effectiveness of the sales force in achieving these goals. At the current time Gottlieb is working to establish an evaluation program for his salespeople.

The field salespeople are responsible for calling on their largest accounts two to five times per week. They are expected to make contact with the remainder of their accounts less frequently; but for those accounts that are seen less, the salesperson is expected to stay in touch through frequent phone contacts. In addition to managing their established accounts, the salespeople must also solicit the business of new accounts. They are also encouraged to bring customer and competitive information back to the sales manager. The phone salespeople have responsibility for servicing the smaller accounts as well as handling all customer-order data entry (their own and that of the outside sales reps) and processing all customer complaints.

The field and phone sales reps are compensated differently. The field reps are given a salary plus a commission, which can amount to as much as 60 percent of their pay. The salary base is the same for all the reps. They can also earn additional incentives in the form of dollars or prizes from Lorrie's suppliers. For example, a supplier may offer $4 for every carton of its product sold. Lorrie would receive $2 and the individual rep would receive the remaining $2. Other suppliers give points for products sold, which then can be turned into vacations or other merchandise by the rep. Phone sales reps are paid a flat salary with no incentives based on sales.

Currently, the evaluation of salespeople is done by Warren Gottlieb on a rather informal basis. Each representative has monthly activity reports indicating the level of sales and profits for their territories. In addition, Gottlieb has recently instituted a monthly chart of personal goals for each rep, which can be compared to actual performance. Gottlieb believes in management by objectives. He counsels his people to set realistic goals and then helps each rep attain those goals.

Gottlieb and Walters both realized that the current evaluation policies were inadequate. They agreed there was a need to establish specific time periods for the evaluations and that these should be tied to an annual review of performance as well as salary. However, the two managers were at odds with each other when it came to deciding what criteria should be used in evaluating the outside salespeople.

As Gottlieb told Walters, "The primary goal should be to tie our reporting of sales and profits into a formal evaluation of the rep. This would become the primary input for considering raises." Gottlieb believed that the salespeople should be evaluated primarily on the basis of sales and profit contribution because that is what drives the company's bottom line. "We just need to formalize what I've been doing all along."

Walters felt that Gottlieb was wrong. In fact, she felt that the salespeople's sales and profit should play a minor role in their evaluations and reward. Rather, she felt that greater weight should be placed on their behaviors. For example, she wanted to include criteria such as the degree to which the rep provides frequent, high-quality customer feedback; cooperates with the phone sales rep; performs the administrative aspects of the job in a timely fashion; and is customer oriented. She argued, "The large percentage of commission pay encourages and rewards them for sales. They don't need any more incentive to sell, but they do need to be motivated to do the more complete selling job. It is these nonselling activities which will help us maintain our position in the marketplace."

Gottlieb didn't buy it. He felt, first, that these criteria were not necessarily related to good sales performance, and, second, that the evaluation of these "behaviors" would be too subjective. More important, he also knew that the administration of such a program would be very costly in terms of both time and money.

Questions:

1. Who is right, Warren Gottlieb or Jennifer Walters?

2. If you were designing the new evaluation program for Lorrie's sales force, what specific criteria would you use to evaluate the performance of the salespeople?

CASE 16-2   SEAL RITE ENVELOPE COMPANY (C)

Evaluation of Telemarketing Reps

After several weeks of considerable discussion with top management about the company's misdirected marketing efforts, Rose Douglas, the company's sales manager, had been given permission to begin a telemarketing program to lower the costs of covering smaller customers. It had been disclosed by an analysis of customer sales volume in relationship to the company's costs of selling to them that the company was spending too much money covering a large number of small accounts while not giving enough attention to the highly profitable large customers.

Seal Rite Envelope Company made and marketed a wide line of envelopes. It sold directly to printers, wholesalers, and corporations with printing facilities. The availability of relatively low-cost printing equipment combined with computer-generated copy had resulted in many companies maintaining in-house printing operations that often were quite large.

Douglas classified the firm's customers into four categories: (1) printers, (2) paper wholesalers, (3) companies buying envelopes for routine mailing purposes, and (4) companies buying envelopes for sales promotional purposes. Companies in the last category required considerable attention, for their needs were diverse and continually changing. A decision had been made to increase the coverage of the larger customers in the last category and make fewer calls on smaller firms in other categories. However, to replace the direct field calls that were being redirected, and to give better support to the entire sales effort, Douglas had been given permission to develop a telemarketing group to handle both outbound and inbound sales programs.

To that end, she had hired six people who were being trained by a telemarketing consultant experienced in such programs. Initially, three of the telephone salespeople would be assigned to handle inbound calls from customers on the company's 800 number line. Such calls would vary from requests to have a sales rep call immediately to deal with some pressing need of the customer to a reorder of some envelope the firm was using. The outbound sales calls would be to customers with frequent needs for envelopes and to smaller customers with infrequent needs.

A callback dating system had been developed. Each customer's usage rate was studied by the sales rep covering that account so that the customer could be contacted a short time before it needed to reorder envelopes.

Douglas was trying to figure out how she was going to evaluate these new telephone sales reps. Could all the reps be evaluated as a group with no distinction between the inbound and outbound telemarketers? Or would she have to evaluate the three inbound people against each other and do the same with the outbound sales reps? She wondered in what way these new telemarketers could be evaluated against the outside sales reps. Would it be a case of trying to compare oranges and apples?

Her boss, Max Chernak, the president, had asked for a complete report on the telemarketing program when Douglas finalized her plans for it. He had specifically mentioned that he was eager to learn how she intended to evaluate the program.

At the company's Christmas party, Rose Douglas had an opportunity to talk with Steve Hunter, the firm's top sales rep, about the telemarketing program that was soon to be online. She chose to sound him out on some of the questions she was pondering. She asked him, "How often do you think the telemarketers should be evaluated?"

Hunter smiled and answered, "How about hourly?"

She retorted, "Seriously, I've got to make some decisions."

"I was serious. It seems to me that one of the real advantages of an inside telephone selling program is that you can continually monitor and evaluate how each person is doing. You can look at each day's efforts and production," Hunter observed.

"I could do that on you guys, too. But when you get too close, random events distort the evaluation. One tough problem during the day could totally ruin a rep's evaluation data. I've got to look over a large enough span of time that I can get a valid reading of the person's performance. I was thinking about monthly evaluations. What do you think?"

"I told you what I think. I'd be evaluating each day's work. A lot of bad things can happen in a month," Hunter said as he left to say hello to Max Chernak.

Rose Douglas wandered over to the corner where the company's controller was trying to look inconspicuous. Somehow the ensuing conversation turned to evaluation programs. They spent some time talking about the different bases on which the new people could be evaluated, such as time on the telephone, calls attempted, calls completed, orders taken, size of orders, total volume, and errors made. Douglas was somewhat bothered by the controller's emphasis on making many short calls. She was more concerned with what she called meaningful calls, that is, that the person talk long enough to the customer to get the job done. It had been her experience as a sales rep that if she kept the customer talking long enough, she received additional orders as the customer thought of other things that were needed. Her experience was that some customers just liked to talk with her. She was reminded of a lecture she once heard about the social aspects of the sales call. The professor had maintained that a sales call was partly a social event at which social amenities should be observed. He had maintained that the sales rep should leave neither too soon nor too late. Douglas wondered if all of this would be changed in telephone selling: Would the customers want to talk, or would efficiency be the order of the day? Should she acquire some mechanical means of measuring the number and length of the telephone calls?

Howie Masters, a foreman in the cutting room, strolled up to Rose Douglas to make idle conversation, but Douglas had other ideas. She knew that Masters was a nut about computers and electronics. She told him about the telemarketing program being developed and asked, "Would it be difficult to record each telephone call so we can tell how the reps are doing and help them improve?"

Masters quickly responded, "No problem at all. All sorts of equipment is available to do the job. You want me to set it up for you?"

"Let me think about it and get back to you. Thanks for offering," Douglas responded. She wondered if any problems would arise if the phone calls were recorded. She knew that there were some laws governing such things, but she speculated that there had to be some way around any legal or ethical problems involved with recording the calls. She had read that other firms did it.

Suddenly, Douglas became somewhat angry with herself, thinking that she was spending too much time contemplating relatively minor matters when she was not certain what she wanted to measure. She admonished herself to focus more on the content of the evaluation program and less on its format.

As Douglas drove home from the party, she put together in her mind everything she wanted to put in her report to Max Chernak. She would write it the next day.

Questions:

1. How often should the telemarketers be evaluated?

2. Should the calls be recorded?

3. On what bases should the telemarketers be evaluated?

4. Should the telemarketers be evaluated against the field sales reps? Against each other?

Ethical and Legal Responsibilities of Sales Managers

17

The likelihood of unethical behavior is directly proportionate to the size of the carrot.

—Michele Marchetti—

Open a newspaper or a business trade journal today and you are likely to find a story about some firm or administrator in trouble with the authorities. Accusations of improprieties are everywhere. The actions of business executives and public officials are now scrutinized as never before. Even if a businessperson is innocent of breaking any law, charges of unethical behavior are hurled, careers are ruined, and family lives are drastically altered. Years of wise leadership and superior performance can be nullified by one unwise decision that leads to a legal or ethical hassle.

An actual case history will show that these words of warning are not merely moralistic hyperbole. The incident concerns a former student of one of your authors. This student, upon graduation, accepted a job as sales representative with a large, well-known corporation to sell certain large equipment to governmental units. He was informed that it was not unknown for sales reps to "share" some of their commissions with the public officials who controlled these purchases. And so the graduate became quite proficient at "sharing" his good fortunes with certain customers, and he prospered.

Unfortunately, one of the public officials got into trouble with the Internal Revenue Service. It seems that the official "forgot" to report his "share" of the commissions. He had also forgotten many other such "shares." The affair was widely publicized in the local papers, forcing state officials to take action, for most people looked on the "shares" as bribes—a violation of state law. When the dust settled, the only person punished was our graduate—who got three years in the state penitentiary. The elected official settled with the IRS and somehow escaped jail. Company executives said, "We had no idea that was going on!" Our graduate's career and life were ruined. When he had been in college, instructors didn't talk or write about such things. Well, now we do.

Business Ethics and Sales Management

Webster's New Collegiate Dictionary defines **ethics** as "the science of moral duty" or "the science of ideal human character." Ethics are moral principles or practices. They are also professional standards of conduct. Thus, to act in an ethical fashion is to conform to some standard of moral behavior.

Sales managers have important ethical responsibilities with regard to their own actions as well as the actions of their salespeople. Sales managers are often faced with ethical dilemmas in hiring, setting quotas, evaluating, and carrying out many other aspects of their managements tasks. They are also responsible for establishing, communicating, and enforcing the ethical standards they expect their salespeople to follow.

Salespeople are exposed to greater ethical pressures than are individuals in many other jobs. They work in relatively unsupervised settings; they are primarily responsible for generating the firm's revenues, which at times can be very stressful; they are continually faced with problems that require unique solutions, which is also stressful; and they are often evaluated on the basis of short-term objectives. The latter, especially, can cause salespeople to promote short-term solutions to customers' problems that may not be in the customers' best interests. A recent survey of sales managers revealed that 49 percent of the managers said their reps have lied on a sales call and that 22 percent said their reps have sold products their customers didn't need. Fifty-eight percent of the managers surveyed said that they have caught reps cheating on an expense report.[1]

The Legal–Ethical Confusion

One often reads in the trade press or hears of such matters as price discrimination, bribes, kickbacks, insider trading, or conflicts of interest. These practices are considered evidence of management's deficient ethical code.

These practices may be unethical, but—more important—they are illegal! It is illegal to take or give bribes. It is illegal to participate in insider trading on the securities exchanges. It is even illegal to pad an expense account—this is called *embezzlement.* Indeed, a large portion of the so-called ethical issues raised by critics of business are not really ethical problems at all. They are law enforcement problems.

In the United States, Americans have standardized a partial common code of ethics based on our complex federal, state, and city statutes—the law. Indeed, there are people for whom the law is their code of ethics: If it is legal, it is ethical. To others, just because something is illegal does not make it unethical. Most speeders, for example, see nothing unethical about their driving habits.

However, most people understand that the law cannot possibly cover and regulate all aspects of life—nor should it attempt to do so. They understand the need for a personal code of ethics beyond that covered by the law.

In this chapter, we focus first on ethical questions and then on legal issues. Nevertheless, understand clearly that the line between ethics and law is murky. Our discussion will continually cross over it, back and forth. For example, many laws governing business practices are seldom enforced. One can violate them rather safely to great personal advantage. One business practice that is unfair—and illegal—is to knowingly lie to a customer about a competitor's situation. Another is to discriminate in price in violation of the Robinson-Patman Act. Yet these practices are widespread. Now one's ethical code comes into play. Will you do something that is illegal but to your advantage if you think it is safe to do so? Bear in mind, for example, that insider trading has been widespread for decades, but the law was not enforced until recently. Many practices that at one time were legal are now illegal. The trend is clearly toward higher and more ethical business standards.

An example of the dilemma faced by businesspeople is the case of an outstanding securities sales manager who was hired as president of a highly publicized small investment company. This firm specialized in over-the-counter and penny stocks. The new president came home at noon of his first day at work and told his family, "I quit! It's a scam. These people are crooks." He bailed out. The hundreds of others in the firm were not so foresighted, nor were they fortunate when the Securities and Exchange Commission and the Federal Bureau of Investigation closed in. As one vice president of sales told a class, "It's not a whole lot of fun to be hauled off to jail in the middle of the night in front of your family." The one sales manager's future was saved by a personal code of ethics that would not allow him to become involved with a firm that was doing what he knew was wrong.

The Pressure to Compromise Personal Ethics

Most of us have our own personal codes of ethics—what we will and will not do. Often we would prefer not to do certain things; but if we are pressed sufficiently hard, our ethical codes may bend. A person's true ethical code surfaces when he or she is tested under difficult conditions. It is easy to be ethical when no hardship is involved—when one is winning and life is going well. The test comes when things are not going so well—when the competitive pressures build up. The pressure brought on by quotas, pay plans, and a fierce competitive environment breeds unethical behavior.

Some business executives believe that in order to advance in an organization, a person must occasionally do something that he or she would prefer not to do. In a recent survey of sales managers, 89 percent of them acknowledge that they or their reps have given gifts in excess of $100 in order to gain favor with potential clients.[2] In a survey of salespeople, nearly half of the respondents admitted to taking part in some illegal or unethical activity, such as deceiving customers, as a result of pressure. The largest number of offenders were from computer and software companies—high-growth, highly competitive industries.[3] This is not to say that individuals involved in such deceptive practices get away with them. Prudential Insurance Company recently agreed to pay a minimum of $425 million to settle a class action suit for using selling practices that deceived customers. Archer Daniels Midland, the United States' largest miller of corn, soybeans, and wheat, paid a $100 million fine for price fixing. One of its executives pleaded guilty to theft, money laundering, conspiracy, and tax evasion.[4]

For executives who ignore the unethical activities of their reps, the consequences are serious—lawsuits, fines, ruined careers, and imprisonment. The damage to their companies is also great in terms of lost customers and potential customers. So, regardless of the pressure to compromise personal standards, all of the recent evidence suggests that it is not in the best interests of salespeople and sales managers to do so.

The Problem of Determining Ethical Standards

As individuals, sales managers usually have their own standards of ethical conduct. And they usually abide by these standards in managing their sales forces. Most of us believe we act ethically by our own standards. However, ethical standards are set by a group—by society—and not by the individual. Thus, the group evaluates what you as an individual think is ethical.

The problem is that the group (society) lacks commonly accepted standards of behavior. What is considered ethical conduct varies from one country to another (see the International Perspective box), from one industry to another, and from one situation to another. Looking to the law or corporate policy for guidance often leads only to more gray areas rather than to clearly defined, specific guidelines.

The moral–ethical–legal framework presents special problems for sales executives, more than for most other managers. Entertaining customers in a gambling house, for example, may be either moral or immoral from an individual's point of view. This entertainment may be considered acceptable (ethical) or not depending on the industry's practice. And it may be legal or illegal, depending on whether it happened in Nevada or California.

In some of the situations discussed in the following sections, it is apparent that it will be difficult at times for the manager to decide whether or not a particular action is ethical.

An International Perspective

Bribery is found in many (perhaps all) cultures and political systems. In fact, in many foreign countries there is no way a company can hope to make sales without paying fees or "commissions" (translate that as *bribes*) to agents in those countries. Bribery is so implanted in many cultures that various languages have slang words to designate it. In Latin America it is called the *mordida* (small bite). It is *dash* in West Africa and *baksheesh* in the Middle East. The French call it *pot de vin* (jug of wine). In Italy there is *la bustarella* (the little envelope) left on a bureaucrat's desk to cut the red tape.

However, under the Foreign Corrupt Practices Act of 1977, it is illegal for U.S. companies to offer bribes to foreign officials or candidates. This law was amended by the Omnibus Trade and Competitiveness Act of 1988. In this amendment a distinction is made between **subordination** and a **facilitation payment.** Subordination involves payment of large sums of money, for which there is not proper accounting, to entice an official to commit an illegal act. This is considered illegal under U.S. law. A facilitation payment, in contrast, involves the payment of relatively small sums of cash to low-ranking officials, where not prohibited by law, to facilitate or expedite the normal, lawful performance of a duty.

It is important to remember that all employees of every U.S. company are subject to the laws of the United States regardless of the country in which they are conducting business. Furthermore, sales managers are held responsible not only for their own actions but also for the actions of their internationally based employees. So any subordination payments made by U.S. companies doing business in any foreign country would be considered illegal and punishable under U.S. law.

These salespeople present a gift to one of their customers.

Ethical Situations Facing Salespeople and Sales Executives

Ethical questions are involved in many of the relationships that sales managers have with their salespeople, their companies, and their customers. A few of these situations are discussed here.

Relations with the Sales Force

A substantial portion of sales managers' ethical problems relates to their dealings with the sales force. Assume, for instance, that a salesperson has built a territory into a highly profitable district. The rep may have even worked under a straight commission compensation plan and paid his or her own expenses. An executive who sees this salesperson's relatively high earnings may decide the territory is too large and therefore must be split. Is this ethical? Yet is it sound management not to split the district if the sales executive believes there is inadequate coverage of an overly large district?

In some companies, management takes over the very large, profitable accounts as *house accounts.* (These customers are sold directly by some executive, and the salesperson in that district usually receives no commission on the account.) The ethics here may be questionable, particularly if the salesperson spent much time and effort in developing the account to a profitable level. Yet management may feel that the account is now so important that an executive should handle it.

Ethical questions often arise in connection with promotions, termination, and references. If there is no likelihood that a sales representative will be promoted to a managerial position, should the rep be told? If the sales manager knows that the rep is working in expectation of such a promotion, to tell him means to lose him. In another instance, when a managerial position opens up in another region, a sales manager may keep a star sales rep in her present territory despite the rep's qualifications and desire for promotion. And what is management's responsibility in giving references for a former salesperson? To what extent is a manager ethically bound to tell the truth or give details about former employees?

Relations with the Company

Changing jobs and handling expense accounts illustrate the ethical problems involved in sales executives' relations with companies. When changing positions, a manager may want to take key customers to the new employer. Ethical and legal questions may arise if this executive tries to move those customers to the new firm.

Many times a sale manager possesses information that could be highly useful to a competitor. Naturally, it is difficult to control the information a manager gives to a new employer. But beyond certain limits, such behavior is clearly unethical.

Ethical questions may arise in the interpretation of expense account policies. Suppose that top management states it will pay only 26 cents a mile to sales reps or sales managers who use their personal cars for company business. Yet a sales manager, knowing that actual expenses are 30 to 35 cents a mile at the minimum, may be tempted to pad mileage and then encourage the reps to do so, too, to make up the difference. The manager may justify this action by rationalizing that the money is really being spent for business purposes and thus the spirit of the expense account is not being violated. Ethical questions include the following: Should sales personnel manipulate expense accounts to protect themselves from the stingy policies of top management? In so doing, they are only recovering money honestly spent in the solicitation of business for the firm. Or should they attempt to get policies changed? Or, failing that, should they change employers rather than commit what they believe are unethical acts?

Relations with Customers

Perhaps the most critical set of ethical questions facing sales managers is associated with customer relations. The major problem areas involve information, gifts, and entertainment.

Information. It is important that salespeople provide their customers with *all* of the information that enables them to make informed decisions. Sometimes salespeople make recommendations that are not in the best interests of their customers. For example, they may neglect to give the customers complete information. To cite one example, several insurance reps were trying to sell new policies to their current policyholders. In doing so, the reps failed to tell their customers that the new policies seemed less expensive than they really were because they were paid for in part by using up the cash value of the older policies.[5]

Sometimes salespeople knowingly sell a higher priced product when a lower priced product would have fulfilled the customer's need just as well. The *Journal of the American Medical Association* claims that pharmaceutical sales representatives are pushing higher priced calcium channel blockers for high blood pressure when cheaper diuretics and beta blockers are just as effective.[6]

Gifts. The practice of giving gifts to customers, especially at the holiday season, is time-honored in American business. But today, perhaps more than ever before, the moral and ethical climate of giving gifts to customers is under careful scrutiny. The practice is being reviewed by both the givers and the receivers of gifts. Some firms put dollar limits on the business gifts they allow their employees to give or receive. The Internal Revenue Service places a limit of $25 a year on the amount that may be deducted for business gifts to any one person. Other firms have stopped the practice of giving Christmas gifts to customers. Instead, some of these firms offer to contribute (in amounts equal to their usual gifts) to their customers' favorite charities.

It is unfortunate that gift giving to customers has become so complicated and so suspect. A reasonably priced, tastefully selected gift can express appreciation for a customer's business. Today the problem lies largely in deciding what constitutes "reasonably priced" and "tastefully selected." The following examples illustrate this problem:

- A box of golf balls may be a reasonable Christmas gift to give a $5,000-a-year customer. But is a $3,000 personal computer a gift or a bribe when given to a million-dollar customer?

- It is customary for appliance manufacturers to reward their distributor-customers with an all-expense-paid incentive trip to the Bahamas. But is it acceptable for a pharmaceutical company to invite its doctor-customers to Jamaica for an all-expense-paid seminar?

- It is a legal and acceptable practice for a manufacturer to give a department store's sales clerks "push money" to promote the manufacturer's brand. But can this manufacturer rightfully give the head buyer a little something extra for first getting the product into the store?

Fortunately, sales executives have some time-tested guidelines to help them avoid gift giving that is unethical or in bad taste:

- Never give a gift before a customer does business with the firm.
- Do not give gifts to customers' spouses.
- Keep the value of gifts low to avoid the appearance of undue influence on future purchase decisions.
- Follow your company's policy on gift giving.
- Walk away from the business if the customer pushes for something that exceeds these guidelines.[7]

Entertainment. Business entertainment is definitely a part of sales work, and a large portion of the expense money is often devoted to it. Reps who spend this money unwisely on accounts with little potential waste time, and their selling costs will be out of line. Indeed, a contributing factor in salespeople's success may be their ability to know the right person to entertain and the nature of the entertainment called for.

Over the years, some useful generalizations have been developed for customer entertainment:

- Entertain to develop long-term business relationships, not one order.

- Keep the entertainment appropriate to the customer and the size of the account.

- Be sensitive to customer attitudes toward types of entertainment.
- Do not rely on entertainment as one of the foundations of the selling strategy—use it only to complement the strategy.

Setting Ethical Guidelines

It is not realistic for a sales manager to construct a two-column list of practices, one headed "ethical" and the other "unethical." A better approach is to depend on time and conscious examples to point out the difference between acceptable and nonacceptable standards of performance. Cite the philosophy followed in the writing and subsequent administration of Section 5 of the Federal Trade Commission Act, which outlaws *unfair competition* but does not state what that term means. The legislators wisely left the task of definition to the commission and the courts. Thus, examples have accumulated through the years as the law has been administered case by case.

Take a Long-Run Point of View

Sales executives should understand that ethical behavior is not only morally right but also, over the long run, realistically sound. Too many sales administrators are shortsighted. They do not see the possible repercussions from their activities and attitudes. Whether or not the buyer was deceived or pressured may seem unimportant so long as the sale is consummated—the brushmark of one immediate sale seems unimportant when the entire canvas is examined. Management often does not recognize that such practices can lose customers or invite public regulation. Figure 17–1 provides some questions that may help a sales executive evaluate the ethical status of proposed actions.

Put Guidelines in Writing

In the mid-1970s, spurred by revelations of bribery at home and in foreign business dealings, many U.S. companies developed **codes of ethics,** which are written ethical guidelines to be followed by all employees. A survey by the Ethics Resource Center showed that 84 percent of the companies surveyed have codes of conduct and 45 percent have ethics offices.[8] Figure 17–2 presents the main points of the Code of Ethics adopted by the American Marketing Association, the largest association of professional marketers in the world.

Writing a code of ethical conduct is no easy task. Critics claim that such a statement usually is public relations window dressing that covers up a bad

---

FIGURE 17-1

Evaluating the ethical status of a business decision

1. Is this sound from a long-run point of view?
2. Would I do this to a friend?
3. Would I be willing to have this done to me? (The Golden Rule)
4. Would I want this action publicized in national media?
5. Would I tell others about it?
6. Who is damaged by the action?

FIGURE 17-2

The American Marketing Association's Code of Ethics

Professional Conduct

Marketers' professional conduct must be guided by:

1. The basic rule of professional ethics: not knowingly to do harm;
2. The adherence to all applicable laws and regulations;
3. The accurate representation of their education, training and experience; and
4. The active support, practice and promotion of this Code of Ethics.

Honesty and Fairness

Marketers shall uphold and advance the integrity, honor and dignity of the marketing profession by:

1. Being honest in serving consumers, clients, employees, suppliers, distributors and the public;
2. Not knowingly participating in conflict of interest without prior notice to all parties involved; and
3. Establishing equitable fee schedules including the payment or receipt of usual, customary and/or legal compensation for marketing exchanges.

Rights and Duties of Parties in the Marketing Exchange Process

Participants in the marketing exchange process should be able to expect that:

1. Products and services offered are safe and fit for their intended uses;
2. Communications about offered products and services are not deceptive;
3. All parties intend to discharge their obligations, financial and otherwise, in good faith; and
4. Appropriate internal methods exist for equitable adjustment and/or redress of grievances concerning purchases.

situation and corrects nothing. Nevertheless, higher levels of ethical behavior have been found in firms where codes of ethics are in place and enforced.[9] An ethical code that is part of the culture of an organization is likely to affect the decision making of that organization's employees. Such codes lessen the chance that executives will knowingly or unknowingly get into trouble, and they strengthen the company's hand in dealing with customers and government officials who invite bribes and other unethical actions. They also strengthen the position of lower-level executives in resisting pressures to compromise their personal ethics in order to get along in the firm.

In addition to providing guidelines for ethical decision making, a code of ethics can contribute to the general ethical climate of an organization if it is endorsed and enforced by top management. Having a code of ethics is a concrete sign that the organization cares about whether or not its employees behave in an ethical manner. Reps who violate the code should be reprimanded; if they don't cease their unethical behavior, they should be fired. In other words, a code of ethics becomes an effective means of guiding behavior only if it is enforced; otherwise, it is meaningless.

Provide a Role Model

Top managers must serve as ethical role models for employees. They must not only verbally endorse ethical behavior but also practice it. Clearly salespeople are not going to take any code of ethics seriously if they see their immediate managers and other executives behaving unethically. Unfortunately, many managers do not serve as role models. A national survey of 4,000 business employees found that 25 percent of those responding felt their companies ignored ethical conduct in order to meet business objectives and that 17 percent believed their companies *encouraged* unethical practices.[10]

Provide Ethical Training

Another means of reducing the occurrence of unethical behavior is for the company to provide ethical training to its employees. Often sales situations are complex, particularly in international situations. Sales managers or salespeople may want to behave in an ethical manner but may not be aware of the ethical implications of some of their decisions; or even if they are aware, they may not know what is the most ethical action to take in a particular situation. Training—through the use of cases, role plays, and games—can simulate ethical dilemmas. This can increase ethical sensitivity and skills.

Public Regulation and Sales Managers

Public regulation at any level of government—federal, state, or local—touches a company's marketing department more than any other phase of the company's operations. This does not imply that regulation of nonselling activities is unimportant. The Securities and Exchange Commission affects corporate financing, minimum-wage legislation influences several aspects of personnel and labor relations, various measures establish safety regulations for offices and factories, local zoning laws affect plant location, and so on. However, the various regulatory measures that affect areas of marketing—such as pricing, advertising, and personal selling—are the ones that will have the greatest impact on the behavior of salespeople and their managers.

As established by the Federal Sentencing Commission for Organizations in 1991, both the employee and the employee's company are responsible for compliance with federal regulations. That is, the government holds the company responsible for preventing misconduct on the part of its employees. It must establish and communicate standards of behavior to employees, monitor employee conduct, allow employees to report criminal activity, punish those who violate the standards, and take steps to prevent further criminal conduct.[11] Sales managers must ensure that their salespeople are aware of their legal responsibilities. To do this, they must provide training with regard to their legal responsibilities and routinely provide updates concerning the most recent legislation and court decisions.

If a manager believes that the behavior of a particular salesperson may lead to legal problems, the sales manager should take action immediately to make the rep cease the questionable behavior.

There are four areas in which sales executives are affected by government regulation of business: price discrimination, unfair competition, the Green River type of municipal ordinance, and cooling-off laws.

Price Discrimination

The Clayton Antitrust Act (1914) and its Robinson-Patman Amendment (1936) are federal laws that generally restrict **price discrimination.** Sales administrators, for example, cannot allow members of their sales force to indiscriminately grant price concessions. Some customers may demand larger discounts than are normally allowed and threaten to take their business elsewhere if their demands are not met. A seller who grants the unusual discount, assuming no corresponding cost differential to justify the transaction, may (along with the buyer) be violating the Robinson-Patman Act.

In another situation, in order to make a sale it may be necessary for a seller to absorb some or all of the freight ordinarily paid by the buyer. Care must be taken to ensure that the move is made in good faith to meet an equally low price of a competitor. Firms normally cannot make price guarantees to some customers without making the same guarantees to other competing customers. Let's assume that a firm wants to grant allowances to customers for such things as cooperative advertising or demonstrators. These attractions must also be offered to all competing customers on a proportionately equal basis.

Unfair Competition

Unfair trade practices that may injure a competitor or the consumer are generally illegal under the Federal Trade Commission Act and its Wheeler-Lea Amendment. No specific examples of **unfair competition** are spelled out in these laws. However, a large body of illustrations has built up through the years as the Federal Trade Commission administered these legislative acts. Offering bribes and providing misleading information to customers have been the focus of many FTC legal actions against firms and their employees.

Bribes

Using **bribes**—the payment of money or gifts to gain or retain a customer—is illegal. Using bribes to gain information about competitors is also illegal. Bribery in selling is an unpleasant fact of life that apparently has existed, in varying degrees, since time immemorial. Blatant bribes, payoffs, or kickbacks may be easy to spot—and they are patently wrong. Unfortunately, today much bribery is done in a sophisticated manner that is not easy to identify. Sometimes the lines are blurred between a bribe, a gift to show appreciation, and a reasonable commission for services rendered.

In sales, the bribe offer may be initiated by the salesperson, or the request may come from the buyer. Usually the buyer's request is stated in a veiled fashion, and it takes a perceptive sales rep to understand what is going on.

Undoubtedly bribery will continue to put sales managers and salespeople to the ethical test. If nothing else, sales executives should realize that "Everyone else is doing it" is not a valid excuse. The penalties can be stiff for those found guilty of taking or giving bribes.

Misleading Information

It is illegal to make false, deceptive, or misleading claims about a product or about the services that accompany that product. If a salesperson makes exaggerated claims about a product and those claims lead to misuse of the product, the seller may also be sued for any property damages or personal injuries arising out of a customer's misuse of the product. In one unusual situation, a group of salespeople from Pacific Bell, which was taken over by Southwestern Bell, filed a complaint with the California Public Utilities Commission. They charged that, after the takeover, their company began forcing them to use deceptive selling practices.[12]

Making false, deceptive, or disparaging statements about a competitor or its products is also illegal. Yet such practices are prevalent.[13] The lies may run from fibs about the competitor's financial stability to personal attacks on its salespeople. Regardless of their nature, these actions all have the same purpose of discrediting the competitor. This is illegal and can lead to prosecution, fines, and imprisonment.

The following guidelines help salespeople minimize the probability of legal proceedings and increase their chances of defending themselves if a legal complaint is brought against them:[14]

- Always make accurate, understandable, and verifiable statements about the product.

- Ensure that customers have the necessary knowledge and skills needed to use the product in the proper manner.

- Caution (in writing) customers against using the product in an improper manner.

- Remind customers to read warning labels.

- Be able to verify any statements made about competitors.

Green River Ordinances

Many cities have enacted **Green River Ordinances,** which restrict the activities of salespeople who represent firms located outside the city. These representatives may sell door-to-door (in-home), or they may call on retailers or other business establishments. Ostensibly, most of these laws were passed to protect local consumers and businesses from the fraudulent, high-pressure, and otherwise unethical selling practices of outlanders. Such measures not only serve this purpose but also tend to insulate local firms from external competition. Generally, these ordinances require salespeople to have a local license to do business in the town. But it often is difficult for representatives from some types of outside firms to get the necessary license. While the constitutionality of these laws is highly questionable, they do serve as a deterrent to unethical sales activity.

Cooling-Off Laws

Legislation at the federal, state, and local levels protects consumers against the sometimes unethical sales activities of door-to-door salespeople. Much of the state legislation and Federal Trade Commission (FTC) administrative rulings are of the "cooling-off" type. That is, the regulations provide for a cooling-off period (usually three days) during which the buyer in a door-to-door (in-home) sale may cancel the contract, return any merchandise, and obtain a full refund.

The 1972 FTC rulings apply to all sales of $25 or more. They require the salesperson to inform the customer orally and in writing about the opportunity to "say no to the company even after you have said yes to the salesperson." By 1973, nearly 40 states, as well as several cities, had passed some type of **cooling-off law.** This poses real problems of compliance for national direct-selling companies, which must deal with many different laws and sales contracts.

Current Problems

The advent and rapid growth of direct-response marketing, telemarketing, and Internet marketing have given rise to some new problems that many people feel have certain ethical overtones. Is it ethical to bother people at home over the telephone, particularly at night? Or is it right to send unsolicited promotional material to prospects over their own fax machines or via e-mail? Some legislation about these practices is pending.

The securities industry is plagued with so-called boiler room operations that use telemarketing techniques to sell financial schemes to people the seller will never know or see. The Securities and Exchange Commission is doing its best to regulate such operations, but it is not an easy task.

A DAY-TO-DAY OPERATING PROBLEM

MAJESTIC PLASTICS COMPANY

MAJESTIC
Plastics Company

Sales Rep Accused of Passing Confidential Information

In their visits to customers' plants, Majestic sales reps were sometimes given confidential information by the customers' personnel about new products, advertising plans, or forthcoming price changes. They also had opportunities to overhear private conversations or to read interoffice correspondence left exposed.

In March, Clyde Brion received a long-distance call from Detroit. Beryl Heckman, president of Northern Foods Company, a packer of fruits and juices, told him angrily: "It *has* to be your salesman who did it! My buyer, Al Resor, assures me that there was no one else in his office but that fellow, Jenner, on the day that Al had my memorandum about our surprise carload sale coming up on April 1! In fact, Al remembered that Jenner walked out with the memo and then brought it back an hour later with the lame excuse that it had gotten caught under a paper clip behind some of *his* papers! Now, of course, it's plain that Orchard Industries, down the street, got the word. They are running the very same offer, two weeks ahead of our jump-off date! We checked, and we know for sure that Jenner called on the buyer at Orchard that same day, right after he left here! And then, to top it all off, Al tells me he knows that Jenner has a criminal record! Did you know that?"

Brion knew that his Detroit sales rep was an ex-convict. Brion had rehired Jenner on the recommen-

dation of Ohio penal officials as a rehabilitation measure. Jenner had been grateful for the chance and had worked hard. His sales record was better than it had been before his conviction, but there was no spectacular upswing. His wife's health had also improved, but Jenner continued to have personal financial problems.

Brion promised Heckman that he would make a thorough investigation. Brion then telephoned Jenner in Detroit and told him of the accusation against him by Northern Foods Company. Jenner readily admitted knowledge of the planned carload sale. He said that Al Resor had shown him the interoffice memorandum containing prices and dates. He added that Resor had used this forthcoming sale as a reason for Jenner to expedite a shipment of bottles. Jenner said he even took down some notes from the memo but denied having given any information to Orchard.

Northern Foods was the largest firm of its industry in the Detroit territory and was growing. However, it had never been a large buyer from Majestic.

Question: What further action should Clyde Brion take in this situation?

Note: See the introduction to this series of problems in Chapter 4 for the necessary background on the company, its market, and its competition.

Summary

Ethics may be defined as moral standards of behavior. Sales managers and salespeople face many different ethical dilemmas. In the United States, many ethical decisions are actually legal questions. Our system of laws standardizes our interpretation of many ethical situations by making them illegal. However, there are still many situations, not covered by the law, in which ethics becomes an important factor.

It is easy to be ethical when it does not cost you anything—when you are winning. The test comes when things are *not* going well. Then there may be real pressure to compromise your personal ethics. There is an increasing awareness and concern over ethics in selling. Adherence to ethical standards is becoming increasingly important.

The problem is to determine what the ethical standards are. Society lacks commonly accepted standards of behavior. Ethical considerations are involved in many of the relationships sales executives have with their sales forces, their companies, and their customers. Customer relations, especially involving information, gifts, and entertainment, can have serious ethical overtones.

When setting ethical standards, it is important to take a long-run perspective. One good ethical guideline to follow is to do what you would feel comfortable explaining to your family, your friends, or even to the public at large on television. A company may help establish an ethical climate by taking a long-run perspective on business decisions, by developing a written code of ethics that managers are expected to enforce, by providing ethical role models through management's words and actions, and by providing ethical training.

Public regulation touches a company's marketing department more than any other phase of the company's operations. Both the employee and the company are responsible for compliance with federal regulations. Government regulation has occurred in several areas that affect sales: price discrimination, unfair competition, Green River Ordinances, and cooling-off laws.

Key Terms

Bribes
Codes of ethics
Cooling-off law

Ethics
Facilitation payment
Green River Ordinances

Price discrimination
Subordination
Unfair competition

Questions and Problems

1. "We always use a manufacturer's rep to open up a new territory; but once that territory is generating enough revenue to support a company rep, we take it away from the rep and put one of our own salespeople in the territory." Is this an ethical policy?

2. "Let's face it. Our product is no different than that of 20 other competitors. It sells for the same price and for the same terms. We all give the same service. It really doesn't matter to the buyer which of us gets the order. So the only way we can get an edge is through our aggressive entertainment and gift program. We work hard at making our buyers happy with us. They enjoy doing business with us." Do you see any ethical problems involved here?

3. You have managed to hire a particularly qualified person to be your assistant sales manager in Los Angeles. The young man moves there with his wife, who yearns for a singing career. The new assistant sales manager is paid a salary that seemed attractive in his former Kansas City area. Economic and culture shock quickly take their toll as the couple learns the

economic facts of life in Los Angeles. They find that the equivalent of their $100,000 Kansas City home sells for $500,000 in West Los Angeles. Moreover, the new assistant's job performance is most unsatisfactory. You are thinking of firing him. What are the ethical considerations involved in this situation?

4. What actions must a company take to ensure its compliance with federal regulation?

5. "Sure we promote our product to fax owners by sending them flyers over their own machines. Why not? We sell fax supplies at great values. If they don't like it, why do they buy so much from us? We're doing great with the program. So a few people complain. So what? Some people will complain if the sun shines while others complain if it doesn't. We're not in business to make everybody happy. Besides, there is no better way to do it." Evaluate the sales manager's statement. Is there any way she could head off such complaints?

6. As a sales manager, you have been asked to recommend someone for a sales management job with another, noncompetitive firm. You have several salespeople who would be excellent for the position, but you don't want to lose them. The other position would be a definite improvement for them; they will never be able to do so well within your own firm. Would you tell them about the opening? Would you recommend them to the other firm?

7. You are one of the newer reps with your company. One of the older reps happens to see your expense report and he says to you, "Don't you think these numbers are low?" When you tell him that this is what you spent, he says, "That may be, but you are so far below the average that you are going to call the rest of us into question." How do you respond?

8. As an American citizen managing a large corporation owned by a large foreign trading company, you have been ordered to do some things that you feel are clearly detrimental to the welfare of the U.S. economy. What concerns, if any, would you have in following those orders?

9. You are a salesperson and you happen to oversee your manager's expense report for a time period during which he was making calls with you. Clearly he has reported some expenses which are fictitious. He has been with the company for a long time and is a respected manager. What should you do about this?

10. Loyalty is a trait highly valued by most executives. They expect their subordinates to be loyal to them and to the company. When might those loyalties conflict? How much loyalty does an employee owe to a superior? To the company?

Experiential Exercises

A. You are a sales manager of a firm that makes printed electronic circuits. You have been requested to write down your policies on entertaining customers, giving gifts, and handling bribery. State your policies in clear, specific terms so that all people concerned know exactly how you will handle each situation.

B. Speak with a sales representative about an ethical issue that he or she faced as part of the job and ask how she or he dealt with the problem. Would you have handled the situation any differently?

Internet Exercises

A. Visit the website of the National Association of Sales Professionals (www.nasp.com) and evaluate this organization's code of conduct in terms of whether or not it is an adequate guide for salespersons' behavior, given the situations that they may face in their jobs.

B. Visit the National Association of Sales Professionals website (listed above) and take the code of ethics test.

References

1. Erin Stout, "Are Your Salespeople Ripping You Off?" *Sales & Marketing Management*, February 2001, p. 59; Michele Marchetti, "Whatever It Takes," *Sales & Marketing Management*, December 1997, pp. 29–38.

2. Melinda Jensen Ligos, "Gimme! Gimme!" *Sales & Marketing Management*, March 2002, p. 34.

3. Marchetti, "Whatever It Takes."

4. Ibid.

5. Ibid.

6. Catherine Arnst, "Is Good Marketing Bad Medicine?" *Business Week* (www.businessweek.com), April 13, 1998.

7. Ligos, "Gimme! Gimme!" pp. 36–38.

8. Marchetti, "Whatever It Takes."

9. Charles H. Schwepker Jr., "Ethical Climate's Relationship to Job Satisfaction, Organizational Commitment, and Turnover Intention in the Sales Force," *Journal of Business Research*, October 2001, p. 40.

10. Ibid., p. 39.

11. United States Sentencing Commission, *Federal Sentencing Guidelines for Organizations*, 1991.

12. "Sales Force Complains about PacBell," Yahoo! News UPI (http://dailynews.yahoo.com/headlin. . . . and_regional_news/capacbell_1.html), April 7, 1998.

13. Melinda Jensen Ligos, "Dirty Rotten Scoundrels," *Sales & Marketing Management*, August 1997, pp. 90–96.

14. Karl A. Boedecker, Fred W. Morgan, and Jeffrey J. Stoltman, "Legal Dimensions of Salespersons' Statements: A Review and Managerial Suggestions," *Journal of Marketing*, January 1991, pp. 70–80.

An Ethical Dilemma:
To Take the "Deal" or Not?

"Every day in every way, I get better and better, I feel happy, I feel healthy, I feel terrific!" Winston (Winnie) Liu repeated the mantra to himself as a young woman wearing a salwarl suit answered the door he had just knocked on. Almost three months after starting his own business selling children's books door-to-door, Winnie was working through a wealthy neighborhood in Edmonton, Alberta. Surrounded by enormous houses and manicured lawns, he reflected for a moment about the promising summer that now found him hungry, lonely, and desperate for a sale.

Anita Howard, a sales manager with the Southwestern Company, recruited Winnie during his first year at the University of Western Ontario (Western). He filled out a card he had received in a chemistry class indicating he was interested in running his own business during the summer. After meeting with Winnie, Anita believed his work ethic, persistence, and friendly personality combined with his passion for education would make him an excellent salesperson. She asked Winnie to consider starting his business selling books, and Winnie agreed, excited about the possibility of being his own boss and making a lot of money. Between January and April, Winnie memorized the prepared sales talks and attended sales training meetings given by students who had sold books before. His enthusiasm for a rewarding summer grew.

The Southwestern Company

The Southwestern Company, located in Nashville, Tennessee, was founded in 1855. The American Civil War exhausted the fortunes of many southwestern American families, and in 1868 the company began helping students finance their school expenses through selling books door-to-door. Over the years the company realized that educational materials were not only more profitable than Bibles but also more consistent with the image of college students.

At present, the educational books and software were sold to families in their homes by students during their summer breaks. Students were independent contractors and had the opportunity to run their own businesses by purchasing products from Southwestern at wholesale and selling them at retail. Students relocated away from home to a different part of the country for the summer, away from distractions that might drain attention and profits from their business.

In 1998 Southwestern recruited 3,000 students from over 300 universities across Canada, the United States, and Europe. The average 1998 summer profits of Southwestern student dealers who sold for three months were:

First-summer students	$ 6,994
Second-summer students	12,891
Third-summer students	17,189
Fourth-summer students	23,364

After the first summer, students could be selected for student management. Many students worked four, five, six, or more summers, gaining invaluable experience by developing their own sales organizations throughout their university careers.

The Books

The two main products sold by the students were the Student Handbook (a four-book set, USA) and the Volume Library, (a three-book set, Canada). These books were study guides designed to complement, not replace, encyclopedias and CD-ROMs. The Student Handbook and the Volume Library contained practical "how-to" information for subjects ranging from math and chemistry to grammar and geography, from the grade 1 to the grade 12 levels. Students in Canada sold the Volume Library set for $320 retail, taking a 40 percent commission from the sales price. Though the prices were only a suggestion from the Southwestern Company, students followed the guidelines for consistency across consumers. Since several students would be selling in every city, it was very likely that friends and relatives might buy the books from different students. Consistency also helped maintain the image of Southwestern, which was critical in this door-to-door sales context.

Sean Barnhart prepared this case under the supervision of Donald W. Barclay solely to provide material for class discussion. The authors do not intend to illustrate either effective or ineffective handling of a managerial situation. The authors may have disguised certain names and other identifying information to protect confidentiality. Ivey Management Services prohibits any form of reproduction, storage or transmittal without its written permission. This material is not covered under authorization from CanCopy or any reproduction rights organization. To order copies or request permission to reproduce materials, contact Ivey Publishing, Ivey Management Services, c/o Richard Ivey School of Business, The University of Western Ontario, London, Ontario, Canada, N6A 3K7; phone (519) 661-3208, fax (519) 661-3882, e-mail cases@ivey.uwo.ca.

Success

The first of two keys to students' success in selling children's books was establishing themselves as legitimate education consultants in the community. Students sought to understand the strengths and weaknesses of the schools and teachers in the community, and the attitudes of parents toward the teachers, schools, and school board. This allowed them to better understand customer needs and to connect quickly during a sales call.

The second key to success was financial planning. Students submitted a high portion of their earnings to the Southwestern Company to secure delivery at the end of the summer (time and experience had demonstrated that students were not good credit risks), so planning was essential to ensure cash flow to cover expenses during the summer.

Winnie's Summer

After a week of sales training at company headquarters in Nashville, Winnie drove to Edmonton, Alberta, with seven other students. He found a place to live with Holden McArthur, who had also just completed his first year at Western, and Seymour Burke, a student from British Columbia, who had sold books during the previous two summers. Winnie and Holden competed against each other daily, not just for sales but also for what they called "feel gooders." These included positive attitude, random acts of kindness, and the number of people they had cheered up during the day.

Winnie had been successful in all ways until the third week of June. He began working in a much wealthier area than he had been in before. His knowledge of local schools, teachers, and students was useless, because these schools and people were unfamiliar and unrecognizable. The children in this neighborhood went to private schools. On Wednesday morning Winnie looked over his sales stats for the past two days: 94 calls, 41 demonstrations, and no sales. Every day without a sale meant stretching his meager food budget a little further. He had been eating peanut butter and jelly for a week straight. For the first time, Winnie allowed himself to think about quitting and going home.

Now Winnie was sitting in the home of Ravish and Kavita Patel, successful stockbrokers and parents of three children. Halfway through the demonstration Ravish asked his wife to bring in the friends they were entertaining in the backyard. The four other couples, all wealthy descendants of hardworking immigrants, lived in the immediate neighborhood, and all had children ranging in age from 7 to 13. All of their children attended Temple, the private school of choice for parents in this neighborhood.

Each of the parents liked the study guides. More important, their children were also enthusiastic about the books. Ravish moved to face Winnie and said, "OK, you've sold us, so no fancy close, Winnie. How much for the set?" Prepared with the no-close close that a fellow salesperson had taught him, Winnie replied confidently, "It's not the hundreds or even thousands that these study guides would cost if you bought them by subject individually. All three books for $320. With tax (7 percent GST) and shipping, the total is only $343. That's pretty good, isn't it?"

Ravish turned to the other four couples and spoke briefly in a language Winnie did not understand but recognized as Hindi. After a brief exchange, Ravish turned to Winnie and said, "Here's the deal. Winnie, what do you make from these, 20 percent? That's $65 per couple here, $325 for you. We'll pay you cash, up front, and cover shipping. Don't charge us tax, and let us pay $310 each. We want just a 10 percent discount. If you don't pay the tax, you only give up $50 and you get five sales now. Boom."

Winnie did the math in his head. Ravish had underestimated his margin by one-half (Winnie normally received 40 percent of the retail price), so Winnie would actually be giving up about $140 for the sale. But the potential profit was still about $500, not the $320 Ravish had calculated.

Winnie responded, less confident now, but sure that Ravish was not objecting to the price. "Everyone pays the same price. There are other students in the city running their businesses and they charge the same price. I've charged the same price to everyone so far and I'm going to charge the same price for the rest of the summer. Besides, wouldn't you feel cheated if you found out your neighbor got 20 percent off? That's why I charge the same price to everyone."

Ravish spoke more slowly now. "No one has to know, Winnie. Think about $1,550 in your pocket right now. For overlooking a silly tax and giving us a small break. You can call it a 'volume discount for Volume Libraries.'" His guests chuckled at Ravish's pun. Ravish continued, "Come on, Winnie. We're salespeople too. This is no big deal." He sat back in his plush chair and sighed softly. "If you don't like the deal, you should leave now."

Winnie considered the offer. The names of these families and their children would open doors in this neighborhood. He desperately needed information about Temple, which these people could give him. Next summer, the Southwestern Company would send students out to work in this area again, just as he was now working in a territory where someone had sold books in the previous summer. The information he collected would benefit them tremen-dously, as would the testimonials they would be able to obtain from five families of book owners.

Ravish was right—no one had to find out about this discount. It was only a small discount. Winnie also felt that the GST was a silly tax. And $500 would end his peanut-butter-and-jelly marathon immediately. He could almost taste a steak dinner and chocolate milkshake. Winnie took a slow deep breath, and spoke to Ravish.

CASE 17-2   AEROSPACE SYSTEMS, INC. (B)

Disclosure of Planned Terminations

More than 10,000 employees of Aerospace Systems had already been terminated as a result of the defense contract cutbacks being experienced by all firms in the defense industry. The company's plight was well reported in the news media.

One of the company's divisions was involved in developing computer networking systems. While its work was not being discontinued, it was being reduced to a level that could be sustained by its nondefense business. Consequently, its sales staff of 56 people had been reduced to 35 sales reps in early 1993. Mark Simpson, the divisional vice president, was meeting with Simon West, the sales manager, about future plans for the sales force. Simpson informed West, "You'll have to let 10 more of your sales reps go on January 1. Give them two weeks' notice and the usual severance package. Try to get rid of the highly paid ones first. Some of your older sales reps are making more than $100,000 a year, while most of the younger people are making $50,000 to $60,000."

West detested what he was being told. He disagreed with the company policies. His silent response to Simpson's orders were "Yeah, they're being paid a lot more than the young ones and for good reason. They make us a lot more money." But Simon West kept his thoughts to himself because he had no place else to work and he enjoyed his $130,000-a-year-plus-benefits salary. He did ask, "Can't we give them more than two weeks' notice?"

Simpson stared coldly at West and said, "You know better than that. Don't you dare tell anyone about our plans. The minute you tell someone, they're history—they quit working for you and start working for themselves. Our obligation is to the company, not to its former employees. We are trying to save this company. It's been good to us. A lot of people are depending on us to do what must be done if the company is to survive. Now, if you don't want to do the job, just say so and . . ."

Simpson did not have a chance to finish his statement before West cut him off. "No, no, I'll do it. I'll have to work out a lot of details about maintaining the coverage of accounts." West said no more and left Simpson's office.

Upon returning to his office, West was met by Bob Lilly, the company's leading sales rep, who also serviced the company's most important commercial account.

After the customary greetings, Lilly said, "I just got off the phone with Mike Markings, who is now president of Spacetech. He wants me to be his sales manager. The pay is about the same as I am making here, but you know that I like it here. I have 20 years of my life invested here, so I don't want to leave. However, the jungle tom-toms have been sending out some messages that there are going to be some more cutbacks coming up in the sales department. If that's true, me and my big salary could be a tempting target. So if I am going to be history around here, then I'll have to leave now to take the Spacetech job. We've been buddies for more than 10 years, Simon. Tell me, is it time to move on? You owe me that much!"

Simon West knew he had to give Bob Lilly an immediate answer. If he didn't, that in itself would be the answer.

Question:

1. What should Simon West say to Bob Lilly?

CASE 17-3   FAIRFAX FILTER FABRICATORS

A Question of Ethics in Selling

"I realize that I'm the new kid on the block and that I may be unduly influenced by my background at Wheelabrator, where our sales policies were highly structured. In that company we really followed the book. Even so, I don't see how Fairfax Filters can continue with the freewheeling selling tactics that some of our guys are using." The speaker was Elsa Brock, the newly hired sales manager for the Fairfax Filter Fabricators Company. Brock was especially concerned about the selling techniques employed by Bernard Nally, one of Fairfax Filter's top salespeople.

Fairfax Filter Fabricators was a Louisiana-based company that produced dust-collector bags—a replaceable part of the equipment used to clean polluted air discharged from smokestacks. These dust-collector bags typically were long, cylindrically shaped pieces of fabric with a closed end. They were produced in a variety of diameters and lengths, depending on the design specified by the filter equipment manufacturers. The bags were available in several fabrics. The particular fabric selected depended on the size of the particulates being filtered, the heat of the discharged air, and how much shock the bags would receive. The most widely used bags were heavy-duty units made from a synthetic felt material with a plastic coating.

Most filter equipment periodically shook the bags or reversed the air flow in order to clean the particulates from the bag so it could be reused. Nevertheless, these bags had to be regularly replaced. The bags were rather simply made and the start-up equipment to manufacture dust-collector bags was relatively inexpensive.

But the market for these bags was big and growing, with all the attention being devoted to reducing air pollution in the United States. Fairfax's annual sales were about $20 million. Its main market was the Louisiana–Texas Gulf Coast, where there was a concentration of petrochemical and other industrial manufacturing plants. In that geographical market, Fairfax was a major supplier of dust-collector bags. In terms of nationwide business, however, Fairfax was not classed as a major firm. Nationally, the big firms were a division of Albany International Company (which in turn was a division of the Carborundum Company), Menardi-Southern Corporation, and P&S Textiles Company.

The bag-replacement industry was very competitive because there was little difference among the products of the various manufacturers. Most firms had experienced sales reps calling on engineers and purchasing agents at the customers' plants. Most of them knew each other from occasional chance meetings at the customers' locations. All reps were familiar with the others' products and selling methods. However, the people at Fairfax believed they had one competitive differential advantage in their primary target market—the Louisiana–Texas Gulf Coast region. In that market Fairfax was the only bag manufacturer that was not a division of a large national company that assigned profit requirements to its bag-replacement division. Fairfax executives felt that this feature allowed them to respond quickly and flexibly to their customers' requirements and requests.

In the past, all the usual activities of a sales manager had been handled by Fairfax's president, Edward Jurgens. Typically, Jurgens had hired male sales reps who had selling experience, though not necessarily in the air-filter industry. Currently the sales force consisted of eight men who averaged four years each with Fairfax. They were paid under a straight-commission compensation plan. Each rep was assigned a sales volume quota based on the sales forecast for his territory. The reps were paid a commission of 3 percent on sales up to their quota and 4 percent for all sales over the quota. The additional 1 percent was calculated at the end of the year and added to the last month's commission check. The average annual pay for the salespeople was $80,000, which was above the industry average.

As Fairfax's market continued to grow, Ed Jurgens realized he could not, and should not, continue to wear two hats—company president and sales manager. Consequently, he established a

Adapted from a case prepared by George W. Kyle, under the direction of Professor William J. Stanton.

separate position of sales manager. For that position Jurgens wanted someone with some technical knowledge of original filter equipment. He hired Elsa Brock, who had been a top-performing sales rep at Wheelabrator-Frye, a major producer of filter equipment. Brock had a bachelor's degree in engineering and an MBA from Louisiana State University. Jurgens felt that Brock knew the petrochemical industry and other industries that constituted Fairfax's primary market. Jurgens's only concern was whether his all-male sales force would work as effectively for Elsa Brock as they had for him.

Fairfax's top rep in terms of sales volume was Bernard Nally, an ex–All American football player from one of the football powers of the Southeastern Conference. Nally's territory included primarily chemical plants and oil companies located along the Mississippi River from Baton Rouge, Louisiana, down to the Gulf of Mexico, plus some firms along the Gulf Coast near the mouth of the Mississippi River.

Nally had a reputation of doing whatever was necessary to get an order. He had been able to operate in this manner because Ed Jurgens had been too busy running the company to establish any policies for sales rep relationships with customers. Elsa Brock, in contrast, came from a highly structured multinational organization with very strict policies covering sales force–customer relations. Consequently, when she arrived at Fairfax, Brock felt that policies in the rep–customer area needed to be established, put in writing, and enforced.

Brock was especially concerned about one relationship that Bernie Nally had established with several of his customers. Nally had what was called the "last look" at competitive bids submitted. Nally, along with competitors' sales reps, submitted a bid on a filter-bag order being placed by a chemical company. After all the bids were in, the purchasing agent for the chemical company gave Nally a last look at all the bids. Then Nally could revise the Fairfax bid to come in with a lower price and consequently get the order. Nally had established this last-look relationship with several customers, and this was a major factor accounting for his high sales volume. Nally had been able to develop these relationships by a mix of (1) his image as a winner, (2) a pleasant personality, (3) entertainment that included football tickets and golf

outings, and (4) the fact that his customers liked the idea of associating with a former All American who was a conference legend.

Elsa Brock then discussed several sales policy situations with Ed Jurgens without spotlighting Bernard Nally's last-look bidding system. Jurgens reminded Brock that she had been hired to run the sales force. He told her to do whatever she thought was necessary as far as sales policies were concerned. He went on to say that he had complete confidence in her decisions. He also agreed that Fairfax was now large enough to need established policies regarding sales tactics and techniques.

Back in her own office, Brock realized that the Nally problem had no really good solution. Any decision she made could easily result in a loss of business, a loss of Fairfax's best sales rep, or a compromise in her belief that Nally's technique was unethical.

Brock decided to have a talk with Nally, and she believed it would be better if this meeting were held someplace outside their offices. She thus used the occasion of a joint sales call with Nally on a new account. After the call, they went to a restaurant for lunch and Brock took that opportunity to discuss the idea of establishing policies to cover various selling situations.

She explained to Nally that she felt the company should have a firm policy to the effect that only one bid would be offered on potential orders. She went on to explain that the company's bid should be based on a predetermined profit margin. She pointed out that even though Nally was the rep with the highest sales volume and dollar profits, his percentage profit margin was the lowest among the entire sales force.

Bernie Nally was very upset with Elsa Brock's proposed change in his method of doing business. He told her that his margins were lower than those of other reps because most of his customers placed orders that were very large and did not allow for a larger margin. He also reminded her that many of his orders were contracts for annual supply for multiplant usage. He reminded her that he had built up his business over several years of hard work and that Ed Jurgens was aware of his practices. Nally went on to say that it would not be fair to the reps to change the rules since the sales force was being paid on a straight commission.

Nally implied that Brock was not qualified to make such sweeping changes. He also suggested that if he lost business because of her policy changes, he could always go with a competitor and take the business with him. Since filter replacement bags were fairly generic, Brock knew that if Nally went, it could have a very negative effect on Fairfax's sales volume.

Brock decided not to press the situation in the restaurant and told Nally she would decide by the next sales meeting what changes would be made. Brock began to doubt her decision to leave Wheelabrator-Frye. She wondered if being a woman had any bearing on the situation involving Nally. She knew that whatever she decided to do in this situation, it must be done soon, and with an appearance of confident firmness.

Questions:

1. What sales policy, if any, should Elsa Brock introduce regarding the bidding practices used by the Fairfax salespeople?

2. Is Bernard Nally's "last-look" bidding technique an ethical selling tactic?

APPENDIX A

Integrative Cases

Integrative Cases: Case-by-Chapter Grid*

								Chapter									
	1	2	3	4	5	6	7	8	9	10	11	12	13	14	15	16	17
Smith & Nephew—Innovex		X	X						X				X				X
A. T. Kearney		X			X	X	X	X	X							X	
Infosystems Technologies Ltd.		X		X				X	X								
Johnson Drug Company	X	X	X		X	X	X	X	X		X						
Hanover-Bates Chemical Corporation												X		X	X	X	
ChemGrow, Inc.														X	X	X	

*The grid indicate for which chapters each case is an appropriate supplement.

CASE A-1 SMITH & NEPHEW—INNOVEX

Evaluating the Use of Sales Agents

At the beginning of March 2000, James Brown, CEO of Smith & Nephew, S. A. (S&N), was in a meeting with Josep Serra, Director of the Medical Division.

Almost six months earlier, on September 29, 1999, they had signed an agency contract with Innovex employees that would promote S&N's moist wound healing (MWH) products Allevyn®, Intrasite® Gel, and Opsite®[1] to primary care centers[2] in Galicia and Astruias (see map in Exhibit 1–5). It was the first time S&N had used the services of a contract or outsourced sales force in Spain.

Among other things, the contact specified that the agreement would expire on March 29, 2000.

Brown and Serra had to assess the results of their collaboration with Innovex and decide not only what to do in Galicia and Asturias but also, more generally, what their policy should be with respect to the sales personnel who promoted the company's MWH products in the rest of Spain.

Smith & Nephew, S. A. (S&N)

Smith & Nephew, S. A. (S&N), was the Spanish subsidiary of the Smith & Nephew group (for information on the group, see Exhibit 1–1).

Founded in Spain in 1963, S&N sold in Spain the health care products manufactured by the Smith & Nephew group in various countries, mainly the United Kingdom and the United States,

though it also imported products from France, Germany and South Africa, among others.

With annual sales of more than 4,000 million pesetas, the Spanish subsidiary had two commercial divisions: a medical division, and a surgical division. Between them these two sold all of the group's product ranges and families except consumer health care products, which were sold almost exclusively in the United Kingdom and some former Commonwealth countries. The company also had an administrative and finance division.

At the beginning of the year 2000, James Brown had been with the Smith & Nephew group for 18 years. He had been appointed CEO of the Spanish subsidiary in 1993. He reported to the Managing Director for Contiental Europe, who, in turn, reported to the Group Commercial Director, who was a member of the Group Executive Committee, along with the chief executive, the three presidents of the group's Global Business Units, and other senior executives.

The Spanish subsidiary had been the official supplier of certain health care products during the 1992 Barcelona Olympics. It had had ISO 9002 certification for several years and had almost finished computerizing its entire sales network.

Since November 1998 S&N had been using the services of a specialized shipping and logistics company, which under contract, took care of the reception of imported goods, storage, stock control, order preparation, and transport and delivery to the customer's address. Given its small workforce of fewer than 100 people, S&N also outsourced certain other services, such as payroll administration and social security paperwork, legal and tax advice, design and execution of advertising materials, organization of sales conventions, etc.

---

[1] Allevyn®, Opsite® and Intrasite® Gel are registered trademarks of T. S. Smith & Nephew Lts. Innovex™ and Quintles™ are registered trademarks of Quintiles Transnational Corporation.

[2] Also known as health centers, basic health areas, or, previously, outpatient clinics. They delivered primary care services to the population covered by Spanish Social Security. There were some 3,000 primary care centers in the country as a whole, each tied to a referral hospital. A hospital and the group of primary care centers tied to it made up what was known as a health management area.

Case of the Research Department at IESE.

Prepared by Professor Lluis G. Renart, May 2000.

It is intended to be used as a basis for class discussion rather than to illustrate either effective or ineffective handling of an administrative situation.

Last edited: 1/16/01

And yet the company had an uneven profit record, and its management faced certain challenges. For example, throughout 1998 and 1999 the pound sterling had steadily appreciated against the peseta, giving rise to a steady income in the peseta cost of the products sold in Spain, most of which were imported from the United States and the United Kingdom.

Selling prices in the Spanish market for health care products were significantly lower than in other European countries. Also, in Spain it was more difficult to raise prices because the Social Security Administration often did its purchasing by a system of open bidding, and because other competitors were less affected by the strength of the dollar and sterling.

CASE EXHIBIT 1-1   The Smith & Nephew Group

This global medical device company, headquartered in London, traced its origins back to 1856 when Thomas James Smith founded a pharmacy in Hull in the United Kingdom.[1] In 1896, the founder brought his nephew Horatio Nelson Smith into the business as a partner, giving rise to the name Smith & Nephew. The company grew rapidly with the addition of products such as elastic adhesive bandages (Elastoplast), plaster casts (Geypsona), and sanitary towels (Lilia), often through acquisitions.

In 1999, the group reported worldwide sales of 1,120 million pounds sterling,[2] with earnings of 171 million pounds[3] before tax and extraordinary income. In that year the group had activities in 90 countries. Geographically, the sales revenues were distributed as follows: 19% in the UK, 20% in continental Europe, 43% in America, and the remaining 17% in Africa, Asia, and Oceania.

The main product ranges or families sold worldwide were: orthopedics and trauma (mainly hip and knee prostheses, and trauma implants, 26%

of worldwide sales); endoscopy (particularly knee and shoulder arthroscopy, 18%); wound management (e.g. Allevyn®, Opsite®, and Intrasite® Gel, 21%); orthosis and rehabilitation, casting and bandaging (bandages and plaster casts), and otology (prostheses and instrumentation for microsurgery of the inner ear) (together, 18%); and consumer health care (17%). In the 1999 annual report, Chris O'Donnell, Chief Executive, declared: "We are concentrating our strategic investment on the three markets of orthopedics [implants and trauma procedures], endoscopy and wound management." Each of these three global business units (GBUs) was headed by a president.

In these three specialties, or in some of their subspecialties, the Smith & Nephew group held first or second place in the global ranking. In its three priority business units it expected to grow both organically and through acquisitions, whereas growth in its other businesses would be basically organic.

The group invested 4% of its sales revenue in research and development. One of its latest developments, precisely in the Wound Management GBU, was Dermagraft, a dressing of human tissue developed through bioengineering processes, which made it possible to heal certain types of chronic ulcers, such as diabetic foot ulcers, in just a few weeks. Although at the beginning of the year 2000 it was already being sold in some countries, Dermagraft was not yet available in Spain.

To summarize, starting from British parent company, the group had evolved to the point where it had a broad range of ever more high-tech health care products that were sold around the globe.

---

[1] In fact, Thomas Southall had founded a pharmacy in Birmingham as early as 1820, and Southalls (Birmingham) Ltd. had been acquired by Smith & Nephew in 1958. So the roots of the company could be said to stretch back even further, to 1820.

[2] Equivalent to approximately 1,800 million dollars or euros, or almost 300,000 million pesetas, at the exchange rates prevailing at the beginning of March 2000. On January 1, 1999, the exchange rate of the peseta had been irrevocably fixed at a rate of 166,386 pesetas per euro. At the beginning on 1999, the euro had traded at 1.18 dollars, but over the year had steadily slipped against the dollar until by the end of February 2000 one euro was practically equal to one dollar. Thus, the peseta was quoted at 166 pesetas per dollar, and 267 pesetas per pound sterling. At the beginning of the year 2000 the pound sterling, the Greek drachma, the Swedish krona, and the Danish krone had not joined the euro.

[3] Data about the group are taken from the Smith & Nephew plc "1999 Annual Report and Accounts." For more information, go to www.smith-nephew.com.

CASE A-1   SMITH & NEPHEW—INNOVEX   (continued)

Commercialization of Health Care Products in Spain

According to EC directives, before a health care product could be commercialized it first had to obtain the "CE marking" from an authorized body in any EU member country. In addition to this, in Spain the company commercializing the product had to submit, generally to the Ministry of Health or the regional government, a "market introduction report." Once these requirements had been met, the product could be marketed and sold.

However, given the way Social Security operated in Spain, the second key required for a product to achieve widespread use was for the product to gain approval from the Social Security Administration as a reimbursable product. Reimbursable products were identified by what was known as the *cupon precinto* or "Social Security coupon."[3] As is explained in greater detail later on, obtaining reimbursable status as certified by the Social Security coupon was critical for sales of a particular product through pharmacies, though not strictly necessary for its use in hospitals.

The Social Security coupon was a rectangle printed on the packaging of each unit of product, with perforated edges to allow it to be detached. On it were printed the initials A.S.S.S. ("Social Security health care"), the commercial name of the product, certain data about the product and manufacturer, and the price.

Health Care Products Sold in Pharmacies

In the case of drugs and health care products sold in pharmacies, patients covered by Social Security had to obtain a prescription from their Social Security physician, who would usually have her office in a primary care center. They could then take the prescription to any pharmacy to obtain the medicine. At the time of purchase, the patient would have to pay 40 percent of the retail price (except for pensioners and the chronically ill, for

whom prescriptions were completely free). Before handing over the product, the pharmacist would cut out the Social Security coupon and staple it to the prescription, so as later to be able to obtain reimbursement of the remaining 60 percent (or 100 percent if sold to pensioner or chronic patient) from the Social Security Administration.

If a drug or health care product was authorized for sale but did not have the Social Security coupon, a patient could still apply to the Social Security Administration's own medical inspection service for reimbursement as an exceptional case, but this was a very laborious procedure with no guarantee of success. The alternative was to pay the full 100 percent of the retail price. In either case use of the product was seriously inhibited, above all if there were alternative health care products on the market that had similar therapeutic qualities and were reimbursable.

Given the pressure to contain health spending in the Spanish state budget, it was quite possible for a more modern and more efficient yet more expensive drug or health care product not to obtain Social Security approval because an alternative product was available which, while not so advanced from a therapeutic point of view and possibly less efficient, could cover the same need.

Health Care Products Used in Hospitals and Primary Care Centers

In hospitals, whether a health care product was reimbursable or not had no direct impact on sales (though it did affect them indirectly, as we shall see later). Private hospitals and clinics purchased health care products in the normal way, paying the price freely agreed with the manufacturer or distributor.

Hospitals and primary care centers belonging to the Social Security Administration, in contrast, used a system of procurement by public bidding. Usually, an individual hospital or primary care center, or all of the hospitals and primary care centers in a particular geographical area, would issue an invitation to tender once a year, specifying the quantity and characteristics of the products they wanted to purchase. All of this would be set out in a bidding document, which would also specify the

---

[3]Only products classed as "medical accessories" (under Royal Decree Legislative 9/1996 of January 15, which regulates the selection of medical accessores, their financing from Social Security funds or government funds earmarked for healthcare, and the basis on which they may be supplied and dispensed to outpatients) could apply for reimbursement.

information and other things required of prospective bidders, the bid closing date, the selection criteria, etc.

Health Care Products for Ulcer and Wound Care

Traditionally, the main wound care products were elastic adhesive bandages, gauzes, and the classic dressings. These constituted what was known as the wet-to-dry method. In the year 2000, wet-to-dry dressings were still commonly used in the management of acute wounds, where it was possible to predict the duration of the healing process. They were products with a low unit value, and so whether they were reimbursable or not was practically irrelevant, as hardly anybody went to the doctor to get a prescription for a roll of plaster.

From the early 80s onward, however, a new method, known as moist wound healing, began to be adopted in the treatment of chronic ulcers.[4] It was found that wounds healed more quickly if they were kept moist and protected from infection, allowing the passage of moisture vapor and maintaining the physiological temperature. Over the years, a variety of products for moist wound healing (MWH) came onto the market, such as polyurethane dressings, hydrocolloids, alginates, hydrocellular dressings, and carbon moist wound dressings.

In Spain, in 1999, the total market for MWH products was worth around 3,200 million pesetas at manufacturer's prices. Of this total, around 1,870 million was sold through pharmacies and around 1,300, to hospitals and clinics. A large proportion of the total MWH market consisted of hydrocolloids.

The main competitors in the MWH product category were C.S. (with a market share of around 35 percent), Danplast (22 percent), and Smith & Nephew (9 percent).[5]

---

[4]Chronic ulcers are ulcers of unpredictable duration. The healing process can easily go on for several months. The most common causes of chronic ulcers are continuous pressure on a particular part of the body (e.g., bedsores) or vascular or circulatory problems. A chronic ulcer can be shallow or deep, and in serious cases can lead to necrosis or gangrene, and may even require amputation of the affected part.

[5]Throughout the case, unless stated otherwise, the market shares of specific products refer to the pharmacies channel, which was monitored by IMS, a market research services company. Market share data for hospitals were difficult to estimate, as they depended on the outcome of the bidding process.

The Medical Division of Smith & Nephew, S. A. (S&N)

Under the overall management of Josep Serra, the medical division's sales and marketing activities were carried out by a sales team and a marketing team. In 1999 the division had total sales in the region of 3,000 million pesetas, shared between three product families: wound care (1,000 million); casting and bandaging; and orthosis, rehabilitation, and aids for everyday living (2,000 million between these last two families).

Of the 1,000 million pesetas in wound care, around 600 million were wet-to-dry and around 400 million, moist wound healing (MWH) products.

At the beginning of the year 2000, S&N competed in only three categories MWH products (in various sizes and varieties):

- Intrasite® Gel, a cleaning hydrogel that regenerated the ulcer, debriding and absorptive, sold in packs of five 15g units. It had the Social Security coupon. In 1999, S&N had sold 130 million pesetas of the product and had a market share in this subcategory in the order of 40 percent of sales through pharmacies.

- The Allevyn® range, a controlled absorption hydrocellular dressing. Three sizes of the range had the Social Security coupon. In 1999, S&N had sold 170 million pesetas of the product and had a market share in this subcategory in the order of 50 percent of sales through pharmacies.

- The Opsite® range, a transparent polyurethane dressing. Six sizes of the range had the Social Security coupon. In 1999, S&N had sold 100 million pesetas of the product and had a market share in this subcategory in the order of 90 percent of sales through pharmacies.

These products had various technical advantages that made the healing of an ulcer or wound faster, safer, and less painful. However, the correct prescription, use, and application of MWH products required certain knowledge that only doctors and nurses were likely to have. This meant that patients and their relatives very rarely influenced the type of product used. Nevertheless, a significant volume of MWH products was sold through pharmacies. It was true that it was always a doctor who prescribed the use of a particular product. But, often, a relative of a housebound chronically ill patient would go to the pharmacy, obtain the product free of charge, and then give it to the nurse who, in the course of a home visit, would apply the dressing.

The management of S&N medical division estimated that slightly over 50 percent of their MWH products were sold through pharmacies. Almost all the remainder, just under 50 percent, was used in hospitals and primary care centers belonging to the Social Security Administration.

S&N Medical Division's Sales and Promotional Activities

The division's *sales* efforts, strictly speaking (i.e., activities undertaken to generate orders and invoices), were conducted in three channels:

1. Sales to Social Security hospitals and primary care centers were made by bidding in yearly auctions.[6] Products that won a contract would be supplied and billed over the course of the year, and were used either in the hospital or primary care center itself, or during home visits.

2. Sales to pharmacies were accomplished through pharmaceutical wholesalers or cooperatives, which replenished their stocks at regular intervals with S&N having to make hardly any effort to sell to them.

3. Lastly, the medical division's own sales representatives sold directly to private hospitals and large private clinics, or indirectly through health care product wholesalers/distributors, to other private hospitals and clinics, geriatric homes and the private practices of doctors and vets.

The division's *promotional* efforts were targeted at doctors and, above all, nurses. The aim was to bring the products to their attention, explain their advantages and how to use them, give the doctors and nurses an opportunity to try them out, and explain to them the differential therapeutic advantages of the company's products compared with older or competing alternatives.

When dealing with health care professionals working in the public health system, the sales representatives' mission was to persuade doctors and nurses to issue favorable reports on S&N's products.

Lastly, an important goal of the promotional effort was to ensure, once a contract had been won and the S&N product was in use in a given health care facility, that the product was always at hand for any doctor or nurse who needed it. As Joseph Serra remarked: "It's a major training and 'merchandising' challenge seeing to it that the products we sell are available on every floor, in every consulting room, on every trolley, and that they are used correctly."

Promotional Tasks Carried Out in the Field by the Medical Division's Own Sales Representatives

The national sales manager supervised two regional sales managers. Between them the two regional sales managers had 18 sales representatives and three commission agents, who did all the sales and promotional work for all the division's products.

This sales team's coverage of the Spanish market as a whole was considered poor, particularly compared with the division's main competitors. It was estimated that it covered almost 100 percent of the hospitals but only 20 percent of the primary care centers. In contrast, Danplast, S. A., was thought to have around 50 sales representatives, and another major competitor, C.S., S.A., more than 40.

S&N's marketing manager estimated that to be able to provide a satisfactory level of promotional and sales service for the medical division's products throughout Spain they would need about 40 sales representatives. Without that number it would be impossible to visit all the primary care centers.

One of the division's sales representatives nominally covered the area of Galicia. But given the size of the region,[7] in practice he only ever had time to visit hospitals, clinics, and health care product wholesalers.

---

[6]In 1999, S&N had bid in almost 500 auctions.

[7]Galicia has an area of 29,575 km^2 and is almost square in shape. In 1998 its population was approximately 2,716,000. Asturias is elongated and narrow in shape, with an area of 10,604 km^2 (approx. 200 × 50 km), and in 1998 had 1,060,000 inhabitants.

In 1999 the medical division's full-time sales representatives had sold an average of 150 million pesetas each, at an average cost per representative of 8.5 million pesetas, including salary, incentives, social security, vacations, and traveling expenses.

The division's three remaining commission agents (previously it had had five or six of them) had between them sold 150 million pesetas. The agent for the region of Extremadura was a company that had been working with S&N for about eight years. The other two agents were individuals. One covered the islands of Majorca and Ibiza, selling only S&N products. The other covered the island of Menorca, offering a very wide range of products by different companies, exclusively to hospitals. Both had been working with S&N for around 20 years, and in both cases the relationship was considered stable.

The commission agents had agency contracts. They visited only hospitals, that is to say, they did not promote the products to primary care centers. According to Serra, "They go for the guaranteed sales, what I mean is, they try to sell the products for which there's already a demand. They don't make much effort to introduce new products. They're undoubtedly more profitable than having full-time representatives of our own in those territories. That would be too expensive, in the case of Extremadura because its so extensive, and in the other cases because they're islands."

When they made a sale without going through a bidding process, the commission agents would close the deal and pass the order on to S&N, which would serve the goods, invoice the customers, and collect payments. The commission agents were only responsible for collecting debts from private (non-public) customers, and earned a commission of between 7 percent and 10 percent. When there was an auction, the commission agents would gather the necessary information, so that S&N executives could prepare the documentation and put in a bid.

Other Promotional Activities Carried Out by the Marketing Department: Advertising, Seminars, "Study Days"

In addition to the sales and promotional activities carried out by the medical division's sales team, the marketing department, consisting of a marketing manager and two product managers, carried out a number of complementary activities. These consisted mainly of:

- Advertising the division's products through inserts in medical journals and through special brochures.

- Attending nursing conferences organized by the professional associations of nurses for particular medical specialities. For example, in 1999 S&N had attended four conferences, including one in Bilbao on gerontological nursing. Attending a medium-sized conference could cost S&N around 3 million pesetas. A conference could be attended and sponsored by some 15–20 companies.

- Study days: These were meetings, organized entirely by S&N and generally held in a hotel, with a specific scientific interest provided by a guest speaker. Following the guest speaker's lecture, an S&N product manager would present the company's products for the application in question. The meeting would end with a colloquium and aperitifs.

In 1999, 23 study days had been held, each of which had been attended by around 65 specially invited nurses. The average cost per study day had been around 300,000 pesetas. To make the most of these occasions, it was vital to carry out close personal follow-up.

Social Security Approval for the Allevyn® Range and First Contacts with Innovex

Up until April 1998, only two of Smith & Nephew, S.A.'s MWH products had the Social Security coupon and were therefore reimbursable: Intrasite® Gel and Opsite®. In fact, hardly any other medical division product had the coupon. In April 1998, after a long wait, S&N's Allevyn® product was finally granted the right to carry the prized coupon. This was an important development, as Allevyn® was potentially a similarly priced but functionally superior substitute for hydrocolloids, which accounted for a large proportion of total market for MWH products.

Allevyn® was already sold by bidding to hospitals and primary care centers. Now, with the Social Security coupon, it seemed set to achieve a significant volume of sales through the pharmacy channel. With sales potential to hospitals and primary care centers currently in the order of 1,100 million pesetas, its potential market could therefore be considered to be augmented by a further 1,600 million or so, in the pharmacy channel, despite the fact that only some of the sizes in which the product was sold were reimbursable by Social Security.

As we said earlier, in order to bid in Social Security procurement auctions, a product did not have to be reimbursable. However, doctors and nurses preferred, when starting treatment of a wound or ulcer in hospital, to use products that *were* reimbursable because that made it much easier for the patient to continue the treatment at home, using the same products as in the hospital.

Conversely, if a particular product was *not* reimbursable, doctors and nurses were sometimes reluctant to use it, even in the hospital, so as not to have to change the patient's prescription on discharge and prescribe a different product that *was* reimbursable and would therefore be free of charge for the patient.

First Fruitless Contact with Innovex

In March 1998, with approval of Allevyn® now imminent, the medical division's top executives contacted Innovex, an international company already established in Spain that specialized in providing contract sales teams for the pharmaceutical and medical devices industry (see Exhibit 1–2 for information on Quintiles Transnational Corporation and its Innovex division). They were keen to explore the possibility of contacting a team of Innovex sales representatives to reinforce the efforts being made by the medical division's own sales team to promote its MWH products to primary care centers.

Smith & Nephew's Spanish subsidiary had never worked with Innovex previously, nor with any other company that offered this kind of contract sales services. But they knew that it was a fairly common practice among their competitors in the health care industry, particularly when launching new products onto the market. Also, colleagues in the group's United Kingdom offices confirmed that they had worked with Innovex and thought highly of the company. One or two other companies that provided services similar to those of Innovex were contacted for the purpose of comparison. In

the end, however, the idea of working with Innovex was dropped for fear that the necessary level of sales and profitability might not be attained.

Developments in the Period April 1998 to February 1999

Between April and June 1998, sales of Allevyn® rose sharply, only to flatten out again in the following months. By February 1999, the management of the medical division were concerned that if they did not take decisive action, Allevyn® was in danger of being sidelined, with a share of only 2 percent or 3 percent of the total MWH market in Spain.

In this situation, they decided that the only course of action was, on the one hand, to intensify and extend the promotional activities aimed at customers already covered by the company's sales team; and on the other, to achieve fuller coverage of primary care centers in the underserved regions of Valencia, Andalusia, Galicia, and Asturias.

The medical division's managers were in a tight spot: there seemed to be a potentially profitable opportunity to promote Allevyn® to primary care centers, but CEO James Brown and his superiors would be reluctant to add to the company's workforce.

Steps toward an Agreement with Innovex

In March 1999 the management of S&N's medical division got back in touch with Innovex to explore the feasibility of contacting a team of medical sales representatives to promote the products of the Opsite®, Intrasite® Gel, and Allevyn® ranges in the regions of Spain hitherto least well covered by the company's own sales staff and commission agents.

In all, they considered the possibility of contracting from Innovex a team of 10 sales representatives and an area manager to serve Galicia (3), Asturias (1), Andalusia (3), and Valencia (3).

Ideally, S&N's management would have preferred to contract a sales team that would devote only 50 percent of its time to promoting S&N's products. Unfortunately, at that time they were unable to find any other company in the health care sector that needed Innovex sales representatives working half-time for precisely the hours that

CASE EXHIBIT 1-2   The Quintiles Transnational Group and Its Innovex Division

Innovex Spain, S. L., was the Spanish subsidiary of Innovex Inc., which in turn was a division of Quintiles Transnational Corp. Both had their headquarters in North Carolina, United States.[1] At the end of 1998 the Quintiles group had more than 18,000 employees in 31 countries and that year reported net revenue of $1,188 million. Of this total, $583 million had been generated in the United States and $340 million in the United Kingdom.

The Quintiles group provided full, outsourced research, sales, marketing, health care policy consulting and information management services to pharmaceutical, biotechnology, medical devices, and health care companies throughout the world.

For example, a pharmaceutical laboratory could turn to the Quintiles group to take care of anything from the basic research needed to synthesize a new molecule or active substance (Phase 1), plus any of the intermediate phases of research and development, clinical trials by physicians and hospitals, data compilation, etc., to the management of the new drug approval and registration process (Phase 4). Then, if it wanted, the laboratory could also hire the Quintiles group to do all the marketing and actually bring the product to market.

Innovex Inc. was a division of the Quintiles group that specialized in sales and marketing services for third parties.

In 1998, Innovex Inc. was present in 19 countries and had more than 7,000 sales representatives, sales managers, and marketing directors. In that year its sales teams had made an average of almost 2 million product presentations per month.

Innovex had been present in Spain since 1996, when it had acquired an existing Spanish company that was already active in the business of providing contact sales teams. Subsequently it had extended, or intended to extend, its services to other areas connected with the commercialization of drugs or medical devices, such as marketing and sales strategy consulting, training, communication, and resource optimization.

As Jesús Polanco, CEO of Innovex's Spanish subsidiary, pointed out: "It's not just a matter of 'getting people out knocking on doors.' In line with the group's general approach, we aim to create value by carefully managing each sales territory, monitoring the costs and results of our actions collecting and compiling the valuable commercial information generated in each territory, and so on." See Exhibit 1–3 for various examples of Innovex's more recent projects in Spain.

At the end of 1999, Innovex's Spanish subsidiary had a team of 152 people. Of these, 17 belonged to the management team, while the remaining 135 made up the sales force that went out "knocking on doors." Seventy-seven of the sales representatives were full-time Innovex employees, with open-ended contracts, while the remaining 58 had temporary contracts linked to a particular job for a client.

---

[1] Data are taken from Quintiles Transnational Corp.'s 1998 annual report. For further details, go to www.corporate. quintiles.com and, www.innovexglobal.com.

---

would fit in the S&N's requirements, in the same geographical areas and for the six-month period S&N envisaged. It was therefore agreed that the sales team contracted from Innovex should devote 100 percent of its time to promoting S&N's MWH products to primary care centers.

In view of the cost this would represent, S&N's management asked Innovex to submit a formal offer for the provision of just two sales representatives to promote S&N's MWH products to primary

care centers in Galicia and Asturias. At that time, Arturo, the company's only sales representative in Galicia, only had time to visit the region's hospitals, so the primary care centers were more or less neglected.

If Innovex's offer was accepted, it would be very much an experiment. After six months, they would decide whether the system should be extended to other areas of Spain where the primary care centers were also relative poorly served, such

CASE EXHIBIT 1-3   Examples of Recent Projects Carried Out by Innovex in Spain in the Field of Contract Sales

Zeneca

Before Zeneca merged with Astra to form Atra-Zeneca, it planned to launch two new products in the same year. To do this, Zeneca's sales force required reinforcement in the form of 65 people hired from Innovex for a period of two years to carry out visits to cardiologists, neurologists, psychiatrists, and general practitioners. The main goal was rapid market share gain to block the entry of competitors. However, it would have been too expensive to keep the 65 people on for a second phase focused on maintaining the products' market presence.

Géminis

Géminis was the new generic pharmaceuticals division of Novaris, which marketed out-of-patent products. As it was a new division, the company did not want to hire extra sales representatives until they had seen what results the new division was capable of achieving. Note that promoting generics requires a different sales approach, both when selling to doctors and when to selling to pharmacies.

The task Innovex undertook between 1998 and 2000 initially required a team of 12 promoters, later expanded to 17.

Pierre Fabre

Pierre Fabre contracted a team of seven "beautician" promoters from Innovex to persuade and educate pharmacists to recommend, for each individual customer, the most appropriate Klorane® product from among a wide range of shampoos and hair creams.

Cardionetics

At the beginning of the year 2000, Innovex was preparing to set up a "virtual" company, i.e., using only temporary employees, to commercialize in Spain an innovative portable ECG device for monitoring and diagnosing abnormal heart rhythms as a person went about his normal daily activities. It would be reasonable for all the functional areas involved in commercialization, including, among other activities, the deployment of a contract sales team.

---

as Valencia and Andalusia. S&N's management chose to conduct the trial in Galicia and Asturias because, of all the poorly covered areas, Galicia was the most suitable.

On July 2, 1999, Jesús Polanco, for Innovex, presented the project to the top managers of S&N's medical division (see Exhibit 1–4 for a summary of his presentation).

On September 29, 1999, after discussing certain details without making any substantial changes, James Brown and Jesús Polanco signed the contract for a term of six months—i.e., to March 29, 2000. Besides the operational details, the contract included clauses regulating confidentiality, contract termination in the event of non-compliance by either of the parties, etc.

Lastly, S&N undertook not to hire any of the Innovex employees involved in the project, and agreed to pay Innovex compensation equal to a percentage of the employee's base salary if it did.

In the case of the sales representatives, the compensation would be equal to 20 percent of 2.8 million pesetas per sales representative per year.

Execution of the Contract

As soon as the contact was signed, Innovex proceeded to select the two sales representatives. S&N gave its approval to the candidates chosen:

- Isabel, the person selected for Galicia, to be based in Vigo, already had some experience of medical sales visits. The S&N products she would have to promote were already known and used in the region, thanks to the hospital work done by Arturo, the local representative, who lived in Corunna. This meant that the new sales representative would have some local support.

- The person chosen for Asturias, Frederico, had little experience but the right profile and

CASE EXHIBIT 1-4

Summary of the Presentation Given on July 2, 1999, by Innovex's Jesús Polanco to the Top Management of Smith & Nephew, S.A.'s Medical Division

- The plan was to conduct a trial campaign to promote the products Opsite®, Interasite® Gel, and Allevyn® in the four provinces of Galicia and in Asturias using a team hired from Innovex, whose target contacts would be nurses. If the trial objectives were achieved, the scheme would be extended to other geographical areas.

- The contract would have a term of six months.

- The team contracted from Innovex would consist of two sales representatives, a project manager, a clerical assistant. The latter two would devote two days a month to the project. The sales representatives would receive five days' training.

- The sales representatives would devote their efforts exclusively to promoting the above-mentioned S&N products.

- The fee per sales representative would be 35,102 pesetas per day actually worked; i.e., neither sick leave nor vacations would be billed.

- The daily cost given above would include:

  - Salary and social security.
  - Health insurance and accident and third-party coverage.
  - Monthly food + travel expenses, including the sales representatives' traveling, parking, and telephone expenses up to a maximum of 80,000 pesetas per person per month.
  - Vacations.
  - All expenses deriving from the vehicles used by Innovex personnel in providing the contracted services.
  - Costs of personnel selection by Innovex (in particular the cost of press advertisements, costs associated with the selection interview, and the costs of hiring). Innovex would only select people who matched the profile and culture required by S&N.

- All aspects of payroll and associated costs, company cars, and the telephone expenses of the project manager.

- The costs of the administration department.

- The following items were not included in the price per day given above:

  - Incentives for the sales representatives.[1]
  - Promotions aimed at doctors and customers.
  - Promotional materials, samples, etc., which would have to be provided by S&N.
  - Trips and field visits by S&N executives.
  - Training costs. S&N would be responsible for all training in products, therapeutic areas, and customers.
  - Innovex would be responsible for managing the sales team. The two companies would agree on the kind of reporting and information S&N thought necessary in order to monitor the team's activities.

- In an appendix, Jesús Polanco's presentation also described:

  - The recommended profile for the sales representatives.
  - The selection process.
  - The functions of the Innovex project manager, who would liase between the two companies.
  - The responsibilities of Innovex's human resources department.
  - The responsibilities of Innovex's finance department.

- Finally, the presentation included a page stressing the advantages of using a sales team contracted from Innovex as opposed to a company-employed sales team.

---

[1] In the end no incentives were established.

plenty of enthusiasm. Asturias has the added disadvantage of having been neglected during the previous two years following the death of S&N's previous sales representative, who had not been replaced. Because of this, in Asturias there had not been the momentary surge in sales registered in other parts of Spain after Allevyn® got the Social Security coupon; and the products Frederico would have to promote were practically unknown in the region.

Both the Innovex sales representatives were given two weeks' training. In the first week they had three days' instruction on the products they would be promoting (given by S&N), and one day on sales techniques (given by Innovex). The second week was given over to on-the-job training, accompanied by one of the S&N regional sales managers. Following this, toward the middle of October 1999, they took up their posts in their respective sales territories and started to visit customers, using a list of primary care centers provided by Innovex and approved by S&N. The centers were ranked on an ABC basis according to their purchasing potential.

The regional sales manager for the central-northern area of S&N's medical division approved the sales routes proposed by Innovex, and after the first week started to accompany the two new representatives on their rounds.

According to the medical division sales manager, "We treated them as if they were our own employees."

It should be said, however, that about two weeks after Isabel, the representative for Galicia, had taken up her post, the marketing department held two study days in Vigo and Corunna, which had already been scheduled from earlier. This gave Isabel a chance to make contacts much more quickly than she could have done without the study days.

In Galicia, Isabel's promotional activities were concentrated in the provinces of Orense (342,000 inhabitants) and Pontevedra (904,000 inhabitants).

Both sales representatives took about three months to adapt to the normal pace of work.

Evaluation of the Results

At the end of February 2000, the director for S&N's medical division, together with his sales manager and marketing manager, analyzed the results on the basis of the data available at the time.

With regard to costs, the average amount billed by Innovex to S&N's had been 810,000 pesetas per sales representative per month.

With regard to sales, they had data from the territorial sales analysis (ATV)[8] for the last quarter of 1999, and internal billing data up to January 2000.

Everybody agreed that the results had been very different in the two areas:

- **In Galicia:** According to the October–December ATV report, the market share of Allevyn® Intrasite® Gel, and Opsite®, in pesetas, for the whole of Galicia had increased from 3.3 percent to 6.4 percent of the total value of MWH products sold. In Orense and in Pontevedra, the increase had been from 5.4 percent to 12 percent. The additional sales revenue (on top of the minimal revenue obtained previously in the region) amounted to around 5,133,000 pesetas in four months (October 1999–January 2000 inclusive).[9] The gross margin had been 1,540,000 pesetas—i.e., 30 percent on average.

- **In Asturias:** The market share of the three products, in the last quarter of 1999, had increased from 0.9 percent to 2.36 percent of total sales, in pesetas, of all MWH products sold by all companies in Asturias. The additional sales revenue amounted to only 1,484,000 pesetas. In four months (October 1999–January 2000 inclusive),[10] with a gross margin of 371,000 pesetas (25 percent).

---

[8]The company IMS conducted a panel study of pharmaceutical retailers. Usually, it only provided aggregate data for the whole of Spain. The territorial sales analysis (*analisis territorial de ventas, ATV*) was a special service that IMS provided, offering the same data broken down by geographical areas similar in size to postal districts.

[9]606,000 pesetas in October; 1,042,000 in November; 1,779,000 in December 1999; and 1,706,000 in January 2000.

[10]134,000 pesetas in October; 252,000 in November; 528,000 in December 1999; and 570,000 in January 2000.

CASE EXHIBIT 1-5   **Map of Spain Showing Autonomous Communities**

The difference in gross margin was due to the fact that the sales representative in Asturias had sold more products that had a lower gross margin. S&N's sales representatives did not know the gross margin of the products they sold. Only indirectly, through marketing actions, were they encouraged to sell higher gross margin products. Essentially, the difference in gross margin between Galicia and Asturias could be said to be due to chance factors.

In response to the low sales in Asturias, the regional sales manager felt that Frederico would have to improve his sales technique, in particular his closing abilities.

Sales Projection

In view of the actual results achieved, the medical division's marketing manager estimated that, if new Innovex sales representatives were introduced in other geographical areas, each one of them could be expected to generate roughly the following sales:

Month 1	450,000 pesetas
Month 2	900,000
Month 3	1,650,000
Month 4	2,225,000
Month 5	2,700,000
Month 6	3,000,000
Month 7 onward	3,000,000

Assuming a gross margin of 30 percent and average Innovex billing steady at 810,000 pesetas per representative per month, breakeven for a representative would be reached in the fifth month ($2,7000,000 \times 30\% = 810,000$ pesetas of gross margin). If these sales and margin forecasts were accurate, from month 6 onward the company would generate new gross income of 90,000 pesetas per month (gross margin less the amount billed by Innovex).

CASE A-1   SMITH & NEPHEW—INNOVEX   (continued)

Other Considerations

The following are comments made by the director of the medical division and his sales marketing managers during their meeting, as they analyzed the facts and figures:

- "Innovex gives us a chance to try things out, to start working with new people and new regions, with a controlled level of risk. Then we can decide whether or not we want to actually hire the people once they've proved they can work profitably."

- "You have to remember that Innovex takes over a whole range of management tasks. During the trial period in Galicia and Asturias all we had to do was approve a bill of 1.6 million pesetas each month. And monitor sales as we wanted. Everything else (payroll, checking the expense sheets, mileage, and so on) was taken care of by Innovex."

- "If the Asturias salesman doesn't perform as well as expected, we can ask Innovex to replace him. And it'll be up to them to carry out the selection, hiring, sales training, etc."

- "Before we replace the salesman, though, we need to be sure it's him who's letting us down, rather than the sales potential of the territory itself, or lack of support on our part."

- "I suspect that Innovex doesn't pay its salespeople very highly. Take our sales representative in Galicia, for example. I'm already starting to worry that one of our competitors will notice our sudden gain of market share, realize that this person is worth her salt, or at least has potential, and offer her a permanent job with better pay."

- "Is it feasible to use Innovex sales representatives in the medium and long term? Or do companies just use them for tactical sales drives that never last more than six or nine months?"

The Decision

Given the results of the trial, Brown and Serra now faced a set of alternatives deriving from the possible combination of three variables:

1. To use salaried sales representatives or to use contract sales representatives employed by Innovex.
2. Level of geographical coverage.
3. Timing: when would be the best moment to do one thing or another?

For example, without trying to be exhaustive, the above three variables could be combined in different ways to generate at least the following possible courses of action:

1. Terminate the contract with Innovex and leave the areas of Galicia and Asturias as they were before, i.e., with a single representative, Arturo, visiting hospitals.

2. Renew the contract with Innovex for another six months, only for Galicia and Asturias, in order to prolong the trial and so obtain more reliable data on sales trends, and to verify whether the sales and financial performance could be consolidated.

3. Terminate the contract with Innovex and proceed immediately to hire:

   3.1 One salaried sales representative for Galicia.
   3.2 Two salaried sales representatives, one for Galicia and one for Asturias.
   3.3 Two or three salaried sales representatives for Galicia and one for Asturias, as in the original plan.

4. Sign a new agreement with Innovex to establish contract sales representatives in all or some of the regions currently lacking coverage: Valencia (two or three representatives) and Andalusia (two or three representatives). The contract could be for six months or one year. Following that, introduce own salaried sales representatives in all or some of those regions, depending on the level of sales and profitability attained in each one.

5. Directly hire a certain number of salaried sales representatives for those same underserved regions.

Finally, if they decided to hire new salaried sales representatives they would have to decide whether

(CASE EXHIBIT 1-6)   Sales Representatives' Legal Status

1. Salaried sales representatives

According to labor legislation in force in Spain in the year 2000, sales representatives who were integrated in a company's workforce had a "labor" contract of employment with that company. In the light of certain court rulings, a worker could be understood to be integrated in a company's workforce when he was unable to organize his professional activity at his own discretion, when his place of work was on the company's premises, and when he was subject to working hours stipulated by the company.

In the event of dismissal, such a sales representative could challenge the company's decision before the labor courts and require them to decide on the "fairness" or "unfairness" of the dismissal. If the dismissal was declared unfair, the company had to pay the worker severance payment or compensation equal to 45 days' salary per year of service up to a maximum of 42 months' salary.

If the company chose to terminate the employment relationship on any of the objective grounds for dismissal specified by the Workers' Statute (Article 52), it had to pay the worker, at the time of notification of termination, compensation equal to 20 days' salary per year of service up to a limit of 12 months' salary. Again in this case, the worker could challenge the dismissal and ask the court to declare it unfair. If in the end the company was unable to demonstrate the existence of objective grounds and the dismissal was declared unfair, the company would have to pay the worker compensation equal to 45 days' salary per year of service up to a maximum of 42 months' salary. Exceptionally, however, if the dismissed worker was hired under the terms of Law 63/1997, which provided for urgent measures to improve the labor market and promote stable employment, the above did not apply. Instead, in such cases, if the dismissal was found to be unfair, the company was obliged to pay compensation equal to 33 days' salary per year of service up to a maximum of 24 months' salary.

2. Sales representatives with an agency contract

According to the Agency Contract Law (Law 12/92 of May 27), a company could decide to establish a commercial relationship with a sales agent.

The features that defined a sales agent's commercial relationship with the company were:

—His place of work was not on the company's premises.

—He was not subject to working hours that were set by the company.

—In his professional activities he acted independently and organized his work as he saw fit.

—He could assume the business risk of the activities he performed, but this circumstance was not considered a defining feature of a commercial agency relationship and therefore was not sufficient by itself to prevent the relationship from being declared one of employment.

Any disputes that might arise between the parties in the execution of the commercial agency contract were resolved by the civil courts.

Unless otherwise expressly agreed by the parties, the company was not obliged to pay any compensation upon termination of the contract. Nevertheless, the commercial agent could claim compensation if by his work he had added new customers to the company's customer base. In any case, whether or not this right arose, and in what circumstances, would depend on the specific content of the agreement between the parties.

Given that the relationship was not one of employment, the company was not obliged to pay Social Security contributions for the sales agent.

CASE A-1 SMITH & NEPHEW—INNOVEX (continued)

it was better for the representatives to work in tandem, as Isabel and Arturo had done in Galicia—i.e., with Arturo visiting mainly hospitals and Isabel visiting primary care centers—or whether it would be better to divide up the territory and for each representative to visit both hospitals and primary care centers in part of the territory assigned to him or her. Obviously, for each of these options they would have to weigh up the costs and the benefits, both in strictly financial terms and in terms of sales and marketing strategy.

In this latter respect, CEO James Brown was starting to get excited at the thought of the strategic possibilities that would be opened up if he ever reached the position of having a sales team fully deployed throughout Spain.

At the same time, however, he needed to make sure that the Smith & Nephew group's Spanish subsidiary reported a profit, as he personally desired and as the company's year 2000 budget demanded.

CASE EXHIBIT 1-7 Reproduction of the Business Cards Used . . .

. . . by a salaried sales representative
employed by
Smith & Nephew

. . . by a salaried sales representative
contracted from
Innovex

Ramón Prats
Sales Representative
Medical Division

Smith & Nephew, S.A.

Fructuós Gelabert, 2 and 4
08970 Sant Joan Despí (Barcelona) Spain
Tel.: 93 373 73 01*
Fax: 93 373 74 53

Smith✛Nephew

Isabel Fernández
Sales Representative
Medical Division

"Employee of Innovex, Spain, S.L."

Smith & Nephew, S.A.

Fructuós Gelabert, 2 and 4
08970 Sant Joan Despí (Barcelona) Spain
Tel.: 93 373 73 01*
Fax: 93 373 74 53
Mobile: 654 918 997

Smith✛Nephew

CASE A-2   A. T. KEARNEY AND THE NEW "DEFINING ENTITY"

Sales Issues Relating to a Merger

It was early Monday morning, September 22, 1996, and Brian Harrison, president of A. T. Kearney (Canada), was in his Chicago office preparing for an upcoming meeting. A. T. Kearney, headquartered in Chicago, Illinois, was one of the world's largest and most respected global management consulting firms. On Friday, Brian was to meet with the rest of the Toronto management team to review the activities of the firm since its acquisition by Electronic Data Systems (EDS) just over a year ago and to discuss the strategic direction of the firm moving forward. Of particular interest to the management team were the challenges A. T. Kearney faced in trying to take advantage of the new relationship it shared with EDS, a leader in the global information services industry.[1]

From a client perspective many new opportunities were created by the acquisition. Clients could take advantage of a much broader range of services. In essence, the new EDS/A. T. Kearney organization was striving to become a "one-stop shop," capable of servicing every client requirement. However, many consultants were concerned about the ability of these two very different organizations, with different skill sets and cultures, to work together in blending their services into a broad, seamless continuum. Senior consultants wondered about the implications it would have to be made for these two companies to benefit fully from the acquisition. Brian prepared himself for what he expected would be a rather lively discussion around this very issue.

Sipping his coffee, Brian smiled as he reviewed the results of a recent A. T. Kearney survey of information technology practices and perceptions at some of the world's largest corporations. Senior executives at Global 1000 companies were interviewed to explore their evolving attitudes toward the role of information technology in their core businesses. Information technology (IT) issues had indeed emerged on the "CEO Agenda." One particular excerpt caught Brian's attention:

> The results suggest a fundamental shift away from the days when information technology was viewed as one tactical item among others used to improve business productivity. No longer is IT just another tool the CEO might use to accomplish cost savings and operational ends. Today, information technology can help solve product problems, set new levels of service and create new distribution and communication channels. It has become sufficiently important to be included in the process of setting a company's strategic objectives.

The study reached the following main conclusions:

- Technology has been integrated into business strategy.
- Technology investments will increase.
- Corporations are embracing the philosophy of restructuring and reengineering.
- Senior management is becoming technology-literate as, across all industries, major corporations increasingly view themselves as "technology-oriented companies."
- Senior management expresses satisfaction with return on technology investment, even in the absence of precise measurements.

These results were no surprise to Brian Harrison, who had played a key role in EDS's acquisition of A. T. Kearney and the subsequent merger of the firm into its new parent. The largest buy-out of a management consulting firm in history had been a bold strategic move for both organizations. The results of the survey highlighted the growing importance of technology as an area of concern and interest among senior management at the world's largest corporations, many of which were clients of A. T. Kearney.

---

[1] According to Consultant News—Chicago Tribune, "Consulting firms are no longer put on the shelf and forgotten," Wednesday, September 27, 1995.

CASE A-2   A. T. KEARNEY   (continued)

Fred Steingraber, A. T. Kearney's CEO since 1983, suggested:

> The days are past when senior management could remain aloof from the adoption of new technology and still expect to increase quality, productivity, market share and profits. Today, every enterprise is a high-technology business to the extent that technology, strategy, and operational decisions must be made simultaneously to ensure a competitive advantage in the marketplace.

Industry

In 1994, general management consulting firms billed an estimated $40 billion of services to corporations around the globe. The world's top 15 consulting companies, with over 91,000 consultants, accounted for $18 billion of this total. In particular, services related to information technology (i.e., IT planning, IT strategy, strategic procurement of hardware and software solutions) and process reengineering accounted for almost half of the total fees billed to clients. This segment was expected to grow faster than any other through the turn of the century at an annual rate of up to 15 percent. Fred Steingraber suggested that total fees for the management consulting industry would double by the year 2000. So why all the growth in consulting?

Many suggested that it had to do with management's need for expert assistance as companies pushed further into the global marketplace and started to rethink strategy for the 21st century. Combined with increasing business uncertainty, senior executives would continue to look for guidance on the way their industries were headed, how to align business processes with strategy, how to empower employees, and how technology could be used to attain competitive advantage. For numerous reasons, it was often more effective for the agent of such changes to come from the outside. Heavy downsizing and cost-cutting efforts by many companies in recent years also played a major role in the continued growth of the consulting industry, since corporations around the world had created their own shortage of capable staff.

Coupled with strong growth, the management consulting industry was also undergoing tremendous change. This transformation was being driven by significant tends in the marketplace, some of which included:

- The convergence of telecommunications, technology, and information services, dramatically altering the structure of business and how companies competed in the global marketplace.
- The rapid pace of technology development and the movement of technology to the "front line" of operations and the desktop.
- The need to rapidly develop, customize, and market new products and services worldwide.

Global clients, accompanied by global issues, were becoming the norm. There was a need to continuously demonstrate greater industry expertise, deep business knowledge, and in-depth thought leadership to guide clients into the future and ensure flexibility in a rapidly changing environment. It was becoming a requirement that leading-edge information technology be incorporated into implemental solutions, as technology and convergence played an increasing role in driving strategy and in restructuring industries.

Engagements were becoming longer and greater emphasis placed on achieving performance targets, and fees increasingly tied to tangible results. Consultants were evolving as "partners" in long-term business relationships. Fred Steingraber:

> For a long time, much of the industry's focus was on single-dimension projects. Now the leading consulting firms must possess multidisciplinary consulting capability to secure meaningful relationships with clients worldwide. The idea that consultants are there for a single project has all but disappeared. Management consulting has new requirements and must develop enhanced capabilities to remain competitive and to be prepared to serve clients effectively in the 21st century.

Competition

The lines between strategy, operations, and information systems consulting continued to blur. A broad range of service capabilities would be required for firms to achieve high-impact, tangible results and the ability to position themselves in the high value-added end of management consulting. An integrated service continuum from strategy formulation to implementation was the direction in which many international players were headed.

(I) The "Big Six"—Classic IT Firms

The "Big Six" accounting firms (Price Waterhouse, Deloitte & Touch, KPMG, Coopers & Lybrand, Ernst & Young, and Andersen) were enjoying annual growth rates in excess of 15 percent. A large part of this growth was supported by their large share of the fast-growing IT/BPR (business process reengineering) consulting market and a strong push into operations consulting as IT became increasingly strategic in nature and instrumental for reengineering.

(II) Operational and Strategic Firms

Traditional consulting firms like McKinsey, BCG, Bain, and Booz Allen & Hamilton, who were best known for their strategic expertise, were broadening their service offerings as they moved aggressively downstream into operations consulting. Both strategy and operational consultants were pushing information technology as clients demanded more implementation capabilities and reengineering required information technology resources.

(III) Systems Integrators and System Vendors

Classical IT firms such as EDS, CSC (Computer Science Corporation), IBM, and Cap Gemini had moved into more traditional management consulting markets, recognizing that IT had become increasingly strategic in nature and critical for reengineering. With the exception of EDS, CSC, and Cap Gemini, these firms had built practices in the business and IT consulting area from the ground up.

(IV) New Information Technology Entrants

Some of the fastest-growing players were the new information technology entrants, such as AT&T and Oracle who, along with Andersen, had spotted the opportunity to consolidate client relationships by selling "upstream" consulting services on top of their core outsourcing and system integration skills. AT&T, for one, started AT&T Solutions in early 1995 to offer end-to-end solutions supplied through various units. They positioned themselves as a "Technology Life Cycle management" company who would increase their value to clients by tying computer and communications solutions to the customer's strategic business objectives. Many of these capital-strong, technology-oriented firms were establishing consulting practices through the acquisition of smaller generalists. Some industry analysts suggested that these IT giants would claim over 15 percent market share before the turn of the century.

Results to date suggested that full-service firms were performing better in terms of growth and profitability (see Exhibit 2–1). Many were expanding and integrating their service portfolio, supporting the belief that technology and high value-added consulting went hand-in-hand. Industry observers had noted several competitors merging practices in convergent industries like telecommunications, media, entertainment, and consumer electronics. Many of the operational, generalist, and IT players continued to evaluate potential merger/alliances to enhance their service portfolio (see Exhibit 2–2).

A. T. Kearney

Founded in 1926, A. T. Kearney had evolved into one of the world's dominant management consulting practices. Its approach was to develop realistic solutions and help clients implement recommendations that generated tangible results and improved competitive advantage. The firm was well known for its ability to deliver value and results throughout the management process, from strategy development to business and market analysis to operations, process, and technology transformation. This mix of strategy and operations, combined with a focus on implementation, had differentiated A. T. Kearney from its competitors and driven the firm's outstanding results for over a decade. The leaders of the firm emphasized strong, lasting relationships (at the CEO level) with fewer, larger clients. To this end A. T. Kearney had been quite successful. Continuously challenging themselves to exceed their clients' expectations, more than 75 percent of their business volume was generated from clients who had used A. T. Kearney's services the previous year.

While striving to help global clients gain and sustain competitive advantage, A. T. Kearney pursued its own goals of globalization, growth, and leadership. Before integrating with Management

CASE EXHIBIT 2-1   Vertically Integrated Firms Perform Better

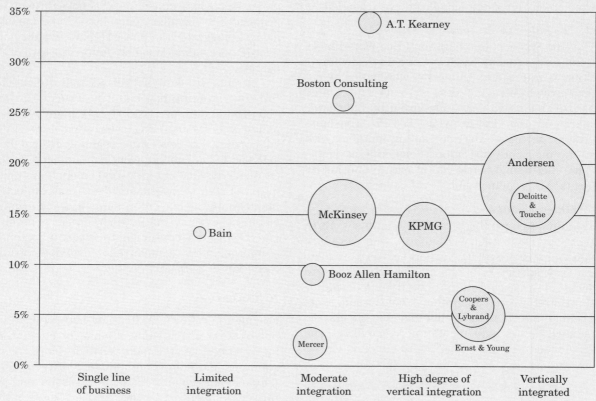

CAGR¹ (Revenues)

Degree of Vertical Integration

Source: *Consultants News*, A. T. Kearney.

¹Growth measured between 1990–1995.

Consulting Services (MCS), EDS's management consulting arm, the firm had 40 offices in 22 countries. It was expected that over 65 percent of A. T. Kearney's revenues would be generated outside of the United States by 1997. This was quite remarkable considering that only 10 percent of revenues came from outside the United States as late as 1980. Accompanying its aggressive move toward globalization, A. T. Kearney had experienced tremendous growth over the last decade. From a staff of only 230 in 1984 to over 1,110 consultants in 1994, the firm had enjoyed double-digit revenue growth for each of the last 13 years. A. T. Kearney

had doubled its size every three years since 1983 and was recently listed in *Consultants News* as one of the five fastest-growing consulting firms in the world. Brent Snell, a principal in the Toronto office, suggested that A. T. Kearney was, in fact, "growth-constrained only by having insufficient number of highly qualified new people at all levels of the organization."

Electronic Data Systems (EDS)

EDS started in 1962 with Ross Perot and a $1,000 investment. The fledgling company began by offer-

CASE EXHIBIT 2-2   **Major Service Offerings of Leading Consulting and Information Technology Services Firms**

Management Consulting Capabilities	Andersen Consulting	AD Little	A.T. Kearney & EDS	Bain & Co.	Booz Allen & Hamilton	Boston Consulting Group	CSC & CSC Index	Coopers & Lybrand	Deloitte & Touche	Ernst & Young	Cap Gemini	IBM	KPMG	McKinsey	Mercer Management	Monitor
Strategic Consulting (enterprise)[1]																
Strategic Consulting (operations improvement)[2]																
Finance																
Marketing & Sales																
HR/benefits																
R&D																
Business Process Reengineering																
• Business Process																
• Organization (change management/design)																
• IT Planning																
IT Strategy																

[1] High-level corporate or business unit strategy (i.e., deciding what business to participate in or to acquire).

[2] Targeted business issue analysis (i.e., deciding how to improve customer service, or deciding on the most effective type of retail delivery system).

Legend:
- ■ Strong
- ▣ Participating
- □ New initiative or small practice
- ☐ Not participating in this area

Sources: A.T. Kearney, Gartner Group

ing routine data processing services for Dallas-area companies on computers it didn't even own. In 1985, a year after Perot sold the information technology giant to General Motors for an estimated $2.5 billion, EDS reported revenues of $3.4 billion, a 264 percent improvement from the previous year. By 1995, as a subsidiary of the auto manufacturer, EDS was making most of its money running the computer networks of its clients more efficiently than they could. It helped customers use information and technology to recast their economics and to identify and seize new opportunities. This translated into 90,000 employees in 41 countries and revenues that were expected to exceed $12 billion. Considered by many to be the inventor of "outsourcing," EDS had established itself as a world leader in information technology services (see Exhibit 2–3).

CASE EXHIBIT 2-3   EDS and Its Major Competitors in the Computer Service Market*

Company	Location	Sales (billions USD)	Net Income (millions USD)	Major Customers
Electronic Data Services	Plano, Texas	$10.50	821.9	GM, Xerox, American Express Bank, Inland Revenue, Bethlehem Steel
Computer Sciences (CSC)	El Sugundo, California	3.37	110.7	General Dynamics, Hughes Aircraft, Lucas Industries, Department of Defense
Andersen Consulting	Chicago, Illinois	3.45	N.A.	Bell Atlantic, LTV, British Petroleum, London Stock Exchange
Integrated Systems Solutions (a unit of IBM)	White Plains, New York	N.A.	N.A.	Bank America, McDonnell Douglas, Amtrak, Eastman Kodak

*Latest fiscal year for each company as of August 1995.   N.A. = Not available.

Sources: The companies, Disclosure Inc.—*The Wall Street Journal*, Tuesday, August 8, 1995.

EDS was very much a part of everyone's world. For soccer's World Cup of 1994, EDS developed the largest and most complex information system of its kind for the world's largest single sporting event (seen more than 31 billion times around the world). Instant information on each match, player biographies, and historical information for every World Cup ever played were available to some 15,000 journalists covering the matches in nine cities across the United States. In 1995 in the United States alone, EDS processed over 2.2 million automated banking machine (ABM) transactions, 1.2 billion credit card authorizations, and 500,000 airline reservations.

EDS defined its business as "shaping how information is created, distributed, shared, enjoyed, and applied for the benefit of businesses, governments, and individuals around the world." Its service offering included four different types of products:

1. *Systems Development*—EDS designed, developed, and implemented systems that supported and improved its clients' business processes and the way they served their customers.

2. *Systems Integration*—EDS became the single point of contact for a client, responsible for directing multiple vendors and ensuring that combinations of hardware, software, communications, and human resources worked together.

3. *Systems Management*—EDS assumed strategic management responsibility for a client's information technology resources.

4. *Process Management*—EDS provided comprehensive management of business processes, such as customer service, insurance claims processing, telemarketing, accounts payable, accounts receivable, and leadership and employee training programs.

By adding these types of information technology services to management consulting, the size of the global market ballooned to an estimated $280 billion. Growth in both industries was expected to be tremendous (see Exhibit 2–4).

Under the leadership of Chief Executive Officer Les Alberthal since 1986, EDS had maintained its reputation as a hard-driving, results-oriented business. It had also lessened the firm's dependence on General Motors from 73 percent of revenues in 1986 to 39 percent in 1993. In 1995, the majority of EDS's revenue (over 75 percent) was generated from systems integration and systems management. A professional sales force focused on long-term contracts, generated over 70 percent of EDS's revenues from clients within the United States and almost 50 percent from corporations whose core business was manufacturing.

But for almost a decade, while EDS was making its fortune running other companies' main-

CASE EXHIBIT 2-4 Estimated Market Size and Growth (in $billions)

Service Continuum	1994	CAGR	1999
Management Consulting	$ 40.0	14.20%	$ 80.0
Systems Development	50.8	6.10	68.3
Systems Integration	56.2	11.90	98.7
Systems Management	120.2	9.10	185.8
Process Management	21.5	35.60	98.3
Estimated Total Market	$288.7		$531

Source: EDS Marketing Strategic Service Unit Market. Analysis, February 1995, Gartner Group.

frame computer operations, competition intensified, and margins began to deteriorate on these traditional lines of business. EDS started to look toward "higher value-added" services rather than data processing. This translated into business-process reengineering and client server technology, two trends that were reshaping the corporate landscape. EDS entered the management consulting industry as part of a strategy to offer business solutions rather than simply IT solutions to its customers.

EDS-Management Consulting Services (MCS)

EDS had been involved in management consulting since 1985 and formalized its efforts by creating MCS in 1993. By leveraging its tradition and strengths, MCS brought a new dimension to EDS. Over a short two-year period, EDS had built MCS into an organization of 1,300 people, with 30 offices in 20 countries, generating an estimated $200 million in revenues. During its first year, MCS services were sold through the EDS sales force to give the firm a chance to get organized internally. During its second year, the consultants were selling on their own. The goals and objectives of the new Strategic Services Unit were simple:

- Grow and be profitable while building a world-class management consulting organization.

- Help grow EDS through leveraged downstream-influenced revenue.

- Act as a catalyst for EDS by bringing in new skills, particularly in relationship management and developing industry knowledge.

Despite the ability to combine expertise and intellectual capital with the delivery capability of EDS, MCS was having difficulties getting off the ground. In 1994 alone, the young organization lost an estimated $23 million. By approaching clients alongside EDS as an IT firm, MCS lacked a clear positioning in the marketplace as a formidable "consulting" practice. One former MCS consultant suggested, "Any company would have had its difficulties turning a profit in such a short period of time, particularly considering the enormous growth rate of MCS." The majority of this growth came internally through a hiring frenzy while the growth in clients was not so quick. "It's hard to achieve profitability with half your staff not billing," commented the ex-MCS consultant. Rapid growth made it difficult for MCS to put in place some of the necessities for success in the global market. Lack of uniform business systems and processes, and inconsistent consulting methodologies, human resources practices, billing rates, and quality measures all translated into an inconsistent positioning in the marketplace. Another struggle for MCS was in establishing its own culture. There were a tremendous number of highly talented people, but coming together so quickly from so many different places made it impossible to establish a unified identity. The firm lacked a sense of cohesion among its broad base of consultants.

CASE A-2   A. T. KEARNEY   (continued)

A. T. Kearney—Acquired by EDS and Merged with MCS (September 1995)

The acquisition of A. T. Kearney was the first significant move by an information technology firm into the upper echelon of the management consulting leagues. EDS had purchased seven management consulting firms over the last two years, but none of this magnitude. Gary Fernandez, EDS vice chairman and new chairman of A. T. Kearney, commented:

> The addition of the A. T. Kearney teams builds on the progress EDS has made to date in creating a world-class management consulting organization. Our enhanced management consulting capability coupled with EDS's traditional information technology and process management expertise represents a powerful combination of business insight, industry experience and global delivery capability to help our clients successfully undertake enterprise-wide transformation initiatives.

EDS agreed to buy A. T. Kearney for $300 million in cash and contingency payments, plus a stock incentive provision of 7 million shares to be earned at a rate of 10 percent a year by A. T. Kearney partners and 100 other key individuals. The total bill was estimated at just over $600 million. It was determined that the MCS practice would be integrated into the new A. T. Kearney, maintaining the brand name, procedures, policies, and standards that had made the Chicago-based firm one of the world's leading management consulting practices. Fred Steingraber would continue to function as the company's CEO. For the first time in EDS's long history, a fully independent subsidiary was created in order to assure the integrity and objectivity of a world-class management consulting firm. This subsidiary provided EDS with a credible, ready-made consulting practice that would have taken far too long for EDS to develop on its own.

This was an excellent match for both A.T. Kearney and MCS as consulting organizations because of the synergistic and complementary industry, functional, and geographic strengths. The operational and technology consulting strengths of MCS complemented the strategy and high value-added operational strengths of A. T. Kearney. The integration provided A. T. Kearney with an influx of new, talented consultants that were necessary for the firm to ramp up its capabilities and reach critical mass in many of its markets. Together, they brought an unparalleled spectrum of capabilities to clients. The combination of locations ensured that a broad and well-positioned global organization was in place to service clients worldwide. Industry coverage was also well matched and balanced; for example, A. T. Kearney was exceptionally strong in manufacturing, while MCS had particular strengths in the communication and electronics industries.

When EDS's information services and technology capabilities were added to the mix, the ability to have a near seamless link of strategy through implementation was created. One competitor suggested:

> The market is demanding integrated business and technology services. I think it will be tough for them, but it's the right move. It's very difficult to do process improvement as A. T. Kearney does and not leverage that into implementing systems.

The combined capabilities brought a range of skills and leading-edge solutions to clients of both A. T. Kearney and EDS. For clients involved in reengineering and transformation, process and functional issues could be addressed concurrently with the enabling technology and implementation issues. In addition, implementation expertise could be tapped into earlier in the development process. The relationship with EDS also helped ensure the availability of major investment resources for A. T. Kearney. It provided the infrastructure to support its rapid growth from both geographic and practice development perspectives. The relationship with A. T. Kearney gave the information technology giant the key high-level perspective on business issues which helped it to sell its outsourcing and systems integration services.

A. T. Kearney was a key part of the EDS vision to become the new "Defining Entity." For A. T. Kearney, the partnership with EDS had placed it in a stronger position to pursue its goals of growth, globalization, and leadership. According to Fred

Steingraber, A. T. Kearney viewed itself as "one of a new breed of management consultancies, rich in resources, global in reach and integrated in solution delivery." Both companies felt the merger had provided them with a tremendous opportunity to take the lead in bringing the "next generation" of professional services capabilities to clients worldwide.

Risks, Challenges, and Obstacles

Despite all of the optimism of A. T. Kearney and EDS, skeptics were lining up to criticize the strategy. Many wondered whether vertically integrating services, so that a single consulting firm offered end-to-end consulting solutions, was an inevitable trend, and even if it was, integrating the existing MCS into A. T. Kearney would be no easy task. One such critic was James Kennedy, publisher of *Consultants News:*

> First you have entirely different cultures. What you are going to get is the propeller heads meeting the button downs. Kearney has been selling top management for decades, while EDS, which has only been in the consulting business since 1993, has been dealing mostly with the systems people. We're talking about two different levels here.

He went on to say:

> Consulting firms are very fragile entities. They cannot be transplanted easily. You have something equivalent to organ rejection when you try to mix and match consultants from one company to another. There are huge egos here.

Referring to the acquisition by the General Motors subsidiary, one A. T. Kearney consultant was quoted as saying, "We would go from being an independent, uninhibited place to being a small piece of the country's largest company. Talk about culture shock." Independence was a major issue for many A. T. Kearney consultants. It was felt that IBM Solutions was essentially created to sell IBM hardware solutions. The relationship between MCS and EDS was not much different. Many consultants feared that A. T. Kearney would be viewed as the front end for EDS. If so, this could have significant implications for A. T. Kearney's ability to both attract and retain good people—the main assets of any professional services firm. Some wondered whether there would be a mass exodus from the Kearney ranks. Clients had parallel concerns. Would A. T. Kearney still be able to maintain its objectivity in helping clients choose the right suppliers? Would clients continue to use A. T. Kearney services, particularly if they competed against EDS or General Motors?

One Year Later (September 1996)

No one would say that the first year had been easy. However, most would argue that it was successful. The integration of MCS into A. T. Kearney had gone smoothly. With 60 offices in over 30 countries, the consulting practice had grown to over 3,500 employees, 2,400 of whom were consultants. In 1995, revenues soared to $650 million, which placed A. T. Kearney as the 11th largest consulting firm in the world (see Exhibits 2–5 and 2–6) and the number two firm in the high value-added segment of the market. The marketplace had received the marriage between A. T. Kearney and EDS with open arms. In fact through June 1996, the two companies partnered on more than 20 successful initiatives resulting in $1.4 billion in new business for EDS and $140 million for A. T. Kearney. Perhaps the most exciting collaboration between the two companies was a 10-year engagement with Rolls-Royce worth over $900 million. Even more remarkable, its independence from EDS and its business systems and culture had been maintained. With almost no turnover of staff throughout the integration and absolutely no turnover of clients, A. T. Kearney had further established itself as a strong and successful player in the management consulting industry.

What Next?

Despite the consulting firm's success to date, Brian Harrison knew that the greatest potential from the merger had yet to be realized. The integration of MCS into A. T. Kearney was the first step. Now EDS and A. T. Kearney sought to take advantage of the synergy created from the merger by leveraging the capabilities of both organizations. While significant revenue had been generated to date from joint clients, most collaborative initiatives had been in response to client demand, or to competitive pressures created by a bidding process. In almost all cases, A. T. Kearney had re-

CASE EXHIBIT 2-5   Top Consulting Firms for 1995 (in $000s)

Rank	Company	Revenues
1	Andersen	$4,200
2	McKinsey & Company	1,800
3	Ernst & Young	1,500
4	KPMG	1,500
5	Deloitte & Touche	1,400
6	Coopers & Lybrand	1,200
7	Mercer Management	1,000
8	Price Waterhouse	1,000
9	Booz Allen & Hamilton	785
10	Towers Perrin[1]	767
11	A. T. Kearney	650
12	Boston Consulting Group	550
13	Cap Gemini	548
14	Arthur D. Little	514
15	Bain	375

[1]Estimate of 1994 revenues only.

Source: *Worldlink*, September/October 1996, pp. 15–25.

acted to opportunities, rather than having taken the initiative and proactively sought them out. One example of this was the Rolls-Royce project. Competing with CSC for the engagement, EDS decided to include its consulting arm in the service mix since the services of CSC Index, CSC's consulting division, had been offered. The selling process was not initiated with both service offerings in mind. Most managers felt that a more proactive approach to similar situations was the ultimate objective of the firm. The question was how to make this happen. Leveraging and combining each other's strengths in the marketplace was a must.

Several courses of action were available to the two organizations in light of the merger. Substantial cross-marketing opportunities were created because of the minimal client overlap. EDS had significant positions in health care, insurance, communications, electronics, and aerospace and defense industries, while A. T. Kearney's strengths resided in manufacturing, consumer products, transportation, and chemical/pharmaceuticals. They shared mutual strengths in industries such as automotive, financial services, energy, and retail. Products and services that had made each company successful in the past could be offered to each other's clients.

Another opportunity was to offer the combined menu of these very same products to a whole new set of clients looking for a "one-stop shop," where A. T. Kearney and EDS were not in a position to service these accounts effectively in the past. Most of the reactive collaborative initiatives to date had taken the form of one of these two approaches.

Brian, however, suggested this was not the primary purpose of the merger. Instead, there was an opportunity to draw on the strengths of both organizations and develop entirely new products. For example, these would be in the category of enterprise-wide transformation initiatives or in the development of technology-enabled strategies. Offered to either existing or new clients, these new products would significantly differentiate the new enterprise from its competition, and generate revenue streams that neither A. T. Kearney nor EDS could have enjoyed without this partnership. This was what Brian considered to be the most attractive opportunity. For example, A. T. Kearney and EDS had recently embarked on the development of a new service called CoSourcing. Once completed,

CASE EXHIBIT 2-6   A. T. Kearney Growth and Performance Unparalleled in the Industry

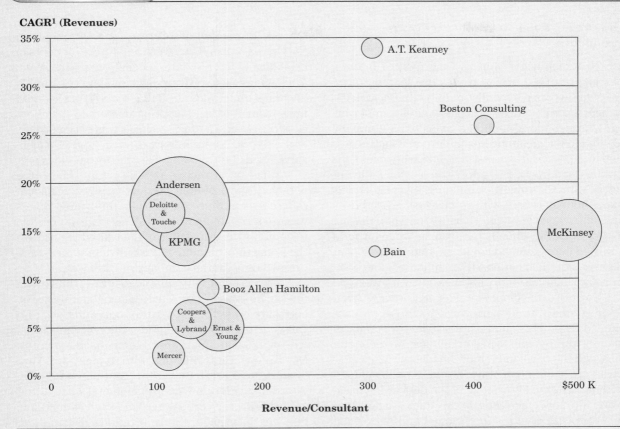

CAGR[1] (Revenues)

Revenue/Consultant

[1]Growth measured between 1990–1995.

Source: *Consultants News*

this would be a collaborative initiative that integrated business process reengineering, information technology, outsourcing, and organizational transformation to deliver significant performance enhancements to prospective clients. However, before this or any other new initiative could possibly work, significant changes to both organizations had to occur, particularly with respect to sales and account management. The objective of these changes would be to create an environment where the two companies could remain apart, but at the same time work together.

Brian sat back in his chair and remembered a comment Fred had made almost a year ago, when the merger was finalized:

> The offer has provided us with a catalyst in terms of looking at the next generation of success criteria that will be critical in this industry in the future. It has caused a lot of people to ponder the future of the consulting industry.

With this in mind, Brian began to prepare for his upcoming meeting on Friday.

CASE A-3   INFOSYS TECHNOLOGIES LTD.

Organizing Sales for Global Software Products

Mr. N. R. Narayana Murthy, Chairman of Infosys, has just returned from a trip to the United States. He is known as a capitalist in mind, but a socialist at heart. Looking tired, with dark circles under his eyes, he is thinking about the vision of his company located in the gleaming headquarters, which is nestled in a 52-acre green oasis within Electronics City, on the outskirts of Bangalore, the silicon valley of India. More than an office building, this place looks like a holiday resort, with rolling lush green lawns and landscaped gardens. There's even a golf putting range. Rock music belts out from an open-air food court, where young people sit and chatter. But theirs is not idle chatter—their animated conversations are all focused on abstruse software topics.

Software development has historically been seen as an art, to be performed by those with advanced technical training. As a result of standardization, improvements in communication technologies, and the development of "high-level" languages, owed application software can now be developed without specific knowledge of the underlying hardware. Moreover, activities in the software development process could be partitioned and performed by people located in different places. In particular, detailed design, coding, and testing could be undertaken anywhere in the world, and therefore a remote software maintenance service was becoming feasible.

Such a phenomenon led to the emergence of companies such as Infosys Technologies Ltd. in India. The company has a rags-to-riches story. In 1981, seven Indians gave up their secure jobs to start this software company with a sum of Rs 10,000 (U.S.$1,000). Their dream was to build a world-class software company.[1] The company initially started by engaging in the development and main-tenance of computer software for their clients in the United States. They were among the pioneers in establishing the offshore concept on a large scale. This means that software development for foreign clients is undertaken in India, by utilizing satellite links instead of sending programmers to the client sites overseas. The early success was based on several factors. First, Infosys had a large English-speaking technical talent. Second, the services provided had an attractive rate structure. Third, the company had a 24-hour productive day. Because of differences in time zones, when the United States went to sleep, India woke up. This made it possible to combine the prime time of the United States with the prime time of India; as a result, it provided compressed time for the company's customers.[2]

Infosys made very significant efforts in wooing foreign business. During a decade of operation, the company grew from a start-up operating out of a garage to a 1,000-person, $12 million organization, with a 125,000-square-foot facility in Bangalore's Electronics City. Starting with typical software maintenance services, porting and patching jobs, the company has moved into high-end, specialized applications for vertical markets such as banking, finance, insurance, transportation, distribution, and retailing. Among its 120 customers are about 30 Fortune 500 companies. Clients include Apple, Boeing, Epson, Intec, JCPenny, Nestlé, Nortel, Reebok, Salomon, and Toshiba. About 90 percent of Infosys revenue is from repeat clients. Almost its entire revenue is from exports.[3]

A project team for a U.S.-based multinational corporation keeps in touch almost constantly with their U.S. colleagues via electronic mail, telephone, and video hookups. Though there is a geographic separation, there is a conscious effort to have the teams work in tandem. All this communication does not come cheap. Each 64K bit/second

---

[1] "The Offshore Advantage," *Asian Business*, August 1999.

[2] "A World-Class Company in India," *Upside*, October, 2000.

[3] Ibid.

This case was written by Dr. Vivek Gupta, Associate Professor, Nayang Technological University, Singapore. It is reproduced with permission.

link has an average annual cost of about $130,000, compared to only $9,000 for domestic leased lines. But U.S. companies still find it less expensive to outsource to overseas firms. In early 1996, Infosys reported that the company provides a cost advantage to their American clients of anywhere from 40 percent to 50 percent.[4]

One of the keys to Infosys's success in software development is its blend of whip-cracking efficiency and fanatic attention to detail. The Carnegie Mellon Software Engineering Institute in Pittsburgh has a rating system for developers that takes into account the ability to produce quality software on time and on budget, called the Capability Maturity Model (CMM). Infosys boasts of having attained the highest grade, CMM Level 5, which means they deliver more than 90 percent of projects on time, compared with the U.S. average of 60 percent to 65 percent.[5]

Infosys had a very interesting account management policy. In 1989 General Electric (GE) became a major customer and, within three years of business, contributed to approximately 40 percent of Infosys's total sales. Attempting to take advantage of its bargaining power as Infosys's largest client, GE began exerting intense pressure on Infosys to reduce its rates. Infosys responded by terminating its relationship with GE. After a one-year transition period, during which all Infosys work at GE was handed over to other companies and in-house IT personnel, Infosys exited the relationship. Apparently Infosys does not want to be dependent on one customer for more than 10 percent of its business. Thus, in financial year 2000, its largest customer accounted for 10 percent, and the five largest customers for 33 percent, of its total sales.[6]

Infosys realizes that its key resource is its employees, and it has created a nurturing environment for them. The company has a strong belief that, in a knowledge industry like software, wealth creation is done by people, and hence they too should be the beneficiaries of that wealth creation. This translates into a generous compensation package, attractive stock options, and a campus-like atmosphere with little hierarchy and flexible hours. The company believes in holistic compen-

sation that has three parts—financial, emotional, and learning. The financial component—salary, loans and stock options—grows and erodes with the industry. The emotional part comes from being part of the Infosys team. And the learning opportunities reward individuals who want to grow in their jobs. Other facilities include a health center and a state-of-the-art gym, a sauna, basketball and volleyball courts, and an excellent child care center. Infosys was also among the first few Indian companies to start an employee stock option plan. Not surprisingly, its employee attrition rate of about 10 percent is about half the industry average. Also, Infosys has been voted the best employer by Hewitt Associates in India.[7]

By the year 2000, Infosys had become a market leader in providing customized software solutions to the world's top companies. It now employed 9,000 people in 30 offices worldwide. Infosys had big plans to maintain high growth. The company wanted to transform itself from a provider of low-cost software fixes for such things as the millennium bug to an InfoTech consulting powerhouse, which would be staffed by programmers and executives to carry projects from design to implementation. It had some success moving up the value chain. Offering cheap solutions to the millennium bug, it built strong client base that include top U.S. companies. It then used those relationships to win contracts for more complex and profitable work such as maintaining and reengineering existing software. The company began making a shift from labor-intensive coding to the development of e-commerce software consulting services. Of course, this required closer contact with customers and a stronger physical presence in markets.

Since March 1999, when Infosys made its debut on the NASDAQ stock exchange, the company's stock prices in the United States have risen more than fivefold. The firm has been consistently rated as India's most admired corporation by the leading financial newspaper for the years 1999 to 2001. This has helped to build the Infosys brand name in the United States and attract talented American executives to work closely with the clients. The listing also helps the company attract global talent by offering dollar-denominated stock options. Infosys is one of the biggest magnets in the

[4]"Look Out, Here Comes India," *Computerworld*, February 26, 1996.

[5]"Passage to India," *Forbes*, October 30, 2000.

[6]Harvard Business School Case no. 9801-445, April 11, 2002.

[7]"A World-Class Company in India."

CASE A-3   **INFOSYS TECHNOLOGIES LTD.** (continued)

talent pool and one of the earliest to move into more sophisticated software work. The company services hundreds of global firms, including Goldman Sachs, Visa, and DHL. It has developed switching software for Cisco, a factory management system for Nestlé, and an inventory tracking application for Nordstrom.[8]

Until 1999 Infosys was organized around nine strategic business units (SBUs). Each SBU was run as a self-contained organization, comprising functions such as sales, marketing, and delivery services. In addition to allowing each area to focus deeply on developing domain expertise, this structure helped the firm develop the next generation of Infosys leaders by giving SBU managers a free hand in leading their SBUs. To take advantage of potential economies of scale across the different business units, in October 1999 the firm was reorganized into practice units (PUs) organized by geography, with dedicated sales and software delivery organizations,[9] although each PU has coordinators for support functions, human resources, finance, and so on.

Future Outlook

Most analysts agree that for Infosys to further succeed in business, it has to transform from its old model to a new model.[10] The old model: (*a*) write code to spec for big clients, (*b*) maintain software for long-distance clients, (*c*) do small portions of large solutions, and (*d*) compete on price. The new model: (*a*) offer software solutions for key customer systems, (*b*) outsource simple code work to cheaper countries, (*c*) create and market software for Western countries, and (*d*) compete on quality.

In the fiscal year ending March 31, 2001, Infosys increased sales by 115 percent and gross profit by 114 percent.[11] But sales growth rates reduced sharply during the fiscal year ending March 2002; the sales total was U.S. $545 million, showing an increase of only 32 percent, and the gross profit was

U.S. $255 million, an increase of 27 percent. The regional sales composition during the year is United States 71 percent, Europe 20 percent, India 2 percent, and 7 percent from the rest of the world. Contribution from offshore business is 51 percent, while the onsite component is 49 percent.[12] The new-customer total for the year was 116, and the company currently has a total of 293 active accounts. Infosys had lost some big-ticket projects to competitors, analysts say. Although it signed up 33 new customers during the last quarter, customers are not expanding initial projects into new work for Infosys. Multinational corporations are not making fast decisions to subcontract or outsource big or new projects, as they decide on a quarter-to-quarter basis.[13]

According to one estimate, there should be a strategy to convert the U.S. slowdown into an opportunity. Last year, 185 of the Fortune 500 companies were outsourcing from India, leaving 315 to do potential business. Infosys believes that even if overall spending by companies goes down, it will continue to garner a greater share of the worldwide IT pie. Since Infosys gets about 70 percent of its revenue from the United States, it is seeking to expand in Europe, Japan, and Asia. A strategy Infosys has is to acquire companies that bring complementary values and new customers. The thinking is that if a company with complementary skills is bought, then it is easier to become a concept-to-execution company. Business analysts expect that in the looming slowdown, large companies with an established client base, good professional management, and deep pockets will survive.

Down a road outside this Indian city jammed with cars, buses, and scooters, inside the industrial park wet now with one of the Bangalore's tropical showers, Mr. Murthy sits down to lunch, as he has probably done a thousand times before. But this time it's not growth miracles the legendary leader of India's bellwether technology company is preparing to discuss. The one-two punch of the U.S. recession and the September 11, 2001, terrorist at-

---

[8]"Passage to India."

[9]Harvard Business School Case no. 9801-445, April 11, 2002.

[10]Company's website (www.infosys.com).

[11]Ibid.

[12]"Infosys Posts 37% Growth in Revenue," *Businessline*, April 11, 2002.

[13]"Asian Trader: IT Slowdown Mows Down Indian Outsourcing Plays," *Barron's* May 21, 2001.

tacks have smacked India's software industry. The strategy Murthy outlines is part vision, part dirty necessity: cut billing rates for volume; lessen dependency on the U.S. market, which buys 60 percent of the company's exports; sell to Old Economy types such as health care companies and government agencies; and expand to offer a range of technology services. Also, the vision is "to be a truly global company, we should raise capital where it is the cheapest, produce software where it is the most cost effective, and sell our services where it is more profitable."[14] As software sales stall, Infosys is struggling to transform itself from a great code-writer to a one-stop technology services provider.

---

[14]"India's Software Guru," *Asian Business*, January 2002.

Questions:

1. How can Infosys increase sales growth in view of the constraints in the U.S. market?

2. In a declining software industry, what recommendations would you provide to Infosys in strategic sales management?

3. Do you think that Infosys's holistic compensation system—financial, emotional, and learning—is an effective way to motivate salespeople?

4. What are the merits and demerits of product-based sales organization versus geography-based organization in context of Infosys? Please refer to SBUs and PUs as described in the case.

CASE A-4   JOHNSON DRUG COMPANY

Implementing a Sales Strategy Change

Late in 1998, Eric Johnson, president of the Johnson Drug Company, a drug wholesaler, was studying the company's sales force. The industry was shifting from an outmoded "product-loading" philosophy to strategies based on consumer needs and wants. "We used to be able to sell individual products to the pharmacist and take orders on a routine basis," Johnson commented, "but now we should sell a complete system which assists the pharmacist in managing as well as selling." The drug wholesaler is increasingly looked upon as a service wholesaler who provides a sophisticated system of information, recording, analysis, and management consulting. Mr. Johnson believed that a redefinition of sales force responsibilities to align them with corporate objectives was critical to this transition. He recognized a need for closer correspondence between the responsibilities and objectives of the sales force and management's long-term commitment to systems selling.

Company Background

The company began its operations in Peoria, Illinois, in 1875. It is a family-owned business that was handed down from grandfather to father to son. Mr. Johnson has served as the chief operating officer for the past 15 years. He oversees the major departments, which are operations, sales and buying, credit, and accounting. Reporting to him are the vice president of merchandise, the secretary-treasurer, the sales manager, the operations manager, and the credit manager. The sales force consists of 10 salespeople, who call on the independent retailers in the Peoria trading area.

The products which the company has distributed for over a century fall into the following product classes: cosmetics, drugs, narcotics, pharmaceuticals, proprietary products, sundries, and toiletries. The market for these commodities comprises physicians and pharmacists located in the hospitals, clinics, and pharmacy departments of both medical and retail institutions. The Johnson Drug Company has three major competitors in the Peoria area. Each has a dollar volume that does not quite equal Johnson's annual sales of $25 million. In addition, recently such mass merchandisers as Revco, SuperX, and Walgreen have competed with the local independents which the drug wholesalers serve. In describing the structure of the company's accounts, Mr. Johnson indicated that, as in many

CASE A-4   JOHNSON DRUG COMPANY (continued)

businesses, 80 percent of the company's profit was attained through 20 percent of its accounts. Many of Johnson's customers, including its larger accounts, are not yet buying the "system." Rather, when the salesperson calls on them, they place periodic orders for the individual product lines. Ideally, Johnson would like to have all of its customers utilizing the "service system."

The Evolution of Drug Wholesaling

From 1940 to 1970, the drug wholesaling industry experienced a "growth-oriented" era, characterized by a surge in consumer demand and rapid growth in competition. During this period, the Johnson Drug Company stressed the sales function and the company's objectives were stated in terms of increased sales volume. By the early 1970s, American pharmaceutical markets had grown considerably, competition for the consumer dollar was acute, and selection of the appropriate distribution channels was becoming increasingly difficult. Drug wholesalers began to identify and respond to the needs of their customers, the retailers and hospitals. The Johnson Drug Company recognized such additional goals as margin contribution and profit maximization. As part of the effort to satisfy its customers' needs, the Johnson Drug Company, like its competitors, placed more emphasis on services—increased delivery scheduling, acceptance of special emergency orders, credit extensions, shelf stocking, discount pricing, and "free goods," for example. This trend played a major role in the transformation of the wholesale drug industry. In fact, some wholesale houses began to refer to themselves as "service drug wholesalers."

The 1980s were characterized by intense product and service competition. Three consequences of this competition were the standardization of products and services, price/profit erosion, and the demand for free services. Standardization resulted because the innovative services which were offered to the customer by a particular drug wholesaler were copied by all of its competitors. Thus, sales personnel were quickly deprived of product/service differentiation as a selling point. Price/profit erosion occurred as retailers "shopped"

wholesale competitors for discounts. Under this pressure to offer discounts, the gross profit margins of wholesale drug companies became uncomfortably thin. Also, retailers began to demand more "free services" (e.g., promotion management and business consultation) by employing the same "shopping" strategy. The combination of these three consequences seriously diminished the profitability of drug wholesaling firms for several years.

In the late 1980s, many business observers began to wonder whether the independent pharmacist was a thing of the past. Chain drugstores, supermarkets, and discounters grew steadily. These larger operations utilized their financial clout to negotiate favorable terms with bankers, developers, and manufacturers. Their advertising stressed discount pricing, ample parking, huge stores, and unlimited product variety. Obviously, neighborhood pharmacies were being threatened by competition more powerful than they could combat. The intense competition, reduced market share, higher costs, and lower margins had retailers and their wholesalers searching for ways to avoid possible extinction. Struggling to survive, the druggist found help by taking advantage of the updated and extended services offered by the drug wholesaler. During the 1990s, the pharmaceutical wholesaler systems have extended the competitive life of the independent retailers as well as that of the wholesaler function.

The Drug Service System

A pharmaceutical system is a sales-generating package comprised of the various health care commodities, computerized order processing equipment, and related merchandising services. Marketed as a complete system, it has the ability to add value to a firm's total product offering. (The added value is derived from the system's contribution to decreasing the customer's overall costs and increasing its revenues.) The system may contribute to decreasing costs in any of the following areas: order replacement decisions (timing, source, and quantity), labor employment, credit policy formulation, bookkeeping, shelf stocking, inventory de-

(**CASE EXHIBIT 4-1**)   **The Pharmaceutical Drug Service**

1. **Order entry**—a handheld computer terminal that contains keyed item code numbers. Memory capacity allows for "recall-and-search" on the display. Dialing a special order entry telephone number and placing the terminal into a transmission "cradle" transmits the order to the wholesale house for processing delivery.
2. **Invoicing**—same-day delivery guaranteed by the purchase invoice for merchandise ordered.
3. **Price labeling**—price stickers preprinted and attached to the merchandise ordered.
4. **Shelf labeling**—the wholesale company product display which indicates item location, item number, and inventory.
5. **Quarterly and annual reports**—the wholesale firm provides performance reports which detail item turnover, expenses, revenues, margin analysis, and other pertinent data.
6. **Retailer accounts receivable**—a periodic compilation of a pharmacist's accounts receivable is prepared and mailed after evaluation by either the pharmacist or the wholesaler.

Systems may also include any combination of the following:

7. **Accounts payable payroll.**
8. **Operating statements.**
9. **Prescription files**—patient profiling and drug interaction and allergy control checking.
10. **Long- and short-term financing.**
11. **Management counseling.**
12. **Automatic reorder plans.**
13. **Drug inventory and pricing services** (microfilm).
14. **Sales and promotional programs.**
15. **Merchandising and advertising programs**—these programs aim "to accent the neighborhood store's competitiveness in the consumer's mind and to fortify the drugstore's position against so-called discounters."

---

cisions, carrying costs, traffic flow, layout structure, financial decision making, and merchandising strategy planning. The system may also contribute to increasing revenues by helping solve problems caused by poor selection of inventory and inconsistent pricing.

The Johnson Drug Company adopted the "system" approach in 1985. Its drug service system offers a complete inventory management system including order entry, price stickers, shelf labeling, microfilm inventory and price files, and annual inventory reports, as well as operating statements, quarterly reports, accounts receivable analysis, and customer billing. As part of the package, Johnson Drug also offers a cooperative promotional program and sponsors centralized group buying from certain manufacturers. (See Exhibit 4–1 for a more detailed description of these services.)

The Sales Force

The field sales manager reports to Eric Johnson. The 10 salespeople are responsible only to the sales manager. The salesperson's duties include

not only selling the system but also selling the individual product lines to those customers who are not on the system, as they have always done. The duties of the sales manager include being a public relations person, a field supervisor of the sales force, a field intelligence person, a troubleshooter, and last but not least, a seller of systems. In his role as an intelligence person, the sales manager serves as a vital link in the communications chain between the marketplace and top management.

Promotion from within the company has been the major source of sales personnel. In terms of qualifications, there are no set policies. Prior experience in sales or in the wholesale drug industry is, of course, considered a "plus" in a new hiree. The level of education has never been an imperative criterion. The major selection tool is the personal interview. Typically, the credit manager or the operations manager conducts an initial interview. Upon the recommendation of these managers, the field sales manager or Eric Johnson will conduct a second interview with an applicant. Both of them have the authority to hire the applicant if the sales force has an opening.

CASE A-4   **JOHNSON DRUG COMPANY** (continued)

Upon selection, each new salesperson is required to work in the warehouse preparing orders until they have been exposed to all of the product areas. This facilitates their understanding of the product groups and the industry language. Second, the salesperson is required to gain a working knowledge of the equipment utilized in the drug service system. The sales manager is responsible for reviewing pertinent company policies with each new recruit. Finally, before being assigned to a territory, the trainee travels with an established salesperson in order to get a "feel" for the job ahead.

As noted earlier, the sales manager is primarily responsible for the field supervision of the salespeople. The manager's only formal sources of information are the monthly sales account reports submitted by each salesperson. The monthly sales account report details the amount of gross profit generated by each account and indicates whether sales were based on a cost-plus discount or the regular price. Sales meetings are held monthly to relay information to the salespeople regarding promotional drives and new products. In terms of territory design, every attempt is made to divide sales volume evenly among the salespersons.

The salespeople are paid a straight commission, based on the gross profit generated by each territory. This gross profit is based on the amount of delivered goods. "Returns" are deducted from total sales, and this affects the total compensation paid. Newly hired people are paid a salary until they reach a predetermined volume of sales, at which time they are switched to a commission basis. The average annual compensation of the salespeople is between $35,000 and $50,000, which is comparable to that paid by Johnson's competitors.

The salespeople pay for their personal expenses and their gas, hotel, and food bills. They are also responsible for telephone charges incurred by clients placing orders to the Peoria warehouses. There are no general sales quotas, but the sales-

people can earn bonuses which are paid by the drug manufacturers. These are offered in conjunction with promotional drives for specific products. A salesperson can earn a 1 percent to 2 percent bonus, depending on the volume of the sales generated by these products.

Eric Johnson stated that selling the "system" was more than just an efficient method of moving product—it represented a new commitment to the customer. "The Johnson Drug Company," he said, "is committed to the profit improvement of its customers." He recognized that this required a thorough knowledge and evaluation of customers' operations in order to locate costs that the system could affect positively and to identify product groups for which higher levels of sales could be achieved. He also recognized that this commitment changed the Johnson Drug Company's basic relationship with the retailer—it transformed the pharmacist from a customer to a client. In turn, the salesperson was responsible not only for the sale of products but, more important, for the management of the system, and thus for the management of profits at the retail level. Mr. Johnson wondered whether his salespeople were adequately prepared for and committed to systems selling and what actions he should take to help them adjust to and fulfill their new roles and responsibilities. Although some customers had accepted the new system, many had been slow to see its advantages. Recognizing that the company's future was likely to be heavily dependent on the success of the customer service system, Mr. Johnson was trying to formulate a strategy for both improving the system and speeding up its implementation.

Question:

1. What changes in the sales management program would you recommend to Eric Johnson to improve the implementation of the "system"?

CASE A-5   HANOVER-BATES CHEMICAL CORPORATION

Evaluating District Performance

James Sprague, newly appointed northeast district sales manager for Hanover-Bates Chemical Corporation, leaned back in his chair as the door to his office slammed shut. "Great beginning," he thought. "Three days into my new job and the district's most experienced sales representative is threatening to quit."

On the previous night, James Sprague, Hank Carver (the district's most experienced sales representative), and John Follett, another senior member of the district sales staff, had met for dinner at Jim's suggestion. During dinner, Jim had mentioned that one of his top priorities would be to conduct a sales and profit analysis of the district's business in order to identify opportunities to improve the district's performance. Jim had stated that he was confident that the analysis would indicate opportunities to reallocate district sales efforts in a manner that would increase profits. As Jim had indicated during the conversation, "My experience in analyzing district sales performance data for the national sales manager has convinced me that any district's allocation of sales effort to products and customer categories can be improved." Both Carver and Follett had nodded as Jim discussed his plans.

Hank Carver was waiting when Jim arrived at the district sales office the next morning. It soon became apparent that Carver was very upset by what he perceived as Jim's criticism of how he and the other district sales representatives were doing their jobs—and more particularly, how they were allocating their time in terms of customers and products. As he concluded his heated comments, Carver had said:

> This company has made it darned clear that 34 years of experience don't count for anything . . . and now someone with not much more than two years of selling experience and two years of pushing paper for the national sales manager at corporate headquarters tells me I'm not doing my job . . . Maybe it's time for me to look for a new job . . . and since Trumbull Chemical (Hanover-Bates's major competitor) is hiring, maybe that's where I should start looking . . . and I'm not the only one who feels this way.

As Jim reflected on the scene that had just occurred, he wondered what he should do. It had been made clear to him when he had been promoted to manager of the northeast sales district that one of his top priorities should be improvement of the district's performance. As the national sales manager had said, "The northeast sales district may rank third in dollar sales but it's our worst district in terms of profit performance."

Prior to assuming his new position, Jim had assembled the data presented in Exhibits 5–1 through 5–7 to assist him in his work. The data had been compiled from records maintained in the national sales manager's office. Although he believed that the data would provide a sound basis for a preliminary analysis of district performance, Jim had recognized that additional data would probably have to be collected when he arrived in the northeast district (District 3). To provide himself with a frame of reference, Jim had also requested data on the north-central sales district (District 7). This district was generally considered to be one of the best, if not the best, in the company. Furthermore, the north-central district sales manager, who was only three years older than Jim, was highly regarded by the national sales manager.

This case was prepared by Professor Robert W. Witt of The University of Texas, Austin. Reproduced by permission.

CASE EXHIBIT 5-1   Summary Income Statements (thousands), 1996 to 2000

	1996	1997	1998	1999	2000
Sales	$39,780	$43,420	$38,120	$43,960	$47,780
Production expenses	23,868	26,994	24,396	27,224	29,126
Gross profit	15,912	16,426	13,724	16,736	18,654
Administrative expenses	5,212	5,774	5,584	5,850	6,212
Selling expenses	4,048	4,482	4,268	4,548	4,798
Pretax profit	6,652	6,170	3,872	6,338	7,644
Taxes	3,024	2,776	1,580	2,852	3,436
Net profit	$ 3,628	$ 3,394	$ 2,292	$ 3,486	$ 4,208

CASE EXHIBIT 5-2   District Sales and Gross Profit Quota Performance (thousands), 2000

District	Number of Sales Reps	Sales Quota	Sales Actual	Gross Profit Quota*	Gross Profit Actual
1	7	$ 7,661	$ 7,812	$ 3,104	$ 3,178
2	6	7,500	7,480	3,000	3,058
3	6	7,300	6,812	2,920	2,478
4	6	6,740	6,636	2,696	2,590
5	5	6,600	6,420	2,620	2,372
6	5	6,240	6,410	2,504	2,358
7	5	5,440	6,210	2,176	2,260
		$47,600	$47,780	$19,040	$18,654

*District gross profit quotas were developed by the national sales manager in consultation with the district managers and took into account price competition in the respective districts.

CASE EXHIBIT 5-3   District Selling Expenses, 2000

District	Sales Rep Salaries*	Sales Rep Commissions	Sales Rep Expenses	District Office	District Manager's Salary	Districts Manager's Expenses	Sales Support	Total Selling Expenses
1	$354,200	$38,852	$112,560	$42,300	$67,000	$22,920	$139,000	$776,832
2	286,440	37,400	101,520	42,624	68,000	24,068	142,640	702,692
3	314,760	34,060	108,872	44,246	70,000†	24,764	140,000	736,722
4	300,960	33,180	98,208	44,008	65,000	22,010	132,940	696,306
5	251,900	32,100	85,440	42,230	66,000	22,246	153,200	653,116
6	249,700	32,530	83,040	41,984	67,000	22,856	134,200	631,310
7	229,700	35,060	89,400	44,970	63,000	23,286	117,500	602,916
								$4,797,830

*Includes cost of fringe benefit program, which was 10% of base salary.

†Salary of Jim Sprague's predecessor.

CASE EXHIBIT 5-4 · District Contribution to Corporate Administrative Expense and Profit, 2000

District	Sales (thousands)	Gross Profit (thousands)	Selling Expenses	Contribution
1	$ 7,812	$ 3,178	$ 776,832	$ 2,401,168
2	7,480	3,058	702,692	2,355,308
3	6,812	2,478	737,058	1,740,942
4	6,636	2,590	696,306	1,893,694
5	6,420	2,372	653,116	1,718,884
6	6,410	2,358	630,752	1,727,248
7	6,210	2,620	600,516	2,019,484
	$47,780	$18,654	$4,797,272	$13,856,648

CASE EXHIBIT 5-5 · District Sales and Gross Profit Performance by Account Category, 2000

District	A	B	C	Total
	Sales by Account Category (thousands)			
Northeast	$1,830	$3,362	$1,620	$6,812
North-central	1,502	3,404	1,304	6,210
	Gross Profit by Account Category (thousands)			
Northeast	$712	$1,246	$ 520	$2,478
North-central	660	1,450	510	2,620

CASE EXHIBIT 5-6 · Potential Accounts, Active Accounts, and Account Call Coverage, 2000

District	Potential Accounts			Active Accounts			Account Coverage (total calls)		
	A	B	C	A	B	C	A	B	C
Northeast	90	381	635	53	210	313	1,297	3,051	2,118
North-central	60	286	499	42	182	216	1,030	2,618	1,299

CASE A-5   HANOVER-BATES CHEMICAL CORPORATION (continued)

The Company and the Industry

The Hanover-Bates Chemical Corporation was a leading producer of processing chemicals for the chemical plating industry. The company's production process was, in essence, a mixing operation. Chemicals purchased from a broad range of suppliers were mixed according to a variety of user-based formulas. Company sales in 2000 had reached a new high of $47,780,000, up from $43,960,000 in 1999. Pretax profit in 2000 had been $7,644,000, up from $6,338,000 in 1999. Hanover-Bates had a strong balance sheet, and the company enjoyed a favorable price-earnings ratio on its stock, which was traded on the over-the-counter market.

Although Hanover-Bates did not produce commodity-type chemicals (e.g., sulfuric acid), industry customers tended to perceive minimal quality differences among the products produced by Hanover-Bates and its competitors. Given the lack of a variation in product quality and the industry-wide practice of limited advertising expenditures, field sales efforts were of major importance in the marketing programs of all firms in the industry.

Hanover-Bates's market consisted of several thousand job shop and captive (i.e., in-house) plating operations. Chemical platers process a wide variety of materials including industrial fasteners (e.g., screws, rivets, bolts, washers), industrial components (e.g., clamps, casings, couplings), and miscellaneous items (e.g., umbrella frames, eyelets, decorative items). The chemical plating process involves the electrolytic application of metallic coatings such as zinc, cadmium, nickel, and brass.

Regardless of the degree of plating precision involved, quality control is of critical concern to all chemical platers. Extensive variation in the condition of materials received for plating requires a high level of service from the firms supplying chemicals to platers. This service is normally provided by the sales representatives of the firm(s) which supply the plater with processing chemicals.

Hanover-Bates and the majority of the firms in its industry produced the same line of basic processing chemicals for the chemical plating industry. The line consisted of a trisodium phosphate cleaner (SPX), anisic aldehyde brightening agents for zinc plating (ZBX), cadmium plating (CBX), and nickel plating (NBX), a protective postplating chromate dip (CHX), and a protective burnishing compound (BUX). The company's product line is detailed in Exhibit 5–7.

Company Sales Organization

The sales organization consisted of 40 sales representatives operating in seven sales districts. Sales representatives' salaries ranged from $28,000 to $48,000 with fringe-benefit costs amounting to an additional 10 percent of salary. In addition to their salaries, Hanover-Bates's representatives received commissions of 0.5 percent of their dollar sales volume on all sales up to their sales quotas. The commission on sales in excess of quota was 1 percent.

In 1998, the national sales manager of Hanover-Bates had developed a sales program based on selling the full line of Hanover-Bates products. Anticipated benefits included the following: (1) sales

CASE EXHIBIT 5-7   Product-Line Data

Container Product	Size	List Price	Gross Margin	Sales (000)
SPX	400 lb drum	$160	$ 56	$7,128
ZBX	50 lb drum	152	68	8,244
CBX	50 lb drum	152	68	7,576
NBX	50 lb drum	160	70	9,060
CHX	100 lb drum	440	180	8,820
BUX	400 lb drum	240	88	6,952

volume per account would be greater and selling costs as a percentage of sales would decrease; (2) a Hanover-Bates sales representative could justify spending more time with such an account, thus becoming more knowledgeable about the account's business and better able to provide technical assistance and identify selling opportunities; (3) full-line sales would strengthen Hanover-Bates's competitive position by reducing the likelihood of account loss to other plating chemical suppliers (a problem that existed in multiple-supplier situations).

The national sales manager's 1998 sales program had also included the following account call frequency guidelines: A accounts (major accounts generating $24,000 or more in yearly sales)—two calls per month; B accounts (medium-sized accounts generating $12,000 to $23,999 in yearly sales)—one call per month; C accounts (small accounts generating less than $12,000 yearly in sales)—one call every two months. The account call frequency guidelines were developed by the national sales manager after discussions with the district managers. The national sales manager had been concerned about the optimum allocation of sales efforts to accounts and felt that the guidelines would increase the efficiency of the company's sales force, although not all of the district sales managers agreed with this conclusion.

It was common knowledge in Hanover-Bates's corporate sales office that Jim Sprague's predecessor as northeast district sales manager had not been one of the company's better district sales managers. His attitude toward the sales plans and programs of the national sales manager had been one of reluctant compliance rather than acceptance and support. When the national sales manager succeeded in persuading Jim Sprague's predecessor to take early retirement, he had been faced with the lack of an available qualified replacement.

Although most of the sales representatives had assumed Hank Carver would get the district manager's job, he had been passed over in part because he would be 65 in three years. The national sales manager had not wanted to face the same replacement problem again in three years and had wanted someone in the position who would be more likely to be responsive to the company's sales plans and policies. The appointment of Jim Sprague as district manager had caused considerable talk, not only in the district but also at corporate headquarters. In fact, the national sales manager had warned Jim that "a lot of people are expecting you to fall on your face. They don't think you have the experience to handle the job, and in particular, to manage and motivate a group of sales representatives most of whom are considerably older and more experienced than you." The national sales manager had concluded by saying, "I think you can handle the job, Jim. I think you can manage those sales reps and improve the district's profit performance, and I'm depending on you to do both."

Questions:

1. Evaluate the performance of the northeast district in comparison with the other Hanover-Bates sales districts.

2. What are the weak spots in the northeast district's performance?

3. What should management do to improve areas of poor performance in the northeast district?

CASE A-6   CHEMGROW, INC.

Evaluating Sales Performance

By September 18, 2002, Mr. John Kee, vice president of agricultural sales, will be presenting his newly conceived Dealer Marketing Plan and Evaluation Program to the president of ChemGrow, Inc., Mr. William Joseph.

Company History

ChemGrow is one of the largest fertilizer manufacturers in the world. It is basic in phosphate rock and manufactures phosphoric acid, anhydrous ammonia, and other mixed fertilizer products. In the past 10 years, the company's production

---

This case was developed by William D. Perreault, Jr., of the University of North Carolina at Chapel Hill and Kevin McNeilly of Miami University. This case is copyrighted by the authors and is reprinted here with their permission.

CASE A-6   CHEMGROW, INC. (continued)

characteristics have shifted dramatically from a manufacturer of specialized NPK (nitrogen, phosphates, and potassium) materials in over 40 plants to the production of high-analysis fertilizers in a few very large capacity installations.

ChemGrow's major production facilities are in Florida, Louisiana, and Arkansas. They are located on or close to river or ocean transportation, and can therefore take advantage of low-cost barge transportation to large terminal points located to supply the market at the lowest possible cost (Exhibit 6–1).

During late 1999 and 2000, ChemGrow evaluated future fertilizer demand and found the need to develop a large-scale expansion program. The $250 million project included a new 425,000-ton-a-year anhydrous ammonia plant at Verdigris, Oklahoma (cost: $35 million), expansion of the phosphate rock mining facilities that it bought from Southern Gas at South Pierce, Florida, and construction of a 400,000-ton phosphoric acid plant near Donaldsonville, Louisiana, as well as sulfuric acid, nitric acid, urea, and granulation facilities, and several formulating facilities.

Much of the ammonia made at Verdigris will start flowing early next year through ChemGrow's own 4,900-mile pipeline that runs from Oklahoma up through the fertilizer-hungry Midwest farm states and into North Dakota, Minnesota, and Ohio. ChemGrow's present expansion activities alone should boost its fertilizer output 50 percent over the 3.7 million tons of products it made in 2000.

The key to capacity growth for ChemGrow has been its control of its raw materials. ChemGrow has enough phosphate rock reserves to maintain its present phosphate production levels for 70 years. For the nitrogen side of its business, ChemGrow signed early last year a 17-year natural gas contract with Oklahoma Natural Gas Company. ChemGrow's expansion program also includes exploration for natural gas in seven offshore Texas and Louisiana tracts.

ChemGrow has been very optimistic about fertilizer growth, but there have been critics of the company—mostly competitors—who believe that ChemGrow's fertilizer expansion is atrociously ill-timed. They feel that after last year's boom, when buyers feared shortages and seized all the fertilizer

CASE EXHIBIT 6-1   ChemGrow's Current Major Production Facilities

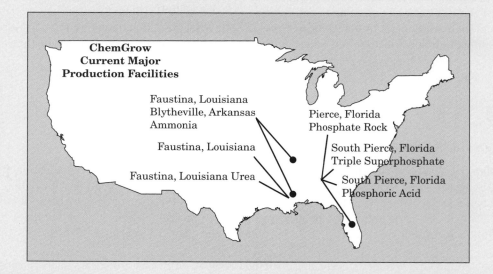

they could find, the industry may now be on the verge of a worldwide glut, perhaps comparable to the agonizing oversupply of 1972–1974.

Management Team

At the headquarters of ChemGrow, Inc., in Tulsa, Oklahoma, Mr. William Joseph has built a winning managerial combination for an industrial empire. Mr. Joseph believes that when it comes to executives, the best are the cheapest for the company in the long run and that you don't make money by being a scrooge.

In selecting top people, he has looked for such qualities as initiative and drive; then he provides his people with the tools with which to work and with an incentive. Money is an incentive, but Mr. Joseph also believes they must have a pride in the company. The job of a chief executive includes creating the atmosphere that these people can operate in successfully. Mr. Joseph has built on the managerial philosophy that in order to succeed in any venture, you don't need a team of people, you need the right man to head up the effort and then he'll develop his own team.

Mr. John Kee, one of Mr. Joseph's leaders, is now in the process of reevaluating and developing his own marketing team. His first step was to define a basic outline for the Dealer Marketing Plan and Evaluation Program. Some of the major aspects of the plan are outlined below:

1. **State ChemGrow's marketing philosophy**—include various statements on channel trade goals, major emphasis products, customer classification and qualifications, and price strategy.

2. **Analyze present position**—use historical sales data, customer/product/territory profiles; define major and minor competition's supply network; describe ChemGrow's strengths and weaknesses compared to each competitor.

3. **Project future environment**—by product tons consumed per acreage, industry projections for product mix, favorable and unfavorable trends, and future competitive programs.

4. **Define marketing regions' goals**—develop goals for product tonnage by account manager for the long and short term; plan strategies to attain these goals by increasing customer growth, increasing the market share in the re-

gion by obtaining new customers, and locating expansion into new areas.

5. **Determine support required to obtain goals**—include manpower requirements, supply and distribution requirements, marketing programs, training programs, and extra services needed.

Mr. Kee felt that the overall basic plan for marketing was specific in terms of the company's primary interests for growth but too general for the region managers to put into action, so another outline was developed for the mechanics of the account manager marketing plan:

1. **Prior to customer call**—outline your territory, locate and identify present customers and their trading area, locate competitor's supply points, and your own, and identify prospective areas of concentration for new customers.

2. **Steps to be completed with customers**—complete sales forecast, update sales history for each customer, and complete customer profile with prospective customers.

3. **Steps to summarize territory marketing plans**—prepare product profile for present customers, prepare marketing plan worksheet, and prepare sales volume forecast for the territory.

4. **Your territory plans**—make up six-month time allocation schedule, make up a monthly calendar, prepare first call action plan for prospective customers, and get regional approval and support for plans and needed help.

Current Issues

Mr. Kee is pleased with the marketing plans which he has outlined, but he knows that getting the appropriate information to complete and implement the plans may be a problem. In the past, efforts at sales analysis had always been done on a "crisis" basis; whenever he absolutely needed a certain form of information, an analyst was assigned to the problem and the answers were developed on a one-time basis. But there was still little *systematic* evaluation of the sales data available in the company. Mr. Kee knows that this void needs to be filled if adequate information is to be available for decisions concerning sales effort planning and control.

CASE A-6   CHEMGROW, INC. (continued)

Mr. Kee's general concern about the present quantitative evaluation program has recently been highlighted by an upcoming deadline. He knows that at the end of the month decisions need to be made involving (1) a special bonus plan for the most productive region, (2) a 10-day vacation to Mexico for the most outstanding salesperson in each region, and (3) a list of "most valuable" customers, who will be invited to participate in a luxury Dealer Council meeting. At the beginning of 2001, when Mr. Kee set up the program which offered these sales promotion incentives, he was intentionally vague about how the customers, salespeople, and regions would be evaluated in arriving at the award decisions. He knows that time is running short and that these evaluations must be made soon. Yet he is also sensitive to the fact that the salespeople and customers alike will be irritated if the award decisions do not appear to be fair. He wants whatever decisions are made to be objective and consistent.

Mr. Kee has expressed to several of his aides his frustration that he is in need of sales analysis information and that once again it must be assembled on a crisis basis. He said in his last staff meeting that he is placing high priority on developing a usable, accessible computerized information system so that problems of this sort do not arise in the future, and so that in the future ongoing sales analysis reports can provide systematic inputs for sales force decision making.

In recent years, all quantitative sales analysis has been done manually under the direction of Mr. Kee's assistant, Richard Evans. Richard never enjoyed these jobs in the past, feeling that he was spending his time on what appeared to be work that was clerical in nature or, worse yet, that could have been done more rapidly, accurately, and completely by computer. This time, however, Richard feels a new sense of intellectual challenge in the job. While he knows that he faces the immediate task of identifying the best performing territory overall, the best salesperson in each territory, and the list of key customers, he also sees that he can have inputs to the design of an integrative sales analysis system. He knows that he can work himself out of this recurring drudgery if he does a good job of figuring out what information is needed and in communicating that need to the computer personnel in the firm. In fact, Mr. Kee has told him that he wants a memorandum from Richard outlining his thoughts on what sales analysis reports they can request starting in the immediate future.

The Available Information

In preparing for his assignment, Richard has talked with several others on the sales management staff and he has been sensitized to the fact that his problem is not a simple one. For example, he has been reminded that each salesperson sells three different products and that each product has a different gross margin associated with it. Moreover, the sales department is concerned with its sales (and margin) growth over time, so Richard wants to be certain that he does not take a static view in evaluating performance.

Unfortunately, the information which he would like is not currently assembled in one place. From the accounting department he is able to get good estimates of the gross margin per ton of sales for each of the three major products (ammonia, phosphate, and potash) sold in this division. These gross margin figures are summarized in Exhibit 6–2.

Richard knows that different salespeople tend to sell these products in different proportions, however. In fact, several months ago this was raised as a concern. Mr. Kee felt that some of the salespeople were selling primarily the products that were easy to sell, rather than a complete product line in general and a profitable mix of products in particular. At that time, Richard had done an analysis on that issue, and it occurs to him that it might be useful for him to check his files for the report he prepared then. With the report in hand, Richard is reminded of what he had done. First, he had tabulated for each salesperson what proportion of his total ton sales were in each of the product lines. The summary table from his report is reproduced here as Exhibit 6–3. He also remembers that he had found the same information across different customers and during different time periods. Richard puts that report to the side, but makes

CASE EXHIBIT 6-2   Dollar Gross Margin Contribution for Each Product

| Product | Gross Margin/Per Ton | | |
	1998	1999	2000
Ammonia	$ 8	$14	$20
Phosphates	12	12	12
Potash	16	9	5

CASE EXHIBIT 6-3   Average Percentage of Total Sales for Each Salesperson

Region	Salesperson	Ammonia	Phosphates	Potash
Eastern	McFee	60%	35%	5%
	Collam	5	20	75
	Parks	80	10	10
	Dow	100	0	0
Central	Thums	80	20	0
	Cook	25	50	25
	Block	20	30	50
	Fowler	75	20	5
Northwest	Vans	70	20	10
	Sciffman	65	20	15
	Lukbore	80	10	10
	Wilkie	20	10	70
Southwest	Goodie	5	5	90
	Stubber	5	15	80
	Holden	0	0	100
	Macke	10	20	70

a mental note that this information can be helpful to him in his current assignment.

Finally, to get sales information on different customers, Richard goes to the accounting department, where he is told, in a pleasant manner, that right now they are in the middle of an audit and will not be able to respond to his requests until after his immediate deadline. However, G. N. Leshades, the head of the accounting department, suggests that the distribution center may have some of the information he needs. At the distribution department, Richard does in fact find some helpful information: an alphabetical computer printout summarizing the total tons of products shipped to each customer in 1998, 1999, and each quarter of 2000.

Back at his office, Richard's secretary volunteers to reorganize the information on the computer printout and to group the different customers according to the salesperson that sells to them and the region in which they are located. The secretary prepares a different summary table for each region, and gives them to Richard. These are summarized here as Exhibits 6–4 through 6–7.

CASE EXHIBIT 6-4   Sales Analysis at the ChemGrow Company: Sales to Each Customer over Time—Eastern Region—Total Tonnage

Obs	Salesperson	Customer	Sales 94	Sales 95	1st Qtr 2000	2nd Qtr 2000	3rd Qtr 2000	4th Qtr 2000
1	Collam	EPF	6,523	4,800	2,800	3,000	2,635	2,635
2	Collam	FEV	3,010	4,550	4,740	10,000	0	0
3	Collam	FSC	1,505	4,100	3,685	5,000	3,025	3,030
4	Collam	HFC	3,261	4,350	3,000	3,000	633	0
5	Collam	M	8,028	13,000	5,000	15,000	3,000	584
6	Collam	PI	2,760	4,650	0	2,948	0	0
7	Dow	CSS	517	2,165	1,000	2,000	500	0
8	Dow	FSC	3,430	5,065	1,500	1,500	0	0
9	Dow	FSI	10,756	8,400	1,050	1,000	1,000	1,000
10	Dow	OSS	7,097	5,470	800	1,200	950	900
11	McFee	CFS	1,395	2,490	950	1,000	723	0
12	McFee	EGS	4,161	6,410	500	4,500	1,500	925
13	McFee	FCS	2,963	3,360	1,485	1,485	1,485	1,485
14	McFee	LAS	15,694	9,030	2,500	1,500	1,500	34
15	McFee	OI	10,076	7,500	1,785	1,783	1,780	1,780
16	Parks	JCS	427	2,800	500	500	500	35
17	Parks	LBC	1,373	7,120	1,605	2,000	500	500
18	Parks	MFS	5,628	4,395	900	1,200	800	170
19	Parks	PFF	12,409	0	3,000	10,000	415	400
20	Parks	SFM	193	3,350	0	1,535	0	0
21	Parks	VT	2,878	5,700	1,640	1,500	1,500	1,500
22	Parks	WT	3,663	6,600	0	0	0	0

CASE EXHIBIT 6-5   Sales Analysis at the ChemGrow Company: Sales to Each Customer over Time—Central Region—Total Tonnage

Obs	Salesperson	Customer	Sales 94	Sales 95	1st Qtr 2000	2nd Qtr 2000	3rd Qtr 2000	4th Qtr 2000
23	Block	CR	8,650	2,940	600	700	700	0
24	Block	LFS	17,350	7,549	200	1,400	1,050	350
25	Block	LSF	8,750	2,526	1,920	400	100	80
26	Block	TCF	5,100	1,623	0	0	0	0
27	Block	WDB	11,400	9,167	3,500	3,000	1,500	1,500
28	Cook	BFH	2,711	3,110	1,000	1,500	1,070	1,000
29	Cook	FFA	2,575	3,730	200	4,000	1,000	284
30	Cook	HD	3,170	3,465	1,500	2,700	2,070	1,500
31	Cook	JC	2,145	6,450	5,000	5,280	0	8,000
32	Cook	PF	1,980	1,190	0	456	0	0
33	Cook	RBR	2,880	1,275	600	675	510	500
34	Cook	TLA	3,375	2,935	3,000	3,855	0	0
35	Fowler	FGC	8,429	7,493	1,020	1,020	0	0
36	Fowler	GFS	9,164	5,994	450	4,245	1,005	800
37	Fowler	MSF	11,284	6,368	1,535	2,480	1,085	960
38	Fowler	RAP	3,843	12,175	0	1,610	0	0
39	Thums	FWM	1,084	2,700	1,260	2,120	1,000	300
40	Thums	WW	3,458	3,100	300	4,000	0	1,004
41	Thums	WWN	3,709	3,400	1,500	1,500	1,420	1,408
42	Thums	YF	15,315	8,660	4,500	9,000	1,200	588>>

CASE EXHIBIT 6-6   Sales Analysis at the ChemGrow Company: Sales to Each Customer over Time—Northwest Region—Total Tonnage

Obs	Salesperson	Customer	Sales 94	Sales 95	1st Qtr 2000	2nd Qtr 2000	3rd Qtr 2000	4th Qtr 2000
43	Lukbore	BAS	6,200	7,444	2,875	3,596	2,485	74
44	Lukbore	MVF	4,800	7,603	1,650	1,550	1,550	1,710
45	Lukbore	SCF	9,300	5,648	2,500	2,500	1,360	0
46	Lukbore	WFL	5,500	3,555	0	6,050	1,460	0
47	Sciffman	HF	11,300	6,764	3,595	3,740	2,460	605
48	Sciffman	JN	2,100	4,194	0	5,000	0	380
49	Sciffman	LS	4,200	1,044	800	820	840	820
50	Sciffman	RM	4,300	3,890	2,160	564	2,010	66
51	Sciffman	VF	5,500	4,747	345	568	327	300
52	Vans	AGC	4,600	2,200	1,550	1,550	0	0
53	Vans	CF	5,900	5,400	1,875	1,875	1,875	1,875
54	Vans	DBI	2,200	2,100	1,265	864	871	0
55	Vans	ECG	8,500	4,620	2,467	3,495	2,140	898
56	Vans	OFC	2,800	6,080	6,591	3,140	719	100
57	Wilkie	ASI	4,800	5,230	2,100	1,565	346	1,889
58	Wilkie	BG	1,150	1,160	3,800	3,800	4,000	3,600
59	Wilkie	CF	4,100	3,700	0	2,600	0	0
60	Wilkie	CI	4,350	15,720	4,860	10,400	5,140	0
61	Wilkie	F&R	13,000	5,720	0	2,250	0	0
62	Wilkie	IO	8,750	2,690	1,200	1,240	1,200	1,200
63	Wilkie	LF	5,100	3,100	1,125	1,695	2,433	2,147>>

CASE EXHIBIT 6-7   Sales Analysis at the ChemGrow Company: Sales to Each Customer over Time—Southwest Region—Total Tonnage

Obs	Salesperson	Customer	Sales 94	Sales 95	1st Qtr 2000	2nd Qtr 2000	3rd Qtr 2000	4th Qtr 2000
64	Goodie	BSF	6,350	4,500	900	700	400	362
65	Goodie	GFF	6,540	8,350	2,465	1,245	1,240	2,500
66	Goodie	KMA	0	0	0	904	0	0
67	Goodie	LCS	3,650	3,840	1,105	1,365	750	981
68	Goodie	PGC	8,510	9,125	2,500	3,262	2,500	2,500
69	Goodie	RGC	19,280	7,240	4,750	20,000	300	671
70	Holden	AGS	2,324	2,505	1,125	3,685	1,038	662
71	Holden	FCS	3,150	5,370	0	5,500	0	0
72	Holden	GF	4,195	5,190	2,531	2,530	2,400	2,664
73	Holden	IFS	5,800	3,340	4,659	3,178	993	0
74	Holden	OFS	2,811	5,935	3,418	8,650	67	0
75	Macke	CE	4,600	2,505	621	652	262	0
76	Macke	CF	3,400	8,670	12,512	3,150	1,013	200
77	Macke	DG	5,900	2,765	850	855	850	855
78	Macke	FER	2,200	2,495	650	650	610	600
79	Macke	SCG	8,500	4,620	2,350	1,240	1,175	1,180
80	Macke	TMN	2,800	3,279	0	5,525	0	0
81	Stubber	BAC	4,505	4,820	1,000	1,000	1,080	1,080
82	Stubber	DPC	2,810	2,600	1,975	1,975	0	0
83	Stubber	GCC	8,125	8,150	5,000	5,000	775	0
84	Stubber	GSS	4,015	3,050	575	685	834	181
85	Stubber	HDS	6,050	5,530	2,475	3,156	1,004	240
86	Stubber	TPS	8,933	6,286	365	2,010	0	83>>

CASE A-6   CHEMGROW, INC. (continued)

Richard knows that more information would be better, but it is not clear that he would be able to get more complete information, even if he had the time to wait. As he sits down to work on his analysis, he focuses on the immediate evaluations that he needs to have completed by the end of the month, but he also writes down his more general thoughts about what computer-generated reports the sales department will want in the future. In fact, he finds that in organizing some of his current analysis he is developing good formats and specifications for the reports that he will suggest in his memorandum to Mr. Kee.

Questions:

1. What decisions would you make with regard to which is the most productive region, who is the most outstanding salesperson, and who are the most valuable customers?

2. What computer reports should be generated on a regular basis to assist the managers in their evaluations?

APPENDIX B

Careers in Sales Management

This appendix provides some insights into the sales manager's job and some ideas about what to do to be a successful sales manager.

A sales manager of an industrial fasteners manufacturer said:

> I wasn't at all certain that I wanted to be sales manager when it was offered to me. After all, I was making real good money in the field, I liked the freedom and the customer contact. I wasn't all that sure I would like managing, let alone be able to do so. Now, as I look back, I can't understand my reluctance to go into management. Working with these people, building the organization, getting things done—I really get a kick out of it. For instance, take a green kid, turn him into a real producer, and you'll know what accomplishment feels like.

The Challenge

People of ability thrive on challenge. Jobs that do not test their capabilities quickly bore them. A key question to ask about an anticipated career is: "Will it offer sufficient challenge to sustain my interest in doing a continually better job?" A sales manager's job has such challenges.

For example, a consumer products company with $14 million sales volume was foundering. Its 1999 losses exceeded $4 million. The firm hired a proven executive from another consumer products company. His experience was in the brand management side of the business, although he had started his career in sales and was widely known in the industry for his selling skills. He was given control over the firm's 40-rep sales force with the mandate to remake it into a reasonably productive unit. The company's average annual sales per salesperson were $350,000, but it was generally felt that a $600,000 average would be more in line with industry standards.

The new sales manager went into the field to work with each of the reps for one day to evaluate their talents. He found most reps not only lacking sales skills but also lacking the desire and ability to develop them. He spotted 20 people he could use; the others were asked to find other employment. With overhead reduced, he set about molding his new crew into a hard-hitting sales force. They put together a new sales plan, and it worked. As the manager later explained, "I used to think that getting out a new product was a challenge. But it's nothing compared to turning a sick operation into a profitable one while giving 20 people more successful careers. It's the toughest job I've ever had, but it made me grow!"

The sales manager is in the front lines, where performance is easily appraised by peers and superiors. While the abilities or contributions of a bookkeeper, personnel manager, or a design engineer may be difficult to assess, the sales manager's effectiveness is quite evident. Such measurable indexes as sales volume, selling expenses, turnover of the sales force, and percentage of market share are potent arguments either for or against the manager's performance. There is no place to hide.

Career Paths in Sales Management

Career paths in sales management vary from company to company as well as from individual to individual within the same company. Different individuals within the same company may take different paths to a top-level executive sales position because they have different professional experiences and education and because they have different preferences.

Typical Career Paths

Figure B-1 depicts the typical positions that individuals may hold during their careers in sales management. As we noted earlier, the path to the top may vary; most individuals will not serve in all of these positions. Sales careers almost always start with a position in sales.

FIGURE B-1   **Typical Sales Management Career Paths**

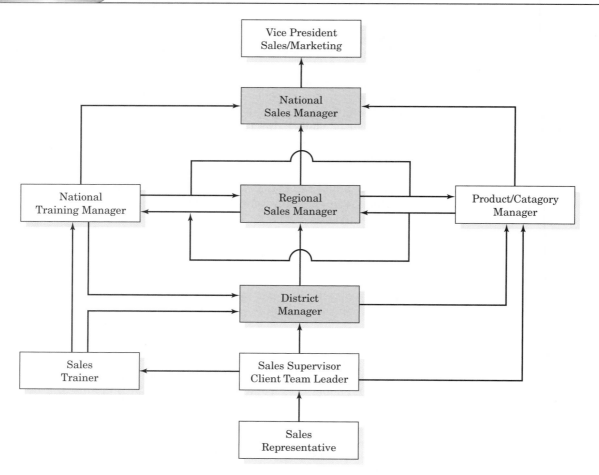

A sales trainee may progress through several levels of increasing sales responsibility such as **sales representative, senior sales representative,** and possibly **national account manager.**

As discussed in Chapter 1, the entry-level sales management position is often as a **sales supervisor,** providing day-to-day supervision to four or five salespeople. In companies where the team approach to selling has been adopted, the first managerial position would be as a **client team leader.** Also, many companies do not have supervisors; then the first management position is typically **district manager.**

As depicted in Figure B-1 by the shaded boxes, some first-line managers may progress in a straight path through all of the line management positions—**regional sales manager, national sales manager,** and finally **vice president of sales** or **vice president of marketing.** This would be likely in a small or medium-sized company.

In most larger companies, the career paths of most managers include assignments in some staff positions. These staff assignments give individuals the experience they need to manage the entire sales and marketing operations. For example, a sales supervisor's next position might be sales trainer. A district manager might move into the position of **national training manager** or a **product** or **category manager,** instead of becoming a **regional manager.** In fact a manager could serve in all three of these positions before moving on to become **national sales manager.**

The following promotion would be into executive management as a **vice president of sales** and/or **marketing.**

Geographic Coverage

The amount of territory the sales manager controls can vary from the whole world to a small city. Prospective sales executives can choose the size of area they prefer. A person who wants to minimize traveling should join an organization whose distribution is limited to a small geographic area. Many such opportunities exist in automobile dealerships, appliance distributorships, business-machine branch organizations, office supply houses, insurance agencies, and local radio, television, and newspaper firms—in general, any retail or wholesale organization that serves a local trading area. Positions with small firms can be as desirable or challenging as those with companies that distribute nationally.

Geographic Location

Sales management positions are located in every section of the country. Prospective sales executives can determine their living environment by getting a job in the area where they want to live. Of course, this limits their bargaining power and choice of firms. However, most sales management positions are located in larger cities and in the more densely populated areas of the country where corporations have their home offices, branches, and sales offices. This does not suggest that there are no firms with headquarters in small towns. The home offices of Maytag Company, for example, are located in a small town in Iowa.

Types of Selling Activities

The sales executive can also choose the type of selling to administer. Each type of sales job requires a varying degree of pressure, different personal qualities, and varying efforts. The job of managing a door-to-door sales organization is different from the task of guiding individuals in selling large industrial installations to top executives. The task of managing a group of automobile salesmen is different from that of administering the activities of a manufacturer's sales force.

The sales job in each industry is unique and has its own characteristics and demands. In planning a sales management career, give considerable thought to what you will be happiest selling. Experience indicates that there are great advantages to staying in one industry throughout a sales career. People who stay in the same industry build a valuable base of knowledge and a strong network of contacts.

The Rewards of a Sales Management Job

Reward systems are important in shaping people's behavior. In several direct and many subtle ways, how much people are paid and the compensation methods influence what they do. The rewards awaiting a sales manager are an important consideration in your job choice.

Direct Monetary Rewards—The Money

According to *Dartnell's 30th Sales Force Compensation Survey*, top sales executives' salaries range from $69,000 to $240,000, with an average of $109,000. The average for a regional sales manager is $85,000 with the highest salaries over $169,000. District sales managers earn an average of $78,000. There is a lot of variability across different-sized companies and industries. In general, smaller companies pay less than larger ones. The fabricated metals industry is relatively high paying, as are insurance and office equipment.[1]

Indirect Monetary Payments

Little is known statistically about the extent of indirect monetary payments for sales managers. These payments include company-paid insurance plans, pension systems, country club memberships, access to company-owned airplanes, and other company-furnished enhancements to a manager's standard of living. However, such indirect payments are important and widely used. At some point in their careers, sales managers may place a high value on deferred compensation, such as stock option plans, pension plans, and insurance policies, which are nontaxable or are tax deferred. A $10,000 country club membership would be worth about $14,000 if it were paid as regular compensation.

These considerations are of particular importance to the sales manager. It is easier to justify to the Internal Revenue Service that the sales manager needs such things as a company-owned airplane or a country club membership than it is to build the same case for the production manager. It is far more likely for the sales executive to be given these benefits than it is for any other executive on the same level in the organization.

Helping your customers is a very rewarding aspect of the sales job.

The Life of a Sales Executive

While it is true that each sales manager's job is unique, there are some common elements:

- **Travel.** Some traveling is required for the performance of any sales management job. However, the amount can vary from an occasional convention trip to an extensive amount of field work with the sales branches or with customers. The amount of traveling sales managers do depends somewhat on their attitudes toward traveling. Many enjoy being on the road and seize every opportunity to get out of the office and into the field.

- **Paperwork.** Inherent in modern management is the nuisance called administrative tasks. No one relishes it, but it goes with the territory—few people who are lax in handling the paperwork advance very far in management. A manager who neglects the paperwork input to the company's information system places a burden, sometimes a difficult one, on other executives who need the information. What constitutes doing paperwork properly? First, paperwork should be done accurately and completely, not haphazardly. Second, it should be done on time.

- **Conferences and meetings.** Sales managers are involved in many decisions which are made with the input of several people. Often these people meet to discuss the issues at hand. For example, the sales manager might frequently be involved in meetings with the product manager, the design engineers, the marketing manager, the research manager, or vice president of human resources. Sometimes these meetings are face-to-face meetings; sometimes they are teleconference or videoconference calls.

  Sales managers also regularly conduct sales meetings for their salespeople. The purposes of these meetings may vary, but they often include training, new program introduction, or information sharing. A capable administrator learns how to participate effectively in such meetings.

- **Work with people.** If there is one common denominator among sales managers, it is that they must deal with people at all levels. In one day, the sales manager may hold conferences with both the sales force and the board of directors or may contact both top executives and a customer's operating staff.
- **Sales.** Some sales managers continue to sell to certain customers; they may retain key accounts. Others go into the field for important sales. Few sales managers ever get very far away from selling.
- **Picking people—talented ones.** We have stressed in this book that the sales manager's most important job is selecting sales personnel. The ability to select individuals who become successful salespeople is critical to the sales manager's own success.
- **Firefighting.** All sorts of problems continually arise that require immediate attention. A customer calls to voice a complaint; something must be done. Corporate counsel requires a deposition in a lawsuit. A sales rep is injured while skiing and cannot cover the trade for a month. There is no anticipating what is going to happen. However, the sales manager must somehow handle each problem presented.
- **Market exposure and opportunity.** Since sales managers continually interface with the market and with the buyers in it, they are in an advantageous position to observe and intercept market opportunities. Many entrepreneurs have used sales management as a springboard into their own enterprises. Such opportunities are hidden from the person who is buried in an office or who does not operate in the market.
- **Above all, managing.** Many super salespeople have failed as sales managers because they did not realize that, above all, they were expected to be managers. A manager manages! A manager leads a group of individuals to accomplish its mission. A manager gets and organizes resources and makes things happen. Responsibility is a key concept. The manager is responsible for the productivity of the group—for recruiting, training, and motivating people within the group.

What It Takes to Be a Successful Sales Manager

Education

Not too many years ago a sales manager needed only successful sales experience to qualify for the job. Today, perusal of the job specifications for a wide range of sales management positions indicates that applicants for these jobs must have college degrees.

Experience

Sales experience is necessary, but you do not have to be an outstanding sales producer to be promoted into a management position. Nevertheless, you have a brighter future as a sales manager if you have performed successfully in a selling job. Such a background provides several advantages.

First, the sales force will have respect for you. They will know that you have been in the field and recognize the problems they face each day. When you tell them to do something, they will have confidence that you know what you are talking about.

Second, sales experience enables you to be realistic in planning activities and in your supervision and control efforts. You are not likely to expect the impossible of the sales force, but you will be able to recognize a loafer when you see one.

Third, the customer contact provided by selling is valuable for any top policy-making executive. Knowing the problems of the customer is essential in developing sound marketing plans. Having personal acquaintances among the firm's customers is also helpful.

More important than sales experience, however, is managerial experience. To become a high-level sales or marketing executive, you must build a base of experience through several lower levels of management experience. It is through the lower level positions that one learns and demonstrates the requisite leadership and administrative skills necessary for top management positions.

Leadership Skills

The ability to lead is so important to sales managers that we devoted an entire chapter to the topic earlier in this book. Sales managers must be effective leaders. The only way they can accomplish their goals is through directing the efforts of others. This requires a change of perspective. Salespeople are primarily concerned about their own efforts to sell and service customers. Managers, in contrast, must be focused on developing and coordinating the efforts of others.

Leaders must also have more of a strategic perspective than salespeople. They should understand the strategic mission of the firm and how the sales strategy contributes to the overall objectives of the firm. Finally, as we noted in the chapter on leadership, the most charismatic manager is one who leads by example.

Administrative Skills

The ability to organize people and activities is a critical dimension of being a successful manager. The best way to learn these skills is to put yourself into positions where you must practice these skills.

For example, a member of the Young Presidents Organization, when questioned about how he had developed his administrative skills, advanced this idea:

> After I got out of college and settled down into my first job, I made it a point to get involved in all sorts of community activities, any group that would take me. Little League, church, neighborhood, you name it and I joined it. I volunteered to do whatever it was that had to be done. I found out that you can learn a great deal about how to get people to do what it is you want them to do—managing them, if you will—in just such activities.
>
> At first I found I was terrible at it. I remember that first year. It was awful. Everything was messed up, nothing flowed right, and I couldn't organize my people. But with experience I learned the ropes. I learned how to organize projects, how to line up things, and how to get things done. I attribute a large part of my success in business to those early years in community activities where I learned to manage people.

That is the way one person developed administrative skills. He learned by doing. He projected himself into situations that required administrative skills and then was perceptive enough to learn them. You can do the same thing while you are still in college by accepting positions of leadership in various campus organizations. Of course you can also seek out such opportunities on the job as well.

The vice president of manufacturing for a large machine tool company used several opportunities on the job to develop administrative skills.

> In my first years with the company I seized every opportunity I could to show some management skills. I remember that first year the boss wanted someone to organize the company picnic. I stepped forward and knocked myself out to make sure that was the best-run picnic the company ever had. And it was! The boss never forgot that. For the next ten years he was continually reminding me of the great job I did on that picnic. Then there was the time we had all of the confusion when the workers struck. We were trying to keep the plant open to get out critical orders and run the place on a skeleton staff. I worked round the clock organizing that effort, and I think more than anything else that was responsible for getting me where I am now. The boss was really impressed with how I held things together during that strike.

Desire

Probably more than anything else, you must want to be a successful sales manager if you are to become one. Your desire must be great enough so that you will apply yourself diligently to all the difficult tasks that lie ahead of you. Many otherwise successful salespeople do not become sales managers simply because they have no desire to do so. If you really want to be a sales manager, you probably will have the opportunity at some point in your career.

Your Strategic Career Plan

At the beginning of most chapters throughout this book, we have included a section on the role of the chapter topic in the firm's strategic market plan. Now it is time for you to think strategically. What is your strategic plan for yourself? What are your goals? How do you plan to achieve them? The members of one of the author's classes were asked about their strategic plans. Their puzzled looks disclosed that few of them had given such plans much thought. Guess what the next assignment was!

The Matter of Goals

It would be folly to suggest that you can now foresee what you will be doing and who you will be at age 50. All evidence clearly shows that fate plays a heavy hand in your career game. Nevertheless, you need goals. You can change goals as you discover new information about yourself and the markets you're dealing in. But you still need ultimate and intermediate goals. Some career specialists suggest that you set goals each year. What do you want to accomplish by this time next year? What do you want to be doing?

One advantage of having goals is that it helps you resist temptations that will lead you into unacceptable situations. For example, assume that you know that you want to have your own business by the time you are 35. Then you might refuse job offers—no matter how attractive otherwise—that would provide little opportunity to acquire the skills you need to be your own boss. If one of your goals is to live in the Sun Belt, then you might shun offers from firms whose bases of operation are in the Northeast. Success with such firms might mean living somewhere you don't want to live.

The bottom line is that you should know what you want in life if you want to maximize your chances of getting it.

What Do You Need to Do to Achieve Your Goals?

We are all imperfect, and our imperfections may block the path to our goals. If you are to achieve your goals, you will have to develop yourself in diverse ways. Identify what you need to learn and what skills you need to acquire to become what you want to be. Then, formulate a plan to remedy your deficiencies. If you see a need for selling skills, go to work for a firm that can give you excellent sales training and sales experience. Think in terms of who knows what you want to know, and then tap that source of knowledge.

Your first few jobs out of school form the base of your credentials for future opportunities. Go where you can acquire the knowledge and skills you'll need to reach your ultimate goals.

What Is Your Level of Aspiration?

Many of you will want to play in the "major leagues"—whatever that may mean to you. It means different things to different people. Others want no part of the fast track. It is best to identify what level of competition you seek early because it is difficult to climb in "class." Coaches wanting to coach in professional football usually do not start out coaching in high schools.

What Is Your Timetable?

You need to achieve a position by a certain time lest you fall behind your competitors. To a somewhat lesser degree, the same thing is true in business. You can become too old for a job just as you can be too young, at least in the mind of the person making the decision about you.

If you are not making normal progression toward your goals, you need to reassess what you are doing. If your boss likes your work and intends to promote you, you will be given some very tangible evidence of that intention. If nothing good is happening on your job, your firm is sending you a message. Look for tangible rewards.

Personal Criteria

You need to give considerable thought to your personal criteria for any job you accept. You need answers to such questions as:

- How much must you earn to consider yourself successful?
- Where do you want to live and work?
- What kind of people do you want to work with?

- What kind of lifestyle do you want?
- How much job security do you need?
- How much power do you need?
- What health limitations do you have?
- What family conditions affect your work?

Unless a job meets your personal criteria, you're not likely to be successful in it for long. Get started right! Don't spend years in a job that cannot give you what you ultimately want.

Final Word

One of your authors has been a sales rep, and all of your authors have worked with and socialized with sales reps and their managers for many years. They cannot recall one instance during that time where the person in sales voiced dissatisfaction with his or her career. To the contrary, they have been and remain excited about their careers, their products, and their customers.

References

1. Christian P. Heide, ed., *Dartnell's 30th Sales Force Compensation Survey* (Chicago: Dartnell Corporation, 1999), pp. 46–48.

Credits

Name Index

Company Index

Subject Index

DealMaker software, 206
Decentralized training, 201–202
Deciders, 96
Delphi technique, 347
Demographics, 23, 36, 231
Demonstration method, 209
Development, 442
Diplomacy Test of Empathy, 166
Direct compensation, 251
Direct cost allocation, 428
Direct costs, 427
Direction, 442
Directories, 60
Direct-response marketing, legal
      issues, 480
Direct selling expense, 453
Discriminant analysis, 132
Discrimination, 321–322
Discrimination charges, 122
Discussion method, 208
Disengagement stage of career, 233
Distinctive manager, 18
Distributors, 101
District manager, 539
District sales manager, 89
Diversity, 23
      minority groups, 139–140
      women, 140
Divisional sales manager, 19
Door-to-door salespeople, 479–480
Driver salespeople, 12
Drug abuse, 170, 318–319
Drug testing, 170
Dual-factor theory, 227–228

Earnings cap, 265–266
E-commerce, 10, 103–104
Economic conditions, 36–37
Economy, importance of sales
      management, 22
Educational background, 158
Edwards Personal Reference
      Schedule, 166
Effort/performance, 229–230
80/20 principle
      and customer classification, 412
      and misdirected marketing effort,
            405–406
      and product sales, 410
Electronic communication, 24
Embezzlement, 469
Employee benefits, in job offer, 172
Employee-owned cars
      miscellaneous expenses, 292
      reimbursement plan, 292–294
      variable costs, 292
Employees
      empowering, 41
      ranking of motivations, 228
Employment agencies, 139

Empowering employees, 41
Encouragement and praise, 238
Energy, 305
Entertainment costs, 284, 295
Environmentalists, 51
Equal Employment Opportunity
      Commission, 122–123, 140, 156
      and sexual harassment, 321–322
Equity theory, 229
Establishment stage of career, 232
Ethical behavior, 25
Ethical guidelines
      codes of ethics, 475–476
      long-run view, 475
      role models, 477
      training, 477
Ethical standards, 471
Ethical training, 477
Ethics, 469
Ethics Resource Center, 475
Ethnic factors, and workload
      capacity, 378
Euro-consumer clusters, 338
European Union, sales forecasting in,
      338
Evaluation, 4; *see also* Performance
      evaluation
Executive ladder
      in personal selling, 19
      in team selling, 20
Executive opinion forecasting
      method, 345–346
Expectancy theory
      effort/performance, 229–230
      performance/reward, 229
      reasons for success or failure, 230
      reward/effort evaluation, 228–229
Expense account auditing policy,
      300–302
Expense account policy, 282
      abuse of, 319–320
      case, 302–303
      characteristics, 285–286
Expense bank account, 295
Expense-quota plan, 289
Expense-to-sales ratio, 453
Experience-based incentives, 234
Experience factor, 232
Experience requirements, 158
Exploration stage of career, 232
Exponential smoothing models,
      350–351
Export intermediaries, 105–106
External environment
      competition, 37
      demography, 36
      economic conditions, 36–37
      political-legal factors, 37
      sociocultural factors, 37
      technology, 37

External referral agencies, 60
Extrinsic rewards, 226

Face-to-face interviews, 163
Facilitation payment, 471
Factory representative, 11
Failure, attributions for, 230
Fair Employment Opportunity Act, 123
Fairness in compensation, 256
Features, product, 65–66
Federal Bureau of Investigation, 470
Federal Sentencing Commission for
      Organizations, 477
Federal Trade Commission, 475,
      479–480
Federal Trade Commission Act, 478
Feedback, on poor performance,
      317–318
Field sales managers, 18
Financial rewards
      compensation, 234
      performance incentives, 234
      sales contests, 235–236
Fixed-allowance plans, 292–293
Fixed costs, 427
Flat-rate mileage plan, 293, 294
Fleet managers, 296
Flexibility, 85
Flexible-allowance plan, 293–294
Follow-up, 71–72
Follow-up inquiry, 62
Foreign assignments, 176
Foreign Corrupt Practices Act, 471
Foreign-country intermediaries,
      106–107
Foreign representatives, 105
Fostering group goals, 309
Fringe benefits, 269–270
Full-cost method, 430–432
Functional organization, 86–87, 89

Gatekeepers, 96
General Sales Aptitude Test, 166
Geographic information system, 381
Geographic organization, 88–90
Gift-giving, 284, 474
Global account management, 94–95
Global positioning systems, 381
Gordon Personnel Profile, 166
Graduated-mileage rate plan, 293
Green River Ordinances, 37, 479
Gross margin goals, 451–452
Gross profit, 451–452
Group goals, 308
Group morale, 316–317
Guerrilla Marketing (Levinson), 208
Guided interview, 161

Halo effect, 454
Hard sell, 40